# Research Methods
## in the
# Social Sciences

### FIFTH EDITION

D0307592

# Research Methods in the Social Sciences

## FIFTH EDITION

### Chava Frankfort-Nachmias

University of Wisconsin, Milwaukee

### David Nachmias

Tel Aviv University
University of Wisconsin, Milwaukee

A member of the Hodder Headline Group
LONDON • NEW YORK • SYDNEY • AUCKLAND

First published in Great Britain 1996 by Arnold
a member of the Hodder Headline Group
338 Euston Road, London NW1 3BH

*British Library Cataloguing in Publication Data*
A catalogue record for this book is available from the British Library

ISBN 0 340 66226 3

6 7 8 9 10

Printed and bound in Great Britain by J W Arrowsmith Ltd, Bristol

# CONTENTS IN BRIEF

# Appendixes

# DETAILED CONTENTS

## Part II ▪ Design and Structure of Research

# Part III ▪ Data Collection

## Part IV ▪ Data Processing and Analysis

---

# Appendixes

# PREFACE

The goal of the Fifth Edition of *Research Methods in the Social Sciences,* as in the previous editions, is to offer a comprehensive, systematic treatment of the scientific approach within the context of the social sciences. We emphasize the relationship between theory, research, and practice, and integrate research activities in an orderly framework so that the reader can more easily comprehend the nature of social science research.

In our view, social science research is a cyclical, self-correcting process consisting of seven major interrelated stages: definition of the research problem, statement of the hypothesis, research design, measurement, data collection, data analysis, and generalization. Each of these stages is interrelated with theory in that it both affects and is affected by it. The text leads the reader through each stage of this process.

## The New Edition

The Fifth Edition incorporates a number of significant revisions:

- A new section on using graphics to describe distributions has been added to Chapter 15, "The Univariate Distribution." The section covers pie charts, bar charts, and histograms.
- Each chapter preview now presents an outline of the material to be studied as well as an example that shows students a real-life application of the chapter topic. The previews are designed to help students focus attention on the material to be covered.
- Summary boxes throughout the text simplify review of important concepts.
- Appendix A, "Introduction to SPSS," has been expanded to include SPSS/PC+ and SPSS for Windows. Appendix A serves to assist students in preparing and executing computerized data analysis utilizing these widely available and often-used software packages. New computer exercises in Chapters 14–19 give students the opportunity to apply SPSS as they analyze a data set.
- A new Appendix B, "Writing Research Reports," gives pointers on report writing for the beginning and advanced student.

The new edition continues to blend a broad range of classic social science research studies with up-to-date examples of contemporary social science issues. The additions and changes reflect the concerns and developments that have surfaced in the field since the publication of the previous edition. The text has also benefitted from the constructive criticism offered by instructors, both users and nonusers, in research methods courses from a variety of disciplines across the country. Following their advice, we have revised the prose to make the tone less formal and the concepts even more accessible for students.

## The Plan of the Book

The book's organization progresses logically from the conceptual and theoretical building blocks of the research process to data analysis and computer applications, offering students a comprehensive and systematic foundation for comprehending the breadth and depth of social science research. The book's self-contained yet integrated chapters promote flexibility in structuring courses, depending upon the individual instructor's needs and interests. The text adapts easily to two kinds of courses: a basic methods course or one that covers methods and statistics sequentially.

Chapter 1 examines the foundations of knowledge, the objectives of scientific research, and the basic assumptions of the scientific approach. Chapters 2 and 3 discuss the basic issues of empirical research and the relationship between theory and research. They cover the topics of concept formation, the roles and types of theories, models, variables, and the various sources for research problems and for the construction of hypotheses. Chapter 4 focuses on ethical concerns in social science research and proposes ways to ensure the rights and the welfare of research participants, including the right to privacy.

Chapters 5 and 6 present the research design stage. A research design is a strategy that guides investigators; it is a logical model for inferring causal relations. Experimental designs are discussed and illustrated in Chapter 5, and quasi- and preexperimental designs are examined in Chapter 6. Chapter 7 is concerned with measurement and quantification. The issues of validity and reliability—inseparable from measurement theory—are also reviewed here, together with the issue of measurement error. In Chapter 8, we present the principles of sampling theory, the most frequently used sampling designs, and the methods for estimating sample size.

In Chapters 9 through 13, we present and illustrate the various methods of data collection available to social scientists. Observational methods, laboratory experiments, and field experimentation are the subjects of Chapter 9. Survey research—particularly the mail questionnaire, the personal interview, and the telephone interview—is examined in Chapter 10. Chapter 11 describes and illustrates methods of questionnaire construction: the content of questions, types of questions, question format, and the sequence of questions. The discussion of the pitfalls of questionnaire construction addresses the issue of bias. Chapter 12 is devoted to the theory and practice of qualitative research, with a particular emphasis on participant observation and field research. In Chapter 13 we discuss major issues of secondary data analysis—the census, unobtrusive data such as private and public documents, and content analysis.

The next five chapters are concerned with data processing and analysis. In Chapter 14 we present the latest techniques of codebook construction, coding schemes and devices, ways to prepare data for computer processing, the use of computers in social science research, and communication network linkages. Chapter 15 introduces the univariate distribution, measures of central tendency and dispersion, and various types of frequency distributions. Chapter 16 examines the central concept of bivariate analysis, concentrating on several measures of nominal, ordinal, and interval relationships, which are discussed and compared. The major topics of multivariate analysis, statistical techniques of control and interpretation, causal inferences, and path analysis are the subjects of Chapter 17. Chapter 18 presents common techniques used in constructing indexes and scales; and in Chapter 19 we discuss strategies of hypothesis testing, the level of significance, the region of rejection, and several parametric and nonparametric tests of significance.

This text, together with the supporting materials, will help readers move through the major stages of the research process.

## Acknowledgments

Our literary debts are testified to throughout the text. Many students, instructors, reviewers, and colleagues have offered useful ideas and comments since the First Edition was published in 1976.

We are particularly grateful to Michael Baer, Bruce S. Bowen, Jeffery Brudney, Gary T. Henry, and Allen Rubin. We are also grateful to the Literary Executor of the late Sir Ronald A. Fisher, F.R.S., to Dr. Frank Yates, F.R.S., to Longman Group Ltd., London, for permission to reprint appendixes from their book *Statistical Tables for Biological, Agricultural, and Medical Research,* Sixth Edition (1974), and to the reviewers of the Fifth Edition: Lydia Andrade, San Jose State University; Claire L. Felbinger, Cleveland State University; Richard Nagasawa, Arizona State University; Marcellina Offoha, Ithaca College; Alfred Powell, University of Texas at San Antonio; John K. Price, Louisiana Tech University; Jules J. Wanderer, University of Colorado at Boulder; and David G. Wegge, St. Norbert College.

We are also grateful to Claire L. Felbinger, Levin College of Public Administration, Cleveland State University, in collaboration with her assistant, Stephen F. Schwelgien, for the preparation of the appendix on SPSS; to Nina Reshef, The Public Policy Program, Tel-Aviv University, who assisted David Nachmias, and whose significant contribution is evident throughout the text; and to Pat Pawasarat, who assisted Chava Frankfort-Nachmias in the revision of the text.

Finally, we wish to express our indebtedness to the staff of St. Martin's Press, especially to Carla Samodulski, who has masterfully crafted the Fifth Edition. We

xxii    PREFACE

also extend our sincere thanks to Sabra Scribner, her conscientious assistant Elizabeth Bast, and Douglas Bell for their patience and support throughout the project.

Chava Frankfort-Nachmias
David Nachmias

# CHAPTER 1
# The Scientific Approach

Can an intractable social problem be solved by a massive research effort? The recently begun Project on Human Development in Chicago Neighborhoods may be such a study. As part of the attempt to draw a detailed picture of what it is like to grow up in Chicago, and thereby understand which ways of growing up lead to delinquency and which to socially acceptable behavior, 11,000 participants in about 75 Chicago neighborhoods will be tracked for over eight years. The study will be interdisciplinary in approach, its researchers looking at individual and family characteristics (the province of psychology) in combination with community influences (the province of sociology). As they analyze their sample and attempt to prove their hypotheses, the researchers will be following the rules of scientific methodology.[1]

IN THIS CHAPTER, WE FIRST DEFINE SCIENCE AND THEN COMPARE the scientific approach with three other approaches to knowledge. We discuss the basic assumptions of science, its aims, and the roles of methodology in the scientific approach. We define the scientific approach, first by its assumptions about nature and experience and then by its methodology relating to communication, reasoning, and intersubjectivity. We then present the ideas of scientific revolutions, discoveries, and progress. Finally, we present a model of the research process, the stages of which are discussed throughout this book.

Throughout this volume, we also ask a number of questions. What benefits can the scientific approach offer to people who take an interest in the problems of society? How can we acquire reliable knowledge about those aspects of the human experience that are considered "social," "political," "economic," and "psychological"? More specifically, how can the scientific approach help us to understand phenomena such as inflation, unemployment, democratic governance, bureaucracy, crime and delinquency, or self-actualization? In other words, how and why are the social sciences members of the family of science?

One way to answer these questions is first to define **science** and then to take a close look at the scientific approach—its assumptions, goals, and attributes—and compare these with other approaches to knowledge.

# What Is Science?

Unfortunately, science is frequently misunderstood. Laypersons, journalists, policymakers, scholars, and scientists themselves employ the term *science* in different ways and in different contexts. To some, science connotes a prestigious undertaking; to others, science implies a body of true knowledge; to still others, it means an objective investigation of empirical phenomena.

1. Ellen K. Coughlin, "Pathways to Crime," *The Chronicle of Higher Education,* (April 27, 1994), pp. A8–A9.

Science is difficult to define primarily because people often confuse the content of science with its methodology. Although science has no particular subject matter of its own, we do not view every study of phenomena as science. For example, astrologists look at the positions of the stars and various events in human life and try to establish relations between them in order to predict future events. These goals and activities do not qualify astrology for admission into the family of science. Even if a prestigious university were to establish a Department of Astrology, recruit faculty, develop a curriculum, and offer a Master of Science degree, astrology would not qualify as a scientific discipline. The reason we reject astrology as a science is not because of its subject matter but, rather, because the methodology used by astrologists is considered to be unscientific. Whenever a branch of what many people accept as factual knowledge is rejected by scientists, that rejection is always based on methodological considerations. Furthermore, much of the content of science is constantly changing: knowledge regarded as scientific today may become "unscientific" in the future. The term *science,* then, does not refer to any general or particular body of knowledge but to a distinct methodology. For these reasons we shall use the term *science* throughout this book to mean all knowledge collected by means of the scientific methodology.

---

# Approaches to Knowledge

The word *science* is derived from the Latin word *scire,* "to know." Throughout history, people have acquired knowledge in various ways. The scientific approach is by no means the only way by which people have attempted to understand their environment and themselves. Three other general modes have served the purpose of acquiring knowledge: the authoritarian mode, the mystical mode, and the rationalistic mode. Major distinctions among these modes lie in the way each vests credibility in the source or producer of knowledge (that is, *Who* says so?), the procedure by which knowledge is produced (*How* do you know?), and the effect of that knowledge (*What difference* does it make?).[2] A brief description of these modes provides a perspective for the comparative evaluation of the scientific approach.

## Authoritarian Mode

In the authoritarian mode, people seek knowledge by referring to individuals who are socially or politically defined as qualified producers of knowledge. These may be oracles in tribal societies, archbishops in theocratic societies (such as the mullahs in contemporary Iran), kings in monarchical societies, and scientists in technocratic societies. Within any society, different authorities may be approached for

---

2. Walter L. Wallace, *The Logic of Science in Sociology* (Hawthorne, N.Y.: Aldine, 1971), p. 11. See also, Anthony O'Hear, *An Introduction to the Philosophy of Science* (New York: Oxford University Press, 1989).

knowledge about different phenomena. To illustrate, for most devout Catholics the Pope has traditionally possessed undisputed authority on religious matters. In another context, during the Cultural Revolution in China (begun in 1965), Chairman Mao Tse–tung and his wife held similar authority on all aspects of life in Mainland China. The *Little Red Book,* containing Mao's aphorisms, served as the "bible" for what was considered to be correct behavior and thought. The mullahs in contemporary Iran are a more recent example. In the authoritarian mode, then, laypersons attribute the ability to generate knowledge to the social, political, or religious authority of the producer. The manner in which the layperson solicits this authority (e.g., ceremony) affects the nature of the authority's response but not the recipient's confidence in the response. Those who wish to discredit, or to delegitimize, the authority of a knowledge producer must repeatedly refute his or her claims and provide an alternate source of knowledge.

## Mystical Mode

In the mystical mode, truth seekers obtain knowledge from authorities on the supernatural, such as prophets, diviners, and mediums. In this sense, the mystical mode is similar to the authoritarian mode. However, it differs in its dependence on manifestations of supernatural events and on the psychophysical state of the knowledge consumer. The mystical mode depends, to a large extent, on the use of ritualistic and ceremonial procedures. For example, the rites surrounding the process of astrological prophecy are aimed at persuading the layperson of the astrologer's supernatural powers.

Moreover, under conditions of acute depression, helplessness, and intoxication, the knowledge consumer is most willing to accept knowledge produced by the mystical mode. The confidence in the knowledge produced in this manner decreases as the number of refutations increases, as the educational level of a society advances, or as one's psychological state improves.

## Rationalistic Mode

According to the school of philosophy known as **rationalism,** the totality of knowledge can be obtained by strict adherence to the forms and rules of logic. The underlying assumptions of rationalism are (1) that the human mind can understand the world independent of its observable phenomena and (2) that forms of knowledge exist that are independent of our personal experiences. In other words, the rationalistic mode is concerned with what must be true in principle and what is logically possible and permissible.

To the rationalist, abstract formal logic presents a model that must be adhered to in order to think scientifically. As such, it is a normative master science— following its rules makes it possible to distinguish scientific claims from unsound thinking. According to classical rationalists, the Greek philosopher Aristotle (384– 322 B.C.E.) made the definitive exploration of the entire subject matter of logic and thus the structure of knowledge and truth. The German philosopher Immanuel Kant (1724–1804) declared:

> Since Aristotle it [i.e., the study of logic] has not had to retrace a single step, unless we choose to consider as improvements the removal of some unnecessary subtleties, or the clearer definition of its matter, both of which refer to the elegance rather than to the solidity of the science. It is remarkable also, that to the present day, it has not been able to make one step in advance, so that, to all appearances, it may be considered as completed and perfect.[3]

The view that knowledge exists a priori and that it is independent of human experience was held way beyond the period of classical rationalism. The supreme embodiment of rationalism in contemporary science is abstract, pure mathematics. Pure mathematics consists of statements that are universally valid, certain, and independent of the empirical world. For example, the statements of pure geometry are considered to be absolute and true by definition. Pure geometry says nothing about reality; its propositions are **tautological,** that is, true by virtue of their logical form alone. Although pure mathematics and formal logic are essential to the scientific approach, their value for the social sciences "exists only in so far as they serve as means to fruitful progress in the subject-matter, and they should be applied, as complex tools always should, only when and where they can help and do not hinder progress."[4]

---

# Basic Assumptions of Science

The scientific approach is grounded on a set of basic **assumptions** that are unproven and unprovable. These fundamental premises are necessary prerequisites for the conduct of scientific discourse. **Epistemology,** the study of the foundations of knowledge, examines the nature of these premises and how they work. By examining these assumptions, we can better understand the scientific approach and its claim of superiority over other approaches to knowledge.

1. *Nature is orderly.* The basic assumption of the scientific approach is that there is a recognizable regularity and order in the natural world; events do not occur randomly. Even within a rapidly changing environment, scientists assume that a degree of order and structure exists and that change is also patterned and can be understood.

The rationalist concept of nature does not refer to omnipotent or supernatural forces. In science, nature encompasses all empirically observable objects, conditions, and events that exist independent of human intervention, including human beings as biological systems. The laws of nature do not prescribe but, rather, describe what is actually happening. However, order and regularity in nature are not

---

3. Immanuel Kant, *Critique of Pure Reason,* trans. Max Muller (London: Macmillan, 1881), p. 688.
4. Kurt Lewin, *Field Theory in Social Science* (Westport, Conn.: Greenwood Press, 1975), p. 12.

necessarily inherent in the phenomena. For example, there is no logically compelling reason why spring should follow winter, winter follow autumn, autumn follow summer, and summer follow spring. But, because they do, and do so regularly, it is concluded that such regularities underlie other observable phenomena.

2. *We can know nature.* The assumption that we can know nature is no more provable than the assumptions that nature is orderly and that laws of nature do exist. It expresses a basic conviction that human beings are just as much a part of nature as other objects, conditions, and events and that, although we possess unique and distinctive characteristics, we can nevertheless be understood and explained by the same methods by which we study other natural phenomena. Individuals and social phenomena exhibit sufficient recurrent, orderly, and empirically demonstrable patterns to be amenable to scientific investigation. That is, the human mind is not only capable of knowing nature but also of knowing itself and the minds of others.

3. *All natural phenomena have natural causes.* The assumption that all natural phenomena have natural causes or antecedents epitomizes the scientific revolution. By rejecting the belief that forces other than those found in nature operate to cause natural events, the scientific approach opposes fundamentalist religion as well as spiritualism and magic. Moreover, until scientists can explain the occurrence of phenomena in natural terms, they reject the argument that some other, supernatural explanation is necessary. This assumption directs scientific research away from a search for omnipotent supernatural forces and toward the discovery of the empirical regularities and order that underlie natural phenomena. Once delineated, such regularities can serve as evidence for cause-and-effect relationships.

4. *Nothing is self-evident.* Scientific knowledge is not self-evident; claims for truth must be demonstrated objectively. Scientists cannot exclusively rely on tradition, subjective beliefs, and common sense to verify scientific knowledge. Scientists accept that possibilities for error are always present and that even the simplest claims call for objective verification. Therefore, scientific thinking is skeptical and critical.

5. *Knowledge is derived from the acquisition of experience.* If science is to help us understand the real world, it must be **empirical;** that is, it must rely on perceptions, experience, and observations. Perception is a fundamental tenet of the scientific approach, and it is achieved through our senses:

> Science assumes that a communication tie between man and the external universe is maintained through his own sense impressions. Knowledge is held to be a product of one's experiences, as facets of the physical, biological, and social world play upon the senses.[5]

However, knowledge is not acquired only through the perceptions transmitted by the five senses of touch, smell, taste, hearing, and sight. Many events cannot be directly experienced or observed. Observation as a mental activity is not "self-evident" or entirely detached from scientific terms, concepts, and theories

---

5. Gideon Sjoberg and Roger Nett, *A Methodology for Social Research* (New York: Harper & Row, 1968), p. 26.

employed by scientists. As the British philosopher of science Sir Karl Popper (1902–1994) wrote:

> The naive empiricist . . . thinks that we begin by collecting and arranging our experiences, and so ascend the ladder of science. . . . But if I am ordered: "Record what you are experiencing," I shall hardly know how to obey this ambiguous order. Am I to report that I am writing; that I hear a bell ringing; a newsboy shouting; a loudspeaker droning; or am I to report, perhaps, that these noises irritate me? . . . A science needs points of view, and theoretical problems.[6]

Historically, the assumption that scientific knowledge should be based solely upon empirical observations was a reaction against the belief that knowledge is innate in human beings or that "pure reason" alone is sufficient to produce verifiable knowledge.

6. *Knowledge is superior to ignorance.* Closely related to the assumption that we can know ourselves as well as nature is the belief that knowledge should be pursued both for its own sake and for the sake of improving the human condition. The argument that knowledge is superior to ignorance does not, however, mean that everything in nature can or will be known. Rather, scientists assume that all knowledge is tentative and changing. Things that we did not know in the past we know now, and current knowledge may be modified in the future. Truth in science is therefore always relative to the evidence, the methods, and the theories employed, and is always open to modification.

The belief that relative knowledge is better than ignorance is diametrically opposed to epistomologies, systems of knowledge based on absolute truth. As Gideon Sjoberg and Roger Nett put it:

> Certainly the ideal that human dignity is enhanced when man is restless, inquiring, and "soul searching" conflicts with a variety of belief systems that would strive toward a closed system, one based on absolute truth. The history of modern science and its clash with absolute systems bears testimony to this proposition.[7]

True believers already "know" all there is to know. Scientific knowledge threatens the old ways of doing things; it is detrimental to tranquility, stability, and the status quo. In exchange, the scientific approach can offer only tentative truth that is relative to the existing state of knowledge. The strengths and weaknesses of the scientific approach rest on the tentative and relative nature of truth:

> It is a strength in the sense that rational man will in the long run act to correct his own errors. It is a weakness in that scientists, not being so confident of the validity of their own assertions as is the general public, may, in those frequent periods when social crises threaten public security, be overturned by absolutists. Science is often temporarily helpless when its bastions are stormed by overzealous proponents of absolute systems of belief.[8]

---

6. Karl R. Popper, *The Logic of Scientific Discovery* (New York: Science Editions, 1961), p. 106.
7. Sjoberg and Nett, *A Methodology for Social Research*, p. 25.
8. Ibid., p. 26.

# Aims of the Social Sciences

Having examined the assumptions of science, we are now in a position to address the question raised earlier: What does science have to offer to people who take an interest in society's problems? The ultimate goal of the social and all other sciences is to produce a cumulative body of verifiable knowledge. Such knowledge enables us to *explain, predict,* and *understand* the empirical phenomena that interest us. Furthermore, a reliable body of knowledge could be used to improve the human condition. But what are scientific explanations? When can we make predictions? When are we justified in claiming that we understand empirical phenomena?

## Scientific Explanation

Why are government expenditures per capita higher in Sweden than in the United States? "Because," someone might respond, "Swedes want their government to spend more." Such an explanation might satisfy the layperson but it would not satisfy social scientists unless they could employ the same reasoning to explain government expenditures per capita in other political systems. In fact, government expenditures per capita in Britain have decreased since the Conservative party won national elections in the 1980s, although it has been reported that most Britons want their government to spend more.

The social scientist's aim is to provide general explanations for "Why?" questions. When scientists ask for an explanation of why a given event or behavior has taken place, they ask for a systematic and empirical analysis of the antecedent factors that caused the event or behavior.

Ever since the Scottish philosopher David Hume (1711–1776) expounded his theories on scientific thinking, this application of the term **explanation** has been considered a matter of relating the phenomenon to be explained with other phenomena by means of *general laws.* General laws comprise the framework from which a particular explanation can be derived. In the words of Richard Braithwaite:

> The function of science . . . is to establish general laws covering the behavior of empirical events or objects with which the science in question is concerned, and thereby to enable us to connect together our knowledge of the separately known events, and to make reliable predictions of events as yet unknown. . . . If science is in a highly developed state, . . . the laws which have been established will form a hierarchy in which special laws appear as logical consequences of a small number of highly general laws. . . . If the science is in an early stage of development, . . . the laws may be merely the generalizations involved in classifying things into various classes.[9]

As scientific disciplines progress, their forms of explanation change. Carl Hempel made an important distinction between two basic types of scientific expla-

---

9. Richard B. Braithwaite, *Scientific Explanation* (New York: Harper & Row, 1960), p. 1.

nation: **deductive** and **probabilistic.** The classification is based on the kinds of generalizations that the explanation employs.[10]

*Deductive Explanations.*   A deductive explanation calls for (a) a universal generalization, (b) a statement of the conditions under which the generalization holds true, (c) an event to be explained, and (d) the rules of formal logic. In a deductive explanation, a phenomenon is explained by demonstrating that it can be deduced from an established universal law. For example, a scientific explanation for the return to earth of an object thrown into the air would be based on the law of gravitation. The scientist might state that if all objects exercise a mutual attraction on one another, any particular object is expected to behave in the same way with reference to the earth. The essential condition for a universal law, then, is that it includes all the cases within its domain.

In deductive reasoning, the premises lead necessarily to the conclusion; that is, if and only if the premises are true, the conclusion must be true. If, however, the premises are not true, the conclusion will not be true. For example, let's say that in democracies, elected officials seek reelection (untrue premise); John Brown is an elected official; therefore, John Brown seeks reelection (untrue conclusion). Deductive explanations are the most powerful type of scientific explanation because their conclusions must be true if their premises are true, and because they explain unique events as well as common behaviors.

*Probabilistic Explanations.*   Not all scientific explanations are based on universal laws. This is particularly the case in the social sciences because few, if any, meaningful universal generalizations can be made. Social scientists use primarily probabilistic or inductive explanations. For example, a political scientist might explain a particular increase in government expenditures in the United States by suggesting that the rise was a response to adverse economic conditions because in the past, increased expenditures have followed severe economic conditions. This explanation links the phenomenon to be explained to an earlier occurrence—the country's economic conditions. The scientist proposes such an explanation because it has been found that there is a relationship between economic conditions and government expenditures. The relationship, however, cannot be expressed by a law in universal form because not every case of adverse economic conditions brings about an increase in government expenditures. The scientist can only suggest that there is a high probability that severe economic conditions will induce increases in government expenditures, or that in a high percentage of all cases investigated, severe economic conditions led to increases in government expenditures. General explanations of this type are referred to as *probabilistic* or *inductive* explanations, and they derive from probabilistic generalizations. In other words, a probabilistic explanation uses generalizations that express either an

10. Carl G. Hempel, *Philosophy of Natural Science* (Englewood Cliffs, N.J.: Prentice-Hall, 1966), ch. 5.

arithmetic ratio between phenomena ($n$ percent of $X = Y$) or generalizations that express tendencies ($X$ tends to cause $Y$).

The major limitation of probabilistic or inductive generalizations, in comparison to universal laws, is that conclusions cannot be drawn about specific cases with complete certainty. If, for instance, you know that 70 percent of the members of an ethnic group have voted for the Democratic party for the past 20 years, you still cannot conclude with absolute certainty that the probability that a particular member of the group voted Democratic is 7/10. Other factors besides membership in the given group for which the generalization is true may influence the behavior of the individual in question. The particular person may also be a member of a social club with a long tradition of Republican political attachment, and this may outweigh the influence of his or her ethnic identification. The logic of inference in scientific research will be further discussed in Chapter 19.

## Prediction

Deductive and probabilistic explanations constitute one important component of scientific knowledge. **Prediction** constitutes the other. In fact, the ability to make correct predictions has been regarded as the outstanding characteristic of science. If knowledge is deficient, prediction is impossible. For example, if you know that 2 times 6 is 12, you can predict the outcome of a count of two combined groups of six objects. If you know that the freezing point of water is 32° F or 0° C, you can predict what will happen to your car if an antifreeze is not added to the water in the radiator during the winter. If you know that governments increase their spending during economic recessions, you can predict that future recessions will bring increases in government spending. If you know that job placement programs solve unemployment problems, you can predict that high rates of unemployment will decline following implementation of such programs.

The expectation that scientific knowledge should lead to accurate predictions is based on the argument that *if* it is known that $X$ causes $Y$ and that $X$ is present, *then* you can predict that $Y$ will occur. Underlying this argument is the assumption that if a universal law or a probabilistic generalization is *both* recognized and true—that the antecedent conditions required for the outcome have been fulfilled—then the only reasons for failing to make an accurate prediction are (1) that the law or the generalization is not in fact true or (2) that the antecedent conditions are incorrectly perceived. Thus let us say, if the problem of unemployment remains unsolved, it is either because the generalization that job placement programs solve unemployment problems is not true or because job placement programs have been erroneously identified as activities aimed at solving unemployment.

Recalling the deductive mode of explanations, we can see that the process of prediction is, logically speaking, the *reverse* of the process of explanation. In the course of prediction, the antecedent observations merely point out that the initial conditions are present. Universal laws or probabilistic generalizations are used to substantiate the prediction that if certain conditions are present, they will be followed by specific consequences.

The logical structure of scientific explanations and predictions can now be explained.[11] This structure consists of the following parts:

1. A statement $E$ describing the specific phenomenon or event to be explained.
2. A set of statements $A_1$ to $A_n$, describing specific relevant conditions that are antecedent or causally related to the phenomenon to be described by $E$.
3. A set of universal laws or probabilistic generalizations $L_1$ to $L_n$, that state: "Whenever events of the kind described by $A_1$ to $A_n$, take place, an event of the kind described by $E$ occurs."

For these three parts to constitute an explanation of the event or the phenomenon, they must fulfill at least two conditions:

1. Statement $E$ must be deducible from statements $A$ and $L$ taken together but not from either set of statements separately.
2. Statements $A$ and $L$ must be true.

The following is a symbolic presentation of the logical structure of scientific explanations and predictions.

$$L_1, \ldots L_n$$
$$A_1, \ldots A_n$$
$$\overline{\text{Therefore, } E}$$

The logical structure of explanation is identical to that of prediction. The difference between them lies in the perspective of the scientist. In the case of explanation, $E$ is a past event relative to the scientist's present vantage point, and he or she seeks the appropriate $L$'s and $A$'s from which to deduce the explanation of the event; in the case of prediction, the scientist already knows the $L$'s and $A$'s and seeks a future event implied by the former.

## Understanding

The third component of social scientific knowledge is understanding. The term *understanding* is used in two radically different ways—***Verstehen*** (or empathic understanding) and predictive understanding. These different usages evolved because the subject matter of the social sciences is human behavior and because social scientists are observers as well as participants in the subject matter of their disciplines. In the words of Hans Zetterberg:

> Symbols are the stuff out of which cultures and societies are made. . . . For example, a sequence of conception, birth, nursing and weaning represents the *biological* reality of parenthood. But in analyzing human parenthood we find, in

11. The following discussion draws on Richard S. Rudner, *Philosophy of Social Science* (Englewood Cliffs, N.J.: Prentice-Hall, 1966), p. 60.

addition to the biological reality, a complex of symbols [e.g., values, norms] dealing with the license to have children, responsibilities for their care and schooling, rights to make some decisions on their behalf, obligations to launch them by certain social rituals. . . . Our language thus contains codifications of what parents are and what they shall do and what shall be done to them, and all these sentences in our language represent the *social* reality of parenthood. Social reality, in this as in other cases, consists of symbols.[12]

But are symbols and, by implication, human behavior amenable to investigation by the same methodology that is used in the natural sciences? Is the subject matter of the social sciences so complex and distinct that a unique scientific methodology ought to be developed? Do social scientists, unlike natural scientists, have to "get inside" their subject matter in order to understand it?

*The* Verstehen *Tradition.*    According to the *Verstehen* (German for "empathy") tradition, the natural and social sciences are distinctive bodies of knowledge because of a divergence in the nature of their subject matter.

Adherents to this tradition contend that natural and social scientists must employ different methods of research. For example, the social scientist must understand both the historical dimension of human behavior and the subjective aspects of human experience. The German sociologist Max Weber (1864–1930) argued that if social scientists are to understand the behavior of individuals and groups, they must learn to "put themselves into the place of the subject of inquiry." They must gain an understanding of the other's view of reality, of his or her symbols, values and attitudes.[13]

More recently, the **interpretive approach** emerged as an offspring of the *Verstehen* tradition. Kenneth Gergen, a proponent of the approach, has stated:

A fundamental difference exists between the bulk of the phenomena of concern to the natural as opposed to the sociobehavioral scientist. There is ample reason to believe that the phenomena of focal concern to the latter are far less stable (enduring, reliable, or replicable) than those of interest to the former. . . . To place the matter squarely, it may be ventured that with all its attempts to emulate natural science inquiry, the past century of sociobehavioral research and theory has failed to yield a principle as reliable as Archimedes' principle of hydrostatics or Galileo's law of uniformly accelerated motion.[14]

The methodology of the *Verstehen* approach is elaborated in Chapter 12.

*Predictive Understanding.*    In contrast to the *Verstehen* tradition, **logical empiricists** take the position that social scientists can attain objective knowledge

12. Hans L. Zetterberg, *On Theory and Verification in Sociology,* 3d enlarged ed. (Totowa, N.J.: Bedminster Press, 1965), pp. 1–2. See also, Kenneth J. Gergen, *Toward Transformation of Social Knowledge* (New York: Springer-Verlag, 1982).

13. Max Weber, *The Theory of Social and Economic Organization,* trans. A. M. Henderson and Talcott Parsons (New York: Free Press, 1964).

14. Gergen, *Toward Transformation of Social Knowledge,* p. 12.

in the study of the social as well as the natural world. They contend that the social and the natural sciences can be investigated by the same scientific methodology. Furthermore, logical empiricists see empathic understanding as a helpful route to discovery. But discoveries must still be validated by empirical observation if they are to be integrated into the scientific body of knowledge. (The idea of discovery versus validation is discussed in greater detail later in this chapter.)

# The Roles of Methodology

The sciences, then, are not united by their subject matter but rather by their methodology. What sets the scientific approach apart from other modes of acquiring knowledge are the assumptions on which it is based and its methodology.

A scientific **methodology** is a system of explicit rules and procedures upon which research is based and against which claims for knowledge are evaluated. This system is neither unchangeable nor infallible. Rather, the rules and procedures are constantly being improved; scientists look for new means of observation, analysis, logical **inference,** and generalization. As these are developed and found to be congruent with the underlying assumptions of the scientific approach, they are incorporated into the system of rules that govern the scientific methodology. Hence, scientific methodology is first and foremost self-correcting:

> Science does not desire to obtain conviction for its propositions at *any* price. [A] proposition must be supported by logically acceptable evidence, which must be weighed carefully and tested by the well-known canons of necessary and probable inference. It follows that the *method* of science is more stable, and more important to men of science, than any particular result achieved by its means. In virtue of its method, the scientific enterprise is a self-corrective process. It appeals to no special revelation or authority whose deliverances are indubitable and final. It claims no infallibility, but relies upon the methods of developing and testing hypotheses for assured conclusions. The canons of inquiry are themselves discovered in the process of reflection, and may themselves become modified in the course of study. The method makes possible the noting and correction of errors by continued application of itself.[15]

The methodology of the social sciences has evolved slowly. Within this evolution, the continuous interchange of ideas, information, and criticism made it possible to firmly establish, or institutionalize, commonly accepted rules and procedures and to develop corresponding methods and techniques. This system of rules and procedures is the *normative* component of the scientific methodology. Because they define the "rules of the game," scientific norms set the standards to be followed in scientific research and analysis. The rules in turn enable communication, constructive criticism, and scientific progress.

15. Morris R. Cohen and Ernest Nagel, *An Introduction to Logic and Scientific Method* (Orlando, Fla.: Harcourt Brace Jovanovich, 1962), pp. 395–396.

## Methodology Provides Rules for Communication

Anatol Rapoport illustrated the general problem of communication between two people who have not shared a common experience with the following anecdote:

> A blind man asked someone to explain the meaning of "white."
> "White is a color," he was told, "as, for example, white snow."
> "I understand," said the blind man. "It is a cold and damp color."
> "No, it doesn't have to be cold and damp. Forget about snow. Paper, for instance, is white."
> "So it rustles?" asked the blind man.
> "No indeed, it need not rustle. It is like the fur of an albino rabbit."
> "A soft, fluffy color?" the blind man wanted to know.
> "It need not be soft either. Porcelain is white, too."
> "Perhaps it is a brittle color, then," said the blind man.[16]

A major function of methodology is to help the blind man "see," to facilitate communication between researchers who either have shared or want to share a common experience. Furthermore, by making the rules of methodology explicit, public, and accessible, a framework for replication and constructive criticism is set forth. **Replication**—the repetition of an investigation in exactly the same way either by the same or other scientists and researchers—is a safeguard against unintentional error, or deception. Constructive criticism implies that as soon as claims for knowledge are made, we can ask the following questions: "Does the explanation (or prediction) logically follow from the assumptions?" "Are the observations accurate?" "What were the methods of observation?" "Was the testing procedure valid?" "Did other factors interfere in drawing conclusions?" "Should the findings be taken as evidence that another explanation is correct?" and so forth. We shall see throughout this book that such questions comprise the criteria for evaluating claims for scientific knowledge, whether old or new.

## Methodology Provides Rules for Reasoning

Although empirical observations are fundamental to the scientific approach, they do not "speak for themselves." Empirical observations or facts must be ordered and related into systematic, logical structures. The essential tool of the scientific approach, along with factual observations, is **logic**—the system of valid reasoning that permits drawing reliable inferences from factual observations. Logical procedures take the form of closely interdependent series of propositions that support each other. By using logic as the foundation of scientific thinking, scientific methodology enhances the internal consistency of the scientific claims for knowledge. That logic, as the study of the foundations and principles of reasoning, is crucial to the scientific approach can be seen in the vestige of its Latin root in the terms for many areas of study—for example, bio*logy,* anthropo*logy,* socio*logy,* crimino*logy,* and geo*logy.*

16. Anatol Rapoport, *Operational Philosophy* (New York: Wiley, 1969), p. 12.

A scientific methodology (or methodologies) therefore requires competence in logical reasoning and analysis. In the following chapters we will discuss the elements of logic—the rules for definition, classification, and forms of deductive and probabilistic (inductive) inferences; theories of probability; sampling procedures; systems of calculus; and rules of measurement—that constitute the methodological tool kit of the social scientist. It is important to remember that through the use of logic, science progresses in a systematic and, sometimes, revolutionary way.

## Methodology Provides Rules for Intersubjectivity

Scientific methodology explains the *accepted criteria* for empirical objectivity (truth) and the methods and techniques for validation. Objectivity and validation are highly interdependent; empirical objectivity depends on validation, so much so that the scientist cannot make claims for objectivity until other scientists have verified his or her findings. **Intersubjectivity,** which involves the sharing of observations and factual information among scientists, is indispensable because logical reasoning alone does not guarantee empirical objectivity.

We have seen that logic is concerned with valid reasoning, not with empirical truth or validated facts. A fact is either certainly or probably true when objective evidence exists to support it. By contrast, a claim for knowledge is valid when it is logically derived, or inferred, from prior assumptions. Thus, scientists can make an erroneous inference from validated facts (truth statements) if they reason incorrectly. However, they can also make an erroneous inference if they reason correctly (logically valid reasoning) but do not employ validated facts: "The truth of an assertion is related to experience; the validity of an assertion is related to its inner consistency or its consistency with other assertions."[17]

Thus, the forms of deductive and probabilistic explanations (predictions) discussed earlier relate only to logically valid reasoning. In other words, the *validity* of their conclusions follows strictly from their antecedent assumptions. However, their *truth* cannot be established or validated solely on logical grounds. Truth has to be validated with empirical evidence. As the following example demonstrates, strict adherence to logical reasoning without studying the empirical facts can lead to what may be an absurd inference, or conclusion:

> All human beings are power-motivated organisms.
> All power-motivated organisms are destructive.
> Therefore, all human beings are destructive.

Given that the criteria for empirical objectivity and the methods for verification are products of the human mind (in contrast to the belief that truth is an absolute given), the term *intersubjectivity* is more appropriate than *objectivity* to describe the process. To be intersubjective, knowledge in general—and the

17. Ibid., p. 18.

scientific methodology in particular—has to be communicable. Thus if one scientist conducts an investigation, another scientist can replicate it and compare the two sets of findings. If the methodology is correct and (we assume) the conditions under which the study was made or the events occurred have not changed, we would expect the findings to be similar. Indeed, conditions may change and new circumstances emerge. But the significance of intersubjectivity lies in the ability of a scientist to understand and evaluate the methods of others and to conduct similar observations so as to validate empirical facts and conclusions. In the words of Abraham Kaplan: "The methodological question is always limited to whether what is reported as an observation can be used in subsequent inquiry even if the particular observer is no longer a part of the context." [18]

# Scientific Revolution

As we have seen in the previous sections, scientific knowledge is knowledge provable by both reason and evidence from the senses (experience). The importance of the scientific methodology is to be found primarily in its provision of a language for communication, rules for reasoning, and procedures and methods for observation and validation. In this sense, methodology is normative—it demands conformity: scientists reject claims for knowledge that do not conform to the rules and procedures prescribed by the methodology. But does methodological conformity hinder new discoveries and, by implication, scientific progress? Furthermore, because scientists are members of scientific communities governed by conventions, norms, rituals, and power relations that may be incompatible with the objective pursuit of knowledge, can scientific communities hinder scientific progress?

Philosophers of science and social theorists have long been concerned with the dangers of conformity and dogma in science. As Scott Greer put it, "If we are lucky and our scientific knowledge accumulates, it may spiral upward; it may also revolve at the same level, a merry-go-round of fashion; or it may spiral downward, from theory to doctrine to dogma." [19] Among the various attempts to describe scientific revolutions from a sociological-political perspective, Thomas Kuhn's theory of scientific communities is particularly provocative and worth outlining in some detail.

## Normal versus Revolutionary Science

Kuhn's theory makes a distinction between *normal science* and *revolutionary science.* **Normal science** is the routine verification of the theory (or paradigm) dominant in any historical period. For this type of science, validation and testing are parts of a puzzle-solving activity. In Kuhn's words:

---

18. Abraham Kaplan, *The Conduct of Inquiry* (New York: Harper & Row, 1968), p. 128.
19. Scott Greer, *The Logic of Social Inquiry* (New Brunswick, N.J.: Transaction Books, 1989), pp. 3–4.

"Normal science" means research firmly based upon one or more past scientific achievements, achievements that some particular scientific community acknowledges for a time as supplying the foundation of its practice. Today such achievements are recounted, though seldom in their original form, by science textbooks, elementary and advanced. These textbooks expound the body of accepted theory, illustrate many or all of its successful applications, and compare these applications with exemplary observations and experiments.[20]

Such scientific texts socialize students and practitioners into the scientific community. They define the kinds of problems to be investigated, the kinds of assumptions and concepts to be employed, and the kinds of research methods to be used. Historically, such texts and research

> were able to do so because they shared two essential characteristics. Their achievement was sufficiently unprecedented to attract an enduring group of adherents away from competing modes of scientific activity. Simultaneously, it was sufficiently open-ended to leave all sorts of problems for the redefined group of practitioners to resolve."[21]

Kuhn terms achievements that share these two attributes **paradigms.** He suggests that paradigms are closely related to the idea of normal science:

> By choosing [the term *paradigm*], I mean to suggest that some accepted examples of actual scientific practice—examples which include law, theory, application, and instrumentation together—provide models from which spring particular coherent traditions of scientific research. . . . The study of paradigm . . . is what mainly prepares the student for membership in the particular scientific community with which he will later practice.[22]

Examples of paradigms might include the dialectical materialism of Marx or Freud's theory of the sexual origins of personality.

Furthermore, because scientists join a professional scientific community whose leaders have all learned the same conceptual and methodological foundations of their discipline from the same sources, their subsequent research will rarely evoke disagreement or criticism over fundamentals. Scientists whose research is grounded in a shared paradigm are psychologically committed to the same rules, norms, and standards of scientific practice: "That commitment and the apparent consensus it produces are prerequisites for normal science, [that is], for the genesis and continuation of a particular research tradition."[23]

Instead of neutral scientists, Kuhn views normal scientific communities as groups of partisans advocating and defending the established paradigm. Yet adherence to a paradigm should not necessarily arrest scientific progress. Paradigms, as organizing principles, are necessary; without them, scientific research could not

20. Thomas S. Kuhn, *The Structure of Scientific Revolutions,* 2d ed. (Chicago: University of Chicago Press, 1970), p. 10.
21. Ibid.
22. Ibid.
23. Ibid., pp. 10–11.

take place as a collective enterprise: "Acquisition of a paradigm and of the more esoteric type of research it permits is a sign of maturity in the development of any given scientific field."[24] However, normal science perpetuates itself and thereby constrains change and innovation.

## Revolutionary Science

In contrast to normal science, Kuhn views **revolutionary science** as the abrupt development of a *rival paradigm*. Paradigm change is revolution in science, and can be accepted only gradually by a scientific community. For example, the paradigm that human intelligence is a product of both the sociocultural environment and genetic processes transformed the earlier paradigm that intelligence is determined entirely by genetic processes. The new paradigm revolutionized the study of personality and human behavior and became the cornerstone of many social, educational, and economic policies.

The process of rejecting a dominant paradigm begins, according to Kuhn, with attempts to verify the paradigm. As scientists empirically test the various dimensions and implications of a dominant paradigm, its congruence with empirical research findings becomes tenuous. Kuhn terms such incongruences *anomalies* and proposes that anomalies become more noticeable as validation or problem-solving activities proceed. At some point a rival paradigm is constructed. Conflict emerges between the supporters of the old paradigm and the supporters of the new. Finally, the scientific community accepts the new paradigm and returns to the activities typical of the normal science. The period of transition from old to new paradigms nonetheless produces uncertainty and cleavages in the scientific community. This period, which may take decades, is characterized by random research, aimless validation, and accidental discoveries, which influence how and when the revolutionary paradigm is enthroned.

Scientific revolutions are therefore rare. Scientists devote most of their time to normal science. They are *not* trying to refute dominant paradigms; they do not perceive anomalies immediately. Perceptions are easily stored in mental categories established long before verification procedures are begun. Scientists, like other professionals, see what they expect to see. For this reason, a dominant paradigm tends to remain the accepted paradigm long after it fails to be congruent with empirical observations.

## A Logic of Discovery?

In Kuhn's view, there can be no *logic* of discovery, only a *sociopsychology* of discovery: anomalies and inconsistencies always abound in science, but a dominant paradigm secures puzzle-solving activities until it is overthrown by a crisis. Is there a rational cause for the appearance of crisis? What makes scientists suddenly aware of one? How is a rival paradigm constructed? Kuhn's thesis does not address these

24. Ibid., p. 11.

questions. For him, there is no logic of discovery but rather group struggle within scientific communities.

In sharp contrast to Kuhn's descriptive view of science is Karl Popper's prescriptive, or normative, theory. Popper maintains that a scientific community ought to be, and to a considerable degree actually is, an "open society" in which no dominant paradigm is ever sacred. Popper states that science has to be in permanent revolution, with criticism at the heart of the scientific enterprise. For him, refutations of claims for knowledge constitute its revolutions:

> In my view the "normal" scientist, as Kuhn describes him, is a person one ought to be sorry for. . . . The "normal" scientist . . . has been badly taught. He has been taught in a dogmatic spirit: he is a victim of indoctrination. He has learned a technique which can be applied without asking for the reason why. . . .[25]

Popper admits that at any moment scientists are "prisoners" caught in their paradigms, expectations, past experiences, and language—with an important qualification:

> We are prisoners in a Pickwickian sense: if we try, we can break out of our framework at any time. Admittedly, we shall find ourselves again in a framework, but it will be a better and roomier one; and we can at any moment break out of it again.[26]

At this point we need to distinguish two contexts of scientific activities: justification and discovery.[27] The **context of justification** refers to the activities of scientists as they attempt to logically and empirically validate claims for knowledge. The scientific method provides the logic of justification, irrespective of how scientists arrive at their insights. The activities of the scientist within the **context of discovery,** however, are not constrained by methodology. Scientific methodologies may facilitate activities that lead toward discovery, but at the initial stages of exploration, no formalized rules or logic can be prescribed as guides. Creativity, insight, imagination, and inspiration are clearly of enormous importance in science. Although these can be nurtured, they cannot be reduced to rules: As John Stuart Mill (1806–1873) said, "There is no science which will enable man to bethink himself of that which will suit his purpose."[28]

# The Research Process

Scientific knowledge is knowledge grounded in both reason and experience (observation). Scientists employ the criteria of logical validity and empirical validation to evaluate claims for knowledge. These two criteria are translated into the

---

25. Karl R. Popper, "Normal Science and Its Dangers," in *Criticism and the Growth of Knowledge,* ed. Irme Lakatos and Alan Musgrave (New York: Cambridge University Press, 1970), p. 53.

26. Ibid., p. 56.

27. See Kaplan, *The Conduct of Inquiry,* pp. 12–18.

28. Ibid., p. 16.

research activities of scientists through the **research process.** The research process is the overall scheme of activities in which scientists engage in order to produce knowledge; it is the paradigm of scientific inquiry.

As illustrated in Figure 1.1, the research process consists of seven main stages: *problem, hypothesis, research design, measurement, data collection, data analysis,* and *generalization.* Each stage affects *theory* and is affected by it as well. In this book, we will discuss extensively each stage as well as the transitions from one stage to the next. For the moment, we will limit ourselves to a general overview of the research process.

The most characteristic feature of the research process is its *cyclic nature.* It usually starts with a problem and ends with a tentative empirical generalization. The generalization ending one cycle is the beginning of the next cycle. This cyclic process continues indefinitely, reflecting the progress of a scientific discipline.

The research process is also *self-correcting.* Scientists test tentative generalizations, or hypotheses, about research problems logically and empirically. If they reject these generalizations, they formulate and test new ones. In the process

**Figure 1.1**
The Main Stages of the Research Process

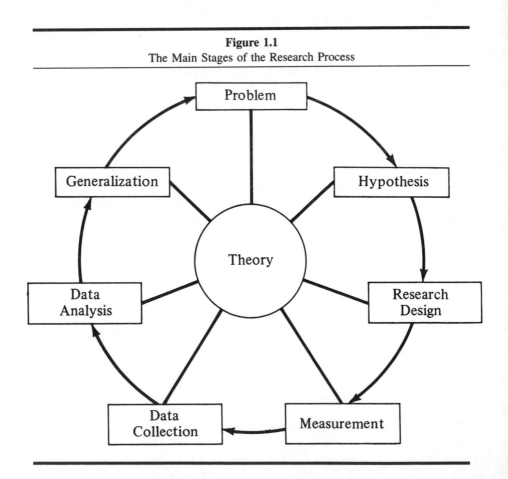

of reformulation, scientists reevaluate all the research operations because a tentative generalization may be rejected not because it is invalid but because of errors in the research operations performed. For example, a researcher will reject the generalization that economic crises lead to increased government spending if it cannot be logically validated and empirically verified. But a generalization can be rejected, *even if it is true,* if the procedures for validation and verification (for example, research design, measurement, or data analysis) are deficient. To minimize the risk of rejecting true generalizations, a scientist reexamines each of the stages in the research process prior to the formulation of new generalizations. This is why scientific methodology is said to be self-correcting. Ideas and theories lack this quality because their purpose is to provide explanations rather than directives for reexamining their basic claims.

Finally, you should be aware that the research process as presented here is somewhat idealized; that is, it is a rational reconstruction of scientific practice:

> The reconstruction idealizes the logic of science only in showing us what it *would* be if it were extracted and refined to utmost purity. . . . [But] not even the greatest of scientists has a cognitive style which is wholly and perfectly logical, and the most brilliant piece of research still betrays its all-too-human divagations.[29]

In practice, the research process occurs

> (1) sometimes quickly, sometimes slowly; (2) sometimes with a very high degree of formalization and vigor, sometimes quite informally, unself-consciously, and intuitively; (3) sometimes through the interaction of several scientists in distinct roles (of, say, "theorist," "research director," "interviewer," "methodologist," "sampling expert," "statistician," etc.), sometimes through the efforts of a single scientist; and (4) sometimes only in the scientist's imagination, sometimes in actual fact.[30]

Therefore, our idealized reconstruction of the research process is not intended to be rigid but rather to convey the underlying themes of social science research.

---

# The Plan of This Book

This book is organized along the major stages of the research process. Chapters 2 and 3 cover the conceptual foundations of empirical research and the relationships between theory and research. They focus on the ideas of concepts, definitions, the functions and structures of theories, models, relations, variables, and the construction of research hypotheses.

Chapter 4 is concerned with ethical and moral questions confronted by social science researchers. In this chapter we deal with issues relating to the rights of research participants, the obligations of scientists, the interactions between par-

29. Ibid., pp. 10–11.
30. Wallace, *The Logic of Science in Sociology,* p. 19.

ticipants and scientists, and professional codes of ethics, which have become increasingly important in planning research projects.

In Chapters 5 and 6, we focus on the research design stage. A research design is the strategy that guides the investigator throughout the process of research. It is a logical model of proof that allows the researcher to draw inferences concerning the causal relations among the phenomena under investigation. As you will see, there are various types of research designs, each of which explains the conditions for accepting or rejecting causal inferences.

Chapter 7 is concerned with the measurement stage of research. During this stage, researchers systematically assign symbols (particularly numbers) to empirical observations. These symbols are in turn amenable to quantitative analyses that reveal information and relations that otherwise could not have been discerned. Numbers can be added, subtracted, percentaged, correlated, and used for describing, explaining, and predicting phenomena.

Typically, scientific generalizations are not based on all the measured observations that might be obtained, but on a relatively small number of cases—a sample. In Chapter 8, we cover the major topics involved with sampling: theory, methods for choosing representative samples, sample size, and sample designs.

The five subsequent chapters cover the data collection stage. In this stage, researchers make and record empirical observations. Data (observations) can be collected by various methods, including structured observation, nonstructured observation, personal interviews, impersonal surveys, public records, or private records. No data collection method is foolproof, nor will one method suit all research problems. Different problems call for different methods, and each method has advantages but also inherent limitations.

Chapter 14 focuses on major topics of data processing, which is the link between data collection and data analysis. During data processing, the observations researchers have gathered in the data collection stage are transformed into a system of conceptual categories. These categories are then translated into coding schemes that also lend themselves to quantitative analysis. These codes can then be recorded and processed by computer. The central issues involved in coding and automatic data processing are also covered in this chapter.

In the next stage of the research process, scientists conduct quantitative, statistical analyses. Statistics are numbers that can be used to summarize, analyze, or evaluate a body of information. It is useful to distinguish between two categories of statistics with their different functions: *descriptive statistics* and *inferential statistics*. Researchers use descriptive statistical procedures to organize, describe, and summarize data. Chapter 15 covers descriptive univariate distributions; Chapter 16, bivariate distributions; and Chapter 17, multivariate data analysis techniques. In Chapter 18, we present methods of index construction and scaling. The second category of statistics, inferential or inductive statistics, makes it possible for researchers to generalize beyond the data in hand, to evaluate differences among groups, and to estimate unknown values. These methods, discussed in Chapter 19, facilitate the conduct of systematic inquiry.

## Summary

**1.** The sciences are united by their methodology, not by their subject matter. What sets the scientific approach apart from other ways of acquiring knowledge is the assumptions on which it is grounded and its methodology.

**2.** The assumptions of the scientific approach are these: nature is orderly, we can know nature, natural phenomena have natural causes, nothing is self-evident, knowledge is derived from the acquisition of experience, and knowledge is tentative but superior to ignorance.

**3.** The methodology of the scientific approach serves three major purposes: it provides rules for communication, rules for logical and valid reasoning, and rules for intersubjectivity (the ability to share knowledge). These three systems of rules allow us to understand, explain, and predict ourselves and our environments in a manner that other systems for producing information (authoritarian, mystical, rationalistic) cannot allow us to do.

**4.** Scientific knowledge is knowledge that can be validated by *both* reason and the evidence of the senses. The scientific method requires strict adherence to the rules of logic and observation. Such adherence discourages dogma because the research process is cyclic and self-correcting. Rational criticism should be at the heart of the scientific enterprise, and science ought to be a permanent revolution. Obviously, scientific communities, like other professional communities, are involved in internal power struggles that are not always conducive to the progress of science. Such power struggles are inevitable. However, claims for knowledge are ultimately accepted only insofar as they are congruent with the assumptions and methodology of science.

## Key Terms for Review

assumptions of science (p. 5)

context of discovery (p. 19)

context of justification (p. 19)

deductive explanation (p. 9)

empirical (p. 6)

epistemology (p. 5)

explanation (p. 8)

inference (p. 13)

interpretive approach (p. 12)

intersubjectivity (p. 15)

logic (p. 14)

logical empiricists (p. 12)

methodology (p. 13)

normal science (p. 16)

paradigm (p. 17)

prediction (p. 10)

probabilistic explanation (p. 9)

rationalism (p. 4)

replication (p. 14)

research process (p. 20)

revolutionary science (p. 18)

science (p. 2)

tautology (p. 5)

*Verstehen* (p. 11)

## Study Questions

1. Compare and contrast the scientific approach with the authoritarian, mystical, and rationalistic modes of knowing.
2. Discuss the assumptions underlying the scientific approach.
3. What are the aims of science as a knowledge-producing system?
4. Describe the research process and its stages.
5. How is science actually carried out, both as a cyclic process of reasoning and observation and as a social institution?

## Additional Readings

Agnew, Neil M., and Sandra W. Pyke. *The Science Game: An Introduction to Research in the Behavioral Sciences.* 6th ed. Englewood Cliffs, N.J.: Prentice-Hall, 1994.

Boulding, Kenneth E. "Science: Our Common Heritage." *Science,* 207 (1980), 831–836.

Cohen, I. Bernard. *Revolution in Science.* Cambridge, Mass.: Belknap Press, 1985.

Fiske, Donald W., and Richard A. Shweder, eds. *Metatheory in Social Science: Pluralisms and Subjectivities.* Chicago: University of Chicago Press, 1986.

Hughes, John A. *A Philosophy of Social Research.* White Plains, N.Y.: Longman, 1980.

Kruskal, William H., ed. *The Social Sciences: Their Nature and Uses.* Chicago: University of Chicago Press, 1986.

Lakatos, Irme. *The Methodology of Scientific Research Programs.* Cambridge: Cambridge University Press, 1978.

O'Hear, Anthony. *An Introduction to the Philosophy of Science.* New York: Oxford University Press, 1989.

Popper, Karl R. In W. W. Bartley, III, ed. *Realism and the Aim of Science.* Lanham, MD: Rowman & Littlefield, 1983.

Scheffler, Israel. *Science and Subjectivity.* 2d ed. Indianapolis: Hackett, 1982.

Taylor, Charles. *Philosophy and the Human Sciences.* New York: Cambridge University Press, 1985.

# CHAPTER 2

# Conceptual Foundations of Research

**Concepts**
Functions of Concepts

**Definitions**
Conceptual Definitions
Operational Definitions
Example: The Definitions of Alienation
The Congruence Problem
Theoretical Import

**Theory: Functions and Types**
What Theory Is Not
Types of Theories
Axiomatic Theory

**Models**
Example: A Model of Policy Implementation

**Theory, Models, and Empirical Research**
Theory before Research
Research before Theory

Can the discovery of an ancient Roman water-driven flour mill in southern France challenge how we conceptualize and subsequently research the life cycles of civilizations? A. Trevor Hodge, a classicist and archaeologist, believes that it can. Archaeologists and historians have traditionally considered slavery to be the cause of the technological decline of the Roman Empire. However, Hodge contends that the mill's size and sophisticated use of waterpower point in another direction. Instead of slavery, he would put greater emphasis on purely technological factors—in this case, the absence of horseshoes and inadequate harnesses—to explain the underutilization of natural resources in the ancient Roman economy.[1]

I N THIS CHAPTER, WE WILL FIRST DISCUSS THE FORMATION OF concepts, the building blocks of theoretical systems. Then, we will distinguish four levels of theory and delineate the models that represent aspects of the real world. Finally, we will explore the links between theory and research.

As we saw in Chapter 1, scientific knowledge is validated by both reason and experience. This implies that social scientists operate at two distinct but interrelated levels—conceptual-theoretical and observational-empirical. Social science research is, then, the outcome of the interaction between these two levels. In this chapter we discuss the basics of the conceptual-theoretical level and the relationships existing among theory, models, and empirical research.

---

# Concepts

Thinking involves the use of language. Language itself is a system of communication composed of symbols and a set of rules permitting various combinations of these symbols. One of the most significant symbols in a language, especially as it relates to research, is the *concept*. A **concept** is an abstraction—a symbol—a representation of an object or one of its properties, or of a behavioral phenomenon. Scientists begin the process of research, then, by forming concepts as a "shorthand" for describing the empirical world. For example, "social status," "role," "power," "bureaucracy," "relative deprivation," and "cohort" are common concepts in political science and sociology. Concepts such as "intelligence," "perception," and "learning" are common among psychologists. Each scientific discipline develops its unique set of concepts. To scientists, these concepts and symbols constitute a professional language. For example, when a social scientist uses the word "cohort," other social scientists immediately know what the term represents: a group of people sharing a demographic characteristic such as age. People untrained in the social sciences would probably consider the term "cohort" to be "jargon."

---

1. A. Trevor Hodge, "A Roman Factory," *Scientific American*, 263(5) (1990): 106–111.

## Functions of Concepts

Concepts serve a number of important functions in social science research. First and foremost, they are the foundation of communication. Without a set of agreed-upon concepts, scientists could not communicate their findings or replicate each other's studies. Communication based on intersubjectivity and shared understanding would be impossible. It is important to remember that concepts are abstracted from perceptions and are used to convey and transmit information. Concepts do not actually exist as empirical phenomena—they are *symbols* of phenomena, not the phenomena themselves. Treating concepts as though they were the concrete phenomena leads to the **fallacy of reification**—the error of regarding abstractions as real rather than the outcome of thinking. For example, it is erroneous to regard a concept such as "power" as having drives, needs, or instincts despite the tendency of some people to speak, or write, as if it did.

Second, concepts introduce a *perspective*—a way of looking at empirical phenomena: "Through scientific conceptualization the perceptual world is given an order and coherence that could not be perceived before conceptualization."[2] The concept enables scientists to relate to some aspect of reality and identify it as a quality common to different examples of the phenomenon in the real world:

> It permits the scientist, in a community of other scientists, to lift his own idiosyncratic experiences to the level of consensual meaning [i.e., intersubjectivity]. It also enables him to carry on an interaction with his environment; he indicates to himself what a concept means and acts toward the designation of that meaning. The concept thus acts as a sensitizer of experience and perception, opening new realms of observation, closing others.[3]

Third, concepts allow scientists to classify and generalize. In other words, scientists structure, categorize, order, and generalize their experiences and observations in terms of concepts. As John McKinney puts it:

> All phenomena are unique in their concrete occurrence; therefore no phenomena actually recur in their concrete wholeness. The meaning of identity is always "identical for the purpose in hand." To introduce *order* with its various scientific implications, including prediction, the scientist necessarily ignores the unique, the extraneous, and [the] nonrecurring, and thereby departs from perceptual experience. This departure is the necessary price he must pay for the achievement of abstract generality. To conceptualize means to generalize to some degree. To generalize means to reduce the number of objects by conceiving of some of them as being identical.[4]

For example, we can overlook the ways in which pine, oak, spruce, fir, palm, and apple differ from one another and grasp their generic resemblance via the concept

2. Norman K. Denzin, *The Research Act,* 3d ed. (Englewood Cliffs, N.J.: Prentice-Hall, 1989), p. 38.
3. Ibid.
4. John C. McKinney, *Constructive Typology and Social Theory* (Norwalk, Conn.: Appleton & Lang, 1966), p. 9.

---

### Four Functions of Concepts

- Concepts provide a common language, which enables scientists to communicate with one another.
- Concepts give scientists a *perspective*—a way of looking at phenomena.
- Concepts allow scientists to classify their experiences and to generalize from them.
- Concepts are components of theories—they define a theory's content and attributes.

---

"tree." "Tree" is the general concept that enables us to grasp a large number of unique characteristics such as color, height, or age, and comprehend them in a given order. "Tree" is also an abstract concept in the sense that the unique attributes of pine, oak, spruce, fir, palm, and apple are lost in the conceptualization process. This process of abstraction and generalization enables scientists to delineate the essential attributes of different types of empirical phenomena. However, once a concept is formed, it is not a perfect, fully encompassing symbol of what it represents—its content is inevitably limited to the attributes the scientist considers essential.

Fourth, concepts serve as components of theories and thus of explanations and predictions. Concepts are the most critical elements in any theory because they define its content and attributes. For example, the concepts "power" and "legitimacy" define the substance of theories of governance. The concepts "individualism" and "Protestantism" define and shape Durkheim's theory of suicide. This theory predicts suicide rates in many Western societies as a function of the relationships between individualism and religion. The concept "relative deprivation" is central to theories of violence, while "supply" and "demand" are the pillars of economic theory. Such concepts, when linked in a systematic and logical way, lead to theories; concept formation and theory construction are therefore closely related.

---

# Definitions

If concepts are to serve the functions of communication, sensitivity to and organization of experience, generalization, and theory construction, they have to be clear, precise, and agreed-upon. Everyday language, however, is often vague, ambiguous, and imprecise. Concepts such as "power," "bureaucracy," and "satisfaction" mean different things to different people and are used in different contexts to designate various things. Usually, this does not create major problems in everyday communication. But science cannot progress with ambiguous and imprecise language.

Because of the need for precision, any scientific discipline is concerned with its vocabulary by necessity. Social scientists have attempted to establish a clear and precise body of concepts (abstractions) to characterize their subject matter. Although many concepts have been invented, used, refined, and discarded, many concepts remain ambiguous and inconsistent. This should not be too surprising. Social scientists face the difficult problem of distinguishing their concepts from those commonly used by the public they want to study. But as the social sciences progress, so will their vocabulary. To achieve clarity and precision in the use of concepts during research, scientists employ two major types of definitions: *conceptual* and *operational*.

## Conceptual Definitions

Definitions that describe concepts by using other concepts are **conceptual definitions.** For example, "power" has been conceptually defined as the ability of an actor (for example, an individual, a group, the state) to get another actor to do something that the latter would not otherwise do. The conceptual definition of "relative deprivation" is an actor's perception of a discrepancy between his or her "value expectations" and his or her "value capabilities."[5]

In these two examples, a number of concepts are used to define other concepts. "Value expectations" and "value capabilities" are themselves concepts. But the process of definition might not stop here. In the case of "relative deprivation," a person unfamiliar with the theory is likely to ask, "What are 'values,' 'capabilities,' 'expectations,' and 'perceptions'?" These concepts call for further clarification. "Expectations," for instance, have been defined as a manifestation of the prevailing norms set by the immediate economic, social, cultural, and political environment. But what is meant by "norms," "immediate," "social," "cultural," "economic," and "political"? These concepts can be defined by still other concepts, and so on.

At a certain point in this process, scientists encounter concepts that cannot be defined by other concepts. These are called **primitive terms.** For example, colors, sounds, smells, and tastes are primitive terms. Primitive terms are not vague and ambiguous. Scientists and laypersons agree on their meaning, which is usually conveyed by clear-cut empirical examples. For example, a scientist can show a real-life behavior and define it as "anger." Technically, this demonstration of the term "anger" is used as an **ostensive definition;** that is, "anger" represents a set of easily observable behaviors. As such, "anger" can be used as a primitive term in theorizing and research.

Conceptual definitions, therefore, consist of primitive terms and derived terms. **Derived terms** are those that can be defined by the use of primitive terms. Thus if there is an agreement on the primitive terms "individual," "interact," and "regularly," we can define the concept "group" (derived term) as two or more

---

5. Ted R. Gurr, *Why Men Rebel* (Princeton, N.J.: Princeton University Press, 1970), p. 24.

individuals who interact regularly. Derived terms are more efficient to use than primitive terms; it is easier to say the word "group" than to constantly repeat the primitive terms that compose the definition of "group."[6]

A crucial point to remember is that conceptual definitions are neither true nor false. As pointed out earlier, concepts are symbols that permit communication. Conceptual definitions are either useful for communication and research, or they are not. While you can criticize the intelligibility of a definition or question whether it is being used consistently, there is no point in criticizing a conceptual definition for not being true. The definition is what the definer says it is.

To summarize, conceptual definitions that enhance communication share the following essential attributes:

- A definition must point out the unique attributes or qualities of whatever is defined. It must include all cases it covers and exclude all cases not covered.
- A definition should not be circular; that is, it must not contain any element of the phenomenon or object being defined. Defining "bureaucracy" as an organization that has bureaucratic qualities or "power" as a quality shared by powerful people does not enhance communication.
- A definition should be stated positively. Defining "intelligence" as a property that lacks color, weight, and character obviously does not enhance communication because there are many other properties that lack color, weight, and character. Positive definitions point to the attributes that are unique only to the concept they define.
- A definition should use clear terms, terms whose meaning is agreed upon by everyone. A term such as "conservative," for example, means different things to different people, and thus it should not be used in a definition.

## Operational Definitions

Often the empirical attributes or events that are represented by concepts cannot be observed directly. Examples include the concepts "power," "relative deprivation," "intelligence," and "satisfaction" and, in general, nonbehavioral properties such as perceptions, values, and attitudes. In such cases, researchers have to infer the empirical existence of the concept. They make inferences of this kind by using operational definitions, definitions that provide concepts with empirical referents.

**Operational definitions** bridge the conceptual-theoretical and empirical-observational levels. An operational definition sets forth a set of procedures that describe the activities a researcher needs to perform to empirically establish the existence, or degree of existence, of a phenomenon described by a concept. That is, they define *what to do* and *what to observe* in order to bring the phenomenon to be studied within the range of the researcher's experience and understanding. Such definitions make the meanings of concepts concrete by laying out the mea-

6. Paul D. Reynolds, *A Primer in Theory Construction* (New York: Macmillan, 1971), pp. 45–48.

suring procedures that provide the empirical criteria for the scientific application of concepts. Operational definitions, therefore, make it possible to confirm the existence of concepts that have no direct observable characteristics.

The idea of operational definitions was developed by the operationist school of thought as exemplified in the works of the physicist P. W. Bridgman. Bridgman's central idea is that the meaning of every scientific concept must be made observable through the use of an operation that tests a specific criterion for applying the concept. The meaning of a concept is fully and exclusively determined by its operational definition. Bridgman explains:

> The concept of length is therefore fixed when the operations by which length is measured are fixed: that is, the concept of length involves as much as and nothing more than the set of operations by which length is determined. In general, we mean by any concept nothing more than a set of operations; *the concept is synonymous with the corresponding set of operations.*[7]

Thus, an operational definition of "length" would specify a procedure involving the use of a ruler for determining the distance between two points. Similarly, the term "harder" as applied, say, to minerals might be operationally defined as follows: "To determine whether mineral $m_4$ is harder than mineral $m_5$, draw a sharp point of a piece of $m_4$ under pressure across the surface of a piece of $m_5$ (test operation); $m_4$ will be said to be harder than $m_5$ only if a scratch is produced (specific test result)."[8] An operational definition of "intelligence" consists of a test to be administered in a certain way in order to measure reasoning ability; the test results are the responses of the individuals tested or a quantitative summary of their responses.

The structure of operational definitions is straightforward. If a given stimulus ($S$) consistently produces a certain reaction ($R$) when applied to an object, the object has the inferred property ($P$). In the last example, an intelligence test (stimulus) is administered to respondents producing test scores ($R$); intelligence ($P$) is inferred from, or defined by, the test scores.

Because the physical manipulation of individuals or events is either impracticable or unethical, many concepts used by social scientists are operationally defined solely on the strength of reactions to specific stimuli, conditions, or situations. Even if we could manipulate individuals through certain operations— say, inducing severe anxiety in a laboratory situation—doing so would involve a number of critical ethical dilemmas, including the right of scientists to do so and the personal rights of the research subjects. (The ethical dilemmas involved in social science research are discussed in Chapter 4.) In such cases, concepts are operationally defined by the subjects' reactions to stimuli such as tests and questionnaires, as well as by aggregate indicators, which will be discussed in later chapters.

7. Percy W. Bridgman, *The Logic of Modern Physics* (New York: Ayer, 1980), p. 5.

8. Carl G. Hempel, *Philosophy of Natural Science* (Englewood Cliffs, N.J.: Prentice-Hall, 1966), p. 89 (edited slightly).

---

### Conceptual and Operational Definitions

- *Conceptual Definitions:* Definitions that describe concepts by using other concepts. Researchers also use *primitive terms,* which are concrete and cannot be defined by other concepts, and *derived terms,* which are constructed by using primitive terms, in conceptual definitions.
- *Operational Definitions:* An operational definition describes a set of procedures a researcher can follow in order to establish the existence of the phenomenon described by a concept. Scientists require the use of operational definitions when a phenomenon cannot be observed directly.

---

What is important to emphasize here is that concepts have both conceptual and operational components. The problem the social scientist faces is that of integrating the two levels. Research can begin either on the conceptual or operational level. But, to stand the test of scientific research and theorizing, the two aspects must support and complement each other. This requirement will be more fully discussed below in the section on congruence.

## Example: The Definitions of Alienation

Let's see how the highly abstract and complex concept "alienation" has been empirically researched. In a pioneering study, Melvin Seeman argued that alienation had been described in the literature as "a sense of the splitting asunder of what was once held together, the breaking of the seamless mold in which values, behavior, and expectations were once cast into interlocking forms."[9] This conceptualization, he suggested, attributes five meanings to alienation, and thus five separate conceptual definitions are called for:

1. *Powerlessness*—the expectation of individuals that their behavior cannot bring about or influence the outcomes they desire.
2. *Meaninglessness*—the perception by individuals that they do not understand decisions made by others or events taking place around them.
3. *Normlessness*—the expectation that socially unacceptable behavior (e.g., cheating) is now required to achieve certain goals.
4. *Isolation*—the feeling of separateness that comes from rejecting socially approved values and goals.
5. *Self-estrangement*—the denial of the image of the "self" as defined by the immediate group or society at large.

In later research, Seeman and other researchers operationally defined these five concepts by constructing questionnaire items for each of the attributes or dimen-

---

9. Melvin Seeman, "On the Meaning of Alienation," in *Continuities in the Language of Social Research,* ed. Paul Lazarsfeld, Ann Pasanella, and Morris Rosenberg (New York: Free Press, 1972), pp. 25–34.

**Figure 2.1**

Transition from the Conceptual to the Observational Level:
The Case of Alienation

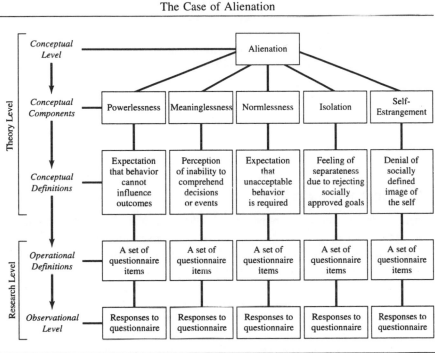

sions referred to by the concepts. The responses of individuals to the entire questionnaire defined the empirical existence of each dimension. For example, researchers used the following question as a means of operationalizing "powerlessness": "Suppose your town was considering a regulation that you believed to be very unjust or harmful. What do you think you could do?" Individuals who responded that they could do nothing were categorized as powerless. Other questions used to define powerlessness operationally were: (1) If you made an effort to change this regulation, how likely is it that you would succeed? (2) If such a case arose, how likely is it that you would actually do something about it? (3) Would you ever try to influence a local decision? (4) Suppose Congress were considering a law that you believed to be very unjust or harmful. What do you think you could do? (5) Would you ever try to influence an act of Congress?[10]

Figure 2.1 illustrates how the researchers transformed the concept of alienation from the conceptual to the observational level. Although "alienation" cannot be directly observed, its empirical existence can, however, be inferred. To establish its empirical existence, researchers first defined its conceptual components or

10. David Nachmias, "Modes and Types of Political Alienation," *British Journal of Sociology*, 24 (1976): 478–493.

dimensions, as we have listed them above. These conceptual definitions indicated that each dimension of alienation referred to different empirical phenomena. For example, the dimensions of powerlessness and normlessness involved an individual's expectations about behavior, whereas isolation involved attitudes toward social goals and beliefs.

Next, researchers constructed operational definitions; in this example, the questionnaire items served as operation definitions. The questionnaire items thus transformed the conceptual definitions into behaviors that could be directly observed. Researchers then administered the questionnaire items (operational definitions). Finally, from the responses to the questionnaire, they were able to infer the extent to which the five dimensions of alienation actually existed on the empirical level.

## The Congruence Problem

When researchers make the transition from the conceptual level to the empirical-observational level, or vice versa, two important issues arise. The first is the degree of **congruence** or agreement between the conceptual and the operational definitions. If "intelligence" is defined conceptually as "the ability to think abstractly" and operationally by an intelligence test, what is the degree of congruence between the two definitions? Does the score achieved by a certain individual in an intelligence test represent everything that the conceptual definition of "intelligence" conveys? Scientists evaluate the degree of congruence between a conceptual definition and an operational definition with the aid of tests of validity, such as those to be discussed in Chapter 7. However, at this stage, we need to emphasize that no absolute criterion has been found for confirming congruence, and there may indeed be situations in which an operational definition does not cover all the elements of a conceptual definition. Improving operational definitions and extending the degree of congruence between them and conceptual definitions constitute important challenges to social scientists.

## Theoretical Import

The second major issue involved in the transition from the conceptual to the observational level arises when concepts cannot be defined operationally; that is, they cannot be observed either directly or indirectly. For example, "ego," "Oedipus complex," "dialectical materialism," "subconscious," "marginal utility," and "public interest" are concepts for which no satisfactory operational definitions have yet been constructed.

According to the orthodox operational approach, a concept that cannot be operationally defined (at least in principle) should not be used in scientific research because it is not amenable to intersubjective verification. In other words, an operational definition is needed in order to enable scientists to replicate each other's research. Without it, the investigator cannot be certain that he or she is observing the same phenomenon. This lack of certainty can lead to inconsistent research. The scientific meaning of a concept can thus be established only by constructing a set of operations (instruments of observation); to know these operations is to understand a concept and to be able to investigate empirically the phenomenon that it represents. Historically, this stringent approach fulfilled the important function of separating empirical science from metaphysics. But when carried to its extreme, the orthodox operational approach becomes problematic.

Scientists should evalute scientific concepts not only in terms of their observability but also in terms of their **theoretical import;** that is, some concepts acquire meaning only in the context of the theory in which they are introduced. For example, the concept "anomie" becomes meaningful in the context of Durkheim's suicide theory, the concept "ego" gains import in the context of psychoanalytic theory, and "public interest" cannot be understood independently from a theory of democracy. Carl Hempel's idea of "systematic import" has influenced current practice:

> Scientific systematization requires the establishment of diverse connections, by law or theoretical principles, between different aspects of the empirical world, which are characterized by scientific concepts. Thus, the concepts of science are the knots in a network of systematic interrelationships in which laws and theoretical principles form the threads. . . .
>
> Empirical import as reflected in clear criteria of application, on which operationalism rightly puts much emphasis, is not the only desideratum for scientific concepts: systematic import is another indispensable requirement. In scientific inquiry, concept formation and theory formation must go hand in hand.[11]

That is, not only are scientific concepts to be evaluated with reference to their observability, but their theoretical import must also be considered. In other words, concepts gain empirical meaning from operational definitions and gain theoretical meaning within the context of the theory within which they are employed. Theory, as indicated in Figure 1.1, plays a vital and central role in the research process. It is not only an important source for the generation of problems and hypotheses, as discussed in Chapter 3, but, just as important, the meaning and significance of key concepts can only be interpreted within the context of a theory.

---

# Theory: Functions and Types

Having discussed concepts, conceptual and operational definitions, and the idea of theoretical import, we can now turn to the place of theory in empirical research. Although social scientists are in agreement that one of the most important functions of empirical research is to contribute to the development and refinement of theory and that theory enhances the goals of science, there is little agreement

11. Hempel, *Philosophy of Natural Science,* pp. 94, 96–97.

on what theory is. George Homans made the following critical observation on the state of theory in sociology:

> Contemporary sociologists have been preoccupied with "theory," yet have seldom tried to make clear what theory *is*. . . . We sociologists show our confusion about the nature of theory both by what we say about theory in general and by what kinds of theories we actually produce.[12]

Since then, similar statements have been made by social scientists in other disciplines.

Theory means different things to different people. Some social scientists would identify theory with any kind of conceptualization. Such concepts as "power," "social status," "democracy," "bureaucracy," and "deviance," when defined and used in interpretations of empirical phenomena, are sometimes equated with theories. In this broad sense, any conceptualization, as opposed to observation, is theory. Other social scientists equate theory with the "history of ideas." Still others view theory in a narrow sense: a *logical-deductive* system consisting of a set of interrelated concepts from which testable propositions can be deductively derived. Before we discuss what theory is and what types of theory are common in the social sciences, it is useful to point out some common misconceptions about theory.

## What Theory Is Not

The layperson usually contrasts "theory" with "practice." The claim that something is "all right in theory but won't work in practice" conveys the idea that theory is impractical. As Arnold Brecht put it, "The relation between practice and theory is well indicated in the popular saying that we learn best through 'trial and error.' Trial is practice; error refers to theory. When theory miscarries in practical trials it needs correction."[13] In principle, there is no contrast between theory and practice. Theory relates to practice; that is, scientists accept a theory (and its practical applications) only when its methodology is logically and explicitly pointed out. A credible theory is the conceptual foundation for reliable knowledge; theories help us explain and predict phenomena of interest and, in consequence, to make intelligent practical decisions.

Another misconception about theory results from people substituting the term "theory" for "philosophy." Thus the writings of classical scholars such as Plato, Aristotle, Locke, Marx, and Pareto are often identified with "theory." In fact, prior to World War II, theory in the social sciences was almost exclusively comprised of philosophy in its various forms, with particular emphasis on moral philosophy— that is, how things *ought* to be. Plato's presentation of the ideal, just polity in which the absolute knowledge of the philosopher-king is the guide for political and social behavior is a familiar example.

12. George C. Homans, "Contemporary Theory in Sociology," in *Handbook of Modern Sociology,* ed. R. E. L. Faris (Chicago: Rand McNally, 1964), p. 951.
13. Arnold Brecht, *Political Theory* (Princeton, N.J.: Princeton University Press, 1959), p. 19.

Moral philosophies state value judgments. They are neither true nor false because they are not empirically verifiable. If you strongly believe that socialism is the best of all economic systems, no amount of empirical evidence can prove or disprove that belief. But unlike philosophical works, scientific theories are abstractions representing certain aspects of the empirical world; they are concerned with the *how* and *why* of empirical phenomena, not with what should be.

## Types of Theories

There is no one simple definition of theory on which all social scientists would agree because there are many different kinds of theories, each serving a different purpose. David Easton, for example, suggested that theories can be classified according to their *scope*—whether they are macro or micro theories; according to their *function*—whether they seek to deal with static or dynamic phenomena, with structure or process; according to their *structure*—whether they are logical systems of thought with closely knit interrelationships, or whether they constitute a more loosely defined set of propositions; or according to their *level*—"by the relationship of the behavioral systems to which they refer as ranked on some hierarchical scale."[14] Our classification, however, is based on the Parsons and Shils distinction among four *levels* of theory: ad hoc classificatory systems, taxonomies, conceptual frameworks, and theoretical systems.[15]

*Ad Hoc Classificatory Systems.*    The lowest level of theorizing is the **ad hoc classificatory system.** It consists of arbitrary categories constructed in order to organize and summarize empirical observations. For example, a researcher might classify responses to the questionnaire item "All groups can live in harmony in this country without changing the system in any way" into four categories: "Strongly Agree," "Agree," "Strongly Disagree," and "Disagree." These categories constitute an ad hoc classificatory system because they are not derived from a more general theory of social order.

*Taxonomies.*    The second level of theory is the *categorical system,* or **taxonomy.** A taxonomy consists of a system of categories constructed to fit empirical observations in such a way that relationships among the categories can be described. Categories may be interdependent. That is, the categories in a taxonomy reflect the reality described. Talcott Parsons's analysis of social action exemplifies this level of theory. He suggested that behavior has four attributes: it is goal-oriented, occurs in group situations, is normatively regulated, and involves an expenditure of energy. When behavior displays all these attributes, it constitutes a social system. Furthermore, social systems take three forms: personality systems,

---

14. David Easton, "Alternative Strategies in Theoretical Research," in *Varieties of Political Theory,* ed. David Easton (Englewood Cliffs, N.J.: Prentice-Hall, 1966), pp. 1–13.
15. Talcott Parsons and Edward A. Shils, *Toward a General Theory of Action* (New York: Harper & Row, 1962), pp. 50–51.

cultural systems, and social structures.[16] Parsons carefully defined these seven categories and then explained their logical interrelations. Ever since Parsons formulated this taxonomy, empirical observations have been fitted to the categories.

Taxonomies basically perform two important functions in social science research. The precise definitions of a taxonomy specify the unit of empirical reality to be analyzed and indicate how the unit may be described (e.g., in Parsons's taxonomy, social systems). The goal of a taxonomy is to provide

> an orderly schema for classification and description. . . . When faced with any subject of research, [one] can immediately identify its crucial aspects or variables by using his taxonomy as a kind of a "shopping list." To "test" his taxonomy, he takes a fresh look at subject $X$ and shows that the general terms defining his dimensions have identifiable counterparts in $X$.[17]

The second function of the taxonomy is to "summarize and inspire descriptive studies,"[18] such as those concerned with the empirical distributions of one or more categories of the taxonomy. However, taxonomies do not provide explanations; they only describe empirical phenomena by fitting them into a set of categories. Knowing the concepts that represent phenomena (for example, "government spending") and their distributions (for example, how much is being spent on various programs) is not equivalent to explaining or predicting those phenomena (for example, why our government spends more on defense than on education).

*Conceptual Frameworks.*    The third level of theory is the **conceptual framework.** In a conceptual framework, descriptive categories are systematically placed in a broad structure of explicit *propositions,* statements of relationships between two or more empirical properties, to be accepted or rejected. Easton's conceptualization of politics is a fruitful example of a conceptual framework. Easton identifies the major functions of political systems as the "authoritative allocation of values."[19] All political systems, whatever their form of government (democracies as well as dictatorships), allocate values authoritatively. Easton uses concepts such as "inputs," "outputs," "environment," and "feedback" (Figure 2.2) to describe and explain empirical observations. These concepts are then interrelated, with "feedback" performing the functions of continuity or change. Easton also offers a variety of propositions to explain how "inputs" (differentiated into "demands" and "supports") are generated, how political decision makers react to "inputs," how the "environment" influences "inputs" and decision makers, and how "outputs" (differentiated into "decisions" and "actions"), through "feedback," change or preserve the nature of "inputs."

16. Ibid., pp. 247–275.

17. Hans L. Zetterberg, *On Theory and Verification in Sociology,* 3d enlarged ed. (Totowa, N.J.: Bedminster Press, 1965), p. 26.

18. Ibid.

19. David Easton, *A System Analysis of Political Life* (Chicago: University of Chicago Press, 1979), pp. 21–32; see also David Easton, *A Framework for Political Analysis* (Chicago: University of Chicago Press, 1979).

**Figure 2.2**
A Conceptual Framework of Political Systems

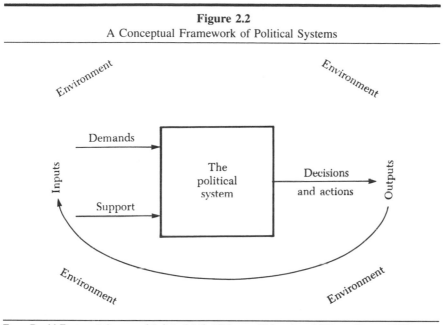

From David Easton, *A System of Political Life* (Chicago: University of Chicago Press, 1979).

This conceptual framework belongs to a higher level than a taxonomy because its propositions summarize behaviors as well as provide explanations and predictions for vast numbers of empirical observations. Much of what is considered theory in the social sciences consists of conceptual frameworks, which can be used to direct systematic empirical research. However, the propositions derived from conceptual frameworks are not established deductively. This dependence on empirical observation in the earlier stages of theorizing and research limits their explanatory and predictive powers and impairs their usefulness for future research.

***Theoretical Systems.*** **Theoretical systems** combine taxonomies and conceptual frameworks by relating descriptions, explanations, and predictions in a systematic manner. This is the highest level of theory and requires the most rigorous definition: a theoretical system is comprised of propositions that are interrelated in a way that permits some propositions to be derived from others. When such a theoretical system exists, social scientists can claim to have explained and predicted the phenomenon at hand.

A theoretical system, such as Durkheim's, provides a structure for an inclusive explanation of empirical phenomena; its scope is not limited to one particular aspect of the event to be explained. It consists of a set of *concepts,* some of which are abstract, showing what the theory is about (for example, "suicide"), while others are measurable empirical properties (for example, "suicide rates"). These empirical properties are termed *variables*. (A detailed discussion of variables and their types is found in Chapter 3.)

A theoretical system also consists of a set of *propositions*. However, contrary to their status within a conceptual framework, these propositions form a *deductive system*. In other words, a set of propositions forms a *calculus* (a method of analysis or calculation using a special symbolic notation). Therefore, by following the rules of their manipulation, scientists can deduce some propositions from others. When propositions are so deduced, they are said to be explained as well as to suggest predictions.

Durkheim's theory of suicide, as presented by George Homans, provides a classic example of a theoretical system:[20]

1. In any social grouping, the suicide rate varies directly with the degree of individualism.
2. The degree of individualism varies with the incidence of Protestantism.
3. Therefore, the suicide rate varies with the incidence of Protestantism.
4. The incidence of Protestantism in Spain is low.
5. Therefore, the suicide rate in Spain is low.

In this example, proposition 3 is deduced from propositions 1 and 2, and proposition 5 is deduced from 3 and 4. Accordingly, if, for example, you did not know what the suicide rate in Bulgaria is but did know that the incidence of Protestantism in the country is low, this observation, together with proposition 3, would allow you to predict that the suicide rate in Bulgaria is also low. Thus the theoretical system provides both an explanation and a prediction of suicide rates.

Finally, some of the propositions of a theoretical system must be *contingent,* dependent on empirical reality, in the sense that "experience is relevant to their truth or falsity or to that of propositions derived from them."[21] Indeed, acceptance of a theoretical system ultimately depends on whether scientists are able to empirically verify its propositions.

## Axiomatic Theory

One theoretical system that deserves special mention is the *formal* or **axiomatic theory.** Axioms are untestable statements or assumptions about the phenomenon in question, that is, they are stated as being true. Axioms describe a direct causal relationship between two concepts. This relationship is considered to be so basic that it requires no further empirical proof. Without such basic assumptions, the process of thinking, conceptualizing, and testing hypotheses becomes impossible. Consequently, an axiomatic theory contains the following:

1. A set of concepts and definitions, both conceptual and operational.
2. A set of statements describing the situations in which the theory can be applied.

20. Homans, "Contemporary Theory in Sociology," p. 959.
21. Ibid.

---

### Four Levels of Theory

- *Ad hoc Classificatory Systems:* Arbitrary categories that organize and summarize empirical data.
- *Taxonomies:* Systems of categories constructed to fit empirical observations. Taxonomies enable researchers to describe relationships among categories.
- *Conceptual Frameworks:* Descriptive categories are systematically placed in a structure of explicit, assumed propositions. The propositions included within the framework summarize and provide explanations and predictions for empirical observations. They are not established deductively, however.
- *Theoretical Systems:* Combine taxonomies and conceptual frameworks by relating descriptions, explanations, and predictions systematically. The propositions of a theoretical system are interrelated in a way that permits some to be derived from others.

---

3. A set of relational statements, divided into
   a. Axioms—untestable statements or assumptions assumed to be true. For example, the axioms in geometry are assumed to be true whether or not they apply to the empirical world.
   b. Theorems—propositions *deduced* from the axioms and amenable to empirical verification.
4. A system of logic employed to
   a. Relate *all* concepts within statements.
   b. Deduce theorems from axioms, combinations of axioms, and other theorems.

Hans Zetterberg's reformulation of Durkheim's theory is an early and often cited example of axiomatic theory. Zetterberg explicated the following ten propositions:[22]

1. The greater the division of labor, the greater the consensus (agreement on basic values and issues).
2. The greater the solidarity (sense of belonging), the greater the number of associates per member (the greater the number of contacts with other members of the group).
3. The greater the number of associates per member, the greater the consensus.
4. The greater the consensus, the smaller the number of rejections of deviants (individuals who do not accept basic values or behave in a manner that is socially disapproved).
5. The greater the division of labor, the smaller the number of rejections of deviants.

---

22. Zetterberg, *On Theory and Verification in Sociology,* pp. 159–160.

6. The greater the number of associates per member, the smaller the number of rejections of deviants.
7. The greater the division of labor, the greater the solidarity.
8. The greater the solidarity, the greater the consensus.
9. The greater the number of associates per member, the greater the division of labor.
10. The greater the solidarity, the smaller the number of rejections of deviants.

Zetterberg then selected the last four propositions as axioms and argued that the remaining propositions can be logically deduced from this combination of axioms.

The most difficult problem in axiomatic theory involves the choice of axioms. What criteria should scientists select when attempting to designate certain propositions as axioms? Why did Zetterberg choose only the last four propositions in the list to constitute his set of axioms? One criterion of selection is *consistency:* axioms should not lead to contradictory theorems. Another criterion is *number*— theorists should select the smallest possible set of axioms from which *all* other theorems can be deduced. This criterion reflects the consensus among scientists that *parsimony* or simplicity should be employed when constructing theories. The third criterion for the selection of axioms—and the one that makes the construction of axiomatic theory in the social sciences most difficult—is to select as axioms only propositions that have achieved the status of laws. However, propositions must have considerable empirical support before they can be considered laws. At present, very few propositions in the social sciences have achieved such a status.

In recent research, scientists have tended to select axioms from among the set of propositions that makes the theory explicit and easy to understand. They achieve this goal by employing propositions that describe a *direct causal* relationship between two concepts as axioms. As Hubert Blalock put it, "An axiom might be stated somewhat as follows: An increase in *X* will produce (cause) an almost immediate increase in *Y;* this increase in *Y* will, in turn, result in further increase in *X,* but with a delayed reaction."[23] Using the rule of direct causal relationships, Blalock restated Zetterberg's four axioms as a causal chain:[24]

1. An increase in the number of associates per member will produce an increase in the division of labor (proposition 9).
2. An increase in the division of labor will produce an increase in solidarity (proposition 7).
3. An increase in solidarity will produce an increase in consensus (proposition 8).
4. An increase in solidarity will produce a decrease in the number of rejections of deviants (proposition 10).

These causal axioms in turn lead to the generation of empirically testable theorems or propositions.

23. Hubert M. Blalock, Jr., *Theory Construction* (Englewood Cliffs, N.J.: Prentice-Hall, 1969), p. 18.
24. Ibid., p. 19.

*Advantages of Axiomatic Theory.*    Because of the complexity of human behavior and the research into that behavior (see Chapter 1), very few propositions
in the social sciences have achieved the status of laws. Why, then, do social scientists continue to construct axiomatic theories?

There are several advantages to axiomatic theory. First, it calls for a careful
description and explanation of the central concepts and assumptions used in a substantive theory. Second, as each concept has to be clearly defined, all its primitive
and derived terms and operational definitions must also be made explicit. Third,
axiomatic theory can provide a parsimonious summary of actual and anticipated
research. Instead of having a large number of propositions, an axiomatic theory
presents only the essential ones. Fourth, an axiomatic theory can be used "to coor-
dinate research so that many separate findings support each other, giving the highest plausibility to the theory per finding."[25] Because the theory consists of a set
of interrelated propositions, empirical support for any one proposition tends to provide support for the entire theory. For example, the accumulated body of empirical
research in social deviance has been carried out on the basis of Durkheim's theory.
Fifth, the axiomatic form allows researchers to systematically examine *all* the
consequences of their axioms; this in turn helps them to determine which parts
of the theory they have verified and which call for further research. This is
particularly useful when researchers go about choosing the research topics that will
contribute most to theory.[26] Finally, the axiomatic form is most compatible for
causal analysis, described in Chapter 17.

# Models

Closely related to the idea of theory as systematic conceptual organization is the
concept of **models.** Theorists often attempt to provide conceptual organization
by using models. As in other disciplines and professions, a *model* can be viewed
as a likeness of something. For example, an engineer might have a model of a
machine, such as a space shuttle. The model is a miniature reproduction of the real
space shuttle, including a scale representation of some of its features—its
structure—but omitting other aspects, such as its control instruments. Because the
model serves as a physical, visual representation of the structure and features of
the space shuttle, it can be used in place of the real space shuttle for experimentation and testing. An engineer might subject the model to the effects of a wind
tunnel (itself a model) to determine the space shuttle's performance in windy
conditions.

In the social sciences, models usually consist of symbols rather than physical
matter; that is, the characteristics of some empirical phenomenon, including its
components and the relationships between the components, are represented as

---

25. Zetterberg, *On Theory and Verification in Sociology,* p. 163.

26. For an excellent application of these advantages, see Gerald Hage, *Theories of Organizations:
Forms, Process, and Transformation* (New York: Wiley-Interscience, 1980).

logical arrangements among concepts. Thus, for social scientists, a *model* is an abstraction from reality that orders and simplifies our view of reality by representing its essential characteristics:

> A characteristic feature in the construction of a model is abstraction; certain elements of the situation may be deliberately omitted because they are judged irrelevant, and the resulting simplification in the description of the situation may be helpful in analyzing and understanding it. In addition to abstraction, model-building sometimes involves a conceptual transference. Instead of discussing the situation directly, it may be the case that each element of the real situation is simulated by a mathematical or physical object, and its relevant properties and relations to other elements are mirrored by corresponding simulative properties and relations . . . ; a city's traffic system may be simulated by setting up a miniature model of its road net, traffic signals, and vehicles.[27]

A model, then, is a representation of reality; it delineates those aspects of the real world the scientist considers to be relevant to the problem investigated, it makes explicit the significant relationships among those aspects, and it enables the researcher to formulate empirically testable propositions regarding the nature of these relationships. After testing, and hopefully achieving a better understanding of some part of the real world, the scientist may decide to change the model to conform with his or her new insights. Models are also used to gain insight into phenomena that the scientist cannot observe directly, such as "power." In policy analysis, for example, researchers construct models of the structures and processes of decision making, and deduce propositions relating to the behavior of the decision makers. They then evaluate these propositions against the empirical data. Policy analysts also use models to estimate the consequences of alternative courses of action that a decision maker might select. The models therefore provide a more systematic basis for policy choices than do subjective judgments.

## Example: A Model of Policy Implementation

Thomas Smith's model of the policy implementation process provides an interesting example of modeling complex aspects of the real world that cannot be observed directly.[28] Many people believe that once a public policy has been decided upon (for example, when Congress passes a bill), implementation of the goals desired by the policymakers will follow naturally and even automatically. But this rarely happens. The technical problems of implementation are widespread, and policies are almost never implemented in the manner originally intended. In addition, public bureaucrats, interest groups, and affected individuals and organizations often attempt to force changes in the original policy during the implementation process.

27. Olaf Helmer, *Social Technology* (New York: Basic Books, 1966), pp. 127–128.
28. Thomas B. Smith, "The Policy Implementation Process," *Policy Sciences,* 4 (1973): 197–209.

Smith's model abstracts certain aspects of the implementation process and focuses on four components:

1. The idealized policy, that is, the idealized patterns of interaction that the policymakers are attempting to induce.
2. The target group, defined as the people obliged to adopt new patterns of interaction by the policy. They are the individuals most directly affected by the policy and who must change to meet its demands.
3. The implementing organization, usually a government agency, responsible for implementation of the policy.
4. The environmental factors influenced by implementation of the policy. The general public and various special-interest groups are included here.

These four components and their postulated relations are diagrammed in Figure 2.3. The policymaking process produces public policies. These policies serve as a tension-generating force in society: implementation causes strain and conflicts among the implementors of the policy as well as the people affected by it. Tensions lead to *transactions,* Smith's term for the responses to these tensions and conflicts. The feedback initiated by transactions and institutions influences the four components of the implementation process as well as future policymaking.

Models, then, are tools for explanation and prediction. If they are well designed, they approximate reality faithfully. But the models themselves are never the reality. Indeed, models are often changed to represent reality more accurately and to incorporate new knowledge. The critical attribute of a scientific model is that it can be tested empirically; that is, it can be proved false and changed or discarded.

**Figure 2.3**
A Model of the Policy Implementation Process

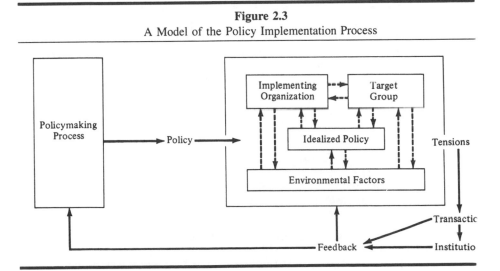

# Theory, Models, and Empirical Research

The social sciences, as scientific disciplines, rest on two major components: theory and empirical research. Social scientists, as scientists, operate in two "worlds": the world of observation and experience and the world of ideas, theories, and models. Establishing a systematic connection between these two worlds enhances the goals of the social sciences—to explain phenomena and to make accurate predictions. But how can we achieve this connection? Should we first construct our theories and models and then move to the world of empirical research? Or should theory *follow* empirical research?

## Theory before Research

According to one major school of thought, theory should come first, to be followed by research; this is often referred to as the **theory-then-research strategy.** Karl Popper (1902–1994) developed this strategy most systematically. He argued that scientific knowledge advances most rapidly when scientists develop ideas (conjectures) and then attempt to refute them through empirical research (refutations).[29] Popper denied the systematic bearing of empirical research on theorizing. He believed that research seldom generates new theories, nor does it serve as a logical method for theory construction. Theories "can only be reached by intuition, based upon something like an intellectual love of the objects of experience."[30]

The theory-then-research strategy involves the following, highly simplified, five stages:[31]

1. Construct an explicit theory or model.
2. Select a proposition derived from the theory or model for empirical investigation.
3. Design a research project to test the proposition.
4. If the proposition derived from the theory is rejected by the empirical data, make changes in the theory or the research project (for example, research, design, measurement; see Figure 1.1) and return to stage 2.
5. If the proposition is not rejected, select other propositions for testing or attempt to improve the theory.

## Research before Theory

In sharp contrast to the theory-then-research strategy, Robert Merton, a proponent of the **research-then-theory strategy,** argued as follows:

29. Karl R. Popper, *Conjectures and Refutations: The Growth of Scientific Knowledge* (New York: Harper & Row, 1968).
30. Karl R. Popper, *The Logic of Scientific Discovery* (New York: Science Editions, 1961).
31. Reynolds, *A Primer in Theory Construction,* pp. 140–144.

It is my central thesis that empirical research goes far beyond the passive role of verifying and testing theory; it does more than confirm or refute hypotheses. Research plays an active role: it performs at least four major functions which help shape the development of theory. It initiates, it reformulates, it deflects, and it clarifies theory.[32]

According to this view, empirical research suggests new problems for theory, calls for new theoretical formulations, leads to the refinement of existing theories, and serves the function of verification. The research-then-theory strategy consists of the following four stages:[33]

1. Investigate a phenomenon and delineate its attributes.
2. Measure the attributes in a variety of situations. (Measurement and measuring procedures are discussed in Chapter 7.)
3. Analyze the resulting data to determine if there are systematic patterns of variation.
4. Once systematic patterns are discovered, construct a theory. The theory may be of any of the types discussed earlier, although a theoretical system is preferred.

Clearly, both strategies regard theory as a manifestation of scientific progress. The real dilemma is over the place of theory in the research process. We contend that no dogmatic commitment to either strategy is necessary for the conduct of research. The social sciences have progressed in spite of this controversy, and scientific undertakings have been pursued under both strategies. In fact, theory and research interact continuously, as suggested by Figure 1.1 in Chapter 1. Furthermore, as Ernest Nagel maintains, the contrast between the two strategies is more apparent than real:

> Distinguished scientists have repeatedly claimed that theories are "free creations of the mind." Such claims obviously do not mean that theories may not be *suggested* by observational materials or that theories do not require support from observational evidence. What such claims do rightly assert is that the basic terms of a theory need not possess meanings which are fixed by definite experimental procedures, and that a theory may be adequate and fruitful despite the fact that the evidence for it is necessarily indirect.[34]

## Summary

**1.** One of the most significant symbols in science is the concept. Science begins by forming concepts to describe the empirical world and advances by

32. Robert K. Merton, *Social Theory and Social Structure,* rev. and enlarged ed. (New York: Free Press, 1968), p. 103.
33. Reynolds, *A Primer in Theory Construction,* pp. 140–144.
34. Ernest Nagel, *The Structure of Science* (New York: Heckett, 1979), p. 86.

connecting these concepts into theoretical systems. Concepts enable effective communication, introduce a point of view, are means for classification and generalization, and serve as the building blocks of propositions, theories, and hypotheses, which will be discussed in Chapter 3.

**2.** To serve their functions effectively, concepts have to be clear, precise, and agreed-upon. This is achieved by means of conceptual and operational definitions. A conceptual definition describes concepts using primitive and derived terms. Operational definitions point out the set of procedures and activities that researchers should perform in order to empirically observe the phenomena represented by concepts. Hence, operational definitions connect the conceptual-theoretical level with the empirical-observational level.

**3.** Although social scientists are in agreement that theory is the ultimate achievement of scientific undertakings, there are divergent views concerning the meaning and structure of theory. At present, scientists distinguish four levels of theory: ad hoc classificatory systems, taxonomies, conceptual frameworks, and theoretical systems. One major form of theoretical system is axiomatic theory. An axiomatic theory contains a set of concepts and definitions, a set of statements, a set of relational statements divided into axioms and theorems, and a logical system used to relate concepts with statements and to deduce theorems from axioms.

**4.** Scientists use models to systematically represent certain aspects of the real world. Models are abstractions that serve the purpose of ordering and simplifying our view of reality while still representing its essential attributes. Scientists also use models to gain insight into phenomena that cannot be observed directly, such as an economic system.

**5.** Scientists have established systematic links between the empirical and the conceptual worlds with the aid of two general strategies: theory-then-research and research-then-theory. Although there is a lively controversy as to which strategy most fruitfully enhances scientific progress, our position is that theory and research should interact constantly and that the contrast between the two strategies is more apparent than real.

---

## Key Terms for Review

---

ad hoc classificatory system (p. 37)
axiomatic theory (p. 40)
concept (p. 26)
conceptual definition (p. 29)
conceptual framework (p. 38)
congruence (p. 34)
derived term (p. 29)
fallacy of reification (p. 27)
model (p. 43)

operational definition (p. 30)
ostensive definition (p. 29)
primitive term (p. 29)
research-then-theory strategy (p. 46)
taxonomy (p. 37)
theoretical import (p. 35)
theoretical system (p. 39)
theory-then-research strategy (p. 46)

## Study Questions

1. Discuss the four functions of concepts in social science research.
2. Distinguish between conceptual definitions and operational definitions, and give an example of each from one of the social sciences you have studied.
3. Discuss the common misconceptions regarding theories. Can you think of any others?
4. Describe and explain the use of models in social science research. Can you give examples from other courses?
5. Discuss the controversy of theory-before-research versus research-before-theory. Which strategy do you think more accurately reflects the process of scientific research? Why?

## Additional Readings

Bartholomew, David J. *Mathematical Models in Social Science.* Reprint. Ann Arbor, Mich.: Books on Demand, 1981.

Blalock, Hubert M., Jr. *Basic Dilemmas in the Social Sciences.* Beverly Hills, Calif.: Sage, 1984.

Braithwaite, Richard B. "Models in Empirical Science." In *Readings in the Philosophy of Science,* ed. Baruch A. Grody. 2d ed. Englewood Cliffs, N.J.: Prentice-Hall, 1989, pp. 268–293.

Isaak, Alan C. *Scope and Methods of Political Science.* 4th ed. Belmont, Calif.: Wadsworth, 1988.

Krathwohl, David R. *Social and Behavioral Science Research.* San Francisco: Jossey-Bass, 1985.

Lave, Charles A., and James G. March. *An Introduction to Models in the Social Sciences.* Reprint. Lanham, Md.: University Press of America, 1991.

Rubinstein, Moshe F., and Kenneth Pfeiffer. *Concepts in Problem Solving.* Englewood Cliffs, N.J.: Prentice-Hall, 1980.

Simon, Herbert A. *The Science of the Artificial.* 2d ed. Cambridge, Mass.: MIT Press, 1981.

Stinchcombe, Arthur L. *Constructing Social Theories.* New York: Harcourt Brace Jovanovich, 1968.

Stinchcombe, Arthur L. *Theoretical Methods in Social History,* New York: Academic Press, 1978.

Sulmer, Martin. *Social Science and Social Policy,* London: Allen & Unwin, 1986.

Weiss, Carol. *Social Science Research and Decision-Making.* New York: Columbia University Press, 1980.

# CHAPTER 3

# Basic Elements
# of Research

**Research Problems**
    Units of Analysis
    The Ecological Fallacy
    The Individualistic Fallacy

**Variables**
    Dependent and Independent Variables
    Control Variables
    Continuous and Discrete Variables

**Relations**
    Kinds of Relations

**Hypotheses**

**Problems and Hypotheses: Some Examples**

**Sources of Research and Hypotheses**
    Bibliographies, Indexes, and Abstracts
    Professional Journals
    Statistical Sourcebooks
    Handbooks

At the beginning of Chapter 1, we discussed an attempt to understand delinquency by conducting a long-term study, involving thousands of people, in Chicago. But what kinds of scientific conclusions can we draw from such a complex study? What is the quality of those conclusions? Can we pinpoint each problem being analyzed? Have the problems been clearly conceptualized and are the procedures used to test hypotheses appropriate? These are the kinds of questions we ask in regard to every research project in the social sciences. They point to just how we use the basic tools of research.

I N THIS CHAPTER, WE EXAMINE HOW SCIENTISTS FORMULATE problems amenable to research and consider two fallacies: the ecological fallacy and the individualist fallacy. We then define variables by type and explore the relations among them. Next, we trace how hypotheses are derived. Finally, we review major guides to published research, including print sources and online databases.

Whether social science research is carried out under the theory-then-research or the research-then-theory strategy, the terms *research problem, variable, relation,* and *hypothesis* crop up with great frequency. They are the basic elements of research, for they help transform an idea into concrete research operations. In this chapter, we define, discuss, and provide examples of the use of these basic terms in the context of the research process.

# Research Problems

In the beginning is the problem. A **research problem** is an intellectual stimulus calling for a response in the form of scientific inquiry. For example, "Who rules America?" "What incentives promote energy conservation?" "How can inflation be reduced?" or "Does social class influence voting behavior?" are all problems amenable to scientific research.

Not all intellectual stimuli can be studied empirically, and not all human behavior is guided by scientific knowledge. In fact, we saw in Chapter 1 that the basic assumptions of science cannot be researched empirically; they are neither proven nor provable. Similarly, questions such as "Will Western civilization disappear?" "Is blue nicer than green?" or "Is Impressionism the most stimulating school of art?" cannot be investigated empirically. In general, problems that cannot be empirically grounded (that is, identified in observable behavior) or that are concerned with subjective preferences, beliefs, values, or tastes are not amenable to empirical research.

The observation that researchers cannot study subjective preferences scientifically does not, of course, imply that social scientists in their roles as concerned citizens, parents, or friends do not have subjective preferences about many things, just like anyone else. However, because preferences or beliefs cannot be empirically validated, they are beyond the realm of scientific knowledge.

Nevertheless, certain subjective preferences or beliefs *can* be studied in the same way that scientists approach other empirical phenomena—as factual problems to be investigated by means of the scientific approach. For example, one can investigate why some people believe that Western civilization will disappear and why others do not share this view, or whether the preference for Impressionism is related to social class or to personality characteristics. We must emphasize, however, that it is not the subjective preferences that are being researched but why people take those positions or, at times, how they will act on the basis of those beliefs.

In addition to being empirically grounded, research problems have to be clearly and specifically articulated. For example, the problem "What incentives promote energy conservation?" is too general and too ambiguous to guide research. It means different things to different people. It does not specify the types of incentives (e.g., economic, social, patriotic) or the sources of energy (e.g., crude oil, gasoline, natural gas, coal). It also fails to distinguish between industrial and residential conservation. A lack of clarity and specificity may lead to ambiguous findings that can be interpreted in contradictory ways.

---

# Units of Analysis

When a social scientist formulates a research problem, he or she must give serious consideration to the **unit of analysis,** the most elementary part of the phenomenon to be studied. The unit (or level) of analysis influences the research design, data collection, and data analysis decisions. Does the research problem call for the study of perceptions, attitudes, or behavior? Should the scientist concentrate on individuals or groups, institutions or societies? Abraham Kaplan called selecting the units of analysis the "locus problem":

> The locus problem may be described as that of selecting the ultimate subject-matter for inquiry in behavioral science, the attribute space for its description, and the conceptual structure within which hypotheses about it are to be formulated. Quite a number of alternatives present themselves, and have been selected in various inquiries: states of conscious acts, actions (segments of meaningful behavior), roles, persons, personalities, interpersonal relations, groups, classes, institutions, social traits or patterns, societies, and cultures. With respect to each of these, there is the associated problem of unit, *that is, of what constitutes the identity of the element selected. Are legal institutions, for example, quite distinct from the institution of the state or part of it, and if so, in what sense of "part"?*[1]

In principle, there are no limitations on the selection of units to be analyzed in a research project. However, once a scientist has made a selection, he or she

---

1. Abraham Kaplan, *The Conduct of Inquiry* (New York: Harper and Row, 1968), p. 78.

must adjust the research procedures, particularly the scope and the level of generalization and theorizing, so that they are congruent with, or suitable to, the units of analysis chosen. This part of the research process is crucial as units of analysis have unique attributes; hence it is often misleading to shift from one unit to another. Generalizations based on individuals as units of analysis and generalizations based on groups can be quite different.

A major reason for such disparities is that similar concepts are often used to refer to attributes that can differ in their observable characteristics depending on the unit of analysis. For example, the concept "survival" is used to explain the behavior of individuals, groups, formal organizations, and nations, each a distinct unit of analysis. But "survival" means different things when applied to these different units. There is no a priori reason to assume that the relationships between "survival" and other attributes will be identical for them all. For example, the behavioral consequences of survival can be similar for individuals, that is, physical survival. However, when organizations are considered, survival may mean the continuing legal status of the firm even if it changes its product line completely. In the case of nations, survival may mean the continuity of political boundaries, an issue illustrated by the civil war in what was formerly Yugoslavia (1993–present).

## The Ecological Fallacy

Researchers need to specify the units of analysis for methodological reasons as well. When relationships are estimated at one unit or level of analysis (e.g., groups) and then extrapolated to another level (e.g., individuals), distortions are likely to result. That is, generalizing directly from a more complex to a simpler unit of analysis, from a higher to a lower level, is inappropriate. This kind of distortion is termed the **ecological fallacy.**

In a classic study, William Robinson effectively demonstrated the consequences of the ecological fallacy.[2] Focusing on the relationship between literacy and place of birth in the 1930s, Robinson compared the geographical regions of the United States. He found that regions with higher percentages of foreign-born people had higher literacy rates than regions with lower percentages of foreign-born persons. But when he subsequently examined the same relationships at the *individual* level, he came up with the *opposite* results: in the same region, native-born individuals were more literate than foreign-born. What explains these contradictory findings? Two possible reasons are (a) significant differences in the quality of public education from region to region—the level of the collective or group, and (b) the tendency for immigrants to settle in regions that happened to have better public education—the level of the individual. Robinson points out that if he had applied only the first of the two explanations, which corresponds to a specific unit of analysis, he would have committed the ecological fallacy.

2. William S. Robinson, "Ecological Correlations and the Behavior of Individuals," *American Sociological Review,* 15 (1950): 351–357.

> **Two Fallacies Researchers Need to Be Aware Of**
>
> - *Ecological Fallacy:* The drawing of inferences about individuals directly from evidence gathered about groups, societies, or nations.
> - *Individualistic Fallacy:* The drawing of inferences about groups, societies, or nations directly from evidence gathered about the behavior of individuals.

## The Individualistic Fallacy

The converse of the ecological fallacy is the reductionist or *individualistic fallacy.* The **individualistic fallacy** results when inferences about groups, societies, or nations are drawn directly from evidence gathered about individuals. For example, if a researcher was to calculate the percentage of individuals in a country who agree with particular statements on democracy and then use this percentage as an indicator of the degree to which the political system in the country is democratic, he or she would be committing the individualistic fallacy. For instance, a political system can have an authoritarian regime even if most of its citizens share democratic values. Furthermore, the concept *democratic* does not mean the same thing at the two levels of analysis. Applied to the individual, it refers to values, attitudes, and behavior; applied to the political system, the concept refers to the system's structure, institutions, and method of decision making. We cannot explain or predict the political system's structure or behavior only from knowledge about its individual members.

---

# Variables

Research problems are conveyed by a set of concepts. We saw in Chapter 2 that concepts are abstractions representing empirical phenomena. In order to move from the conceptual to the empirical level, concepts are converted into *variables.* It is in the form of variables that our concepts appear in hypotheses and are tested.

Concepts are converted into variables by *translating* or *mapping* them into a set of values. For example, when researchers assign numbers (one type of values) to objects, they are mapping the objects into a set of numbers. A **variable** is an empirical property that can take on two or more values. That is, if a property can change, either in quantity or quality, it can be regarded as a variable. For example, "social class" is a variable because it can be differentiated into at least five distinct values: lower, lower middle, middle, upper middle, and upper. Similarly, "expectations" is a variable because it can be assigned at least two values: "high" and "low."

A variable that can have only two values is called a *dichotomous variable.* Researchers have also found it important to make an analytic distinction among dependent, independent, and control variables, and between continuous and discrete variables.

## Dependent and Independent Variables

The variable that the researcher wishes to explain is the **dependent variable.** The variable the researcher expects will explain change in the dependent variable is referred to as the **independent variable.** The independent variable is also called the **explanatory variable;** it is the presumed cause of changes in the values of the dependent variable; the dependent variable is expected to be caused or influenced by the independent variable. (Dependent variables are also called *criterion variables;* independent variables are also called *predictor variables.*)

In the language of mathematics, the dependent variable is the variable that appears on the left-hand side of an equation. For example, if we write $Y = f(X)$, we are considering $Y$ to be the dependent and $X$ the independent variable. In this case, we say that $Y$ is a *function* (indicated by $f$) of $X$—that changes in the values of $X$ are associated with changes in the values of $Y$, or that $X$ yields $Y$.

For example, a researcher might want to explain why some people participate in politics more than others. Based on the theory of social stratification, the researcher may deduce that the higher an individual's social class, the more likely that person is to participate in politics. In this case, the researcher hypothesizes that political participation (the dependent variable) is the outcome of social class; social class (the independent variable) is presumed to cause variations in political participation.

It should be stressed that the distinction between dependent and independent variables is analytic and relates *only* to the study's purpose. In the real world, variables are neither dependent nor independent: the researcher decides how to view them, and that decision is based on the research objective. An independent variable in one investigation may be a dependent variable in another, and the same researcher, working on different projects, may classify the same variables in different ways. If you want to explain variations in political participation, political participation will be the dependent variable. One variable that explains variations in political participation is social class, which will be regarded as an independent variable. But if you want to explain variations in social class (for example, why some individuals are in the lower class and others in the middle), social class will now be regarded as the dependent variable. One variable that may be hypothesized to explain variations in social class is political participation, which will now be regarded as an independent variable.

Most of the phenomena that social scientists investigate require them to assess the effects of several independent variables on one or more dependent variables. This occurs because social phenomena are so complex. One independent variable usually explains only a certain amount of the variation in the dependent variable, and additional independent variables have to be introduced by the researcher in order to explain more of the variation. For example, when political participation is studied as a dependent variable, social class explains why some people participate in politics more than others. This explanation is incomplete, however, because other factors also explain variations in political participation. Among these additional factors, or independent variables, are age, gender, educational attainment, and a sense of political efficacy (the extent to which individuals believe that their participation will affect political outcomes).

## Control Variables

Scientists use **control variables** in empirical research to reduce the risk of attributing explanatory power to independent variables that are not in fact responsible for the variation found in the dependent variable. Control variables are used to test the possibility that an empirically observed relation between an independent and a dependent variable is *spurious*. A **spurious relation** is a relation that can be explained by variables other than those stated in the hypothesis. In other words, if the influence of all other variables is eliminated (or controlled for) and the empirical relation between the independent variable and the dependent variable is maintained, then the relation is nonspurious. By using control variables, the researcher can ensure that there is an inherent, causal link between the variables, as stated in the hypothesis, and that the observed relation is not based on an unforeseen connection with some other phenomenon.

For example, suppose that you observe that the number of firefighters present at the site of a fire is related to the amount of fire damage. That is, our hypothesis can state that the more firefighters appearing at the site of a fire, the greater the amount of fire damage. Generally, firefighters are not considered to be the direct cause of the damage. Accordingly, the amount of fire damage (dependent variable) should not be explained by the number of firefighters (independent variable) at the site but by another variable, namely, the size of the fire. Large fires call forth more firefighters and also cause more damage. Thus the original observed relation between the number of firefighters at the fire site and the amount of fire damage is spurious because a third factor, the size of the fire, explains it. In this case, the size of the fire is employed as a control variable to test the validity of the original relation. Without the influence of the control variable, the relation observed between the number of firefighters and the amount of fire damage would be spurious. This is illustrated in Figure 3.1.

Another example illustrating the significance of control variables is the empirical relation observed between political participation and government expenditure. Is the amount of government expenditure (dependent variable) caused by the extent of political participation (independent variable)? Seemingly yes. However, a great body of research has shown that the empirical relation between political participation and government expenditure vanishes when the control variable of economic development is introduced.[3] The level of economic development influences *both* government expenditure and political participation. Without the influence of economic development, the observed relation between political participation and government expenditure would continue to appear valid. Control variables thus serve the important purpose of testing whether or not the

3. For the first breakthrough study on this issue, see Hayward R. Alker, *Mathematics and Politics* (New York: Macmillan, 1965).

**Figure 3.1**
Importance of a Control Variable

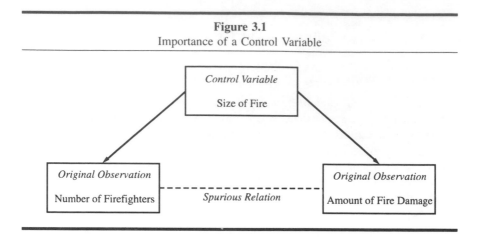

observed relations between independent and dependent variables are spurious (for more on spurious and nonspurious relations, see Chapter 5).

## Continuous and Discrete Variables

Another important attribute of variables is whether they are continuous or discrete. This attribute, as we shall see in later chapters, affects research operations, particularly measurement procedures, data analysis, and methods of statistical inference and logical generalization.

A **continuous variable** does not have a minimum-sized unit a priori. Length is an example of a continuous variable because there is no minimum unit of length to be found in nature. A particular object may be at least 10 inches long, it may be 10.5 inches long, or it may be 10.5431697 inches long. In principle, we can speak of a tenth of an inch, a ten-thousandth of an inch, or a ten-trillionth of an inch. Although we cannot measure all possible length values with absolute accuracy (some values will be too small for any measuring instrument to register), it is conceptually possible for objects to exist at an infinite number of lengths.

Unlike continuous variables, **discrete variables** do have a minimum-sized unit. The amount of money in your bank account at the moment is an example of a discrete variable because currency has a minimum unit. You can have $101.21 or $101.22, but not $101.21843. Different amounts of money cannot differ by less than the minimum-sized unit, in this case, one cent. The number of children in a family is another example of a discrete variable because the minimum unit is one child. Families may have three or four children but not 3.5 children. If some quantity of a variable cannot be subdivided, the variable is discrete. You should be aware that when you read, for example, that the average American family has, say, 2.2 children or 1.8 cars, this figure does not mean that the discrete unit of analysis, the child or automobile, can be further divided in real life. The numbers 2.2 and 1.8 are, after all, statistics—products of mathematical manipulation (see Chapters 7 and 14, in particular, for further explanations).

---

### Kinds of Variables

- *Dependent Variable:* The variable the researcher is trying to explain.
- *Independent Variable:* The variable that causes a change in the dependent variable.
- *Control Variable:* Researchers use these variables to test the possibility that the relation between the dependent and independent variables is *spurious*—in other words, that it can be explained only by the presence of another variable.
- *Continuous Variable:* A variable that does not have a minimum-sized unit, such as length.
- *Discrete Variable:* A variable that does have a minimum-sized unit, such as the number of children in a family.

---

# Relations

In earlier chapters, we saw that scientific explanations and predictions involve *relating* the phenomenon to be explained (dependent variable) to other phenomena (explanatory or independent variables) by means of general laws or theories. But what is a relation?

A **relation** in research always refers to a relation between two or more variables. When we say that variable $X$ and variable $Y$ are related, we mean that there is something *common* to both variables. For example, if we say that education and income are related, we mean that the two "go together," that they covary, or change together in a systematic way. **Covariation** is what education and income have in common: individuals with higher education have higher incomes. Establishing a relation in empirical research therefore consists of determining whether the values of one variable covary with values of one or more other variables, and measuring those values. The researcher systematically pairs values of one variable with values of other variables. For example, the two sets of observations given in Table 3.1

**Table 3.1**
Relation between Education and Income

| Observations | Years of Schooling | Income |
|---|---|---|
| Dan | 16 | $35,000 |
| Ann | 15 | 30,000 |
| Marie | 14 | 27,000 |
| Jacob | 13 | 19,000 |
| Phillip | 12 | 15,000 |
| Suzanne | 11 | 12,000 |

report the values of education (operationally defined by years of schooling) and income of six individuals. The table expresses a relation because the two sets of values have been linked in an orderly way—they covary: higher education is linked with higher income and lower education with lower income.

## Kinds of Relations

We say that two variables are related when changes in the values of one systematically bring about changes in the values of the other. In the last example, changes in years of schooling brought about changes in income. Scientists are always concerned with two properties of these relations when doing empirical research: direction and magnitude.

*Direction.*    When we speak of *direction,* we mean that the relations between variables are either positive or negative. A **positive relation** means that as values of one variable increase, values of the other also increase. For example, the relation between education and income is positive because increases in years of schooling lead to higher income. There is also a positive relation between interest in politics and political participation: as individuals become more interested in politics, they tend to participate more in political activities. Studies have also revealed a positive relation between economic development and government expenditures, as pointed out earlier.

A **negative** (or *inverse*) **relation** indicates that as values of one variable increase, values of the other decrease. High values for one variable are associated with low values for the other. For instance, the interest rate for a home mortgage is inversely related to the number of new home loans: as the interest rate increases, the number of new home loans decreases. An inverse relation also exists between education and racial prejudice: people with higher levels of education tend to be less prejudiced. An inverse relation has also been found between bureaucratization and political participation: as political systems become more bureaucratized, the level of political participation declines.

We can illustrate the relation between an independent variable and a dependent variable with the aid of orthogonal axes (see Figure 3.2). Following the custom in mathematics, $X$, the independent variable, is represented by the horizontal axis, and $Y$, the dependent variable, by the vertical axis; $X$ values are laid out on the $X$ axis, $Y$ values on the $Y$ axis. A very common way to observe and interpret a relation is to plot the pairs of $XY$ values, using the $X$ and $Y$ axes as a frame of reference. Let us suppose that in a study of academic achievement we have two sets of measures: $X$ measures the number of hours a student devotes to studying each day, and $Y$ measures the number of excellent grades attained by a student in a given semester. Hypothetical data for nine students on the two measures are presented in Table 3.2, and the measures are plotted in Figure 3.2.

The line graph in Figure 3.2 makes the relation between the number of daily hours of study (independent variable) and the number of excellent grades (dependent variable) visible: high values on the $X$ axis are related to high values on

**Table 3.2**
Number of Hours of Study per Day and
Number of Excellent Grades (Hypothetical Data)

| Number of Hours of Study per Day ($X$) | Number of Excellent Grades ($Y$) |
|:---:|:---:|
| 8 | 5 |
| 7 | 5 |
| 6 | 4 |
| 5 | 3 |
| 4 | 2 |
| 4 | 1 |
| 3 | 1 |
| 2 | 0 |
| 1 | 2 |

the $Y$ axis, medium values on the $X$ axis are related to medium values on the $Y$ axis, and low values on the $X$ axis are related to low values on the $Y$ axis. When illustrated in this way, the relation between the independent variable ($X$) and the dependent variable ($Y$) is termed the *joint distribution of the values*. The straight

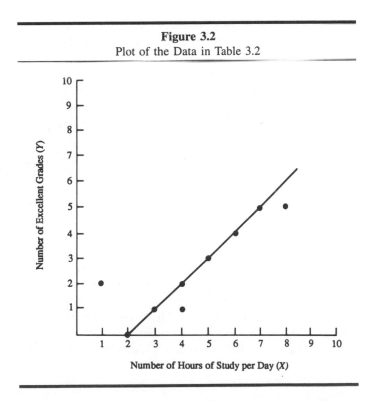

**Figure 3.2**
Plot of the Data in Table 3.2

line passing through the points representing pairs of values indicates the direction of the relation. Furthermore, a researcher can use information about the characteristics of the straight line (its slope and the intercept), to predict the values of the dependent variable according to the values of the independent variable. (For methods of calculating the slope and the intercept, see Chapter 16.) In other words, if you know the slope of the straight line and the value of the point at which it intersects the $Y$ axis, you can predict how many daily hours of study will produce how many excellent grades.

*Magnitude.*    Relations between variables are characterized not only by direction but also by *magnitude*. The **magnitude of a relation** is the extent to which variables covary positively or negatively. The highest magnitude of relation is a *perfect relation*. If a relation between two variables is perfect, the value of one or more independent variables exactly determines the value of the dependent variable. Physical laws such as $E = mc^2$ (Einstein's Law of Relativity) are almost perfect relations because very few exceptions to the rule have been found. The hypothetical example in Table 3.1 displays a perfect relation: there are no exceptions to the rule that increases in years of schooling produce increases in income.

At the other extreme is the lowest magnitude of relation, the *zero relation*. No systematic covariation between the values of an independent variable and a dependent variable can be discerned; that is, the variables are not related. Changes in the values of one variable do not affect the values of the other.

The relations studied in the social sciences, as in other sciences, range in magnitude between zero and perfect. The relation between education and income is positive but not perfect: individuals who have acquired higher levels of education *tend* to have higher incomes, but there are many exceptions. The relation between education and racial prejudice is inverse but not perfect: not all highly educated persons are unprejudiced, and not all persons with lower education are prejudiced. (Precise measures of magnitude, such as coefficients of correlations, are discussed in Chapters 16 and 17.)

Having discussed variables and relations, the basic ingredients of the research problem, we are now in a position to elaborate more fully on the presentation of the answer: the hypothesis and its characteristics.

# Hypotheses

A **hypothesis** is a tentative answer to a research problem, expressed in the form of a clearly stated relation between the independent and the dependent variables. Hypotheses are *tentative* answers because they can be verified only *after* they have been tested empirically. When proposing a hypothesis, the researcher does not know whether it will be verified or not. A hypothesis is constructed and then tested. If it is rejected, another one is put forward; if it is accepted, it is incorporated into the body of scientific knowledge.

Researchers derive hypotheses either deductively from theories, inductively on the basis of direct observations, by using intuition, or by using a combination of these approaches. The sources from which researchers derive their hypotheses are of little significance in comparison to the way in which they reject or fail to reject them. For example, some scientists believe that an apple falling from a tree led Sir Isaac Newton (1642–1727) to propose his hypothesis about gravitation. In a scene from the televised movie *And The Band Played On,* Dr. Don Francis of the Centers for Disease Control realizes that the HIV invades receptor cells in the blood by watching his colleague, Dr. Harold Jaffe, play PacMan.[4] However, neither of these episodes, despite their imaginative appeal, convinced scientists to accept the hypotheses they may have inspired—acceptance came only after they were supported by empirical data.

Research hypotheses share four common characteristics. They are *clear, specific, amenable to empirical testing with the available research methods,* and *value-free.* Examining these characteristics in greater detail will help you construct your own hypotheses and evaluate the hypotheses of others.

1. *Hypotheses must be clear.* In order to test a hypothesis empirically, one has to define all the variables in the hypothesis. Conceptual and operational definitions, as discussed in Chapter 2, help clarify hypotheses. The professional literature and experts' opinions can be of great help when constructing hypotheses and defining the variables. Suppose your hypothesis states that alienation (your independent variable) is inversely related to political participation, your dependent variable. By examining the professional literature, you will discover how other researchers defined the variables. Among these definitions, you are likely to find one suitable to your research hypothesis. If not, you can always build on others' experience while defining the variables in a way more appropriate to your research needs. In any case, your operational definitions must be specific and precise enough to make observation and replication possible.

2. *Hypotheses are specific.* The investigator has to point out the expected relations among the variables in terms of direction (positive or negative) and the conditions under which the relations will hold. A hypothesis stating that $X$ is related to $Y$ is too general. The relation between $X$ and $Y$ can be positive or negative. Furthermore, relations are not independent of time, space, or the unit of analysis. As we saw earlier, the observed relations between variables may vanish when we change the unit of analysis (for example, the ecological fallacy). Thus the relations between, say, education and political participation can be studied at the individual, group, or electoral district level. These different levels of analysis require different conceptualizations and different operational definitions for the variables being researched.

The hypothesis should also explicitly state the conditions under which the relations will be observed. Here theory becomes especially important in generating researchable and fruitful hypotheses.

4. John D. Piette, "Review Symposium, 'Playing It Safe,' " *Journal of Health Politics, Policy and Law,* 19(2) (1994): 453.

3. *Hypotheses are testable with available methods.* A researcher can arrive at clear, value-free, and specific hypotheses and find that there are no research methods to test them. How, for example, are we to test the hypothesis that object *A* is 3 inches longer than object *B* without a ruler? Or how are we to test the hypothesis that the secretions of microbe *C* have a positive relation to disease *D* without an instrument permitting the identification of the microbe? Or how are we to test the relation between education and political participation without instruments to observe these variables?

The simplicity of these examples should emphasize the point that scientists cannot evaluate hypotheses unless they have methods for testing them. Indeed, progress in science is dependent on the development of new research methods, methods of observation, data collection, and data analysis and on their being made available to as many researchers as possible.

Some social scientists attach little value to methods for fear of being enslaved by them. It is possible, of course, to become entrapped by a method of research if the investigator employs it dogmatically, without regard to the research problem at hand, or if he or she regards the method as an end rather than a means. Hypotheses that lack methods of testing may still have a place in the scientific approach if they are innovative. However, their validation depends on the ability to test them, which depends on the availability of methods of research.

4. *Scientific hypotheses are value-free.* In principle, the researcher's own values, biases, and subjective preferences have no place in the scientific approach. However, given that research in the social sciences is to a certain extent a social activity whose problems are affected by its milieu, the researcher must be aware of his personal biases and make them as explicit as possible. As Gunnar Myrdal (1898–1987) wrote in a classic investigation of racial relations:

> The attempt to eradicate biases trying to keep out the valuations themselves is a hopeless and misdirected venture. . . . There is no other device for excluding biases in the social sciences than to face the valuations and to introduce them as explicitly stated, specific, and sufficiently concretized value premises.[5]

# Problems and Hypotheses: Some Examples

Problems pose general questions about relations among variables; hypotheses posit tentative, concrete, and testable answers. A few examples will further clarify the distinction between problems and hypotheses and illustrate how hypotheses are constructed and expressed.

The following examples of research questions derive from the more general problem of how to govern a democratic country:

- Who rules America?
- What causes inflation?

5. Gunnar Myrdal, *The American Dilemma* (New York: Harper, 1944), p. 1043.

---

### Characteristics of Research Hypotheses

- *Hypotheses must be clear.* The researcher must define all of the variables conceptually and operationally.
- *Hypotheses are specific.* The researcher points out the expected relations among the variables in terms of direction (positive or negative) and the conditions under which the relations will hold.
- *Hypotheses are testable with available methods.* The evaluation of a hypothesis depends on the existence of methods for testing it.
- *Scientific hypotheses are value-free.* Because research in the social sciences takes place in a social milieu, the researcher must be aware of personal biases and make them as explicit as possible.

---

- Why does bureaucracy threaten democracy?
- Are affirmative action programs achieving their objectives?
- Does school integration enhance educational attainment?
- What factors determine urbanization?
- What causes political violence?

The research process requires that the scientist operationalize such general questions into a series of hypotheses—tentative answers—in order to enable their investigation. For example, Ted Gurr has conceived of a series of hypotheses, including the following, as tentative answers to the question on political violence:[6]

- The potential for group violence increases as the intensity and scope of relative deprivation among members of a group increases.
- The potential for political violence varies strongly with the intensity and scope of normative justifications [i.e., justifications provided by a commonly held moral standard] for political violence among members of a group.
- The potential for specifically political violence varies strongly with the potential for group violence generally.
- The magnitude of political violence varies strongly with the potential for political violence.

Another example of hypothesis construction is from Gibbs and Martin's often-cited study on the causes of urbanization.[7] The authors advanced these hypotheses:

- The degree of urbanization in a society varies directly with the dispersion [i.e., distribution over a wide physical area] of objects of consumption.
- The degree of urbanization in a society varies directly with the division of labor.

6. Ted R. Gurr, *Why Men Rebel* (Princeton, N.J.: Princeton University Press, 1970), pp. 360–367.
7. Jack P. Gibbs and Walter T. Martin, "Urbanization, Technology, and the Division of Labor: International Patterns," in *Urbanism, Urbanization and Change,* ed. Paul Meadows and Ephraim H. Mizruchi, 2d ed. (Reading, Mass.: Addison-Wesley, 1976), pp. 132–145.

- The division of labor in a society varies directly with the dispersion of objects of consumption.
- The degree of urbanization in a society varies directly with technological development.
- Technological development in a society varies directly with the dispersion of objects of consumption.

Gerald Hage's attempt to synthesize theory and research in the field of complex organizations is an excellent illustration of hypotheses arrived at deductively.[8] Hage translated some key ideas in Max Weber's theory of bureaucracy into variables. For example, Hage restated the concept of "hierarchy of authority" as the variable "degree of organizational centralization" and restated the concept of "rules and procedures" into the variable "degree of formalization" (how much the behavior involved with every job is codified into rules and regulations). This enabled him to construct three major hypotheses:

- The greater the centralization in organizations, the greater the volume of production, and vice versa.
- The greater the centralization, the greater the efficiency, and vice versa.
- The greater the centralization, the greater the formalization, and vice versa.

# Sources of Research and Hypotheses

Research problems and hypotheses can be derived in many ways—from theories, directly from observation, intuitively—singly or in combination. Probably the best source for stimulating the statement of problems and hypotheses is the professional literature. A critical review of the professional literature familiarizes the researcher with the current state of knowledge; with concepts, theories, major variables, and conceptual and operational definitions; with problems and hypotheses that others have studied; and with the research methods used. Basing new research on the knowledge described in the professional literature contributes to the cumulative nature of scientific knowledge.

Reviewing the professional literature is no longer a simple task due to the ever-growing wealth and complexity of the material available. This is true for the professional researcher as well as for the student. Inasmuch as thousands of articles and books in the social sciences are published every year, it is best to begin any search with one of the guides to published literature. These guides, which include bibliographies, indexes, and abstracts, are becoming increasingly computerized.

The Appendix on Report Writing (Appendix B) will present some guidelines on how to incorporate past research in your own presentation of hypothesis and research findings.

8. Gerald Hage, *Theories of Organizations: Forms, Process, and Transformation* (New York: Wiley-Interscience, 1980), pp. 36–40.

## Bibliographies, Indexes, and Abstracts

The following are useful basic reference books, bibliographies, and indexes for published professional literature in the social sciences. Libraries are increasingly purchasing computerized reference material in the form of CD-ROMs (Compact Disk-Read Only Memory) or subscribing to online databases such as DIALOG. CD-ROMs are similar in their hardware configuration to music CDs. Consequently, adjustments must be made to the hardware and programming of a PC in order to use them. These electronic media store massive amounts of information in a highly accessible manner. The terms "online," "CD-ROM," and "microfiche" indicate the nonprint availability of the sources indicated.

- Sheehy, Eugene P., ed. *Guide to Reference Books.* 10th ed. Chicago: American Library Association, 1986.
- Balay, Robert, ed. *Guide to Reference Books.* Supplement to the 10th ed. Chicago: American Library Association, 1992.
- The library card catalog and subject guide. (Many universities have computerized their card catalogs with online database programs. If your university has done so, you can use a terminal to quickly check bibliographic information and to find out whether the library owns the item.)
- The following reference works list the complete publication information necessary to find the book or article you are seeking. All are available in print format.

*Biography Index*
(also: online, CD-ROM)
*Book Review Index*
(also: microfiche, online)
*Cumulative Book Index*
(also: online, CD-ROM)
*Education Index*
(also: online, CD-ROM)
*Index of Economic Articles in Journals and Collective Volumes*
(also: online)

*International Bibliography of the Social Sciences*
(also: online)
*National Union Catalog*
(also: microfiche)
*PAIS International*
(also: online, CD-ROM)
*Social Sciences Citation Index (SSCI)*
(also: online, CD-ROM)
*Social Sciences Index*
(also: online, CD-ROM)

- Abstracts contain short summaries of the works cited.

*Current Contents: Social and Behavioral Sciences (CC: S&BS)*
(also: online)
*Dissertation Abstracts*
(also: microfiche, online, CD-ROM)

*Historical Abstracts*
(also: online, CD-ROM)
*International Political Science Abstracts*
*Journal of Economic Abstracts*
(also: microform, online, CD-ROM)

*Political Science Abstracts*
*Psychological Abstracts*
  (also: online, CD-ROM)
*Resources in Education (RIE)*
  (also: microform, online,
  CD-ROM)
*Sage Public Administration*
  *Abstracts*

*Sage Urban Studies Abstracts*
*Social Work Abstracts*
  (also: microform, online,
  CD-ROM)
*Sociological Abstracts*
  (also: online, CD-ROM)

## Professional Journals

The plethora of social science journals, many of which are highly specialized, make it necessary to use abstracts, indexes, and other guides to efficiently locate the article on the subject of interest. In order to assist you in your first research attempts, we list below some of the major journals, arranged by academic discipline. The references listed above index articles published in journals by author's last name, specialization, or a key word in the title.

### Political Science

*American Journal of Political*
  *Science*
*American Political Science Review*
*American Politics Quarterly*
*British Journal of Political*
  *Science*
*Canadian Journal of Political*
  *Science*
*Canadian Journal of Political and*
  *Social Theory*
*Comparative Political Studies*
*Comparative Politics*
*European Journal of Political*
  *Research*

*International Studies Quarterly*
*Journal of Policy Analysis and*
  *Management*
*Journal of Political Philosophy*
*Journal of Politics*
*Policy Sciences*
*Policy Studies Journal*
*Policy Studies Review*
*Political Science Quarterly*
*Polity*
*Public Interest*
*Public Opinion Quarterly*
*Urban Affairs Quarterly*
*World Politics*

### Sociology

*American Journal of Sociology*
*American Sociological Review*
*British Journal of Sociology*
*Canadian Review of Sociology and*
  *Anthropology*
*Human Relations*
*International Journal of*
  *Comparative Sociology*

*Journal of Mathematical Sociology*
*Journal of Social Issues*
*Social Forces*
*Social Problems*
*Social Psychology Quarterly*
*Social Science Quarterly*
*Sociological Quarterly*

## Psychology

American Behavioral Scientist
Canadian Journal of Experimental
   Psychology
Journal of Applied Behavioral
   Research
Journal of Applied Psychology

Journal of Applied Social
   Psychology
Journal of Personality and Social
   Psychology
Psychological Bulletin
Psychological Review

## Public Administration and Management

Academy of Management Journal
Administration and Society
Administrative Science Quarterly
Advanced Management Journal
American Review of Public
   Administration
Canadian Journal of
   Administrative Sciences

Decision Sciences
Evaluation Review
Harvard Business Review
Management Science
Public Administration Review
Public Personnel Management

## Economics and Business

American Economic Review
Econometrica
Economic Journal
Fortune Magazine
Journal of Political Economy

Quarterly Journal of Economics
Rand Journal of Economics
Review of Economics and
   Statistics
Socio-economic Planning Sciences

## Social Work

Criminology
Journal of Social Service Research
Social Service Review

Social Work
Social Work Abstracts
Social Work Research

# Statistical Sourcebooks

The following are useful statistical sourcebooks and government publications.

- ■ U.S. Bureau of the Census. *Historical Statistics of the United States.* Washington, D.C.: U.S. Government Printing Office. Published irregularly. Arranged in 26 chapters: population; vital statistics and health and medical care; migration; labor; prices and price indexes; national income and wealth; consumer income and expenditures; social statistics; land, water, and climate; agriculture; forestry and fisheries; minerals; construction and housing; manufactures; transportation; communication; power; distribution and services; foreign trade and other international transactions; business enterprise; productivity and technological development; banking and finance; government; colonial statistics. Index of names and subjects.

- U.S. Bureau of the Census. *Statistical Abstract of the United States.* Washington, D.C.: U.S. Government Printing Office. Published annually. Arranged in 33 sections: population; vital statistics, health, and nutrition; immigration and naturalization; education; law enforcement, federal courts and prisons; area, geography, and climate; public lands, parks, recreation, and travel; labor force, employment, and earnings; national defense and veterans affairs; social insurance and welfare services; income, expenditures, and wealth; prices; elections; federal government finances and employment; state and local government finances and employment; banking, finance, and insurance; business enterprise; communications; power; science; transportation—land; transportation—air and water; agriculture—farms, land, and finances; agriculture—production, marketing, and trade; forests and forest products; fisheries; mining and mineral products; construction and housing; manufactures; distribution and services; foreign commerce and aid; outlying areas under the jurisdiction of the United States; comparative international statistics. Six appendixes. Index of names and subjects. (Also available online.)
- U.S. Bureau of the Census. *Census of Population.* Washington, D.C.: U.S. Government Printing Office. Published every ten years. Contains the following information for most urban places of 2,500 inhabitants or more: population by sex; major occupational groups by sex; color of population by sex; age of population by sex; years of school completed; marital status of males and females, 14 years of age and older; country of birth of foreign-born whites.
- Murray, Toni, ed. *The Federal Data Base Finder.* 4th ed. Kensington, Md.: Information USA, 1995.
- U.S. Superintendent of Documents. *Monthly Catalog of United States Government Publications.* Washington, D.C.: U.S. Government Printing Office. Published monthly. (Available: print, microfiche, online, CD-ROM.)
- Taylor, Charles L., and David Jodice. *World Handbook of Political and Social Indicators.* 3d ed. New Haven, Conn.: Yale University Press, 1983. 2 vol. set. An extensive compilation of 75 variables for 133 countries based on indexes covering human resources, government and politics, communication, wealth, health, education, family and social relations, distributions of wealth and income, and religion.
- U.S. Bureau of the Census. *County and City Data Book.* Washington, D.C.: U.S. Government Printing Office. Published irregularly. Includes numerous tables for each county and cities with 25,000 inhabitants or more. Contains tables on such areas as labor force, income, elections, banking and finance, business enterprises, and education. (Available: print, microfiche, online, CD-ROM.)
- *Municipal Year Book.* Washington D.C.: International City-County Management Association. Published annually. Authoritative reference book on municipal governments. Includes information about the role of city governments (including education, housing, welfare, and health) making it possible to compare the cities listed on hundreds of variables.

- *American Statistics Index.* Bethesda, Md.: Congressional Information Service. Published monthly. A comprehensive index of statistical publications from more than 400 agencies of the U.S. government. (Also available: online, CD-ROM.) [CD-ROM title: *Statistical Masterfile.*]
- *Statistical Reference Index.* Bethesda, Md.: Congressional Information Service. Published monthly. Information on state government publications and on statistical studies by universities and independent research organizations. (Also available: online, CD-ROM.) [CD-ROM title: *Statistical Masterfile.*]
- *Index to International Statistics.* Bethesda, Md.: Congressional Information Service. Published monthly. This is an index of international and intergovernmental organizations. (Also available: online, CD-ROM.) [CD-ROM title: *Statistical Masterfile.*]

## Handbooks

Several excellent handbooks are available that describe, in great detail, the sources of problems, hypotheses, and data available to social scientists. They include the following:

- Bart, Pauline, and Linda Frankel. *The Student Sociologist Handbook.* 4th ed. New York: McGraw-Hill, 1986.
- Holler, Fredrick L. *Information Sources of Political Science.* 4th ed. Santa Barbara, Calif.: ABC-Clio, 1986.
- Miller, Delbert C. *Handbook of Research Design and Social Measurement.* 5th ed. Newbury Park, Calif.: Sage Publications, 1991.
- Murphy, Thomas P., ed. *Urban Indicators: A Guide to Information Sources.* Detroit: Gale Research, 1980.
- Wasserman, Paul, and Jacqueline O'Brien. *Statistics Sources.* 18th ed. Detroit: Gale Research, 1994.

## Summary

**1.** Research problems are intellectual stimuli calling for an answer in the form of a scientific inquiry. Problems amenable to research are empirically grounded, clear, and specific. In the problem formation stage, researchers also give serious consideration to the units of analysis. Making inferences about a unit of analysis on the basis of research on a unit at a different level can lead to either of two fallacies, the ecological or the individualistic.

**2.** Researchers move from the conceptual to the observational level when they convert concepts into variables by mapping or translating them into a set of values. A variable is an empirical property that can have two or more values. For purposes of research, scientists make a distinction between independent, dependent, and control variables. An independent variable is the presumed cause of the dependent variable, and a dependent variable is the presumed outcome of the influence of the independent variable. Researchers use control variables to test whether the observed relations between independent and dependent variables are spurious. Variables can also be continuous or discrete. A discrete variable has a minimum-sized unit; a continuous variable does not have a minimum-sized unit.

**3.** A relation in empirical research always means an association between two or more variables. When we say that two variables are related, we mean that there is something common to them. Researchers establish the presence of a relation by determining whether values of one variable covary with values of other variables. Two properties of relations should be stressed: direction and magnitude. When we speak of direction, we mean that the relation between the variables is either positive or negative. The magnitude of a relation is the extent to which variables covary positively or negatively.

**4.** Hypotheses are tentative answers to research problems. They are expressed in the form of a relation between dependent and independent variables. Research hypotheses have to be clear, specific, value-free, and amenable to empirical testing with the available research methods.

**5.** Research problems and hypotheses can be deductively derived from theories, directly from observation, intuitively, or from a combination of these methods. The greatest source of problems and hypotheses is the professional literature. The social scientist should be informed of the major guides to published research, including reference books, bibliographies, indexes, abstracts, journals, and statistical sourcebooks. Most university libraries now offer online (computerized) database search services.

---

## Key Terms for Review

---

continuous variable (p. 58)
control variable (p. 57)
covariation (p. 59)
dependent variable (p. 56)
discrete variable (p. 58)
ecological fallacy (p. 54)
explanatory variable (p. 56)
hypothesis (p. 62)
independent variable (p. 56)

individualistic fallacy (p. 55)
magnitude of a relation (p. 62)
negative relation (p. 60)
positive relation (p. 60)
relation (p. 59)
research problem (p. 52)
spurious relation (p. 57)
unit of analysis (p. 53)
variable (p. 55)

---

## Study Questions

---

1. Identify two empirical social science problems.
2. What is the ecological fallacy? What is the individualistic fallacy? How can a researcher avoid these fallacies?

3. Write three researchable hypotheses and identify their independent, dependent, and control variables.
4. Using the same three hypotheses, clearly indicate expected changes in the magnitude and direction of the dependent and independent variables.
5. What are some major sources of information regarding the research problems identified in Question 1?

---

## Additional Readings

---

Alker, Hayward R. "A Typology of Ecological Fallacies." In *Quantitative Analysis in the Social Sciences,* ed. Mattei N. Dogan and Stein Rokkam. New York: Cambridge University Press, 1969.

Bailey, Kenneth D. *Methods of Social Research.* 4th ed. New York: Free Press, 1994.

Bronowski, Jacob. *The Origins of Knowledge and Imagination.* New Haven, Conn.: Yale University Press, 1979.

Gilreath, Charles L. *Computerized Literature Searching: Research Strategies and Data Bases.* Boulder, Colo.: Westview Press, 1984.

Harris, Cooper M. *Integrating Research: A Guide to Literature Review.* Newbury Park, Calif.: Sage, 1989.

Johnson, Janet B. *Political Science Research Methods.* 2d ed. Washington, D.C.: CQ Press, 1991.

Kramer, Jerald H. "The Ecological Fallacy Revisited: Aggregate versus Individual Level Findings on Economics and Elections and Sociotropic Voting." *American Political Science Review,* 77 (1983): 92–111.

Reason, Peter, and John Rowan, eds. *Human Inquiry: Developments in New Paradigm Research.* Thousand Oaks, Calif.: Sage, 1989.

Williams, Martha E., Lawrence Lannon, and Carolyn G. Robins, eds. *Computer-readable Databases: A Directory and Data Sourcebook.* Ann Arbor, Mich.: Books on Demand, a Division of University Microfilms, 1985.

# CHAPTER 4

# Ethics in Social Science Research

Suppose you wanted to prevent or lower the incidence of skin cancer in the population? How would you go about it? Consider the case of the Tel Aviv school system. Concerned about the potential effects of Israel's Mediterranean climate and sun-loving lifestyle on the incidence of this disease, the school system decided to test whether a cancer awareness program could be effective in changing behavior. An evaluation test of such a program was conducted in 1991. The program included information about recommended times and how to dress when playing in the sun, the use of sun screens, and so forth. The researchers chose eight junior high schools; after being tested for information and physical condition, the children in four schools were taught the program while the children in the other four were not. A year later, in 1992, all the children were retested on their knowledge and behavior in order to ascertain the differential effects of the program. The results were then used to devise a program to be taught throughout the school system.

Despite its scientific framework and health-promoting objectives, such a test procedure nonetheless raises important issues: Is it ethical to deny important information to some of the research participants during the conduct of the research, even for a short time? How can the social scientist confront such an issue without jeopardizing his or her research goals?[1]

T HIS CHAPTER DISCUSSES THE ETHICS OF CONDUCTING SOCIAL science research and ways to ensure the rights and welfare of persons and communities that are the subjects of scientific studies. First, we review the reasons for recent concerns with research ethics. Next, we present three case studies—on obedience to authority, police behavior, and the attitudes of college students—as examples of some central ethical concerns. We then discuss the ethical dilemma of social scientists—the conflict between the right to conduct research and the right of research participants to self-determination, privacy, and dignity. We also suggest a cost-benefit framework for making ethical decisions in particular situations. Informed consent and the right to privacy are important ethical issues; we discuss them next. Finally, we examine professional codes of ethics and present a composite code for social scientists.

In Chapter 1, we argued that the social sciences are scientific and humanistic disciplines, and that social scientists are observers as well as participants in the research process. We also noted that social science research is not conducted in isolation. Researchers are constantly interacting with a complex and demanding sociopolitical environment that influences their research decisions both formally and informally. One critical way of coping with these influences is by following the guidelines of ethics in research.

1. Michael Fadida, Menashe Hadad, and Rafael Shafir, *Sun Exposure Among Junior High School Students in Tel Aviv—Jaffo: Knowledge, Attitudes and Behavior,* Research and Surveys (No. 67), (Tel Aviv—Jaffo: The Center for Economic and Social Research, 1994).

# Why Research Ethics?

As the scope of the social sciences has expanded and as our methods of research and analysis have become more sophisticated and penetrating, concern over the ethics of conducting social science research has grown. Issues related to research participants' rights and welfare and researchers' obligations have been discussed in each of the social science professions, and most scientific associations have adopted ethical codes that cover their particular domains.

Obviously, conducting research that may violate the rights and welfare of research participants is neither the intent nor the major interest of social scientists. The sole objective of research is to contribute to the development of systematic, verifiable knowledge. The research process, as discussed earlier (see Figure 1.1), provides the overall scheme of activities enabling scientists to produce such knowledge. However, each of the stages of the research process may involve ethical, in addition to purely scientific, considerations.

Ethical issues arise from the kinds of problems social scientists investigate and the methods used to obtain valid and reliable data. They may be evoked by the research problem itself (e.g., genetic engineering, determinants of intelligence, program evaluation), the setting in which the research takes place (hospitals, prisons, public schools, government agencies), the procedures required by the research design (exposure of the experimental group to conditions that may have negative effects on the participants), the method of data collection (covert participant observation), the kinds of persons serving as research participants (the poor, children, people with AIDS, politicians), and the type of data collected (personal information, recruitment practices in public agencies). The following three studies provide concrete examples of these ethical issues.

## Obedience to Authority Study

The Milgram study is an important and controversial case worth describing in some detail. Stanley Milgram conducted a controlled laboratory experiment to identify the conditions under which individuals would fail to obey instructions from a person in a position of authority.[2]

Two people came to a psychology laboratory to work together in a study of learning processes. One was to be a "teacher" and the other a "student." The real experimental participant was the teacher, who was told that the objective of the experiment was to study the effect that punishment would have on learning. However, the student, who was seated in a chair with an electrode attached to his wrist and his arms strapped to prevent movement, had been instructed beforehand on how to react. The individual conducting the experiment told the student that he

---

2. The following discussion is based on Stanley Milgram, *Obedience to Authority* (New York: Harper & Row, 1975).

was to learn a list of pairs of words. If he made an error, he would receive a shock. The teacher observed all this and was then taken into the main experimental room and instructed on how to use an impressive-looking shock generator that had an array of 30 switches labeled from 15 to 450 volts. The switches were also labeled from "slight shock" to "danger—severe shock"; at level 28 (420 volts), the label was marked "XXX" in red.

The teacher was then told that he would "teach" the person in the other room by reading him a list of paired words such as *"nice—day"* or *"blue—box."* The teacher was then to read one of the words—the stimulus term—followed by four possible responses. The student was to indicate which of the possible responses was correct by pressing one of four switches. If the response was correct, the teacher went on to the next set. If the response was incorrect, he was to administer a shock to the student. The teacher was also instructed to move one level higher on the shock generator whenever a wrong response was given. However, unknown to the teacher, *no actual shocks were ever given to the student.*

The primary dependent variable in these experiments was obedience—the willingness of the teacher to follow the instructions of the person in authority, the investigator, who encouraged him to continue to administer increasingly severe shocks to the student, who continued to make errors or failed to respond. The instructions took the form of statements such as: "You must go on. The experiment requires that you go on. I'll take the responsibility." The student continued to give similar responses to the experimental procedure. He indicated no discomfort until the 75-volt shock, at which time he gave a little grunt. He continued to grunt at the 90-volt and the 105-volt shocks, but at the 120-volt shock, the student yelled that the shocks were painful. At 135 volts, he groaned loudly, and at 150 volts he shouted that he wanted to be released and refused to continue. He gave similar responses but with greater intensity to subsequent shocks, and at 180 volts he cried out that he couldn't stand the pain. At 270 volts he screamed in agony, and at 300 volts he refused to continue giving answers. After 330 volts, the student was no longer heard from.

The findings of these experiments defied common morality: many research participants were obedient and continued to administer what they thought were painful and dangerous shocks to the student in compliance with the experimenter's instructions. In one experiment, 26 of the 40 research participants continued the shocks to the maximum of 450 volts, 5 reached 300 volts before quitting, and 8 reached between 315 and 360 volts.

Another important finding in this study was the extent to which the experimental experience induced a high level of stress for the *teacher* rather than for the student, who was never actually shocked. According to Milgram, "Subjects [i.e., the teachers in the experiment] were observed to sweat, bite their lips, groan, and dig their fingernails into their flesh. These were characteristic, rather than exceptional, responses to the experiment."[3] There was substantial evidence that the

3. Stanley Milgram, "Behavioral Study of Obedience," *Journal of Abnormal and Social Psychology,* 67 (1963): 375.

stress for the research participants, usually those who were obedient, was extreme. Such stress was acknowledged by both the teachers and the experimenters. Aware of the possibility that the research procedures might have long-term negative consequences on the participants, the research team took two measures. First, they later provided all participants with a complete, true description of the purposes and the mechanics of the experiment and arranged a friendly meeting between the teacher and the student. Second, one year after the experiment, a psychiatric interview was conducted with a sample of the participants; no negative effects were detected.

The experiment aroused a number of ethical criticisms concerning the way it was conducted. First, the teachers were under the false impression that they were inflicting pain on another individual. That is, the participants were *initially deceived* about the true purpose of the research. Thus, their right to full and truthful information about the experiment had been denied. Second, the participants suffered extreme stress; they became seriously upset and nervous, and some even had uncontrollable seizures. Third, some critics charged that as the results were made known, participants might be overwhelmed with guilt when they realized what the results might have been had they really administered electric shocks. Fourth, the experiment was criticized on the grounds that "it could easily effect an alteration in the subject's ability to trust adult authorities in the future"; in other words, it could undermine the participants' trust in authority. Finally, some critics maintained that because the participants derived no benefit from being in the obedience study, the experiments should not have been carried out.[4] Although Milgram has responded to these ethical concerns, the issues raised continue to be valid and important.[5]

## Police Behavior Study

In the 1960s, charges of police brutality were frequent in communities throughout the United States. Until then, such charges and actual police behavior toward the public in general had not been studied systematically. Albert Reiss decided to observe how police treated citizens. He knew, however, that if the individual police officers being observed had known the true purpose of the study, they would have curtailed any brutality. Therefore, Reiss led the officers to believe that the study mainly concerned the reactions of citizens to the police. In the course of the study, Reiss recorded a substantial amount of mistreatment and brutality on the part of the police.[6]

This study raised three important ethical issues. First, Reiss had used deception to gain access to observations that he would otherwise have been denied. (The

4. For a more detailed discussion of these criticisms, see Diana Baumrind, "Some Thoughts on Ethics of Research: After Reading Milgram's Behavioral Study of Obedience," *American Psychologist,* 19 (1964): 421–423.

5. For Milgram's responses, see his *Obedience to Authority,* pp. 193–202.

6. Albert J. Reiss, *The Police and the Public* (New Haven, Conn.: Yale University Press, 1971), and "Police Brutality: Answers to Key Questions," *Transaction,* 5 (1968): 10–19.

individual police officers had not known the true purpose of the study, nor had they known that *they* were the primary units of observation and analysis.) Second, and relatedly, the police officers had not agreed to participate in the study. They had not given their fully informed consent because they had not been told that they were the true subjects of the research. And third, studies of this type could generate distrust among potential research participants, such as police officers, to the extent that future investigators would find it difficult to obtain information or to gain the cooperation of participants.

## College Student Attitudes Study

A study that increased the awareness of ethical issues in survey research was the American Council of Education project on the social and political attitudes of college students.[7] Designed in the 1960s during the period of student unrest on college campuses, its purpose was to provide information on the attitudes and behavior of college undergraduates during and after their college years. This longitudinal study involved repeated surveys of the same students, as well as hundreds of thousands of other respondents. Controversy over the project was heightened when researchers included questions related to political orientation and activism in the survey questionnaire. Critics drew substantial attention to the question of the possible uses of the data and to the suspicion that school administrators or government agencies might be able to identify student activists through their access to the questionnaire. In this case, the major ethical issue was the anonymity of the participants and the confidentiality of the data. These issues are closely related to concerns over participants' rights and welfare, which we will discuss later in the chapter.

---

# Balancing Costs and Benefits

These three studies illustrate that important ethical issues arise before and after the conduct of research in the social as well as other sciences. Research that employs **deception** as a part of an experiment has become commonplace because it offers methodological and practical advantages. Researchers sometimes collect data without the knowledge of the observed individuals; and some investigators are not always scrupulous about guarding the confidentiality of survey data.

In many cases, social scientists face a conflict between two rights: the right of the scientist to conduct research and to acquire knowledge and the right of individual research participants to self-determination, privacy, and dignity. A decision not to conduct a planned research project because it interferes with the participants' welfare imposes limitations on the researcher's rights. A decision to conduct research despite an ethically questionable practice (for example, deception) denies

---

7. See Robert F. Boruch, "Education Research and the Confidentiality of Data: A Case Study," *Sociology of Education*, 44 (1971): 59–85, and J. Walsh, "A.C.E. Study on Campus Unrest: Questions for Behavioral Scientists," *Science*, 165 (1969): 1243–1245.

the participants' rights. This conflict is the essence of the **ethical dilemma** of social science research.

There are no absolute right or wrong answers to this dilemma. The values people attach to the benefits and costs of social science research depend heavily on their background, convictions, and experience. For example, whereas policy analysts emphasize the benefits that can result from accurately predicting the effects of public policies, civil libertarians are always alert to possible dangers to individual freedom, privacy, and self-determination. They tend to doubt that the benefits of any study justify taking even a small risk of invading individual rights.

In planning a research project, researchers have the obligation to carefully weigh the potential benefits or contributions of a project against its costs to the individual participants. Such costs may include affronts to dignity, anxiety, embarrassment, loss of trust in social relations, loss of autonomy and self-determination, and lowered self-esteem. For the scientist, the benefits of a study are potential advances in theoretical or applied knowledge; for the participant, the gains include monetary compensation, satisfaction in making a contribution to science, and better understanding of the researched phenomena.

The process of balancing potential benefits against possible costs is necessarily subjective. Scientists formulate or select research procedures in accordance with professional and personal values. Because our choices are related to our values, scientists, just like anyone else, should weigh these values carefully when making ethical decisions. Furthermore, ethical decisions have to be made individually, in each case, because the process of reaching decisions is as important as the final choice. The ethical researcher "is educated about ethical guidelines, carefully examines moral alternatives, exercises judgment in each situation, and accepts responsibility for his choice."[8] Within this context of costs versus benefits, two central problems that most often concern investigators are those of informed consent and privacy.

# Informed Consent

There is a wide consensus among social scientists that research involving human participants should be performed with the **informed consent** of the participants. Informed consent is absolutely essential whenever participants are exposed to substantial risks or are asked to forfeit personal rights. In fact, the U.S. Department of Health and Human Services guidelines governing research supported by its grants require that a researcher obtain signed consent forms from research participants who are to be placed "at risk."[9] Major universities have voluntarily agreed

8. Eduard Diener and Rick Crandall, *Ethics in Social and Behavioral Research* (Chicago: University of Chicago Press, 1978), pp. 4–5.
9. U.S. Department of Health, Education and Welfare, Public Health Service and National Institutes of Health, *The Institutional Guide to D.H.E.W. Policy on Protection of Human Subjects,* DHEW Publication (NIH): 72–102 (December 2, 1971). See also, Arturo Gandara, *Major Federal Regulations Governing Social Science Research* (Santa Monica, Calif.: Rand, 1978).

to comply with federal guidelines in reviewing all research conducted in their institutions, whether funded by the federal government or not. The informed consent policy does not preclude the conduct of social science research that involves risk, but it does require the use of informed participants. When research participants are to be exposed to pain, physical or emotional injury, invasion of privacy, or physical or psychological stress, or when they are asked to temporarily surrender their autonomy (for example, in drug research), informed consent must be fully guaranteed. Participants should know that their involvement is voluntary at all times, and they should receive a thorough explanation beforehand of the benefits, rights, risks, and dangers involved with their participation in the research project.

## Reasons for Informed Consent

The idea of informed consent derives from both cultural values and legal considerations. It is rooted in the high value we attach to freedom and to self-determination. We believe that people should be free to determine their own behavior because freedom is a cherished value. Advocates of this view might even argue, like John Locke, that being free is a natural right, and that restrictions on freedom must be carefully justified and agreed to. When the individuals involved in research risk limitation of their freedom, they must be asked to agree to this limitation.

Furthermore, asking individuals whether they wish to participate in a research project reflects a respect for the right of self-determination. Another reason for consent is based on the argument that informed individuals are best able to promote their own well-being. Because people will protect their own interests, allowing them freedom of choice about their participation provides a safeguard against hazardous research procedures.[10] Finally, from the researchers' perspective, informed consent shifts part of the responsibility to the participants for any negative effects that might occur in the course of the study. It also reduces the legal liability of the researcher because participants will have voluntarily agreed to take part in the research project.

## The Meaning of Informed Consent

Although the principle of informed consent has enjoyed widespread acceptance, researchers have yet to implement it consistently. This is mainly a result of disagreements about what informed consent means in specific cases. Questions like these—"What is an informed participant?" "How do we know that a person understands the information given?" "How much information should be given?" "What if it is extremely important that participants do not know whether they are in the experimental or control group?"—are obviously difficult, and there are no standard answers. It is possible and useful, however, to clarify the intent of the

10. Diener and Crandall, *Ethics in Social and Behavioral Research*, p. 36.

informed consent principle. We do so in order to point out its major elements and to discuss some issues involved in its implementation.

Eduard Diener and Rick Crandall define informed consent as "the procedure in which individuals choose whether to participate in an investigation after being informed of facts that would be likely to influence their decision."[11] This involves four elements: competence, voluntarism, full information, and comprehension.

*Competence.*    The underlying assumption of the principle of informed consent, the assumption of **competence,** is that any decision made by a responsible, mature individual *who is given the relevant information* will be the correct decision. However, because many persons are not mature or responsible, the problem becomes one of systematically identifying them.

In general, persons are incapable of providing consent if they have impaired mental capacity or a questionable ability to exercise self-determination. Persons generally considered incompetent include young children, comatose medical patients, and mental patients. When participation in a research project (for example, tests of a therapeutic treatment) may provide direct benefits to the subjects, it is considered appropriate for the guardians, parents, and others responsible for such incompetent individuals to make decisions for them. When direct benefits are not expected and there is some risk of negative effects, many would suggest that the research should be prohibited altogether.[12]

*Voluntarism.*    An investigator who complies with the principle of informed consent ensures the freedom of participants to choose whether or not to take part in a research project and guarantees that exposure to known risks is undertaken voluntarily. But establishing the conditions under which individuals can decide on the basis of free will is a complex task. In research situations that involve institutional settings such as prisons, mental institutions, hospitals, or public schools, persons in positions of authority exercise substantial influence over the participants. For example, a patient in the care of a physician-researcher may consent to a treatment because he or she is physically weak or is under the influence of the physician in some way. Although the ethics of medical experimentation emphasize voluntary consent, researchers did not face the subtle nature of some infringements on that **voluntarism** until after World War II. The *Nuremberg Code,* devised after the gruesome evidence of Nazi medical experimentation came to light, sets forth the researcher's responsibility to carefully explain the conditions of the research as a prerequisite to receiving truly voluntary consent:

> This means that the person involved should have legal capacity to give consent; [the person] should be so situated as to be able to exercise free power of choice,

---

11. Ibid., p. 34.
12. Paul D. Reynolds, *Ethical Dilemmas and Social Science Research* (San Francisco: Jossey-Bass, 1979), p. 91.

without the intervention of any element of force, fraud, deceit, over-reaching, or other ulterior form of constraint or coercion.[13]

In order to establish the conditions conducive to voluntary consent, some observers have suggested that the researcher establish an egalitarian relationship with the participants and view the research endeavor as a joint adventure in the exploration of the unknown.[14] Other scientists suggest that the presence of a neutral third party during the informed consent procedure will minimize possibilities for coercion. Still others advise that participants be allowed to consult with others after a request for consent is made but before a decision is reached.

*Full Information.*     To be acceptable, consent must be *voluntary* and *informed.* Consent may be uninformed yet given voluntarily or fully informed yet involuntary.

In practice, it is impossible to obtain fully informed consent, as this would require the researcher to communicate numerous technical and statistical details as well as undermine the usefulness of a control group. Furthermore, in many situations scientists themselves do not have full information about the consequences associated with the research procedures. If, in Paul Reynolds's words, "there were full information, there would be no reason to conduct the research—research is only of value when there is ambiguity about a phenomenon."[15] This, however, should not imply that the informed consent philosophy is totally inapplicable. Instead, scientists have adopted the strategy of **reasonably informed consent.**

The federal guidelines are based on the idea of reasonably informed consent. The guidelines call for researchers to communicate six basic elements of information in order for consent to be reasonably informed:[16]

1. A fair explanation of the procedures to be followed and their purposes.
2. A description of the attendant discomforts and risks reasonably to be expected.
3. A description of the benefits reasonably to be expected.
4. A disclosure of appropriate alternative procedures that might be advantageous to the participant.
5. An offer to answer any inquiries concerning the procedures.
6. An instruction that the person is free to withdraw consent and to discontinue participation in the project at any time without prejudice to the participant.

Some of the elements of information included in these guidelines are obviously controversial. For example, disclosure of the research purpose could invalidate the findings; this was the case in the Milgram experiments and the Reiss study. Scientists also disagree over how much information must be disclosed. In fact, a study by H. R. Resnick and T. Schwartz illustrates a situation in which giv-

13. Ibid., p. 436.
14. Ibid., p. 93.
15. Ibid., p. 95.
16. HEW, *Institutional Guide to D.H.E.W. Policy,* p.7.

ing complete information can be undesirable. Resnick and Schwartz told potential participants in a verbal conditioning study everything about the experiment before it began, giving them a lengthy, detailed explanation about the research procedures. Many participants never showed up for the study. And, contrary to the findings from other similar studies, those who did participate did not learn. The study showed that giving participants too much information can have destructive effects on the research outcomes.[17]

Questions concerning the criteria for deciding what information should be given to participants have taken on crucial importance. One criterion is the legal framework of what a "reasonable and prudent person" would want to know. Researchers must fully disclose all aspects of the study that a person concerned about his or her own welfare would need to know before making a decision. Research participants should always be informed of any possible negative physical or psychological consequences or of any rights to be lost during the study.

A more easily applied method to determine what information may be relevant to participants is to let a committee representing potential participants or both investigators and participants make the selection. Another procedure is to interview surrogate participants systematically and allow them to determine what information is relevant.[18]

*Comprehension.*    The fourth element of informed consent, **comprehension,** refers to "confidence that the participant has provided knowing consent when the research procedure is associated with complex or subtle risks."[19] Clearly, an elaborate description of the project, even if it is provided in nontechnical language, may be difficult to fully comprehend.

A number of ways have been suggested to ensure complete comprehension by participants. These include the use of highly educated participants who are most likely to understand the information, the availability of a consultant to discuss the study with the participant, and a time lag between the request for participation and the decision to take part in the study. A common procedure used to independently measure comprehension consists of directly questioning the participants or asking them to respond to questionnaires that test whether they understand the information.[20]

## The Responsibility of the Scientist

The practice of ensuring informed consent is the most general solution to the problem of how to promote social science research without encroaching on individual rights and welfare. If all the conditions associated with informed consent—

17. H. J. Resnick and T. Schwartz, "Ethical Standards as an Independent Variable in Psychological Research," *American Psychologist,* 28 (1973): 134–139.
18. For this and other procedures, see Reynolds, *Ethical Dilemmas and Social Science Research,* pp. 95–96.
19. Ibid., p. 97.
20. Ibid.

competence, voluntarism, full information, and comprehension—are present, the scientist can be relatively confident that the rights and welfare of research participants have received appropriate attention.

The principle of informed consent should not, however, be made an absolute requirement for all social science research. Although desirable, it is not an absolute necessity in studies where no danger or risk is involved. The more serious the risk to research participants, the greater the obligation to obtain informed consent. At the same time, investigators remain responsible for possible negative effects on participants, even if the latter have consented to take part in the research.

# Privacy

Invasions of privacy are of great concern to all, especially in an era when computerized databanks, both governmental and commercial, are so accessible. The **right to privacy**—"the freedom of the individual to pick and choose for himself the time and circumstances under which, and most importantly, the extent to which, his attitudes, beliefs, behavior, and opinions are to be shared with or withheld from others"[21]—may easily be violated during a study or after its completion.

In the investigation of the attitudes of college students conducted by the American Council on Education, we saw that respondents were requested to give private, sensitive information that could have been used by campus administrators and government authorities to identify campus activists. The data were placed in computer storage and made available to anyone willing to pay a small user's fee, a practice more and more common today. To protect their research participants, the researchers separated the identity of the participants from their responses in the databank. But, at the time, the possibility that the authorities might subpoena the information was quite real. In this study, the researchers requested private information from students, but they could not guarantee confidentiality in the pervading political climate. In order to protect their privacy, the researchers subsequently made the sensitive information "subpoena-free" by storing the code that linked the data to individual respondents. Although this technique has been implemented in many scientific studies, the protection of the respondent's privacy is still problematic.

## Dimensions of Privacy

Three different dimensions of privacy have been identified: the sensitivity of information being given, the setting being observed, and dissemination of the information.[22] Before discussing a few methods for safeguarding privacy, it is useful to discuss each of the three dimensions.

21. M. O. Ruebhausen and Oliver G. Brim, "Privacy and Behavioral Research," *American Psychologist,* 21 (1966): 432.
22. Diener and Crandall, *Ethics in Social and Behavioral Research,* pp. 55–57.

*Sensitivity of Information.*    **Sensitivity of information** refers to how personal or potentially threatening the information is that the researcher wishes to collect. As a report by the American Psychological Association states, "Religious preferences, sexual practices, income, racial prejudices, and other personal attributes such as intelligence, honesty, and courage are more sensitive items than 'name, rank, and serial number.' "[23] The greater the sensitivity of the information, the more researchers are obligated to provide safeguards to protect the privacy of the research participants. For example, until the November 1993 Joseph Steffan decision, Pentagon policy had barred gay people from serving as soldiers and sailors under any circumstances.[24] If information about a soldier's sexual preferences had been transmitted during a research project, the investigators would have to be doubly scrupulous in ensuring his or her privacy.

*Settings Being Observed.*    The setting of a research project may vary from very private to completely public. For example, the home is considered one of the most private settings in our culture, and intrusions into people's homes without their consent are forbidden by law. However, the extent to which a particular setting is public or private is not always self-evident and thus may lead to ethical controversies. For example, in order to study the nature of the activities of male homosexuals engaging in brief, impersonal sexual encounters in public locations (restrooms), Laud Humphreys assumed the role of a covert observer. He adopted the voyeuristic role of a "watch queen" (warning participants of approaching police, teenagers, or heterosexual males), thus gaining the confidence of the participants and access to the setting in which they could be observed. He also recorded the license plate numbers of 134 vehicles used by the participants, and interviewed 50 of these people in their homes as part of a legitimate public health survey conducted one year later.[25] Critics charged that although the study was conducted in a public restroom, the participants did not initiate sexual activities ("private acts") until they were assured that the public setting was temporarily "private." Humphreys was therefore accused of invading their privacy.

*Dissemination of Information.*    The third aspect of privacy concerns the ability to match personal information with the identity of research participants. For example, information about income remains relatively private if only the investigator has access to it. But when such information, including amounts and names, is publicized through the media, privacy is seriously invaded. The greater the number of people who can learn details of the information, the more concern there must be about privacy.

---

23. American Psychological Association, *Ethical Principles in the Conduct of Research with Human Subjects* (Washington, D.C.: Ad Hoc Committee on Ethical Standards in Psychological Research, American Psychological Association, 1973), p. 87.
24. David A. Kaplan and Daniel Glick, " 'Into the Hands of Bigots'," *Newsweek,* November 29, 1993, p. 43.
25. Laud Humphreys, *Tearoom Trade: Impersonal Sex in Public Places* (Hawthorne, N.Y.: Aldine, 1975).

It is not uncommon for a whole town or a small community to be able to identify participants in a research project even when fictitious names are used. For example, in *Small Town in Mass Society,* Arthur Vidich and Joseph Bensman described the intimate and sometimes embarrassing details of the lives of the residents in a small town in upstate New York.[26] Although the town and the residents were given fictitious names in the book, the individual descriptions were easily recognized by those involved. Not only was this aspect of the study severely criticized,[27] but the townspeople staged a parade in which each wore a mask bearing the fictitious name given to him or her by the researchers—a clear indication that the whole town knew the identity of the participants in the book. At the end of the parade came a manure spreader, with an effigy of the researcher looking into the manure.[28]

Researchers must consider all three aspects—sensitivity of the information, the setting of the project, and the extent of the dissemination of information obtained—when deciding how private certain information is and what safeguards must be used to protect research participants.

Like most rights, privacy can be voluntarily relinquished. Research participants may voluntarily give up their right of privacy by either allowing a researcher access to sensitive information and settings or by agreeing that the research report may identify them by name. In the latter case, the informed consent of participants is necessary.

---

# Anonymity and Confidentiality

Two common methods researchers use to protect participants are anonymity and confidentiality. The obligation to protect the anonymity of research participants and to keep research data confidential is all-inclusive. It should be fulfilled at all costs unless the researcher makes arrangements to the contrary with the participants in advance. As in the case of privacy, the spread of computer networks such as INTERNET and advanced satellite communications are making the ability to safeguard anonymity and confidentiality more technically complicated and morally necessary.

## Anonymity

Researchers provide **anonymity** by separating the identity of individuals from the information they give. A participant is considered anonymous when the researcher or other persons cannot identify particular information with a particular participant. That is, if the information is given anonymously, with the researcher unable to associate a name with the data, then the identity of the participant is secured even though sensitive information may be revealed. For example, researchers can

26. Arthur J. Vidich and Joseph Bensman, *Small Town in Mass Society* (Garden City, N.Y.: Doubleday, 1960).
27. Urie Bronfenbrenner, "Freedom and Responsibility in Research: Comments," *Human Organization,* 18 (1959): 49–52.
28. Diener and Crandall, *Ethics in Social and Behavioral Research,* p. 62.

maintain anonymity in a mail survey (discussed in Chapter 10) by removing identification numbers from questionnaires after they are returned. On the other hand, a respondent to a personal interview cannot be considered anonymous because the respondent is identifiable to the interviewer.

One procedure for ensuring anonymity is simply not to acquire names and other means of identifying participants in a research project. Alternatively, researchers may ask participants to use an alias of their own choosing or to transform well-remembered identification numbers (for example, by subtracting the numerals of their birthday from their social security number). Anonymity may be enhanced if names and other identifiers are linked to the information by a code number. While preparing the data for analysis, researchers can maintain anonymity by separating identifying information from the data itself. Further safeguards include the prevention of duplication of records, passwords to control access to data, and automatic monitoring of the use of files.[29]

## Confidentiality

Participants in social science research are often told that the information they provide will be treated as confidential, that is, that even though the researchers are able to identify a particular participant's information, they will not reveal it publicly. Although investigators have a strict moral and professional obligation to keep the promise of **confidentiality,** there are circumstances in which it may be difficult or even impossible to do so. One of the most important of these situations arises when information is subpoenaed by judicial authorities or legislative committees.

In the data collection stage, researchers should clearly and accurately inform the participants about the meaning and limits of confidentiality, preferably by written statements. The greater the jeopardy posed by the information itself and the greater the chances of subpoena or audit of individual data, the more explicit the explanation given to participants should be. Donald Campbell and his coauthors offer suggestions for possible explanations. However, when the material solicited involves no obvious jeopardy to respondents, a general promise of confidentiality is sufficient, for example:

> These interviews will be summarized in group statistics so that no one will learn of your individual answers. All interviews will be kept confidential. There is a remote chance that you will be contacted later to verify the fact that I actually conducted this interview and have conducted it completely and honestly.[30]

Where full and honest answers to research questions could jeopardize a respondent's interests, as in the case of subpoena, the respondent should be so informed, for example:

29. For an excellent discussion of these and other procedures, see Reynolds, *Ethical Dilemmas and Social Science Research,* pp.167–174.

30. Donald T. Campbell et al., "Protection of the Rights and Interests of Human Subjects in Program Evaluation, Social Indicators, Social Experimentation, and Statistical Analyses Based upon Administrative Records: Preliminary Sketch." Northwestern University, mimeographed, 1976.

These interviews are being made to provide average statistical evidence in which individual answers will not be identified or identifiable. We will do everything in our power to keep your answer completely confidential. Only if so ordered by Court and Judge would we turn over individually identified interviews to any other group or government agency.[31]

In order to permit outsiders' access to data without compromising the confidentiality requirement, a number of techniques have been developed. These include the following:[32]

1. *Deletion of identifiers*—for example, deleting the names, social security numbers, and street addresses from the data released on individuals.
2. *Crude report categories*—for example, releasing county rather than neighborhood (or census-tract) data, year of birth rather than specific date, profession but not professional specialization, and so on.
3. *Microaggregation*—that is, constructing "average persons" from data on individuals and releasing these data rather than the original data on individuals.
4. *Error inoculation*—deliberately introducing errors into individual records while leaving the aggregate data unchanged.

---

# Professional Codes of Ethics

Regulations guiding social science research now exist at several levels. Legal statutes, ethics review committees in research universities and institutions, ethical codes of the professional associations, and the personal ethics of the individual researcher are all important regulatory mechanisms. Here we will explore the issue of professional codes of ethics and present a composite ethical code for social scientists.

The major professional societies have developed **codes of ethics** to assist their members. Ethical codes are written to cover the specific problems and issues that scientists frequently encounter in the types of research carried out within a particular profession. Codes sensitize the researcher to obligations and to problem areas where there is agreem:nt about proper ethical practice. These codes therefore reflect the consensus regarding values within the profession. They help the individual researcher because they state and explain what is required and what is forbidden.

Paul Reynolds has put together a useful composite code of ethics based on statements appearing in 24 separate codes related to the conduct of social science research. Most of these codes have been adopted by national associations of social scientists. Reynolds's composite code is reported in Exhibit 4.1. (The figure after each item indicates how many of the 24 ethical codes included such a statement.)

---

31. Ibid.
32. See Henry W. Riecken and Robert F. Boruch, *Social Experimentation* (Orlando, Fla.: Academic Press, 1979), pp. 258–269.

---

**Exhibit 4.1**

A Code of Ethics for Social Scientists

---

## Principles

*General Issues Related to the Code of Ethics*

1. The social scientist(s) in charge of a research project is (are) responsible for all decisions regarding procedural matters and ethical issues related to the project whether made by themselves or subordinates (7).

2. Teachers are responsible for all decisions made by their students related to ethical issues involved in research (1).

3. All actions conducted as part of the research should be consistent with the ethical standards of both the home and host community (1).

4. Ethical issues should be considered from the perspective of the participant's society (2).

5. If unresolved or difficult ethical dilemmas arise, assistance or consultation should be sought with colleagues or appropriate committees sponsored by professional associations (2).

6. Any deviation from established principles suggests: (a) that a greater degree of responsibility is being accepted by the investigator, (b) a more serious obligation to seek outside counsel and advice, and (c) the need for additional safeguards to protect the rights and welfare of the research participants (2).

*Decision to Conduct the Research*

7. Research should be conducted in such a way as to maintain the integrity of the research enterprise and not to diminish the potential for conducting research in the future (3).

8. Investigators should use their best scientific judgment for selection of issues for empirical investigation (1).

9. The decision to conduct research with human subjects should involve evaluation of the potential benefits to the participant and society in relation to the risks to be borne by the participant(s)—a risk-benefit analysis (2).

10. Any study which involves human subjects must be related to an important intellectual question (4).

11. Any study which involves human subjects must be related to an important intellectual question with humanitarian implications, and there should be no other way to resolve the intellectual question (2).

12. Any study which involves human participants must be related to a very important intellectual question if there is a risk of permanent, negative effects on the participants (2).

13. Any study involving risks as well as potential therapeutic effects must be justified in terms of benefits to the client or patient (2).

14. There should be no prior reason to believe that major permanent negative effects will occur for the participants (1).

15. If the conduct of the research may permanently damage the participants, their community, or institutions within their community (such as indigenous social scientists), the research may not be justified and might be abandoned (2).

*Conduct of the Research*

16. All research should be conducted in a competent fashion, as an objective, scientific project (4).

---

**Exhibit 4.1** *(continued)*

---

17. All research personnel should be qualified to use any procedures employed in the project (7).

18. Competent personnel and adequate facilities should be available if any drugs are involved (4).

19. There should be no bias in the design, conduct, or reporting of the research—it should be as objective as possible (4).

## Effects on and Relationships with the Participants

*Informed Consent*

General

20. Informed consent should be used in obtaining participants for all research; investigators should honor all commitments associated with such agreements (10).

21. Participants should be in a position to give informed consent; otherwise it should be given by those responsible for the participant (2).

22. Informed consent should be used if the potential effects on participants are ambiguous or potentially hazardous (7).

23. If possible, informed consent should be obtained in writing (1).

24. Seek official permission to use any government data, no matter how it was obtained (1).

Provision of Information

25. Purposes, procedures, and risks of research (including possible hazards to physical and psychological well-being and jeopardization of social position) should be explained to the participants in such a way that they can understand (7).

26. Participants should be aware of the possible consequences, if any, for the group or community from which they are selected in advance of their decision to participate (1).

27. The procedure used to obtain the participant's name should be described to him or her (1).

28. Sponsorship, financial and otherwise, should be specified to the potential participants (2).

29. The identity of those conducting the research should be fully revealed to the potential participants (2).

30. Names and addresses of research personnel should be left with participants so that the research personnel can be traced subsequently (1).

31. Participants should be fully aware of all data gathering techniques (tape and video recordings, photographic devices, physiological measures, and so forth), the capacities of such techniques, and the extent to which participants will remain anonymous and data confidential (2).

32. In projects of considerable duration, participants should be periodically informed of the progress of the research (1).

33. When recording videotapes or film, subjects should have the right to approve the material to be made public (by viewing it and giving specific approval to each segment) as well as the nature of the audiences (1).

Voluntary Consent

34. Individuals should have the option to refuse to participate and know this (1).

35. Participants should be able to terminate involvement at any time and know that they have this option (3).

36. No coercion, explicit or overt, should be used to encourage individuals to participate in a research project (6).

*Protection of Rights and Welfare of Participants*

General Issues

37. The dignity, privacy, and interests of the participants should be respected and protected (8).

38. The participants should not be harmed; welfare of the participants should take priority over all other concerns (10).

39. Damage and suffering to the participants should be minimized through procedural mechanisms and termination of risky studies as soon as possible; such effects are justified only when the problem cannot be studied in any other fashion (8).

40. Potential problems should be anticipated, no matter how remote the probability of occurrence, to ensure that the unexpected does not lead to major negative effects on the participants (1).

41. Any harmful aftereffects should be eliminated (4).

42. The hopes or anxieties of potential participants should not be raised (1).

43. Research should be terminated if danger to the participants arises (3).

44. The use of clients seeking professional assistance for research purposes is justified only to the extent that they may derive direct benefits as clients (1).

Deception

45. Deceit of the participants should only be used if it is absolutely necessary, there being no other way to study the problem (3).

46. Deception may be utilized (1).

47. If deceit is involved in a research procedure, additional precautions should be taken to protect the rights and welfare of the participants (2).

48. After being involved in a study using deception, all participants should be given a thorough, complete, and honest description of the study and the need for deception (5).

49. If deception is not revealed to the participants, for humane or scientific reasons, the investigator has a special obligation to protect the interests and welfare of the participants (1).

Confidentiality and Anonymity

50. Research data should be confidential and all participants should remain anonymous, unless they (or their legal guardians) have given permission for release of their identity (15).

51. If confidentiality or anonymity cannot be guaranteed, the participants should be aware of this and its possible consequences before involvement in the research (4).

52. Persons in official positions (studied as part of a research project) should provide written descriptions of their official roles, duties, and so forth (which need not be treated as confidential information) and be provided with a copy of the final report on the research (1).

53. Studies designed to provide descriptions of aggregates or collectivities should always guarantee anonymity to individual respondents (1).

54. "Privacy" should always be considered from the perspective of the participant and the participant's culture (1).

55. Material stored in databanks should not be used without the permission of the investigator who originally gathered the data (1).

56. If promises of confidentiality are honored, investigators need not withhold information on misconduct of participants or organizations (1).

---

## Exhibit 4.1 *(continued)*

---

57. Specific procedures should be developed for organizing data to ensure anonymity of participants (1).

*Benefits to Participants*

58. A fair return should be offered for all services of participants (1).

59. Increased self-knowledge, as a benefit to the participants, should be incorporated as a major part of the research design or procedures (1).

60. Copies or explanations of the research should be provided to all participants (2).

61. Studies of aggregates or cultural subgroups should produce knowledge which will benefit them (1).

*Effects on Aggregates or Communities*

62. Investigators should be familiar with, and respect, the host cultures in which studies are conducted (1).

63. Investigators should cooperate with members of the host society (1).

64. Investigators should consider, in advance, the potential effects of the research on the social structure of the host community and the potential changes in influence of various groups or individuals by virtue of the conduct of the study (1).

65. Investigators should consider, in advance, the potential effects of the research and the report on the population or subgroup from which participants are drawn (1).

66. Participants should be aware, in advance, of potential effects upon aggregates or cultural subgroups which they represent (1).

67. The interests of collectivities and social systems of all kinds should be considered by the investigator (1).

## Interpretations and Reporting of the Results of the Research

68. All reports of research should be public documents, freely available to all (4).

69. Research procedures should be described fully and accurately in reports, including all evidence regardless of the support it provides for the research hypotheses; conclusions should be objective and unbiased (14).

70. Full and complete interpretations should be provided for all data and attempts made to prevent misrepresentations in writing research reports (6).

71. Sponsorship, purpose, sources of financial support, and investigators responsible for the research should be made clear in all publications related thereto (3).

72. If publication may jeopardize or damage the population studied and complete disguise is impossible, publication should be delayed (2).

73. Cross-cultural studies should be published in the language and journals of the host society, in addition to publication in other languages and other societies (2).

74. Appropriate credit should be given to all parties contributing to the research (9).

75. Full, accurate disclosure of all published sources bearing on or contributing to the work is expected (8).

76. Publication of research findings on cultural subgroups should include a description in terms understood by the participants (2).

77. Whenever requested, raw data or other original documentation should be made available to qualified investigators (1).

78. Research with scientific merit should always be submitted for publication and not withheld from public presentation unless the quality of research or analysis is inadequate (1).

Reprinted with permission from Paul Davidson Reynolds, *Ethical Dilemmas and Social Science Research* (San Francisco: Jossey-Bass, 1979), pp. 443–448.

## Summary

1. Because the social sciences are both scientific and humanistic, a fundamental ethical dilemma exists: How are we to develop systematic, verifiable knowledge when research procedures may infringe on the rights and welfare of individuals? There are no absolute right or wrong answers to this dilemma.

2. The values that we attach to the potential benefits and costs of social science research depend on our backgrounds, convictions, and experience. The ethical researcher is educated about ethical guidelines, thoroughly examines the costs and potential benefits of the research project, exercises judgment in each situation, and accepts responsibility for his or her choice.

3. Within this ethical decision-making framework, two common issues are informed consent and privacy. Informed consent is the most general solution to the problem of how to promote social science research without encroaching on individual rights and welfare. It is the procedure whereby individuals choose whether to participate in a research project after being informed of the facts that would be likely to influence their decision. Informed consent involves four basic aspects: competence, voluntarism, full information, and comprehension. The more serious the risk to research participants, the greater the researcher's obligation to obtain informed consent.

4. The right to privacy can be easily violated during a study or after its completion. In deciding how private given information is, the researcher considers three criteria: the sensitivity of the information, the setting being observed, and the extent of dissemination of the information. Two common ways to protect the privacy of research participants are to maintain their anonymity and to keep the data confidential.

5. A broad consensus regarding ethical issues has been emerging, as is evident from the adoption of ethical codes by professional societies. These codes state what is required and what is forbidden. Although they sensitize researchers to their obligations and to problem areas where there is agreement about proper ethical practice, there is no substitute for the personal code of ethics of the individual investigator.

## Key Terms for Review

anonymity (p. 88)
codes of ethics (p. 90)

competence (p. 83)
comprehension (p. 85)

confidentiality (p. 89)
deception (p. 80)
ethical dilemma (p. 81)
informed consent (p. 81)

reasonably informed consent (p. 84)
right to privacy (p. 86)
sensitivity of information (p. 87)
voluntarism (p. 83)

---

## Study Questions

---

1. Why do ethical concerns often arise in the conduct of research? Do you think there is a way of avoiding them in social science research?
2. List several costs and benefits of research that an investigator must weigh in deciding whether the benefits of a research project outweigh its costs to participants. Relate these costs and benefits to a specific research topic.
3. Discuss in detail the nature of informed consent. Have you participated in a research project that required informed consent? If so, how did you make your decision?
4. How can we protect the privacy of individuals when dealing with sensitive research topics? Do you have additional suggestions?
5. Distinguish between the issues of anonymity and confidentiality for research participants. Which of the two do you consider to be more problematic for the social science researcher?

---

## Additional Readings

---

Beauchamp, Tom L., et al., eds. *Ethical Issues in Social Science Research.* Baltimore: Johns Hopkins University Press, 1982.

Bermant, Gordon, Herbert C. Kelman, and Donald P. Warwick, eds. *The Ethics of Social Intervention.* New York: Wiley, 1978.

Boruch, Robert F., and Joe S. Cecil. *Assuring the Confidentiality of Social Research Data.* Philadelphia: University of Pennsylvania Press, 1979.

Faden, Ruth R. *A History and Theory of Informed Consent.* New York: Oxford University Press, 1986.

Gubrium, Jaber F., ed. *The Politics of Field Research: Beyond Enlightenment.* Newbury Park, Calif.: Sage, 1989.

Kelman, Herbert C. *A Time to Speak: On Human Values and Social Research.* San Francisco: Jossey-Bass, 1968.

Kimmel, Allan J. *Ethics and Values in Applied Social Research.* Newbury Park, Calif.: Sage, 1988.

Lappe, M. "Accountability in Science." *Science,* 187 (1975): 696–698.

Lee, Raymond, *Doing Research on Sensitive Topics.* Newbury Park, Calif.: Sage, 1993.

Punch, Maurice. *The Politics and Ethics of Field Work.* Newbury Park, Calif.: Sage, 1985.

Sieber, Joan E., ed. *The Ethics of Social Research.* New York: Springer-Verlag, 1982.

Sieber, Joan E. *Planning Ethically Responsible Research: A Guide for Social Science Students.* Newbury Park, Calif.: Sage, 1992.

# CHAPTER 5

# Research Designs: Experiments

"Who Are the Whites?"[1] This is the question guiding a 1992 study of color classifications in the 1980 Brazilian census. Unlike the United States, where race is defined through lines of descent, in Brazil individuals classify themselves by color using a combination of physical and socioeconomic characteristics. Thus children may be classified differently than their parents or siblings. The researchers in this study noted that the forced-choice, four-category color question on the Brazilian census used an obscure term for the mixed-color, or "brown," category. They argued that the use of this term caused people to reject the mixed-color option and identify themselves as either black or white, inflating the number of people counted in these categories (the fourth category, yellow, was seldom chosen). They hypothesized that if the obscure term were changed to a term more commonly used, more people would identify themselves as being of mixed color, reducing the number of both blacks and whites and more accurately reflecting the way individuals would classify themselves in a free-choice description of their color. The researchers tested a sample of the population using a pretest-posttest design and found support for their hypothesis. Based on their findings, they argued that studies using 1980 census data to compare the life experiences of Brazilian blacks and whites are flawed because many people of mixed color are included in both the black and white census categories. In turn, researchers who have used census data in their studies will be examining the design and implementation of the color-classification study to evaluate the validity of the findings. The design and implementation of such experimental studies and the factors that influence validity are the subjects of this chapter.

IN THIS CHAPTER WE DISCUSS THE RESEARCH DESIGN AS A logical model of causal inference and distinguish among several research designs. In the first section, we give an example of how an experimental research design is implemented. In the second section, we explain the structure of experimental designs. We then examine the four components of research designs: comparison, manipulation, control, and generalizability. Finally, we present some commonly used experimental designs.

Once the research objectives have been determined, the hypotheses explained, and the variables defined, the researcher confronts the problem of constructing a research design that will make it possible to test the hypotheses. A research design is the program that guides the investigator as he or she collects, analyzes, and interprets observations. It is a logical model of proof that allows the researcher to draw inferences concerning causal relations among the variables under investigation. The research design also defines the domain of generalizability, that is, whether the obtained interpretations can be generalized to a larger population or to different situations.

1. Marvin Harris, Josildeth Gomes Consorte, Joseph Lang, and Bryan Byrne, "Who Are the Whites?: Imposed Census Categories and the Racial Demography of Brazil," *Social Forces,* 72 (1993): 451–462.

# The Research Design: An Example

Any researcher who is about to test a hypothesis faces some fundamental problems that must be solved before the project can be started: Whom shall we study? What shall we observe? When will observations be made? How will the data be collected? The **research design** is the "blueprint" that enables the investigator to come up with solutions to these problems and guides him or her in the various stages of the research.

Our purpose here is to describe the processes involved in designing a study and to demonstrate how the specific research design that a scientist decides to use helps to structure the collection, analysis, and interpretation of data. We will describe research based on an experimental design summarized in the book *Pygmalion in the Classroom* by Robert Rosenthal and Lenore Jacobson.[2] This study was an attempt to test the effect that others' expectations have on a person's behavior. The central idea of the study was that one person's expectations for another's behavior may serve as a self-fulfilling prophecy. This is not a new idea, and we can find many anecdotes and theories to support it. The most notable example is George Bernard Shaw's play *Pygmalion* (1916), which was later adapted as the musical *My Fair Lady*. To use Shaw's own words:

> You see, really and truly, apart from the things anyone can pick up (the dressing and the proper way of speaking, and so on), the difference between a lady and a flower girl is not how she behaves, but how she's treated. I shall always be a flower girl to Professor Higgins, because he always treats me as a flower girl, and always will; but I know I can be a lady to you, because you always treat me as a lady, and always will.

Many studies of animal behavior support Shaw's shrewd observations. In these studies, when experimenters believed their animal subjects were genetically inferior, the animals performed poorly. However, when the experimenters thought the animals were genetically superior, the animals excelled in their performance. In reality, there were no genetic differences between the two groups of animals.

Rosenthal and Jacobson, who conducted the *Pygmalion in the Classroom* study, argued that if animal subjects believed to be brighter actually became brighter because of their trainers' expectations, then it might also be true that schoolchildren believed by their teachers to be brighter would indeed become brighter because of their teachers' expectations.

To test this hypothesis, the investigators selected one school—Oak School—as a laboratory in which the experiment would be carried out. Oak was a public elementary school in a lower-class community. On theoretical grounds, the study

2. Robert Rosenthal and Lenore Jacobson, *Pygmalion in the Classroom* (New York: Holt, Rinehart and Winston, 1968); see also E. Y. Babad, J. Inbar, and R. Rosenthal, "Pygmalion, Galatea, and the Golem: Investigations of Biased and Unbiased Teachers," *Journal of Educational Psychology,* 74 (1982): 459–474.

should have examined the effects of teachers' favorable or unfavorable expectations on their pupils' intellectual competence. However, because of ethical concerns, only the hypothesis that teachers' favorable expectations will lead to an increase in intellectual competence was tested.

The independent variable of the study was the expectations held by the teachers. The investigators manipulated the expectations by using the purported results of a standard nonverbal test of intelligence. This test was described to the teachers as one that would predict intellectual "blooming." At the beginning of the school year, following schoolwide pretesting, the teachers were given the names of the students in their classrooms who were among the 20 percent of Oak School's children who in the academic year ahead would supposedly show dramatic intellectual growth. These predictions were allegedly made on the basis of the children's scores on the "intellectual blooming" test. However, the names of the potential bloomers were actually chosen randomly. Thus the difference between the potential bloomers and their classmates was only in the mind of the teacher.

The dependent variable was the intellectual ability of the children. It was measured by using the standard IQ test that allegedly predicted intellectual growth. All the children of Oak School were retested with the same test after a full academic year. Rosenthal and Jacobson computed gains in IQ from the first to the second testing for the potential bloomers and for all the other children. The researchers defined the advantage resulting from positive teachers' expectations by the degree to which IQ gains by the "special" children exceeded gains by all other children. After the first year of the experiment, a significant gain was observed among the potential bloomers, especially those in the first and second grades.

In interpreting the results of the experiment, Rosenthal and Jacobson concluded that the teachers' favorable expectations for the potential bloomers accounted for their significant gain in IQ. In their summary of the results, the investigators attempted to account for this process:

> We may say that by what she said, by how and when she said it, by her facial expression, postures, and perhaps by her touch, the teacher may have communicated to the children of the experimental group that she expected improved intellectual performance. Such communications together with possible changes in teaching techniques may have helped the child learn by changing his self-concept, his expectations of his own behavior, and his motivation, as well as his cognitive style and skills.[3]

In the next section, we first introduce some of the key terms employed in discussions of experimental research designs. We then discuss the structure of the classic experimental research design using the *Pygmalion* experiment to illustrate the components of this design. Finally, we discuss the importance of the classic experimental design as a model to which other research designs can be compared.

---

3. Rosenthal and Jacobson, *Pygmalion in the Classroom,* p. 180.

# The Classic Experimental Design

The **classic experimental design** consists of two comparable groups: an **experimental group** and a **control group.** These two groups are equivalent except that the experimental group is exposed to the independent variable (also termed the treatment) and the control group is not. Assignment of cases (or subjects) to either the experimental or the control group is based on chance—cases are randomly assigned to the groups. To assess the effect of the independent variable, researchers take measurements on the dependent variable, designated as *scores,* twice from each group. One measurement, the **pretest,** is taken for all cases prior to the introduction of the independent variable in the experimental group; a second, the **posttest,** is taken for all cases after the experimental group has been exposed to the independent variable. The difference in measurements between posttest and pretest is compared between the two groups. If the difference in the experimental group is significantly larger than in the control group, it is inferred that the independent variable is causally related to the dependent variable.

## The Structure of the Classic Experimental Design

The classic design is often diagrammed as in Table 5.1, where $X$ designates the independent variable; $O_1$, $O_2$, $O_3$, and $O_4$, the measurements on the dependent variable; $R$, the random assignment of subjects to the experimental group and the control group; and $d_e$ and $d_c$, the difference between the posttest and the pretest in each group.

To illustrate the structure and application of the classic experimental design in a social setting, let us examine again the Rosenthal and Jacobson study on the self-fulfilling prophecy. All the Oak School children participated in the experiment. The children defined by the investigator as potential bloomers were in the *experimental group,* and all the other children were in the *control group.* The researchers determined who would be in either group randomly (designated $R$ in Table 5.1). Twenty percent of the Oak School children were in the experimental group, and all the rest were in the control group. All the children were pretested (designated $O_1$, and $O_3$) with the standard nonverbal test of intelligence. Following the pretest, each of the participating teachers was given the names of the children

**Table 5.1**
The Classic Experimental Design

| Group | | Pretest | | Posttest | Difference |
|---|---|---|---|---|---|
| Experimental | $R$ | $O_1 \longrightarrow$ | $X \longrightarrow$ | $O_2$ | $O_2 - O_1 = d_e$ |
| Control | $R$ | $O_3 \longrightarrow$ | | $O_4$ | $O_4 - O_3 = d_c$ |

who were purportedly expected to show intellectual growth. These predictions, allegedly made on the basis of an intellectual blooming test, generated the teachers' expectations, the independent variable in the study (designated $X$ in Table 5.1). All the children in the two groups were retested (posttested) with the same intelligence test after one year ($O_2$ and $O_4$), and gains in intelligence were measured. The changes in intelligence were defined as the dependent variable. The researchers found a significant difference between the pretest and the posttest only among the children of the experimental group. This finding led the investigators to conclude that the positive expectations of teachers accounted for the intellectual growth of the children in the experimental group.

Another interesting example based on an experimental design, this time in the area of policy research, is the Manhattan Bail Project, initiated by the Vera Institute in New York City.[4] The Vera Institute sought to furnish criminal court judges with evidence that many persons could be safely released prior to trial and without bail provided they had strong links to the community through employment, family, residence, and friends. The population examined included persons accused of felonies and misdemeanors; individuals charged with more serious crimes were excluded from the experiment. New York University law students and Vera staff members reviewed the defendants' employment records, families, residences, references, current charges, and previous records to decide whether a pretrial release without bail should be recommended to the court. The recommendees were split randomly into experimental and control groups, and recommendations were made to the judge only for persons in the experimental group. The independent variable was pretrial releases granted, and the dependent variable was the default rate.

In the majority of cases, judges accepted the recommendation for pretrial release without bail for the experimental group. The results of the experiment were clear-cut. Between 1961 and 1964, when the experiment ended, less than 1 percent of the experimental group failed to show up in court for trial—a rate considerably lower than that for similarly charged defendants who had posted bail. The results suggest that relaxing the bail requirement did not result in unacceptable default rates. Following this experiment, the New York Probation Department extended this program to criminal courts in all five boroughs of the city.

## Why Study Experiments?

The classic experimental design is usually associated with research in the biological and physical sciences. We are used to associating experiments with studies in the natural sciences rather than with the study of social phenomena such as discrimination, gang behavior, religion, or social attraction. Why, then, do we spend considerable time discussing experiments in the social sciences? The rea-

---

4. This account draws on Bernard Botein, "The Manhattan Bail Project: Its Impact in Criminology and the Criminal Law Process," *Texas Law Review,* 43 (1965): 319–331.

sons are twofold. First, the classic experimental design helps us understand the logic of *all* research designs; it is a model against which we can evaluate other designs. Second, an experiment allows the investigator to draw causal inferences and observe, with relatively little difficulty, whether or not the independent variable caused changes in the dependent variable. With other research designs, this causal relation cannot be easily determined. Thus when we understand the structure and logic of the classic experimental design, we can also understand the limitations of other designs.

Generally, social scientists use the experiment less widely than natural scientists primarily because its rigid structure often cannot be adapted to social science research. Thus social scientists frequently use designs that are weaker for drawing causal inferences but are more appropriate to the type of problems they examine. Designs identified as quasi-experiments (discussed in Chapter 6) are more common in social science research.

Yet, as we see from the *Pygmalion* and The Manhattan Bail Project examples, experiments certainly are used in the social sciences. As a matter of fact, in some social science fields such as social psychology, experiments are the predominant design. Moreover, the use of experiments has become more widespread in policy analysis and evaluation research.

---

# Causal Inferences

Both the *Pygmalion* experiment and the Manhattan Bail Project are tests of causal hypotheses. Indeed, at the heart of all scientific explanations is the idea of causality; that is, an independent variable is expected to produce a change in the dependent variable in the direction and of the magnitude specified by the theory. However, if a scientist observes that whenever the independent variable varies, the dependent variable varies too, it does not necessarily mean that a cause-and-effect relationship exists.

Consider, for instance, crime control policies. A major objective of such policies is to deter crime. Now, does the observation that a person does not commit a crime imply that he or she has been effectively deterred from doing so by a government policy? The answer depends on whether the individual was inclined to engage in criminal behavior in the first place. Furthermore, even if the person was inclined to commit a crime, was he or she deterred by the possibility of apprehension and punishment or by other factors such as the lack of opportunity or peer group influence? Accordingly, even if researchers observe that when the government enacts more aggressive crime control policies, the frequency of crimes actually committed declines, they cannot safely conclude that the two are causally related.

In practice, the demonstration of causality involves three distinct operations: demonstrating covariation, eliminating spurious relations, and establishing the time order of the occurrences.

## Covariation

**Covariation** simply means that two or more phenomena vary together. For example, if a change in the level of education is accompanied by a change in the level of income, you can say that education covaries with income, that is, that individuals with higher levels of education have higher incomes than individuals with lower levels of education. Conversely, if a change in the level of education is not accompanied by a change in the level of income, education does not covary with income. In scientific research, the notion of covariation is expressed through measures of relations commonly referred to as *correlations* or *associations*. Thus in order to infer that one phenomenon causes another, a researcher must find evidence of a correlation between phenomena. For example, if poverty is not correlated (does not covary) with violence, it cannot be the cause of violence.

## Nonspuriousness

The second operation requires the researcher to demonstrate that the covariation he or she has observed is *nonspurious*. As explained in Chapter 3, a nonspurious relation is a relation between two variables that cannot be explained by a third variable. If the effects of all relevant variables are controlled for and the relation between the original two variables is maintained, the relation is nonspurious. When researchers establish that a relation is nonspurious, they have strong evidence that there is an inherent causal link between variables and that the observed covariation is not based on an accidental connection with some associated phenomena. As we saw in Figure 3.1, the observed covariation between the number of firefighters at a fire and the amount of fire damage is spurious because a third variable—the size of the fire—explains the covariation.

## Time Order

The third operation, *time order*, requires the researcher to demonstrate that the assumed cause occurs first or changes prior to the assumed effect.

For example, a number of studies have shown that the covariation between urbanization and democratic political development is nonspurious. To establish

---

**The Logical Model of Proof: Three Necessary Components**

- *Covariation:* Two or more phenomena vary together.
- *Nonspuriousness:* The effects of all relevant variables are controlled for and the relation between the original two variables is maintained.
- *Time Order:* The assumed cause occurs first or changes prior to the assumed effect.

that urbanization is causally related to democratic development, a researcher must also demonstrate that the former precedes the latter. The implicit assumption here is that phenomena in the future cannot determine phenomena in the present or the past. It is usually not difficult to determine the time order of phenomena. The status of parents influences the educational expectations of their children, and not vice versa; an interest in politics precedes political participation; and depression precedes suicide. In other cases, however, the time order is harder to determine. Does urbanization precede political development, or does political development occur prior to urbanization? Does achievement follow motivation, or does a change in the level of motivation follow achievement? We shall discuss the methods employed to determine the time order of events in Chapters 6 and 17, but at this point we merely want to stress the significance of the time order criterion when formulating causal explanations.

---

# Components of a Research Design

The classic research design consists of four components: comparison, manipulation, control, and generalization. The first three are necessary to establish that the independent and dependent variables are causally related. Comparison allows us to demonstrate covariation, manipulation helps in establishing the time order of events, and control enables us to determine that the observed covariation is nonspurious. Generalization, the fourth component, concerns the extent to which the research findings can be applied to larger populations and different settings.

## Comparison

The process of comparison underlies the concept of covariation or correlation. A **comparison** is an operation required to demonstrate that two variables are correlated. Suppose that we wanted to demonstrate a correlation between cigarette smoking and lung cancer: that the smoking of cigarettes is associated with a greater risk of getting lung cancer. To examine this, a researcher might compare the frequency of cancer cases among smokers and nonsmokers or, alternatively, compare the number of cancer cases in a population of smokers before and after they started smoking. Or suppose that we believe that television viewing contributes to sexist views of the roles of men and women among adolescents. We should then expect to find covariation of television viewing with sexist attitudes. That is, adolescents who spend more time watching television will exhibit traditional sex role stereotypes. To estimate the covariation of television viewing and sex role conceptions, we could compare groups of light and heavy viewers, or we could compare one group's sex role conception before and after viewing a television program that portrays traditional sex role images. In other words, to assess covariation, we evaluate the adolescents' scores on the dependent variables before and after the introduction of the independent variable, or we compare a group that is exposed to the independent variable with one that is not. In the former case, a group is compared with itself; in the latter case, an experimental group is compared with a control group.

## Manipulation

The notion of causality implies that if $Y$ is caused by $X$, then an induced change in $X$ will be followed by a change in $Y$. It is hypothesized that the relations are asymmetrical: that one variable is the determining force and the other is a determined response. In order to establish causality, the induced change in $X$ would have to occur prior to the change in $Y$, for what follows cannot be the determining variable. For example, if a researcher is attempting to prove that participation in an alcohol treatment group decreases denial of drinking problems, he or she must demonstrate that a decrease in denial took place after participation in the treatment group. The researcher needs to establish some form of control over (**manipulation of**) the assignment to the treatment group so that he or she can measure the level of denial of drinking problems before and after participation in the group. In experimental settings, especially in laboratory experiments, researchers can introduce the experimental treatment themselves; in natural settings, however, this level of control is not always possible. In both cases, the major evidence required to determine the time sequence of events—that is, that the independent variable precedes the dependent variable—is that a change occurred only after the activation of the independent variable.

## Control: The Internal Validity of Research Designs

**Control,** the third criterion of causality, requires that the researcher rule out other factors as rival explanations of the observed association between the variables under investigation. Such factors could invalidate the inference that the variables are causally related. Donald Campbell and Julian Stanley have termed this issue the problem of **internal validity.** In order to establish internal validity, a researcher must answer the question of whether changes in the independent variable did, in fact, cause the dependent variable to change.[5] The effort to attain internal validity is the guiding force behind the design and implementation of a research project.

The factors that may jeopardize internal validity can be classified as those that occur prior to the research operation—extrinsic factors—and those that are intrinsic to it and impinge on the results during the study period.

*Extrinsic Factors.*     Ethical considerations and issues of practicality sometimes prevent the random assignment of research participants to the experimental and control groups in social science research. When researchers must use some other means of assignment, possible biases—selection effects—can be introduced into the experiment because **extrinsic factors** may have produced differences

5. Donald T. Campbell and Julian C. Stanley, *Experimental and Quasi-experimental Designs for Research* (Skokie, Ill.: Rand McNally, 1963), p. 3.

between the experimental and control groups *prior to* the research operation. When the two groups differ at the outset of the experiment, it is difficult for researchers to separate selection effects from the effects of the independent variable. For example, in an evaluation of the effectiveness of employment programs for welfare recipients, the Manpower Demonstration Research Corporation compared welfare recipients who participated in federal job programs with other welfare recipients. They found that these programs increased the employment and earnings of participants and reduced welfare costs for taxpayers. However, a rival explanation for the observed changes in employment and earnings is that the program participants were initially different from other welfare recipients; perhaps they differed in their motivation to seek employment, and this initial difference could have accounted for their high level of employment and earnings.

Selection effects are especially problematic in cases in which the individuals themselves decide whether to participate in an experiment. In such cases, the investigator cannot tell whether the independent variable itself caused the observed differences between the experimental and control groups or whether other factors related to the selection procedures were responsible for the observed effects. In fact, many social programs are available on a self-selection basis to a larger target population. Researchers find it difficult to assess the effectiveness of such programs because of selection effects, among other things. Selection factors must be controlled before the investigator can rule them out as rival explanations. Later in this chapter we discuss methods for controlling selection factors.

*Intrinsic Factors.*     **Intrinsic factors** include changes in the individuals or the units studied that occur during the study period, changes in the measuring instrument, or the reactive effect of the observation itself. The following are the major intrinsic factors that might invalidate a causal interpretation given to research findings.[6]

1. *History.* **History** refers to all events that occurred during the time of the study that might affect the individuals studied and provide a rival explanation for the change in the dependent variable. For example, in a study attempting to assess the effect of an election campaign on voting behavior, the hypothesis might be that information about a candidate to which voters are exposed during the campaign is likely to influence their voting. Investigators compare the voting intentions of individuals before and after exposure to the information. Differences in the voting intentions of the two groups—the one that has been exposed to information and the other that has not—could be the result of differential exposure to the information or, alternatively, of events that occurred during this period. Perhaps a governmental conflict has happened, an international crises has erupted, the rate of inflation has increased, or an incumbent has proposed additional taxes. The longer the time lapse between the pretest and the posttest, the higher the probability that events other than the independent variable will become potential rival hypotheses.

6. Ibid.

2. *Maturation.* **Maturation** involves biological, psychological, or social processes that produce changes in the individuals or units studied with the passage of time. These changes could possibly influence the dependent variable and lead to erroneous inferences. Suppose that one wants to evaluate the effect of a specific teaching method on student achievement and records the students' achievement before and after the method was introduced. Between the pretest and the posttest, students have gotten older and perhaps wiser; this change, unrelated to the teaching method, could possibly explain the difference between the two tests. Maturation, like history, is a serious threat to the validity of causal inferences.

3. *Experimental mortality.* **Experimental mortality** refers to dropout problems that prevent the researcher from obtaining complete information on all cases. When individuals drop out selectively from the experimental or control group, the final sample on which complete information is available may be biased. In a study of the effect of the media on prejudice, for instance, if most dropouts were prejudiced individuals, the results could give the impression that exposure to media reduced prejudice, whereas in fact it was the effect of experimental mortality that produced the observed shift in opinion.

4. *Instrumentation.* **Instrumentation** designates changes in the measuring instruments between the pretest and the posttest. To associate the difference between posttest and pretest scores with the independent variable, researchers have to show that repeated measurements with the same measurement instrument under unchanged conditions will yield the same result. If they cannot show the same result, the observed differences could be attributed to the change in the measurement instrument and not necessarily to the independent variable. The stability of measurement is also referred to as *reliability,* and its absence can be a threat to the validity of experiments (see Chapter 7). For example, if a program to improve cognitive skills were evaluated by comparing preprogram and postprogram ratings by psychologists, any changes in the psychologists' standard of judgment that occurred between testing periods would bias the findings.

5. *Testing.* The possible reactivity of measurement is a major problem in social science research. In other words, the process of testing may itself change the phenomena being measured. The effect of being pretested might sensitize individuals and improve their scoring on the posttest. A difference between posttest and pretest scores could thus be attributed not necessarily to the independent variable but rather to the experience gained by individuals while taking the pretest. It is known, for example, that individuals may improve their scores on intelligence tests by taking them often. Similarly, when they take a pretest, individuals may learn the socially accepted responses either through the wording of the questions or by discussing the results with friends. They might then answer in the expected direction on the posttest.

6. *Regression artifact.* The **regression artifact** is a threat that occurs when individuals have been assigned to the experimental group on the basis of their extreme scores on the pretest that measures dependent variables. When this happens and measures are unreliable, individuals who scored below average on the pretest will appear to have improved on retesting. Conversely, individuals who

scored above average on the pretest would appear to have done less well on re-testing. We are all familiar with this problem from our own experience in test taking. Most of us have sometimes performed below our expectations on an academic test because of factors beyond our control that had nothing to do with our academic ability. We may have had a sleepless night just before taking the test or were distracted by some serious personal problems. It is very likely that if we were to take the test again, our performance would improve without any additional studying. Viewed more generally, regression artifact can become a threat to the validity of a study whenever the treatment is expected to produce a change in individuals whose scores on the dependent variable are extreme to begin with.

For example, the Job Corps is considered a successful program for disadvantaged out-of-school youth, providing remedial education, vocational training, and health care. But if enrollees were chosen to participate in the program on the basis of their extremely low scores on an unreliable test, it is possible that they will show improvement when retested even without being directly affected by the program simply because the unreliability of the test would cause their scores to change and they cannot get any worse. There is a risk, then, that their improvement will be erroneously attributed to the effect of the program.

7. *Interactions with selection.* Many of the intrinsic factors that pose a threat to the internal validity of experiments can interact with selection factors and present added threats to the validity of the study. The factors that are most commonly cited are *selection-history* and *selection-maturation.*

The selection-history interaction poses a threat when the experimental group and the control group are selected from different settings so that each setting might affect their response to the treatment. Suppose, for example, that investigators designed a study to test the effect of personnel training on the transition of the hardcore unemployed into nonsubsidized jobs. Participants in the program (the experimental group) were inadvertently selected from regions where several industrial plants had closed down just when the training program terminated, making it very difficult for program graduates to obtain employment. Thus it would seem that the program had no effect, whereas it was the interaction of the specific economic condition in the region and the selection of participants from that region that produced these results.

Selection-maturation interaction occurs when the experimental group and the control group mature at a different rate. For example, suppose that the cognitive development of males and females is compared at pretest and posttest. It is possible that the rate of development for females is faster than for males, and this might account for their better performance on the posttest.

## Procedures of Control

Extrinsic and intrinsic factors that threaten the internal validity of causal inferences may be controlled by several procedures. Scientists employ two methods of control to counteract the effect of extrinsic factors. The first, matching, controls for variables that are known to the investigator prior to the research operation. The second, randomization, helps to offset the effect of unforeseen factors. Using a control group helps counteract the effects of intrinsic factors.

*Matching.*   **Matching** is a way of equating the experimental and control groups on extrinsic factors that are known to be related to the research hypothesis. Two methods can be used to match the experimental and control groups: *precision matching* and *frequency distribution*. With precision matching (also known as pairwise matching), for each case in the experimental group, another case with identical characteristics is selected for the control group. As a means of controlling the effect of age, for example, for every individual in a specific age category in one group, there should be one in the same category in the second group, as illustrated in Figure 5.1. Having matched on the extrinsic variables, the investigator can conclude that any difference found between the experimental and control groups cannot be due to the matched variables.

The main drawback in this method is the difficulty in matching a large number of factors. For example, if we wanted to control for age, gender, race, and education, for every Asian male 30 years old with a college degree in the experimental group, we would have to find an individual with the same combination of characteristics for the control group. Therefore, when there are many relevant characteristics that need to be controlled, it is difficult to find matching pairs. Indeed,

**Figure 5.1**
Precision Matching

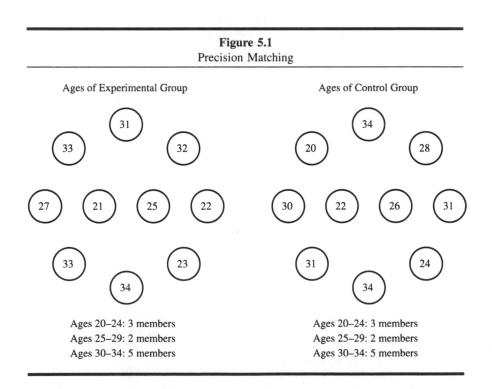

Ages of Experimental Group

Ages 20–24: 3 members
Ages 25–29: 2 members
Ages 30–34: 5 members

Ages of Control Group

Ages 20–24: 3 members
Ages 25–29: 2 members
Ages 30–34: 5 members

researchers using precision matching often lose about 90 percent of the cases for which an appropriate match cannot be found.

An alternative and more efficient method of matching is frequency distribution. With this method, the experimental and control groups are made similar for each of the relevant variables *separately* rather than in combination. Thus instead of a one-to-one matching, the two groups are matched on central characteristics. For example, when one is matching for age, the average age of one group should be equivalent to that of the other. If gender is controlled, care should be taken that the two groups have the same proportion of males and females. As Figure 5.2 shows, the two groups are matched separately for each extrinsic factor. Although somewhat less precise, frequency distribution matching is much easier to execute than precision matching and enables the investigator to control for several factors without having to discard a large number of cases.

The most basic problem in using matching as a method of control is that ordinarily the investigator does not know which of *all* the relevant factors are critical in terms of explaining the independent-dependent variable relationship. Furthermore, researchers can never be certain that they have considered all relevant factors.

***Randomization.*** Matching is a method of controlling for a limited number of predefined extrinsic factors. However, even if it were possible to eliminate the

**Figure 5.2**
Frequency Distribution Matching

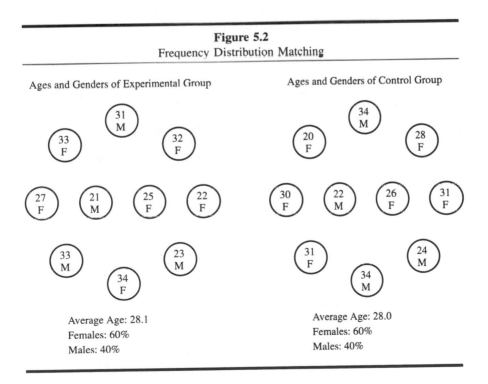

Ages and Genders of Experimental Group

Average Age: 28.1
Females: 60%
Males: 40%

Ages and Genders of Control Group

Average Age: 28.0
Females: 60%
Males: 40%

effects of all the factors, investigators can never be sure that all of them have been isolated. Other factors of which the investigator is unaware may lead to erroneous causal interpretations. Researchers avoid this problem by using **randomization,** another process whereby cases are assigned to the experimental and control groups. Randomization can be accomplished by flipping a coin, by using a table of random digits, or by any other method that ensures that any of the cases has an equal probability of being assigned to either the experimental group or the control group.

Suppose that a researcher is examining the hypothesis that the participation of workers in the decision-making process of their place of work is conducive to production. Workers are divided into experimental and control groups; the experimental group is allowed to participate in decisions concerning the work schedule and its organization. The production level of both groups is measured at the beginning and at the end of the experiment. The objective is to see whether workers who took part in the decisions are significantly more productive than workers in the control group. However, a difference in the production level can be accounted for by numerous factors other than participation in the decision-making process, the factor whose effect is being directly examined. Obviously, a number of personal factors, such as age, physical fitness, intelligence, and motivation, could account for the difference. The highly motivated, the more intelligent, the more physically fit, and the younger workers could be more productive. Without a controlled assignment of the workers to the groups, perhaps the most motivated, intelligent, and fit among the younger participants would volunteer for the experimental group, a fact that might account for the improved production level.

One way to counteract the effect of these variables is by pairwise matching (Figure 5.1). Another is to randomize the groups by flipping a coin or using a table of random digits (see Appendix D) to decide which workers are assigned to the experimental group and which to the control group. Coin flipping is a simple process whereby the heads go into one group and the tails into another. A table of random digits may be used in many ways for different purposes—see page 186 for a description of how the table works. Randomization ensures that motivation, intelligence, physical fitness, and average age will have similar distributions in the two groups. Consequently, any difference in production between the groups can be attributed to the fact that workers in the experimental group participated in the decision-making process. In other words, randomization cancels out the effect of any systematic error due to extrinsic variables that may be associated with either the dependent variable (productivity) or the independent variable (participation in decision making). The advantage of this method is that it controls for numerous factors simultaneously even when the researcher is unaware of what they are. With this method, the investigator can equalize the experimental and control groups on *all* initial differences between them.

*The Control Group.*    Researchers control intrinsic factors by using a control group from which they withhold the experimental stimulus. Ideally, the control and experimental groups have been selected randomly or by matching so that they will have exactly the same characteristics. The groups also experience identical conditions during the study except for their differential exposure to the independent variable. Thus features of the experimental situation or external events that occur during the experiment are likely to influence the two groups equally and will not be confounded with the effect of the independent variable.

By using a control group, the researcher controls most of the intrinsic factors that could threaten the validity of the experiment. History does not become a rival hypothesis because the control and experimental groups are both exposed to the same events occurring during the experiment. Similarly, maturation is neutralized because the two groups undergo the same changes. Including a control group does not necessarily avoid the mortality problem because one group might lose more cases than the other and bias the results. The acceptable procedure is for researchers to include in the final sample only cases for which complete information is available, provide information on mortality, and discuss its implications. Researchers can also avoid the influence of instrument change by using a control group; if the change between posttest and pretest scores is a result of the instrument's unreliability, this will be reflected in both groups. Only when the groups are exposed to identical testing conditions does this method of control provide a solution to the instrumentation problem, however. Using a control group is also an answer to the matter of testing. The reactive effect of measurement, if present, is reflected in both groups and leaves no grounds for misinterpretation.

The use of a control group will help in counteracting the effects of factors that interact with selection (e.g., selection-maturation, selection-history, and other interactions) only if researchers use it in conjunction with methods that control for extrinsic factors, such as matching and randomization. Such methods assure that the group being treated and the control group have the same properties and that they experience identical conditions during the experiment.

## Generalizability: External Validity

While internal validity is indeed a crucial aspect of social research, an additional significant question concerns the extent to which the research findings can be generalized to larger populations and applied to different social or political settings. Most research is concerned not only with the effect of one variable on another in the particular setting studied but also with its effect in other natural settings and on larger populations. This concern is termed the **external validity** of research designs. The two main issues of external validity are the representativeness of the sample and the reactive arrangements in the research procedure.

*Representativeness of the Sample.* To ensure the external validity of a study, the characteristics of the subjects must reflect the characteristics of the population the researcher is investigating. Although randomization contributes to the internal validity of a study, it does not necessarily ensure that the sample is representative of the population of interest. Results that prove to be internally valid might be specific to the group selected for the particular study. This possibility

---

### Components of the Classic Research Design

- *Comparison:* The operation that determines whether two variables covary (are correlated).
- *Manipulation:* The operation that controls the assignment to the treatment group, so that the researcher can determine the time sequence to make sure that the independent variable changes *before* the dependent variable changes.
- *Control:* The operation that enables the researcher to rule out rival explanations for the change in the dependent variable. Investigators must control *extrinsic,* or selection, factors and *intrinsic* factors such as history and maturation.
- *Generalization:* The extent to which the research findings can be generalized to larger populations and applied to different settings.

---

becomes likely in situations where it is difficult to recruit cases to the study. Consider an experiment on college students that is carefully planned yet is based on volunteers. Investigators cannot assume that this group is representative of the student body, let alone the general population. To make possible generalizations beyond the limited scope of the specific study, researchers must take care to select the sample using a sampling method that assures representation. Probability methods such as random sampling make generalizations to larger and clearly defined populations possible, as discussed in Chapter 8. In theory, the experimental and control groups should each constitute a probability sample of the population. In practice, however, drawing a probability sample for an experiment often involves problems such as high cost and a high rate of refusal to cooperate.

*Reactive Arrangements.*    External validity can be compromised when the experimental setting or the experimental situation does not reflect the natural setting or situation to which researchers wish to generalize. When a study is carried out in a highly artificial and contrived situation, such as a laboratory, features of the setting might influence the subjects' response. For example, Muzafer Sherif designed a well-known study to examine how group norms—guidelines for behavior— influence individuals placed in an unstable situation in which all external bases of comparison are absent.[7] Sherif created the unstable situation and removed external bases of comparison experimentally by using the autokinetic effect, which occurs when a single stationary ray of light is introduced into a completely dark room. The ray of light seems to move erratically from place to place due to a lack of external reference points. Sherif found that participants' reports of movement were influenced by the responses of other group members. However, it can be claimed that an experimental situation in which persons are placed in a dark room and are required to respond to a ray of light does not represent ordinary social

---

7. Muzafer Sherif, "An Experimental Approach to the Study of Attitudes," *Sociometry,* 1 (1937): 90–98.

situations and that the observed results might very well be specific to the artificial situation alone.

Various other features in the setting might be reactive and affect the external validity of the study. For example, the pretest may influence the way individuals respond to the experimental stimulus; its observed effect would thus be specific to a population that has been pretested. The attitude or behavior of an experimenter can influence the way subjects respond because subjects generally desire to give the response they think the experimenter expects. In survey research it is particularly important to develop questions that are neutrally worded to avoid influencing responses (see Chapter 11).

# Design Types

Research designs can be classified by the extent to which they meet the criteria we have discussed so far. Some designs allow researchers to manipulate variables but fail to employ methods of control or to provide an adequate sampling plan; others may include control groups but give the researcher no control over the manipulation of the independent variable. Accordingly, four major design types can be distinguished: *experimental, quasi-experimental, cross-sectional* and *pre-experimental*. In experimental designs, individuals or other units of analysis are randomly assigned to the experimental and control groups and the independent variable is introduced only to the experimental group. Such designs allow for comparison, control, manipulation, and, usually, generalizability. Quasi-experimental and cross-sectional designs ordinarily include combinations of some of these elements but not all of them. Typically, these designs lack possibilities for manipulation and randomization. Preexperimental designs include even fewer safeguards than quasi-experimental and cross-sectional designs, and in this sense they provide the least credibility in determining whether two or more variables are causally related. Some commonly used experimental designs are discussed in this chapter; preexperimental, quasi-experimental, and cross-sectional designs will be presented in Chapter 6.

## Controlled Experimentation

The classic experimental design presented in Table 5.1 is one of the strongest logical models for inferring causal relations. The design allows for pretest, posttest, and control group-experimental group comparisons; it permits the manipulation of the independent variable and thus the determination of the time sequence; and most significant, by including randomized groups, it controls for most sources of internal validity. However, the external validity of this design is weak, and it does not allow researchers to make generalizations to nontested populations. Two variations of the classic experimental design are stronger in this respect: the Solomon four-group design and the posttest-only control group design.

## The Solomon Four-Group Design

The pretest in an experimental setting has advantages as well as disadvantages. Although pretesting provides an assessment of the time sequence as well as a basis of comparison, it can have severe reactive effects. By sensitizing the sampled population, a pretest might in and of itself affect posttest scores. For example, measuring public attitudes toward a government policy prior to its implementation may sensitize individuals to respond differently on a posttest from nonpretested persons because the pretest may have caused them to consider and research the possible implications of policy implementation. Furthermore, there are circumstances under which a premeasurement period is not practical. In education, for instance, researchers often experiment with entirely new methods of teaching for which pretests are impossible.

The Solomon four-group design, presented in Table 5.2, contains the same features as the classic design plus an additional set of control and experimental groups that are not pretested. Therefore, the reactive effect of testing can be directly measured by comparing the two experimental groups ($O_2$ and $O_5$) and the two control groups ($O_4$ and $O_6$). These comparisons will indicate whether $X$ has an independent effect on groups that were not sensitized by a pretest. If the comparisons show that the independent variable had an effect even with the absence of the pretest, the results can be generalized to populations that were not measured prior to exposure to $X$. Moreover, as Campbell and Stanley suggest,

> not only is generalizability increased, but in addition, the effect of $X$ is replicated in four different fashions: $O_2 > O_1$, $O_2 > O_4$, $O_5 > O_6$, and $O_1 > O_3$. The actual instabilities of experimentation are such that if these comparisons are in agreement, the strength of the inference is greatly increased.[8]

***An Example: The Selling of the Pentagon.*** An interesting application of the four-group design was a study on the effect of public affairs television in politics.[9] Throughout the early 1960s, most political scientists clung to the theory of minimal consequences, which relegated television and all mass media to a position of relative impotence. This position began to change late in the decade when, during the war in Vietnam and the student demonstrations, people focused their attention on television journalism. Robinson's study addressed the issue of network news programs and politics. It asked several questions: Does television news reporting affect the national political ethos? Has it fostered cynicism, feelings of inefficacy? Has it influenced a national election?

Robinson adopted the Solomon four-group design to test the impact of a CBS documentary, *The Selling of the Pentagon,* on individual opinions about the military, the administration, and the media. (Actually, there were two sets of experiments—one set for testing the effects of the program, the other set for testing

8. Campbell and Stanley, *Experimental and Quasi-experimental Designs,* p. 25.
9. Michael J. Robinson, "Public Affairs Television and the Growth of Political Malaise: The Case of 'The Selling of the Pentagon,'" *American Political Science Review,* 70 (1976): 409–432.

**Table 5.2**
The Solomon Four-Group Design

| | Pretest | | Posttest |
|---|---|---|---|
| $R$ | $O_1$ | $X$ | $O_2$ |
| $R$ | $O_3$ | | $O_4$ |
| $R$ | | $X$ | $O_5$ |
| $R$ | | | $O_6$ |

the effects of the commentary presented at the end of the program. We shall discuss only the first set of experiments.)

To test the program effects, the design included two experimental groups and two control groups. A pretest was administered to some, but not all, of the participants. Posttests were administered to the experimental groups immediately following presentation of *The Selling of the Pentagon*. Control groups were tested just prior to exposure. A follow-up test was administered to all groups two months later. The design is presented in Table 5.3. The pretest and posttest were in the form of a questionnaire designed to measure opinions about the behavior and credibility of (1) social and political institutions, (2) public officials, (3) private citizens, and (4) news organizations. The follow-up questionnaire addressed similar issues but was shorter.

The analysis of the results demonstrates some of the practical realities involved in social science research. Robinson originally selected the Solomon design because it provides an effective way to control virtually all potential factors that might provide alternative explanations for the results. But including an experimental and a control group that were not pretested raised some serious problems. It turned out that members of group B and group D, who were not pretested, were far less likely to return for the follow-up test than those who had been pretested. Thus the dropout rate from these two groups was so serious that the investigator had to rely on only the pretested group for the analysis of the results.

**Table 5.3**
The *Selling of the Pentagon* Experiment

| | Pretest (Nov. 1971) | Mode of Exposure | Posttest (Dec. 1971) | Follow-Up (Feb. 1972) |
|---|---|---|---|---|
| Group A | Yes | Program | Yes | Yes |
| Group B | No | Program | Yes | Yes |
| Group C | Yes | Control | Yes | Yes |
| Group D | No | Control | Yes | Yes |

Adapted from Michael J. Robinson, "Public Affairs Television and the Growth of Political Malaise: The Case of 'The Selling of the Pentagon,'" *American Political Science Review*, 70 (1976): 412.

The results confirmed that *The Selling of the Pentagon* changed beliefs about the behavior of the American military, rendering those beliefs less positive. The experimental groups perceived the military as more likely to get involved in politics and more likely to seek special political advantage than these subjects had previously believed. The control group showed no significant change on any of the items. The experimentally induced change is significant because it was in the direction of "disloyalty," that is, change in beliefs about governmental misconduct.

## The Posttest-Only Control Group Design

Although the Solomon four-group design is a strong experimental design, it is often impractical or too costly to implement, or the pretests it requires might be reactive. The posttest-only control group design is a variation of both the classic design and the Solomon design; it omits the pretested groups altogether. The design is diagrammed in Table 5.4. It is identical to the last two groups of the Solomon four-group design, which are not pretested. Individuals are randomly assigned to either the experimental or the control group and are measured during or after the introduction of the independent variable.

For example, suppose that a researcher examining the effects on attitude change of an educational session about the AIDS virus selects a sample of people who are randomly assigned to either of the two groups. One group participates in a four-hour-long educational program on AIDS; later, both groups are interviewed and their responses are compared. Attitudes about safer sex in the experimental group are compared with attitudes in the control group. A significant difference will indicate that the educational session had an effect on changing attitudes. The researcher can infer the time order from the fact that the individuals were assigned to the different groups randomly. This procedure removes any initial differences between the groups, and it can therefore be inferred that any observed difference was caused by the educational program.

The posttest-only control group design controls for all intrinsic sources of invalidity. With the omission of the pretest, testing and instrumentation become irrelevant sources of invalidity. The remaining intrinsic factors are controlled because both groups are exposed to the same external events and undergo the same maturation processes. In addition, the extrinsic factor of selection is controlled by the random assignment of individuals, which prevents an initial bias in either group.

**Table 5.4**
The Posttest-Only Control Group Design

|  |  | Posttest |
| --- | --- | --- |
| $R$ | $X$ | $O_1$ |
| $R$ |  | $O_2$ |

## Experimental Designs to Study Effects Extended in Time

In all the experimental designs we have described so far, the effect of the independent variable on the dependent variable can be observed immediately or within a very short period of time. But sometimes we can expect long-range effects that are spread out over time. Such effects are particularly evident in policy studies and in research in which the dependent variable is an attitude.

Suppose that we want to study the integration of race and gender into the curriculum and its effect on sexism and racism among students. It is unlikely that the effect of a curriculum integration project will be immediately observed, and thus the observation of possible changes in attitudes should be spread out over a long period of time. Or say that we wanted to examine the effect of restricting abortion on voting for pro-choice political candidates. The central concern in research on this topic would be to test and specify the conditions under which persons change their voting behavior as a response to more restrictive abortion policies. Yet the change cannot be expected to occur immediately, and thus the assessment of changes in voting behavior will have to be of longer duration.

One solution to the problem of a delayed-effect study would be to introduce additional posttest periods, for example, six months or a year later. When the research is taking place in school settings, for instance, additional posttest periods are a convenient solution, especially since grades would be collected anyway. However, as Campbell and Stanley have indicated,

> when the posttest measures are introduced by the investigator, the repeated measurements on the same subjects could have the same invalidating effect as the pretest would. Therefore, a better solution would be to set up separate experimental and control groups for each time delay for the posttest.[10]

An illustration is presented in Table 5.5.

The same duplication of the experimental group can be incorporated into other research designs.

**Table 5.5**
An Experimental Design for Delayed Effect

|   | Pretest |   | Posttest | Posttest |
|---|---------|---|----------|----------|
| R | $O_1$ | X | $O_2$ |   |
| R | $O_3$ |   | $O_4$ |   |
| R | $O_5$ | X |   | $O_6$ |
| R | $O_7$ |   |   | $O_8$ |

10. Campbell and Stanley, *Experimental and Quasi-experimental Designs*, p. 32.

## Factorial Designs

In all the designs we have discussed so far, there was only one independent variable (the treatment), which was introduced in the experimental group and withheld from the control group. The independent variables have been an educational program, a film, and a social policy, and in each example the effect of only a single variable was observed systematically. Often, however, researchers might gain more insight by studying the effect of two or more independent variables simultaneously. For example, research on organizations suggests that the size of the organization is related to the members' morale. Larger organizations are more likely to present their members with situations that lead to stress and lowered morale. However, although size is an important determinant of morale, investigators cannot consider it independent of other organizational variables. The effect of size will be different in different types of organizations. Large organizations vary in structure, and some organizations minimize the negative effects of size through decentralization.

Examining the effect of more than one independent variable requires a large number of experimental groups and a **factorial design.** Suppose that we use size and decentralization as our independent variables and morale as the dependent variable. If each independent variable has only two possible values (dichotomous variables), we will need four experimental groups to study all combinations of these two variables; we can diagram the combinations as in Table 5.6.

The four possible combinations are: (1) large size and high decentralization, (2) small size and high decentralization, (3) large size and low decentralization, and (4) small size and low decentralization. Any of the designs discussed previously can be applied to this problem. For example, in Table 5.7 the posttest-only control group design is applied. The four different combinations illustrated in Table 5.6 are represented by $X_1$ to $X_4$, and $O_1$ to $O_4$ are posttest measures of morale. As usual, the cases have been randomly assigned to the four groups.

***External Validity of Factorial Designs.***    The chief advantage of factorial designs is that they may considerably broaden the range of generalizability. Instead of "controlling for everything," as in single-variable experiments, the researcher

### Table 5.6
Possible Combinations in a Two-Independent-Variable Design

|  |  | Size | |
|---|---|---|---|
|  |  | Large | Small |
| Decentralization | High | 1 | 2 |
|  | Low | 3 | 4 |

**Table 5.7**
A Factorial Design to Test the Effects of Size and
Decentralization on Morale

|     |         | Posttest |
| --- | ------- | -------- |
| $R$ | $X_1$   | $O_1$    |
| $R$ | $X_2$   | $O_2$    |
| $R$ | $X_3$   | $O_3$    |
| $R$ | $X_4$   | $O_4$    |

introduces additional relevant variables, each at two or more different levels. Consequently, the researcher is not restricted by some constant level of each of these relevant variables when generalizing about the effect of an independent variable. Rather, the investigator is able to infer that the effect (morale) occurs similarly across several levels of the variables or, alternatively, that the effect is different at different levels of one or another of these variables. For example, large, highly decentralized firms may produce morale levels similar to those found in small firms with low decentralization. Or, decentralization may significantly improve morale in large firms but have little effect in small firms. Factorial designs, then, increase the external validity of experiments because, as Ronald A. Fisher has suggested:

> Any conclusion . . . has a wider inductive basis when inferred from an experiment in which the quantities of other ingredients have been varied than it would have from any amount of experimentation in which these had been kept strictly constant. The exact standardization of experimental conditions, which is often thoughtlessly advocated as a panacea, always carries with it the real disadvantage that a highly standardized experiment supplies direct information only in respect of the narrow range of conditions achieved by standardization. Standardization, therefore, weakens rather than strengthens our ground for inferring a like result, when, as is invariably the case in practice, these conditions are somewhat varied.[11]

***Interaction Effects in Factorial Designs.***    Another advantage of the factorial design is that it allows us to assess systematically how two (or more) independent variables interact. Variables interact when the effect of one independent variable on the dependent variable depends on the value of the second independent variable.

For example, if large organizational size is associated with low morale of members *only* in organizations that are low on decentralization, it means that size and decentralization interact. Conversely, if large size leads to lowered morale whether or not the organization is more or less decentralized, the effect of size on morale is independent of decentralization, and there is no interaction. The test for interaction makes it possible to expand greatly our understanding of the effect of

11. Ronald A. Fisher, *The Design of Experiments,* 8th ed. (New York: Hafner Press, 1971), p. 106.

independent variables on the dependent variable. It allows us to qualify our conclusions about their effects in an important way because we study the simultaneous operation of the two independent variables.

---
## Summary
---

**1.** The research design is the program that guides the investigator in the process of collecting, analyzing, and interpreting observations. It allows inferences concerning causal relations and defines the domain of generalizability.

**2.** The classic research design consists of four components: comparison, manipulation, control, and generalization. Comparison is an operation that enables researchers to demonstrate that the independent and dependent variables are related. Manipulation involves some form of control over the introduction of the independent variables, so that the investigator can determine the time order of the variables. The control component allows researchers to rule out other factors as rival explanations of the observed associations between the independent and dependent variables. The fourth component, generalization, requires that the findings of research be applicable to the natural settings and populations the researcher is investigating.

**3.** The process of control is related to the internal validity of the research design. To establish internal validity the researcher must rule out rival explanations for the change occurring in the dependent variable. Factors that may jeopardize internal validity are intrinsic or extrinsic to the research operation. Extrinsic factors are called selection effects. They are biases resulting from the differential recruitment of respondents to the experimental and control groups. Intrinsic factors are history, maturation, experimental mortality, instrumentation, testing, regression artifact, and factors that interact with the selection effects caused by differential assignment of subjects to the experimental and control groups.

**4.** Two methods of control are employed to counteract the effect of extrinsic factors. Matching allows investigators to control for variables that are known to them prior to the research operation, and randomization helps to offset the effects of foreseen as well as unforeseen factors. Intrinsic factors are controlled by using a control group.

**5.** Generalization addresses the problem of the external validity of research designs. It concerns the extent to which the research findings can be generalized to larger populations and applied to different settings.

**6.** Experimental research designs are the strongest models of proof because they permit the manipulation of the independent variables and provide maximum control over intrinsic and extrinsic factors. Two variations of the classic experimental design are the Solomon four-group design and the posttest-only control group design. Other designs allow the study of effects extended in time, and factorial designs permit researchers to examine the effects of more than one independent variable. The advantage of factorial designs is that they strengthen the external validity of the study and allow the investigator to assess the interaction between the independent variables.

## Key Terms for Review

classic experimental design (p. 101)
comparison (p. 105)
control (p. 106)
control group (p. 101)
covariation (p. 104)
experimental group (p. 101)
experimental mortality (p. 108)
external validity (p. 113)
extrinsic factors (p. 106)
factorial design (p. 120)
history (p. 107)

instrumentation (p. 108)
internal validity (p. 106)
intrinsic factors (p. 107)
manipulation (p. 106)
matching (p. 110)
maturation (p. 108)
posttest (p. 101)
pretest (p. 101)
randomization (p. 112)
regression artifact (p. 108)
research design (p. 99)

## Study Questions

1. Describe the elements of the classic experimental design.
2. Distinguish between external and internal validity.
3. What operations are involved in the demonstration of causality?
4. List and describe the different methods of controlling threats to the internal validity of research.
5. What are three important variants of the classic experimental design? What are their advantages and disadvantages?

## Additional Readings

Aronson, Elliot, Marilyn Brewer, and James Carlsmith. "Experimentation in Social Psychology." In *The Handbook of Social Psychology,* ed. Lindzey Gardner and Elliot Aronson. New York: Random House, 1985.

Berkowitz, L., and E. Donnerstein. "External Validity Is More than Skin Deep: Some Answers to Criticisms of Laboratory Experiments." *American Psychologist,* 37 (1982): 245–257.

Brewer, Marilynn B., and Barry E. Collins, eds. *Scientific Inquiry and the Social Sciences.* San Francisco: Jossey-Bass, 1981.

Brinberg, David, and Joseph McGrath. *Validity and the Research Process.* Newbury Park, Calif.: Sage, 1985.

Campbell, Donald T., and Thomas D. Cook. *Quasi-experimentation.* Skokie, Ill.: Rand McNally, 1979.

Davis, J. A. *The Logic of Causal Order.* Newbury Park, Calif.: Sage, 1985.

Kirk, R. E. *Experimental Design: Procedures for the Behavioral Sciences.* 2d ed., Pacific Grove, Calif.: Brooks/Cole, 1982.

Martin, David W. *Doing Psychology Experiments.* 2d ed. Pacific Grove, Calif.: Brooks/Cole, 1991.

Miller, Stephen H. *Experimental Design and Statistics.* 2d ed. New York: Methuen, 1989.

Monk, Melvin M., and Thomas D. Cook. "Design of Randomized Experiments and Quasi-experiments." In *Evaluation Research Methods,* ed. Leonard Ruttman. Newbury Park, Calif.: Sage, 1984.

Ray, William, and Richard Ravizza, *Methods toward a Science of Behavior and Experience.* 2d ed. Belmont, Calif.: Wadsworth, 1993.

CHAPTER 6

# Research Designs: Cross-Sectional and Quasi-Experimental Designs

Are men better physicians than women? Researchers have found that they should be if mean scores on the National Board of Medical Examiners Part I Examination are valid indicators of success in the practice of medicine.[1] The Board examination, administered to medical students two years prior to expected graduation, consists of 900 to 1,000 questions covering seven different science subjects salient to physicians. Because scores on the Board exam are an important factor in students' promotion and placement in residency programs, it is important that the test be both valid and unbiased. To study whether this is the case, in the month of June in 1986, 1987, and 1988, researchers categorized all students taking the test by race and ethnicity. Because the researchers could not manipulate the independent variables—gender and race or ethnicity—they could not employ an experimental design to answer their research question. Instead, using a cross-sectional design, they found that the mean score of white students was consistently higher than the mean scores of Asian, Hispanic, and black students. In all groups women scored lower than their male counterparts. Because medical schools have been actively recruiting women and minorities for the past two decades, and in some cases have lowered admission standards for these groups, the researchers controlled for differences in undergraduate preparation for medical education. They found that prior academic experience and performance explained a large part of the difference between the mean scores of white, Hispanic, and black students, but did not explain the lower mean scores of Asians and women.

The authors indicate that cultural differences may cause Asians to perform more poorly than expected on the exam, and they suggest that teachers may not encourage women to excel in the areas this test measures. The findings of this study led the researchers to suggest both extra educational measures to better prepare minorities for the Board exam and further research to determine whether scores on the examination actually predict the quality of a physician's performance in the practice of medicine.

Alternatives to the experimental design—such as the one employed by these researchers—are the subject of this chapter.

ALTHOUGH THE EXPERIMENTAL DESIGN, DISCUSSED IN Chapter 5, is the strongest model of logical proof, many phenomena that are of interest to social scientists are not amenable to the straightforward application of experimental designs. In this chapter we present a number of designs that are more common in the social sciences. First, we look at the relation between the types of variables we study and the research designs we employ. We then dis-

1. Beth Dawson, Carrolyn K. Iwamoto, Linette Postell Ross, Ronald J. Nungester, David B. Swanson, and Robert L. Volle, "Performance on the National Board of Medical Examiners Part I Examination by Men and Women of Different Race and Ethnicity," *Journal of the American Medical Association,* 272.9 (1994): 674–679.

cuss cross-sectional designs, quasi-experimental designs, and preexperimental designs. We also discuss combined designs, and we end by comparing the strengths and weaknesses of the various designs.

The controlled experiment allows the most unequivocal evaluation of causal relations between two or more variables. However, as we saw in Chapter 5, social scientists often cannot control one or more of the variables they wish to study. Furthermore, social, political, and ethical considerations may discourage or prevent researchers from conducting controlled experiments. Although we can induce fear in laboratory situations and experimentally manipulate individuals, the question of whether we have the right to do so, even for the sake of science, is extremely important. In general, researchers cannot employ the experimental design if they cannot guarantee randomization and experimental control.

The designs we will discuss in this chapter offer social scientists alternatives to the classic experimental design. Each has advantages and disadvantages, but all of them allow researchers to study variables in a real life setting. Before we describe the different designs, however, we need to consider the types of variables scientists usually study.

---

# Types of Relations and Designs

In Chapter 5, we discussed research examples in which the researcher could manipulate the independent variables. Unfortunately, we cannot manipulate many of the variables we study in the social sciences. We cannot manipulate the race or gender of our subjects, nor can we make them younger or older when we wish to study the effect of these variables on some dependent variables. In the social sciences, we usually study property-disposition relationships. A **property-disposition relationship** is the relationship between some characteristic or quality of a person *(property)* and a corresponding attitude or inclination *(disposition),* for example, the relation between social class and an attitude such as political tolerance or the relation between race and prejudice. In contrast, in fields characterized more often as experimental, the relationships studied are of the *stimulus-response* type. **Stimulus-response relationships** are characterized by an independent variable that can be manipulated by the researcher. For example, a researcher might induce stress or expose subjects to an advertising campaign. The dependent variable would then be a direct response to the independent variable. It could be a certain psychological reaction to stress or an increase in consumption patterns following the advertising campaign.

Whereas stimulus-response relationships are well suited for experimental investigation, property-disposition relationships are not. This is because the two types of relationships differ in four ways: time interval, degree of specificity, the nature of comparison groups, and the time sequence of events.[2]

---

2. Morris Rosenberg, *The Logic of Survey Analysis* (New York: Basic Books, 1968), Chap. 1.

1. *Time interval.* In a stimulus-response relationship, the time interval between the introduction of the independent variable and the response to it is relatively short. In a property-disposition relationship, the time interval can extend over a long period. For example, a researcher can observe the response to a drug or an advertising campaign within a short period, but the effects of properties such as age, race, and social class can take a long time to develop.

2. *Degree of specificity.* The second difference is the degree of specificity of the independent variable. A stimulus is usually easy to isolate and identify, and its effect can be concretely delineated. However, a property such as social class is more general and incorporates various factors, including prestige, occupation, and education, each exerting its relative influence. Therefore, with this type of variable, researchers often find it difficult to define the relevant causes and to manipulate them experimentally.

3. *Nature of comparison groups.* When studying a stimulus-response relationship, a researcher can compare two similar groups, one that has been exposed to the stimulus—the experimental group—and one that has not—the control group, or the same group both before and after exposure to the stimulus. When studying a property-disposition relationship, however, a before-after comparison is practically impossible, especially with properties that do not change, such as gender and race. Similarly, it is difficult to assume that two groups having different properties are comparable in any other respect. Indeed, a lower-class group and an upper-class group differ in various aspects other than class: values, orientations, child-rearing practices, voting behavior, and so on. When researchers employ cross-sectional or quasi-experimental designs, they commonly refer to comparison groups, rather than experimental and control groups, to indicate that statistical analysis has been substituted for the experimental criteria of manipulation and control.

4. *Time sequence of events.* With the stimulus- response kind of relation, the direction of causation is relatively clear, especially when the research design allows the researcher to make before-after comparisons. But the time sequence is harder to establish with some properties. When properties are permanent, such as race and gender, researchers establish causal direction based on the fact that these can only be determining factors, not determined effects. For example, gender may influence attitudes toward capital punishment, but not vice versa. However, properties that are acquired, including intelligence, education, and political orientation, can both determine and be determined by other factors, which makes it difficult for researchers to establish time order.

Because of these four difficulties, social scientists cannot apply the components of research designs—comparison, manipulation, and control—to property-disposition relations in the pure experimental sense. Not all the phenomena that are of interest to social scientists can be experimentally manipulated by them. Moreover, they cannot always randomly assign units of analysis to experimental and control groups, and many social, political, and economic processes can be studied only after a relatively long period of time. Yet social scientists try to approximate the experimental model by employing specialized data analysis techniques that compensate for the limitations inherent in studying property-disposition relations. (These techniques are discussed in Chapter 17.)

---

# Cross-Sectional Designs

The **cross-sectional design** is perhaps the most predominant design employed in the social sciences. This design is often identified with survey research, a method of data collection common in many social science fields. In survey research (discussed in more detail in Chapters 10 and 11) scientists usually ask a random sample of individuals to respond to a set of questions about their backgrounds, past experiences, and attitudes. In most cases, survey research yields data that scientists use to examine relationships between properties and dispositions. Although numerous studies are concerned with establishing causal relations between these properties and dispositions, in many other studies researchers are simply trying to describe the pattern of relation before any attempt at causal inference is made.

As an example of a typical problem a researcher might examine by using a cross-sectional design, consider the question of who supports nuclear power production. Attitudes toward nuclear power have important implications for the environment and human safety.[3] Many studies have consistently found that a large "gender gap" exists in attitudes toward nuclear power production, with females less supportive than males.

A researcher would conduct a cross-sectional study by obtaining a representative random sample of males and females and asking them to respond to a number of questions about their attitudes toward nuclear power production. Because of the nature of the variables being investigated—especially the independent variable, gender—this research problem would be classified as a property-disposition type. Since the researcher cannot manipulate the independent variable to make a before-after comparison, this question is not amenable to experimental investigation. Moreover, the time interval in which gender shapes attitudes toward nuclear power extends over a relatively long period. Because of these limitations, it would be difficult to incorporate into a research design the components of manipulation and control, which are necessary to establish causality. This design may be diagrammed as in Figure 6.1, where the dotted $X$ indicates gender and $O_1$ indicates attitudes toward nuclear power production. Obviously, such a design would suffer from serious methodological limitations, especially with regard to its internal validity.

To overcome the methodological limitations of cross-sectional designs, researchers use statistical analysis to approximate some of the operations that are naturally built into an experimental design. In a study of attitudes toward nuclear power production, the researcher would first need to establish that gender and

---

3. This example is drawn from Lawrence S. Solomon, Donald Tomaskovic-Devey, and Barbara J. Risman, "The Gender Gap and Nuclear Power: Attitudes in a Politicized Environment," *Sex Roles,* 21 (1989): 401–414.

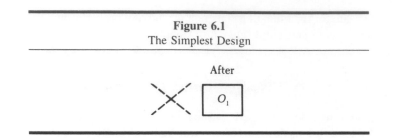

**Figure 6.1**
The Simplest Design

After

attitudes toward nuclear power production are interrelated. Table 6.1 presents the results of a statistical analysis designed to assess the relationship between these two variables. By using statistics to organize, describe, and summarize our observations, we can see that 59 percent of men but only 29 percent of women support nuclear power; a gender gap of 30 percent. This observation is based on data analysis techniques called *cross-tabulation* and *bivariate percentage analysis,* which will be discussed in detail in Chapter 16.

By using these data analysis techniques, we have improved our design to approximate the posttest-only control group design (described in Chapter 5). This improved cross-sectional design is diagrammed in Figure 6.2. The dotted cell—$O_2$—indicates extra information we obtained during the data analysis stage. When the data is organized and summarized by category as in Table 6.1, we are able to make a number of comparisons between the different groups.

Though the cross-sectional design as presented in Figure 6.2 would allow us to assess the relation (or correlation) between gender and support for nuclear power production, we cannot conclude that these two variables are causally related, nor do we understand why females are less likely than males to support nuclear power production. There are a number of possible explanations for the gender gap; for example, the women in the study may have been less knowledgeable about technological matters and therefore more reluctant to support nuclear power. Or perhaps women's greater concern with safety would lead them to oppose nuclear power more than men.

**Table 6.1**
Gender and Attitudes toward Nuclear Power

|  | Male | Female |
|---|---|---|
| Support | 59% | 29% |
| Oppose | 41% | 71% |
|  | 100% | 100% |

Adapted from Lawrence S. Solomon, Donald Tomaskovic-Devey, and Barbara J. Risman, "The Gender Gap and Nuclear Power: Attitudes in a Politicized Environment," *Sex Roles,* 21 (1989): 407.

**Figure 6.2**
The Cross-Sectional Design

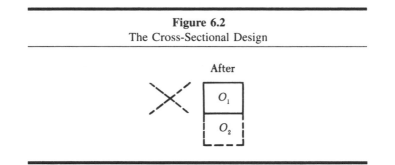

When an experimental design is employed, these factors are controlled through randomization and the use of a control group. When researchers employ a cross-sectional design, they must control these factors statistically. In cross-sectional designs, multivariate methods of statistical analysis—such as elaboration by cross-tabulation, multiple regression, and path analysis—are the most common alternatives to experimental methods of control and the drawing of causal inferences. (For further elaboration on this issue and a discussion of these methods, see Chapter 17.)

It is important to note, however, that researchers cannot perform statistical analyses to establish the time order of the variables in a cross-sectional design. Researchers must establish the time sequence on the basis of theoretical or logical considerations. In our nuclear power example, gender may logically produce differences in attitudes toward the production of nuclear power, but attitudes toward nuclear power production cannot change gender, which is a permanent property.

The main advantage of cross-sectional studies is that they may be carried out in natural settings and permit researchers to employ random probability samples. This allows researchers to make statistical inferences to broader populations and permits them to generalize their findings to real-life situations, thereby increasing the external validity of the study.

# Quasi-Experimental Designs

Using the classic experimental design as a model of logical proof, scientists have developed a number of quasi-experimental designs. As in cross-sectional designs, these designs are weaker on internal validity than experimental designs, and researchers must depend on data analysis techniques as a method of control. Quasi-experimental designs often allow researchers to randomly select samples from the population, but they do not require the random assignment of individual cases to the comparison groups. They are superior, however, to cross-sectional designs because they usually involve the study of more than one sample, often over an extended period of time. In the following sections we explore the most important quasi-experimental designs in current use.

## Contrasted Groups Designs

A common problem in social science research is that in many cases the researcher cannot randomly assign individuals or other units of analysis to comparison groups. For example, researchers cannot assign individuals to a race, gender, social class, or religion, to name just a few. At times, researchers use intact comparison groups either at the pretest phase only or at the posttest phase only. Causal inferences concerning the independent variables are especially vulnerable when researchers cannot use randomization to assign cases to groups that are known to differ in some important attributes: for example, when they are comparing poor communities with relatively well-to-do ones, groups from different ethnic backgrounds, or males with females. If a researcher uses a posttest-only design with such contrasted groups, differences on the posttest measures are likely to be due to initial differences between the groups rather than to the impact of the independent variable. Nevertheless, when researchers need to assess differences among such contrasted groups, several possible modifications in the research design can act as safeguards against the intrusion of influences other than that of the independent variable.

The least elaborate design for **contrasted groups** is one in which individuals or other units of analysis are regarded as members of *categoric groups*. Categoric group members share some attribute that assigns them to an identifiable category, such as males, Democrats, or Catholics. Members of each group are measured with respect to the dependent variables. For example, a researcher could compare the reading performance of children residing in different communities. This design can be symbolized in the following way, where $O_1 \ldots O_k$ represent measures on the dependent variable by grouping category:

$$O_1$$
$$O_2$$
$$O_3$$
$$O_4$$
$$.$$
$$.$$
$$.$$
$$O_k$$

Researchers can perform straightforward comparative statistical analyses on the differences in measurement scores obtained for the $k$ groups. For example, they can examine the difference between means—average scores—of the groups. However, because contrasted groups differ from one another in many ways, difficulties arise when researchers attempt to assess the causes for the observed differences. Relatedly, the groups might differ because of problems with the measurement procedures rather than because of any real differences among them. For instance, studies have repeatedly shown that measurements based solely on personal interviews are affected by the interviewers' backgrounds and that black and white interviewers elicit different answers from black respondents. (A more detailed discussion of this and other problems with interviews appears in Chapter 10.)

Researchers can reduce the risk of being wrong when making causal inferences based on contrasted groups designs by obtaining supplementary evidence over time regarding the differences they have predicted in their hypothesis. If they obtain the same finding in other settings and make comparisons on a number of measures concerning the dependent variables, such supplementary evidence can increase the inferential powers of a contrasted groups design.

A more elaborate design for contrasted groups is one in which researchers compare two or more intact groups before and after the introduction of the treatment variable. In this design—the nonequivalent control group design—statistical techniques are used to test for comparability between the contrasted groups before causal inferences are drawn.

A recent study evaluating an undergraduate course on AIDS provides an example of this design.[4] The researchers set out to evaluate how a college course about AIDS had an impact on AIDS-relevant knowledge, attitudes, and behavior by comparing two groups of subjects. The experimental group consisted of students recruited from the course "AIDS: The Modern Plague." The control group consisted of students recruited from a different course, "Astronomy: The Nature of the Universe."

The researchers administered a pretest and a posttest: students in both classes were asked to fill out a self-administered questionnaire at the beginning and at the end of each course. The design used in this study is shown in Table 6.2. Since it was impossible to randomly assign students to the experimental and control groups, the evaluation of the course's impact had important methodological limitations. A critical issue, for example, was the fact that both groups were self-selected. If students in the experimental group had preexisting concerns about AIDS, they might have been more likely to adopt safer sexual practices whether or not they took the AIDS course. Therefore, the researchers had to make special efforts to approximate comparability between the experimental and control groups. One strategy was to pick a comparison group that would be as similar as possible to the experimental group. Relevant criteria for selecting the control group included (1) cohort effect (both courses were offered during the same quarter so history was not a factor), (2) discipline (both courses were listed in the science curriculum), (3) open enrollment, and (4) popularity (both courses had popular appeal on campus).

**Table 6.2**
A Nonequivalent Control Group Design

| Pretest | | Posttest |
|---------|---|----------|
| $O_1$ | $X$ | $O_2$ |
| $O_3$ | | $O_4$ |

4. Paul R. Abramson, Joan C. Sekler, Richard A. Berk, and Monique Y. Cloud, "An Evaluation of an Undergraduate Course on AIDS," *Evaluation Review*, 13 (1989): 516–532.

In addition, using multivariate statistical techniques (discussed in Chapter 17), the researchers equated the experimental and control groups on age, gender, ethnicity, class, and the pretest, thus ruling out the alternative explanation that pre-existing differences in those factors accounted for differences between the two groups on the posttest. The results of the study suggest that the course on AIDS had a beneficial impact on attitudes, knowledge, and behavior relevant to the transmission of the AIDS virus. We must, however, stress again the limitation of this design. Because of the absence of random assignment of subjects to the experimental and control groups, the internal validity of the study is jeopardized.

In some cases in which social scientists compare contrasted groups, measures are available on a number of occasions before and after the introduction of the independent variable. In such cases, researchers can obtain multiple measures before and/or after exposure. Such supplementary data provide a measure of the amount of normal variation in the dependent variable from time to time, irrespective of the independent variable's impact. Suppose that researchers wish to evaluate the effectiveness of a new approach to teaching reading implemented through the fifth grade in school E. They can compare achievement test scores in reading for children in the third through seventh grades in that school and in another school (C) in the same community that did not use the new approach. The study is conducted retroactively for students who are currently in the seventh grade and have remained in school from the third grade up to that time. Because schools administer achievement tests each year, the researchers can obtain comparable measures for each of the five years. Evidence for a program effect when there are multiple measures over time consists of a sharp difference in the level of the dependent variable from before to after implementation of the program for the units being compared, as illustrated in Figure 6.3. Notice that the scores on the dependent variable increase steadily for school C—the school where the program was not implemented. In contrast, the scores for school E rise sharply between the fourth and fifth year and then level off.

Unlike the hypothetical results in Figure 6.3, the findings shown in Figure 6.4 indicate that the independent variable had no effect at all on the individuals in group E beyond what could be expected from the usual course of events, as evidenced in group C. The apparent change in group E is illusory because it is matched by a proportional change in group C.

## Planned Variation Designs

When researchers use **planned variation** designs, they expose individuals to stimuli that have been systematically varied in order to assess their causal effects. The Head Start Planned Variation (HSPV) is an excellent policy-relevant example of such a design. HSPV was a three-year investigation designed to compare the effects that different kinds of Head Start centers were having on the development of the academic skills of children from relatively poor families. The study was developed on the assumption that by selecting a number of "sponsors"—schools, agencies, or voluntary organizations that took on management responsibilities—

**Figure 6.3**
Comparison of Two Contrasted Groups Indicating That the
Independent Variable Had a Definite Effect

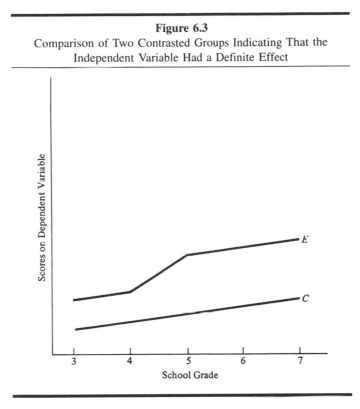

for different types of programs, and by systematically varying the kinds of programs offered to children, the researchers could discover which kinds of programs most benefited which kinds of children.[5]

The sponsors selected to participate in the investigation varied substantially in terms of their goals and their teaching programs. During the 1971–1972 academic year, 11 sponsors were distributed over a total of 28 neighborhood sites scattered throughout the country. For purposes of comparison, 11 of the 28 sites also had "nonsponsored" classrooms managed directly by Head Start staff. In addition, three sites had comparison groups of children who were not enrolled in any program. Children selected for this comparison group were contacted by direct recruitment and from Head Start waiting lists. Each sponsor operated two, three, or four sites. Each site had a different number of classrooms run by the specific sponsor. Some sites contained both sponsored and regular, nonsponsored Head Start classrooms; other sites had only sponsored classrooms.

One major shortcoming of this research design was that a number of important variables were not equally distributed across the sponsored sites. As Herbert I.

5. The following account draws on Herbert I. Weisberg, *Short-Term Cognitive Effects of Head Start Programs: A Report on the Third Year of Planned Variation, 1971–1972* (Cambridge, Mass.: Huron Institute, 1973).

**Figure 6.4**
Comparison of Two Contrasted Groups Indicating That an
Independent Variable Had No Effect

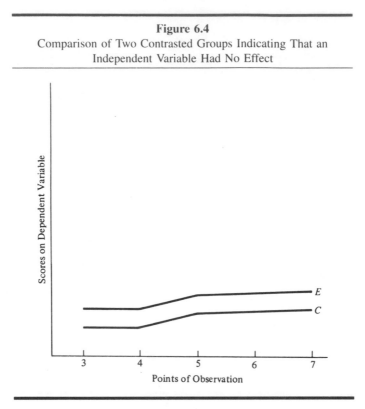

Weisberg pointed out, race, age, prior preschool experience, and socioeconomic background were all unequally distributed. For example, one sponsor had almost no black children at his site, whereas another sponsor had almost no white children. In spite of this serious source of reduced validity, the researchers drew three general inferences: (1) overall, both the sponsors' programs and the regular Head Start programs tended to accelerate certain kinds of specific academic performance, such as number and letter recognition; (2) pooling the 11 sponsored sets of classrooms and comparing them with the regular, nonsponsored Head Start classrooms showed no large differences; and (3) when the sponsored sets of classrooms were compared among themselves, some differences in performance emerged on several of the cognitive tests the children were given. In other words, certain types of curricula seemed to enhance different kinds of cognitive development.

Obviously, as we have implied, these conclusions are suggestive at best because of the unequal distributions of important variables across the sponsors. That is, because important variables were present in an unsystematic way, the researchers could not claim a high degree of validity or consequent applicability of the conclusions they drew. This example demonstrates that researchers can increase confidence in the findings obtained with planned variation designs when they can guarantee that important variables are equally distributed among the test groups, and if the dependent variables are measured on a number of occasions both before and after exposure to an independent variable.

## Panels and Time-Series Designs

Some quasi-experiments are extended over time to allow researchers to examine changes in the dependent variable. Time poses a dilemma for social scientists for the following reasons. First and foremost, humans and the social environment are not static entities. They change in response to internal processes and external events, few of which can be willfully controlled by the researcher. Therefore, the variables the scientist wishes to investigate may be modified over time. This tendency may undermine the appropriateness or accuracy of the researcher's procedures and the validity of his or her conclusions. Methodologically then, as time cannot be controlled in real life, methods must be adopted to control for its effects on the empirical data. We shall discuss two major designs that incorporate time: *panels* and *time-series designs.*

*Panels.*    A more rigorous solution to the time dilemma in cross-sectional studies and correlational designs is the **panel,** in which the same sample is examined at two or more time intervals. Panel studies allow researchers to approximate the before-after condition of experimental designs more closely by studying a group at two or more points in time before and after exposure to the independent variable.

A good illustration of the panel design is a study, begun in the 1980s, that investigated the effects of children leaving home on parental well being.[6] Most studies of the effects of the child-leaving phase on a parent's life rely on cross-sectional designs. This method limits the analysis of change in parental well-being associated with the child's leaving by treating the departure as a unique event in a single unit of time. The research cited is based on a national sample interviewed in 1980 and again in 1983 and 1988. The investigators followed a sample of 402 parents of older children and compared changes in marital happiness and life satisfaction between those who did and did not empty their nest. The main advantage of such a study plan was that it enabled the researchers to determine the direction of causation. That is, by comparing measures taken among the same respondents before and after their children left home, they could ascertain whether parental well-being was a cause or a result of the child's leaving. By comparing measures of parental well-being of the same respondents taken before and after the critical event, the researchers could determine the order of influence.

The main problem with panels is obtaining an initial representative sample of respondents who are willing to be interviewed at set intervals over an extended period. Moreover, even if a researcher succeeds in obtaining their commitment, some respondents usually drop out, either because they refuse to continue to coop-

6. Lynn White and John N. Edwards, "Emptying the Nest and Parental Well-being: An Analysis of National Panel Data," *American Sociological Review, 55* (1990): 235–242.

erate or because difficulties arise in tracing those who move or change jobs. A serious consequence of this decline in participation is that the researcher cannot determine if these respondents changed in a way different from those who remained in the study. This uncertainty may affect the representativeness and validity of the findings. Another problem occurring when investigators repeatedly interview the same group is *panel conditioning*—the risk that repeated measurements may sensitize the respondents to give a given set of answers. For example, members of a panel may try to appear consistent in the views they express on consecutive occasions. In such cases, the panel may become atypical of the population it was selected to represent. One possible safeguard to panel conditioning is to give members of a panel only a limited panel life (i.e., participation period) and then to replace them with persons taken randomly from a reserve list of the same general population.[7]

*Time-Series Designs.*    In cases when no comparison or control group is available for assessing cause-and-effect relations, investigators can use **time-series designs**—research designs in which pretest and posttest measures are available on a number of occasions before and after the activation of an independent variable. Usually, the investigator attempts to obtain at least three sets of measures before and three sets after the introduction of the independent variable. A typical time-series design can be represented as follows:

$$O_1 \; O_2 \; O_3 \; x \; O_4 \; O_5 \; O_6$$

By employing a time-series design, researchers can separate reactive measurement effects (see Chapter 5) from the effects of an independent variable. A time-series design also enables the researcher to see whether an independent variable has an effect over and above the reactive effects. If the reactive effect shows itself at $O_3$, this measure can be compared with $O_4$. An increase at $O_4$ above the increase at $O_3$ can be attributed to the independent variable. Researchers can also estimate whether the changes caused by introducing the independent variable are greater than those due to the passage of time, thus guarding against the maturation source of invalidity.

A classic illustration of the advantages as well as the problems involved with time-series designs is Campbell's evaluation study of the Connecticut crackdown on speeding following a record number of traffic fatalities in 1955.[8] At the end of 1956, 284 traffic deaths were registered in Connecticut, compared with 324 the year before, a reduction of 12.3 percent. The results are graphically displayed in Figure 6.5, which intentionally magnifies the differences. Referring to these data, the authorities concluded that "the program is definitely worthwhile." As this

7. For a detailed analysis of the advantages and disadvantages of panels, see Robert F. Boruch and Robert W. Pearson, "Assessing the Quality of Longitudinal Surveys," *Evaluation Review,* 12 (1988): 3–58.
8. Donald T. Campbell, "Reforms as Experiments," *American Psychologist,* 24 (1969): 409–429.

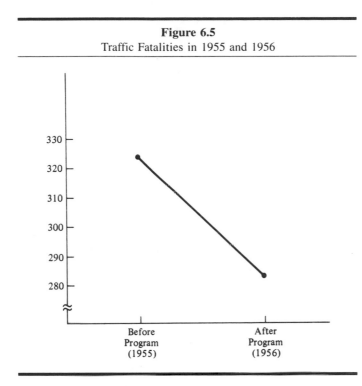

**Figure 6.5**
Traffic Fatalities in 1955 and 1956

inference is based on a type of pretest-posttest design, a number of plausible rival interpretations could also be advanced. For instance, 1956 might have been a particularly dry year, with fewer accidents caused by rain or snow.

The researchers could have made more valid causal inferences if the data were presented as part of an *extended time series,* as illustrated in Figure 6.6. This time-series design controls for maturation. These data, gathered over a number of years prior to the crackdown, permitted the rejection of a rival interpretation suggesting that traffic death rates were already going down year after year. The latter could be a plausible interpretation if the fatalities had been measured only one year before and one year after implementation of the program.

Although the **extended time-series design** takes into account three observations before introduction of the program and three observations after its implementation, it nevertheless fails to control for the effects of other potential sources of invalidity; for example, history remains a plausible rival explanation. In such a case, one strategy for strengthening the credibility of the conclusion is to make use of supplementary data when available. For example, researchers can examine weather records to evaluate the rival interpretation that weather conditions were responsible for the decline in traffic deaths.

But time-series data are sensitive to time-related change, as noted earlier, even when no independent variables are being introduced. The degree of this normal

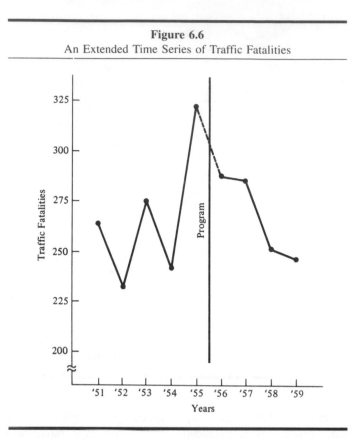

**Figure 6.6**
An Extended Time Series of Traffic Fatalities

instability is, according to Campbell, "the crucial issue, and one of the main advantages of the extended time-series is that it samples this instability."[9] In the Connecticut case, the authorities had in fact implied that all the change from 1955 to 1956 was due to the crackdown policy. However, as Figure 6.6 indicates, the relatively high preprogram instability makes the policy look ineffective: "The 1955–1956 shift is less than the gains [in lower fatality rates] of both 1954–1955 and 1952–1953. It is the largest drop in the series, but it exceeds the drops of 1951–1952, 1953–1954, and 1957–1958 by trivial amounts."[10] Accordingly, another scientist could legitimately argue that the 1955–1956 drop is merely an outcome of the instability of the data series. Notwithstanding this plausible interpretation, notice that after the crackdown there are no year-to-year increases, suggesting that the character of the time series has changed.

Regression artifacts, which are statistical results based on unusual, extreme data values (see Chapter 5), also present a serious threat to the validity of time-series designs, especially when the data are unstable. As a rule, with any highly

9. Ibid., p. 413.
10. Ibid.

variable time-series, if one selects a point that is the "highest" or "lowest" so far, the next point, on the average, will be nearer to the general trend. In the Connecticut example, the most dramatic shift in the whole series is the upward shift just prior to the crackdown. Thus it is plausible that this increase motivated the implementation of the program rather than, or in addition to, the program's expected effectiveness in causing a decline in traffic fatalities. Therefore, at least part of the 1956 drop is an artifact of the 1955 extremity; that is, the number of fatalities could be expected to drop anyway. The research problem then becomes to determine how much.

Figure 6.7 illustrates a case from which it can be concluded that an independent variable had no effect on the dependent variable. The curve goes up before the introduction of the independent variable, and continues to do so after its introduction. However, what is important is that the curve was going up at the same rate both before and after the independent variable was introduced.

It is even more difficult to interpret the hypothetical data presented in Figure 6.8. The curve began rising before the introduction of the independent variable, as it does after its implementation. However, the great variations observed before and after its introduction prevent researchers from making causal inferences with any degree of confidence.

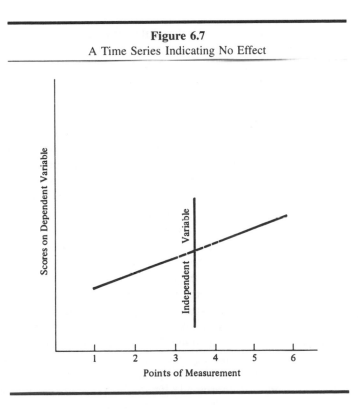

**Figure 6.7**
A Time Series Indicating No Effect

**Figure 6.8**
A Time Series Illustrating an Illusory Causal Effect

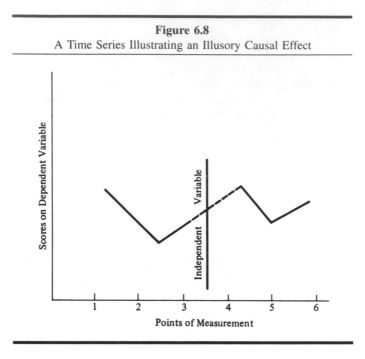

Figures 6.7 and 6.8 illustrate only two different types of findings that could be obtained from a time-series study. They do, however, demonstrate again that time-series designs, like other quasi-experimental designs devoid of a comparison group, provide only partial evidence concerning cause-and-effect relations.

## Control-Series Designs

We have already pointed out that one of the major obstacles in constructing experimental designs is the difficulty of applying random selection procedures when assigning individuals or other units of analysis to experimental and comparison groups. Procedures for matching the members of the two groups may also be vulnerable if the researcher lacks evidence regarding significant external factors. However, when nonequivalent comparison groups are used in time-series designs, they provide more reliable evidence on causal effects. Such designs are called **control-series designs** because they attempt to control aspects of history, maturation, and test-retest effects that are shared by the experimental and comparison groups.

Figure 6.9 illustrates these points for the Connecticut speeding crackdown, adding evidence from the fatality rates of neighboring states (the comparison group). To make the two series comparable, Campbell presented the data as population-based fatality rates. The control-series design shows that downward trends were present in the neighboring states for 1955–1956 owing to history and maturation (weather, automative safety devices, and so on). However, the data also indicate a general trend for Connecticut's fatality rates to approach those of the

**Figure 6.9**
A Control-Series Design Comparing Connecticut Traffic
Fatalities with Those of Four Other States

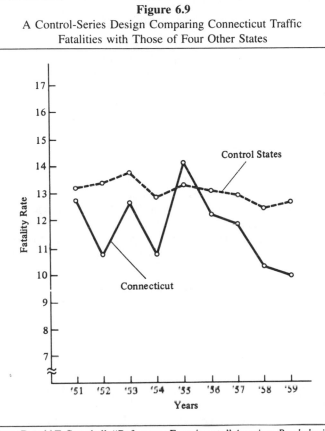

From Donald T. Campbell, "Reforms as Experiments," *American Psychologist,*
24 (1969): 419. Reprinted by permission.

other states prior to 1955, and to drop steadily and more rapidly than the other
states from 1956 onward. Based on such evidence, the researcher can infer that
the program did have some effect over and above the regression artifact.

# Combined Designs

So far, we have focused on the most important of the many possible quasi-
experimental designs.[11] Designs such as the classic controlled experiment, discussed in Chapter 5, are much stronger in controlling for intrinsic factors (e.g.,

11. For other types of quasi-experimental designs, see Thomas D. Cook and Donald T. Campbell,
*Quasi-experimentation: Design and Analysis Issues for Field Settings* (Skokie, Ill.: Rand McNally,
1979), and E. A. Suchman, *Evaluation Research* (Englewood Cliffs, N. J.: Prentice-Hall, 1987).

## Quasi-Experimental Designs

Quasi-experimental designs involve the study of more than one sample, often over a period of time. They have lower internal validity than classically controlled experiments and depend on data analysis techniques as a method of control.

- *Contrasted Group Designs:* Individuals or other units of analysis are treated as members of categoric groups (e.g., women, Democrats).
- *Planned Variation Designs:* In these designs, individuals are exposed to systematically varied stimuli (e.g., educational teaching methods) in order to assess the causal effects of the stimuli.
- *Panels:* In these studies, researchers estimate before-after conditions by examining the same sample over a number of time periods.
- *Time-Series Designs:* In these research designs, a number of measures, at least three, are taken before and after the introduction of an independent variable (such as a new traffic ordinance).
- *Control-Series Designs:* These designs combine a time-series method with the collection of similar data on a nonequivalent comparison group in order to control for the influence of history, maturation, and test-retest effects.

history, maturation, regression artifacts) that might invalidate causal inferences. The weakest quasi-experimental designs, such as the contrasted group design, introduce a greater measure of ambiguity regarding the validity of the inferences they might support.

Each of the designs discussed can provide valid information, but they differ both in the kind of data that they generate and in the limitations they impose on inferring causation. To overcome these difficulties, researchers often employ a multimethod approach. This approach improves their ability to make causal inferences by systematically combining two or more designs in a single study.[12]

Perhaps one of the most instructive field studies that used **combined designs** (i.e., combining several *features* of different research designs) to assess causal effects is that of the Salk vaccine against paralytic poliomyelitis, first tested in 1954.[13] In the initial design, the idea was to give the vaccine only to second graders whose parents volunteered them for study, and not to give it to first and third graders, who comprised the comparison groups. Presumably, by comparing results for the experimental group and the comparison groups, researchers might learn whether or not the vaccine was effective. Such a research design was highly vulnerable, however, because polio occurred more frequently in more sanitary neighborhoods than in unsanitary ones, and the more sanitary neighborhoods were

12. John Brewer and Albert Hunter, *Multimethod Research: A Synthesis of Styles* (Newbury Park, Calif.: Sage, 1989).

13. The following account draws on Paul Meier, "The Biggest Health Experiment Ever," in *Statistics: A Guide to the Unknown,* ed. Judith M. Tamur, et al. (Oakland, Calif.: Holden Day, 1972), pp. 2–13, and K. A. Brownlee, "Statistics of the 1954 Polio Vaccine Trials," *Journal of the American Statistical Association,* 50 (1955): 1005–1013.

associated with higher socioeconomic status. People of higher socioeconomic status tend to volunteer more than people of lower socioeconomic status, so that most second graders could be expected to come from this population. Consequently, it could be expected that volunteers in the second grade would have been more prone to contract the disease in the first place compared to second graders in general and to the average of the first and third graders. This bias could have invalidated the comparison. Furthermore, if only second graders were vaccinated, physicians might have suspected that some of them had caught paralytic polio because of exposure to the vaccine itself, so that there might have been significant differences in the frequency of positive diagnoses in the volunteer and nonvolunteer groups.

Aware of these problems, some state public health officials recommended a controlled field experiment that randomized the distribution of the vaccine among volunteers from all grade groups. Half the volunteers would receive the vaccine and half a saltwater injection (placebo), so that the "blindness" (that is, the inability to identify the experimental or control group members) of the diagnoses could be protected, thereby shielding physicians from their own expectations of the outcome when making a diagnosis.

Some states applied the original design; others, the randomized controlled design. The results of the latter conclusively showed a reduction in the paralytic polio rate from about 57 per 100,000 among the comparison groups to about 16 per 100,000 in the experimental group. In the states where only the second-grade volunteers were vaccinated, the experimental group had about the same rate (17 per 100,000) as those vaccinated with a placebo in the comparison neighborhoods. The expected bias of an increased rate for volunteers compared with nonvolunteers appeared among the whole group. Among those receiving the placebo, the volunteers had the highest rate (57 per 100,000), while those who did not volunteer had a rate of about 36 per 100,000. In the states using the initial quasi-experimental design, the first and third graders, who were not asked to volunteer and were not vaccinated, had a rate between the two extremes, 46 per 100,000. In the Salk vaccine investigation, then, the two research designs were used simultaneously, and they supported each other.

In many other situations, the use of a quasi-experimental design alone does not provide sufficient confidence in the results. When complex problems are studied, one or more of the major components of the problem can frequently be studied experimentally, while the remaining components may be amenable to quasi-experimental designs. The choice of the component factors of a combined design depends on the specific problem investigated and the creativity of the researchers.

# Preexperimental Designs

Preexperimental designs are not suitable for experimental manipulations and do not allow researchers to randomly assign cases to an experimental group and a control group. In fact, most often these designs do not include a comparison group

In addition, in preexperimental studies, respondents are not randomly se-
~~lected~~ from a larger representative population, nor are multivariate statistics used
as a substitute for experimental control. Preexperiments are, therefore, the weakest
research designs since most of the sources of internal and external validity are not
controlled for. The risk of error in drawing causal inferences from preexperimental
designs is extremely high, and they are primarily useful as a basis for pretesting
some research hypotheses and for exploratory research. An example of a preexperimental design is the one-shot case study.

## The One-Shot Case Study

A **one-shot case study** involves an observation of a single group or event at a single
point in time, usually subsequent to some phenomenon that allegedly produced
change. For example, the study might be an observation of a community after an
urban renewal program, a political system after general elections, or a school after
it has been exposed to an innovative teaching method.

The case of Head Start vividly illustrates the pitfalls of the one-shot case study.
In January 1965, President Lyndon B. Johnson informed the public that a preschool
program named Head Start would be established as part of the Community Action
Program. Initially, the government intended to commit $17 million for the summer
of 1965 to enable 100,000 children to participate in the program.[14] The publicity
given Head Start generated a large volume of demands for funds from numerous
localities. The Office of Economic Opportunity (OEO) met these demands by
committing $103 million to provide places for 560,000 children during the summer
of 1965. Later in the year, Head Start became a permanent part of the antipoverty
program. According to President Johnson, Head Start had been "battle-tested" and
"proven worthy," and as a result, it was expanded to include a full-year program.
In 1968, $330 million was allocated to provide places for 473,000 children in
summer programs and another 218,000 in full-year programs, turning Head Start
into the largest single component of the Community Action Program.

As late as mid-1967, no reliable evidence existed regarding the effectiveness of the program. Members of Congress, the Bureau of the Budget, and OEO
officials were pressing for evidence. Consequently, the evaluation division of the
Office of Research, Plans, Programs and Evaluations (RPP&E) proposed a one-
shot case study design for Head Start in which children who had participated in
the program and were currently in the first, second, and third grades would be
observed through a series of cognitive and affective tests. The children's performance on these tests would serve as evidence of the effectiveness of Head Start.

Head Start officials opposed the proposed study on the grounds that such a
design cannot provide solid evidence for inferring causality. Numerous rival explanations and hypotheses can explain differential performance in cognitive and

14. This account draws on Walter Williams and John W. Evans, "The Politics of Evaluation: The Case
of Head Start," *Annals of the American Academy of Political and Social Science,* 385 (September
1969): 118–132.

affective tests. They argued that observations made only at the testing period would have no meaningful basis of comparison, and comparison is an essential component of making causal inferences. Furthermore, this design fails to provide any evidence of whether the program had *any* impact on the children. In order to draw valid causal inferences, it is necessary to make observations *prior to* implementation of the program. The one-shot case study design has no control over extrinsic and intrinsic factors. It also does not allow for before-after or control group-experimental group comparison. The one-shot case study cannot be used for testing causal relations.

The one-shot case study is useful in exploratory research, however. It may lead to insights that could in turn be studied as research hypotheses. But in the case of Head Start, this weak design was used to test the effectiveness of the program, and when the research findings were made available they were ignored precisely because of "problems in research design."[15]

Despite these limitations, for many policy questions—especially on controversial issues, when it is difficult to implement a quasi-experimental or experimental design—the one-shot case study may be the only available technique.

As the number of case studies on a certain topic grows, it is important to attempt to integrate the findings of the various studies in order to overcome the limitation of a single-case study. Michael Berger has suggested a method of integrating case studies. This technique, the case survey method, involves analyzing the content of case studies, aggregating the various case experiences, and then making generalizations about the studies as a whole.[16]

---

# A Comparison of Designs

In Chapter 5 and this chapter, we have focused on two basic problems of scientific research: inferring causation and generalizing the findings. These problems pose a basic dilemma: to secure unambiguous evidence about causation (internal validity), you frequently sacrifice generalizability (external validity). Designs that are strong on internal validity, such as experimental designs, tend to be weak on external validity. However, designs that are weak on internal validity, such as the one-shot case study, are, by definition, also weak on external validity because without internal validity, no generalizations can be made.

Perhaps the most serious threat to the internal validity of research designs is the lack of adequate control of extrinsic and intrinsic factors. In order for the results of a study to be generalizable, the design must allow researchers to study a sample that accurately represents the population in a real social setting or situation. External validity is sometimes increased by increasing the heterogeneity of the

15. David Nachmias and Gary T. Henry, "The Utilization of Evaluation Research: Problems and Prospects," in *The Practice of Policy Evaluation,* ed. David Nachmias (New York: St. Martin's Press, 1980), pp. 461–476.

16. Michael A. Berger, "Studying Enrollment Decline (and Other Timely Issues) via the Case Survey," *Evaluation Studies,* 11 (1986): 720–730.

sample and of the experimental situation. However, as researchers increase realism and heterogeneity, they may be forced to sacrifice control.

This is the point where we can compare the weaknesses and advantages of the various designs. Whereas experiments are strong on control and weak on rep-

---

## Advantages and Disadvantages of Research Designs Used in the Social Sciences

### Experimental Designs

*Advantages*
- Experiments enable researchers to exert a great deal of control over extrinsic and intrinsic variables, strengthening the validity of causal inferences (internal validity).
- Experiments enable researchers to control the introduction of the independent variable so they may determine the direction of causation.

*Disadvantages*
- External validity is weak because experimental designs do not allow researchers to replicate real-life social situations.
- Researchers must often rely on volunteer or self-selected subjects for their samples. Therefore, the sample may not be representative of the population of interest, preventing researchers from generalizing to the population and limiting the scope of their findings.

### Cross-Sectional and Quasi-Experimental Designs

*Advantages*
- They allow researchers to carry out studies in natural, real-life settings using probability samples, thus increasing the external validity of their studies.
- They do not require the random assignment of individual cases to comparison groups. While this limits the internal validity of studies employing these designs, it does enable researchers to study situations where the assignment of individuals to either a control or an experimental group might be unethical or impossible.

*Disadvantages*
- The lack of adequate control over rival explanations makes it difficult for researchers to make unambiguous inferences.
- Because researchers often cannot manipulate the independent variable, the direction of causation must be logically or theoretically inferred.

### Preexperimental Designs

*Advantages*
- They may allow researchers to gather information when no other research design can be applied, or may allow researchers to show that further, more valid, research would be valuable.

*Disadvantages*
- They are very weak on both internal and external validity and do not allow researchers to make causal inferences.

resentation, quasi-experiments and cross-sectional designs are strong on representation but weak on control. Experiments have several advantages. First and foremost, they enable scientists to make valid causal inferences by exerting a great deal of control—particularly through randomization—over extrinsic and intrinsic variables. The second advantage is that experiments allow researchers to control the introduction of the independent variable, thus permitting them to determine the direction of causation. The major shortcomings of quasi-experiments, cross-sectional designs, and especially preexperiments are that they do not provide these advantages. Lack of adequate control over rival explanations and difficulties in manipulating the independent variable prevent the researcher from drawing unambiguous inferences.

However, although the experiment is accepted as the scientific method par excellence, it too has several shortcomings. The most frequent criticism of experiments, especially laboratory experiments, is that they are artificial and removed from real-life situations. Critics maintain, as we shall see in Chapter 9, that reality cannot be replicated in experimental settings and, hence, that important issues cannot be analyzed there. A second problem concerns the sample design. In experimental designs, it is difficult to represent a specified population. Many experiments include volunteers or have an incidental sample at best. Nonrepresentative samples prevent the investigator from generalizing to populations of interest and limit the scope of the findings. Conversely, most cross-sectional designs are carried out in natural settings and permit the employment of probability samples. This allows scientists to make statistical inferences to broader populations and permits them to generalize their findings to real-life situations.

Because no design can solve the problems of control and representation simultaneously, the investigator faces a difficult choice. Although in practice the nature of the study dictates this choice, scientists generally accept the rule that the attainment of internal validity is more crucial than the attainment of external validity. Still, experiments, cross-sectional studies, and quasi-experiments can be improved. Scientists using experiments can increase external validity by clearly defining the population to be studied and by drawing sampling units from this population following a probability sample design. Scientists using cross-sectional studies and quasi-experiments can greatly improve internal validity by including auxiliary information as a control against rival hypotheses. Moreover, by using more sophisticated statistical techniques such as path or causal analysis, researchers using cross-sectional studies and quasi-experiments can improve the quality of causal inferences.

---

## Summary

---

**1.** Randomization, together with careful experimental control, gives scientific research strength and persuasiveness that cannot ordinarily be obtained by other means. However, property-disposition relations are not readily amenable to experimentation, and social, political, and ethical considerations may discourage or prevent the use of experimental designs with stimulus-response relations.

**2.** Cross-sectional designs, most predominant in survey research, are used to examine relations between properties and dispositions and attempt to approximate the posttest-only control group design by using statistical data analysis techniques.

**3.** Quasi-experimental designs are similar to cross-sectional designs in that they are weaker on internal validity than experimental designs and depend on statistical data analysis techniques as a method of control. They are superior to cross-sectional designs, however, because they usually involve the study of more than one sample, often over an extended period of time. Contrasted groups designs and planned variation designs are quasi-experiments; panel and time-series designs are quasi-experiments that are extended over time.

**4.** Traditionally, preexperimental research designs, such as the one-shot case study, were used when experimentation was impossible. Preexperiments are the weakest research designs since researchers cannot control for most of the sources of internal and external validity.

---

## Key Terms for Review

---

combined designs (p. 144)
contrasted groups (p. 132)
control-series design (p. 142)
cross-sectional design (p. 129)
extended time-series design (p. 139)
one-shot case study (p. 146)

panel (p. 137)
planned variation (p. 134)
property-disposition relationship
  (p. 127)
stimulus-response relationship (p. 127)
time-series design (p. 138)

---

## Study Questions

---

1. Describe the kinds of relationships that lend themselves to study with experimental or quasi-experimental designs. Provide an example of each kind.
2. Develop a quasi-experimental design to study the effect of sex education programs on teenage pregnancy rates. Be sure to explain your logic and the advantages and disadvantages of your research design.
3. Differentiate among combined designs, cross-sectional designs, and panel designs in terms of their strengths and weaknesses.
4. Discuss the limitations of preexperimental designs.
5. Discuss why designs with high internal validity tend to have low external validity.

---

## Additional Readings

---

Berk, Richard A., et al. "Social Policy Experimentation." *Evaluation Review,* 9 (1985): 387–429.

Brewer, John, and Albert Hunter. *Multimethod Research: A Synthesis of Styles.* Newbury Park, Calif.: Sage, 1989.

Coleman, James S. *Longitudinal Data Analysis.* New York: Basic Books, 1981.

Cook, Thomas D. "Quasi-experimentation: Its Ontology, Epistemology and Methodology." In *Beyond Method: Strategies for Social Research,* ed. G. Morgan. Newbury Park, Calif.: Sage, 1983.

Cook, Thomas D., and Donald T. Campbell. *Quasi-experimentation.* Skokie, Ill.: Rand McNally, 1979.

Cronbach, Lee J. *Designing Evaluations of Educational and Social Programs.* San Francisco: Jossey-Bass, 1982.

Feinberg, Stephen B., and Judith M. Tamur. "The Design and Analysis of Longitudinal Surveys: Controversies and Issues of Costs and Continuity." In *Designing Research with Scarce Resources,* ed. Robert F. Boruch and Robert W. Pearson. New York: Springer-Verlag, 1987.

Hedrick, Terry E., Leonard Bickman, and Debra J. Rog. *Applied Research Design: A Practical Guide.* Newbury Park, Calif.: Sage, 1993.

Hausman, Jerry A., and David A. Wise. *Social Experimentation.* Chicago: University of Chicago Press, 1985.

Kish, Leslie. "Some Statistical Problems in Research Design." *American Sociological Review,* 24 (1959): 328–338.

Lazarsfeld, Paul F. "Some Episodes in the History of Panel Analysis." In *Longitudinal Research on Drug Abuse,* ed. D. B. Kandel. New York: Hemisphere, 1978.

McCleary, Richard, and Richard A. Hay. *Applied Time-Series Analysis for the Social Sciences.* Newbury Park, Calif.: Sage, 1980.

Nachmias, David. *Public Policy Evaluation.* New York: St. Martin's Press, 1979. See especially Chapter 3.

Rossi, Peter H., and H. Freeman. *Evaluation: A Systematic Approach.* 3d ed. Newbury Park, Calif.: Sage, 1993.

Suchman, E. A. *Evaluation Research.* Englewood Cliffs, N. J.: Prentice-Hall, 1987.

Trochim, William M. K. *Research Design for Program Evaluation: Regression-Discontinuity Approach.* Newbury Park, Calif.: Sage, 1984.

# CHAPTER 7

# Measurement

**The Nature of Measurement**
Defining Measurement
Structure of Measurement

**Levels of Measurement**
Nominal Level
Ordinal Level
Interval Level
Ratio Level

**Data Transformation**

**Measurement Error**

**Validity**
Content Validity
Empirical Validity
Construct Validity

**Reliability**
Test-Retest Method
Parallel-Forms Technique
Split-Half Method

How can an economist know whether or not the social security, welfare, or pension benefits paid in Illinois are comparable to those paid in Mississippi, or in France? What the economist needs is an instrument that measures the cost of goods and services, one that can be used consistently in almost any modern economy. Such an instrument is the cost of living index. This index provides the mathematical tools for computing and comparing changes in prices independent of the currency used. It is effective because it is precise, reliable, and valid. Before it was devised, economists could never accurately estimate which areas of the economy were contributing to inflation, nor were government agencies able to properly adjust payments to the needy. Because social scientists rely extensively on measuring instruments such as the cost of living index, they must pay close attention to how accurately such tools represent reality. How they determine the accuracy of their instruments is one of the topics of this chapter.

I N THIS CHAPTER WE EXPLORE THE NATURE OF MEASUREMENT in the social sciences and discuss the concept of *isomorphism,* which concerns how measurement instruments relate to the reality being measured. We then present the four levels of measurement: nominal, ordinal, interval, and ratio. Next we discuss the issue of measurement error. The chapter concludes with descriptions of the concepts of validity—whether an instrument measures what it is supposed to measure—and reliability—whether and by how much measurements are consistent from one observation to the next.

Once scientists decide on a research problem and begin to specify the hypotheses to be tested, they are immediately confronted with two problems—how to design the study, and how to measure the variables. In Chapters 5 and 6, we discussed issues of research design. This chapter focuses on measurement, its nature and structure, levels of measurement, as well as the validity and reliability of measuring instruments. The major point to recognize about measurement is that, in the classic words of Norbert Wiener, "things do not . . . run around with their measures stamped on them like the capacity of a freight car: it requires a certain amount of investigation to discover what their measures are."[1] In some cases, this investigation will involve a search for a measure already developed and reported in the professional literature; in other cases, the researcher has to develop measures that will convert empirical observations into the form required by the research problem and the research design. In addition, researchers have to provide evidence that the measures chosen are valid and reliable.

1. Norbert Wiener, "A New Theory of Measurement: A Study in the Logic of Mathematics," *Proceedings of the London Mathematical Society,* 19 (1920): 181. Quoted in *Research Methods: Issues and Insights,* ed. Billy J. Franklin and Harold W. Osborne (Belmont, Calif.: Wadsworth, 1971), p. 118.

# The Nature of Measurement

**Measurement** is closely tied to the concept of operational definitions discussed in Chapter 2. Operational definitions are measurement procedures bridging the conceptual-theoretical level with the empirical-observational level. More specifically, measurement is a procedure in which a researcher assigns numerals—numbers or other symbols—to empirical properties (variables) according to rules.[2] Suppose you intend to purchase a new car. Having found that the difference in price among the various compact cars is minute, you decide to make the purchase on the basis of which model best meets the following requirements: design, economical operation, and service. These three features vary. For example, one model may be well designed and economical to operate, but the service supplied by the manufacturer may be unsatisfactory. Accordingly, you decide to rank each of the three features on a scale of five numbers: 10, 11, 12, 13, and 14. Number 10 indicates total dissatisfaction, and number 14 stands for complete satisfaction. Numbers 11, 12, and 13 indicate increasing degrees of satisfaction with the feature being examined. You then evaluate the five models. Table 7.1 summarizes the evaluation of each model according to the three criteria you set. After examining the scores, you decide to purchase car C because it received the highest score on all three counts. This indicates that car C is the model providing the highest degree of satisfaction possible according to the three criteria.

This car-rating system is an extremely simplified instance of measurement, but it conveys the basic idea expressed in the definition—you assigned numerals to properties according to rules. The properties or variables, the numerals, and the rules for assignment were contained in instructions that you also specified. You might then use the numerals, which are the end product of measurement, for comparing, evaluating, and assessing relations between the various properties measured. For example, you could compute measures of relation between design and economy or between design and service.

**Table 7.1**
**Preference Ranking**

|       | Design | Economy | Service |
|-------|--------|---------|---------|
| Car A | 10     | 11      | 10      |
| Car B | 13     | 14      | 12      |
| Car C | 14     | 14      | 14      |
| Car D | 14     | 12      | 13      |
| Car E | 10     | 12      | 14      |

2. S. S. Stevens, "Mathematics, Measurement and Psychophysics," in *Handbook of Experimental Psychology,* ed. S. S. Stevens (New York: Wiley, 1951), p. 8.

## Defining Measurement

We need to clarify the three basic concepts used to define measurement—numerals, assignments, and rules. A *numeral* is a symbol of the form I, II, III, . . . , or 1, 2, 3, . . . . A numeral has no quantitative meaning unless you give it such a meaning. Numerals can be used to identify phenomena, objects, or persons; thus we can use numerals to designate months, driving licenses, streets, books, variables, or football players. Numerals that are given quantitative meaning become numbers; as such, they enable researchers to use mathematical and statistical techniques for purposes of description, explanation, and prediction. In other words, numbers are amenable to quantitative analyses, which may reveal new information about the phenomena being studied.

In the definition of measurement, the term *assignment* means mapping. Numerals or numbers are mapped onto objects or events. Figure 7.1 illustrates the mapping idea in measurement: in the assortment of circles and squares, 1 is mapped onto the circles, and 2 is mapped onto the squares.

The third concept used to define measurement is that of *rules*. A rule specifies the procedure a researcher uses to assign numerals or numbers to objects or events. A rule might say: "Assign the numerals 10 through 15 to political systems according to how democratic they are. If a political system is very democratic, assign the number 15 to it. If a political system is not at all democratic, assign the number 10 to it. To political systems between these limits of democracy, assign numbers between the numerical limits." Or suppose that a group is composed of three Democrats and two Republicans. An investigator might use the following mapping rule: "If an individual is a Democrat, assign the numeral 1; if a Republican, assign the numeral 2." The application of this rule is illustrated in Figure 7.2.

## Structure of Measurement

Measurement, then, is the assignment of numerals or numbers to objects, events, or variables according to rules. Rules are the most significant component of the

**Figure 7.1**
Assignment or Mapping

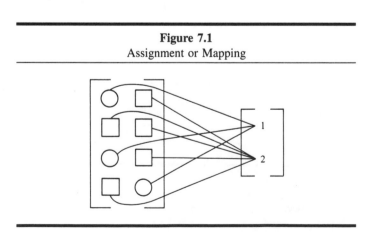

**Figure 7.2**

Assignment in Application of a Rule

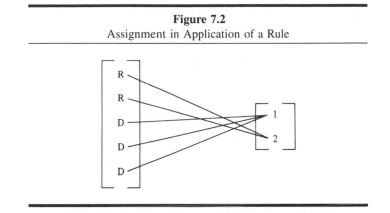

measurement procedure because they determine the quality of measurement. Poor rules make measurement meaningless. Measurement is meaningless when it is not tied to reality, when it lacks an empirical basis. The function of rules is to tie the measurement procedure to reality. For example, suppose that you are measuring the softness of three objects. If object A can scratch B and not vice versa, then B is softer than A. Similarly, if A can scratch B and B can scratch C, then A can probably scratch C. You would then deduce that object C is softer than object A. As these are observable conditions, you can assign numbers indicating the degree of softness to each object after performing a few scratch tests. In this case, the measurement procedure and the number system are isomorphic to reality.

**Isomorphism** means "similarity or identity of structure." In measurement, the crucial question to be asked is whether the numerical system used is similar in structure to the structure of the concepts being measured. To the physical scientist, the problem of isomorphism is often of secondary concern because the relation between the concepts being observed and the numbers assigned to the observations is quite direct. In contrast, the social scientist must always be alert to the fact that this similarity may be neither obvious nor clear-cut:

> In order for him to be able to make certain operations with numbers that have been assigned to observations, the structure of his method of mapping numbers to observations must be isomorphic to some numerical structure which includes these operations.[3]

When we say that two systems are isomorphic, we mean that they have similar structures and that the relations among their internal parts, or the operations they allow for, are also identical. Thus, when a researcher assigns numbers to objects or systems and then manipulates these numbers by, say, adding them, he or she is implying that the structure of this system of measurement is isomorphic to the relationships within, or between, the phenomena under study.

3. Sidney N. Siegel, *Nonparametric Statistics for the Behavioral Sciences* (New York: McGraw-Hill, 1988), p. 22.

Frequently, social scientists measure **indicators** of concepts. Concepts such as democracy, motivation, hostility, and power cannot be observed directly; researchers must infer their presence by measuring their empirical, observable indicators. If elections are held regularly in a political system, a political scientist may infer that this is one indicator of democracy. If someone achieves a certain score in a motivation test, a psychologist may infer something about this person's level of motivation. In these examples, some identifiable behavior is used as an indicator of an underlying concept. Often, researchers must develop multiple indicators to represent abstract concepts. Important concepts in the social sciences are multifaceted and thus require the use of multiple indicators, each reflecting a distinct aspect of the concept involved. For example, democracy entails much more than elections. Fairness of elections, freedom of the press, freedom to organize, and the rights of minorities are other essential attributes. Consequently, the regularity of elections is, by itself, an insufficient indicator of the degree of democracy in a society. Each attribute serves as an additional indicator of the total process.

Indicators should not be selected arbitrarily. They should be grounded in both theory and the empirical world. The indicators used to measure democracy in the previous example derive from both democratic theory and the actual behavior of political systems. Although the process of measuring directly observable concepts is identical to the one for measuring indicators of concepts, the rules in the latter case are more difficult to formulate because the process of measuring indicators calls for a greater degree of inference. The validity of the inferences made depends, in turn, upon the methodology used and the internal logic of the theory that guides the research. Finally, measurement acquires scientific meaning only if it can be related to explanatory theory.

In sum, indicators are specified by operational definitions; after researchers observe the indicators, they substitute numerals or numbers for the values of the indicators and perform quantitative analyses. The numerical structure of the measuring instrument must be similar, in its relations and operations, to the structure of the indicators; that is, the two must be isomorphic.

---

# Levels of Measurement

Because the numerical systems and the empirical properties (or indicators) measured must be isomorphic, scientists distinguish among different ways of measuring or, in technical terminology, distinct levels of measurement. (The term *scales* is sometimes used instead of *levels of measurement*. A scale may be thought of as a tool for measuring; a speedometer is a scale, as is a ruler or a questionnaire.) The mathematical and statistical operations that a researcher can perform on a given set of numbers are dependent on the level of measurement attained. We will discuss the four principal levels of measurement—nominal, ordinal, interval, and ratio—and the rationale behind the operations permitted on each level.

# Nominal Level

The lowest level of measurement is the **nominal level.** At this level, numbers or other symbols are used to classify objects or observations into a number of categories. These numbers or symbols constitute a nominal, or classificatory, scale. By means of the symbols 1 and 2, for instance, it is possible to classify a given population into males and females, with 1 representing males and 2 standing for females. The same population can be classified by religion; Christians might be represented by the numeral 6, Jews by 7, and Moslems by 8. In the first case, the population was classified into two categories; in the second, into three. As a rule, when a set of objects can be classified into categories that are exhaustive (that is, that include all cases of that type) and mutually exclusive (that is, with no case that can be classified as belonging to more than one category), and when each category is represented by a different symbol, a nominal level of measurement is attained. Gender, nationality, ethnicity, religion, marital status, place of residence (e.g., urban or rural), and party identification are all nominal variables.

Mathematically, the basic property of the nominal level of measurement is that the properties of objects in one category are designated as identical for all its cases, that is, for all the cases covered by a similar category. For example, all the residents of Canada and the United States are considered to be members of the nominal category of residents of the North American continent, notwithstanding their citizenship. Similarly, all the citizens of the 50 states belong to the same nominal category for the purpose of federal tax collection; their specific address determines whether they will also be included in other nominal categories, such as the tax rolls of a particular state or municipality.

At the nominal level, scientists can classify objects by utilizing any set of symbols. The investigator can also change the symbols without altering any information, if he or she does so consistently and completely. Accordingly, only statistics that are unaffected, that is, remain unchanged by such transformations, are permissible at the nominal level. These statistics include the mode, measures of qualitative variation, and appropriate measures of associations, which are discussed in Chapters 15 and 16.

# Ordinal Level

Social scientists study many variables that are not only classifiable but also exhibit some kind of relation. Typical relations are "higher," "greater," "more desired," "more difficult," and so on. Such relations may be designated by the symbol >, which means "greater than." In reference to particular properties, > may be used to designate "is higher than," "is greater than," "is more desired than," and so forth. For instance, it can be hypothesized that France is more democratic than Russia but less so than England. In general, if (in addition to equivalence) the relation > holds for all sets of observations that generate a complete ranking of objects (e.g., from "the most" to "the least"), an **ordinal level** of measurement is attained. The equivalence relation holds among cases of the same rank, whereas the > relation holds between any pair of ranks.

The > relation is irreflexive, asymmetrical, and transitive. Irreflexivity is a logical property holding for any $a$, *it is not true that $a > a$*. Asymmetry means that if $a > b$, then $b \not> a$. Transitivity means that if $a > b$ and $b > c$, then $a > c$. In other words, if a variable such as "conservatism" is measured on the ordinal level, one can infer that if a person in group A is more conservative than a person in group B, and if group B is more conservative than group C, then a person in group A is more conservative than a person in group C, and that the > relation is maintained with regard to all the individuals in each of the respective three groups.

As an example of measurement at the ordinal level, consider the common practice of measuring attitudes. Researchers measure attitudes by means of a series of questions, whose alternative answers are ranked in ascending or descending order. For instance, one of the statements used to measure political alienation is "People like me have a lot of influence on government decisions." The respondent is asked to mark the number representing his or her degree of agreement or disagreement with this statement. Table 7.2 illustrates a possible correspondence between the numbers and the answers. Additional questions about the same attitude are presented to the respondent, who can then be ranked according to his or her responses to all the statements.

Suppose that a researcher employs ten statements in all, each permitting four alternative responses: 1 standing for "agree strongly," 2 for "agree," 3 for "disagree," and 4 for "disagree strongly." The highest score a respondent can achieve in this case is 40 (that is, a score of 4 on each of the ten statements); similarly, the lowest is 10. To simplify matters, we assume that the respondents reply to all ten statements. A respondent whose score is 40 will be regarded as the most alienated and will be ranked first on a scale of degree of alienation. Another, whose score is nearest to 40—say, 36—will be ranked second, and so on for each individual in the group. The ranking process ends when all the respondents are ranked by their scores on the political alienation questionnaire. Table 7.3 displays these hypothetical scores and associated rankings of seven respondents. According to the data presented in the table, respondent $S_6$ is the most alienated and respondent $S_1$ the least.

The ordinal level of measurement is amenable to any monotonic transformation no matter how the numbers are manipulated; that is, the information

**Table 7.2**
Ordinal Ranking Scale

| Rank | Value |
|------|-------|
| 1 | Agree strongly |
| 2 | Agree |
| 3 | Disagree |
| 4 | Disagree strongly |

**Table 7.3**
Individuals Ranked by Their Scores on a Questionnaire
about Political Alienation

| Respondent | Score | Rank |
|------------|-------|------|
| $S_1$ | 10 | 7 |
| $S_2$ | 27 | 3 |
| $S_3$ | 36 | 2 |
| $S_4$ | 25 | 4 |
| $S_5$ | 20 | 5 |
| $S_6$ | 40 | 1 |
| $S_7$ | 12 | 6 |

obtained does not change. Nor does it matter what numbers the researcher assigns
to a pair of objects or to a category of objects so long as he or she is consistent.
As a matter of convenience, researchers generally use lower numbers for the
"higher" ranks, just as we usually refer to superior performance as "first class"
and to progressively inferior performances as "second class" and "third class."
Besides attitudes, other ordinal variables commonly studied by social scientists are
social class, school grades, military ranks, hierarchical positions in organizations,
and political party participation. Whenever you can evaluate a phenomenon or a
process along a range such as excellent to terrible (for films, let us say) or highest
to lowest (when referring to social class), you have an ordinal measurement.

The numbers assigned to ranked objects are called *rank values*. Researchers
assign rank values to objects according to the following rule: the object at one
extreme (largest or smallest) is assigned 1; the next in size, 2; the third in size,
3; and so forth up to the object at the other extreme, which is assigned the last
number in the series. In the example in Table 7.3, $S_6$ was assigned 1, $S_3$ was
assigned 2, $S_2$ was assigned 3, $S_4$ was assigned 4, $S_5$ was assigned 5, $S_7$ was
assigned 6, and $S_1$ was assigned 7. It is important to stress that ordinal numbers
indicate rank order and nothing more. The numbers do not indicate that the intervals between the ranks are equal, nor do they indicate absolute quantities. You
cannot assume that because the numbers are equally spaced, the properties they
represent are also equally spaced. If two respondents have the ranks 7 and 5 and
two others are ranked 4 and 2, you cannot infer that the differences between the
two pairs are equal.

Transformations that do not change the order of properties are permissible at
the ordinal level. Accordingly, researchers can perform any mathematical and statistical operations that do not alter the order of properties. For example, a statistic
that describes the central tendency of ordinal numbers is the median. The median
is not affected by changes in any numbers above or below it so long as the number
of ranked observations above and below remains the same. Other statistics appropriate for the ordinal level, discussed in Chapters 15 and 16, are the range,
gamma, and tau-*b*.

## Interval Level

If, in addition to being able to rank a set of observations in terms of the > relation, you also know the exact distance between each of the observations and this distance is constant, then you have reached an **interval level** of measurement. In addition to saying that one object is greater than another, you can now specify by exactly how many units the former is greater than the latter. For example, with interval measurement it is possible to say not only that Sue earns more than Mike, but also that Sue earns, say, $5,000 more than Mike. To make these quantitative comparisons, you must have a precise unit of measurement. An interval level of measurement, then, is characterized by a common and constant unit of measurement that assigns a real number to all pairs of objects in the ordered set. In this kind of measurement, the ratio of any two intervals (distances) is independent of the unit of measurement. Let us say that we were to change an 800-point grading system from nominal units to percentages. The ratio between the score of 66% and 99% would be the same as between, say, scores of 528 and 792, i.e., 2:3. The qualitative distance between the two measuring systems would remain the same. Examples of variables measured at the interval level are income, intelligence quotient (IQ), SAT scores, voter turnout, and crime rates.

At the interval level of measurement, the differences between observations are isomorphic to the structure of arithmetic. When researchers assign numbers to the positions of the objects on the scale used, they can then meaningfully apply several arithmetic operations to the differences between these numbers. The following formal properties characterize the interval level of measurement:

1. Uniqueness: if $a$ and $b$ stand for real numbers, then $a + b$ and $a \times b$ represent one and only one real number.
2. Symmetry: if $a = b$, then $b = a$.
3. Commutation: if $a$ and $b$ denote real numbers, then $a + b = b + a$, and $ab = ba$.
4. Substitution: if $a = b$ and $a + c = d$, then $b + c = d$; and if $a = b$ and $ac = d$, then $bc = d$.
5. Association: if $a$, $b$, and $c$ stand for real numbers, then $(a + b) + c = a + (b + c)$, and $(ab)c = a(bc)$.

Any change in the numbers assigned to the observations must preserve not only their ordering but also their relative differences. Thus the information you obtain at this level is not altered if, for example, you multiply each number by a positive constant and then add a constant to the product. All descriptive and inferential statistics are applicable to interval data.

## Ratio Level

Variables that have natural zero points (i.e., such as the point at which water freezes) can be measured on the **ratio level** of measurement. Variables such as weight, time, length, and area have natural zero points and are measured at the

---

### The Four Levels of Measurement

- *Nominal Level:* At the nominal level, numbers or symbols are used to classify objects or observations. Phenomena in one classificatory category are equal to each other, but not to phenomena in any other category (i.e., the nominal level has the property of equivalence).
- *Ordinal Level:* When variables exhibit a relation to each other, they can be measured at the ordinal level. Such relations can be designated by the symbol > (greater than). The ordinal level of measurement also has the property of equivalence.
- *Interval Level:* When the exact distance between each of the observations is known and constant, measurement is carried out at the interval level. Phenomena of this level also display the property of equivalence, and one observation can be greater (or smaller) than another.
- *Ratio Level:* When variables have natural zero points, they can be measured at this level. The ratio level also has the property of equivalence, relations in which one variable can be greater than another, and a fixed interval.

---

ratio level. At this level, the ratio of any two numbers is also independent of the unit of measurement. The interval and the ratio levels are similar, and the rules by which numbers are assigned are the same, with one exception. For a ratio level of measurement, we apply the arithmetic operations and numbers to the total amount measured from an absolute zero point; for an interval level, we apply the operations to differences from an arbitrary point. A ratio level of measurement, most commonly encountered in the physical sciences, is achieved only when it is possible to attain all four of these relations: (1) equivalence, (2) greater than, (3) known distance of any two intervals, and (4) a true zero point.[4]

---

# Data Transformation

Variables that can be measured at the ratio level can also be measured at the interval, ordinal, and nominal levels. As a rule, properties that can be measured at a higher level can also be measured at lower levels, but not vice versa. A variable such as party affiliation can be measured only at the nominal level. The formal properties that characterize each level of measurement are summarized in Table 7.4. For example, whereas the equivalence property exists at each of the four levels, a natural zero is found only on the ratio level.

Earlier, we pointed out the kinds of numerical operations and statistics that are, in a strict sense, legitimate and permissible with each level. Some researchers

---

4. For more details on levels of measurement, see Siegel, *Nonparametric Statistics,* which informed much of our discussion.

**Table 7.4**
Levels of Measurement and Their Characteristic Properties

| Level | Equivalence | Greater Than | Fixed Interval | Natural Zero |
|---|---|---|---|---|
| Nominal | Yes | No | No | No |
| Ordinal | Yes | Yes | No | No |
| Interval | Yes | Yes | Yes | No |
| Ratio | Yes | Yes | Yes | Yes |

tend to deemphasize this point. The issue, however, is significant enough to warrant a few additional comments.

Mathematics and statistics are contentless languages. They deal with numbers and are not concerned with whether the numbers represent the empirical world. They are useful because of their precision and because they enable researchers to reveal information about phenomena that would otherwise remain hidden. A question such as "To what extent are a series of variables related?" can be meaningfully and precisely answered by computing measures of relations. By assigning numbers, researchers can perform any kind of statistical operation. Remember that social scientists are concerned with empirical phenomena; hence, they use numbers and statistics chiefly to gain a better understanding of the relations among these phenomena. Unless they employ numerical systems and statistics that are isomorphic to the structure of empirical phenomena, however, the outcomes of their efforts are of little use in advancing our knowledge.

# Measurement Error

Measurement procedures are used by scientists to assign numerals, numbers, or scores to properties. Once scores are assigned, they can attribute differences in the scores obtained during repeated observations to two sources. One source is the extent to which the variables exhibit *real differences* in the properties being measured. The other source of difference in the scores is the extent to which the measure itself, or the setting in which measurement takes place, influences the scores. In this case, the measures reveal illusory differences. Perfect measures reveal only real differences between the properties. However, measures are seldom perfect and often indicate not only real differences but also *artifact differences,* variations produced by the measuring procedure itself. Differences in measurement scores that are due to anything other than real differences are termed **measurement errors.**

There are several common sources of measurement errors. First, the scores obtained may be related to an associated attribute, that is, an attribute that the researchers did not intend to measure. For example, respondents may require a certain level of intelligence and social awareness to interpret and answer a question measuring moral development. The responses of individuals to this question will, in effect, reflect real differences in moral development, but also the effect of differences in intelligence and social awareness. The influence of associated attributes is a measurement error. Second, measurement errors may result from differences in temporary conditions, such as health or mood, that may affect a person's responses to a questionnaire or a person's behavior. Third, differences in the setting in which the measure is used contribute to measurement errors. For example, the age, race, and gender of interviewers influences the answers of survey respondents. Fourth, differences in the administration of the measuring instrument (e.g., poor lighting, noise, tired interviewers) can lead to measurement errors. Fifth, measurement errors also result from differences in processing (e.g., when different coders code similar answers to a question differently). The last major source of distortion occurs when different people interpret the measuring instrument in different ways.

The errors that arise from these sources are either systematic or random errors. *Systematic errors* are produced whenever the measuring instrument is used, and they are constant between cases and studies. They consistently introduce a measure of invalidity to the findings. *Random errors,* by contrast, affect each usage of the measuring instrument in a different way. The seriousness of the issues of validity and reliability are issues that prompted the introduction of techniques for reducing measurement errors.

---

# Validity

**Validity** is concerned with the question "Am I measuring what I intend to measure?" The problem of validity arises because measurement in the social sciences is, with very few exceptions, indirect. Under such circumstances, researchers are never completely certain that they are measuring the variable for which they designed their measurement procedure. For example, does voter turnout truly measure political development? If a respondent agrees with the statement "This world is run by a few people in power, and there is not much the little guy can do about it," is his or her response a genuine indicator of the presence of the variable "alienation"? To answer such questions, the researcher must provide supporting evidence that a measuring instrument does, in fact, measure what it appears to measure.

We can distinguish three basic kinds of validity, each of which is concerned with a different aspect of the measurement situation: content validity, empirical validity, and construct validity. Each includes several kinds of evidence and has special value under certain conditions.

## Content Validity

There are two common varieties of content validity: face validity and sampling validity. **Face validity** rests on the investigator's subjective evaluation of the validity of a measuring instrument. In practice, face validity does not relate to the question of whether an instrument measures what the researcher wishes to measure;

rather, it concerns the extent to which the researcher believes that the instrument is appropriate. For example, an investigator intends to measure the variable "liberalism" by means of a questionnaire consisting of ten statements. After constructing the questionnaire, the researcher reviews each statement to assess the extent to which it is related to "liberalism." To do so, he or she might consult a number of specialists (judges). If there is agreement among the judges, the researcher will propose that the questionnaire has face validity and that, consequently, it measures "liberalism." If the judges disagree, however, their lack of consensus would impair the face validity of a measuring instrument.

The main problem with face validity is that there are no precise, replicable procedures for evaluating the measuring instrument. As it is extremely difficult to precisely repeat the evaluation procedure, the researcher has to rely entirely on subjective judgments.

The primary concern of **sampling validity** is whether a given population (i.e., the total set of cases in the real world) is adequately sampled by the measuring instrument in question. In other words, do the statements, questions, or indicators— the content of the instrument—adequately represent the property being measured? The underlying assumption of sampling validity is that every variable has a *content population* consisting of a large number of items (which can be expressed as statements, questions, or indicators) and that a highly valid instrument constitutes a representative sample of these items. In practice, problems arise with the definition of a content population, for this is a theoretical, not an empirical, issue. (We discuss these problems further in Chapter 8, in which we present sampling techniques.) These problems impair the effectiveness of sampling validity as a test of an instrument's overall validity. However, sampling validity serves an important function: it necessitates familiarity with all the items of the content population. It follows that sampling validity is especially useful in exploratory research, where investigators attempt to construct instruments and employ them for the first time. After their initial use of the instrument, they can compare its validity with other tests.

## Empirical Validity

**Empirical validity** is concerned with the relationship between a measuring instrument and the measurement outcomes. Scientists assume that if a measuring instrument is valid, there should be a strong relation between the results produced by applying the instrument and the real relationships existing among the variables measured. For example, an educator might want to know if the scores obtained by the IQ test he or she was using really reflect the intelligence of the subject. Investigators gather evidence to support the existence of a relation by using measures of correlation appropriate to the level of measurement. (A correlation coefficient is an index of the degree of relation between two measures or variables; details can be found in Chapter 16.) Of the various tests designed to evaluate empirical validity, predictive validity is the most widely used. For this reason, we shall discuss it at some length.

Researchers estimate **predictive validity** by predicting the results they expect to obtain in reference to an external measure, referred to as a *criterion,* and by checking their measuring instrument against outcomes obtained by other measuring instruments. In other words, predictive validity is the degree of correlation, known as the correlation coefficient, between the results of a given measurement and an external criterion. For example, an investigator can validate an intelligence test by first obtaining the test scores of a group such as college students and by then obtaining the grade point averages that these students achieved in their first year of college (the criterion). The researcher then computes a correlation coefficient between the two sets of measurements. This particular correlation coefficient is called the *validity coefficient.* Other criteria that could be used to validate intelligence tests are social outcomes of adjustment tests and ratings of performance.

Figure 7.3 illustrates the process by which the predictive validity of an instrument is evaluated. A variable ($V$) is measured by a certain measuring instrument ($I$). To assess the predictive validity of the instrument, the researcher employs a criterion ($C$) whose validity is agreed upon. The measurements obtained by $I$ are correlated with the measurements obtained by $C$. The size of the validity coefficient ($r_{IC}$) indicates the predictive validity of the instrument.

In order to apply the test of predictive validity, researchers need to consider two general issues. One concerns the need to use a measuring instrument instead of only a criterion; for example, most colleges compare SAT scores (the measuring instrument) to past grade averages (the criterion) to predict the future achievement of potential students. The other issue relates to the validity of the criterion.

Regarding the first issue, a problem may arise if the criterion is too difficult or expensive to use: for instance, testing the quality of every computer board that comes off the assembly line is very expensive; therefore, only a sample is tested. In other cases, investigators may have to make initial measurements of a variable before deciding upon and then applying a criterion. Scholastic abilities is such a variable—it must first be measured before being selected as a criterion for success in a course of study.

As far as the second issue is concerned, two common methods are used to establish the validity of the criterion. One method relies on the agreement among researchers that a certain criterion is valid for evaluating a measuring instrument.

**Figure 7.3**
Evaluating Predictive Validity

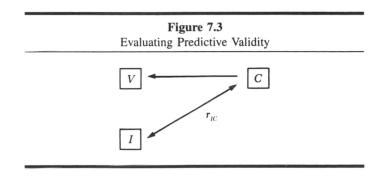

This agreement is subject to tests of face validity and sampling validity. A somewhat different method is to determine the percentage of individuals (or other units of analysis) who would be correctly classified by the instrument according to their known characteristics and to express the relationship between the instrument and the criterion in terms of this percentage.[5]

Suppose that a researcher needs to evaluate the validity of an instrument designed to measure political conservatism. If there are theoretically sound reasons for arguing that people in the lower class are more conservative than people in the middle class, the researcher can compare membership in the two classes as a check of predictive validity. In this case, social class serves as an indirect criterion for the predictive validity of the instrument. If, however, the empirical findings reveal that persons in the lower class are as conservative as persons in the middle class, the measurement instrument lacks predictive validity. Conversely, a relatively high correlation between social class and degree of conservatism would validate the instrument. However, a high correlation is a necessary but not a sufficient condition to establish the predictive validity of an instrument because the indirect criterion (social class) may also be related to variables other than political conservatism (e.g., education). The instrument might be measuring variables other than political conservatism per se. An indirect criterion, then, is more useful for revealing that an instrument is not valid than for validating it.

## Construct Validity

Researchers establish **construct validity** by relating a measuring instrument to a general theoretical framework in order to determine whether the instrument is tied to the concepts and theoretical assumptions they are employing. Lee J. Cronbach, an early proponent of construct validity, observed that "whenever a tester asks what a score means psychologically or what causes a person to get a certain test score, he is asking what concepts may properly be used to interpret the test performance."[6] Theoretical expectations about the variable being measured lead the investigator to postulate various kinds and degrees of relationships between the particular variable and other specified variables. To demonstrate the construct validity of a measuring instrument, an investigator has to show that these relationships do in fact hold. We shall illustrate the utility of construct validity through Milton Rokeach's famous research on dogmatism.[7]

On the basis of theoretical reasoning, Rokeach constructed a dogmatism questionnaire. This instrument consisted of statements assumed to measure closed-mindedness, a personality trait associated with adherence to any belief system or

5. C. G. Helmstadter, *Research Concepts in Human Behavior* (Englewood Cliffs, N. J.: Prentice-Hall, 1970).

6. Lee J. Cronbach, *Essentials of Psychological Testing,* 4th ed. (New York: Harper & Row, 1984), p. 121.

7. Milton Rokeach, *The Open and the Closed Mind* (New York: Basic Books, 1960).

ideology, regardless of its content. Rokeach argued that individuals' ideological orientations are related to their personalities, thought processes, and behavior. Consequently, he predicted, among other things, that dogmatism is related to being strongly opinionated. Rokeach conducted a number of studies aimed at testing his theory and the construct validity of the measuring instruments he employed. In one study, he used the **known-groups technique.** In this method, the investigator administers a measuring instrument to groups of people with known attributes in order to predict the direction of differences among the groups. Rokeach asked college professors and graduate students to select friends who they thought to be open-minded or closed-minded. The dogmatism questionnaire clearly differentiated the two groups. This finding provided supporting evidence of the construct validity of the dogmatism measure.

Cronbach and Meehl describe the logical process of construct validation in the following way: first, a scientist offers the proposition that an instrument measures a certain property (say, property A); second, he or she inserts the proposition into the present theory regarding property A; third, in working through the theory, the investigator predicts which properties should be related to the instrument and which should exhibit no relation to the instrument; finally, he or she collects data that will empirically confirm or reject the predicted relations. If the anticipated relationships are found, the instrument is considered valid. If the predictions fail, the explanation lies in at least one of three possible causes: (1) the instrument does not measure property A, (2) the theoretical framework that generated the predictions is flawed, or (3) the research design failed to test the predictions properly. The researcher must then decide which of these three conditions is applicable. Such a decision is based on a careful reconstruction of each of the four steps constituting the validation process.[8]

Campbell and Fiske suggested another method of construct validation involving correlation matrices.[9] This is the *convergent-discriminant* conception of validity, or the *multitrait-multimethod matrix* technique. This method is derived from the idea that different methods of measuring the same property should yield similar results, whereas different properties should yield different measurement results regardless of the measuring instrument. Operationally, this means that correlation coefficients among scores for a given property measured by different instruments should be higher than correlation coefficients among scores for different properties measured by similar instruments. In order to obtain evidence of the construct validity of an instrument, a researcher must make use of both a convergent principle—two measures of the same property should correlate highly with each other even though they represent different methods—and a discriminant principle—two measures of different properties should not correlate highly with each other even though a similar instrument is used.

8. Lee J. Cronbach and Paul Meehl, "Construct Validity in Psychological Tests," *Psychological Bulletin,* 52 (1955): 281–302.

9. Donald T. Campbell and Donald W. Fiske, "Convergent and Discriminant Validation by the Multitrait-Multimethod Matrix," *Psychological Bulletin,* 56 (1959): 81–105.

---

### Three Kinds of Validity

- *Content Validity:* The relevance of an instrument to the characteristics of the variable it is meant to measure is assessed by *face validity*—the researcher's subjective assessment of the instrument's appropriateness—and *sampling validity*—the degree to which the statements, questions, or indicators constituting the instrument adequately represent the qualities measured.
- *Empirical Validity:* If a measuring instrument is valid, there should be a strong relationship between the results it predicts and the results it obtains when measuring the same or related variables. Empirical validity can be supported by comparisons with measurements made by other instruments.
- *Construct Validity:* This kind of validity is established by relating the measuring instrument to a general theoretical framework.

---

In view of the distinctions among the three types of validity, which test should we use when evaluating the validity of a given measuring instrument? This is a significant problem, and it has no simple solution. Therefore, a team of experts from different disciplines recommended that a thorough examination of a measuring instrument include information about all three types of validity.[10] Thus, when researchers begin to construct a measurement instrument, they first evaluate theories that could serve as a foundation for the instrument (construct validity); next, they define a content population of items from which a representative sample is to be drawn (content validity); finally, they assess the predictive (empirical) validity of the instrument by correlating it with an external criterion.

---

# Reliability

Reliability is of central concern to social scientists because the measuring instruments they employ are rarely completely valid. In many cases, evidence of validity is almost entirely lacking; instead, the researcher has to evaluate the measuring instrument with respect to other characteristics and assume its validity. A method frequently used by social scientists for evaluating an instrument is its degree of reliability.

**Reliability** refers to the extent to which a measuring instrument contains *variable errors,* that is, errors that appear inconsistently from observation to observation during any one measurement attempt or that vary each time a given unit is measured by the same instrument. For example, if you measure the length of a desk at two points in time with the same instrument—say, a ruler—and get

---

10. See American Psychological Association Committee on Psychological Tests, "Technical Recommendations for Psychological Tests and Diagnostic Techniques," *Psychological Bulletin Suppl.,* 51 (1954), pt. 2: 1–38, and Donald T. Campbell, "Recommendations for APA Test Standards Regarding Construct, Trait, or Discriminant Validity," *American Psychologist,* 15 (1960): 546–553.

slightly different results, the instrument contains variable errors. Because measurement in the social sciences is primarily indirect, the number of errors that occur when social variables are measured tends to be greater than when physical variables are measured. Factors such as a respondent's momentary distraction when completing a questionnaire, ambiguous instructions, and technical difficulties (e.g., a pencil breaks while the respondent is filling in a questionnaire) may cause the introduction of variable measurement errors.

Each measurement, then, consists of two components: a *true component* and an *error component*. Reliability can therefore be defined as the ratio of the true-score variance to the total variance in the scores as measured.[11] (The variance is a measure of the spread of observations, or scores; it is a description of the extent to which the observations differ from each other; that is,

$$\sigma^2 = \frac{\sum_{i=1}^{N}(x_i - \bar{x})^2}{N}$$

See Chapter 15 for a detailed presentation.) Algebraically, each person's observed score can be represented as

$$x_i = t_i + e_i \tag{7.1}$$

where $x_i$ = score actually obtained by person $i$

$t_i$ = true score for person $i$

$e_i$ = amount of error that occurred when obtaining the score for person $i$ at the time the measurement was made

Expressed in variance terms, we get

$$\sigma_x^2 = \sigma_t^2 + \sigma_e^2$$

where $\sigma_x^2$ = variance of observed scores

$\sigma_t^2$ = variance of true scores

$\sigma_e^2$ = variance of errors

Reliability, defined as the ratio of true-score variance to observed-score variance, can be expressed as

$$\text{Reliability} = \frac{\sigma_t^2}{\sigma_x^2} = \frac{\sigma_x^2 - \sigma_e^2}{\sigma_x^2} \tag{7.2}$$

From Equation (7.2) we can see that if the measurement involves nothing but error, then $\sigma_x^2 = \sigma_e^2$ and the reliability is zero. However, when there is no variable error at all, $\sigma_e^2 = 0$, and the ratio defined as reliability becomes

$$\frac{\sigma_x^2}{\sigma_x^2} = 1$$

11. This definition and the following presentation are based on C. G. Helmstadter, *Research Concepts,* pp. 169–176.

Therefore, the **reliability measure** varies on a scale from 0 to 1, having the former value when the measurement involves nothing but error and reaching 1 when there is no variable error at all in the measurement.

In practice, it is impossible to compute the true score independently of all the error that occurs in any particular measurement. Consequently, the ratio $\sigma_t^2/\sigma_x^2$ has to be estimated. There are three common ways of estimating reliability: the test-retest method, the parallel-forms technique, and the split-half method.

## Test-Retest Method

The **test-retest method** derives directly from the conceptual definition of reliability. The researcher administers the measuring instrument to the same group of persons at two different times, and computes the correlation between the two sets of observations (scores). The coefficient that the researcher obtains is the *reliability estimate*. With this method, error is defined as anything that leads a person to get a different score on one measurement from the score that person obtained on another measurement. Symbolically,

$$r_{xx'} = \frac{S_t^2}{S_x^2}$$

(7.3)

where $x$ = performance on the first measurement

$x'$ = performance on the second measurement

$r_{xx'}$ = correlation coefficient between $x$ and $x'$

$S_t^2$ = estimated variance of the true scores

$S_x^2$ = calculated variance of the observed scores

The correlation $r_{xx'}$ provides an estimate of reliability defined as a ratio of the true variance to the observed variance. (For methods of computing the correlation coefficient, see Chapter 16.)

The test-retest method has two main limitations. First, measurement on one occasion may influence measurements on subsequent occasions. If, for example, the instrument is a questionnaire, a respondent may remember specific questions and give the same answer as on the first occasion, thus yielding a high but overstated reliability estimate. Second, since many phenomena constantly change, it is possible that changes may have occurred in the measured variable during the period between the two tests (the measurement interval), thus lowering the obtained estimate of reliability. The test-retest method, then, may either overestimate or underestimate the true reliability of the instrument, and in many cases it is difficult to determine which has occurred.

## Parallel-Forms Technique

One way to counter the two limitations of the test-retest method is to use the **parallel-forms technique.** In order to use this technique, a researcher needs to develop two parallel versions of a measuring instrument. He or she then administers both forms to the same group of persons, and then correlates the two sets of measures (scores) to obtain an estimate of reliability. With this technique, however, the problem arises as to whether or not the two forms of an instrument are in fact parallel. Although scientists have developed statistical tests to determine whether the forms are parallel in terms of statistical measures, researchers must still rely on their judgment when evaluating the results.[12]

## Split-Half Method

The **split-half method** estimates reliability by treating each of two or more parts of a measuring instrument as a separate scale. Suppose that the measuring instrument is a questionnaire. The questionnaire is separated into two sets, using the odd-numbered questions for one set and the even-numbered questions for the other. Each of the two sets of questions is treated separately and scored accordingly. The two sets are then correlated, and this is taken as an estimate of reliability. To adjust the correlation coefficient obtained between the two halves, the following formula, known as the Spearman-Brown prophecy formula, may be applied:

$$r_{xx'} = \frac{2r_{oe}}{1 + r_{oe}} \tag{7.4}$$

where $r_{xx'}$ = the reliability of the original test

$r_{oe}$ = the reliability coefficient obtained by correlating the scores of the odd statements with the scores of the even statements

This correction assumes that an instrument that is $2n$ questions long will be more reliable than an instrument that is $n$ questions long. Because the length of the instrument has been halved by dividing it into odds and evens, and each part has been scored separately, the complete instrument will have a higher reliability than either half had it been applied alone.

Cronbach, Rajaratnam, and Glesser have introduced a revision to the traditional concept of reliability.[13] These authors maintain that the chief concern of reliability theory is to answer the question "To what universe of potential measurements do we wish to generalize?" Thus, instead of reliability, they have introduced the idea of generalizability. **Generalizability** implies that what scientists really want to know about is to what extent, and with respect to what properties, one set of measurements is like other sets of measurements that researchers might have taken from a given universe of potential measurements. The same applies to differences among the sets of measurements that might be drawn from that universe of potential measurements. When scientists ask questions about the likeness or difference of potential measurements, they are asking about the limits of their ability to generalize based on the results of any one set of measurements. Whether

12. See Harold Gulliksen, *Theory of Mental Tests* (New York: Wiley, 1962).

13. Lee J. Cronbach, Nageswars Rajaratnam, and Goldine C. Glesser, "A Theory of Generalizability: A Liberalization of Reliability Theory," *British Journal of Statistical Psychology*, 16 (1963): 137–163.

we consider a particular relation among measurements to be evidence of reliability or generalizability depends on how we choose to define likeness and difference of conditions and measures. Just how researchers construct a list of items or properties that are the same or different in each set of measurements depends, of course, on the research problem. [14]

---

## Summary

**1.** Measurement is the assignment of numerals to variables, properties, or events according to rules. The most significant concept in this definition is "rules." The function of a rule is to tie the measurement procedure to reality, that is, to establish isomorphism between a certain numerical structure and the structure of the variables being measured. If they can establish isomorphism, researchers can perform quantitative analyses with the numerals that stand for the properties.

**2.** Isomorphism between numerical systems and empirical properties enables the researcher to distinguish between four levels of measurement: nominal, ordinal, interval, and ratio. In general, the level of measurement determines which quantitative analyses can be performed on a given set of numbers.

**3.** Measurement procedures are highly sensitive to data transformation and measurement error. Properties that can be measured at a higher level of precision can also be measured at a lower level, but not vice versa. That is, some data can be transformed from the ratio level to the nominal level, but not all data can be transformed from the nominal to the ratio level.

**4.** Measurement error refers to the accuracy and consequent consistency of the measuring instrument itself. The source of the error may lie in a misunderstanding of what is actually being measured (e.g., intelligence rather than attitudes) or in the measure's sensitivity to the measurement setting (e.g., a respondent's ability to concentrate in a noisy testing room). In any case, the error reflects problems of measurement and not real differences in the variable being measured.

**5.** The concepts of validity and reliability are inseparable from measurement. They underlie the sources of measurement error. Validity is concerned with the question of whether researchers are measuring what they think they are measuring. Traditionally, three basic types of validity have been distinguished, each of which relates to a different aspect of the measurement situation: content validity, empirical validity, and construct validity. To validate a certain measuring instrument, the researcher must look for information geared to each of these three types.

**6.** Reliability indicates the extent to which a measure contains variable errors. Operationally, it is assumed that any measure consists of a true component and an error component; the proportion of the amount of variation in the true compo-

---

14. For the statistical expression of the generalizability index, see ibid., and Goldine C. Glesser, Lee J. Cronbach, and Nageswars Rajaratnam "Generalizability of Scores Influenced by Multiple Scores of Variance," *Psychometrika*, 30 (1965): 395–418.

nent to the total variation indicates the measure's reliability. Researchers estimate reliability by one or more of the following methods: test-retest, parallel-forms, and split-half. The notion of generalizability implies that the main concern of reliability is with the extent to which a set of measurements is similar to other sets of measurements that might have been drawn from a given universe of potential measurements.

---

## Key Terms for Review

---

construct validity (p. 168)
empirical validity (p. 166)
face validity (p. 165)
generalizability (p. 173)
indicator (p. 158)
interval level (p. 162)
isomorphism (p. 157)
known-groups technique (p. 169)
measurement (p. 155)
measurement errors (p. 164)
nominal level (p. 159)

ordinal level (p. 159)
parallel-forms technique (p. 172)
predictive validity (p. 167)
ratio level (p. 162)
reliability (p. 170)
reliability measure (p. 172)
sampling validity (p. 166)
split-half method (p. 173)
test-retest method (p. 172)
validity (p. 165)

---

## Study Questions

---

1. Define measurement and explain why measurement is important to scientific research.
2. What are the various levels of measurement? Why are the differences between the levels of measurement important? Give an example of data that can be transformed from one level to another, and another example of data that cannot be transformed.
3. Define the concept "validity" and explain how to distinguish among the three major types of validity.
4. Define the concept "reliability" and discuss the ways of assessing it.
5. How is validity related to reliability? Can you give an example?

---

## Additional Readings

---

Achen, Christopher H. "Toward Theories of Data: The State of Political Methodology." In *Political Science: The State of the Discipline, No. II,* rev. ed., ed. Ada Finifter. Washington, D.C.: American Political Science Association, 1993.

Allen, Mary J. *Introduction to Measurement Theory.* Pacific Grove, Calif.: Brooks/Cole, 1979.

Blalock, Hubert M., Jr. *Conceptualization and Measurement in the Social Sciences.* Newbury Park, Calif.: Sage, 1982.

Bohrnstedt, George W., and Edgar F. Borgatta, eds. *Social Measurement.* Newbury Park, Calif.: Sage, 1981.

Bohrnstedt, George W., and David Knoke. *Statistics for Social Data Analysis.* 2d ed. F. E. Peacock: 1988.

Carley, Michael. *Social Measurement and Social Indicators.* Boston: Allen & Unwin, 1981.

Ghiselli, Edwin E., and Sheldon Zedeck. *Measurement Theory for the Behavioral Sciences.* New York: Freeman, 1981.

Kidder, Louise H. "Face Validity from Multiple Perspectives." In *New Directions for Methodology of Social and Behavioral Science: Forms of Validity,* ed. David Brimberg and Louise Kidder. San Francisco: Jossey-Bass, 1982.

Schwartz, Norman, et al. "Rating Scales: Numeric Values May Change the Meaning of Scale Labels." *Public Opinion Quarterly,* Winter (1991): 570–582.

Shively, W. Phillips. *The Craft of Political Research.* 3d ed. Englewood Cliffs, N. J.: Prentice-Hall, 1990.

Sullivan, John L., and Stanley Feldman. *Multiple Indicators.* Newbury Park, Calif.: Sage, 1979.

Zeller, Richard A., and Edward G. Carmines. *Measurement in the Social Sciences.* New York: Cambridge University Press, 1980.

CHAPTER 8

# Sampling and Sample Designs

"Trial heat" polls for predicting results just prior to major elections have been popular for some time. During the 1992 campaign, these polls greatly overestimated the margin of Clinton's victory while they greatly underestimated Perot's strength. What do these inaccuracies in estimation say about polling and the sampling procedures used? By investigating how these trial heat polls were conducted, Richard Lau has come to some important methodological conclusions about polling in general.[1] According to Lau, variations in results, as well as errors, occur because of inconsistent sample sizes; the specific population included in the sampling frame, for example, "registered voters" versus "likely voters"; inconsistently determined nonresponse rates, especially as the time of day or day of the week when the poll was conducted effectively limits the inclusion of certain groups; the proportion of "undecideds"; and how many days before the election the poll was taken. If these factors influence trial heat polls, how do they influence polls about the other subjects investigated with the use of samples?

The factors that Lau isolated all have to do with the problem of obtaining a sample that represents the population a researcher is studying. That problem is the subject of this chapter.

I N THIS CHAPTER, WE COVER THE FUNDAMENTALS OF SAMPLING theory, the how and why of sample selection. In the first section, we discuss the aims of sampling. We then move on to definitions and a discussion of central concepts—population, the sampling unit, sampling frame, and the sample—as well as the procedures of probability and nonprobability sampling designs. Next, we discuss the considerations involved in determining the sample size. Finally, we present procedures for estimating nonsampling errors.

Researchers collect data in order to test hypotheses and to provide empirical support for explanations and predictions. Once investigators have constructed their measuring instruments in order to collect sufficient data pertinent to the research problem, the subsequent explanations and predictions must be capable of being generalized to be of scientific value. As we emphasized in Chapter 1 (Figure 1.1), generalizations constitute a major stage of the research process. Generalizations are important not only for testing hypotheses but also for descriptive purposes. For example, questions such as "What is the level of political trust among Americans?" or "Are voters more concerned with the environment now than they were a decade ago?" call for descriptive generalizations.

Typically, generalizations are not based on data collected from *all* the observations, *all* the respondents, or *all* the events that are defined by the research problem. Instead, researchers use a relatively small number of cases (a sample) as the basis for making inferences about all the cases (a population). Election polls

1. Richard R. Lau, "An Analysis of the Accuracy of 'Trial Heat' Polls During the 1992 Presidential Election," *Public Opinion Quarterly*, 58 (1994): 2–20.

are a familiar example. Based on the responses of a relatively small group of respondents, pollsters forecast how the entire population of voters would vote if the election were held at the time the poll was taken; they also attempt to predict how those voters will vote when the actual election is held. Social scientists, as well as pollsters, apply various criteria in selecting their samples. These considerations in turn influence how they make inferences from a sample to a population.

# Aims of Sampling

Empirically supported generalizations are usually based on partial information because, as stated above, it is often impossible, impractical, or extremely expensive to collect data from all the potential units of analysis covered by the research problem. Researchers can draw precise inferences on all the units (a set) based on a relatively small number of units (a subset) when the subsets accurately represent the relevant attributes of the whole set. Marketing researchers, for example, use the preferences expressed by a small subset of households to target new products to millions of customers. The Environmental Protection Agency uses a small number of automobiles of various models to obtain data on performance. The data collected from the subset are used to define and regulate the performance standards of all automobiles.

The entire set of relevant units of analysis, or data, is called the **population.** When the data serving as the basis for generalizations is comprised of a subset of the population, that subset is called a **sample.** A particular value of the population, such as the median income or the level of formal education, is called a **parameter;** its counterpart in the sample is termed a **statistic.** The major objective of sampling theory is to provide accurate estimates of unknown values of the parameters from sample statistics that can be easily calculated.

To accurately estimate unknown parameters from known statistics, researchers have to effectively deal with three major problems: (1) the definition of the population, (2) the sample design, and (3) the size of the sample.

# Population

Methodologically speaking, a population is the "aggregate of all cases that conform to some designated set of specifications."[2] For example, by the specifications "people" and "residing in Britain," we can define a population consisting of all the people who reside in Britain. Similarly, by employing the specifications "students" and "enrolled in state universities in the United States," we define a population consisting of all students enrolled in state universities in the United States. You may similarly define populations consisting of all the households in

---

2. Isidor Chein, "An Introduction to Sampling," in Claire Selltiz, et al., *Research Methods in Social Relations,* 4th ed. (New York: Holt, Rinehart and Winston, 1981), p. 419.

a given community, all the registered voters in a particular precinct, or all the books in a public library. A population may be composed of all the residents in a specific neighborhood, legislators, houses, records, and so on. The specific nature of the population depends on the research problem. If you are investigating consumer behavior in a particular city, you might define the population as all the households in that city. Or, if you are focusing on a particular product, let us say dog food, your population would be composed only of those having dogs as pets.

Therefore, one of the first problems facing a researcher who wishes to estimate a population value from a sample value is how to determine the population involved. If a political scientist is interested in voting behavior in Britain and wishes to draw a sample so as to predict how an election will turn out, the sample should exclude individuals under 18 because they do not have the right to vote. Nevertheless, "all British subjects 18 years of age or older" is still an inadequate definition of the population of voters because individuals have to meet certain legal requirements before the election is held. Individuals who do not meet such criteria are ineligible to vote; hence, they should be excluded from the sampling population. The population, then, has to be defined in terms of (1) content, (2) extent, and (3) time—for example, (a) all residents over 18 years of age living in permanent residential units, (b) in England, (c) as of May 1, 1995.

## The Sampling Unit

A single member of a sampling population (e.g., a voter, a household, an event) is referred to as a **sampling unit.** Usually, sampling units have numerous attributes, one or more of which are relevant to the research problem. For example, if the population is defined as all third graders in a given town attending public schools on a particular day, the sampling units are all third graders. Third graders, however, have many traits (variables), including grades, habits, opinions, and expectations. A research project may examine only one variable, such as arithmetic grades, or relations among several variables, for example, arithmetic grades, IQ scores, and formal education of parents.

A sampling unit is not necessarily an individual. It can be an event, a university, a city, or a nation. For example, in a study of conflict behavior within and between nations, Rudolph J. Rummel collected data on 22 measures of foreign and domestic conflict behavior (such as assassinations, guerrilla warfare, purges, riots, revolutions, military actions, wars) for 77 nations over a three-year period.[3] In his study, the sampling units were nations, but not all nations were selected. The sampling units had to meet two criteria to be included in the study: (1) sovereign statehood for at least two years, as evidenced by diplomatic relations with other countries and the existence of a foreign ministry, and (2) a minimum population of 800,000.

3. Rudolph J. Rummel, "Dimensions of Conflict Behavior within and between Nations," in *Macroquantitative Analysis: Conflict, Development and Democratization,* ed. J. V. Gillespie and B. A. Nesvold (Newbury Park, Calif.: Sage, 1971).

## Finite and Infinite Populations

A population may be finite or infinite, depending on whether the sampling units are finite or infinite. By definition, a *finite population* contains a countable number of sampling units, for example, all registered voters in a particular city in a given year. An *infinite population* consists of an endless number of sampling units, such as an unlimited number of coin tosses. Sampling designed to produce information about particular characteristics of a finite population is usually termed *survey sampling*.

## Sampling Frame

Once researchers have defined the population, they draw a sample that adequately represents that population. The actual procedures involve selecting a sample from a **sampling frame** comprised of a complete listing of sampling units. Ideally, the sampling frame should include all the sampling units in the population. In practice, a physical list rarely exists; researchers usually compile a substitute list. For example, in large national studies, it is impossible to obtain a complete and accurate listing of all individuals residing in the United States. This difficulty is regularly encountered even by large research organizations, such as the Bureau of the Census, which counts the entire nation every decade. The 1990 census, which cost an estimated $2.6 billion, required 277 million forms. The Bureau of the Census collected an estimated 3.3 billion individual answers, which were processed by nearly 480,000 census workers over the period 1988–1991. These workers compiled and checked address lists, and gathered and processed vital information on approximately 250 million people and 106 million housing units in the United States and its territories. The Census also hired 35,000 temporary employees to go door-to-door during 1988–1989. They compiled a list of about 43 million addresses of housing units, many outside metropolitan areas. In addition, the Census Bureau purchased about 55 million residential addresses in large metropolitan areas from commercial mailing list companies. Census and Postal Service workers checked and updated the address lists before the Census Bureau produced mailing labels for the questionnaire envelopes.[4] Yet, for all its efforts, it is estimated that the census missed approximately 5 million of the nation's residents. As in the 1980 census, the increasingly mobile lifestyle in the United States made it difficult to compile a complete mailing list.

In smaller-scale studies, the sampling frame may be based on telephone directories, city directories, or membership lists of private and public organizations.

The researcher should ensure that there is a high degree of correspondence between a sampling frame and the sampling population. The accuracy of a sample depends, first and foremost, on the sampling frame. Indeed, every aspect of the sample design—the population covered, the stages of sampling, and the actual selection process—is influenced by the sampling frame. Prior to selecting a sam-

---

4. From *Census '90 Basics* (U.S. Department of Commerce, Bureau of the Census, December 1985), p. 1.

ple, the researcher has to evaluate the sampling frame for potential problems. Leslie Kish provides a useful classification of typical problems in sampling frames: incomplete sampling frames, clusters of elements, and blank foreign elements.[5]

***Incomplete Frames.***    The problem of incomplete sampling frames arises when sampling units included in the real population are missing from the list. For example, if the population includes all new residents in a community, a sampling frame based on the real estate multiple-listing service in the community would be incomplete because the service registers new homeowners (sellers and buyers) but excludes renters.

When the sampling frame is incomplete, one option might be to use supplemental lists. For example, it may be possible to compile a list of all new renters in the community by using the city directory if it identifies new residents in the community as homeowners or renters.

***Clusters of Elements.***    The second potential problem of a sampling frame is clusters of elements. This problem occurs when sampling units are listed in clusters rather than individually. For example, the sampling frame may consist of city blocks, whereas the study focuses on individuals. A possible solution to this problem would be for the investigator to take a sample of blocks and then list all the individual households in each of the selected blocks. The researcher would then select individuals from each household (most households include more than one individual) according to prespecified criteria, such as individuals over 18, or only heads of households.

***Blank Foreign Elements.***    The problem of blank foreign elements is quite common. It occurs when some sampling units in the sampling frame are not included in the research population, such as the case where the population is defined as consisting only of eligible voters whereas the frame contains a number of individuals who are too young to vote. This problem often crops up when the listing used as a frame is outdated. Another example, often encountered when researchers use city directories, results when the directory lists an address but fails to list its residents. This does not necessarily mean that no one lives at that address; the residents may have recently moved there and have yet to be included in the periodic listing. These cases should be treated as blanks and *simply omitted* from the sample. It is a good practice to select a slightly larger sample initially in order to compensate for such omissions.

## Errors in Sampling Frames: The 1936 Presidential Election

Our discussion of errors in sampling frames could not be complete without mentioning the best-known example of sampling failure, the 1936 *Literary Digest* poll. In 1936, Franklin Delano Roosevelt, completing his first term of office as

5. Leslie Kish, *Survey Sampling* (New York: Wiley, 1965), sect. 2.7.

president of the United States, was running against the Republican candidate, Alf Landon of Kansas. The *Literary Digest* magazine, in a poll consisting of about 2.4 million individuals, the largest in history, predicted a victory for Landon by 57 percent to 43 percent. Despite this decisive prediction, Roosevelt won the election by a huge landslide—62 percent to 38 percent.[6]

Despite the very large sample size, the error was enormous, the largest ever made by any polling organization. The major reason for the error was found in the sampling frame. The *Digest* had mailed questionnaires to 10 million people whose names and addresses were taken from sources such as telephone directories and club membership lists. In 1936, however, few poor people had telephones, nor were they likely to belong to clubs. Thus the sampling frame was incomplete as it systematically excluded the poor. This omission was particularly significant because in that year, 1936, the poor voted overwhelmingly for Roosevelt whereas the well-to-do voted mainly for Landon.[7] That is, the sampling frame did not accurately reflect the actual voter population.

# Sample Designs

In the previous section, we discussed sampling problems in relation to the definition of the population and the sampling frame. The second sampling problem arises when researchers attempt to secure a **representative sample.** The essential requirement of any sample is that it be as representative as possible of the population from which it is drawn. A sample is considered to be representative if the analyses made using the researcher's sampling units produce results similar to those that would be obtained had the researcher analyzed the entire population.

## Probability and Nonprobability Sampling

In modern sampling theory, a basic distinction is made between probability and nonprobability sampling. The distinguishing characteristic of **probability sampling** is that for each sampling unit of the population, you can specify the probability that the unit will be included in the sample. In the simplest case, all the units have the same probability of being included in the sample. In **nonprobability sampling,** there is no way of specifying the probability of each unit's inclusion in the sample, and there is no assurance that every unit has some chance of being included. If a set of units has no chance of being included in the sample, this implies that the definition of the population must be restricted; that is, if the traits of this set of units remain unknown, then the precise nature of the population cannot be known.[8] Returning to the 1936 election forecast, the voting intentions

---

6. David Freedman, Robert Pisani, and Roger Purves, *Statistics* (New York: Norton, 1978), pp. 302–307.

7. Ibid.

8. Chein, "An Introduction to Sampling," p. 421.

of the poor were unknown. Accordingly, only probability sampling can be used in representative sampling designs.

A well-designed sample ensures that if a study were to be repeated on a number of different samples drawn from a given population, the findings from each sample would not differ from the population parameters by more than a specified amount. A probability sample design thus makes it possible for researchers to estimate the extent to which the findings based on one sample are likely to differ from what they would have found by studying the entire population. When a researcher is using a probability sample design, it is possible for him or her to estimate the population's parameters on the basis of the sample statistics calculated.

Although researchers can make accurate estimates of the population's parameters only with probability samples, social scientists do use nonprobability samples. They employ this option for reasons of convenience and economy, which, under certain circumstances (e.g., exploratory research), may outweigh the advantages of using probability sampling. Social scientists also use nonprobability samples when a sampling population cannot be precisely defined or when a list of the sampling population is unavailable. For example, no list can be compiled of drug addicts or of illegal residents in the United States.

## Nonprobability Sample Designs

Three major designs utilizing nonprobability samples have been employed by social scientists: convenience samples, purposive samples, and quota samples.

*Convenience Samples.*    Researchers obtain a convenience sample by selecting whatever sampling units are conveniently available. Thus a college professor may select students in a class; or a researcher may take the first 200 people encountered on the street who are willing to be interviewed. The researcher has no way of estimating the representativeness of convenience samples, and therefore cannot estimate the population's parameters.

*Purposive Samples.*    With purposive samples (occasionally referred to as judgment samples), researchers select sampling units subjectively in an attempt to obtain a sample that appears to be representative of the population. In other words, the chance that a particular sampling unit will be selected for the sample depends on the subjective judgment of the researcher. Because it is usually impossible to determine why a researcher judges the sampling unit selected as representative of the sample, it is difficult to determine the probability of the inclusion of any specific sampling unit in the sample. Nevertheless, social scientists have used purposive samples with some success in attempts to forecast election turnout. In the United States, for example, researchers select a number of small election districts in each state whose election returns in previous years approximated the overall state returns. All the eligible voters in the selected districts are interviewed as to their voting intentions, and the forecast is based on these reports. The underlying (and indeed risky) assumption is that the selected districts continue to be representative of their respective states.

*Quota Samples.*    The chief aim of a quota sample is to select a sample that is as similar as possible to the sampling population. For example, if it is known that the population has equal numbers of males and females, the researcher selects an equal number of males and females in the sample. If it is known that 15 percent of the population is black, 15 percent of the total sample will be black. In quota sampling, interviewers are assigned quota groups characterized by specific variables such as gender, age, place of residence, and ethnicity. For example, an interviewer may be instructed to interview 14 individuals, of whom 7 live in the suburbs and 7 in the central city. Seven have to be men and 7 women; of the 7 men, exactly 3 should be married and 4 single. The same allocation would apply for women. From the example, it is obvious that disproportions between the sample and the population are likely to occur in variables that the researchers have not specified in the interviewers' quotas. As with other nonprobability samples, we cannot estimate the parameters of the population accurately from quota samples.

Pollsters frequently used quota samples until the presidential election of 1948, when the polls incorrectly predicted that Thomas E. Dewey would be elected president.[9] Three major polls predicted the outcome of the election, and all three declared Dewey the winner. Yet on election day, President Harry S Truman won with almost 50 percent of the popular vote, whereas Dewey received just over 45 percent.

All three polls used quota samples, taking into consideration variables that they assumed influenced voting such as place of residence, gender, age, ethnicity, and income. Although their assumption about the importance of these variables was reasonable, many factors other than the ones considered influenced voting in that election. Most significantly, no quota was set on Republican or Democratic votes because the distribution of political opinion was exactly what these polling organizations did not know and were trying to find out. Finally, perhaps the most problematic element in the 1948 polls was that the interviewers were free to choose whomever they pleased within the assigned quotas. This left a lot of room for discretion, which in turn created a significant bias.[10]

## Probability Sample Designs

Earlier we pointed out that in contrast to nonprobability sampling, probability sample designs permit the researcher to specify the probability of each sampling unit's being included in the sample in a single draw from the population. Here we present four common designs of probability samples: simple random sampling, systematic sampling, stratified sampling, and cluster sampling.

9. Freedman et al., *Statistics,* pp. 302–307.
10. Ibid., pp. 305–307.

***Simple Random Samples.***    **Simple random sampling** is the basic probability sampling design, and it is incorporated into all the more elaborate probability
sampling designs. Simple random sampling is a procedure that gives each of the
total sampling units of the population (noted by the letter "$N$") an equal and known
nonzero probability of being selected. For example, when you toss a perfect coin,
the probability that you will get a head or a tail is equal and known (50 percent),
and each subsequent outcome is independent of previous outcomes. Scientists
usually use computer programs or tables of random digits to select random samples. A table of random digits is reproduced in Appendix D. Such a table is quite
simple to use. First, list each sampling unit of the population and give it a number,
from 1 to $N$. Then, start reading the table of random digits at some random starting
point. Each digit that appears in the table is read in order (up, down, or across;
the direction does not matter, as long as it is consistent). Whenever a digit that
appears in the table of random digits corresponds to the number of a sampling unit
in your list, select that sampling unit for your sample. Continue this process until
you reach the desired sample size. When using this method, the selection of any
given sampling unit is random, that is, independent of the selection of previous
sampling units. You have consequently eliminated bias in the selection procedure,
and you can then estimate parameters with the confidence that they are representative of the real values you would find in the total population.

Random selection procedures ensure that every sampling unit of the population has an equal and known probability of being included in the sample; this
probability is $n/N$, where $n$ stands for the size of the sample and $N$ for the size
of the population.[11] For example, if the population consists of 50,389 eligible
voters in a town and a simple random sample of 1,800 is to be drawn, the probability of each sampling unit of the population's being included in the sample is
1,800/50,389, or .0357 (See Exhibit 8.1.).

---

### Exhibit 8.1
How to Draw a Random Sample

---

The Problem

In a cost containment study of a regional hospital, patients' records are to be examined.
There are $N = 100$ patients' records from which a simple random sample of $n = 10$ is to
be drawn.

1.  We can number the accounts, beginning with 001 for the first account and ending
    with 100 for the hundredth account. Notice that we have assigned a three-digit
    number to each record in our population. If the total number of records were 1,250,

---

11. For the mathematical proof, see Kish, *Survey Sampling,* pp. 39–40.

we would need four-digit numbers. In this case, we need to select three-digit random numbers in order to give every record the same known chance of selection.

2. Now refer to Appendix D and use the first column. You will notice that each column contains five-digit numbers. If we drop the last two digits of each number and proceed down the column, we obtain the following three-digit numbers:

| | | | |
|---|---|---|---|
| 104 | 854 | 521 | 007* |
| 223 | 289 | 070* | 053* |
| 241 | 635 | 486 | 919 |
| 421 | 094* | 541 | 005* |
| 375 | 103 | 326 | 007 |
| 779 | 071* | 293 | 690 |
| 995 | 510 | 024* | 259 |
| 963 | 023* | 815 | 097* |
| 895 | 010* | 296 | |

The last number listed is 097 from line 35 (column 1). We do not need to list more numbers since we already have ten different numbers that qualify for our sample (007 appears twice but is selected only once). The starred numbers are the records chosen for our sample because they are the only numbers that fall between the range we specified, 001–100.

We now have ten records in our simple random sample:

| | | |
|---|---|---|
| 094 | 070 | 005 |
| 071 | 024 | 097 |
| 023 | 007 | |
| 010 | 053 | |

3. We need not start with the first row of column 1. We can select any starting point, such as the seventh row of column 2. We can also choose to progress in any way we want down the columns, across them, or diagonally as long as we decide ahead of time what our plan will be.

---

*Systematic Samples.* **Systematic sampling** consists of selecting every $K$th sampling unit of the population after the first sampling unit is selected at random from the total of sampling units. Thus if you wish to select a sample of 100 persons from a population of 10,000, you would take every hundredth individual ($K = N/n$ $= 10,000/100 = 100$). The first selection is determined by some random process, such as the use of a table of random digits. Suppose that the fourteenth person were selected; the sample would then consist of individuals numbered 14, 114, 214, 314, 414, and so on.

Systematic sampling is more convenient than simple random sampling. When interviewers untrained in sampling techniques have to conduct their sampling in the field, it is much simpler to instruct them to select every $K$th person from a list than to have them use a table of random digits. Systematic samples are also more amenable for use with very large populations or when large samples are to be selected (See Exhibit 8.2.).

---

**Exhibit 8.2**
How to Draw a Systematic Sample

---

The Problem

A social scientist is interested in investigating the relationship between parents' occupations and the grade point averages of students on a large urban campus ($N$ = 35,000). As the information needed can be obtained from the students' records, a sample of $n$ = 700 records will be selected. Although we could select a simple random sample (see Exhibit 8. 1), this would require a great deal of work. Alternatively, we could use the following procedure.

1. The first step is to determine the sampling interval, $K$. As $N$ = 35,000 and the sample size $n$ = 700, $K$ is 35,000/700; that is, $K$ = 50.
2. We now select the first record at random from the first $K$ = 50 records listed and then select every fiftieth record thereafter until we have reached the sample size of 700. This method is called a 1-in-50 systematic sample.

---

With systematic sampling, each sampling unit in the population has a $1/K$ probability of being included in the sample. However, there may be a pattern in the data systematically occurring at every $K$th unit. This phenomenon will bias the sample. For example, you may be doing a study of the average size of one-family homes in a city, and the first house chosen is a corner house. However, you may not be aware that every $K$th house on your list is also a corner house. This might introduce a bias since corner houses tend to be larger. If you are aware of a systematic pattern in the population of sampling units, and if you can shuffle the list thoroughly first, you can minimize problems.[12]

***Stratified Samples.*** Researchers use **stratified sampling** primarily to ensure that different groups of a population are adequately represented in the sample so as to increase their level of accuracy when estimating parameters. Furthermore, all other things being equal, stratified sampling considerably reduces the cost of execution. The underlying idea in stratified sampling is to use available information on the population "to divide it into groups such that the elements within each group are more alike than are the elements in the population as a whole."[13] That is, you create a set of homogeneous samples based on the variables you are interested in studying. If a series of homogeneous groups can be sampled in such a way that when the samples are combined they constitute a sample of a more heterogeneous population, you will increase the accuracy of your parameter estimates.

For example, suppose that it is known that there are 700 whites, 200 blacks, and 100 Mexican-Americans in a given population. If a random sample of 100

---

12. For some other procedures for avoiding problems caused by systematic patterns in populations, see William Cochran, *Sampling Techniques,* 3d ed. (New York: Wiley, 1977).
13. Morris H. Hansen, William N. Hurwitz, and William G. Madow, *Sample Survey Methods and Theory* (New York: Wiley, 1953), p. 40.

persons were drawn, you would probably not get exactly 70 whites, 20 blacks, and 10 Mexican-Americans; the proportion of Mexican-Americans in particular might be relatively too small. A stratified sample of 70 whites, 20 blacks, and 10 Mexican-Americans would ensure better representation of these groups. Stratification does not violate the principle of random selection because a probability sample is subsequently drawn within each stratum.

The necessary condition for dividing a sample into homogeneous strata is that the criteria for its division be related to the variable the researcher is studying. A second consideration is that the criteria used should not require so many subsamples that they increase the total size of the sample over that required by a simple random sample. Suppose that you want to estimate the median family income in a small town and you know the traits of the families in the population. As it has already been established that income correlates with occupation, education, ethnicity, age, and gender, these would become logical bases for stratification of your samples. However, if all these bases were used, the value of stratified sampling would diminish, for the number of subsamples would become enormous.

Consider what would happen if there were four categories of occupation, three of education, three of ethnicity, three of age, and two of gender. The number of subsamples would then equal $4 \times 3 \times 3 \times 3 \times 2$, or 216. Because a statistically satisfactory frequency in the smallest cell cannot be less than ten cases, you would need a minimum of 2,160 cases, assuming that the frequencies in all cells were equal. No one would consider such a large number as an appropriate sample of a small town. To solve this problem, we assume that many such stratification bases occur as associated factors (i.e., characteristics that appear together). Thus if social status is chosen to stand for occupation, education, and ethnicity, the number of subsamples can be reduced to 4 (social-status groups) × 3 (age groups) × 2 (gender groups) = 24 subsamples with a total of 240 cases. This is a more usable sample design, and it would represent the population better than a simple random sample.

Sampling from the different strata can be either proportional or disproportional. If you select the same number of sampling units from each stratum, or a uniform sampling fraction ($n/N$), the sample is known as a *proportionate stratified sample* because the sample size drawn from each stratum ($n$) is proportional to the population size of the stratum ($N$). However, if the total number ($N$) in each stratum is different, that is, if there are variable sampling fractions, the sample is a *disproportionate stratified sample*. In other words, when the total number of people characterized by each variable (or stratum) is different, we need to choose the size of each sample of each stratum according to our research requirements. As a rule, disproportionate stratified samples are used either to compare two or more particular strata or to analyze one stratum intensively. When researchers use a disproportionate stratified sample, they have to weight the estimates of the population's parameters by the number belonging to each stratum[14] (see Exhibit 8.3).

---

14. See Kish, *Survey Sampling*, pp. 77–82, for methods of weighting.

---

**Exhibit 8.3**
How to Draw a Stratified Sample

---

The Problem

In a study of revitalization in an urban neighborhood, we plan to examine the attitudes of new residents toward their community. We anticipate that the attitudes of homeowners may differ from those of renters. Therefore, as a means of ensuring the proper representation of both groups, we will use a proportional stratified random sample with two strata: new homeowners and new renters.

1. The population consists of $N = N_1 + N_2$, with $N_1$ denoting new homeowners and $N_2$ new renters. $N_1 = 200$ and $N_2 = 300$. Therefore, $N = 500$. We decide to select a proportional sampling fraction of 1/10 from each stratum. Thus $N_1 = 20$ homeowners and $N_2 = 30$ renters will be included in the sample.
2. We then apply the simple random sampling procedure (see Exhibit 8.1) separately to each list.

---

*Cluster Samples.* The fourth type of probability sampling used by social scientists is **cluster sampling.** It is frequently used in large-scale studies because it is the least expensive sample design. Cluster sampling involves first selecting larger groupings, called *clusters,* and then selecting the sampling units from the clusters. The clusters are selected by a simple random sample or a stratified sample. Depending on the research problem, researchers can include all the sampling units in these clusters in the sample or make a selection from within the clusters using simple or stratified sampling procedures.

   Suppose that the research objective is to study the political attitudes of adults in the various election districts of a city. No single list containing the names of all the adult residents is available, and it is too expensive to compile such a list. However, a map of the election districts does exist. First, we can randomly select a number of election districts from the list (first-stage cluster sampling). Then, within each of the districts, we can select blocks at random (second-stage cluster sampling) and interview all the persons on these blocks. We may also use a simple random sample within each block selected. In such a case, we would be constructing a three-stage cluster sample. (This sampling method is also called *area probability sampling* or just *area sampling.*) Similarly, a survey of urban households may use a sample of cities; within each city selected, a sample of districts; and within each selected district, a sample of households (see Exhibit 8.4).

---

**Exhibit 8.4**
How to Draw a Cluster Sample

---

The Problem

The purpose of the study is to interview residents of an urban community. No list of resident adults is available, and thus cluster sampling is used as the sampling design.

Stage 1

1. Define the area to be covered using an up-to-date map. Boundaries are marked, and areas that do not include dwelling units are excluded.
2. Divide the entire area into blocks. Boundary lines should not bisect dwellings and should be easily identifiable by fieldworkers.
3. Next, number the blocks, preferably serially and in serpentine fashion.
4. Finally, select a simple random or systematic sample of blocks, using the appropriate procedure.

Stage 2

1. List and number all dwelling units in each of the selected blocks. The delineation sometimes requires fieldworkers to ensure that all new constructions are listed.
2. Select a simple random or systematic sample of dwelling units.
3. Finally, interview selected individuals within each selected dwelling unit. The selection usually follows the investigator's guidelines.

Based in part on Matilda White Riley, *Sociological Research: Exercises and Manual* (Orlando, Fla.: Harcourt Brace Jovanovich, 1963), vol. 2, p. 172.

---

The choice of clusters depends on the research objectives and the resources available for the study. Households, blocks, schools, districts, and cities have all been used as clusters. In fact, as Leslie Kish points out:

> The population of the United States may be alternatively regarded as an aggregate of units which are entire counties; or of cities, towns, and townships; or of area segments and blocks; or of dwellings; or, finally, as individual persons. Indeed, all those sampling units are employed in turn for area samples of the United States.[15]

## Probability Sampling: A Summary

The four designs of probability sampling that we have described are the basic designs most commonly used by social scientists. However, they do not exhaust the range of probability sampling procedures, and you are advised to consult the additional readings listed at the end of this chapter for further information. By way of a summary, the box on page 192 gives a brief description of the four designs.

## Probability Sampling: An Example

To illustrate the entire sampling process, we shall examine the procedures employed by the Institute for Social Research (ISR) at the University of Michigan in its national surveys.[16] The sampling procedure involves three sampling designs: cluster sampling, stratified sampling, and simple random sampling.

15. Ibid., p. 150.
16. Survey Research Center, *Interviewer's Manual*, rev. ed. (Ann Arbor: Institute for Social Research, University of Michigan, 1976), Chapter 8.

---

### Description of Four Probability Samples

- *Simple Random Sample:* Assign a unique number to each sampling unit; select sampling units by use of a table of random digits.
- *Systematic Sample:* Determine the sampling interval $(N/n)$; select the first sample unit randomly; select remaining units according to the interval.
- *Stratified Sample:* (Proportionate) Determine the strata; from each stratum, select a random sample proportionate to the size of the stratum in the population. (Disproportionate) Determine the strata; from each stratum, select a random sample of the size dictated by analytical considerations.
- *Cluster Sample:* Determine the number of levels of clusters; from each level of clusters select a sample randomly; the basic units of analysis are groups within the sampling populations.

Based on Russell Ackoff, *The Design of Social Research* (Chicago: University of Chicago Press, 1953).

---

ISR is among the largest university-based social science research organizations in the United States. Research projects conducted by the institute are sponsored by government agencies, private business, and public service organizations. Many of the studies involve large nationwide samples. Listed here are the steps roughly followed by the ISR in drawing a national sample[17] (see Figure 8.1).

1. The entire geographic area of the United States is divided into small areas, each called a *primary sampling unit* (PSU). The PSUs are generally counties or metropolitan areas. Out of the entire list of PSUs, researchers select 74 by stratified random sampling to ensure that rural areas, large and middle-sized cities, and regions are adequately represented.

2. Each of the 74 selected PSUs is further subdivided into smaller areas. For example, a hypothetical PSU consisting of two large cities, six medium-sized towns, and the rural remainder of the county would be divided into three strata: (1) large cities, (2) smaller cities and towns, and (3) rural areas. Units within these strata are called *sample places.* One or more sample places are selected within each stratum.

3. Each sample place is further divided into *chunks.* A chunk is defined as an area having identifiable boundaries: for example, in urban areas, a chunk is equivalent to a block; in rural areas, it is bounded by roads or county lines. Within each sample place, chunks are selected randomly.

4. At this stage, the interviewers play a major role in the sampling process. They visit each chunk, listing all the dwelling units, and suggest how the chunk can be divided into areas containing 4 to 12 dwelling units each. These areas are called *segments.* Segments are then randomly selected from each chunk.

---

17. Ibid.

**Figure 8.1**
Drawing a National Sample

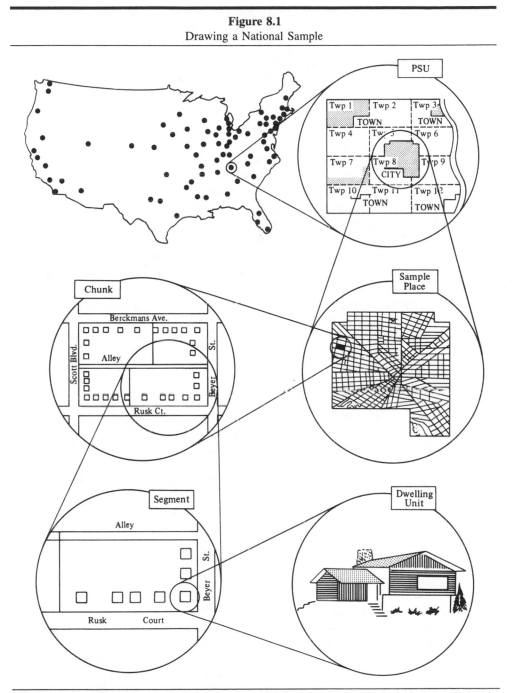

From Survey Research Center, *Interviewer's Manual,* rev. ed. (Ann Arbor: Institute for Social Research, University of Michigan, 1976), p. 8–2.

5.  At the last stage, researchers select the dwelling units to be included in the final sample from each segment. The procedure for selecting dwelling units varies. When a segment includes only a few dwelling units, all are included in the study. If the segment contains many dwelling units, only a specified fraction of the dwellings in that segment will be included in the study.

---

# Sample Size

A *sample* is any subset of sampling units from a population. A **subset** is any combination of sampling units that does not include the entire set of sampling units that has been defined as the population. A sample may include only one sampling unit, all but one sampling unit, or any number in between. How do we determine the size of a sample?

There are several misconceptions about the necessary size of a sample. One is that the sample size must be a certain proportion (often set at 5 percent) of the population; another is that the sample should total about 2,000; still another is that any increase in the sample size will increase the precision of the sample results. These are faulty notions because they do not derive from sampling theory. To estimate the adequate size of the sample properly, researchers need to determine what level of accuracy is expected of their estimates; that is, how large a standard error is acceptable.

## Standard Error

The concept of **standard error** (some people use the terms *error margin* or *sampling error*) is central to sampling theory and to determining the size of a sample. It is one of the statistical measures that indicates how closely the sample results reflect the true values of a parameter. We will illustrate the idea of standard error by making computations from a small hypothetical population from which simple random samples will be drawn.

Our hypothetical population consists of five students earning $500, $650, $400, $700, and $600 per month, so the population's mean monthly income (denoted by $\mu$) is $570.[18] Say that we draw a sample of two with the purpose of estimating $\mu$, and that we select the two students earning $500 and $400, respectively. The sample mean ($\bar{x}$) is therefore ($500 + $400)/2 = $450, which we take as the estimate of $\mu$, the population mean. Since we already know that the population mean is $570, we can easily see that the estimate of $450 is inaccurate. Had we selected the two students earning $650 and $700, the sample mean would have been $675, which is also an inaccurate estimate of the population mean. In a similar manner, we can draw all the samples of size $n = 2$ from this population.

Table 8.1 presents the ten possible samples and their means, the estimates of $\mu$, derived from each. None of these samples accurately estimates $\mu$. However,

---

18. See Chapter 15 for a discussion of the mean and the standard deviation.

**Table 8.1**

Estimates of the Population's Mean

| Possible Samples of $n = 2$ (incomes of students selected, in $) | $\bar{x}$ (estimate of $\mu$, in $) |
|---|---|
| 500 and 650 | 575 |
| 500 and 400 | 450 |
| 500 and 700 | 600 |
| 500 and 600 | 550 |
| 650 and 400 | 525 |
| 650 and 700 | 675 |
| 650 and 600 | 625 |
| 400 and 700 | 550 |
| 400 and 600 | 500 |
| 700 and 600 | 650 |
| Total | 5,700 |

some sample means (for example, $500 and $650) are closer to the population mean than others. If we continue indefinitely to draw samples of $n = 2$, each of the samples in Table 8.1 would be selected more than once. We can then plot the distribution of all the sample means. The distribution that results from the value of the sample mean ($\bar{x}$) derived from an *infinite* number of samples is termed *the sampling distribution of the mean* or *mean distribution*. In our example, each of the ten samples has an equal chance of being drawn (it is a simple random sample), and if we continue the selection indefinitely, samples would be drawn an equal number of times. Consequently, the mean of the estimates derived from *all* the possible samples is $5,700/10 = 570$, which equals the population mean.

In general, the mean distribution of an infinite number of samples is assumed to equal the mean of the population. The more sample mean values deviate from the population mean, the greater the variability of findings obtained from each sample, and the greater the risk of making a large error in estimating a parameter of the population from one or a limited number of samples.

Because the population in our hypothetical example was small, we knew the population mean and could compare it with the means obtained from the samples. In reality, the population mean is unknown, and the researcher draws only a single sample (not an infinite number of samples) in order to estimate the population parameter. The distribution of the values obtained from a single sample serves as an indicator of the entire sampling distribution, and the dispersion of those values within the single sample is measured by the standard deviation, $s$ (see Chapter 15). The distribution of all the sample means about the mean of the total of those samples is termed the standard error ($S.E.$).

We can calculate the standard deviation and then estimate the $S.E.$ (see Chapter 15). We cannot calculate the $S.E.$ directly because we cannot draw the infinite number of samples necessary for its calculation. It is assumed that the dispersion of the variable's value within a single randomly selected and representative sample indicates its dispersion within the sampling population.

The standard deviation of the sampling distribution in our example is calculated as:

$$[(575 - 570)^2 + (450 - 570)^2 + (600 - 570)^2 + (550 - 570)^2$$
$$+ (525 - 570)^2 + (675 - 570)^2 + (625 - 570)^2 + (550 - 570)^2$$
$$+ (500 - 570)^2 + (650 - 570)^2]/10 = \sqrt{4,350} = 65.95$$

We then estimate the S.E. by dividing the standard deviation of the sample by the square root of the sample size ($n$):

$$S.E. = \frac{s}{\sqrt{n}}$$

where $s$ = standard deviation

$n$ = sample size.

If the population is small, the factor $1 - n/N$, a statistical procedure called the finite population correction has to be included in the equation:

$$S.E. = \sqrt{\frac{s^2}{n}\left(1 - \frac{n}{N}\right)}$$

where $s^2$ = sample variance

$n$ = sample size

$N$ = population size.

In this formula, note that $n/N$ is subtracted from 1 because the population is small. In our example, $N = 5$ and $n = 2$, so

$$s^2 = \frac{(500-570)^2 + (650-570)^2 + (400-570)^2 + (700-570)^2 + (600-570)^2}{4}$$
$$= \frac{58,000}{4} = 14,500$$

Therefore, the standard error of the sample means is calculated as

$$S.E. (\bar{x}) = \sqrt{\left(\frac{14,500}{2}\right)\left(\frac{5-2}{5}\right)} = \sqrt{4,350} = 65.95$$

which is identical to the previous result.

## Confidence Intervals

Before presenting the method for determining the sample size, we need to discuss one more concept, the **confidence interval.** We have pointed out that the population mean equals the mean of all the sample means that can be drawn from a population and that we can compute the standard deviation of these sample means. If the distribution of sample means is normal or approximates normality, we can use the properties of the normal curve to estimate the location of the population mean.[19] If we knew the mean of all sample means (the population mean) and the standard deviation of these sample means (standard error of the mean), we could compute $Z$ scores and determine the range within which any percentage of the sample means can be found. Between $-1Z$ and $+1Z$, we would expect to find 68 percent of all sample means; between $-1.96Z$ and $+1.96Z$, we would expect to find about 95 percent of all sample means; and between $-2.58Z$ and $+2.58Z$, we would expect to find 99 percent of all sample means. However, as we do not know the mean of the population, we have to estimate on the basis of a single sample.

We can use the normal curve for this purpose (see Figure 8.2). A sample mean that is $+1.96Z$ scores, or approximately 2.0 standard errors above the population mean, has a .025 probability of occurrence; in other words, 95.5 percent of all sample means will deviate by less than $\pm1.96$ from the mean. If it is a rare event for a sample mean to be 1.96 or more than 2.0 standard errors above the population mean, it is just as rare for the population mean to be 2.0 standard errors below a given sample mean (i.e., $-1.96Z$). But we do not know whether the sample mean is larger or smaller than the true mean of the population. Nevertheless, if we construct an interval of $-1.96$ to $+1.96Z$ about the sample mean, we can be confident that 95.5 percent of the population is located within that interval. We do not expect that the sample mean will in fact be as far as $\pm2.0$ standard errors away from the population mean, and we are fairly confident that the population mean is no farther than this from the sample mean.

If we construct a confidence interval of $\pm1.96Z$ scores, or approximately 2.0 standard errors from the mean about the sample mean, we expect the population mean to lie within this interval with about 95 percent confidence. This means that there is a 5 percent chance that we are wrong, that is, that the population mean does not fall within the interval. If you do not wish to run a 5 percent risk of being incorrect, you can use a different confidence interval. The chance that the population mean will be within $+2.58$ and $-2.58Z$, or approximately 3.0 standard errors of the sample mean, is 99 out of 100; this is termed the 99 percent confidence interval. In Figure 8.2, for illustrative purposes, we indicate that 3 standard errors cover 100 percent of the sample when the sample population is large. The width of the confidence interval around the sample mean to be employed is chosen by the researcher on the basis of the required level of predictive accuracy. In other words, the width of the confidence interval is determined by how much the researcher is willing to risk being wrong. The researcher could even use an interval of $\pm.68$ standard errors of the mean and have only a 50 percent chance of being correct in assuming that the population mean is within the interval.

To sum up, if a given sampling distribution is known to be approximately normal, we can infer that about 68 percent of the sample estimates of which it is comprised will lie between its mean and one standard error, about 95 percent

19. The concept of normalcy, expressed in the normal curve, points to assumptions about the distribution of a variable in the general population. See pages 000–000 for a detailed discussion of the normal curve and its properties.

---

**Figure 8.2**
Normal Curve: Percent Areas from the Mean to Specified
Standard Error Distances

---

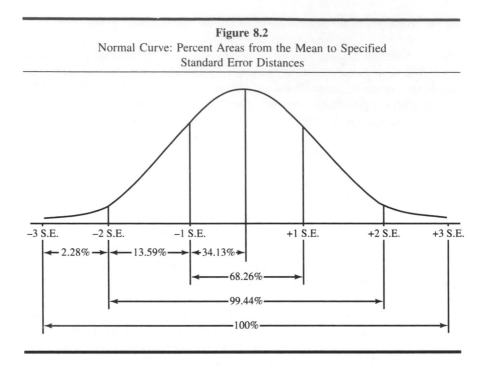

---

between its mean and 2.0 standard errors. Confidence levels and standard errors are routinely used in surveys and opinion polls. Without these statistical checks, pollsters could never be sure if their election outcome projections were valid, nor could marketing executives be sure of a new product's degree of success.

## Determining the Sample Size

Now we can estimate the size of samples. If cost and other practical limitations do not enter into the decision about sample size, there is no difficulty in determining the desired size. Recall the formula for the standard error of the mean:

$$S.E. = \frac{s}{\sqrt{n}}$$

where $s$ = standard deviation of the variable under study

$n$ = sample size.

Inverting, we then have

$$n = \frac{s^2}{(S.E.)^2}$$

To calculate the sample size, $n$, we have to have some idea of the standard deviation in the population and must also decide how large a standard error we can tolerate. If, for example, a random sample is to be drawn from a population consisting of

10,000 sampling units, $s^2 = .20$, and the desired $S.E. = .016$, the estimated sample size is

$$n = \frac{.20}{.000256} = 781.25$$

If the sample size is too large relative to the population, the finite population correction is added. In this case, $n/N$ is added to 1. The final sample size is thereby calculated by

$$n' = \frac{n}{1 + (n/N)}$$

where $N$ = population size

   $n$ = sample size

   $n'$ = optimal sample size

In our example, if $N = 10,000$, then

$$n' = \frac{781.25}{1 + \dfrac{781.25}{10,000}} \cong 725$$

In practice, decisions concerning the sample size are more complicated. First of all, researchers must decide how precise they want their sample results to be, that is, how large a standard error is acceptable. Second, they must determine the way the results are to be analyzed. Third, if researchers are studying more than one variable at the same time, they should ascertain whether a sample that is adequate for one variable is also satisfactory for another variable.[20]

---

# Nonsampling Errors

Sampling theory is concerned with the error introduced by the sampling procedure. In a perfect design, this type of error is minimized for an individual sample. The error in our estimates draws attention to the difference between what is expected in the long run and what is attained if a researcher follows a particular set of procedures throughout the study. However, even if the sampling error is minimized, there are other sources of error, for example, measurement error (see Chapter 7). In survey research, however, the most pervasive error is the **nonresponse error.** Nonresponse is defined as observations that are not carried out because of reasons such as refusal to answer, absence, and lost forms. Nonresponse can introduce a substantial bias into the findings.

Recall the *Literary Digest* poll of 1936. We discussed the errors made by the *Digest* in the process of selecting the sampling frame. The *Digest* made additional important errors later on, when it based its estimates on a very low response rate.

---

20. For further details, see Kish, *Survey Sampling;* and C. A. Moser and Graham Kalton, *Survey Methods in Social Investigation,* 2d ed. (New York: Basic Books, 1972).

The results of the poll were based on the response of 2.4 million people, out of 10 million originally selected to be included in the sample.[21] This biased the results considerably because, during the polling, there was evidence showing that the non-respondents tended to vote for Roosevelt whereas, among the respondents, over half favored Landon.

Generally, the amount and kind of bias is related to the following conditions:

1. The greater the nonresponse proportion, the greater the biasing effects. The response proportion can be computed as follows:

$$R = 1 - \frac{n-r}{n}$$

where $R$ = response rate

$n$ = sample size

For example, if the original sample size is 1,200, and 1,000 responses are actually obtained, the response rate is $1 - (1,200 - 1,000)/1,200 = .83$, and the nonresponse rate is .17, or 17 percent.

2. The seriousness of the nonresponse bias depends on the extent to which the population mean of the nonresponse stratum in the sample differs from that of the response stratum.[22]

3. Each of the following nonresponse types influences the sample results in a different way. (These types apply to entire interview schedules as well as to parts of an interview or questionnaire as well as to single questions).[23]

- *Uninterviewables:* people who are ill, illiterate, or have language barriers.
- *Not found:* people who have moved and are inaccessible, for instance, those with whom the interviewer cannot make an appointment.
- *Not-at-homes:* people who are out when the interviewer calls but are reached later, and their responses are subsequently added.
- *Refusals:* people who refuse to cooperate or to answer all the survey questions. Refusals may vary with the type of question being asked.

The proportion of nonrespondents depends on factors such as the nature of the population, the data collection method, the kinds of questions being asked, the skill of the interviewers, and the number of callbacks that can be made. A poorly designed and/or administered interview schedule will result in a very high nonresponse rate.

To estimate the effect of nonresponse, an interviewer can collect information about the nonrespondents on callbacks, then make certain estimates. Suppose that voters in a small community are surveyed to estimate the proportions of the population that identify with one party or another, and that the survey has a 10 percent nonresponse rate. This information can be corrected with additional information

21. Freedman et al., *Statistics,* pp. 302–307.

22. Moser and Kalton, *Survey Methods in Social Investigation,* pp. 166–167.

23. Dennis J. Palumbo, *Statistics in Political and Behavioral Science,* rev. ed. (New York: Columbia University Press, 1977), p. 296.

on the education or income of the nonrespondents. Suppose that 10 percent amounts to 300 voters and that of these, you can confirm from other sources that 70 percent have incomes of about $25,000 a year. If you knew that, in general, 90 percent of the people in this income level are Democrats, you might estimate that 189 of the nonrespondents are Democrats ($.70 \times 300 \times .90 = 189$). However, because there is no way of computing the possible error of this estimate, such estimates should be used to correct for nonresponse only if the response rate is relatively low.

## Summary

**1.** In this chapter, we focused on how we draw population estimates from sample statistics. To arrive at accurate estimates of parameters, the researcher has to deal effectively with three problems: (1) definition of the population, (2) selection of a representative sample, and (3) determination of the sample size.

**2.** A population has to be defined in terms of content, extent, and time. A sample is any subset of sampling units taken from the population. A sample may range from one sampling unit to all but one sampling unit, or any number in between.

**3.** After the definition of a population and the estimation of the size of the sample, a representative sampling design has to be selected. A sample is representative if the analyses made on its units produce results equivalent to those that would be obtained had the entire population been analyzed. Researchers use probability sampling designs most often in situations where they can specify the probability of each unit of the population's being included in the sample. The characteristics of four basic probability samples—simple random, systematic, stratified, and cluster—are summarized in the box on page 192.

**4.** The determination of a sample size is directly dependent on the value of the standard error and on the width of the confidence interval that is set by the researcher. The confidence interval can be made extremely narrow, if the researcher is willing to run a large risk of being wrong, or extremely wide, if the researcher opts to run a negligible risk.

**5.** In survey research, in addition to sampling error, nonresponse error is pervasive. Nonresponse is defined as measurements that are not carried out because of refusal to answer, absence, lost forms, and so on. Nonresponse can introduce a substantial bias into the findings. Consequently, researchers have to apply one of the techniques mentioned to compensate for this type of bias if the response rate is low.

## Key Terms for Review

cluster sample (p. 190)  
confidence interval (p. 196)  
nonprobability sample (p. 183)  
nonresponse error (p. 199)

parameter (p. 179)
population (p. 179)
probability sample (p. 183)
representative sample (p. 183)
sample (p. 179)
sampling frame (p. 181)
sampling unit (p. 180)

simple random sample (p. 186)
standard error (p. 194)
statistic (p. 179)
stratified sample (p. 188)
subset (p. 194)
systematic sample (p. 187)

## Study Questions

1. Why can samples be used to describe populations? List the different types of samples and give examples.
2. Distinguish between probability and nonprobability sampling, and explain the advantages and disadvantages of each. What sorts of social problems are amenable to the different sampling procedures?
3. Discuss the major types of probability sampling, cite their strengths and weaknesses, and explain how to select a sample using each method.
4. Discuss the idea of sampling error and how it allows researchers to construct confidence intervals around their sample estimates. Give examples of how this information could influence your anticipated survey results.
5. What factors could introduce nonsampling error into a survey?

## Additional Readings

Alreck, Pamela L., and Robert B. Settle. *The Survey Research Handbook.* Homewood, Ill.: Irwin, 1984.

Granovettes, Mark. "Network Sampling: Some First Steps." *American Journal of Sociology,* 81 (1976): 1287–1303.

Hess, Irene. *Sampling for Social Research Surveys, 1947–1980.* Ann Arbor: Institute for Social Research, University of Michigan, 1985.

Jaeger, Richard M. *Sampling for Education and the Social Sciences.* White Plains, N.Y.: Longman, 1984.

Kalton, Graham. *Introduction to Survey Sampling.* Newbury Park, Calif.: Sage, 1983.

Kruskal, William H., and Frederick Mosteller. "Ideas of Representative Sampling." In *New Directions for Methodology in Social and Behavioral Science,* ed. Donald W. Fiske. San Francisco: Jossey-Bass, 1981, pp. 3–24.

Stuart, Alan. *The Ideas of Sampling.* 3d ed. New York: Oxford University Press, 1987.

Wainer, Howard. *Drawing Inferences from Self-selected Samples.* New York: Springer-Verlag, 1986.

Yates, Frank. *Sampling Methods for Censuses and Surveys.* 4th ed. London: Griffin, 1981.

# CHAPTER 9
# Observational Methods

The fragrance industry, and the new field of aromatherapy, are based on the assumption that people respond to pleasing aromas in a positive way. Few of us, however, have paid much systematic attention to how fragrances influence the way we feel or act. But Drs. Robert Baron and Marna Bronfen[1] have done just that. In a recent study, they investigated whether introducing pleasant fragrances into the work setting increases task performance, or productivity, while reducing stress. Baron and Bronfen set up two controlled situations in which a task, a fragrance, and a gift were experimentally manipulated. Their study raises two methodological issues every experimenter has to face: First, is experimental realism truly evoked within the laboratory setting, that is, is the situation experienced as real and meaningful by the participants? Second, does the experiment reflect mundane realism? Does it contain elements similar to what the participants are likely to find in the real world? In other words, what is the connection between the laboratory and life, and does the quality of the linkage affect the validity of a researcher's findings?

I N THIS CHAPTER WE FIRST DISCUSS THE FOUR FORMS OF DATA collection used in the social sciences and exemplify the idea of triangulation—the practice of using more than one form to test a hypothesis. Next we discuss the reasons for and ways of using the first form, observation, in social science research. We then discuss the types of behavior that researchers observe and present strategies for conducting direct observations and recording data. The chapter concludes with a discussion of controlled observation in the laboratory and the field.

Having decided on the *what* and the *how* of an investigation, we can proceed to the data collection stage. Social science data are obtained when investigators or others record observations about the phenomena being studied. Four general forms of data collection may be distinguished: observational methods, survey research, secondary data analysis, and qualitative research. Researchers employ a number of distinctive methods for each form, the most common of which are discussed in the following chapters. It should be emphasized at the outset, however, that each of these four forms has certain unique advantages but also some inherent limitations. For example, if an investigator asks respondents to identity the most influential member in their work group (survey research), the findings yielded may be quite different from the data he or she might have obtained from direct observation. This example points to the fact that there is a certain degree of "method specificity" in each form of data collection used by social scientists. Consequently, researchers find it advantageous to **triangulate** methods whenever feasible, that is, they use more than one form of data collection to test the same hypothesis.

---

1. Robert A. Baron and Marna I. Bronfen. "A Whiff of Reality: Empirical Evidence Concerning the Effects of Pleasant Fragrances on Work-Related Behavior," *Journal of Applied Social Psychology,* 24 (1994): 1179–1203.

# Triangulation

Data in the social sciences are obtained in either formal or informal settings and involve verbal (oral and written) or nonverbal acts or responses. The combination of the two settings and the two types of responses results in the four major forms of data collection: observational methods, survey research (personal interviews and questionnaires as discussed in Chapters 10 and 11), secondary data analyses (for example, analysis of existing documents as discussed in Chapter 13), and qualitative research (discussed in Chapter 12). At the one extreme, when researchers wish to study nonverbal actions in informal settings, they often use participant observation—a form of qualitative research. At the other extreme, when researchers focus on verbal (oral and written) acts in formal, structured settings, the most commonly used forms of data collection are laboratory experiments and structured questionnaires.

As we pointed out, each of these data collection methods has certain advantages as well as some inherent limitations. For example, if we observe behavior as it occurs (direct observation), we may miss the reasons for its occurrence (which may be understood from responses to structured questionnaires). Similarly, if we ask respondents to report on their behavior verbally (interviewing), we have no guarantee that their actual behavior (studied by direct observation or existing records) is identical to their reported behavior. For example, in a study aimed at ascertaining the validity of welfare mothers' responses to interview questions on voting, Carol Weiss reported:

> On the voting and registration questions, 82 percent of the welfare mothers answered accurately. Sixteen percent overreported their registration and 2 percent underreported. The amount and direction of response error are similar to those of the largely middle-class populations whose voting self-reports have been validated in previous studies.[2]

In voting behavior as in other behavior, there is often a discrepancy between people's verbal reports and their actual behavior.

To a certain degree, research findings are affected by the nature of the data collection method used. Findings that are very strongly affected by the method used could be *artifacts* (i.e., products of the data analysis methods; see below and Chapter 5) rather than empirical facts. As Donald Fiske points out:

> Knowledge in social science is fragmented, is composed of multiple discrete parcels. . . . The separateness or specificity of those bodies of knowledge is a consequence, not only of different objects of inquiry, but also of method specificity. Each method is one basis for knowing, one discriminable way of knowing.[3]

2. Carol Weiss, "Validity of Welfare Mothers' Interview Responses," *Public Opinion Quarterly,* 32 (1968): 622–633.

3. Donald W. Fiske, "Specificity of Method and Knowledge in Social Science," in Donald W. Fiske and Richard A. Shweder, *Metatherapy in Social Science* (Chicago: University of Chicago Press, 1986), p. 62.

To minimize the degree of specificity of certain methods to particular bodies of knowledge, a researcher can use two or more methods of data collection to test hypotheses and measure variables; this is the essence of triangulation. For example, a structured questionnaire could be supplemented with in-depth interviewing, existing records, or field observations. If the findings yielded by the different data collection methods are consistent, the validity of those findings is increased. In addition, as a research strategy, triangulation has the benefit of raising social scientists "above the personal biases that stem from single methodologies. By combining methods in the same study, observers can partially overcome the deficiencies that flow from employing one investigator or one method."[4]

# Roles of Observation

Social science research is rooted in observation. Political scientists observe, among other things, the behavior of occupants of political roles; anthropologists observe rituals in simple societies; and social psychologists observe interactions in small groups. In a sense, all social science research begins and ends with empirical observations.

The main advantage of observation is its *directness;* it enables researchers to study behavior as it occurs. The researcher does not have to ask people about their own behavior and the actions of others; he or she can simply watch as individuals act and speak. This in turn enables the investigator to collect data firsthand, thereby preventing contamination of the factors standing between him or her and the object of research. For example, when people are asked to report their past behavior, distortions in memory may significantly contaminate the data, whereas memory has no effect at all on behavioral data collected through observational methods.

Moreover, whereas other data collection methods introduce elements of artificiality into the research environment, data collected by observation describes the observed phenomena as they occur in their *natural settings.* An interview, for instance, is a form of face-to-face interaction. As such, it is subject to unique problems because of the lack of consensus surrounding the roles of the researcher and the respondent. In such a situation, respondents might behave in an uncharacteristic manner (see Chapter 10). Such artificiality can be reduced in observational studies, especially when the subjects are not aware that they are being observed, or when they become accustomed to the observer and do not regard him or her as an intruder.

Some studies focus on individuals who are unable to give verbal reports or to articulate themselves meaningfully. For example, researchers are required to use observation in most studies of children because it is difficult for children to be introspective, to verbalize, and to remain attentive to lengthy tasks. David Riesman and Jeanne Watson, in an intriguing sociability study, used observational methods

---

4. Norman K. Denzin, *The Research Act: A Theoretical Introduction to Sociological Methods,* 3d ed. (Englewood Cliffs, N.J.: Prentice-Hall, 1989), p. 236.

because the persons studied "had no language for discussing sociable encounters, no vocabulary for describing parties except to say that they were 'good' or 'bad,' no way of answering the question 'What do you do for fun?' "[5]

Researchers can also use observational methods when people are unwilling to express themselves verbally. Observation, compared to verbal reports, demands less active involvement on the part of those being studied. Furthermore, through observation, researchers can validate verbal reports by comparing them with actual behavior. Finally, because the relationship between a person and his or her environment is not altered in observational studies, the researcher can observe the impact of the environment on researched individuals. This facilitates analysis of the *contextual background* of behavior.

It is important to remember that observation takes many forms. It includes casual experiences as well as sophisticated laboratory devices such as one-way-vision screens and video cameras. Such multiplicity makes observation a suitable method for a variety of research purposes. Researchers employ observational methods in exploratory research in order to gain insights that will subsequently be tested as hypotheses. They can also employ such methods when collecting supplementary data for use in interpreting or qualifying findings obtained by other methods, or as the primary methods of data collection in descriptive studies.

Observation, therefore, ranges in versatility. It may take place in natural settings or in the laboratory, thereby enabling an investigator to study phenomena, such as patterns of learning, as they occur in real-life situations (e.g., the classroom or playground) or in a controlled experimental setting. At the same time, observational procedures are highly flexible. Some are guided only by the progress of research on a general problem. Others can be totally specific, with structured instruments designed in advance for unique contexts. Researchers may themselves participate in the activities of the group they are observing (participant observation); they may be viewed as members of the group but minimize their participation; they may assume the role of an observer without being part of the group; or their presence may be concealed entirely from the people they are observing. Nevertheless, whatever the purpose of the study or the observational procedure used, researchers must deal with three major considerations to ensure that the data obtained are systematic and meaningful—what to observe, when to observe and how to record, and how much inference is required.

---

# Types of Behavior

The first significant consideration concerns *what should be observed.* Suppose a social scientist interested in studying the relation between frustration and aggression hypothesizes that frustration leads to aggression. To test this hypothesis, the

5. David Riesman and Jeanne Watson, "The Sociability Project: A Chronicle of Frustration and Achievement," in *Sociologists at Work,* ed. Phillip E. Hammond (New York: Basic Books, 1964), p. 313.

scientist must observe frustration and aggression. To make observation possible, the scientist must formulate clear and precise operational definitions of the two variables. The measurement of such variables can be based on nonverbal, spatial, extralinguistic, or linguistic behavior.[6]

## Nonverbal Behavior

**Nonverbal behavior** is "the body movements of the organism" and "consists of motor expressions . . . , [that] may originate in various parts of the body."[7] Facial expressions, in particular, convey a whole range of emotions, including fear, surprise, anger, disgust, and sadness. Social scientists have studied nonverbal behavior extensively, and it has been repeatedly shown to be a valid indicator of social, political, and psychological processes. Paul Ekman suggests that observations of nonverbal behavior generate data that can serve "to repeat, contradict, or substitute for a verbal message, as well as accent certain words, maintain the communicative flow, reflect changes in the relationship in association with particular verbal messages and indicate a person's feeling about his verbal statement."[8] Scientists, therefore, often study nonverbal behavior as a means of validating other responses made by respondents in the research situation.

## Spatial Behavior

**Spatial behavior** refers to the attempts of individuals to structure the physical space around them. For example, people move toward or away from a person or object; they maintain closeness or distance. The range, frequency, and outcomes of such movements provide significant data for a variety of research goals. Violations of personal space frequently produce stress. People whose personal space is violated report feeling tense and anxious. The physiological signs of stress include increases in galvanic skin response, pulse rate, and blood pressure.[9] Scientists can use these responses as indicators of culturally oriented spatial norms and include them in research on interperson behavior in a number of physical settings, such as crowds.

For example, there are distinct patterns in the way people use the space that immediately surrounds them when interacting with others. Every culture develops

6. The following discussion draws from Karl E. Weick, "Systematic Observational Methods," in *The Handbook of Social Psychology,* 3d ed., ed. Gardner Lindzey and Elliot Aronson (New York: Random House, 1985).

7. Paul Ekman, "A Methodological Discussion of Nonverbal Behavior," *Journal of Psychology,* 43 (1957): 14, 136.

8. Paul Ekman, "Communication through Nonverbal Behavior: A Source of Information about Interpersonal Relationship," in *Affect, Cognition, and Personality,* ed. Silvan S. Tomkins and Carroll E. Izard (New York: Springer, 1965), p. 441, and Paul Ekman and W. Friesen, "The Repertoire of Nonverbal Behavior: Categories, Origins, Usage and Coding," *Semiotica,* 1 (1969): 1–20.

9. S. Worchel, and C. Teddlie, "The Experience of Crowding: A Two-Factor Theory," *Journal of Personality and Social Psychology,* 34 (1976): 30–40.

unwritten codes regulating how closely individuals can approach each other: South Americans have narrower personal spaces than do North Americans, Germans, and the English. Cultural variations in personal space can have serious implications in culturally heterogeneous societies or cities. An individual from a German background may find it uncomfortable to interact with a South American because the two of them have difficulty establishing a satisfactory interpersonal space with each other. Friction may develop between the two because each may view the other as rude. Actually, they are both attempting to establish spacing that is comfortable and acceptable in their respective cultures. Furthermore, differences in personal space norms can even vary within one society. Aiello and Thompson found that at young ages, blacks interact more closely than whites. However, adolescent blacks interact at greater distances than do adolescent whites.[10]

## Extralinguistic Behavior

Words, linguistic content, make up only a small portion of observable behavior. The noncontent aspects of behavior, such as rate of speaking, loudness, tendency to interrupt, and pronunciation peculiarities, constitute a fruitful source of data, generally referred to as **extralinguistic behavior** or **paralanguage.** The contemporary concept of "body language" essentially refers to the same phenomena.

Social scientists have documented the significance of paralanguage in human behavior in numerous studies. For example, a vocal characteristic such as pitch accurately measures emotional states.[11] The average duration of spontaneous speech increases as the size of the group increases.[12] Frequency of interruption reflects differences in personal power. People express passive emotions such as sadness through slow speech, lower volume, and pitch; they communicate active emotions such as anger by fast, loud, and high-pitched speech. These examples only hint at the range of applications for which scientists can utilize extralinguistic indicators in the study of behavior. They can only begin to point to the potential significance of this type of behavior for a variety of social research purposes.

## Linguistic Behavior

**Linguistic behavior** refers to the manifest content of speech and the various attributes of verbal communication. The study of these characteristics can be applied to a number of research goals. Investigators have made extensive use of measures of linguistic behavior particularly in studies on social interaction. Robert Bales, for example, devised a well-known system for organizing and coding the

10. A. J. Aiello and E. D. Thompson, "Personal Space, Crowding, and Spatial Behavior in a Cultural Context," in *Human Behavior and Environment,* ed. I. Altman et al. (New York: Plenum, 1980).

11. William F. Soskin and Paul E. Kauffman, "Judgment of Emotion in Word-free Voice Samples," *Journal of Communication,* 11 (1961): 73–80.

12. William F. Soskin and John P. Vera, "The Study of Spontaneous Talk," in *The Stream of Human Behavior,* ed. Roger C. Baker (Norwalk Conn.: Appleton & Lang, 1963).

---

### Types of Behavior

- *Nonverbal Behavior:* Body movements such as facial expressions.
- *Spatial Behavior:* People's attempts to structure the space around them, such as through the control of the amount of personal space.
- *Extralinguistic Behavior:* The formal aspects of speech, such as the rate of speaking and the tendency to interrupt.
- *Linguistic Behavior:* The content of speech and the structural characteristics of talking.

---

process of interaction in groups involved in problem-solving activities. Bales's system, Interaction Process Analysis, or IPA, contains 12 kinds of distinctive behaviors that can be used for coding and analyzing interaction within groups (see Exhibit 9.1). In addition, scholars of political culture can employ linguistic variables in studying leadership styles as well as subcultures.

---

# Timing and Recording

The second major consideration in observational studies concerns the timing and recording of observations. Obviously, as it is impossible to make an infinite number of observations, researchers make a decision as to when to observe. One accepted approach to this problem is to follow a *time-sampling schedule*. **Time sampling** refers to the process of selecting observation units at different points in time. This technique ensures the representativeness of the chosen ongoing activities. Regarding the observation units, researchers select these units in systematic ways in order to ensure representation of a defined population of behavior. For example, a researcher might make observations during a 15-minute period of each hour randomly selected after stratifying the sample by day of the week and hour of the day. Another useful sampling procedure is *individual sampling,* also referred to as *specimen records.* In this case, the researcher selects one individual and records all behavior and events involving that individual. For example, an observer might select one child and record all instances of physical aggression between that child and other classmates for a specified period of time. Every 30 minutes, a different child would be selected and observed. The total of data collected would then represent the behavior of all the children in the class.

In developing a time-sampling design, the researcher must also develop a coding system for recording the observations. In order to transform the complexity of ongoing events into data that can be expressed numerically and quantified, the researcher must first categorize the data and assign a code for each category. Such a coding system can be constructed by applying either a deductive approach or an inductive approach. When using a deductive approach, the researcher begins with a conceptual definition, specifies indicators of the behavior to be observed,

**Exhibit 9.1**
IPA Code of Categories

| | | |
|---|---|---|
| Social-emotional area: Positive reactions | A | 1. Shows solidarity, raises other's status, gives help, reward |
| | | 2. Shows tension-release, jokes, laughs, shows satisfaction |
| | | 3. Agrees, shows passive acceptance, understands, concurs, complies |
| Task area: Attempted answers | B | 4. Gives suggestion, direction, implying autonomy for other |
| | | 5. Gives opinion, evaluation, analysis, expressive feeling, wish |
| | | 6. Gives orientation, information, repeats, clarifies, confirms |
| Task area: Questions | C | 7. Asks for orientation, information, repetition, confirmation |
| | | 8. Asks for opinion, evaluation analysis, expression of feeling |
| | | 9. Asks for suggestion, direction, possible ways of action |
| Social-emotional area Negative reactions | D | 10. Disagrees, shows passive rejection, formality, withholds help |
| | | 11. Shows tension, asks for help, withdraws out of field |
| | | 12. Shows antagonism, deflates other's status, defends or asserts |

a  b  c  d  e  f

| Key: | a. | Problems of orientation | d. | Problems of decision |
|---|---|---|---|---|
| | b. | Problems of evaluation | e. | Problems of tension-management |
| | c. | Problems of control | f. | Problems of integration |

From Robert F. Bales, *Interaction Process Analysis,* by permission of the University of Chicago Press. Copyright © 1976 The University of Chicago Press.

and then standardizes and validates the resulting instrument. When implementing this approach, the investigator assigns observations to prespecified categories at the time the record is made. In contrast, the inductive approach requires the researcher to select indicators at the first stage of data collection and to postpone the construction of definitions until he or she identifies a pattern. Each approach involves some risk. With the deductive approach, it is difficult to foresee whether the conceptual definition is precise. On the other hand, the inductive (or empirical) approach poses difficulties in interpreting the observations (see Chapter 14). The ideal way to reduce these risks is to combine the two approaches. Karl Weick suggests that

> in the ideal sequence, the observer would start with the empirical approach, obtain extensive records of natural events, induce some concepts from the records, and then collect a second set of records which are more specific and pointed more directly at the induced concept.[13]

Regardless of whether researchers use a deductive or an inductive approach, the categories to which they assign observations must exhibit certain characteristics. The *category system* construct must

> limit the observation to one segment or aspect of . . . behavior, and construct a finite set of categories into one and only one of which every unit observed can be classified.[14]

Put briefly, the categories must be explicit, exhaustive, and mutually exclusive. (For an in-depth discussion of categorization, see Chapter 14).

---

# Inference

The third major consideration in structured observational studies relates to the degree of inference required of the observer. Most data collection by observation involves inferences. When an investigator observes a certain act or behavior, he or she must process this observation and infer as to whether or not the behavior indicates a certain variable. Some observational systems require a low degree of observer inference, for example, the recording of straightforward acts such as "asks a question," "suggests a course of action," and "interrupts another group member." Many acts, however, require a greater degree of inference. Suppose that the researcher observes an adult striking a child. An inference has to be made whether this act represents "aggression," "aggressive behavior," "hostility," "violence," or some other variable. The validity of such an inference depends to a large extent on the competence of the observer. Well-trained observers are likely to make more reliable inferences, other things being equal.

As a means of increasing the reliability of inferences, researchers have designed training programs appropriate to various observational situations. Typically, a program begins with an exposition of the theory and the research hypotheses involved in a given study, as well as an explanation of the category and coding systems constructed to record the observations. After the trainees have had an opportunity to raise questions, they practice application of the category system in a real-life situation. Only after this trial experience does the actual data collection begin.

13. Weick, "Systematic Observational Methods," p. 102.
14. Donald M. Medley and Harold E. Mitzel, "Measuring Classroom Behavior by Systematic Observation," in *Handbook of Research on Teaching,* ed. Nathaniel L. Gage (Skokie, Ill.: Rand McNally, 1963), p. 298.

# Types of Observation

We can distinguish between controlled and noncontrolled observational systems by the extent to which decisions regarding behavior, timing, recording, and inference are systematically and rigorously implemented. A controlled observational system is typified by clear and explicit decisions as to what, how, and when to observe; a noncontrolled system is considerably less systematic and allows great flexibility. For example, in **controlled observation,** a time sample is usually drawn prior to observation; in **noncontrolled observation,** samples are rarely taken. The choice between controlled and noncontrolled observation depends to a large extent on the research problem and research design; that is, researchers use controlled observation most frequently with experimental research designs but seldom with preexperimental designs or qualitative studies. We will discuss controlled observational systems in this chapter; noncontrolled observation (qualitative research) is presented in Chapter 12.

# Controlled Observations

Controlled observations can be carried out in the laboratory as well as in the field. In both settings, the investigator wishes to infer causality by maximizing control over extrinsic and intrinsic variables while employing one of a variety of experimental research designs and systematically recording observations.

# Laboratory Experimentation

*Laboratory experimentation* is the most controlled method of data collection in the social sciences. It involves the creation of conditions in an environment, the laboratory, whose characteristics can be adjusted by the researcher, that is, a controlled environment. The laboratory setting permits simulation of certain features of a natural environment along with the manipulation of one or more elements, the independent variables, in order to observe the effects produced.

Solomon Asch's experiments on interpersonal influence are classic examples of laboratory experimentation. Asch's objective was to examine the social and personal factors that induce individuals to yield to or resist group pressures when the group's perceived behaviors are contrary to fact. Asch developed a procedure for placing individuals in intense disagreement with their peers and for measuring the effect of this relationship upon them. In one such experiment, eight individuals were instructed to match the length of a given line with one of three unequal lines and to announce their judgments aloud. During the test, one individual would suddenly be contradicted by the other seven members of the group, because Asch had instructed them to respond with wrong judgments at certain points. The errors of the majority were obvious, ranging between 1/2 inch and 1 3/4 inches.

The eighth individual confronted a situation in which the group unanimously contradicted the evidence of his or her senses. This individual, commonly referred to as the *critical subject,* was the true object of investigation. Asch also used a control group in which the errors introduced by the majority were not of the same order encountered under the experimental conditions. One of the interesting findings was a marked movement toward the majority within the experimental group:

> One third of all the estimates [of the critical subject] in the critical group were errors identical with or in the direction of the distorted estimates of the majority. The significance of this finding becomes clear in the light of the virtual absence of errors in the control group.[15]

The Asch experiment exemplifies the two major advantages of laboratory experimentation: it allows rigorous control over extrinsic and intrinsic factors, and it provides unambiguous evidence about causation. Asch eliminated the effects of many variables that might have caused critical subjects to yield to or to resist group pressure. This increased the probability that the differences observed were due to changes purposely introduced by the experimental treatment. Moreover, Asch could unambiguously specify what caused the movement of his critical subjects toward the majority opinion because he himself controlled and manipulated the independent variable—the seven members of the group who were told when to respond with wrong judgments. Furthermore, Asch varied the experimental treatment in a systematic way, thus allowing for the precise specification of important differences. Finally, Asch constructed the experiment in a way that enabled him to clearly detect the effects of the experimental treatment: the critical subjects had to state their judgments aloud. By declaring themselves and taking a definite position vis-à-vis their peers, they could not avoid the dilemma created within the experimental situation.

The complexity of Asch's experiments can only hint at the scope of experimental options. Laboratory experiments do, in fact, vary in complexity and design, depending on the research problem and the ingenuity of the experimenter. Experimenters also have to construct a set of procedures that capture the meaning of their conceptualization of the research problem as well as enable the testing of their hypotheses. This requirement in turn demands the invention of measuring tools and consideration of the influence of the tools on the behavior of the research participants. In other words, the experimenter must construct a setting within which the manipulations of the independent variables make sense and the measurements are valid and reliable.

## Experimental and Mundane Realism

Because the laboratory does not represent a real-world situation, you may have questions about the meaningfulness of laboratory experimentation. In the Asch experiment, critical subjects were, after all, judging a very clear physical event (the

---

15. Solomon E. Asch, "Effects of Group Pressure upon the Modification Distortion of Judgments," in *Readings in Social Psychology,* ed. Eleanor Maccoby, Theodore Newcomb, and Eugen Hartley (New York: Holt, Rinehart and Winston, 1958), p. 177.

length of lines) when they were contradicted by their peers. In everyday life, however, a situation where the unambiguous evidence of one's senses is contradicted by the unanimous judgments of one's peers is unlikely.

This problem has led scientists to distinguish between two senses in which any given experiment can be said to be realistic.[16] In the first sense, an experiment is realistic if the situation is experienced as real by the research participants, that is, if it involves them and affects them. This kind of realism is commonly termed **experimental realism.** In the Asch experiment, the critical subjects exhibited signs of tension and anxiety. They were reacting to a situation that was as real for them as any of their experiences outside the lab.

The second sense of realism refers to the extent to which events occurring in a laboratory setting are likely to occur in the real world. This type of realism is called **mundane realism.** An experiment that is high on mundane realism and low on experimental realism does not necessarily yield more meaningful results than one that is high on experimental realism and low on mundane realism. Had Asch observed interpersonal influences in the real world, he probably would not have found a situation so clearly structured for observing the effects of group pressure on individual members. Moreover, if we assume that such a situation could have been found, because the researcher could not have controlled for the effects of intrinsic and extrinsic factors, the findings obtained could have been ambiguous and inconclusive. Therefore, by employing both forms of realism, the experimenter increases the internal validity of the experiment by producing more significant effects within the experimental situation.

## Sources of Bias in Laboratory Experiments

Notwithstanding the advantages of laboratory experiments, they do have certain inherent limitations. These can be classified into three types: bias due to the demand characteristics of the experimental situation itself, bias due to the unintentional influence of the experimenters, and measurement artifacts.

*Demand Characteristics.*    Bias due to **demand characteristics** may occur when individuals know that they are in an experimental situation, are aware that they are being observed, and believe that certain responses are expected from them. Consequently, they may not respond directly to the experimental manipulation. Instead, their responses may reflect their interpretation of the behavior these manipulations are intended to elicit. Even if the experimenter announces that there are no right or wrong responses, subjects may continue to assume that certain behaviors are expected and may try to comply with those expectations.[17] Subjects

16. The following discussion is based on Elliot Aronson, Marilynn B. Brewer, and James Carlsmith, "Experimentation in Social Psychology," in *The Handbook of Social Psychology,* 3d ed., ed. Gardner Lindzey and Elliot Aronson (New York: Random House, 1985), pp. 481–483.
17. M. T. Orne, "Demand Characteristics and the Concept of Quasi-controls," in *Artifacts in Behavioral Research,* ed. Robert Rosenthal and R. L. Rosnow (Orlando, Fla.: Academic Press, 1969).

may also discover the research hypothesis and respond in a manner consistent with it in an attempt to please the experimenter. One practice experimenters commonly use to counteract these sources of bias is to reduce the participants' awareness of being observed during the experimental situation. Another strategy is to discuss only general rather than specific research objectives with the participants. The logic behind this method is that if some subjects modify their behavior so as to support, or refute, what they erroneously believe to be the research hypothesis, the results relating to the true hypothesis may not be affected in a systematic way.[18]

*Experimenter Bias.*    Behavior on the part of the experimenter that is not intended to be part of the experimental manipulation, but that nevertheless influences the participants, is termed **experimenter bias** or the *experimental expectancy effect*. Experimenters may unintentionally communicate their expectations of the subjects' behavior in various ways, such as showing tension or relief or by nodding when responses are made. Robert Rosenthal and his colleagues found that when 8 of 12 experimenters using the same methodology received biased data from their first two subjects (who were accomplices of Rosenthal and his colleagues) these early returns influenced the data they collected from subsequent true research participants. The four experimenters who received hypothesis-confirming data from their first two participants recorded the strongest confirming data from the naïve participants who followed the planted participants. The four experimenters who received disconfirming data from their first two planted participants recorded the most disconfirming data from their naïve participants. The comparison group of experimenters, who tested only naïve participants, obtained values ranging between those obtained by the other two groups of experimenters. Accordingly, the authors concluded that early returns bias subsequently obtained data.[19] Experimenter bias is thus the outcome of the observers' motivations.

By using tape recorders, television cameras, or other automated procedures to minimize interactions between experimenters and research participants, researchers can eliminate the communication of expectations and thereby minimize unintentional experimenter bias. Researchers have also mitigated bias effects by using experimenters who have differing expectations of the outcome of the investigation. In one study, the researchers included expectations about the effects of the manipulated variables as one of the variables in the experimental design. In this case, the researchers assessed whether their own differing expectations produced different outcomes.[20] Another recommendation offered for reducing experimenter bias is the use of more than one observer or data gatherer. This technique

18. For a comprehensive discussion of bias-reducing methods, see Aronson et al., "Experimentation in Social Psychology."

19. Robert Rosenthal et al., "The Effects of Early Data Returns on Data Subsequently Obtained by Outcome-biased Experimenters," *Sociometry,* 26 (1963): 487–493.

20. J. Merrill Carlsmith, Barry E. Collins, and Robert L. Helmreich, "Studies in Forced Compliance: I. The Effect of Pressure for Compliance on Attitude Change Produced by Face-to-Face Role Playing and Anonymous Essay Writing," *Journal of Personality and Social Psychology,* 4 (1966): 1–13.

---

### Three Sources of Bias in Experiments

- *Demand Characteristics:* When individuals know they are part of an experiment and try to respond in the way they think the experimenter wants them to.
- *Experimenter Bias:* When an experimenter unintentionally communicates his or her expectations to participants.
- *Measurement Artifacts:* Measurement procedures may give participants hints about what is really going on in the experiment. Measuring instruments such as cameras or test schedules can also affect participants and bias results.

---

modifies the effect of researchers' personality traits, physical characteristics, and subtle differences in their treatment of participants.

*Measurement Artifacts.*    Measurement is a crucial part of the research process. In laboratory experiments, where the effects of an independent variable may be small, short, and sensitive, precise measurement is needed. Moreover, measurement procedures are not independent of other research design problems. Measurement procedures may invite biased interpretations of the data by giving experimental participants hints about the true purpose of the experiment, by giving them the opportunity to make a favorable impression, and so on.

Measuring instruments themselves may be reactive in the sense that they may change the phenomenon being measured. For instance, if researchers are using cameras to record responses, the individuals being studied might behave atypically just because they are aware of the cameras. Exposure to the measuring instrument in a pretest may sensitize individuals and affect their posttest scores. Even the timing of measurement may produce misleading results. A researcher may measure for the effects of independent variables before they have had sufficient time to affect the dependent variable or after their effects have already waned, thus concealing their actual effect. In their pioneering study, Carl Hovland and his associates found that discredited public speakers had no *immediate* persuasive effect on their listeners but may have had a significant effect a month later, unless the listeners were reminded of the source.[21]

## Recording Observations

The above discussion should sensitize us to the importance of recording observations. Observations in the laboratory are recorded on the spot during the experimental session. Mechanical devices such as video or movie cameras, tape recorders, and television are often used to obtain an overall view of the occur-

---

21. Carl I. Hovland, Irving L. Janis, and Harold H. Kelley, *Communication and Persuasion* (New Haven, Conn.: Yale University Press, 1953).

rences. Next, the units of observation are assigned to a well-structured classificatory system such as the one reproduced in Exhibit 9.1. Categorization may take place during the experimental session if the system of recording has been prepared and pretested well in advance. With a well-prepared system of recording and training observers, the degree of inference required of the observers is minimal.

# Field Experimentation

As the terms imply, the major difference between laboratory experimentation and experiments in the field is the setting. In laboratory experimentation, researchers introduce controlled conditions into the environment that simulate certain features of a natural environment. By contrast, in **field experimentation,** because the research takes place in a *natural* situation, the investigator manipulates one or more independent variables under conditions that are as carefully controlled as the situation permits. In terms of research design, the contrast between the laboratory experiment and the field study is not sharp (see Chapter 5). However, the difficulties involved in controlling intrinsic, and especially extrinsic, factors are considerably greater in field experiments.

An intriguing example of field experimentation is the oft-cited Piliavin, Rodin, and Piliavin study on helping behavior—altruism.[22] The researchers conducted a field experiment to study the effects of several variables on helping behavior, using the express trains of the New York Eighth Avenue Independent Subway as a laboratory on wheels. Four teams of students, each consisting of a victim, a model, and two observers, staged standard collapses in which the type of victim (ill or drunk), the race of victim (black or white), and the presence or absence of a model were varied. Data were recorded on the number and race of bystanders, the inherent propensity to help (or latency of the helping response), the race of helper, the number of helpers, the movement out of the "critical area," and spontaneous comments. Figure 9.1 illustrates the setting of this field experiment.

The researchers found that (1) an apparently ill person is more likely to receive assistance than one who appears to be drunk; (2) the race of victim has little effect on the race of helper except when the victim is drunk; (3) men are considerably more likely to help than women; and (4) the longer the emergency continues without help being offered, the more likely it is that someone will simply leave the area of the emergency.

In this study, the investigators relied primarily on systematic observation within a naturally occurring setting. The experimenters did not control their setting but introduced a systematic variation—the behavior of an experimental accomplice—in order to study the helping behavior of bystanders in the largely uncontrolled context of a subway train. Researchers conducting field experiments

22. Irving M. Piliavin, Judith Rodin, and Jane Allyn Piliavin, "Good Samaritanism: An Underground Phenomenon?" *Journal of Personality and Social Psychology,* 13 (1969): 289–299.

**Figure 9.1**
Scheme of the Field Experiment

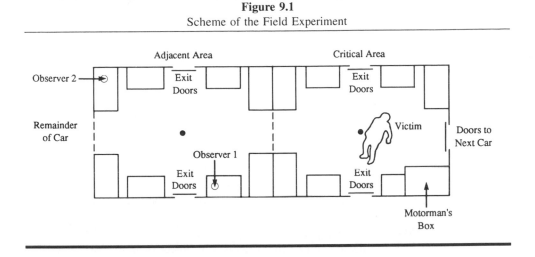

can therefore construct different experimental situations as well as introduce experimental variations within natural settings. In yet other cases, the researcher does not manipulate the independent variables directly but rather selects the stimuli that represent the theoretical concept of interest within the naturally recurring situations.

As we pointed out earlier, the main appeal of field experiments is that they permit the investigation of complex interactions, processes, and change in a natural setting. Their major weakness lies in the area of control: experimenters cannot control intrinsic and extrinsic sources of validity as systematically as in laboratory experiments. Participant self-selection is a pervasive problem, and randomization is often impossible. As a means of estimating the effects of noncontrollable elements, a pilot study is often carried out. Pilot studies enable the investigator to make a convincing case that the research participants are not likely to systematically differ on any relevant factors other than their responses to the causal process of interest.[23]

Ethical issues are, of course, a major concern in field experiments. Is it ethical to expose innocent bystanders to someone who collapses and pretends to be seriously ill? In laboratory experiments, the rights of the participants are protected by informed consent and by debriefing; research participants are aware that they are taking part in research. Even if the participants enter the experimental session with no information of the experiment's objective, they know that they will be informed by the time the session is over. In field experiments, individuals are often unaware that they are participating in research. In such situations, the researcher has to ensure that the privacy of the affected individuals is not violated and that

23. For other methods used to minimize validity problems, see Aronson et al., "Experimentation in Social Psychology."

they will be protected from undue embarrassment or distress. (Methods for ensuring privacy and confidentiality are discussed in Chapter 4.)

## Summary

**1.** Observation is considered the archetypical method of scientific research. If you want to understand, explain, and predict what exists, you can simply go and observe it. But if your findings are to be systematic, the observations must be carried out with reference to three crucial issues: what to observe, where and when to observe, and how much to infer when recording observations.

**2.** The research problem requires, first and foremost, the designation of what type of behavior is to be observed—nonverbal, spatial, extralinguistic, or linguistic.

**3.** How to carry out your observations is the focus of the research problem and the research design. When the researcher's objective is to test a hypothesis experimentally, the units of observation are explicitly defined; a setting is chosen—the laboratory or field; a time sample is drawn; and the observations are systematically recorded. The operational procedures should involve as little observer inference as possible. These operations typify controlled observations. When recording and categorizing the observations, researchers employ triangulation, the use of two or more data collection methods to study the same phenomenon, to further enhance the validity of the findings.

**4.** It is helpful to distinguish between experimental realism—the extent to which an experimental situation is experienced as real to the research participants—and mundane realism—the relevance of an experimental situation to the real world. Systematic bias may be introduced in experiments as a result of demand characteristics, experimenter bias, and measurement artifacts.

**5.** The field experiment presents challenges to the researcher because of the difficulties involved in controlling the setting (the natural environment), participant selection, and the manipulation of the independent variable. Ethical issues are a major concern because the participants are unaware that they are involved in an experimental situation.

## Key Terms for Review

controlled observation (p. 213)

demand characteristics (p. 215)

experimental realism (p. 215)

experimenter bias (p. 216)

extralinguistic behavior (p. 209)

field experimentation (p. 218)

linguistic behavior (p. 209)

mundane realism (p. 215)

noncontrolled observation (p. 213)

nonverbal behavior (p. 208)

paralanguage (p. 209)

spatial behavior (p. 208)

time sampling (p. 210)

triangulation (p. 204)

## Study Questions

1. Why would a researcher choose to triangulate? Is triangulation more important in a controlled or field setting?
2. List a set of research goals and match them with the various forms of observation you think most appropriate. Explain your choice.
3. Describe the major techniques for timing and recording observations.
4. Discuss the strengths and weaknesses of laboratory experiments versus field experiments as modes of observation.
5. List the advantages and drawbacks of field experimentation.

## Additional Readings

Bales, Robert F., and Stephen P. Cohen. *SYMLOG: A System for the Multiple Level Observation of Groups.* New York: Free Press, 1979.

Bonacich, Philip, and John Light. "Laboratory Experimentation in Sociology." *Annual Review of Sociology,* 4 (1978): 145–170.

Brewer, John, and Albert Hunter. *Multimethod Research: A Synthesis of Styles.* Newbury Park, Calif.: Sage, 1989.

Emerson, Robert M. "Observational Field Work." *Annual Review of Sociology,* 7 (1981): 351–378.

Iyengar, Shanto, Mark D. Peters, and Donald R. Kinder. "Experimental Demonstrations of the 'Not-So-Minimal' Consequences of Television News Programs." *American Political Science Review,* 76 (1982): 848–888.

Ray, William, and Richard Ravizza. *Methods toward a Science of Behavior and Experience.* Belmont, Calif.: Wadsworth, 1993.

Rosenthal, Robert. *Experimenter Effects in Behavioral Research.* New York: Irvington, 1976.

Saxe, Leonard. *Social Experiments: Methods for Design and Evaluation.* Newbury Park, Calif.: Sage, 1981.

Suen, Hoi K. *Analyzing Quantitative Behavioral Observation Data.* Hillsdale, N.J.: Erlbaum, 1989.

Vargas, Marjorie F. *Louder Than Words: An Introduction to Nonverbal Communication.* Ames: Iowa State University Press, 1986.

# CHAPTER 10

# Survey Research

E-mail (electronic mail) is becoming an increasingly popular method of communication between parties with access to computers equipped with modems. Information and messages sent via e-mail reach their destination in minutes rather than days, as may be the case with conventional mail, and users can send fairly large files at a reasonable cost. Researchers looking for new methods of conducting surveys may soon find e-mail to be an alternative to traditional mail and telephone surveys. Professor Samuel Brown of Fordham university recently tested the viability of e-mail as a method of securing survey responses.[1] Using a different name and posing as a student needing information for a class project, he sent messages to 150 e-mail service subscribers living in Abilene, Texas. Although he had selected Abilene simply because it was at the top of an alphabetical list of cities, Brown described it as the "ideal" city and asked people for their views on the attributes of the city. Brown was somewhat surprised by the response to his message. Some of the potential respondents contacted their local newspaper to report that Abilene had been selected as an ideal city. When the newspaper checked the credentials of the researcher, they discovered the student did not exist and uncovered Brown's deception. Nevertheless, Brown says he received about 30 responses to his survey and intends to have the members of his sociology class perform e-mail surveys.

In this chapter we discuss the advantages and disadvantages of more traditional survey methods. As you read the chapter, think about the possible advantages and disadvantages of e-mail as a data collection technique.

S OCIAL SCIENCE RESEARCHERS CAN CHOOSE FROM AMONG three methods of gathering data with surveys: mail questionnaires, personal interviews, and telephone interviews. In this chapter, we explore the activities involved in conducting the three different types of surveys and discuss the advantages and disadvantages of each. We conclude the chapter by comparing the three methods.

Observational methods of data collection are suitable for investigating phenomena that researchers can observe directly. However, not all phenomena are accessible to the investigator's direct observation; very often, therefore, the researcher must collect data by asking people who have experienced certain phenomena to reconstruct their experiences. Keeping in mind budget restrictions and the availability of staff, the researcher must determine the survey method that will elicit the most complete responses from a sample of individuals presumed to have experienced the phenomenon of interest. The responses constitute the data on which the research hypotheses are examined.

---

1. Richard Perez-Pena, "Professor's Plan Backfires: E-Mail Project Was Hoax," *New York Times,* July 11, 1994: p. B2.

# Mail Questionnaire

The **mail questionnaire** is an impersonal survey method. Under certain conditions and for a number of research purposes, an impersonal method of data collection can be useful. As with any method, however, mail questionnaires have both advantages and disadvantages.

## Advantages of the Mail Questionnaire

1. *Low cost.* Economy is one of the most obvious appeals of mail questionnaires. The mail questionnaire does not require a trained staff of interviewers; all it entails is the cost of planning, sampling, duplicating, mailing, and providing stamped, self-addressed envelopes for the returns. Processing and analysis are usually also simpler and cheaper than for other survey methods. The lower cost of administering a mail questionnaire is particularly evident when the population under study is widely spread over a large geographic area. Under such circumstances, the cost of interviewing could become prohibitive, and the mail questionnaire may be the only practicable instrument.

2. *Reduction in biasing error.* The use of a mail questionnaire reduces *biasing errors* that might result from the personal characteristics of interviewers and variability in their skills. Personal interview situations are fraught with possibilities for bias due to the nature of the interaction between the interviewer and the respondent. Investigators can avoid this pitfall by using a mail questionnaire.

3. *Greater anonymity.* The absence of an interviewer also provides greater anonymity for the respondent. The assurance of anonymity that a mail questionnaire provides is especially helpful when the survey deals with sensitive issues, such as sexual behavior or child abuse. People in the sample are more likely to respond to sensitive questions when they do not have to face an interviewer or speak to someone directly.

4. *Considered answers and consultations.* Mail questionnaires are also preferable when questions demand a considered (rather than an immediate) answer or if answers require respondents to consult personal documents or other people.

5. *Accessibility.* Finally, the mail questionnaire permits wide geographic contact at minimal cost. When a survey requires wide coverage and addresses a population that is dispersed geographically, interviewing would involve high travel costs and large investments of time.

## Disadvantages of the Mail Questionnaire

1. *Requires simple questions.* Researchers can use the mail questionnaire as an instrument for data collection only when the questions are straightforward enough to be comprehended solely on the basis of printed instructions and definitions.

2. *No opportunity for probing.* The answers have to be accepted as final; researchers have no opportunity to probe beyond the given answer, to clarify ambiguous answers, or to appraise the nonverbal behavior of respondents.

3. *No control over who fills out the questionnaire.* With a mail questionnaire, researchers have no control over the respondent's environment; hence they cannot be sure that the appropriate person completes the questionnaire. An individual other than the intended respondent may complete it.

4. *Low response rate.* The final disadvantage of a mail questionnaire—and perhaps its most serious problem—is that it is often difficult to obtain an adequate response rate. The **response rate** is the percentage of respondents in the sample who return completed questionnaires. For many mail surveys, the reported response rates are much lower than for personal interviews. The typical response rate for a personal interview is about 95 percent, whereas the response rate for a mail survey without follow-up is between 20 and 40 percent. Researchers who use mail questionnaires must almost always face the problem of how to estimate the effect the nonrespondents may have on their findings. (The response rate is of great significance when making generalizations; see Chapter 19.) Nonrespondents are usually quite different from those who answer a questionnaire. Often they are the poorly educated who may have problems understanding the questions, the elderly who are unable to respond, or the more mobile who cannot be located. Consequently, the group of respondents is not likely to accurately represent the population originally defined by the investigators, and this will undoubtedly introduce bias into the study.

---

### Advantages and Disadvantages of Mail Questionnaires

**Advantages**

- The cost is low compared to other methods.
- Biasing error is reduced because respondents are not influenced by interviewer characteristics or techniques.
- Questionnaires provide a high degree of anonymity for respondents. This is especially important when sensitive issues are involved.
- Respondents have time to think about their answers and/or consult other sources.
- Questionnaires provide wide access to geographically dispersed samples at low cost.

**Disadvantages**

- Questionnaires require simple, easily understood questions and instructions.
- Questionnaires do not offer researchers the opportunity to probe for additional information or to clarify answers.
- Researchers cannot control who fills out the questionnaire.
- Response rates are low.

# Factors Affecting the Response Rate of Mail Questionnaires

Researchers use various strategies to overcome the difficulty of securing an acceptable response rate to mail questionnaires and to increase the response rate.

*Sponsorship.*    The sponsorship of a questionnaire has a significant effect on respondents, often motivating them to fill it out and return it. Therefore, investigators must include information on sponsorship, usually in the cover letter accompanying the questionnaire. Sponsorship affects the response rate by convincing the respondent of the study's legitimacy and value as well as the perceived sanctions of a failure to reply. For example, the U. S. Bureau of the Census is successful in obtaining a response rate of nearly 95 percent on its National Health Interview Survey because it is government sponsored—which lends legitimacy and implies sanctions—and health is an important issue to the public. At the other extreme, only 5 percent of the sample responds in some mail surveys.[2] In general, government-sponsored questionnaires obtain high response rates while relatively little-known commercial organizations get low response rates.

*Inducement to Respond.*    Researchers who use mail surveys must appeal to the respondents and persuade them that they should participate by filling out the questionnaires and mailing them back. Several methods can be used, but they vary in their degree of effectiveness. One method is to appeal to the respondents' goodwill, telling them that the researchers need their help. For example, a student conducting a survey for a class project may mention that his or her grade may be affected by the response to the questionnaire.[3]

Another widely used method is to offer the respondent a reward, such as a prize or a nominal sum of money. The problem with offering money is that some respondents will be indignant that the researchers consider the respondent's time worth so little and thus may not respond at all.[4] However, most often respondents see the reward as a symbolic gesture, and they cooperate because they consider the study worthwhile.

Other inducements to respond include letters of support from professional associations and advertisements of the coming survey in publications of professional associations. But perhaps the most effective strategy is to appeal to the respondents' altruistic sentiments and to convince them of the significance of the study. In the following example from a cover letter accompanying a questionnaire, the writer emphasizes the importance of the study and the respondents' potential contribution to its success:

> As you know, public service employment is a major part of the federal, state, and
> local strategy to overcome the employment and income problems of economically

2. Floyd J. Fowler, Jr., *Survey Research Methods* (Newbury Park, Calif.: Sage, 1989), p. 48.
3. Kenneth D. Bailey, *Methods of Social Research* (New York: Free Press, 1987), p. 156.
4. Ibid., p. 157.

disadvantaged unemployed people. There is no question that the program is needed throughout the country . . . You are probably also aware . . . that public service employment programs are quite controversial and their future may be in jeopardy. Part of the reason that these programs are so controversial is that no systematic evaluation of the benefits of these programs for the individuals employed and the communities served has been conducted.

Because this specific evaluation has significant national implications, I strongly urge you to give this enclosed questionnaire your prompt attention and thank you for your cooperation in this evaluation.[5]

*Questionnaire Format and Methods of Mailing.*    Designing a mail questionnaire involves several considerations: typography, color, and length and type of cover letter. A slightly larger investment in format and typography (e.g., high-quality paper and adequate spacing) will pay off in a higher response rate. The use of unusual colors is not recommended because it may have a negative effect.[6]

*Cover Letter.*    Another factor to be considered in designing the questionnaire is the cover letter. The cover letter must succeed in convincing the respondents to fill out the questionnaire and mail it back. It should therefore identify the sponsor of the study, explain its purpose, tell the respondents why it is important that they fill out the questionnaire, and assure them that the answers will be held in strict confidence. The investigator must choose between a formal or a semipersonal letter. Studies have shown that a semipersonal letter generates a slightly higher response rate than a formal form letter.

*Type of Mailing.*    An important consideration is the type of mailing to be used. Questionnaires that are not accompanied by a postpaid return envelope obtain few responses. It is unreasonable to expect the respondent not only to fill out the questionnaire but also to find an envelope and then go to the post office to have it weighed and stamped. Hence it is a common practice to enclose a stamped, self-addressed envelope. (An official-looking business reply envelope tends to reduce the response rate.)

*Timing of Mailing.*    The timing of mailing has been shown to affect the response rate of mail questionnaires. For example, because summer and holidays produce the lowest response rate, it is not advisable to conduct the first wave of a mailing during those times.

*The Total Design Method (TDM).*    In recent years, researchers have improved data collection with mail surveys considerably by applying the *total design*

---

5. Mickey L. Burnim, *An Evaluation of the Public Service Employment Projects in Florida Created under Title VI of the Comprehensive Employment and Training Act of 1973* (Tallahassee: Florida Department of Community Affairs, 1978), p. 164.

6. Pamela L. Alreck and Robert B. Settle, *The Survey Research Handbook* (Homewood, Ill.: Irwin, 1985).

*method,* a standardized set of step-by-step procedures[7] that is divided into two parts: questionnaire construction and survey implementation.

The principles researchers follow in constructing TDM questionnaires include paying particular attention to details such as the outside of the envelope that contains the questionnaire, the front cover of the questionnaire, and the order of the questions. Researchers using TDM try to make sure that the questionnaire will be immediately differentiated from junk mail.

The TDM implementation procedures focus primarily on **follow-up**. The most common follow-up strategy is to send a reminder postcard to respondents who have not replied one week after the first mailing. The second follow-up consists of another reminder letter and a replacement questionnaire with a return envelope sent at the end of the third week. After seven weeks, another letter with a replacement questionnaire is sent, preferably by certified mail, to all of the individuals who have not responded.

Researchers tested the effectiveness of these follow-up methods on large statewide samples of the general population in four states. Table 10.1 shows the average and the cumulative response rates at the end of each step of the follow-up procedure. The results reveal the importance of a *multiwave follow-up*. Observe that each wave increases the response rate substantially in the most cost-effective manner. Postcards, the least expensive type of follow-up mailing, are sent to the greatest number of people. Certified mailings, the most expensive type of mailing, go out to the fewest people. Indeed, "with a mail methodology available which will consistently provide a high response, poor return rate can no more be excused than can inadequate theory or inappropriate statistics."[8] Recently, critics have suggested that the use of certified mail has some important drawbacks.[9] Respondents may feel coerced by the requirement of signing for receipt, and the cost in time and money may be even greater if the recipient has to go to the post office to retrieve the questionnaire. As an alternative, the final follow-up by certified mail may be replaced by a telephone reminder, which is as effective as certified mail in reducing nonresponse.

Although follow-up is clearly an important mechanism in raising the response rate, it creates several problems. First, because researchers send follow-up letters and questionnaires only to respondents who have not replied, it is necessary to identify all respondents; thus anonymity cannot be maintained. Researchers can get around this difficulty by assuring respondents that the replies will be held in strict confidence. Another limitation is that the quality of the responses declines with successive mailings. Individuals who do not respond the first time might be

---

7. Donald A. Dillman, "Mail and Other Self-administered Questionnaires," in *Handbook of Survey Research,* ed. Peter H. Rossi, James D. Wright, and Andy B. Anderson (Orlando, Fla.: Academic Press, 1983), and Anton J. Nederhof, "Effects of a Final Telephone Reminder and Questionnaire Cover Design in Mail Surveys," *Social Science Research,* 17 (1988): 353–361.

8. Donald A. Dillman, James A. Christensen, Edward H. Carpenter, and Ralph M. Brooks, "Increasing Mail Questionnaire Response: A Four-State Comparison," *American Sociological Review,* 39 (1974): 755.

9. Nederhof, "Effects," p. 354.

**Table 10.1**
Average and Cumulative Response Rates to Four Mailings

| Mailing | Time | Average Response Rate | Cumulative Response Rate |
|---|---|---|---|
| 1. First mailing | Week 1 | 23.8% | 23.8% |
| 2. Postcard follow-up | Week 2 | 18.2 | 42.0 |
| 3. First replacement questionnaire | Week 4 | 17.0 | 59.0 |
| 4. Second replacement sent by certified mail | Week 7 | 13.4 | 72.4 |

Adapted from Donald A. Dillman, James A. Christensen, Edward H. Carpenter, and Ralph M. Brooks, "Increasing Mail Questionnaire Response: A Four-State Comparison," *American Sociological Review*, 39 (1974): 755, and Donald A. Dillman and D. E. Moore, "Improving Response Rates to Mail Surveys: Results from Five Surveys," paper presented at the annual meeting of the American Association for Public Opinion Research, Hershey, Pa., 1983.

less likely to take the study seriously and thus may return incomplete questionnaires, or their answers may be unreliable. Researchers can examine bias due to this reason by comparing the responses of people who reply immediately with the responses of people who return the questionnaire after one or more follow-up steps are taken.[10]

*Selection of Respondents.* The selection of respondents is largely determined by the nature of the study and the characteristics of the population. Thus beyond the definition of the sampling population, there is very little a researcher can do in the selection process to increase the response rate. However, certain characteristics of potential respondents are associated with a high or low response rate. Recognizing this can help a researcher determine if a mail questionnaire should be used to begin with or whether to use other strategies to increase the response rate. The most significant dimension a researcher needs to consider in selecting respondents is whether they consist of a heterogeneous or a homogeneous group. Heterogeneous groups consist of individuals who differ from one another in some way that might influence the phenomenon of interest. For example, a heterogeneous group could consist of individuals from various ethnic and racial backgrounds, with different levels of income, or from urban and rural locations. Homogeneous groups, by contrast, consist of individuals with similar characteristics. Heterogeneous groups are typically used in opinion polls, whereas in more specialized studies, questionnaires are sent to select groups, for example, to physicians, legislators, city managers, university professors, or members of the local chamber of commerce. The response rate for select groups is usually higher than it is for the general population because members of these groups are more likely to identify with the goals of the study and thus will be more motivated to respond. Beyond this distinction, certain background characteristics are associated with differences in response rates. Respondents who are more educated are more likely to fill out

10. Fowler, *Survey Research Methods,* p. 54.

and return questionnaires. Interest in or familiarity with the topic under investigation is another important factor in determining the rate of return. Finally, in general, professionals tend to have the highest response rate among all occupations.

Table 10.2 ranks the various procedures discussed so far according to their relative effectiveness in increasing the rate of return of questionnaires. The ranks were determined on the basis of various studies estimating the possible increase

**Table 10.2**
Techniques for Increasing Response Rate

| Method | Rank (High to Low) | Optimal Conditions |
|---|---|---|
| Follow-up | 1 | More than one follow-up. Telephone could be used for follow-up. |
| Inducement | 2 | Questionnaires containing a token monetary reward produce better results than ones without. However, the population and the type of the questionnaire have to be considered. |
| Sponsorship | 3 | People the respondent knows produce the best result. |
| Introductory letter | 4 | An altruistic appeal seems to produce the best results. |
| Method of return | — | A regular stamped envelope produces better results than a business reply envelope. |
| Format | — | Aesthetically pleasing cover; a title that will arouse interest; an attractive page format. |
| Selection of respondents | — | • Nonreaders and nonwriters are excluded from participation.<br>• Interest in or familiarity with the topic under investigation is a major factor in determining the rate of return.<br>• The better educated are more likely to return the questionnaires.<br>• Professionals are more likely to return questionnaires. |

Adapted from Delbert C. Miller, *Handbook of Research Design and Social Measurement,* 5th ed. (Newbury Park, Calif.: Sage, 1991); Pamela L. Alreck and Robert B. Settle, *The Survey Research Handbook* (Homewood, Ill.: Irwin, 1985); and Francis J. Yammarino, Steven J. Skinner, and Terry L. Childers, "Understanding Mail Survey Response Behavior: A Meta-Analysis," *Public Opinion Quarterly,* 55 (1991): 613–639.

of total return for each procedure. Rank could not be determined for the last three procedures.

## Evaluating the Response Rate

What is an acceptable response rate for a mail questionnaire? Most investigators attempt to maximize the response rate by using some or all of the strategies just discussed. Yet despite these efforts, many mail surveys achieve a response rate no larger than 50 percent. Nonresponse is a serious problem because nonrespondents differ considerably from respondents. Studies have shown that mail questionnaires addressed to the general population are likely to result in an upward bias in education: better-educated people tend to respond more quickly to mail questionnaires.[11] Therefore, the bias resulting from nonresponse may limit the investigator's ability to make generalizations about the entire population.

The question of what constitutes an acceptable response rate cannot be answered easily because scientists do not agree on a standard for a minimum response rate. For example, surveys done under contract to the federal government are expected to yield a response rate higher than 75 percent. But whereas academic survey organizations are usually able to achieve that level, the response rates for surveys conducted by more obscure organizations are considerably lower.

Finally, there is some evidence that response rates to mail questionnaires have been improving with the increased standardization of follow-up techniques.[12]

Indeed, in recent years, survey research has become a widely used tool, not only of research and marketing organizations but also of national and local government. Some citizens, though dedicated and loyal to the goals of research, may find themselves trying to decide which and how many of the questionnaires they receive each year deserve a response. The satirical questionnaire for questioners reprinted in Exhibit 10.1 is an attempt to sensitize the questioners to this problem.

# Personal Interview

The personal interview is a face-to-face, interpersonal role situation in which an interviewer asks respondents questions designed to elicit answers pertinent to the research hypotheses. The questions, their wording, and their sequence define the structure of the interview.

## The Schedule-Structured Interview

The least flexible personal inteview form is the **schedule-structured interview.** In scheduled interviews the number of questions and the wording of the questions are identical for all of the respondents. Thus interviewers should not reword ques-

---

11. Ibid., pp. 355–356.
12. Nederhof, "Effects," p. 356.

## Exhibit 10.1
### Questionnaire for Questioners

Dear Questioner:

You are no doubt aware that the number of questionnaires circulated is rapidly increasing, whereas the length of the working day has, at best, remained constant. In order to resolve the problem presented by this trend, I find it necessary to restrict my replies to questionnaires to those questioners who first establish their *bona fide* by completing the following questionnaire.

1. How many questionnaires, per annum, do you distribute? _____
2. How many questionnaires, per annum, do you receive? _____
3. What fraction of the questionnaires you receive do you answer? _____
4. What fraction of the questionnaires you distribute are answered? _____
5. Do you think the ratio of the fraction 3:4 should be greater than 1, less than 1, any other value? (Please explain.) _____
6. What fraction of your time (or effort) do you devote to:
    a. Compiling questionnaires? _____
    b. Answering questionnaires? _____
    c. Examining the replies to your own questionnaires? _____
    d. Examining the replies to other people's questionnaires? _____
    e. Drawing conclusions from questionnaires? _____
    f. Other activities? _____
    (a+b+c+d+e+f should add up to 100 percent. If not, please explain.)
7. Do you regard the ratio of (a+b+c+d+e)/f as:
    a. too small? _____
    b. too large? _____
    c. any other? _____ (check one only)
8. Do you ever distribute questionnaires exclusively to people who you know distribute questionnaires? _____
9. Do you expect answers to questionnaires from people who themselves distribute questionnaires about questionnaires? _____
10. Do you consider it would be of value to distribute a questionnaire regarding answers to questionnaires to those individuals who receive questionnaires about the distribution of questionnaires?
    Yes _____
    No _____ (check one only)
    Any other answer? please explain.

Replies to this questionnaire must be signed. As you may surmise, they are not suitable, nor will they be used for statistical purposes.

From Samuel Devons, "A Questionnaire for Questioners," *Public Opinion Quarterly,* 39 (1975): 255–256.

tions or provide explanations of the questions if the respondent asks for clarification. In a structured interview the sequence in which the questions are asked is the same in every interview. The schedule-structured interview combines these two elements. Researchers use the schedule-structured interview to make sure that any variations between responses can be attributed to the actual differences between the respondents and not to variations in the interview. The researcher attempts to reduce the risk that changes in the way questions are worded, for example, might elicit differences in responses. The schedule-structured interview is based on three crucial assumptions:

1. That for any research objective "the respondents have a sufficiently common vocabulary so that it is possible to formulate questions which have the same meaning for each of them."[13]
2. That it is possible to phrase all questions in a form that is equally meaningful to each respondent.
3. That if the "meaning of each question is to be identical for each respondent, its context must be identical and, since all preceding questions constitute part of the contexts, the sequence of questions must be identical."[14]

## The Focused Interview

The second basic personal interview form is the *non-schedule-structured* or **focused interview.** This form has four characteristics:[15]

1. It takes place with respondents known to have been involved in a particular experience.
2. It refers to situations that have been analyzed prior to the interview.
3. It proceeds on the basis of an interview guide specifying topics related to the research hypotheses.
4. It is focused on the subjects' experiences regarding the situations under study.

Although the encounter between the interviewer and respondents is structured and the major aspects of the study are explained, respondents are given considerable liberty in expressing their definition of a situation that is presented to them. For example, in her study of women's best friends and marriage, Stacey Oliker employed a focused interview that was "malleable enough to follow emergent leads and standardized enough to register strong patterns."[16] The focused interview

---

13. Stephen Richardson, Barbara S. Dohrenwend, and David Klein, *Interviewing: Its Forms and Functions* (New York: Basic Books, 1965), p. 40.
14. Ibid., p. 43.
15. Robert K. Merton and Patricia L. Kendal, "The Focused Interview," *American Journal of Sociology,* 51 (1946): 541–557.
16. Stacey J. Oliker, *Best Friends and Marriage* (Berkeley: University of California Press, 1989), p. xvi.

permits the researcher to obtain details of personal reactions, specific emotions, and the like. The interviewer, having previously studied the situation, is alert and sensitive to inconsistencies and omissions of data that may be needed to clarify the problem.

## The Nondirective Interview

The most flexible form of personal interviewing is the *nonstructured* or **nondirective interview.** Here the researcher does not employ a schedule to ask a prespecified set of questions, nor are the questions asked in a specified order. With little or no direction from the interviewer, respondents are encouraged to relate their experiences, to describe whatever events seem significant to them, to provide their own definitions of their situations, and to reveal their opinions and attitudes as they see fit. The interviewer has a great deal of freedom to probe various areas and to raise specific queries during the course of the interview. Eleanor Miller's study of female street hustlers is based on such nondirective interviews:[17]

> Seventy women agreed to taped interviews with me during which they shared with me the details of their lives. Special attention was paid to the initiation of these women into street hustling and the development of a career line as a street hustler. Although the same broad topics were introduced during each interview, many of my questions changed over time. Initial taped interviews were played again and again after being recorded. Tentative hypotheses and emergent behavior categories arose out of these hours of listening. During subsequent interviews, . . . I would introduce questions to test these tentative hypotheses.[18]

---

### Exhibit 10.2
### The Schedule-Structured Interview

---

*Interviewer's explanation to the respondent:* We are interested in the kinds of problems teenagers have with their parents. We need to know how many teenagers have conflicts with their parents and what those conflicts are. We have a checklist here of some of the kinds of things that happen. Think about your own situation, and put a check mark to show which conflicts you have had and about how often they have happened. Be sure to put a check in every row. If you have never had such a conflict, put the check in the first column, where it says, "Never."

(Hand respondent the first card dealing with conflicts over the use of the automobile, saying, "If you don't understand any of the things listed or have some other things you would like to mention about how you disagree with your parents over the automobile, let me know and we'll talk about it.")

---

17. Eleanor M. Miller, *Street Woman* (Philadelphia: Temple University Press, 1986).
18. Ibid., p. 26.

**Exhibit 10.2** *(continued)*

| AUTOMOBILE | Never | Only Once | More Than Once | Many Times |
|---|---|---|---|---|
| 1. Wanting to learn to drive | | | | |
| 2. Getting a driver's license | | | | |
| 3. Wanting to use the family car | | | | |
| 4. Using it too much | | | | |
| 5. Keeping the car clean | | | | |
| 6. Repairing the car | | | | |
| 7. Driving someone else's car | | | | |
| 8. Want to own a car | | | | |
| 9. The way you drive your own car | | | | |
| 10. Other | | | | |

(When the respondent finishes all rows, hand him or her card number 2, saying, "Here is a list of types of conflicts teenagers have with their parents over their friends of the same sex. Do the same with this as you did with the last list.")

Adapted from Raymond L. Gorden, *Interviewing: Strategy, Techniques, and Tactics*, 3d. ed. (Homewood, Ill.: Dorsey, 1980), pp. 49–50.

Exhibits 10.2, 10.3 and 10.4 illustrate the differences in interviewing styles in the three types of interviews. All three are concerned with the same research problem. The purpose of the study is to discover the types of conflict between parents and teenagers and the relationship between these conflicts and juvenile crime. The interviews are conducted with two groups of children. One consists of teenagers who have committed no crimes, and the second consists of teenagers who have been known to commit several juvenile crimes.

**Exhibit 10.3**
The Focused Interview

*Instructions to the interviewer:* Your task is to discover as many specific kinds of conflicts and tensions between child and parent as possible. The more *concrete* and detailed the account of each type of conflict, the better. Although there are four areas of possible conflict that we want to explore (listed in question 3 below), you should not mention any area until after you have asked the first two questions in the order indicated. The first question takes an indirect approach, giving you time to build up rapport with the respondent.

1. What sorts of problems do teenagers have in getting along with their parents? (Possible probes: Do they always agree with their parents? Do any of your friends have "problem parents"?)

2. What sort of disagreements do you have with your parents? (Possible probes: Do they cause you any problems? In what way do they try to restrict you? Do they like the same things you do?)
3. Have you ever had any disagreement with either of your parents over:
   a. using the family car?
   b. friends of the same sex?
   c. dating?
   d. smoking?

Adapted from Raymond L. Gorden, *Interviewing: Strategy, Techniques, and Tactics*, 3d ed. (Homewood, Ill.: Dorsey, 1980), pp. 48–49.

---

**Exhibit 10.4**
The Nondirective Interview

---

*Instructions to the interviewer:* Discover the kinds of conflicts that the teenager has had with the parents. Conflicts should include disagreements; tensions due to past, present, or potential disagreements; outright arguments; and physical conflicts. Be alert for as many categories and examples of conflicts and tensions as possible.

Adapted from Raymond L. Gorden, *Interviewing: Strategy, Techniques, and Tactics*, 3d ed. (Homewood, Ill.: Dorsey, 1980), p. 48.

---

An interview may be completely structured or nonstructured, as illustrated in the exhibits. Alternatively, an interview may combine structured and nonstructured elements, depending on the purpose of the study. For example, a researcher may use the schedule-structured interview for most questions but rely on the nondirective format for questions that are particularly sensitive.

---

# Personal Interview versus Mail Questionnaire

## Advantages of the Personal Interview

1. *Flexibility.* The interview allows great flexibility in the questioning process, and the greater the flexibility, the less structured the interview. Some interviews allow the interviewer to determine the wording of the questions, to clarify terms that are unclear, to control the order in which the questions are presented, and to probe for additional information and detail.

2. *Control of the interview situation.* One major advantage of the interview is that it gives the researcher greater control over the interviewing situation. An interviewer can ensure that the respondents answer the questions in the appropriate sequence or that they answer certain questions before they are asked subsequent questions. Moreover, in an interview situation, researchers can standardize the

environment in order to ensure that the interview is conducted in private; thus respondents do not have the opportunity to consult one another before giving their answers. It is also possible to record the exact time and place of the interview; this allows the researcher to interpret the answers more accurately, especially when an event occurring around the time of the interview could have influenced the respondent's answers.[19]

3. *High response rate.* The personal interview results in a higher response rate than the mail questionnaire. Respondents who would not ordinarily take the time to reply to an impersonal mail questionnaire will often respond to a request for a personal interview. This is also true of people who have difficulties reading or writing or do not fully understand the language.

4. *Collection of supplementary information.* An interviewer can collect supplementary information about respondents. This may include background information about the respondents' personal characteristics and their environment that can aid the researcher in interpreting the results. Moreover, an interview situation often yields spontaneous reactions that the interviewer can record and that might be useful in the data analysis stage.

## Disadvantages of the Personal Interview

1. *Higher cost.* The cost of interview studies is significantly higher than that of mail surveys. Costs are involved in selecting, training, and supervising interviewers; in paying them; and in the travel and time required to conduct interviews. Furthermore, the cost of recording and processing the information obtained in nonstructured interviews is especially high.

2. *Interviewer bias.* The very flexibility that is the chief advantage of interviews leaves room for the interviewer's personal influence and bias. The lack of standardization in the data collection process also makes interviewing highly vulnerable to interviewer bias. Although interviewers are instructed to remain objective and to avoid communicating personal views, they nevertheless often give cues that may influence respondents' answers.[20] Even when he or she avoids verbal cues, interviewers can fail to control nonverbal communication. Sometimes even the interviewer's race or gender can influence respondents who may give socially admirable but potentially misleading answers because they are trying to please the interviewer.

3. *Lack of anonymity.* The interview lacks the anonymity of the mail questionnaire. Often the interviewer knows all or many of the potential respondents (or at least their names, addresses, and telephone numbers). Thus respondents may feel threatened or intimidated by the interviewer, especially if a respondent is sensitive to the topic or some of the questions.

19. Bailey, *Methods of Social Research,* p. 174.

20. John B. Williamson, David A. Konk, and John R. Dalphin, *The Research Craft* (Boston: Little, Brown, 1977).

---

### Advantages and Disadvantages of the Personal Interview

**Advantages**

- *Flexibility in the questioning process.* Interviews can range from highly structured to nonstructured depending on the research problem under examination. In focused and nondirective interviews the interviewer can clarify questions and probe for additional information.
- *Control of the interview situation.* Interviewers determine who answers questions, where the interview is conducted, and the order in which questions are answered.
- *High response rate.*
- *Fuller information.* Interviewers are able to collect supplementary information from respondents, including background information and spontaneous reactions.

**Disadvantages**

- *Higher cost.* Interviews can be expensive to implement, especially when respondents are widely dispersed geographically.
- *Interviewer bias.* Innate characteristics of interviewers and differences in interviewer techniques may affect respondents' answers.
- *Lack of anonymity.* The presence of the interviewer may make the respondent feel threatened or intimidated.

---

# Principles of Interviewing

We now turn to a more detailed discussion of the principles and procedures of interviewing. The first step in the interviewing process is getting the respondent to cooperate and to provide the desired information. Three factors help in motivating the respondent to cooperate.[21]

1. *The respondents must feel that their interaction with the interviewer will be pleasant and satisfying.* It is up to interviewers to make respondents feel that they will be understanding and easy to talk to.

2. *The respondents need to see the study as being worthwhile.* The respondents should feel not only that the study may benefit them personally but also that it deals with a significant issue and that their cooperation is important. Interviewers should interest the respondents in the study by pointing out its significance and the contribution that the respondents can make by cooperating.

3. *Barriers to the interview in the respondents' minds need to be overcome.* Interviewers must correct misconceptions. Some respondents may be suspicious of the interviewers, seeing them as salespeople or as representatives of the gov-

---

21. Survey Research Center, *Interviewer's Manual* (Ann Arbor, Mich.: Institute for Social Research, University of Michigan, 1976), p. 3-1.

ernment. The interviewers should explain, in a friendly manner, the purpose of the study, the method of selecting respondents, and the confidential nature of the interview.

The Survey Research Center of the University of Michigan's Institute for Social Research provides some useful pointers on how interviewers should introduce themselves to respondents:[22]

1. Tell the respondent who you are and who you represent.
2. Tell the respondent what you are doing in a way that will stimulate his or her interest.
3. Tell the respondent how he or she was chosen.
4. Adapt your approach to the situation.
5. Try to create a relationship of confidence and understanding (rapport) between yourself and the respondent.

After the initial introduction, the interviewer is ready to begin the interview. There are specific techniques that the interviewer can use in this process:[23]

1. *The questionnaire should be followed, but it can be used informally.*

2. *The interview should be conducted in an informal and relaxed atmosphere, and the interviewer should avoid creating the impression that what is occurring is a cross-examination or a quiz.*

3. *The questions should be asked exactly as worded in the questionnaire.* This is of particular importance, for even slight changes in the way the questions are presented may change the responses. Various studies have shown that even small omissions or changes in the phrasing of questions can distort the results.

4. *Read each question slowly.* Studies have shown the ideal reading pace to be two words per second. A slow pace helps interviewers to enunciate more clearly and allows respondents time to understand the question and formulate an answer.

5. *Questions should be presented in the same order as in the questionnaire.* The researcher has planned the question sequence to provide continuity and to make sure that either the respondents' answers will not be influenced by their responses to previous questions or that each respondent is subject to the same influence.

6. *Ask every question specified in the questionnaire.* Sometimes respondents provide answers to questions before they are asked. When this occurs, the interviewer should still ask the question at the appropriate time while acknowledging the respondent's earlier answer. For example, "I know you answered this question earlier, but. . . ."

7. *Questions that are misinterpreted or misunderstood should be repeated and clarified.* In most cases, respondents will not have any problem interpreting or understanding a question. At most, some people will need more time before they

22. Ibid. (edited slightly).

23. Survey Research Center, *Interviewer's Manual,* rev. ed. (Ann Arbor, Mich.: Institute for Social Research, University of Michigan, 1976), pp. 11–13 (edited slightly).

respond to a particular question. But occasionally, respondents who have language or hearing problems will have difficulties in understanding a question. The interviewer should then repeat the question. Only on rare occasions should the interviewer reword the question, and then only if convinced that otherwise the respondent would misinterpret it.

## Probing

In the *Interviewer's Manual* of the University of Michigan Survey Research Center, **probing** is defined as

> the technique used by the interviewer to stimulate discussion and obtain more information. A question has been asked and an answer given. For any number of reasons, the answer may be inadequate and require the interviewer to seek more information to meet the survey objectives. Probing is the act of getting this additional information.[24]

Probes have two major functions: they motivate the respondent to elaborate on or clarify an answer or to explain the reasons behind the answer, and they help focus the conversation on the specific topic of the interview.

In general, the less structured the interview, the more important probing becomes as an instrument for eliciting and encouraging further information.

The following exchange shows an interviewer probing to elicit additional information by "repeating the respondent's statements without including a direct question." [25]

> RESPONDENT: The main reason I came to Antioch College was because of the combination of high academic standards and the work program. It appealed to me a lot.
> INTERVIEWER: It appealed to you a lot?
> RESPONDENT: That's right.
> INTERVIEWER: Could you tell me a little more exactly why it had this appeal for you?
> RESPONDENT: I don't know—it was just that the place sounded less stuffy and straightlaced than a lot of places with just as good an academic program.
> INTERVIEWER: You don't like places that are stuffy and straightlaced?
> RESPONDENT: You can say that again. A lot of places spend most of their time trying to work out a way of controlling the students, assuming that they are completely incapable of self-control. . . .
> INTERVIEWER: Why do you suppose Antioch has less supervision by the administration?
> RESPONDENT: Well, it is part of the educational philosophy. . . .

24. Survey Research Center, *Interviewer's Manual* (Ann Arbor, Mich.: Institute for Social Research, University of Michigan, 1976), p. 5-1.

25. Raymond L. Gorden, *Interviewing: Strategy, Techniques, and Tactics,* 3d ed. (Homewood, Ill.: Dorsey: 1980), p. 436.

INTERVIEWER: Let me see if I have grasped the whole picture—you like a school with high academic standards, but one that is not too straightlaced and operates on the assumption that college students can exercise self-control. . . .
RESPONDENT: That hits it on the head.

---

# Telephone Interview

The telephone interview, also called the *telephone survey,* can be characterized as a semipersonal method of collecting information. Not too long ago, social scientists viewed telephone surveys with skepticism or outright distrust. Some texts explicitly warned their readers to avoid them.[26] The primary reason for this reluctance to use telephone interviewing was the high likelihood of a serious sampling bias. When a substantial proportion of the population had no access to telephones, the sample tended to overrepresent those who were relatively well-off and could afford a telephone. More recently, however, telephone surveys have gained general acceptance as a legitimate method of data collection in the social sciences.

The main rationale for employing telephone surveys more extensively today is that investigators are able to reach more than nine-tenths of the population. In 1958, only 72.5 percent of U.S. households had access to telephones; by the end of the 1980s, the figure was close to 98 percent. In addition, financial pressures have made the telephone survey more attractive. Increasing salaries and fuel costs make the personal interview extremely costly. In comparison, the telephone is convenient, and it produces a very significant cost saving. Moreover, the telephone interview results in a higher response rate than the personal interview. In some metropolitan areas, people are quite nervous about opening their doors to strangers. Finding respondents at home has also become increasingly difficult with the greater participation of married women in the labor force.

Technological changes and improvements in telephone equipment have also made telephone interviewing easier. It has become possible to draw a random sample of telephone numbers by a process called **random-digit dialing (RDD).** To use this method, the researcher first identifies all working telephone exchanges in the targeted geographic area. He or she then creates a potential telephone number by randomly selecting an exchange and then appending a random number between 0001 and 9999. Additional numbers are created by repeating these two steps. Nonresidential telephones and nonworking numbers are excluded during the interviewing process. Computers have made the process of random-digit dialing faster and easier because they can be programmed to randomly select both the exchange and the final digits, dial the number for the interviewer, and delete from future selections any numbers for which an interview has been completed or those that are nonresidential or nonworking.

---

26. William R. Klecka and Alfred J. Tuchfarber, "Random Digit Dialing: A Comparison to Personal Survey," *Public Opinion Quarterly,* 42 (1978): 105–114. Many details of our discussion derive from this source.

Although the telephone survey provides the obvious advantages of low cost and speed, there remains the question of whether telephone surveys are an alternative to face-to-face interviewing. In the first major experiment designed to answer this question, William Klecka and Alfred Tuchfarber replicated a large, personal interviewing survey by means of an RDD telephone survey.[27] The personal interview survey on crime victimization had been conducted by the U.S. Bureau of the Census in 1974. Klecka and Tuchfarber compared the two samples on demographic-characteristic measures of crime victimization and attitudes toward crime and the police. The results were very similar, indicating that random-digit dialing is an accurate and cost-effective alternative to the personal interview. More recent studies that compared answers to the same questions in mail, telephone, and personal interviews likewise found little difference in their validity.[28]

Aside from its relative accuracy, telephone interviewing tends to increase the quality of the data. In most cases, telephone interviewers are working from a central office, and supervisors can monitor their work constantly. This helps ensure that interviewers are asking the questions correctly and that researchers can identify and correct problems immediately.

One of the latest developments in telephone surveys is the use of computerized questionnaires. In **computer-assisted telephone interviewing (CATI),** the interviewer sits at a computer terminal and, as a question flashes on the screen, asks it over the telephone. The interviewer types and codes the respondents' answers directly on a disk, and the next question then comes up on the screen. Among the advantages of CATI are its speed and the use of complex instructions, programmed in advance. For instance, in good CATI systems, coders are not allowed to input incorrect or out of range scores. The screen prompts them to put in a correct one. However, CATI is not suitable for open-ended questions.[29]

However, the weaknesses of telephone interviewing cannot be ignored. Telephone interviewing has created a new kind of nonresponse—the "broken-off" interview. In about 4 percent of the calls, respondents terminate the interview before it is completed—a rare occurrence in personal interviews.[30] Telephone interviews also produce less information; interviewers cannot describe the respondents' characteristics or their environment in detail. Moreover, proportionately more telephone respondents indicate that they feel uneasy about discussing some topics, especially financial status and political attitudes, over the telephone.

In summary, telephone interviewing should be used as an alternative to personal interviewing under certain circumstances—especially when the interview schedule is relatively simple. However, the question of whether personal and telephone interviews are interchangeable remains to be answered. In the future, most

27. Ibid.
28. Seymour Sudman and Norman M. Bradburn, Asking Questions (San Francisco: Jossey-Bass, 1982).
29. Ibid.
30. Institute for Social Research, University of Michigan, *Newsletter,* 4 (Autumn 1976).

---

### Advantages and Disadvantages of Telephone Interviews

**Advantages**

- *Moderate cost.*
- *Speed.* Telephone interviewers can reach a large number of respondents in a short time. Interviewers can code data directly into computers, which can later compile the data.
- *High response rate.* Telephone interviews provide access to people who might be unlikely to reply to a mail questionnaire or refuse a personal interview.
- *Quality.* High quality data can be collected when interviewers are centrally located and supervisors can ensure that questions are being asked correctly and answers are recorded properly.

**Disadvantages**

- *Reluctance to discuss sensitive topics.* Respondents may be hesitant to discuss some issues over the phone.
- *The "broken-off" interview.* Respondents can terminate the interview before it is completed.
- *Less information.* Interviewers cannot provide supplemental information about the respondents' characteristics or environment.

---

surveys may be conducted totally by telephone; others may combine telephone and personal interviews so that the two can complement each other to provide greater precision and increased response rate.

---

# Comparing the Three Survey Methods

In deciding which survey method is best suited for your research, you have to determine which criteria are most significant to the research objective. For example, if you plan to conduct long interviews with a representative sample of the general population and wish to control for nonverbal behavior, and if sufficient funds are available, a form of a personal interview is preferable.[31] Conversely, if the interview can be simplified, and if funds and speed are concerns, the telephone survey can be used to collect the information. If you are using a rather lengthy questionnaire or one that includes threatening or sensitive questions, and especially if the population to be investigated is relatively dispersed geographically or is a selective population, the mail questionnaire can be considered as an alternative.

Table 10.3 presents some of the comparative advantages and limitations of the three methods of survey research.

---

31. A sample is representative if the measurements made on its units produce results equivalent to those that would be obtained had the entire population been measured. See Chapter 8.

**Table 10.3**
Evaluation of Three Survey Methods

| Criterion | Personal Interview | Mail | Telephone |
|---|---|---|---|
| Cost | High | Low | Moderate |
| Response Rate | High | Low | High |
| Control of interview situation | High | Low | Moderate |
| Applicability to geographically dispersed populations | Moderate | High | Moderate |
| Applicability to heterogeneous populations | High | Low | High |
| Collection of detailed information | High | Moderate | Moderate |
| Speed | Low | Low | High |

# Conclusion

The survey method is one of the most important data collection methods in the social sciences, and as such it is used extensively to collect information on numerous subjects of research. In recent years, with public demands for government accountability, the emphasis on survey instruments has increased. Survey research is becoming a widely used tool of various government organizations. Studies of local governments indicate that 50 percent of cities with populations over 100,000 and counties with populations over 250,000 have used some form of survey. With the growth in the number of surveys conducted, the method has become the subject of increased criticism. Comments such as "Getting things right in social science research is not easy," "The sample of potential respondents was a hodgepodge of various procedures," and "I wouldn't trust any survey with a response rate like that," are typical. Although sometimes these remarks are justified, often they are not based on facts and simply pay "lip service" to the spirit of criticism. Yet there is no denying that we need a set of criteria that will help us evaluate the usefulness of surveys, detect and control errors in them, and compensate for these errors wherever possible.[32]

Half a century ago, Edward Deming wrote an article, now a classic, called "On Errors in Surveys."[33] In this article, Deming lists 13 potential errors researchers should consider when planning a survey and evaluating its results. The most important factors that might become potential errors in surveys were discussed in this chapter: interviewer bias, low response rate, and difficulty in asking sensitive questions. Reuben Cohen made the following remarks regarding these

32. Gregory Daneke and Patricia Klobus Edwards, "Survey Research for Public Administrators," *Public Administration Review,* 39 (1979): 421–426.
33. W. Edward Deming, *Some Theory of Sampling* (New York: Wiley, 1950).

potential errors in a presidential address to the American Association for Public Opinion Research:

> Some 30 years ago, I was handed a reprint of W. Edward Deming's list of errors in surveys. The message was pretty obvious: Now that you know about them don't make them. With my relative inexperience, and my eternal optimism, I accepted the challenge. My first approach was to try to do the perfect survey. I am still trying, but I should know better. I quickly discovered Murphy's Law—if anything can go wrong, it probably will. But I also discovered something else. Even without the time and budget constraints that most of us complain about, there are no perfect surveys. Every survey has its imperfections. The world is not ideally suited to our work. The best we can do is think through the ideal approach to a survey design, or implementation, or analysis problem—what we would do if we had our druthers—then get as close to the ideal as we can within the constraints of time and budget which govern much of our work.[34]

And to readers who might be discouraged by these less than perfect goals, we offer the following advice:

> Practical work consists in good part of guessing what irregularities, where, and how much one can afford to tolerate. . . . The same is true for survey research. It should be done well. It can and should conform well, even if not perfectly, to an ideal approach.[35]

## Summary

**1.** In this chapter, we discussed the survey as a method of data collection. Three methods were described: the mail questionnaire, the face-to-face interview, and the telephone interview.

**2.** The mail questionnaire is an impersonal survey method. Its major advantages are low cost, relatively small biasing error, anonymity, and accessibility. Its disadvantages are a low response rate, no opportunity for probing, and lack of control over who fills out the questionnaire.

**3.** Because of the difficulty of securing an acceptable response rate to mail questionnaires, researchers use various strategies that are known to increase the response rate. Among those, the most effective are the use of follow-up mailings, sponsorship of the survey, and the appeal of the questionnaire. The format of the questionnaire and the methods of mailing an investigator uses will also affect the response rate.

**4.** The personal interview is a face-to-face situation in which an interviewer asks respondents questions designed to obtain answers pertinent to the research hypotheses. The schedule-structured interview is the most structured form. The

---

34. Reuben Cohen, "Close Enough for All Practical Purposes," *Public Opinion Quarterly,* 43 (1979): 421–422.
35. Ibid., p. 424.

questions, their wording, and their sequence are fixed and identical for every respondent. The focused interview follows an interview guide specifying topics related to the research hypothesis. It gives respondents considerable liberty to express their views. Finally, nondirective interviews are the least structured, employing no prespecified set of questions. The interviewer has a great deal of freedom to probe various areas and to raise specific queries during the course of the interview.

5. Telephone interviewing has gained general acceptance as a substitute for personal interviewing. The telephone survey is convenient and cost-effective. In addition, it sometimes results in a higher response rate than the personal interview. Technological changes and improvements in telephone equipment have also made telephone interviewing easier, especially when researchers use random-digit dialing and computer-assisted telephone interviewing.

---

## Key Terms for Review

computer-assisted telephone
   interviewing (CATI) (p. 243)
focused interview (p. 234)
follow-up (p. 229)
mail questionnaire (p. 225)

nondirective interview (p. 235)
probing (p. 241)
random-digit dialing (RDD) (p. 242)
response rate (p. 226)
schedule-structured interview (p. 232)

---

## Study Questions

1. Describe the basic techniques of survey data collection.
2. Discuss the advantages and disadvantages of mail questionnaires, telephone interviews, and personal interviews.
3. List and describe the basic principles of interviewing.
4. What type of survey research would you use to study drug users? Defend the logic of your choice.
5. Suppose you are engaged in a research project to determine the attitudes in a small town toward welfare. You are planning to use a mailed questionnaire, and you have chosen a sample. Write the cover letter.

---

## Additional Readings

Babbie, Earl. *Survey Research Methods.* Belmont, Calif.: Wadsworth, 1990.
Backstrom, Charles, and Gerald Hursh. *Survey Research.* 2d ed. New York: Wiley, 1981.
Bainbridge, William Sims. *Survey Research: A Computer-assisted Introduction.* Belmont, Calif.: Wadsworth, 1989.
Banaka, William H. *Training in Depth Interviewing.* New York: Harper & Row, 1971.

Call, Vaughn, Luther B. Otto, and Kenneth 1. Spenner. *Tracking Respondents: A Multi-method Approach.* Lexington, Mass.: Lexington Books, 1982.

Cannell, Charles F., P. V. Miller, and L. Oksenberg. "Research on Interviewing Techniques." In *Sociological Methodology,* ed. Reinhardts. San Francisco: Jossey-Bass, 1981.

Converse, Jean M. *Survey Research in the United States.* Los Angeles: University of California Press, 1987.

De Vaus, D. A. *Survey in Social Research.* London: Allen & Unwin, 1986.

Dillman Don A., Kristen K. West, and Jon R. Clark. "Influence of an Invitation to Answer by Telephone on response to Census Questionnaires." *Public Opinion Quarterly,* 58 (1994): 557–569.

Fowler, Floyd J., Jr. *Survey Research Methods.* Newbury Park, Calif.: Sage, 1989.

Frey, James H. *Survey Research by Telephone.* Newbury Park, Calif: Sage, 1983.

Gorden, Raymond L. *Interviewing: Strategy, Techniques, and Tactics.* 3d ed. Homewood, Ill.: Dorsey, 1980.

Groves, Robert M., "Theories and Methods of Telephone Surveys," In *Annual Review of Sociology,* vol 16, ed. W. Richard Scott and Judith Blake. Palo Alto, Calif.: Annual Reviews, Inc., 1990, pp. 221–240.

Hyman, Herbert H., and Eleanor Singer. *Taking Society's Measure: A Personal History of Survey Research.* New York: Russell Sage Foundation, 1991.

Jolliffe, F. R. *Survey Design and Analysis.* London: Ellis Horwood, 1986.

Marsh, Catherine. *The Survey Method.* London: Allen & Unwin, 1982.

Schuman, Howard, and Graham Kalton. "Survey Method." In *The Handbook of Social Psychology,* 3d ed., ed. Gardner Lindzey and Elliot Aronson. New York: Random House, 1985.

Tocker, C. "Interviewer Effects in Telephone Surveys." *Public Opinion Quarterly,* 47 (1983): 84–95.

Wentland, Ellen J., and Kent W. Smith. *Survey Responses: An Evaluation of Their Validity.* San Diego, Calif.: Academic Press, 1993.

Yammarino, Francis J., Steven J. Skinner, and Terry L. Childers. "Understanding Mail Survey Response Behavior: A Meta-Analysis." *Public Opinion Quarterly,* 55 (1991): 613–640.

# CHAPTER 11

# Questionnaire Construction

**The Question**

**Content of Questions**
Factual Questions
Questions about Subjective Experiences

**Types of Questions**
Closed-Ended and Open-Ended Questions
Contingency Questions

**Question Format**
Rating
Matrix Questions
Semantic Differential
Ranking

**Sequence of Questions**
Funnel Sequence
Inverted Funnel Sequence

**Avoiding Bias: Pitfalls in Questionnaire Construction**
Wording
Response Set
Leading Questions
Threatening Questions
Double-Barreled Questions

**Cover Letter**

**Instructions**

**Constructing a Questionnaire: A Case Study**

How would you answer this question: "Does it seem possible or does it seem impossible to you that the Nazi extermination of the Jews never happened?" How many times did you have to read the question before you could answer it? Are you sure your answer really expresses your belief? If the question confused you, you are not alone. According to an article in the *New York Times,* the responses to this question led researchers at the Roper polling organization to conclude that one in five Americans thought the Holocaust never happened.[1] Was their conclusion correct? Probably not. According to Roper, their effort to provide an unbiased question resulted in such clumsy wording that it confused many respondents and caused them to answer inappropriately. The Gallup organization conducted an independent survey to test the validity of the Roper poll and found that when respondents were presented with a clearer question, less than three percent of Americans doubted the Holocaust happened. Roper has conducted a new poll using a more clearly worded question, and they have publicly apologized for their mistake.

Because the findings of surveys often influence policy decisions that have an impact on people's lives and may be the only source of information on an issue available to the public, survey questions must be carefully constructed and ordered to elicit accurate data. As you will see in this chapter, question construction is not as easy as it may seem.

I N THIS CHAPTER, WE FOCUS ON THE QUESTIONNAIRE AS THE main instrument in survey research. We start by discussing the foundation of all questionnaires—the question. We then look at the content of questions; differentiate between closed-ended, open-ended, and contingency-type questions; and analyze their format and sequencing. Next we explore possible biases in the wording of questions, as well as leading, double-barreled, and threatening questions. Finally, we give important pointers on the cover letter accompanying the questionnaire and the instructions included in it.

---

# The Question

The foundation of all questionnaires is the **question.** The questionnaire must translate the research objectives into specific questions; answers to such questions will provide the data for hypothesis testing. The question must also motivate the respondent to provide the information being sought. The major considerations involved in formulating questions are their content, structure, format, and sequence.

---

1. John Kifner, "Pollster Finds Error on Holocaust Doubts," *New York Times,* May 20, 1994: A12.

# Content of Questions

Survey questions may be concerned with facts, opinions, attitudes, respondents' motivation, and their level of familiarity with a certain subject. Most questions, however, can be classified in either of two general categories: factual questions and questions about subjective experiences.

## Factual Questions

**Factual questions** are designed to elicit objective information from the respondents regarding their backgrounds, environments, habits, and the like. The most common type of factual question is the background question, which is asked mainly to provide information that can be used to classify respondents. Background questions include such items as gender, age, marital status, education, or income. Such classifications may in turn aid in explaining differences in behaviors and attitudes. The following is an example of such a question:

What was the last grade you completed in school? (Please check one.)
____ 8th grade or lower
____ 9th or 10th grade
____ 11th or 12th grade: high school graduate? ___Yes ___No
____ 1 to 2 years of college
____ 3 to 4 years of college: college graduate? ___Yes ___No
____ 5 or more years of college

Other kinds of factual questions are intended to provide information about the respondent's social environment ("Would you please tell me, who are the people living in your household?"), means of transportation ("How do you generally get to work?"), or leisure activities ("How often do you go to the movies?").

People often think that factual questions are easier to design than other types of questions. However, even factual questions can present the researcher with problems. How accurately people report depends on what and how they are being asked. There are four reasons why respondents give less than accurate answers to factual questions:[2]

1. They do not know the information.
2. They cannot recall the information.
3. They do not understand the question.
4. They are reluctant to answer.

The researcher can take several steps to increase accuracy, including encouraging respondents to consult other members of the household, asking more than one question about the matter, repeating questions, and making respondents feel comfortable when asking about events that they may find embarrassing.

2. Floyd J. Fowler, Jr., *Survey Research Methods* (Newbury Park, Calif.: Sage, 1989), p 91.

## Questions about Subjective Experiences

Subjective experience involves the respondents' beliefs, attitudes, feelings, and opinions.[3] Surveys conducted in the social sciences, particularly those designed to explore property-disposition relationships (see Chapter 6), often include questions about attitudes. **Attitudes** are general orientations that can incline a person to act or react in a certain manner when confronted with certain stimuli. Here is an example of a question about attitudes toward abortion. This question is included in the General Social Survey (GSS):

> Please tell me whether or not *you* think it should be possible for a pregnant woman to obtain a *legal* abortion if there is a strong chance of serious defects in the baby.
>
> 1. Yes
> 2. No
> 3. Don't know
> 4. No answer

Individuals express their attitudes through speech or behavior only when they perceive the object of the attitude. A person may have strong attitudes for or against abortion, but these are aroused and conveyed only when that person encounters some issue connected with abortion or is confronted with a stimulus such as a question in an interview.

Attitudes can be described by their content (what the attitude is about), their direction (positive, neutral, or negative feelings about the object or issue in question), and their intensity (an attitude may be held with greater or lesser vehemence). To one person, abortion may be of but passing interest; to another, it may be of great significance and lead that person to join a pro-choice or pro-life organization. The latter person would be expected to agree or disagree more strongly than the former on questions dealing with, say, whether the legislature should pass a constitutional amendment that would make abortion illegal.

In general, we are interested in measuring attitudes because they account for the respondent's general inclination. The study of opinion is of interest only insofar as the opinion is a symbol of an attitude. The main difference between asking for opinions and measuring attitudes is that researchers generally measure an **opinion** by estimating the proportion of the surveyed population that would say they agree with a single opinion statement. They measure attitudes using attitude scales consisting of five to two dozen or more attitude statements, with which the respondent is asked to agree or disagree. An essential requirement of attitude measurement is that such attitude statements be scaled, that is, that the researcher select the statements and put them together from a much larger number of attitude statements according to certain techniques. These techniques are discussed in Chapter 18.

The construction of survey questions about opinions and attitudes presents more problems than survey questions about facts. It is relatively simple to obtain

3. Royce Singleton, Jr., Bruce C. Straits, Margaret M. Straits, and Ronald J. McAllister, *Approaches to Social Research* (Oxford: Oxford University Press, 1988), p. 272.

accurate information on whether a person is married or single. The researcher may reasonably assume that the respondent knows if he or she is married. With opinions or attitudes, researchers cannot always make the assumption that respondents know what they think. Respondents may not have an attitude toward making abortions illegal, or if they do, it might be latent. Moreover, because many attitudes have numerous aspects or dimensions, the respondent may agree with one aspect and disagree with another. This is why attitudes cannot be measured by a single question. For example, if a person strongly disagrees with the statement "Abortions should be available to any woman who wants one," this does not imply a broad antiabortion attitude. This person's view may be different if the woman's life is in danger, if the pregnancy resulted from incest or rape, or if a doctor has determined that the baby will be severely deformed. By using several attitude statements, a researcher can more accurately ascertain both the strength of a respondent's attitude and the conditions under which his or her attitude may change.

Finally, answers to opinion and attitude questions are more sensitive to changes in wording, emphasis, and sequence than answers to factual questions. This reflects, in part, the multidimensionality of many attitudes. Questions presented in different ways sometimes reflect different aspects of the attitude and thus elicit different answers.

---

# Types of Questions

The content of the questions is only one important aspect of constructing survey questionnaires. The researcher must also consider the structure of the questions and the format of the response categories that accompany them. We will discuss three types of question structures: closed-ended questions, open-ended questions, and contingency questions.

## Closed-Ended and Open-Ended Questions

Questions on a questionnaire can be either closed-ended or open-ended. In a **closed-ended question,** respondents are offered a set of answers and asked to choose the one that most closely represents their views. For example, to measure respondents' degree of satisfaction with family life, the General Social Survey—a public opinion poll conducted yearly by the National Opinion Research Council—used the following closed-ended question:

Tell me the number that shows how much satisfaction you get from your family life.

1. A very great deal     6. Very little
2. A great deal     7. None
3. Quite a bit     8. Don't know
4. A fair amount     9. No answer
5. A little

Answers to closed-ended questions can be more elaborate, like the following question taken from a survey about women's and men's attitudes about a woman's place and role.[4]

> Suppose both a husband and wife work at good and interesting jobs and the husband is offered a very good job in another city. Assuming they have no children, which one of these solutions do you think they would be inclined to favor?
>
> - Husband should turn down the job
> - Wife should quit and relocate with husband
> - Husband should take new job and move/wife should keep her job and stay
> - Don't know
> - No answer

Closed-ended questions are easy to ask and quick to answer, they require no writing by either respondent or interviewer, and their analysis is straightforward. Their major drawback is that they may introduce bias, either by forcing the respondent to choose from given alternatives or by offering the respondent alternatives that might not have otherwise come to mind.

**Open-ended questions** are not followed by any kind of specified choice, and the respondents' answers are recorded in full. For instance, the question "What do you personally feel are the most important problems the government in Washington should try to take care of?" is an open-ended question used frequently in questionnaires designed to study public opinion. The virtue of the open-ended question is that it does not force the respondent to adapt to preconceived answers. Once respondents understand the intent of the question, they can express their thoughts freely, spontaneously, and in their own language. If the answers to open-ended questions are unclear, the interviewer may probe by asking the respondent to explain further or to give a rationale for something stated earlier. Open-ended questions enable the interviewer to clear up misunderstandings, and they encourage rapport. However, open-ended questions are difficult to answer and still more difficult to analyze. The researcher has to design a coding frame in order to classify the various answers; in this process, the details of the information provided by the respondent might get lost (see Chapter 14).

The appropriateness of either closed-ended or open-ended questions depends on a number of factors. Some years ago, Paul Lazarsfeld suggested that researchers use the following considerations to determine appropriateness:[5]

1. *The objectives of the questionnaire.* Closed-ended questions are suitable when the researcher's objective is to lead the respondent to express agreement or disagreement with an explicit point of view. When the researcher wishes to learn how the respondent arrived at a particular point of view, an open-ended question is likely to be more appropriate.

---

4. Rita J. Simon and Jean M. Landis, "Report: Women's and Men's Attitudes about a Woman's Place and Role," *Public Opinion Quarterly,* 53 (1989): 265–276.
5. Paul F. Lazarsfeld, "The Controversy over Detailed Interviews: An Offer for Negotiation," *Public Opinion Quarterly,* 8 (1944): 38–60.

2. *The respondent's level of information about the topic in question.* Open-ended questions provide opportunities for the interviewer to ascertain a lack of information on the part of the respondent, whereas closed-ended questions do not. Obviously, it is futile to raise questions that are beyond the experiences of respondents.

3. *The extent to which the topic has been thought through by the respondent.* The open-ended question is preferable in situations where respondents have not yet crystallized their opinions. Using a closed-ended question in such situations involves the risk that in accepting one of the alternatives offered, respondents may make a choice that is quite different from the opinion they would otherwise have expressed had they gone through the process of recalling and evaluating their past experiences.

4. *The ease with which respondents can communicate the content of the answer or the extent to which respondents are motivated to communicate on the topic.* The closed-ended question requires less motivation to communicate on the part of the respondent, and the response itself is usually less revealing (and hence less threatening) than in the case of the open-ended question. The researcher who uses closed-ended questions tends to encounter refusals to respond less frequently.

Sometimes there may be good reasons for asking the same question in both open-ended and closed-ended form. For example, an open-ended answer to the question "Who rules America?" will provide a clear idea of the respondent's perception of the political system and the significance that the person attaches to different power groups. Although this datum is most valuable, it might not allow the researcher to compare one group of respondents with another. Furthermore, the researcher cannot be sure that the respondent has mentioned all information of importance; factors such as the inability to articulate thoughts or a momentary lapse of memory may cause the respondent to omit significant points. Therefore, the researcher can ask the same question again, later in the interview, but this time in closed-ended form.

## Contingency Questions

Frequently, questions that are relevant to some respondents may be irrelevant to others. For example, the question "Check the most important reasons why you will be going to college" obviously applies only to high school students who are planning to go to college. It is often necessary to include questions that might apply only to some respondents and not to others. Some questions may be relevant only to females and not to males, others will apply only to respondents who are self-employed, and so on.

A **contingency question**—a special-case closed-ended question—applies only to a subgroup of respondents. The investigator determines the relevance of the question to this subgroup by asking all respondents a preceding **filter question.** For example, in a news media survey, the filter question might read, "Do you regularly follow the news in the papers?" The contingency question could be, "What recent event do you remember reading about? (Give a brief description.)" The relevance of the second question to the respondent is contingent on his or her response to the filter question. Only respondents who answered "Yes" to the filter question will find the contingency question relevant. Therefore, the response categories of the filter questions will be "1. Yes (answer the following question); 2. No (skip to question 3)."

The formats for filter and contingency questions vary. One alternative is to write directions next to each response category of the filter question. Another common format is to use arrows to direct the respondent either to skip to another question or to answer the contingency question, as in the following example:

Is this the first full-time job you have held since you graduated from college?

   1. Yes
   2. No————⌐

What happened to the job you had before—were you promoted, laid off, or what? (Check one.)

     1. Company folded
     2. Laid off or fired
     3. Job stopped; work was seasonal
     4. Quit voluntarily
     5. Promoted; relocated
     6. Other

---

### Exhibit 11.1
Contingency Question

---

ANSWER QUESTIONS BELOW IF YOU ARE A SENIOR PLANNING TO GO TO COLLEGE NEXT FALL. NONSENIORS SKIP TO QUESTION 144.

137. Did you take the College Entrance Board Exams?
     _____ yes
     _____ no

138. Do you definitely know which college you will attend?
     _____ yes
     _____ no

---

Another format is to box the contingency question and set it apart from the ordinary questions to be answered by everybody. An example of such a format appears in Exhibit 11.1. When the questionnaire is addressed to several subgroups and several contingency questions apply to each subgroup, it is useful to indicate by number which questions the respondent should answer. The instructions are written next to the appropriate response categories in the filter question. This is demonstrated in the following example:

---

**Three Types of Questions**

- *Closed-Ended Questions:* Respondents are given a set of responses and asked to choose the one that most closely describes their attribute or attitude.
- *Open-Ended Questions:* Respondents are not given a specific set of responses. They are asked to describe their attributes or attitudes in their own words, and their answers are recorded in full either by the respondent or by an interviewer.
- *Contingency Questions:* A type of closed-ended question applicable to a subgroup of respondents. The subgroup may be identified by a filter question, which directs them to answer other relevant questions, or instructions may be provided that direct members of the subgroup to answer a question or set of questions and nonsubgroup members to skip to another question.

---

22. Are you looking for another job at this time?

_____ yes
_____ no
_____ don't know     } Go to question 25.
_____ inappropriate

With computer-assisted telephone interviewing (CATI), the computer is pre-programmed to do the skipping automatically. If a respondent answered "no," "don't know," or "inappropriate" to the preceding question, question 25 would automatically appear on the screen.

---

# Question Format

Researchers use several common techniques to structure the response categories of closed-ended questions. The general format is to present all possible answers and have the respondents choose the appropriate categories. The respondents can either circle or write the number of the answer or check a box or a blank, as shown here:

What is your marital status?

| | | | | | |
|---|---|---|---|---|---|
| _____ Married | | ☐ Married | | 1. Married |
| _____ Single | *or* | ☐ Single | *or* | 2. Single |
| _____ Divorced | | ☐ Divorced | | 3. Divorced |
| _____ Widowed | | ☐ Widowed | | 4. Widowed |

Of course, respondents need specific directions as to whether they are to circle a number or check a blank or a box. Among the three methods shown, the least recommended is the one with blanks because respondents may check between the blanks, making it difficult to tell which category was intended. Circling a code number is preferable because the code number can be easily transferred to a computerized storage device.

## Rating

One of the most common formats for questions asked in social science surveys is the rating scale. Researchers use a **rating** scale whenever they ask respondents to make a judgment in terms of sets of ordered categories, such as "strongly agree," "favorable," or "very often"; for example:

> Police should be allowed to conduct a full search of any motorist arrested for an offense such as speeding.
>
>   1. Agree strongly
>   2. Agree
>   3. Neither agree nor disagree
>   4. Disagree
>   5. Disagree strongly

The response categories of such questions are termed **quantifiers;** they reflect the *intensity* of the particular judgment involved. The following sets of response categories are quite common:

| | | |
|---|---|---|
| 1. Strongly agree | 1. Too little | 1. More |
| 2. Agree | 2. About right | 2. Same |
| 3. Depends | 3. Too much | 3. Less |
| 4. Disagree | | |
| 5. Strongly disagree | | |

The numerical codes that accompany these categories are usually interpreted to represent the intensity of the response categories, so that the higher the number, the more intense the response. Although we assume that the quantifiers involved are ordered by intensity, this ordering does not imply that the distance between the categories is equal. Indeed, rating scales such as these are most often measured on ordinal levels, which only describe whether one level is higher or lower than another level but do not indicate how much higher or lower, as discussed in Chapter 7.

Despite the difficulty in estimating intensities, we cannot typically ask respondents for exact responses because most of them would find this task to be very difficult. Although most respondents would find it relatively easy to report how many hours of television they had watched in the past week, they would find it much more difficult to give exact responses to questions dealing with issues that have low salience to them, such as attitudes about foreign policy.[6]

## Matrix Questions

The **matrix question** is a method of organizing a large set of rating questions that have the same response categories. The following is an example of such a device:

6. Norman M. Bradburn and Seymour Sudman, *Improving Interview Method and Questionnaire Design* (San Francisco: Jossey-Bass, 1974), pp. 152–162.

Indicate your reaction to each of the following statements.

| | I strongly agree | I agree | It depends | I disagree | I strongly disagree |
|---|---|---|---|---|---|
| My vote gives me all the power I want in governmental affairs. | ☐ | ☐ | ☐ | ☐ | ☐ |
| If I complained to the people at a city agency, they would fix up whatever was wrong. | ☐ | ☐ | ☐ | ☐ | ☐ |
| I've sometimes wished that government officials paid more attention to what I thought. | ☐ | ☐ | ☐ | ☐ | ☐ |

## Semantic Differential

The **semantic differential** is another type of rating scale. It measures the respondents' reaction to some object or concept by asking them to indicate a rating on a bipolar scale defined by contrasting adjectives at each end:[7]

| | Very | Fairly | Slightly | Neither | Slightly | Fairly | Very | |
|---|---|---|---|---|---|---|---|---|
| Good | ___ | ___ | ___ | ___ | ___ | ___ | ___ | Bad |

The question below is an example of an application of the semantic differential:[8]

Here is a list of pairs of words you might use to describe civil servants. Between each pair is a measuring stick of seven lines. Taking the first pair of words—i.e., "good/bad"—as an example, the line on the extreme left would mean that the civil servant is very good, the next line would mean he or she is fairly good, and so on. The words at the top of your card will help you choose the line you think is appropriate.

Now will you tell me which line you would use to describe civil servants?

| | Very | Fairly | Slightly | Neither | Slightly | Fairly | Very | |
|---|---|---|---|---|---|---|---|---|
| Good | ___: | ___: | ___: | ___: | ___: | ___: | ___: | Bad |
| Honest | ___: | ___: | ___: | ___: | ___: | ___: | ___: | Dishonest |
| Efficient | ___: | ___: | ___: | ___: | ___: | ___: | ___: | Inefficient |
| Deep | ___: | ___: | ___: | ___: | ___: | ___: | ___: | Shallow |
| Active | ___: | ___: | ___: | ___: | ___: | ___: | ___: | Passive |

7. David R. Heise, "The Semantic Differential and Attitude Research," in *Attitude Measurement*, ed. Gene F. Summers (Skokie, Ill.: Rand McNally, 1970), p. 235.

8. David Nachmias and David H. Rosenbloom, *Bureaucratic Culture: Citizens and Administrators in Israel* (New York: St. Martin's Press, 1978), pp. 110–115.

## Ranking

Researchers use **ranking** in questionnaires whenever they want to obtain information regarding the degree of importance or the priorities that people give to a set of attitudes or objects. For instance, in a survey on the quality of life, respondents were asked to rank various dimensions they consider important.

> "I would like you to tell me what you have found important in life. Please look at this card and tell me which of these is most important to *you* as a goal in *your* life, which comes next in importance, which is third, and which ranks fourth."

|  | Rank | | | |
|---|---|---|---|---|
| A prosperous life (having a good income and being able to afford the good things in life) | 1 | 2 | 3 | 4 |
| A family life (a life completely centered on my family) | 1 | 2 | 3 | 4 |
| An important life (a life of achievement that brings me respect and recognition) | 1 | 2 | 3 | 4 |
| A secure life (making certain that all basic needs and expenses are provided) | 1 | 2 | 3 | 4 |

Ranking is a useful device because it provides some sense of relative order among objects or judgments. This is particularly important because many properties that social scientists measure (for example, "quality of life," "status") cannot be given any precise numerical value. However, with the use of ranking we can at least obtain information regarding their relative order. As with rating scales, however, ranking does not provide any information about the distance between the ranks. The difference between rank 1 and rank 2 may not be the same as the difference between rank 2 and rank 3.

---

# Sequence of Questions

After the researcher has determined the question format, he or she must consider the order in which the questions are placed on the questionnaire. Researchers have found two general patterns of question sequence that are most appropriate for motivating respondents to cooperate: the *funnel sequence* and the *inverted funnel sequence.*

## Funnel Sequence

In the funnel sequence, each successive question is related to the previous question and has a progressively narrower scope. For example, if you were interested in finding out how respondents' views of political, economic, and social problems are related to the newspapers they read, you might want to know what sorts of issues the respondents think of as problems, what the perceived relative significance of each problem is, how much information they have on the topic, what their sources of information are, and whether certain newspapers have influenced their thinking on the problem. The following questions form a funnel sequence:

1. What do you think are some of the most important problems facing the nation?
2. Of all the problems you have just mentioned, which do you think is the most important one?
3. Where have you obtained most of your information about this problem?
4. Do you read the *Washington Post?*

When the objective of the survey is to obtain detailed information and when the respondent is motivated to supply that information, the funnel approach helps the respondent recall details more efficiently. Furthermore, by asking the broadest questions first, the researcher can avoid imposing a frame of reference before obtaining the respondent's perspective. When the objective of the survey is to discover unanticipated responses, interviewers should pursue broader questions first.[9]

## Inverted Funnel Sequence

In the inverted funnel sequence, narrower questions are followed by broader ones. When the topic of the survey does not strongly motivate the respondents to communicate—either because the topic is not important to them or because their experiences are not recent enough to be vivid in their memories—it may be helpful to begin with the narrow questions, which are easier to answer, and reserve the broader (and more difficult) ones until later. If the purpose is to obtain a generalization in the form of a judgment regarding a concrete situation and if the researcher is unfamiliar with the facts but the respondent knows them, narrower questions aimed at establishing specific facts should precede questions requiring an overall judgment.[10]

In the following example, the researcher is attempting to obtain the respondents' judgment regarding the effectiveness of rescue operations during a disaster. To help people make an unbiased judgment, the researcher felt that it was better to deal with the specifics first, asking for the generalization later.[11]

1. How many people were killed in the tornado?
2. How many do you suppose were injured so seriously that they had to go to the hospital?
3. How long was it before most of the injured got to the hospital?
4. Did you see anyone administer first aid by giving artificial respiration or stopping bleeding? Who was it?
5. In general, how well do you think the first aid and rescue operations were carried out?

9. Raymond L. Gorden, *Interviewing: Strategy, Techniques, and Tactics,* 3d. ed. (Homewood, Ill.: Dorsey, 1980), pp. 415–416.
10. Ibid.
11. Ibid.

Studies have shown that the order in which the questions are presented affects the type of response given. For example, there is evidence that answers to attitude questions in surveys can vary markedly, depending on the preceding items in the questionnaire. In a recent study, more than 1,100 respondents were asked about target issues such as abortion, defense spending, and welfare.[12] In one version of the questionnaire, target questions were preceded by related context questions; in others, the target questions were preceded by neutral questions. For example, the abortion target question "Do you favor or oppose the Supreme Court's decision that legalized abortion?" was preceded in the first version by a number of context questions about traditional values and rape. Respondents were generally affected by related context questions, especially when they held conflicting beliefs about the target issue. There is also evidence that the position of an item in a list has a significant impact on its being chosen. Respondents most often choose items that appear first on the list.[13] It has been shown, too, that when respondents are asked to assign numerical values to a set of items (for example, according to their degree of importance), items appearing first tend to receive a higher rank.

In the following question, respondents are more likely to assign the first rank to the first category than to the last one simply because it is listed first.

> Among the items below, what does it take to get to be important and looked up to by the other students here at school? (Rank from 1 to 6.)
>
> _____ Coming from the right family
> _____ Leader in activities
> _____ Having a nice car
> _____ High grades, honor roll
> _____ Being an athletic star
> _____ Being popular

This problem may arise especially in situations where the questions are subjective statements like attitudes, which are not central or salient to the respondent. In such situations, the item appearing first tends to form a point of reference for all items that follow. Researchers can overcome this problem by acquainting respondents with the list of items before respondents are asked to evaluate them. Alternatively, researchers can randomize the order of presentation so that the order effects will be randomized, too, and will not result in any systematic bias.[14]

Finally, questions that are presented first in the questionnaire should put the respondent at ease; the initial questions in an interview should help create rapport between the interviewer and the respondent. Thus the opening question should be easy to answer, interesting, and noncontroversial. For example, questions about

12. Roger Tourangeau, Kenneth A. Rasinski, Norman M. Bradburn, and Roy D'Andrade, "Carryover Effects in Attitude Surveys," _Public Opinion Quarterly,_ 53 (1989): 495–524.

13. William A. Belson, "The Effects of Reversing the Presentation Order on Verbal Rating Scales," _Journal of Advertising Research,_ 6:4 (1966): 30–37.

14. Edwin H. Carpenter and Larry G. Blackwood, "The Effects of Question Position on Responses to Attitudinal Questions," _Rural Sociology,_ 44 (1979): 56–72.

the respondent's drinking habits or sex life, if placed at the beginning, will in all likelihood increase the refusal rate. It is also recommended that open-ended questions be placed later, for they usually require more time and thought and thus may reduce the respondent's initial motivation to cooperate if they appear at the beginning.

---

# Avoiding Bias:
# Pitfalls in Questionnaire Construction

## Wording

The question must be worded so that the respondent understands it. For example, the researcher's vocabulary might include a word such as *synthesize* that might not be understood by most other people. If the respondents come from all walks of life, the interviewer should use words that can be understood by the average sixth grader. Furthermore, researchers should either avoid or qualify words that are open to interpretation. For example, the question "Are you a liberal?" is too broad. You might be referring to the person's education, politics, profession, or sex life. But a question such as "Do you consider yourself liberal? Politically, I mean," instructs the respondent to use the political frame of reference in answering the question. Each question should be worded so that the respondent understands its meaning and so that the question has the same meaning to each respondent.

## Response Set

A *response set* is the tendency to answer all questions in a specific direction regardless of their content.[15] This problem may arise when a set of questions is presented together with the same response format, especially when the questions all refer to the same topic. For example, if a set of questions reflects a pro-choice attitude regarding abortion, respondents who are against abortion may check all the same response categories (for example, all "strongly disagree," or all "strongly agree") simply because they assume that these categories all express objection to abortion. Investigators can avoid creating a response set by changing the question format, either by varying the response categories for each question or by distributing questions on a topic throughout the questionnaire instead of placing them all together.

## Leading Questions

A **leading question** is a question phrased in such a manner that it seems to the respondent that the researcher expects a certain answer. A question designed to elicit general attitudes toward legal abortions might read, "Do you favor or oppose

---

15. Kenneth D. Bailey, *Methods of Social Research* (New York: Free Press, 1987), p. 133.

legal abortions?" The same question phrased in leading form might read, "You wouldn't say that you were in favor of legal abortion, would you?" A more subtle form of leading question might be, "Would you say that you are not in favor of legal abortions?" This last question makes it easier for respondents to answer yes than no because most people feel more comfortable agreeing with the language of the question and not contradicting the interviewer.

Respondents also tend to agree with statements that support accepted norms or that are perceived as socially desirable. Respondents endorse statements that reflect socially undesirable behavior or attitudes less frequently than those high on the scale of social desirability. Similarly, the way that issues are labeled and enhanced can have a substantial effect on public support for some issues. Analyses of variations in question wording in the General Social Survey showed significant differences in responses when the same issue was labeled differently. For example, when a question on welfare spending read "Are we spending too much, too little, or about the right amount on welfare?" 23 percent said too little. But when the question was worded "Are we spending too much, too little, or about the right amount on assistance to the poor?" almost 63 percent said too little.[16]

A 1994 ABC/*Washington Post* poll contained the following question: "Is Clinton an old-style, tax-and-spend Democrat or a new-style Democrat who will be careful with the nation's money?" In a criticism of the national press, Jeff Faux points out that this question is both biased and leading.[17] Because the question labels liberals negatively and conservatives positively, it suggests that if the respondent is dissatisfied with Clinton's performance, it must be because he or she is an old-style liberal Democrat. A more value-free question, such as "Is Clinton a liberal Democrat or a conservative Democrat?" might elicit a different response.

Researchers who are looking for undistorted responses should avoid leading questions. Under certain circumstances, however, leading questions may serve the research objective. The question "Would you favor sending food overseas to feed the starving people of India?" was used to determine the number of people who were so strongly opposed to shipping food to other countries that they rejected the idea even within the strong emotional context of "starving people."[18]

## Threatening Questions

Often it is necessary to include questions on topics that the respondent may find embarrassing and thus difficult to answer. Such **threatening questions** are, according to Norman Bradburn and coauthors, "anxiety-arousing questions about, for example, behaviors that are illegal or contra-normative or about behaviors that,

16. Kenneth A. Radinski, "The Effect of Question Wording on Public Support for Government Spending," *Public Opinion Quarterly,* 53 (1989): 388–394.

17. Jeff Faux, "Hey, Big Spender." *The Nation,* 31 Oct, 1994: 480.

18. Robert I. Kahn and Charles F. Cannell, *The Dynamics of Interviewing* (New York: Wiley, 1957), p. 129.

though not socially deviant, are not usually discussed in public without some tension."[19] Threatening questions may inquire about such subjects as the respondents' gambling habits, drinking, or sexual preferences.

There is considerable empirical evidence that threatening questions lead to response bias—respondents either deny the behavior in question or underreport it. In general, as the degree of threat in a question increases, respondents' tendency to report certain behaviors decreases. When they are presented with a threatening question, respondents are caught in a conflict between the role demands of the "good respondent," who responds truthfully to all the questions, and the tendency for people to present themselves positively. Respondents usually resolve the conflict not by refusing to answer but by reporting that they did not engage in the particular activity when, in fact, they did.[20]

Because threatening questions may elicit biased responses, it is important for researchers to first determine whether or not certain questions are threatening. Norman Bradburn and Seymour Sudman suggest that the best method for determining the relative threat of questions is by asking respondents to rate question topics as to how uneasy they thought most people would feel in talking about them.[21] Interviewers can also ask respondents about their reactions to the questions or rate the degree of difficulty the topics caused in the interview.

Once researchers have identified threatening questions, what should they do about them? In a comprehensive study dealing with response effects to threatening questions in survey research, Bradburn and Sudman determined that the way questions are constructed makes a great deal of difference.[22] Perhaps their most significant finding was that the accuracy of the response is considerably increased by using a long introduction to the question rather than asking short questions, by employing an open-ended rather than a closed-ended format, and, to a lesser extent, by letting the respondents choose their own words when talking about sensitive topics. Bradburn and Sudman's questionnaire contained an item about the number of times in the past year the respondent had become intoxicated. In the short, closed form, the item read: "In the past year, how often did you become intoxicated while drinking any kind of beverage?" Respondents were asked to classify their response into one of the following categories: never, once a year or less, every few months, once a month, every few weeks, once a week, several times a week, and daily. In the open-ended, long form, the respondents were first asked to provide their own word for intoxication: "Sometimes people drink a little too much beer, wine, or whiskey so that they act different from usual. What word do you think we should use to describe people when they get that way, so that you will know what we mean and feel comfortable talking about it?" The intoxication

19. Norman M. Bradburn, Seymour Sudman, Ed Blair, and Carol Stocking, "Question Threat and Response Bias," *Public Opinion Quarterly,* 42 (1978): 221–222.
20. Ibid., pp. 221–234.
21. Bradburn and Sudman, *Improving Interview Method and Questionnaire Design,* p. 165.
22. Ibid., pp. 14–25.

item then read: "Occasionally people drink on an empty stomach or drink a little too much and become (respondent's word). In the past year, how often have you become (respondent's word) while drinking any kind of alcoholic beverage?" No response categories were provided for these questions.[23]

## Double-Barreled Questions

**Double-barreled questions** combine two or more questions in one. Here is an example from an opinion poll about domestic violence:

> Domestic violence and AIDS are the most serious problems facing America today.
>
> _____ Agree        _____ Disagree
> _____ Depends       _____ Strongly disagree

The problem with such a question is that it might confuse respondents who agree with one aspect of the question—say, domestic violence—but disagree with the other, AIDS. Many questions that contain _and_ are very likely doubled-barreled. Questions with _and_ can be used, however, if the dimensions separated by _and_ are mutually exclusive and the respondent is asked to select one or to rank them according to some criterion, for instance:

> At the present time, the country is faced with two major problems: the environment and domestic violence. Which of these two problems would you say is the more important?
>
> _____ The environment
> _____ Domestic violence

# Cover Letter

After the researcher has constructed the questionnaire, the next step is to write an introductory statement (for a personal or telephone interview) or a cover letter (for a mail questionnaire) to explain the purpose of the survey to the respondents and to encourage a high response rate. The content of the cover letter is particularly important in mail questionnaires, where the difficulty of securing a high response rate, especially when the researcher needs to ask more than a few simple questions, is well documented (see Chapter 10).

A cover letter must succeed in overcoming any resistance or prejudice the respondent may have against the survey. It should (1) identify the sponsoring organization or the persons conducting the study, (2) explain the purpose of the study, (3) tell why it is important that the respondent answer the questionnaire, and (4) assure the respondent that the information provided will be held in strict confidence.

23. Ibid., p 18.

In general, the cover letter for a mail questionnaire needs to be more detailed than the introductory statement in a personal interview. In an interview, the interviewer is always there to explain or persuade the respondent should that become necessary. With a mail questionnaire, the cover letter is all there is, and thus its function is very significant.

Two examples of cover letters used in various mail surveys are presented here. The first, shown in Exhibit 11.2, was used with a mail questionnaire designed by the Institute of Social Research at Florida State University under the auspices of the State Department of Manpower Planning of Florida to evaluate the Public Service Employment and Training Act, Title VI (CETA).[24]

---

**Exhibit 11.2**
Florida Questionnaire Cover Letter

---

To Program Operators:

The Office of Manpower Planning, Department of Community Affairs, in conjunction with the State Manpower Services Council, has funded a special evaluation of public service employment projects authorized under Title VI of the Comprehensive Employment and Training Act. This evaluation is being conducted by Dr. M. L. Burnim in the Institute for Social Research at Florida State University. The purpose of the evaluation is to determine the impact of public service employment projects on unemployed persons in Florida and to measure the benefit of these projects to the communities in which they are conducted.

As you know, public service employment is a major part of the federal, state, and local strategy to overcome the employment and income problems of economically disadvantaged, unemployed people. There is no question that the program is needed throughout the country to create jobs and training opportunities for the large numbers of people who remain unemployed. You are probably also aware, however, that public service employment programs are quite controversial and their future may be in jeopardy. Part of the reason that these programs are so controversial is that no systematic evaluation of the benefits of these programs for the individuals employed and the communities served has been conducted.

Because this specific evaluation has significant national policy implications, I strongly urge you to assist the research team in compiling the necessary data. It is very important that you complete the survey questionnaire transmitted to you as soon as possible.

Thank you for your cooperation.

Sincerely,

Edward A. Feaver, Director
Office of Manpower Planning

---

24. Mickey L. Burnim, *An Evaluation of the Public Service Employment Projects in Florida Created under Title VI of the Comprehensive Employment and Training Act of 1973* (Tallahassee: Florida State University, 1978), p. 164.

---

## Exhibit 11.3
### Wisconsin Questionnaire Cover Letter

---

Dear Friend:

We are conducting a survey sponsored by the University of Wisconsin-Milwaukee and assisted by the American Civil Liberties Union (ACLU). Our purpose is to learn more about how people like yourself feel about certain aspects of civil liberties and how beliefs are related to behavior. You have been selected at random to participate in this survey—thus your opinions will represent the opinions of thousands of people much like yourself.

Enclosed find a copy of our questionnaire. While it is a bit lengthy and will require about 20 minutes to complete, we hope that you will take the time to complete it and return the questionnaire to us in the enclosed self-addressed envelope. The information you provide will contribute to an important study and may also be used to influence ACLU policy.

A bit about confidentiality. We promise you confidentiality under the academic ethics standards of the American Political Science Association. Your name will not be revealed or associated with your response nor will anyone outside of the project staff here at the University of Wisconsin-Milwaukee be allowed to see your response. Thus, while the ACLU may be interested in the policy implications of our study, they will not be furnished with any information which in any way identifies you as an individual. Please note the number in the upper right-hand corner of the questionnaire. This number allows us to temporarily identify you. By referring to this number we will know that you responded to the questionnaire and will not send you the follow-up mailing we will have to send to nonrespondents.

We appreciate your willingness to help us in our research effort. If you would like a copy of our completed study please indicate this on the last page of the questionnaire. We will make certain that you receive a copy of our results. We believe that you will find the questionnaire both interesting and provocative and look forward to receiving your reply.

Sincerely yours,

Richard D. Bingham                                          James L. Gibson
Assistant Professor                                         Associate Professor

Note: If by some chance you recently received and responded to this particular questionnaire, please return the blank questionnaire to us indicating "duplicate" on the first page.

---

The second example, reprinted in Exhibit 11.3, is from a study on commitment to civil liberties conducted by investigators at the University of Wisconsin at Milwaukee.[25] The letter emphasizes the confidentiality of the study and explains in detail how the individual responses will be used.

25. Richard D. Bingham and James L. Gibson, "Conditions of Commitment to Civil Liberties," unpublished (Milwaukee: Department of Political Science, University of Wisconsin, 1979).

Finally, researchers must carefully choose an appropriate style for the cover letter, that is, whether to make it a formal or a semipersonal letter. In the two examples, researchers sent out a form letter to all respondents included in the sample. As an alternative, the researcher might choose to personalize the letter by inserting the respondent's name and address rather than addressing the letter to "Dear Friend" or "Dear Respondent." Most word processing programs can personalize letters automatically and inexpensively if the letter and the mailing list are both computerized, and it has been shown that a more personal letter generates a slightly higher response rate than a form letter.[26]

# Instructions

Another element researchers must consider when constructing a questionnaire is the instructions that go with each question or with a set of questions. Instructions should be included with any questions that are not self-explanatory; the instructions may range from very simple ones such as "circle the appropriate category" to more complex guidelines that explain how to rank a set of priorities. When an interviewer administers a questionnaire, the instructions are usually written for him or her and thus are often short and concise, instructing the interviewer what to do when the respondent provides a certain answer, when to probe for a more detailed answer, or how to clarify a certain question. The following is an example of instructions written for an interviewer:

Who was your employer on your last job?
(PROBE FOR CORRECT CATEGORY)

☐ Private
☐ City
☐ County
☐ State
☐ Federal
☐ Self-employed
☐ Public, nonprofit
☐ Other _____ (specify)
☐ Doesn't know

When a personal or telephone interview is used, the interviewer is available to answer any questions that the respondent may raise, but this is not the case with mail questionnaires, where any questions that are vague or unclear are likely to be answered incorrectly, if at all. Therefore, providing clear instructions is extremely important. They can vary from general instructions introducing the questionnaire or its subsections to specific details preceding individual questions.

26. Michael T. Matteson, "Type of Transmittal Letter and Questionnaire Color as Two Variables Influencing Response Rates in a Mail Survey," *Journal of Applied Psychology,* 59 (1974): 532–536.

The following is an example of general instructions given at the beginning of a questionnaire on attitudes toward civil liberties:[27]

INSTRUCTIONS: For each of the following questions please mark the answer that comes closest to the way you feel about the issue. There are no "right" or "wrong" answers—please answer the questions as honestly as possible. Answer each of the questions in the order in which it appears. If you wish to make additional comments on any of the specific questions or on the issues in general, use the space at the end of the questionnaire. Your opinions are extremely important for understanding these complex civil liberty issues—we greatly appreciate your cooperation!

The next example, taken from the General Social Survey, introduces a question presented in a ranking scale format:

INSTRUCTIONS: Some people think that the government in Washington ought to reduce the income differences between the rich and the poor, perhaps by raising the taxes of wealthy families or by giving income assistance to the poor. Others think that the government should not concern itself with reducing this income difference between the rich and poor.

Here is a card with a scale from 1 to 7. Think of a score of 1 as meaning that the government ought to reduce the income differences between rich and poor, and a score of 7 meaning that the government should not concern itself with reducing income differences. What score between 1 and 7 comes closest to the way you feel? (CIRCLE ONE):

| HAND |
| CARD O |

GOVERNMENT SHOULD DO                          GOVERNMENT SHOULD
SOMETHING TO REDUCE                             NOT CONCERN ITSELF
INCOME DIFFERENCES                              WITH INCOME
BETWEEN RICH AND POOR.                          DIFFERENCES.

```
 |____|____|____|____|____|____|
 1    2    3    4    5    6    7
```

Finally, here is an example is of a specific instruction for replying to a single question.

About how many states have you lived in during your life? (Count only those states that you lived in for at least one year.)

# Constructing a Questionnaire: A Case Study

Many stages are involved in the construction of a questionnaire. The researcher begins with the research problem and goes through the process of formulating the questions and considering the format and the type of questions to be used. To

27. Bingham and Gibson, "Conditions of Commitment to Civil Liberties."

illustrate these stages, we present in Exhibit 11.4 a questionnaire based on an actual study conducted by the Institute for Social Research at the University of Michigan.[28]

The objective of the study was to explore the attitudes and perceptions related to urban problems and race relations in 15 northern cities in the United States. The investigators sought to define the social and psychological characteristics as well as the aspirations of the black and white urban populations. Researchers selected a black sample and a white sample in each of the cities in the study. Approximately 175 black and 175 white respondents were interviewed in each city. In addition, 366 whites were interviewed in two suburban areas. Altogether, 2,809 black respondents and 2,950 white respondents were interviewed. Respondents were between the ages of 16 and 69 and lived in private households.

The researchers used two questionnaire forms, one for whites and one for blacks. The questions about background characteristics were almost identical in the two forms. The attitudinal questions were also identical in both interview forms, but a greater number of questions were addressed exclusively to one racial group or to the other. The questionnaires contained attitudinal questions probing the respondents' satisfaction with neighborhood services, their feelings about the effectiveness of the government in dealing with urban problems, their interracial relationships, their attitudes toward integration, and their perception of the hostility between the races. The questionnaire in Exhibit 11.4 is a shortened version of the original questionnaire addressed to blacks.

Notice that the questionnaire starts off with identification numbers for the person being interviewed as well as his or her location. There is also room for the interviewer to provide information on when the interview began. Question 1 is an example of an attitude question on degree of satisfaction with services provided by the city. The researcher used a matrix format for this question. Note also that instructions are provided both for the interviewer ("Code A below, and ask B through E") and the respondent.

Question 2 has a closed-ended and open-ended component (2A). Item 2A is also a contingency question. Questions 3, 5, 6, and 7 are likewise contingency questions. The first part is the filter question, and the second is the contingency question, which applies only to respondents who have checked specific categories in the first part. All questions use a numerical code, which is checked off by the interviewer.

The final section of the questionnaire demonstrates the relative advantage of an interview over other modes of filling out questionnaires (mail, telephone). The interviewer can provide detailed information on the general attitude of the respondents, which can help researchers interpret their response pattern.

28. Based on Angus Campbell and Howard Schuman, *Racial Attitudes in Fifteen American Cities* (Ann Arbor, Mich.: Social Science Archive, 1973).

## Exhibit 11.4
## Urban Problem Study Questionnaire

| TIME INTERVIEW BEGAN: _____ A.M. P.M. |
|---|

City Number ☐☐ v.3

Segment Number ☐☐☐ v.9

DULS Line Number ☐☐☐☐ v.10

Person Number ☐ v.19

FOR OFFICE USE ONLY

☐☐☐☐☐ v.2

1. First, I'd like to ask how satisfied you are with some of the main services the city is supposed to provide for your neighborhood. What about the quality of public schools in this neighborhhod—are you generally satisfied, somewhat dissatisfied, or very dissatisfied?

(CODE A BELOW, AND ASK B THROUGH E)

|  | Generally satisfied | Somewhat satisfied | Very dissatisfied | Don't know |
|---|---|---|---|---|
| A. Quality of public schools | 1 | 2 | 3 | 8 |
| B. Parks and playgrounds for children in this neighborhood | 1 | 2 | 3 | 8 |
| C. Sports and recreation centers for teenagers in this neighborhood | 1 | 2 | 3 | 8 |
| D. Police protection in this neighborhood | 1 | 2 | 3 | 8 |
| E. Garbage collection in this neighborhood | 1 | 2 | 3 | 8 |

2. Thinking about city services like schools, parks, and garbage collection, do you think your neighborhood gets better, about the same, or worse services than most other parts of the city?

Better ....(ASK A) ....1
About same ..........2
Worse ....(ASK A) ....3
Don't know ...........8

A. IF BETTER OR WORSE: What is the reason this neighborhood gets (better/worse) services?

3. If you have a serious complaint about poor service by the city, do you think you can get city officials to do something about it if you call them?

RECODED VALUES

Yes ......(ASK A) ......1
No ......(ASK A) ......5
Don't know ..(ASK A) ..8

A. Have you ever called a city official with a complaint about poor service?

Yes ..........1
No ..........5

4. In general, do you think (CITY) city officials pay more, less, or the same attention to a request or complaint from a black as from a white person?

More ................1           1
Less ................2           3
Same ................3           2
Don't Know ..........8           8

Now let's talk about the problems of (CITY) as a whole.

5. Do you think the Mayor of (CITY) is trying as hard as he/she can to solve the main problems of the city, or that he/she is not doing all he/she could to solve these problems?

> Trying as hard as he/she can ......1
> Not doing all he/she could (ASK A) X
> Don't know .................... 8

A. IF NOT DOING ALL HE/SHE COULD: Do you think he/she is trying fairly hard to solve these problems, or not hard at all?

> Fairly hard .............2
> Not hard at all ..........3

---

6. How about the state government? Do you think they are trying as hard as they can to solve the main problems of cities like (CITY), or that they are not doing all they could to solve these problems?

> Trying as hard as they can ........1
> Not doing all they could (ASK A) .X
> Don't know .................... 8

A. IF NOT DOING ALL THEY COULD: Do you think they are trying fairly hard to solve these problems, or not hard at all?

> Fairly hard .............2
> Not hard at all ..........3

---

7. How about the federal government in Washington? Do you think they are trying as hard as they can to solve the main problems of cities like (CITY), or that they are not doing all they could to solve such problems?

> Trying as hard as they can ........1
> Not doing all they could (ASK A) .X
> Don't know .................... 8

A. IF NOT DOING ALL THEY COULD: Do you think they are trying fairly hard to solve these problems, or not hard at all?

> Fairly hard .............2
> Not hard at all ..........3

---

8. A black mayor has been elected in Cleveland and also in Gary, Indiana. What effect do you think this will have on solving city problems in Cleveland and Gary? Do you think it will make things better, worse, or won't there be much change?

> Better.........................1
> Worse.........................2
> Not much change .............3
> Don't know ....... (ASK A) .......8

A. IF DON'T KNOW: What would you *guess* the effect would be—to make things better, worse, or won't there be much change?

> Better...................1
> Worse...................2
> Not much change ........3

## Exhibit 11.4 *(continued)*

Now I want to talk about some complaints people have made about the (CITY) police.
9. First, some people say the police don't come quickly when you call them for help. Do you think this happens to people in this neighborhood?

            Yes . . . . . . . . . . (ASK A) . . . . . . . . . .1
            No . . . . . . .(GO TO Q. 10) . . . . . . .5
            Don't know. . . . . . .(ASK A). . . . . .8

A. IF YES OR DON'T KNOW: Has it ever happened to you?
            Yes . . . . . . . . (ASK B & C) . . . . . . . .1
            No . . . . . . . . . .(ASK C) . . . . . . . . .5

   B. IF YES TO A: How long ago was that (the last time)?
                                    _____ years ago
   C. IF YES OR NO TO A: Has it happened to anyone you know?

                        Yes . . . . . . . . . . . . . . . . . . . .1
                        No . . . . . . . . . . . . . . . . . . . .5

10. Some people say the police don't show respect for people or they use insulting language. Do you think this happens to people in this neighborhood?

            Yes . . . . . . . . . . (ASK A) . . . . . . . . . .1
            No . . . . . . .(GO TO Q. 11) . . . . . . .5
            Don't know. . . . . . .(ASK A). . . . . .8

A. IF YES OR DON'T KNOW: Has it ever happened to you?
            Yes . . . . . . . . (ASK B & C) . . . . . . . .1
            No . . . . . . . . . .(ASK C) . . . . . . . . .5

   B. IF YES TO A: How long ago was that (the last time)?
                                    _____ years ago
   C. IF YES OR NO TO A: Has it happened to anyone you know?

                        Yes . . . . . . . . . . . . . . . . . . . .1
                        No . . . . . . . . . . . . . . . . . . . .5

RECODED
VALUES

11. Some people say the police frisk or search people without good reason. Do you think this happens often to people in this neighborhood?

            Yes . . . . . . . . . . (ASK A) . . . . . . . . . .1
            No . . . . . . .(GO TO Q. 12) . . . . . . .5
            Don't know. . . . . . .(ASK A). . . . . .8

A. IF YES OR DON'T KNOW: Has it ever happened to you?
            Yes . . . . . . . . (ASK B & C) . . . . . . . .1
            No . . . . . . . . . .(ASK C) . . . . . . . . .5

   B. IF YES TO A: How long ago was that (the last time)?
                                    _____ years ago
   C. IF YES OR NO TO A: Has it happened to anyone you know?

                        Yes . . . . . . . . . . . . . . . . . . . .1
                        No . . . . . . . . . . . . . . . . . . . .5

12. Some people say the police rough up people unnecessarily when they are arresting them or afterwards. Do you think this happens to people in this neighborhood?

```
Yes . . . . . . . . . .(ASK A) . . . . . . . . . .1
No . . . . . . .(GO TO Q. 13) . . . . . . .5
Don't know. . . . . . .(ASK A). . . . . . .8
```

A. IF YES OR DON'T KNOW: Has it ever happened to you?

```
Yes . . . . . . . .(ASK B & C) . . . . . . . .1
No . . . . . . . . .(ASK C) . . . . . . . . .5
```

B. IF YES TO A: How long ago was that (the last time)?

_____ years ago

C. IF YES OR NO TO A: Has it happened to anyone you know?

```
Yes . . . . . . . . . . . . . . . . . . . .1
No . . . . . . . . . . . . . . . . . . . .5
```

---

13. Do you think black citizens are generally given better treatment by black police officers, by white police officers, or that it doesn't make much difference?

```
Black police officers (ASK A) . . . . . .1          1
White police officers (ASK A) . . . . .2          2
Not much difference . . . . . . . . . . . .3          2
Don't know. . . . . . . . . . . . . . . . . . .8          8
```

A. IF BLACK OR WHITE POLICE OFFICERS: Why do you think this is?

---

14. In general, do you think judges in (CITY) are usually harder on blacks, harder on whites, or that there is not much difference?

```
Harder on blacks . . . . . . . . . . . . . . .1          1
Harder on whites. . . . . . . . . . . . . . .2          3
Not much difference . . . . . . . . . . . .3          2
Don't know. . . . . . . . . . . . . . . . . . .8          8
```

---

15. Do you personally feel safer from crime now than you did two or three years ago, or is there no change, or do you feel less safe?

```
Safer today . . . . . . . . . . . . . .1
No change. . . . . . . . . . . . . .2
Less safe . . . . . . . . . . . . . .3
```

---

16. Here are some complaints you hear sometimes about stores and merchants. Would you tell me if these things ever happen *to you* when you shop in stores in or near this neighborhood?

## Exhibit 11.4 *(continued)*

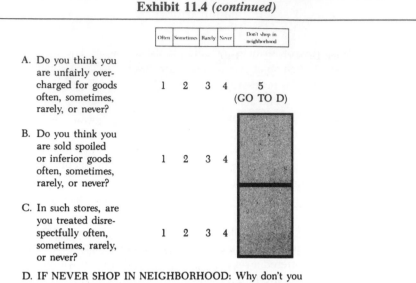

| | Often | Sometimes | Rarely | Never | Don't shop in neighborhood |
|---|---|---|---|---|---|

A. Do you think you are unfairly over-charged for goods often, sometimes, rarely, or never?    1    2    3    4    5 (GO TO D)

B. Do you think you are sold spoiled or inferior goods often, sometimes, rarely, or never?    1    2    3    4

C. In such stores, are you treated disre-spectfully often, sometimes, rarely, or never?    1    2    3    4

D. IF NEVER SHOP IN NEIGHBORHOOD: Why don't you shop around here?

### FILL IN ITEMS BELOW IMMEDIATELY AFTER LEAVING RESPONDENT

A. Total length of interview:

_____ Minutes

B. Cooperativeness of respondent:

Very cooperative . . . . . . . .1
Somewhat cooperative . . .2
Not cooperative . . . . . . .3

C. Interest of respondent in racial issues:

Great interest . . . . . . . . . .1
Ordinary interest . . . . . . .2
Little interest . . . . . . . . . .3

D. Respondent's understanding of questions:

Good understanding . . . .1
Fair understanding . . . . . .2
Poor understanding . . . . .3

E. What persons over 14 years of age were present during interview? CIRCLE *ALL* THAT APPLY.

v.63        None . . . . . . . . . . . . . . . .0
Spouse . . . . . . . . . . . . . . .1
Parent . . . . . . . . . . . . . . .2
Child over 14 . . . . . . . . . .3
Other relative or friend . . .4
Other (SPECIFY) . . . . . . .5

F. Neatness of home interior:

v.64        Very neat and clean . . . . .1
Fairly neat and clean . . .2
Fairly messy . . . . . . . . . . .3
Very messy . . . . . . . . . . . .4

G. Date of Interview: _____

v.69

H. Interviewer's Signature:

I. Please give here a brief description of the respondent, and of any special conditions that affected the interview.

## Summary

**1.** The foundation of all questionnaires is the question. The questionnaire must translate the research objectives into specific questions. The answers to these questions will provide the necessary data for hypothesis testing.

**2.** Most questions can be classified as either factual questions or questions about subjective experiences. Factual questions are designed to elicit objective information from the respondent. Subjective questions are concerned with inclinations, preferences, prejudices, ideas, fears, and convictions. In general, subjective questions are much more complex and difficult to construct than questions about personal facts. Answers to subjective questions are more likely to change with changes in wording, emphasis, and sequence than are answers to factual questions.

**3.** Three types of question structure can be distinguished: closed-ended questions, open-ended questions, and contingency questions. In closed-ended questions, respondents are offered a set of response categories from which they must choose the one that most closely represents their view. Open-ended questions are not followed by any kind of choice, and the respondents' answers are recorded in full. A contingency question applies only to a subgroup of respondents. The relevance of the question to this subgroup is determined by the answer of all respondents to a preceding filter question.

**4.** One of the most common formats researchers use to ask questions in surveys is the rating scale, whereby the respondent makes judgments in terms of sets of ordered categories. There are several types of rating scales, including the semantic differential. The matrix question is a method of organizing a large set of rating questions that have the same response categories. Ranking is used in questionnaires when the objective is to obtain information regarding the degree of importance or the priorities that people apply to a set of attitudes or objects.

**5.** Questions must be worded so that all respondents can comprehend them. The way a *leading question* is phrased makes it appear to the respondent that the researcher expects a certain answer. *Threatening questions* raise the anxiety level of the respondents. Both types of questions may lead to response bias. Researchers should avoid leading questions and construct threatening questions with great sensitivity, using special techniques such as a long introduction to the question and an open-ended rather than a closed-ended format.

## Key Terms for Review

attitude (p. 252)
closed-ended question (p. 253)
contingency question (p. 255)
double-barreled question (p. 266)

factual question (p. 251)
filter question (p. 255)
leading question (p. 263)
matrix question (p. 258)

open-ended question (p. 254)        ranking (p. 260)
opinion (p. 252)                    rating (p. 258)
quantifiers (p. 258)                semantic differential (p. 259)
question (p. 250)                   threatening question (p. 264)

---

## Study Questions

---

1. Discuss the various ways in which questions can be used to get factual information, opinions, and attitudes from respondents.
2. Explain the uses of closed-ended, open-ended, and contingency questions.
3. List and describe the formats used to ask questions for various purposes.
4. Discuss the importance of question sequencing in a questionnaire.
5. List the various problems that may arise while constructing questionnaires.

---

## Additional Readings

---

Abramson, Paul R., and Charles W. Ostrom. "Question Wording and Partisanship: Change and Continuity in Party Loyalties during the 1992 Election Campaign." *Public Opinion Quarterly,* 58, (1994): 21–49.

Bailey, Kenneth D. *Methods of Social Research.* New York: Free Press, 1987.

Bishop, G. F., R. W. Oldendick, and Alfred J. Tuchfarber. "Effects of Filter Questions in Public Opinion Surveys." *Public Opinion Quarterly,* 47, (1983): 528–546.

———. "What Must My Interest in Politics Be If I Just Told You 'I Don't Know?'" *Public Opinion Quarterly,* 46 (1982): 510–519.

Gaskell, George D., Colm A. O'Muircheartaigh, and Daniel B. Wright. "Survey Questions about Frequency of Vaguely Defined Events: The Effects of Response Alternatives." *Public Opinion Quarterly,* 58 (1994): 241–255.

Gorden, Raymond L. *Interviewing: Strategy, Techniques, and Tactics.* 3d ed. Homewood, Ill.: Dorsey, 1980.

Kahn, Robert I., and Charles F. Cannell. *The Dynamics of Interviewing.* New York: Wiley, 1957.

Rasinski, Kenneth A., David Mingay, and Norman M. Bradburn. "Do Respondents Really 'Mark All That Apply' on Self-Administered Questions?" *Public Opinion Quarterly,* 58 (1994): 400–409.

Schuman, Howard, and Stanley Presser. *Questions and Answers in Attitude Surveys.* Orlando, Fla.: Academic Press, 1981.

Singleton, Royce, Jr., Bruce C. Straits, Margaret M. Straits, and Ronald J. McAllister. *Approaches to Social Research.* Oxford: Oxford University Press, 1988.

Sudman, Seymour, and Norman M. Bradburn. *Asking Questions.* San Francisco: Jossey-Bass, 1982.

Tourangeau, Roger, and Kenneth A. Rasinski. "Cognitive Processes Underlying Context Effects in Attitude Measurement." *Psychological Bulletin,* 103 (1988): 299–314.

# CHAPTER 12

# Qualitative Research

**Field Research**

**Participant Observation**
Complete Participant
Participant-as-Observer

**The Practice of Field Research**
Selecting a Research Topic
Choosing a Site and Gaining Access
Establishing Relations with Members
Finding Resourceful and Reliable Informants
Leaving the Field
Recording Observations
Analyzing Data

**The Theory of Field Research**

**Blue-Collar Community: An Example of Field Research**
Choosing the Research Topic and the Research Site
Gaining Access
Establishing Relations with Members
Leaving the Field

**Ethical and Political Issues of Fieldwork**

What goes on behind the scenes at a university rape crisis center and how do you find out? Amy Fried was interested in how the beliefs volunteer counselors bring to their work shape and modify the goals of the organization and influence the counseling offered to victims of rape.[1] Fried chose to study a newly forming rape crisis center by becoming a volunteer counselor. Along with 15 other women and 4 men who served as the staff of the center, she attended training sessions and organizational meetings and observed the interaction among the other volunteer members, concentrating on how members defined rape and the language they used to describe victims. She found that two distinct subcultures emerged within the group. One subculture held what she called the political perspective. This faction consisted of feminists who believed rape was the result of the social power men hold over women. Their goal was to empower the victims of rape and ultimately effect social change. The other faction held a service perspective. They believed that both sex and power issues were involved in rape, but that the goal of the organization should be to help people—both women and the significant men in their lives—overcome the pain associated with being victimized by rape. Generalizing from her findings, Fried argues that the clash between these two subcultures weakens the ability of feminists to reform society and suggests that, perhaps, feminists need to form their own organizations to meet their mission. Fried employed qualitative methods to gather the data for her study. Her participant observer role allowed her to discover how meanings and beliefs enter into organizational goals.

I N THIS CHAPTER, WE FOCUS ON FIELD RESEARCH FOR QUALItative study, concentrating on complete participant and participant-as-observer roles. We discuss how researchers select their topics, identify and gain access to their subjects, establish relationships, and record their observations. We also consider how field researchers develop grounded theory based on their data using the process of analytic induction. Finally, we consider the ethical and political dilemmas of field research.

So far we have discussed methods of data collection designed primarily for quantitative analyses. In this chapter, we describe the prototype of qualitative research—field research. Qualitative research, as a method of data collection and analysis, derives from the *Verstehen* tradition described in Chapter 1. Scientists must gain an empathic understanding of societal phenomena, and they must recognize both the historical dimension of human behavior and the subjective aspects of the human experience. In his study of asylums, Erving Goffman describes the process of actively participating in the daily life of the observed and the gaining of insights by introspection in the following way:

---

1. Amy Fried, "'It's Hard to Change What We Want to Change,'" *Gender & Society,* 8:4 (1994): 562–583.

My immediate object in doing field work at St. Elizabeth's was to try to learn about the social world of the hospital inmate, as this world is subjectively experienced by him. . . . It was then and still is my belief that any group of persons—prisoners, primitives, pilots, or patients—develop a life of their own that becomes meaningful, reasonable, and normal once you get close to it, and that a good way to learn about any of these worlds is to submit oneself in the company of the members to the daily round of petty contingencies to which they are subject.[2]

Qualitative researchers attempt to understand behavior and institutions by getting to know the persons involved and their values, rituals, symbols, beliefs, and emotions. Applying such a perspective, researchers would, for example, study poverty by immersing themselves in the life of the poor rather than collecting data with a structured interview schedule.

---

# Field Research

Field research is the most central strategy of data collection associated with qualitative methodology. In general terms, **field research** is defined as "the study of people acting in the natural courses of their daily lives. The fieldworker ventures into the worlds of others in order to learn firsthand about how they live, how they talk and behave, and what captivates and distresses them."[3] More explicitly, field-work is characterized by its location and by the manner in which it is conducted.[4] With respect to location, fieldwork is carried out in *natural* settings, for example, anthropologists living with remote tribes or sociologists sharing in and observing the daily life of a local community. Field research is also a way of empathizing with and understanding the subjective meanings of the people being studied. Typically, fieldworkers attempt to incorporate these two characteristics in their studies.

Contemporary sociological fieldwork has its origins in the social reform movement of the turn of the twentieth century. Reformers believed that descriptions of the conditions in which the poor lived would call attention to their plight and lead to social change and improvement in those conditions. The reform movement found its strongest academic expression in the Chicago School in the early 1920s. The Chicago School sociologists were intensely involved in the social reform movement centered outside the university. Robert Park, a leading figure in the Chicago School, saw in the city a critical area for sociological research and urged his students to observe life in its various enclaves firsthand:

Go and sit in the lounges of the luxury hotels and on the doorsteps of the flop-houses; sit on the Gold Coast settees and on the slum shake-downs; sit in

---

2. Erving Goffman, *Asylums* (Garden City, N.Y.: Doubleday, 1961), pp. ix–x.
3. Robert M. Emerson, ed., *Contemporary Field Research* (Boston: Little Brown, 1983), p. 1.
4. Ibid.

Orchestra Hall and in the Star and Garter Burlesk. In short, gentlemen, go get the seat of your pants dirty in real research.[5]

At that time, the methodology of qualitative research was limited to assembling a variety of personal documents—autobiographies, life histories, letters, and diaries. Qualitative researchers had only a limited conception of how to participate in the lives of the people they were studying. During the following two decades, as fieldwork became more established in sociology, its methodology came to emphasize participation in the lives of those studied so that researchers could share, and consequently better understand, the subjective perspectives of the subjects.

# Participant Observation

The method of data collection most closely associated with contemporary field research is **participant observation,** whereby the investigator attempts to attain some kind of membership in or close attachment to the group that he or she wishes to study.[6] In doing so, the participant observer attempts to adopt the perspectives of the people in the situation being observed. The participant observer's role is that of "conscious and systematic sharing, insofar as circumstances permit, in the life activities, and on occasion, in the interests and effects of a group of persons."[7] Direct participation in the activities of the observed often entails learning the language, habits, work patterns, leisure activities, and other aspects of their daily lives. The researcher assumes either a complete participant role or a participant-as-observer role.

## Complete Participant

In a **complete participant** role, the observer is wholly concealed; the research objectives are unknown to the observed, and the researcher attempts to become a member of the group under observation. The complete participant interacts with the observed "as naturally as possible in whatever areas of their living interest him and are accessible to him."[8]

For example, Festinger, Riecken, and Schachter studied a group of persons who predicted the destruction of the world. The nature of the group led the investigators to believe that if they presented themselves as researchers, they would not

5. John C. McKinney, *Constructive Typology and Social Theory* (Norwalk, Conn.: Appleton & Lang, 1966), p. 71.

6. Rosalie H. Wax, "Participant Observation," *International Encyclopedia of Social Sciences* (New York: Macmillan, 1968), p. 238.

7. Florence Kluckhohn, "The Participant-Observer Technique in Small Communities," *American Journal of Sociology,* 46 (1940): 331.

8. Raymond L. Gold, "Roles in Sociological Field Observation," *Social Forces,* 36 (1958): 219.

be allowed to observe the activities of the group. Consequently, they posed as individuals who shared the beliefs of the group and became full-fledged members trying to be "nondirective, sympathetic listeners, passive participants who were inquisitive and eager to learn whatever others might want to tell us."[9] Richard Mitchell, Jr., describes some of the difficulties he and his fellow researchers encountered in a field investigation of paramilitary survivalists.[10] In order to penetrate the secrecy surrounding the activities of most paramilitary survivalist groups, the researchers took advantage of the survivalist desire for new members by posing as potential recruits. Although they found themselves overdressed when they arrived for their first weekend among the survivalists, they were accepted and praised for their enthusiasm even though their costumes made it difficult to blend in. To gain membership in the group, the researchers had to participate in physical and social activities antithetical to their personal beliefs. Mitchell describes an occasion when he was required to tell a story proposing a solution to something the group considered to be a social problem.

> As I began a new man joined us. He listened to my idea and approved, introduced himself, then told me things not everyone knew, about plans being made, and actions soon to be taken. He said they could use men like me and told me to be ready to join. I took him seriously. Others did, too. He was on the FBI's "ten most wanted" list.[11]

Mitchell's story was good enough to gain him admittance to the inner circle of the group, but his success was not without cost. There was a possibility that his proposed solution, repulsive as it was to him, would be implemented by the survivalist. He tells how he felt about this.

> If there are researchers who can participate in such business without feeling, I am not one of them nor do I even hope to be. What I do hope is someday to forget, forget those unmistakable sounds, my own voice, my own words, telling that . . . story.[12]

Complete participation has been justified on the grounds that it makes possible the study of inaccessible groups or groups that do not reveal to outsiders certain aspects of their lives. Presumably, the fieldworker is treated as just another member of the group. Despite this research advantage, some researchers have severely criticized the complete participant role on methodological and ethical grounds. Kai Erikson, for example, rejects all field studies in which the researchers do not make

9. Leon Festinger, Henry Riecken, and Stanley Schachter, *When Prophecy Fails* (New York: Harper and Row, 1956), p. 234.

10. Richard Mitchell, Jr. "The Secrecy and Disclosure in Field Work," in *Experiencing Field Work: An Inside View of Qualitative Research,* eds. William B. Shaffir and Robert A. Stebbins (Newbury Park, Calif.: Sage, 1991), pp. 97–108.

11. Ibid., p. 107.

12. Ibid., p. 107.

their role and the intent of the study known beforehand. He maintains that such studies constitute an invasion of privacy and may harm the observed:

> The sheer act of entering a human transaction on the basis of deliberate fraud may be painful to the people who are thereby misled; and even if that were not the case, there are countless ways in which a stranger who pretends to be something else can disturb others by failing to understand the conditions of intimacy that prevail in the group he has tried to invade.[13]

Erikson points to the difficulties that may arise when a researcher takes on a complete participant role and uses as an illustration an incident reported in the Festinger, Riecken, and Schachter study, *When Prophecy Fails:*

> At one point in the study, two observers arrived at one of the group's meeting places under instructions to tell quite ordinary stories about their experience in Spiritualism in order to create as little commotion as possible. A few days afterwards, however, the leader of the group was overheard explaining that the two observers had appeared upset, excited, confused, and unsure of their errand at the time of their original visit, all of which helped confirm her suspicion that they had somehow been "sent" from another planet. In one sense, of course, this incident offered the observers an intriguing view of the belief structure of the cult, but in another sense, the leader's assessment of the situation was very shrewd: after all, the observers *had* been sent from another world, if not another planet, and she may have been quite right to sense that they were a bit confused and unsure of their errand during their early moments in the new job. "In both cases," the report informs us, the visits of the observers "were given as illustrations that 'strange things are happening.'" Indeed, strange things *were* happening; yet we have no idea how strange they really were. It is almost impossible to evaluate the reaction of the group to the appearance of the pair of observers because we do not know whether they were seen as ordinary converts or as extraordinary beings. And it makes a difference, for in the first instance the investigators would be observing a response which fell within the normal range of the group's experience, while in the second instance they would be observing a response which would never have taken place had the life of the group been allowed to run its own course.[14]

The complete participant role poses several methodological problems. First, observers may become so self-conscious about revealing their true selves that they are handicapped when attempting to perform convincingly in the pretended role. Or they may "go native," that is, incorporate the pretended role into their self-conception and lose the research perspective.[15] Second, it is difficult for the researcher to decide what to observe because he or she cannot evoke responses or behavior and must be careful not to ask questions that might raise the suspicions of the persons observed. Third, recording observations or taking notes is impos-

---

13. Kai T. Erikson, "A Comment on Disguised Observation in Sociology," *Social Problems,* 14 (1967): 368.
14. Ibid., pp. 371–372.
15. Gold, "Roles in Sociological Field Observation," p. 220.

---

**Two Types of Field Research**

■ *Complete Participant:* Observers become participating members of the group of interest without revealing their identities or research goals to the group.
■ *Participant-as-Observer:* Observers become participants in the activities of the group by revealing their identities and the goals of their research.

---

sible on the spot; these have to be postponed until the observer is alone. However, time lags in recording observations introduce selective bias and distortions through memory.

## Participant-as-Observer

In view of these limitations, contemporary fieldworkers most often assume the **participant-as-observer** role. When researchers adopt this type of role, they inform the group being studied that there is a research agenda. Researchers make long-term commitments to becoming active members of the group and attempt to establish close relationships with its members who subsequently serve as both informants and respondents. John Van Maanen's research on police training illustrates the process of taking this role.

> While a graduate student at the University of California . . . , I began contacting police officials across the country seeking permission to conduct a one man field study inside a large, metropolitan law-enforcement agency. . . . Although I encountered some initial difficulties in locating a department willing to tolerate my planned foray into its organizational spheres, eventually I managed to gain access to one police organization. . . . Throughout the study I worked in the fashion of a traditional ethnographer or participant observer, made no attempt to disguise my scholarly aim or identity, and met with little overt hostility from the men whose everyday affairs were the explicit subject of my investigation. In most respects I felt my mode of inquiry approximated both the substance and spirit of Evans-Pritchard's classic formulation of the ethnographic technique: "to get to know well the persons involved and to see and hear what they do and say."[16]

As this example demonstrates, the participant-as-observer role differs from complete participation in that the research goal is explicitly identified. Yet membership and participation in the observed group is still an important dimension in this form of research. With this method, the fieldworker gains a deeper appreciation of the group and its way of life and may also gain different levels of insight by actually participating rather than only observing.[17]

---

16. John Van Maanen, "The Moral Fix: On the Ethics of Fieldwork," in *Contemporary Field Research,* ed. Emerson, pp. 269–270.
17. Ibid., p. 270.

# The Practice of Field Research

## Selecting a Research Topic

The first step in doing field research is to select a topic for investigation. Very often, the selection of a topic is influenced by personal interests or concerns. Such concerns may be related to the researcher's job, personal relationships, family history, social class, or ethnic background. Lofland and Lofland, in their useful guide to doing qualitative research, describe this process as "starting where you are."[18] This practice originated in the 1920s with the Chicago School, where many well-known qualitative studies arose out of the unique experiences of students with little background in doing social research. Everett Hughes has described the beginning of this tradition in the following way:

> Most of these people didn't have any sociological background. . . . They didn't come in to become sociologists. They came in to learn something and Park picked up whatever it was in their experience which he could build on. . . . He took these people and he brought out of them whatever he could find there. . . . They might be Mennonites who were just a little unhappy . . . about wearing plain clothes . . . , girls who didn't like to wear long dresses and funny little caps; . . . or children of Orthodox Jews who really didn't like to wear beards anymore. . . . And he got hold of people and emancipated them from something that was inherently interesting but which they regarded as a cramp. And he turned this "cramping orthodoxy" into something that was of basic and broad human interest. And that was the case for a lot of these people. He made their pasts interesting to them, much more interesting than they ever thought they could be.[19]

Field research requires that the investigators first determine what they care about independent of scientific considerations. This emotional involvement in their work provides a meaningful link between the personal and emotional lives of the researchers and the rigorous requirement of the social scientific endeavor; not only does this emotional attachment make the involvement in social research more personally rewarding but it helps researchers to cope with problems that are inevitable in every research project.[20]

## Choosing a Site and Gaining Access

Once a researcher has chosen a research topic, the next stage of field research is to select and gain access to an appropriate research site. To a large extent, the choice of a topic determines the range of appropriate sites. For example, Festinger and his colleagues were interested in how religious sects deal with prophetic

---

18. John Lofland and Lyn H. Lofland, *Analyzing Social Settings* (Belmont, Calif.: Wadsworth, 1984), p. 7.
19. Ibid., pp. 9–10.
20. Ibid.

failure.[21] This interest necessarily limited their choice to a contemporary research site where prophecies likely to fail had been made about events in the near future. They chose a religious sect that predicted a natural disaster on a given date. This allowed them to make observations *before* the predicted disaster and *after* the date of the failed prophecy. In this case, substantive and theoretical interest dictated the choice of setting.

Very often, geographic or other practical considerations will dictate the choice. Moreover, it is tempting to choose a site that is easily accessible, where a researcher has an influential contact or is a member. However, in situations where would-be observers are close to the group and thus have easy access, they must find ways to distance themselves emotionally when they engage in their analysis. Conversely, investigators who are outsiders to the research setting may have more difficulty gaining access and need to determine how much to reduce distance after entering the research site. When the researcher reduces the distance too much, he or she runs the risk of "going native." Researchers who "go native" internalize the lifestyle of the group being studied and lose their objectivity, which compromises the findings of the research project. Some researchers even abandon their research projects to protect their adopted group. If researchers maintain too much distance, however, they are unable to fully understand or empathize with the group being studied.

The ascriptive characteristics of the investigator are another important consideration in gaining access to a setting. For example, the gender, age, race, or ethnicity of the observers, if different from the observed, may create serious barriers in gaining access or in communication.[22]

In the words of Rosalie Wax:

> Many tribal or folk societies not only maintain a strict division of labor between the sexes and ages, but the people who fall into these different categories do not converse freely or spontaneously with each other. . . . I, as a middle aged woman, was never able to converse openly or informally with either the old or the young Indian men at Thrashing Buffalo. The older men, even when I knew them fairly well, would tend to deliver lectures to me; the younger men, as was proper, were always too bashful or formally respectful to say much. With the Indian matrons, on the other hand, I could talk for hours.[23]

On the basis of her experience in the field, Wax concluded that a biased view of "whole" cultures can be avoided by using research teams whose members have a variety of personal attributes similar to those of the group being studied.

The problems that confront young female fieldworkers in gaining access to male-dominated settings were discussed by Lois Easterday and her associates:

> One of us established rapport with the photographers of a special military photography programme by being a photographer and knowing their language.

---

21. Festinger et al., *When Prophecy Fails.*
22. Lofland and Lofland, *Analyzing Social Settings.*
23. Rosalie H. Wax, "The Ambiguities of Fieldwork," in *Contemporary Field Research,* ed. Emerson, pp. 194–195.

The relationship was sustained by insisting that the researcher not be photo-graphed as a model, but rather that she be "one of the boys" on the other side of the lens. In an attempt to gain approval for the study from the programme's director, the researcher was denied full access with the statement, "It won't work. The men in the programme are a close bunch, and the talk is rough. They wouldn't be themselves if you are there."[24]

While these examples demonstrate that the status and gender of the researcher may be a handicap in field research, there are situations where differences have definite advantages. Blanche Geer wrote about women:

The most handicapped observer is the one doing people and situations he/she is closest to. Hence, women are in luck in a male-run world. They can see how few clothes the emperor has on, question the accepted, what is taken for granted.[25]

In other words, being an outsider can sometimes seem less threatening to the ob-served, help a researcher gain access to the field, and contribute to the percep-tiveness that the researcher brings to the field.

## Establishing Relations with Members

The ease with which a researcher establishes relationships with members of a group depends to a large extent on the nature of the group and the skills of the researcher. Edward Evans-Pritchard gives an example:

Azande would not allow me to live as one of themselves; Nuer would not allow me to live otherwise. Among Azande I was compelled to live outside of the community; among Nuer I was compelled to be a member of it. Azande treated me as a superior; Nuer as an equal.[26]

Contemporary field researchers have emphasized that the phase of estab-lishing social relations is perhaps the most central aspect of fieldwork: "Good fieldwork . . . depends crucially upon discovering the meaning of social relations, and not just those characterizing the natives' relations with each other. It depends equally upon discovering the meanings of anthropologists' relations with people they study."[27]

One basic requirement, significant especially when studying subcultures, is that the observer understand the jargon used by the particular group. Eleanor Miller, who studied "street women," describes her frustration in her initial en-counter with the women she interviewed:

---

24. Lois Easterday, Diana Papedemas, Laura Schorr, and Catherine Valentine, "The Making of a Female Researcher: Role Problems in Fieldwork," in *Field Research: A Sourcebook and Field Manual,* ed. Robert G. Burgess (London: Allen & Unwin, 1982), pp. 63–64.

25. Ibid., p. 66.

26. Edward E. Evans-Pritchard, *The Nuer* (Oxford: Clarendon, 1940), p. 15.

27. Ivan Karp and Martha B. Kendall, "Reflexivity in Field Work," in *Explaining Human Behavior: Consciousness, Human Action, and Social Structure,* ed. Paul F. Secord (Newbury Park, Calif.: Sage, 1982), p. 250.

I remember very well my first visit to Horizon House. I had been invited to dinner after which I was to describe my study and recruit informants. Dinner was being served, so I sat down. There were, perhaps, eight others seated as well, mostly black women. . . . People talked and joked and occasionally sang along with the radio. I couldn't understand half of what was being said. With a sinking feeling I started to question whether or not I could ever be comfortable enough personally to do this study.[28]

The kinds of social relations that develop between the observer and the observed have several aspects. Rosalie Wax has noted that the identity that is chosen by the fieldworker and the role playing that takes place in the field are central to this social process. She suggests that in a well-balanced relationship, the fieldworker "strives to maintain a consciousness and respect for what he is and a consciousness and respect for what his hosts are."[29] The tendency to assume a "native" identity is one of the most serious errors that a fieldworker can commit. Ned Polsky, in his study of criminals, stresses the danger of "going native":

In doing field research on criminals you damned well better not pretend to be "one of them," because they will test this claim out and one of two things will happen: either you will . . . get sucked into participant observation of the sort you would rather not undertake, or you will be exposed, with still greater negative consequences. You must let the criminals know who you are; and if it is done properly it does not sabotage the research.[30]

There are no magic formulas for learning the ropes, and field researchers generally recommended that the researcher begin by participating in the daily life of the observed, a process described as "hanging around."[31] Learning the ropes and establishing relationships involve adopting a variety of roles. These roles are sometimes spontaneously invented and blend with the demands of the particular research setting. Rosalie Wax describes her experiences while conducting a field-work study of the Japanese relocation centers during the Second World War:

I would not have been able to do field work in Gila and Tule Lake if my respondents and I had not been able, jointly, to invent and maintain many of these relationships. Some Japanese Americans felt more comfortable if they could treat me like a sympathetic newspaper reporter. I knew very little about how a reporter behaved (indeed, I had never seen or spoken with one), but I responded and we were able to converse more easily. In Tule Lake the superpatriots and agitators found it easier to talk to me once they convinced themselves that I was German *Nisei*, "full of the courageous German spirit." I found this fantasy personally embarrassing, but I did not make a point of denying my German ancestry. Finally, I was not a geisha, even though a shrewd Issei once suggested that it was because I functioned as one that I was able to find out so much of what happened at

28. Eleanor Miller, *Street Woman* (Philadelphia: Temple University Press, 1986), pp. 221–222.
29. Wax, "Ambiguities of Fieldwork," p. 197.
30. Ned Polsky, *Hustlers, Beats, and Others* (Hawthorne, N.Y.: Aldine, 1967), p. 124.
31. William B. Shaffir, Robert A. Stebbins, Allan Turowetz, eds., *Fieldwork Experience: Qualitative Approaches to Social Research* (New York: St. Martin's Press, 1980), p. 113.

Tule Lake. His explanation was that Japanese men—and especially Japanese politicians—do not discuss their plans or achievements with other men or with their wives, but they are culturally conditioned to speak of such matters with intelligent and witty women.[32]

As this example shows, learning the ropes and adopting the range of research roles is a flexible process that requires the researcher to exercise ingenuity and demonstrate sensitivity to the personalities and perceptions of the research participants.

## Finding Resourceful and Reliable Informants

Once participant observers have established relationships with members of the group, they are regarded as provisional group members. They learn how to behave in the group and "teach" the observed how to act toward them. Next, observers are accepted as *categorical members* of the group. By this time, rapport will have been established, areas of observation will be agreed on, and **informants** will be providing information. William Whyte's experiences illustrate several phases in this process:

> I began with a vague idea that I wanted to study a slum district. . . . I made my choice on very unscientific grounds: Cornerville best fitted my picture of what a slum district should look like. . . . I learned early in my Cornerville period the crucial importance of having the support of the key individuals in any groups or organizations I was studying. Instead of trying to explain myself to everyone, I found I was providing far more information about myself and my study to leaders such as Doc than I volunteered to the average corner boy. I always tried to give the impression that I was willing and eager to tell just as much about my study as anyone wished to know, but it was only with group leaders that I made a particular effort to provide really full information. . . . Since these leaders had the sort of position in the community that enabled them to observe much better than the followers what was going on and since they were in general more skillful observers than the followers, I found that I had much to learn from a more active collaboration with them.[33]

Intimate relationships with informants may, however, bias the researcher's reports, as Whyte himself has observed:

> Doc found this experience of working with me interesting and enjoyable, and yet the relationship had its drawbacks. He once commented: "You've slowed me up plenty since you've been down here. Now, when I do something, I have to think what Bill Whyte would want to know about it and how I can explain it. Before, I used to do things by instinct.[34]

32. Wax, "Ambiguities of Fieldwork," p. 200.

33. William F. Whyte, *Street Corner Society,* 2d ed. (Chicago: University of Chicago Press, 1955), pp. 279–358.

34. Ibid., p. 301.

## Leaving the Field

The social complexity of field research is not limited to gaining access and establishing relationships. Leaving the field is no less problematic. This stage depends on the agreement the observer and the observed reached when the study began and on the kind of social relationships that developed during the research process. The research requirement of "getting involved" during the fieldwork itself presents a problem when it is time to leave, as Wax notes:

> Being by that time experienced fieldworkers, Murray and I had planned to stay six months in the field and spend six months writing our report. But rough as life was, I had become so attached to some of my Indian friends that I talked Murray into staying an extra month—even at temperatures of 30 below zero. I did not want to leave but I had to.[35]

Another problem in leaving the field is how it affects the subjects themselves. "As they see it, they stand to gain little, if anything, from our research findings and may even lose. A related reason for their reluctance is their impression that our work will add little to their own lives."[36]

Field exit processes range from the quick and sharply defined to the gradual and drawn out. Leaving can be a recurring phenomenon when research needs require the researcher to leave and come back numerous times. In the end, the procedure the researcher selects is a function of the commitment he or she made while conducting the research.[37]

## Recording Observations

In field research, the primary sources of data are what people say and do. Researchers may record the behavior they observe by writing notes, tape recording, and on occasion photographing or videotaping. In some cases when the researcher's identity and purpose are known to the observed, recording can be done on the spot, during the event. In most cases, however, the researcher wants the members of the group to forget they are being observed so that their behavior and interaction remains natural. Recording in the presence of the group serves as a reminder of the researcher's agenda, which may influence the behavior of the group and also may limit the researcher's ability to participate in group activities. When the researcher's identity and purpose are unknown to the observed, it is usually impossible to document events as they occur.

When researchers cannot overtly document observations, they must use devices to help them remember events as they occurred so they can be fully docu-

35. David R. Maines, William B. Shaffir, and Allan Turowetz, "Leaving the Field in Ethnographic Research: Reflections on the Entrance Exit Hypothesis," in *Fieldwork Experience*, ed. Shaffir, et al., p. 277.
36. Shaffir et al., *Fieldwork Experience*, p. 258.
37. Maines et al., "Leaving the Field," p. 273.

mented at the earliest possible opportunity. Many researchers use moments of privacy—such as regular use of the rest room—to jot down key words that will help them to remember the sequence of events, relevant behaviors, and valuable quotations. When privacy is impossible, researchers may rely on mnemonic devices to help them remember. The key to mnemonic devices is the association of the things to be remembered with things that are familiar and easily recalled.

When researchers cannot fully document their observations immediately, the possibility of distortion and unintentional misrepresentation increases. The longer the researcher must wait to record observations, the greater the possibility for flawed recall. It is helpful to employ certain notational conventions to minimize distortions. For example, a researcher could use quotation marks around recorded material to indicate exact recall; data with no quotation marks around it would be based on impressions or inferences. Such a recording practice is vulnerable because of observer inference, however. Lofland and Lofland suggest asking the following questions before the data is written up:[38]

1. Is the report firsthand?
2. What was the spatial location of the observer?
3. Did the research participant have any reason to give false or biased information?
4. Is the report internally consistent?
5. Can the report be validated by using other independent reports?

Although information gained from these questions does not guarantee that a report is true, it helps the researcher to assess the reliability of the data.

## Analyzing Data

Data analysis in qualitative field research is an ongoing process. Observers formulate hypotheses and note important themes throughout their studies. As the research progresses, some hypotheses are discarded, others are refined, and still others are formulated. Bogdan and Taylor give an example of such a process:

> In the job training program study, the observer had an early hunch that men trainees clearly differentiated "women's factory work" from "men's factory work." The hunch came after one of the staff personnel had reported the following to the observer: "When the men saw women doing the work (soldering) on the assembly line, they didn't want any part of it." Since this sex differentiation would have important implications for the potential success of the program and for the meanings of work, the researcher presented his hunch on later visits to the setting. He found that, although men and women differed in the types of work they valued, men did not reject certain work as "women's work." For example, they expressed little pride in doing physical labor and openly avoided jobs that were dangerous

38. Lofland and Lofland, *Analyzing Social Settings,* p. 51.

or "too hard." The observer dropped his earlier hypothesis and turned to the pursuit of others.[39]

An important aspect of data analysis during the period of data collection is establishing files and coding fieldnotes (see Chapter 14 for more information on inductive coding). Essentially, this is a process of dissecting fieldnotes. In the early stages of fieldwork, a researcher may develop simple categories based on the characteristics of the people being observed and the events that occur. For example, a researcher might classify members of the group as leaders, followers, and renegades. Field notes pertaining to the actions of each type of group member are filed or coded under the appropriate classification. Interactions between different types of group members are filed under both classifications. As the fieldwork progresses, researchers use what they have learned to refine and, sometimes, redefine their categories. After each refinement the researcher must review and refile all relevant field notes. It is during the process of categorization that researchers develop tentative hypotheses.

Researchers can create files by actually cutting apart a copy of their fieldnotes and filing the pieces of paper into file folders, or they can use a word processing program to excerpt portions of the fieldnotes into separate data files. The labels on the file folders or data files reflect the categories the researcher has developed.

Becker and Geer, in their study of a medical school, found it useful to prepare data for analysis by making a running summary of their field notes. They coded the data into separate incidents, summarizing for each incident their observation of a student's action. First, they tentatively identified the major areas or categories during the fieldwork process. Then, when going through a summarized incident, they marked it with a number standing for each area into which it could be classified. The following examples from their field notes and their subsequent analysis illustrates this process:

> "Mann says that now that he and the other students have found out what Dr. Prince, the staff physician, is like, they learn the things they know he's going to try to catch them on and keep him stumped that way." This incident contains some reference to student-faculty relations and would accordingly be coded under that category. It also refers indirectly to the phenomenon of student cooperation on school activities and would be coded under that category as well. The next stage in the analysis would be to inspect the various items coded under one area, and formulate a more detailed statement of the content of this area or perspective citing examples of actions and statements that characterize it.[40]

Once researchers have identified actions and statements that support their emerging hypotheses, their next step is to look for **negative cases**—instances that

39. Robert Bogdan and Steven J. Taylor, *Introduction to Qualitative Research Methods* (New York: Wiley, 1975), pp. 80–81.
40. Howard S. Becker and Blanche Geer, "Participant Observation: The Analysis of Qualitative Field Data" in *Field Research*, ed. Burgess, p. 245.

refute the hypotheses. Researchers must compare positive and negative cases to determine whether the hypothesis can be modified to better fit all of the data or if the hypothesis must be rejected entirely. In addition, the range of the perspective is checked, that is, how widely the items of data were distributed through a number of different situations.

When analyzing qualitative data, it is useful to look for certain regularities or patterns that emerge from the numerous observations made during the fieldwork stage. A researcher can perform this task by posing a number of questions:[41]

1. What type of behavior is it?
2. What is its structure?
3. How frequent is it?
4. What are its causes?
5. What are its processes?
6. What are its consequences?
7. What are people's strategies?

The written report is the culmination of the field-research study. The final report describes the background for the study, the theoretical framework guiding it, and the design and methodology of the study. It provides a detailed analysis and interpretation of the data and also explores what the findings imply in terms of further analysis or public policy decisions.

# The Theory of Field Research

When researchers engage in quantitative research, their goal is to either falsify, modify, or provide support for existing theory. They accomplish this goal deductively by deriving hypotheses from theory and using the data they collect to statistically test the hypotheses. Qualitative field research moves in the opposite direction, using a process call **analytic induction.** Researchers collect data, formulate hypotheses based on the data, test their hypotheses using the data, and attempt to develop theory. The theory they develop is called **grounded theory** because it arises out of and is directly relevant to the particular setting under study:

> While in the field, the researcher continually asks questions as to fit, relevance, and workability about the emerging categories and relationships between them. By raising questions at this point in time the researcher checks those issues while he still has access to the data. As a result, he continually fits his analysis to the data by checking as he proceeds.[42]

Researchers must approach the field with an open mind to ensure that their ultimate theory is grounded. Because field research is based on observation, preconceived ideas and rigid hypotheses may influence the observations a researcher

41. Lofland and Lofland, *Analyzing Social Settings,* p. 94.
42. Barney G. Glaser, *Theoretical Sensitivity* (Mill Valley, Calif.: Sociology Press, 1978), p. 39.

chooses to record for analysis, which can compromise the resultant theory. Since most researchers do not spend all of their time in the field, they may, however, use very loosely defined hypotheses to decide when and how to make their initial observations. Subsequently, researchers will use observations to refine, reject, and reformulate hypotheses throughout the research process. Blanche Geer exemplifies this method in the following excerpt:

> My use of hypotheses falls roughly into three sequential types. The first operation consisted of testing a crude yes-or-no proposition. By asking informants or thinking back over volunteered information in the data . . . I stated a working hypothesis in the comments and began the second operation in the sequence: Looking for negative cases or setting out deliberately to accumulate positive ones. . . . Working with negatively expressed hypotheses gave me a specific goal. One instance that contradicts what I say is enough to force modification of the hypothesis. . . . The third state of operating with hypotheses in the field involves two-step formulations and eventually rough models. Hypotheses take the form of predictions about future events which may take place under specific conditions or changes in informants over time in conjunction with events.[43]

Theory building in analytic induction consists of finding and delineating relationships between categories of observations. Often, researchers attempt to distinguish a core category and explain how various subcategories influence the core category. The researcher's goal in developing grounded theory is to produce a set of propositions that explains the totality of the phenomenon. Qualitative researchers use examples of their observations and quotations from members of the group under study to support their theories. In some cases, researchers can use grounded theory to develop empirically testable hypotheses amenable to statistical analysis.

A classic instance of field research using analytic induction is Donald Cressey's study of embezzlement.[44] Cressey defined embezzlement as the phenomenon of accepting a position of trust in good faith and then violating this trust by committing a crime. He initially formulated a hypothesis that these violations of trust occurred when embezzlers conceived of the thefts as "technical violations" but rejected this hypothesis after finding embezzlers who said they knew their behavior had been wrong and illegal. Cressey next hypothesized that violators defined the illegal use of funds as an emergency that could not be met by legal means. But he revised this hypothesis again when he observed violators who did not report an emergency or who noted an even greater emergency in the past. Next Cressey noted that violators were individuals who felt they needed to use "secret means." But again, he had to reformulate this hypothesis when he discovered deviant cases. The final hypothesis, according to Cressey, is the one that accounts for all cases observed:

43. Blanche Geer, "The First Days in the Field," in *Sociologists at Work,* ed. Phillip Hammond (Garden City, N.Y.: Doubleday, 1967), pp. 389–390.
44. Donald R. Cressey, *Other People's Money: A Study in the Social Psychology of Embezzlement* (New York: Free Press, 1953).

Trusted persons became trust violators when they conceive of themselves as having a financial problem which is non-shareable, are aware that this problem can be secretly resolved by violation of the position of financial trust, and are able to apply to their own conduct in that situation verbalizations which enable them to adjust their conceptions of themselves as trusted persons with their conceptions of themselves as users of the entrusted funds or property.[45]

# Blue-Collar Community:
# An Example of Field Research

Before concluding our discussion of field research, it is useful to illustrate the various stages with one inclusive study, *Blue-Collar Community,* conducted by William Kornblum in South Chicago.[46] Kornblum used a variety of methods to gather data, including discussions with community residents, archival records, census data, interviewing, and attending community meetings. However, the study leans primarily on Kornblum's firsthand involvement and participation in the life of the community. As such, it is a good example of a field study employing participant observation as the main method of analysis.

## Choosing the Research Topic and the Research Site

The general topic was suggested to Kornblum by his professors in graduate school, who were interested in sponsoring a study of Chicago's south Slavic ethnic groups. Kornblum conducted some research on local community organizations in Yugoslavian communities and was interested in the general question of how Yugoslav immigrants adapted in the United States. He decided to focus on the south Slavic settlement in South Chicago and on the Pulaski-Milwaukee section on the Northwest side and started interviewing Croatian and Serbian immigrants. He also visited the immigrant coffee shops, soccer clubs, and taverns and was gradually drawn toward the steel mill neighborhoods of South Chicago. Kornblum describes his choice of the community in the following way:

> South Chicago fascinated me. I had never seen such heavy industry at close range, and I was awed by the immensity of the steel mills and the complexity of the water and rail arteries which crisscrossed the area's neighborhoods. In the people's faces and in their neighborhoods I saw more of the spectrum of cultural groups which had settled and built the community. Thus, I was beginning to see that my study would have to concern itself as much with the larger community as it would with the cultural and social adaptations of Serbian and Croatian settlers.[47]

Kornblum found a Serbian immigrant restaurant where he was introduced to some of the regular patrons. The majority of them were Serbian immigrant men

45. Ibid,, p. 273.
46. William Kornblum, *Blue-Collar Community* (Chicago: University of Chicago Press, 1974).
47. Ibid., p. 232.

in their mid-thirties to early forties, most of whom were steelworkers. Although it was a congenial spot, the restaurant was socially peripheral because its patrons were mostly recent immigrants. At this point, Kornblum wanted to make contacts with American-born Serbian and Croatian residents, so he began looking for a place to settle in the community.

## Gaining Access

Soon after moving into the community, Kornblum started attending public meetings to identify local leaders and to arrange an introductory meeting with them. He identified himself as a researcher only to a few; to most residents he said he was teaching at the nearby Indiana University while his wife was a student at the University of Illinois in the central city and that the neighborhood was a halfway point for both of them.

Gradually, Kornblum became friendly with a larger number of political activists and leaders, in particular with a group of steelworkers who ran the local union at one of the mills. He began to feel that it was necessary to make more of a commitment to South Chicago's lifestyle:

> I felt like a knowledgeable outsider who was missing some of the most important experiences of life in the community. . . . A friend whose opinion I highly valued, the Serbian president of a local steel union, confronted me with a serious challenge, "How can you really understand what goes on here . . . if you've never spent any time inside a steel mill?"[48]

Subsequently, Kornblum was hired as a subforeman in the steel mill that became the focus of his study.

## Establishing Relations with Members

Kornblum's job as a subforeman proved to be an ideal position from a research perspective. As subforeman he had to understand how the work at his end of the mill fit with the overall division of labor in the entire plant. As a manager he could walk freely throughout the mill and converse informally with workers. This made him sensitive to the interactions that took place in the mill, especially to the meaning of unionism. He began to understand how steel production creates an occupational community inside the mill.

Kornblum was particularly interested in understanding the community's political leaders, especially unionist politicians. At that time, the community was involved in choosing the leaders of its central institutions. Therefore, many of his friends and informants were actively involved in politics and were sometimes members of opposing factions. This created a problem that is quite typical of field research. Kornblum notes:

48. Ibid., pp. 235–236.

I began to feel that I could not remain aloof from political commitment when all the people I cared for had so much more at stake than I did. Aside from the personal aspect of this decision, there are very real limitations to what one can learn about political processes through informants. If one wishes actually to watch decisions being made in a competitive political system, it is often necessary to become part of the decision-making body itself. I did this by taking highly partisan although "behind the scenes" roles in most of the political campaigns reported in this study. The liabilities of this strategy are numerous and deserve some attention. First, it is obvious that the more committed one is to a particular faction, the less one can learn, at first hand, about others. . . . In consequence of this, whenever I committed myself to a given faction I attempted to function as much as possible in capacities which would require little public exposure. In order to keep up with events in opposing factions I attempted to explain my affiliations as frankly as possible to friends on opposite sides, in much the same terms as any other resident of the community would. In this way it was possible to act as a partisan and still communicate with friends in opposing factions who acted as my informants. . . . Another problem in taking on partisan roles as a researcher is that it almost inevitably causes bias in favor of those to whom one is committed. In my case, again, the answer to this problem was to maintain close informants on opposing sides, and to try, in the analysis of events, to be on guard against my own partialities so that I might correct them or use them knowingly.[49]

## Leaving the Field

Kornblum and his family moved from South Chicago to Seattle, where the study was written. Periodically, he returned to South Chicago to continue his involvement in local political life.

---

# Ethical and Political Issues of Fieldwork

Because fieldwork is characterized by long-term and intimate participation in the daily life of the people being studied, it is associated with a number of ethical, legal, and political dilemmas. Two ethical issues are associated with fieldwork: the problem of potential deception and the impact the fieldwork may have on the lives of those studied.[50]

Earlier in this chapter, we saw that fieldworkers sometimes conduct their study under a false identity in order to gain access to the field and that this kind of fieldwork has generated considerable controversy and criticism. However, some field researchers defend the use of disguised observation; they claim that it is the only way to gain access to important research sites. Furthermore, they argue that covert methods have never directly harmed the people studied in any significant way.

49. Ibid., pp. 240–241.
50. Emerson, *Contemporary Field Research,* p. 255.

Obviously, this is a serious controversy that cannot be easily resolved. We must stress, however, that anyone planning to use disguised identity in a field study should be aware of the serious ethical implications of doing so. If at all possible, the researcher should examine alternative ways of gaining access to the research site.

Another important ethical issue is the unanticipated effect that any kind of fieldwork may have on the people being studied. Very often the fieldworkers have more power than their hosts. Subjects may perceive fieldworkers as sources of material resources, political connections, and social prestige. For example, in a study conducted in New Guinea, the Papuan settlers (mistakenly) credited the fieldworkers with getting the government to change certain land policies.[51] Obviously, such a perception could be very harmful to the relations between the researcher and the study population, especially if the fieldworker fails to perform in ways that the people expect.

The research community has become more concerned with the political issues associated with field research as governments and other political groups have become increasingly interested in who gets studied and in what ways.[52] This concern has particular relevance in cases where the results of research dealing with disadvantaged groups may have political and social implications. In addition, many of these groups are now claiming the right to review both research proposals and prepublication drafts of research reports.

In spite of these ethical and political concerns, qualitative field research can yield rich descriptions of cultures that cannot be attained through quantitative research. When we have little or no information about a group or subculture, field research can serve as an exploratory tool in the development of quantitative measures. Researchers who engage in field research must act responsibly to ensure that social scientists do not lose the opportunity to use this valuable tool.

---

## Summary

---

**1.** Field research is the most central strategy of data collection associated with the qualitative method. Scientists conduct field research in natural settings in an effort to understand subjectively the people being studied.

**2.** The method of data collection most closely associated with field research is participant observation, the process through which the investigator attempts to obtain membership in or a close attachment to the group he or she wishes to study. The researcher can assume either a complete participant role or a participant-as-observer role. Complete participants conceal their identities and do not make their research objectives known, whereas participants-as-observers make their presence known to the group being studied.

51. Ibid.
52. Ibid., p. 266.

**3.** The practice of field research can be divided into the following distinct stages: selecting a research topic, choosing an appropriate research site and obtaining access, establishing relations with members of the group and finding reliable informants, and leaving the field and analyzing the data.

**4.** The goal of field research is to develop grounded theory using the method of analytic induction. The researcher constructs analytic categories from the data and develops hypotheses based on the relationships between categories. Both the analytic categories and the hypotheses are revised and refined as the research progresses by comparing positive and negative cases.

**5.** Fieldwork is associated with a number of ethical and political dilemmas. The first problem is the potential for deception, which is especially likely in studies in which the observer disguises his or her identity. The unanticipated consequences of the research are a second important ethical issue. Subjects may perceive researchers as sources of material resources, political connections, and social prestige, resources that are unrelated to the research process or its objectives.

## Key Terms for Review

analytic induction (p. 294)
complete participant (p. 282)
field research (p. 281)
grounded theory (p. 294)

informant (p. 290)
negative case (p. 293)
participant-as-observer (p. 285)
participant observation (p. 282)

## Study Questions

1. Discuss the main differences between qualitative and quantitative research.
2. Compare and contrast the *complete participant* and *participant-as-observer* roles.
3. Describe the difficulties associated with gaining access to a research site.
4. What is analytic induction?
5. What are the major ethical and political issues of fieldwork?

## Additional Readings

Agar, Michael H. *Speaking of Ethnography.* Newbury Park, Calif.: Sage, 1986.
Berg, Bruce L. *Qualitative Research Methods.* Boston: Allyn & Bacon, 1989.
Burgess, Robert G., ed. *Field Research: A Sourcebook and Field Manual.* London: Allen & Unwin, 1982.
Emerson, Robert M., ed. *Contemporary Field Research.* Boston: Little, Brown, 1983.
Golde, Peggy, ed. *Women in the Field: Anthropological Experience.* 2d ed. Berkeley: University of California Press, 1986.

Gorden, Raymond, L. *Interviewing: Strategy, Techniques, and Tactics.* 3d ed. Homewood, Ill.: Dorsey, 1980.

Lofland, John, and Lyn H. Lofland. *Analyzing Social Settings.* Belmont, Calif.: Wadsworth, 1984.

McCracken, Grant. *The Long Interview.* Newbury Park, Calif.: Sage, 1988.

Miles, Matthew B., and Michael A. Huberman. *Qualitative Data Analysis.* Newbury Park, Calif.: Sage, 1983.

Patton, Michael Quinn, *Qualitative Evaluation and Research Methods.* 2d ed. Newbury Park, Calif.: Sage, 1990

Shaffir, William B., and Robert A. Stebbins, eds. *Experiencing Fieldwork: An Inside View of Qualitative Research.* Newbury Park, Calif.: Sage, 1991.

Shaffir, William B., Robert A. Stebbins, and Allan Throwetz, eds. *Fieldwork Experience: Qualitative Approaches to Social Research.* New York: St. Martin's Press, 1980.

Smith, Robert B., and Peter K. Manning, eds. *Handbook of Social Science Methods: Vol. 2. Qualitative Methods.* Cambridge, Mass.: Ballinger, 1982.

Strauss, Anselm, and Juliet Corbin. *Basics of Qualitative Research: Grounded Theory, Procedures, and Techniques.* Newbury Park, Calif.: Sage, 1990.

Strauss, Anselm L. *Qualitative Analysis for Social Scientists.* New York: Cambridge University Press, 1987.

Van Maanen, John. *Tales of the Field.* Chicago: University of Chicago Press, 1988.

——, ed. *Qualitative Methodology.* Newbury Park, Calif.: Sage, 1983.

Wax, Rosalie H. *Doing Fieldwork: Warnings and Advice.* Chicago: University of Chicago Press, 1971.

# CHAPTER 13
# Secondary Data Analysis

Art can sometimes follow science, as in the case of Umberto Eco's novel *Foucault's Pendulum*.[1] Jacopo Belbo, an eccentric but intriguing editor, is running for his life and has asked his good friend Casaubon for help. In order to solve the personal and intellectual mysteries surrounding Belbo's plight, Eco, the Italian linguist, provides his characters with tools that combine fantasy with the important empirical methodology of content analysis. He sends Casaubon on a chase for clues through volumes of ancient texts, including biographies, as well as through computer files whose entry codes must first be cracked. Casaubon searches for recurring phrases, for shared themes, and for references to specific events. As would any good social scientist, he checks the validity of these sources against the empirical facts of history and his hypotheses concerning motivation to solve the puzzle and help his friend. In the following chapter, we will stick to empirical reality and present guidelines for the systematic use of secondary data analysis.

I N THIS CHAPTER, WE FIRST DISCUSS THE REASONS FOR THE INcreased use of secondary data; we then point out the advantages and inherent limitations of secondary data analysis. Next we examine the major sources of secondary data, including the census, special surveys, simple observation, and archival data. Finally, we present content analysis as a method for systematically analyzing data obtained from archival records, documents, and newspapers.

The data collection methods that we have discussed so far generate *primary* data. Such collection takes place in a contrived or natural setting (for example, field experimentation), in which the research participants are often unaware of being studied, and in which the researcher either collects the data personally or has trained observers or interviewers do so. Increasingly, however, social scientists are making use of data previously collected by *other* investigators, usually for purposes that *differ* from their own research objectives. *Secondary data analysis* thus refers to research findings based on data collected by others. For example, social scientists have used census data collected by governments for administrative and public policy purposes to investigate, among other things, the structures of households; income distribution and redistribution; immigration and migration patterns; characteristics of racial and ethnic groups; changes in family composition; occupational structures; social mobility; and attributes of rural, urban, and metropolitan areas. Data collected by Gallup and other national survey research organizations have been used to study a variety of issues such as changes in public opinion, political attitudes, and voting patterns and their determinants.

1. Umberto Eco, *Foucault's Pendulum* (London: Pan Books, 1990).

# Why Secondary Data Analysis?

Secondary data analysis has a rich intellectual tradition in the social sciences. Emil Durkheim examined official statistics on suicide rates in different areas and found that the suicide rates in Protestant countries were higher than in Catholic countries.[2] Karl Marx used official economic statistics to document his "class struggle" thesis and argue for economic determinism.[3] Max Weber studied the official ideologies of early Protestant churches and other historical documents to rebut Marx's analysis by suggesting that religion rather than economic determinism was the source of sociopolitical behavior.[4]

Social scientists are increasingly using data collected by other investigators and institutions for research purposes that differ from the original reasons for collecting the data. Referring specifically to survey research, Norval Glenn has observed that

> an almost revolutionary change in survey research would seem to be occurring. Until recently, survey data were analyzed primarily by the persons who designed the surveys, but there seems to be a rather strong trend toward separation of survey design from data analysis. One can almost envision a time when some survey researchers will specialize in survey design and others will specialize in data analysis.[5]

There are three basic explanations for this increased use of secondary data: conceptual-substantive reasons, methodological reasons, and economic reasons.

## Conceptual-Substantive Reasons

From a conceptual-substantive point of view, secondary data may be the only data available for the study of certain research problems. Social and political historians, for example, must rely almost exclusively on secondary data.

In research on more contemporary issues, as Herbert Hyman points out, the investigator searches through a wide range of materials covering different areas and eras, which may result in greater scope and depth than is possible when using a single primary data research project.[6] With the aid of such secondary sources,

2. Emile Durkheim, *Suicide* (New York: Free Press, 1966). Originally published 1897.

3. Karl Marx, *Capital* (New York: International Publishers, 1967). Originally published 1867.

4. Max Weber, *The Protestant Ethic and the Spirit of Capitalism,* trans. Talcott Parsons (New York: Scribner, 1977). Originally published 1905.

5. Norval D. Glenn, "The General Social Surveys: Editorial Introduction to a Symposium," *Contemporary Sociology,* 7 (1978): 532.

6. Herbert H. Hyman, *Secondary Analysis of Sample Surveys* (Middletown, Conn.: Wesleyan University Press, 1987), Chapter 1.

we can better understand the historical context; by analyzing data collected in different times on similar issues, we can also describe and explain change. For example, the Interuniversity Consortium for Political and Social Research (ICPSR) at the University of Michigan has systematic survey data on American national elections held since 1952.[7] Social scientists have utilized these data to describe and explain stability and change in ideology, trust, party identification, and voting over time.

Secondary data can also be used for comparative purposes. Comparisons within and between nations and societies may enlarge the scope of generalizations and provide additional insights. For example, the ICPSR has data from election studies conducted in European democracies. Since these studies measured many variables similar to those covered in the U.S. studies, this databank makes it possible to compare issues such as political participation and the structures of conflict and consensus, both nationally and internationally. As Hyman suggests, particularly in regard to survey research:

> Secondary analysis of a series of comparable surveys from different points in time provides one of the rare avenues for the empirical description of long-term changes and for examining the way phenomena vary under the contrasted conditions operative in one [or several] society[ies] at several points.[8]

## Methodological Reasons

There are several methodological advantages to secondary analysis. First, secondary data, if reliable and accurate, provides opportunities for *replication*. A research finding gains more credibility if it appears in a number of studies. Rather than conduct several studies personally, a researcher can use data collected by others in addition to his or her own. Second, the availability of data over time enables the researcher to employ longitudinal research designs. One can find baseline measurements in studies conducted decades ago and locate similar data collected more recently. Indeed, when researchers compare their primary data with those collected in earlier studies, they essentially conduct a follow-up to the original research. Third, secondary analysis may improve measurement by expanding the scope of independent variables employed in the operationalization of concepts. In Hyman's words, the secondary analyst

> must examine a diverse array of concrete indicators, assorted specific manifestations of behavior or attitude. . . . He is likely to be more exhaustive in his definition of a concept, to think about it not only in his accustomed ways, but in all sorts of odd ways.[9]

---

7. Warren E. Miller et al., *American National Elections Studies Data Sourcebook, 1952–1978* (Cambridge, Mass.: Harvard University Press, 1980).

8. Hyman, *Secondary Analysis*, p. 17.

9. Ibid., p. 24.

This expansiveness enables the researcher to gain new insights. Fourth, by using secondary data we can increase the sample size, its representativeness, and the number of observations that could lead to more encompassing generalizations. Finally, secondary data can be used for triangulation, increasing the validity of research findings obtained with primary data.

## Economic Reasons

Primary research is a costly undertaking. A survey of a national sample of 1,500 to 2,000 individuals can cost $200,000 or more. This is a prohibitive sum for university professors, independent researchers, and graduate students, particularly with the retrenchment in research support and funding opportunities. It is considerably cheaper to use existing data rather than to collect new data.

# Public Opinion and Public Policy: An Example

What effects, if any, does public opinion have on government policy? To study this important question, Benjamin Page and Robert Shapiro examined several hundred surveys of U.S. national samples conducted between 1935 and 1979 by Gallup, the National Opinion Research Center, and the Center for Political Studies' Survey Center at the University of Michigan.[10] They created a file of 3,319 questionnaire items about policy preferences, of which some 600 were repeated in identical form at two or more points in time. Then the authors identified every instance in which there was a significant change in opinion from one survey to another (6 percent or more in samples of 1,500 with fairly even divisions of opinion). They found 357 such instances of change in Americans' policy preferences, encompassing a wide range of foreign and domestic issues, such as taxation, spending, regulation, trade, and military action.

For each of these instances of opinion change, Page and Shapiro measured indicators of policy outputs beginning two years before the initial opinion survey was conducted and ending four years after the final survey. Using these two sets of data, the authors coded agreements and disagreements between the instances of opinion change and the policy indicators. Upon analyzing the data, they found a great deal of congruence between changes in policy and changes in opinion during the half century they studied. Furthermore, congruence was more frequent when the policymaking process had time to react to changes in public opinion. The authors concluded that "public opinion, whatever its sources and quality, is a factor that genuinely affects government policies in the United States."[11]

10. Benjamin I. Page and Robert Y. Shapiro, "Effects of Public Opinion on Policy," *American Political Science Review,* 77 (1983): 175–190.

11. Ibid., p. 189.

# Limitations of Secondary Data Analysis

Like other data collection methods, secondary data analysis has certain inherent limitations. Perhaps the most serious problem in using secondary data is that often they only approximate the kind of data that the investigator would like to employ for testing hypotheses. There is an inevitable gap between primary data the investigator collects personally with specific research purposes and intentions in mind and data others collect for other purposes. Differences are likely to appear in sample size and design, question wording and sequence, the details of the interview schedule and technique, and the setup of laboratory experiments.

A second problem in using secondary data is access to such data. Although thousands of studies are available in data archives, it may be difficult to find the ones with the variables of interest. Sometimes the relevant data may be inaccessible because the original investigator will not release them. Researchers are not, after all, required to make their data available for secondary analysis. This problem often prods researchers into a creative use of their skills in locating relevant secondary data and measuring variables.

A third problem with secondary data analysis may emerge if the researcher has insufficient information about how the data was collected. This information is important for determining potential sources of bias, errors, or problems with internal or external validity. The ICPSR, for example, deals with this problem by classifying data into four classes according to the amount of information, documentation, and effort devoted by the original investigators as well as its staff in standardizing and checking the data (see Exhibit 13.1).

---

**Exhibit 13.1**
ICPSR Data Classes

---

The ICPSR currently employs two systems to describe the extent of processing undergone by data collections. The first, repeated below, categorizes the collections according to the extent of processing performed by the ICPSR on the original data. The second system, implemented in 1992, replaces the data class system with codes describing the discrete processing steps performed on the data either by ICPSR, the principal investigators, or the data producers.

All ICPSR collections undergo some basic checks to determine that the data and documentation correspond and that confidential or sensitive information, such as names or dates, have been recoded to protect anonymity. A codebook containing bibliographic citations and introductory materials describing the data collection is also supplied.

Class I

Class I data sets have been checked, corrected if necessary, and formatted to ICPSR specifications. The data may also have been recoded and reorganized in consultation with the investigator to maximize their utilization and accessibility. A machine-readable codebook is available. This codebook fully documents the data and may include descriptive statistics such as frequencies or means. Class I studies are often available in multiple technical formats, and SAS and SPSS data definition statements have been prepared for many Class I collections.

## Class II

Class II studies have been checked and formatted to ICPSR specifications. Most non-numeric codes have been removed. Many studies in this class are available in multiple technical formats, often with corresponding SAS and SPSS data definition statements. Any peculiarities in the data are indicated in the documentation.

## Class III

Class III studies have been checked by the ICPSR staff for the appropriate number of records per case and accurate data locations as specified by the investigator's codebook. Frequency checks on these data have often been made. Known data discrepancies and other problems, if any, are communicated to the user at the time the data are requested.

## Class IV

The Class IV studies are distributed in the form received by the ICPSR from the original investigator. The documentation for Class IV studies is reproduced from the material originally received.

From Inter-university Consortium for Political and Social Research, *Guide to Resources and Services, 1994–1995* (Ann Arbor: University of Michigan, Institute for Social Research, Center for Political Studies, 1994), p. xxiii.

---

# The Census

A *census* is defined as the recording of the demographic data describing a population in a strictly defined territory carried out by the government at a specific time and at regular intervals. A census, or population enumeration, should, in principle, be universal, including every person who lives in the designated area.[12]

12. William Peterson, *Population* (New York: Macmillan, 1975).

There are some indications that censuses date back to 3800 B.C.E. in Babylonia, to about 3800 B.C.E. in China, and to 2500 B.C.E. in Egypt. Reports have also been cited of population enumerations made in ancient Greece and Rome and by the Incas. Modern censuses, however, were first undertaken in Canada in 1666 and in the United States in 1790. A decennial (every ten years) census has taken place in both countries ever since.[13]

The primary reason behind population enumerations in early as well as modern times was to collect data that would facilitate government activities associated with domestic policies such as taxation, induction into the military, appropriation of government aid, and apportionment of elected officials. The scope of the contemporary census has been enlarged, and data collected can also provide information for research by government, by industry, and by the academic community.[14]

## The U.S. Census

The first U.S. census was conducted in 1790 by U.S. marshals under the supervision of Thomas Jefferson. In 1902, Congress established a permanent census office, the Bureau of the Census, which today is responsible for enumerating the population every ten years. In addition, the Census Bureau conducts numerous ongoing surveys of population; housing and construction; business and industry; federal, state, and local governments; and foreign trade.

The Census Bureau has introduced or participated in devising a number of statistical and technological innovations. Among the most important are population sampling, which increased the scope of the census; development of the first computer designed for mass data processing; and, most recently, the development of the Topologically Integrated Geographic Encoding and Referencing (TIGER) system. TIGER is an automated geographic database that provides coordinate-based digital map information, including political and statistical area boundaries and codes, for the entire United States, including its commonwealths and territories. Users can obtain census and other statistical data separately and add them to the TIGER database with appropriate software to assist them in such tasks as drawing new political, administrative, and service-area boundaries; delineating high-crime areas; and plotting projected population growth in their jurisdictions.[15]

The census of population and housing taken every ten years is called a **complete count census** and is intended to reach every household in the country. The decennial census uses two questionnaires: a short form that asks for basic demographic information on each member of the household plus a few questions about the housing unit, and a long form, or sample questionnaire, which contains additional questions on socioeconomic status and housing. The complete count

13. Mortimer Spiegelman, *Introduction to Demography* (Cambridge, Mass.: Harvard University Press, 1968).

14. Ibid.

15. For further discussion, see *TIGER: The Coast-to-Coast Digital Map Data Base* (Washington, D.C.: U.S. Department of Commerce, Bureau of the Census, November, 1990).

census is conducted using the short form. In addition, a population sample, consisting of 17 percent of all households surveyed, completes the longer questionnaire. In April 1990, the date of the most recent complete count census of the United States, a long form was sent to 17.7 million out of an estimated 106 million housing units.

A complete count of the U.S. population is necessary because census statistics determine the number of seats apportioned to each state in the House of Representatives. Moreover, federal funds to state and local governments are distributed on the basis of decennial census data. In addition, only a complete count census can provide information on small geographic areas such as a small town or a **census block**—the smallest geographic area for which census data is collected. However, as a complete count census is prohibitively expensive and its administration is complex, it is used to collect only the most basic type of information. Population sampling (questions to be asked of only a portion of the surveyed population) is also employed as it has a number of advantages over a complete count census. It is more economical, more efficient, and faster to complete; therefore, it reduces the time expended between the collection of data and the publication of initial results. Moreover, the use of sampling allows the Census Bureau to expand the scope and detail of the data gathered regarding the population's housing and employment status. In addition, some of the sample surveys conducted by the Census Bureau are designed to collect information regarding the population's attitudes toward a wide variety of issues.

Census data are generally provided for two types of geographic clusters: political units such as states, counties, or congressional districts; and statistical areas, which are regions defined for statistical use on the basis of primarily geographic criteria. Among the most common statistical areas are **Metropolitan Statistical Areas (MSA)**, **Census Designated Places (CDP)**, and **census tracts.** An MSA is defined as one or more counties, including a large population nucleus and nearby communities, that have a high degree of interaction.[16] The designated CDPs are densely settled population centers lacking legally defined corporate limits or powers.[17] Census tracts are small, locally defined statistical areas in metropolitan areas and some other counties with an average population of 4,000.[18]

## Errors in Census Statistics

The modern census constitutes an important source of reliable statistical information. However, errors in census enumerations do occur, and users need to be aware of the methodological limitations of the data.

Census data are prone to two types of errors: errors in coverage and errors in content. *Errors in coverage* means that a person or group is either not counted at all or counted twice. Duplicate counts are less serious than undercounts. The

16. From *Census '90 Basics* (Washington, D.C.: U.S. Department of Commerce, Bureau of the Census, December, 1985), p. 5.

17. Ibid.

18. Ibid.

phenomenon of undercounting the population has long been of concern to elected officials, researchers, and the public because uncounted individuals (and especially groups such as the homeless and migrant workers) often lose their ability to be represented in national, state, and local governments.

One category of undercounted individuals consists of persons who cannot be located due to their lack of a permanent address. Another is made up of people who deliberately avoid detection, such as illegal residents. It is difficult for the Census Bureau to estimate error in this case because illegal residents are not likely to appear in other official records, such as those kept by the Social Security Administration, which can be used to verify census statistics.

*Errors in content* occur whenever information is incorrectly reported or tabulated. Apart from errors due to carelessness, errors in content often occur because the persons surveyed may deliberately give inaccurate responses to questions measuring social status. For example, individuals have been misclassified into higher or lower income, occupation, or education categories as a result of their misleading responses. Such errors can have serious consequences for the validity of research findings pertaining to domestic policy-making.

## Census Products

Census products are available from the Census Bureau in various formats: printed reports, computer tapes, microfiche, and more recently CD-ROM laser disks. Printed statistical reports are convenient and readily available. Data in printed reports are presented in the form of tables showing specific sets of data for a specified geographic area. These reports are released in various series. Some series provide information for all the levels—the nation as a whole, the states, MSAs, urban areas, cities, and counties. The *Small Area* series presents block and census tract statistics. The subject series summarize data on selected subjects at the national level.

Subject reports focus primarily on housing and on population issues, but each publication centers on a particular aspect within these general areas. For example, one report, entitled "Journey to Work: Metropolitan Community Flows," contains statistics on local and national commuting patterns for each of the MSAs in the United States as well as information about the places where workers live and work. Another report, "Living Arrangements of Children and Adults," which is useful for studies of the American household, has national-level statistics about the living arrangements of children and adults. It provides this information for children in various age groups according to their relationship to the householder and the marital status of the parents.

For users needing census statistics in greater detail or for smaller geographic and statistical units than are available in the various printed reports, the Census Bureau provides census data on computer tapes in two forms—Summary Tape Files (STFs), which contain summary tables in greater detail than those presented in the printed reports, and Public-Use Microdata Sample files (PUMS), consisting of a small sample of unidentified households and containing all census data collected about each person in the household. PUMS files enable users to prepare specialized tabulations and cross tabulations of items on the census questionnaire. These are of great value to academic researchers interested in a more-detailed study of some characteristics.[19]

Microfiche containing statistics for a subset of census blocks from the 1980 census are also available. The microfiche present a subset of the tabulations for blocks found in STF 1B. In 1990, the entire nation was "blocked" for the first time. This has increased the number of blocks for which the Census Bureau provides data from 2.5 million (in 1980) to about 7 million (in 1990). The cost and storage of block data of this magnitude would be prohibitive if they were published in printed reports.[20]

CD-ROM—compact disk-read only memory, a type of optical or laser disk— is the most recently developed technology for data storage and retrieval. One 4¼-inch CD-ROM can hold the contents of approximately 1,500 flexible diskettes, or three or four high-density tapes.[21] Special peripherals enable CD-ROMs to be used on personal computers. Due to its enormous capacity and facility of use, we expect more and more census data to be made available in this form.

## Other Data Collected by the Census Bureau

Although the decennial census of population and housing is the main source of information about the American population, it cannot cover every subject of interest. In addition, after a few years it may become outdated for many purposes. Hence, the Census Bureau conducts a number of ongoing special censuses and sample surveys. Here we describe a few that may be of particular interest to social scientists.

*Current Population Survey (CPS).*   The Current Population Survey is a monthly sample survey of the civilian noninstitutionalized population (i.e., excluding soldiers, prisoners, long-term patients) of the United States. Its primary aim is to produce statistics on unemployment and present information on the personal characteristics of the labor force, such as age, sex, race, marital and family status, and educational background. The survey also provides information on other subjects that are periodically added to the basic list of items surveyed. The Census Bureau publishes a number of reports based on these data under the title *Current Population Reports.*

*American Housing Survey (AHS).*   Every two years, as part of the AHS program, the Census Bureau interviews respondents in a representative sample of all housing units in the United States. The American Housing Survey includes extensive household-level data on housing quality, reasons for housing choices, and evaluations of public services and the general quality of life in the neighborhood. This survey contributes to the measurement of changes in the housing

19. Ibid., p. 13.
20. Ibid., p. 16.
21. Ibid., p. 16.

inventory resulting from losses, new construction, mobile home placement, and demographic characteristics of the occupants.[22]

*Consumer Expenditure Survey.* Consumer Expenditure Surveys are designed to monitor changes in prices. Data from these surveys are essential for measuring the extent of the U.S. inflation rate and its impact on the cost of living. Data from this survey are also used by the Bureau of Labor Statistics to update the monthly Consumer Price Index (CPI). Consumer Expenditure Surveys take three forms: *The Quarterly Interview Survey, The Diary Survey,* and the *Point of Purchase Survey.*

*The Quarterly Interview Survey* is conducted monthly through household interviews and provides data on living expenses incurred during the three months prior to the interview.[23]

*The Diary Survey,* also conducted monthly, collects data on the daily living expenses of individuals living in households over two consecutive one-week periods.[24] The information is recorded on special "diary" forms, hence the name of the survey.

The annual *Point of Purchase Survey* is conducted to identify the kinds of stores and other establishments frequented by consumers as they purchase a variety of goods and services. It is particularly useful for the analysis of economic trends and commercial planning activities.

The Census Bureau publishes several useful guides: the *1990 Census User's Guide* is the primary guide for use of 1990 census data; the *Census and You* is the Census Bureau's monthly newsletter for data users; and the *Census Catalog and Guide* provides a comprehensive list of all new publications, computer tape files, special tabulations, and products available from the bureau. In addition to its main headquarters in Washington, D.C., the Census Bureau operates 12 regional offices throughout the United States that are staffed by information services specialists who answer questions by telephone, in person, or through correspondence. Databanks can be purchased by universities, major city libraries, and other large organizations dealing with research.

---

# Searching for Secondary Data

With thousands of studies available in this country and abroad, how do you locate the precise data of interest? William Trochim offers some guidelines for data search:[25]

---

22. From *Census Surveys: Measuring America* (Washington, D.C.: U.S. Department of Commerce, Bureau of the Census, December, 1985), p. 6.

23. Ibid., p. 12.

24. Ibid.

25. William M. K. Trochim, "Resources for Locating Public and Private Data," in *Reanalyzing Program Evaluations,* ed. Robert F. Boruch (San Francisco: Jossey-Bass, 1981), pp. 57–67.

1. *Specify your needs:* examine subject indexes of archive holdings and identify relevant keywords.
2. *Familiarize yourself:* search the guides, catalogs, and data archives or organizations' listings that may have the desired data.
3. *Make initial contacts:* first contact people familiar with the archive and obtain information on using the data.
4. *Make secondary contacts:* use professional staff to verify information and learn how to formally request the data.
5. *Check accessibility:* obtain information on possible problems from people who have used the data.
6. *Analysis and supplemental analyses:* Obtain additional data if needed after conducting your initial analysis.

The main resources available to secondary data analysts searching for data are catalogs, guides, directories of archives, and organizations established to assist researchers. Useful catalogs of archives are *Statistics Sources,* 17th Edition, ed. P. Wasserman (Detroit: Gale Research Co., 1994); and *Research Centers Directory,* 14th Edition, ed. A. M. Palmer (Detroit: Gale Research Co., 1989). Major guides to government databases include *A Framework for Planning U.S. Federal Statistics* and *The Directory of Computerized Data Files and Related Software,* both published by the U.S. Department of Commerce; and *Federal Information Sources and Systems: A Directory for the Congress.*

The ICPSR at the University of Michigan and the Roper Center at the University of Connecticut are the largest archives of secondary data in the United States. The ICPSR publishes a yearly *Guide to Resources and Services.* The Association of Public Data Users publishes a *Data File Directory.* Other major organizations include the Bureau of Applied Social Research, Columbia University; the Laboratory for Political Research, Social Science Data Archive, University of Iowa; the National Opinion Research Center (NORC), University of Chicago; and the European Association of Scientific Information Dissemination Centers.[26]

This selection can only hint at the cornucopia of databanks and published information sources. Their steady growth in number and quality requires that students and researchers be in constant touch with the information services centers within universities, government offices, and other organizations.

# Unobtrusive Measures

An **unobtrusive measure** (also known as a *nonreactive measure*) is any method of data collection that directly removes the researcher from the interactions, events, or behavior being investigated. For example, perusing public archival documents is an unobtrusive measure because the researcher has no influence on the condi-

26. See also ibid., p. 65, and Catherine Hakim, *Secondary Analysis in Social Research: A Guide to Data Sources and Methods with Examples* (Boston: Allen & Unwin, 1982).

tions under which the data are collected. Unobtrusive measures avoid the data contamination that might arise when investigators and research participants meet in data collection situations. With unobtrusive measures, the individual "is not aware of being tested, and there is little danger that the act of measurement will itself serve as a force for change in behavior or elicit role-playing that confounds the data."[27] These measures range from consulting private and public archives to simply observing people at work or play, from physical trace analysis to contrived observations. For example, physical traces and evidence left behind by a population are generated without the producer's knowledge of their future use by researchers.

Eugene Webb and his coauthors make a distinction between two broad classes of physical evidence: erosion measures and accretion measures.[28] **Erosion measures** are the signs left after use of an object. For example, the wear on library books is an index of their popularity, and the number of miles accumulated by police officers in their patrol cars is a measure of their daily activity. Thus a researcher can confirm the verbal reports of daily activities made by police officers by checking the number of miles accumulated in their patrol cars.

**Accretion measures** constitute the evidence deposited by a population in the course of their activities. In this case, the researcher examines remnants that are suggestive of some human behavior. For example, the amount of dust on machines has been taken by investigators as an indicator of the frequency of their use; similarly, an investigator can estimate the popularity of different radio stations by noting the settings on car radios when cars are brought in for servicing.

Both the time needed for collection and the dubious quality of the data make physical trace analysis problematic. Even more important, in many instances the researcher lacks sufficient information on the population from which these measures are collected to draw valid generalizations.

## Simple Observation

**Simple observations** are another basic nonreactive measure. They are used in situations "in which the observer has no control over the behavior or sign in question, and plays an unobserved, passive and unobtrusive role in the research situation."[29] Although researchers making simple observations use the methodology of other observational methods in all other respects, simple observation is a distinct method because the researcher does not intervene in the production of the data (compare with the experimental observation methodologies described in Chapter 8). There are four basic types of simple observation: observation of exterior body and physical signs, analysis of expressive movement, physical location analysis, and observation of language behavior.

27. Eugene J. Webb et al., *Nonreactive Measures in the Social Sciences* (Boston: Houghton Mifflin, 1981), p. 175.
28. Ibid., pp. 35–52.
29. Webb et al., *Nonreactive Measures,* p. 112.

*Observation of Exterior Body and Physical Signs.*    In this type of simple observation, researchers observe the exterior body and physical elements as indicators or signs of behavior patterns and attitudes. Examples of such signs are tattoos, hairstyles, clothing, ornamental items such as jewelry, and other objects. The signs posted in public places are included in this category. For example, a change in the language of store signs serves as a measure of social change because it indicates the settlement of immigrant groups in the neighborhood.

*Analysis of Expressive Movement.*    A second type of simple observation is the analysis of expressive movement. Observers focus on the self-expressive features of the body and how these movements indicate social interactions. People communicate many feelings as well as social norms through body language—how close together people stand, how much they look at each other, and how often they touch.

When researchers investigate facial and body gestures, they confront a major problem: determining what particular gestures convey. For instance, a smile may mean relief or happiness. The observer's role is to determine the meaning of that gesture for both the person expressing it and the recipient within the context in which the gesture is used. The same movement may, after all, convey different emotions in different situations.

*Physical Location Analysis.*    The main purpose of **physical location analysis** is to investigate the ways in which individuals use their bodies in a naturally occurring social space. For example, before the demise of the Soviet empire, observers of Russian internal politics always took note of who stood next to whom on the dais when the Soviet leadership observed the May Day parade in Red Square. Their positions served as clues of stability or change in the power elite. Another example is protocol—its rules essentially institutionalize the physical representation of status. The researcher should therefore be sensitive to variations in the proximity of leading figures to each other when measuring changes in political or social status.

*Observation of Language Behavior.*    This fourth form of simple observation focuses on conversations and the interrelationship of speech patterns to locale, to social categories, and to time of day. The analysis combines the study of physical locations with that of expressive movements. In her popular books, Dr. Deborah Tannen makes effective use of language behavior in analyzing how relationships between people are structured and maintained. Based on close observation of conversations, she notes that men are more sensitive to "messages," the obvious meaning of what is said; women are more sensitive to "metamessages," the information implicit in what is said that conveys attitudes about what is being said and about the people talking or listening.[30]

---

30. Deborah Tannen, *You Just Don't Understand, Women and Men in Conversation* (New York: Ballantine Books, 1990), p. 32.

*Problems with Simple Observations.* The main advantage of simple observation is that the researcher has no responsibility for structuring the observation situation and remains unobserved throughout. This eliminates the bias that might otherwise be introduced (see Chapters 5 and 9). Simple observation, however, does have its own problems. First, the recorded observations may not represent a wide enough population, thus limiting the scope of generalizations. Second, bias might be introduced by the observer if he or she becomes more or less attentive, adept, or involved as time goes by. Biases may, then, be introduced as a result of unintended, uncontrolled changes in the way observation is carried out. Third, if the observer is to remain unnoticed, the settings most accessible to simple observation are public, which limits the scope of behaviors amenable to such observation. Fourth, much of the data collected by simple observation do not automatically invite clearcut explanations: "The data . . . don't offer the 'why,' but simply establish a relationship."[31] This ambiguity limits the applicability of simple observations and the validity of their interpretation, even though the situations observed may be easily replicated.

---

# Archival Records

Archival records are another form of unobtrusive data. These data are collected from diverse sources such as actuarial records, electoral and judicial records, government documents, the mass media, and private records such as autobiographies, diaries, and letters. Some of these records have been compiled for more general use, whereas others have been prepared specifically for purposes of research. Hence, a large amount of data in the form of public and private archival records is readily available to social scientists.

## Public Records

Four basic kinds of public records may be distinguished. First are **actuarial records,** which describe the personal demographic characteristics of the population served by the recordkeeping agency, such as birth and death statistics and records of marriages and divorces. Second are judicial and other official records concerning court decisions, legislators' activities, public votes, budget decisions, and the like. Third are governmental and quasi-governmental documents such as crime statistics, records of social welfare programs, hospitalization records, and weather reports. Fourth are the various reports, news items, editorials, and other information produced or transmitted by the mass media. Each of these four types of public records has been used as sources for numerous and varied research purposes.

31. Webb et al., *Nonreactive Measures,* p. 127.

*Actuarial Records.*    Most societies maintain records of births, deaths, marriages, and divorces. Social scientists use such data for both descriptive and explanatory purposes. For example, Russell Middleton examined fertility levels with two sets of data: fertility values expressed in magazine fiction and actuarial fertility levels for three different time periods: 1916, 1936, and 1956. Middleton first estimated fertility values by observing the size of fictional families in eight American magazines. When he compared these values with population data for the same years, the results showed that shifts in the size of fictional families closely paralleled shifts in the actual fertility level of the United States.[32]

Lloyd Warner used a number of official records in his original study on death and its accoutrements in an American city. Warner investigated official cemetery documents to establish a social history of the dead. He indeed found the social structure of the city was mirrored in its cemetery. For example, the father was most often buried in the center of the family plot, and headstones of males were larger than those of females. Moreover, a family that had raised its social status moved the graves of its relatives from less prestigious cemeteries to more prestigious ones.[33]

*Judicial and Other Official Records.*    Political scientists have used voting statistics widely to study electoral behavior and the voting patterns of legislators. Collections such as *A Review of Elections of the World,* issued biennially by the Institute of Electoral Research in London, and the volumes of *America at the Polls: A Handbook of American Presidential Election Statistics, 1920–1965* edited by Richard M. Scammon (Salem, N.H.: Ayer, 1976) and *Kennedy to Clinton, 1960–1992* by Alice V. McGillivray and Richard M. Scammon (Washington D.C.: Congressional Quarterly Inc., 1994) provide useful historical data on voting. *The Congressional Quarterly Almanac* gives information on the U.S. Congress, including data on the backgrounds of members of Congress, information on major items of legislation, tabulations of roll-call votes, and a survey of political developments. In the *World Handbook of Political and Social Indicators* (New Haven, Conn.: Yale University Press, 1983), Charles L. Taylor and David Jodice report transnational data on 148 political and social measures, such as electoral participation, counts of riots by county per year, numbers of irregular government changes, and inequalities in income distribution. Harold W. Stanley and Richard G. Niemi, in *Vital Statistics on American Politics,* 3d Edition (Washington, D.C.: Congressional Quarterly Inc., 1991), present useful time-series data on political institutions, public opinion, and government policies.

The *Congressional Record* contains information that can be used to study the behavior not only of members of Congress but also of people outside Congress. For example, it is a common practice for members of Congress to insert in the

32. Russell Middleton, "Fertility Values in American Magazine Fiction, 1916–1956," *Public Opinion Quarterly,* 24 (1960): 139–143.

33. Lloyd W. Warner, *The Living and the Dead: A Study of the Symbolic Life of Americans* (New Haven, Conn.: Yale University Press, 1965).

*Record* newspaper columns that reflect their personal points of view. In an early study of political columnists, Eugene Webb employed these data to estimate conservatism and liberalism among Washington's columnists. Webb assigned a score on a liberal-conservative continuum to individual members of Congress by evaluating their voting records as published by two opposing groups—the Conservative Americans for Constitutional Action and the Liberal Committee on Political Action of the AFL-CIO. He then ranked columnists vis-à-vis the mean score of the members of Congress who had placed their articles in the *Record*.[34]

***Governmental Documents.***   Just as the analysis of birth and death records can be fruitful, other governmental and quasi-governmental documents may also serve as sources of data. Lombroso, for instance, was interested in discovering what, besides economic or human resources, might contribute to scientific creativity. He used governmental documents to study the effect of weather and time of year on scientific creativity. After drawing a sample of 52 physical, chemical, and mathematical discoveries, he noted the time of their occurrence. His evidence showed that 22 of the major discoveries occurred in the spring, 15 in the autumn, 10 in the summer, and 5 in winter.[35]

City budgets are fertile sources for much of the research in the social sciences. Robert Angell used such data in his unique research on the moral integration of American cities. He constructed a "welfare effort index" by computing local per capita expenditures for welfare; he combined this with a "crime index," based on FBI data, to arrive at an "integration index."[36] Budgets have also been used as indicators of policy commitments. The expenditure side of the budget shows "who gets what" in public funds, and the revenue side tells "who pays the price." Most important, the budgetary process provides a mechanism for reviewing governmental programs, assessing their cost, relating them to financial sources, making choices among alternative expenditures, and determining the financial effort that a government has expended on these programs. In their classic study, Otto Davis, M. A. H. Dempster, and Aaron Wildavsky examined the federal budget in consecutive periods and identified two variables that explain the greatest portion of budgetary allocations in any year:

> 1. The agency's yearly budget request is comprised of a fixed percentage of the Congressional appropriation in the previous year plus a random component for the current year. 2. The Congressional appropriation for an agency in a certain year is a fixed percentage of the agency's request in that year plus a component representing a deviation from the usual relationship between the Congress and the agency for the previous year.[37]

34. Eugene J. Webb, "How to Tell a Columnist," *Columbia Journalism Review,* 2 (1963): 20.

35. Webb et al., *Nonreactive Measures,* p. 72.

36. Robert C. Angell, "The Moral Integration of American Cities," *American Journal of Sociology,* 57 (1951): 1–140.

37. Otto A. Davis, M. A. H. Dempster, and Aaron Wildavsky, "A Theory of the Budgetary Process," *American Political Science Review,* 60 (1966): 529–547.

*The Mass Media.*    The mass media constitute the most easily available source of social science data. The mass media record people's verbal communications; researchers analyze these communications to test propositions. The introduction of content analysis, to be discussed later in this chapter, enabled researchers to expand their use of the mass media as a primary source of data. Accordingly, research using data obtained from the mass media is voluminous.[38] We will cite only one recent example. Gina Daddario studied TV sportscasters' descriptions of and commentaries on women's events during the 1992 Winter Olympics. Her data indicate that the style of the commentaries and the language used attempt to present the female athlete as an adolescent ideal rather than a serious role model despite the onscreen depiction of physically challenging events, activities that contradict stereotypical images of femininity. She concluded that sportscasters' use of masculine imagery maintained the marginalization of female sports.[39]

## Private Records

Private records are more difficult to obtain than public records. Nevertheless, they can be of great value to researchers who wish to gain insights by inspecting an individual's own definition of a situation or an event. Private records include auto-biographies, diaries, letters, essays, and the like. *Autobiographies* are the most frequently used private record; they reflect the author's interpretation of his or her personal experiences. The *diary* is a more spontaneous account, as its author tends to be unconstrained by the sense of mission that often controls the production of autobiographies. Both autobiographies and diaries are initially directed to one person—the author. *Letters,* in contrast, have a dual audience—the writer and the recipient—from the outset, and often reflect the interaction between them.[40] These three categories of private records focus on the author's personal experiences and express his or her personal reflections. As such, they are usually produced at the author's own initiative.

One of the major problems in using private documents is the question of their **authenticity.** There are two kinds of unauthentic records: records that have been produced by deliberate deceit and records that have been unconsciously mis-represented. Records may be falsified or forged for the sole purpose of gaining prestige or material rewards. For example, writers who claim to have an intimate knowledge of the subject's life can more easily sell an alleged biography to a publishing company; such was the case with a fake biography of the eccentric billionaire Howard Hughes, sold in 1972 to a reputable publisher under false pretenses.

38. For studies using the mass media as a source of unobtrusive data, see Webb et al., *Nonreactive Measures.*
39. Gina Daddario, "Chilly Sciences of the 1992 Winter Games: The Mass Media and the Marginalization of Female Athletes," *Sociology of Sports Journal,* 11 (1994): 275–288.
40. Norman K. Denzin, *The Research Act: A Theoretical Introduction to Sociological Methods,* 3d ed. (Englewood Cliffs, N.J.: Prentice-Hall, 1989), Chapter 8.

As a means of guarding against unauthenticity, several procedures can be employed. First, the investigator needs to examine authorship critically. Second, he or she must establish the date of the document and verify the other dates mentioned. For instance, if the author refers to a particular event, say, a flood, this event can be verified by checking another source, such as contemporary accounts in newspapers. If the writer refers to an event that had not yet taken place at the time the document was purportedly written, the investigator has grounds to suspect the record's legitimacy.

The second kind of unauthenticity is much more difficult to detect. Although documents may not be false, they may nevertheless misrepresent the truth for the following reasons: the authors of letters, diaries, or autobiographies may not remember the facts clearly; or they may be trying to please or amuse their readers by exaggerating; or, perhaps, they may be constrained by social norms and conventions and thus forced to present a somewhat distorted picture. Stuart Chapin has suggested that a researcher answer the following critical questions before accepting a document as an authentic record:[41]

1. What did the author mean by a particular statement? Is its real meaning different from its literal meaning?
2. Was the statement made in good faith? Was the author influenced by sympathy or antipathy? By vanity? By public opinion?
3. Was the statement accurate? Was the author a poor observer because of a mental defect or abnormality? Was he or she badly situated in time and place to observe, or negligent or indifferent?

When the investigator has obtained answers to these questions, he or she is in a better position to evaluate records and accept only the credible ones.

***Autobiographies.***    The uniqueness of the autobiography is that it provides a view of a person's life and experiences uncontaminated by another person's analysis of the events. The investigator may thus gain an understanding of a person's life in its natural setting, presumably directly communicated and free of intervening influences.

Gordon Allport distinguished three major types of autobiographies, each of which may serve different research objectives.[42] The first is the *comprehensive autobiography,* which covers a full cycle of the person's life from his or her earliest memory and integrates a large number of experiences. Helen Keller's accounts of her life as a blind deaf-mute exemplify the comprehensive autobiography. The second type is the *topical autobiography,* which focuses on a limited aspect of the person's life. For example, Edwin Sutherland studied only one phase of the life of a professional thief:

41. Stuart F. Chapin, *Field Work and Social Research* (New York: Ayer, 1979), p. 37. Originally published 1920.
42. Gordon W. Allport, *The Use of Personal Documents in Psychological Research* (New York: Social Science Research Council, 1942).

The principal part of this book is a description of the profession of theft by a person who had been engaged almost continuously for more than twenty years in this profession. This description was secured in two ways: first, the thief wrote approximately two-thirds of it on topics and questions prepared by me; second, he and I discussed for about seven hours a week for twelve weeks what he had written, and immediately after each conference I wrote in verbatim form . . . all that he had said in the discussion.[43]

The third type is the *edited autobiography,* which is an edited version of the person's account. The investigator selects only experiences that are relevant to the research purpose. Through editing, the researcher clarifies and organizes the material so that it illuminates the points relevant to the research hypotheses.

*Diaries.*   A diary provides a firsthand account of the writer's life experiences. Written close to the time the events occurred, it conveys immediate experiences undistorted by memory. People who write diaries are not inhibited by the fear of public exposure; therefore, they reveal details of events and experiences that they considered significant at the time of their occurrence.

Diaries have been classified into three types. The *intimate journal* is a continuous record of a person's subjective perception of his or her experiences over a long period of time. The second type, the *memoir,* is rather impersonal and is written in a relatively short time; it resembles an objective record of the individual's affairs. The third type, the *log,* is also impersonal and contains a record of events, meetings, visits, and other activities engaged in by the individual during a limited period of time. Nevertheless, it usually lacks the individual's interpretations or details of the context in which the events occurred.

Some social scientists find the intimate journal useful because it contains authentic expressions of a person's perceptions over a prolonged period of time. For example, one biography of the poet Dylan Thomas contains portions of his personal diary, notes he kept on poems he was writing, reflections on his financial status, and comments on his relations with the artistic world.[44] The intimate journal not only chronicles a person's subjective perceptions over an extended period but also allows the investigator to compare various time periods in a person's life and to note continuities and changes.

*Letters.*   Historians and literary critics have made extensive use of letters when attempting to reconstruct the lives of historical and literary figures. One of the earliest attempts to employ letters as a source of data in scientific social research was William Thomas and Florian Znaniecki's study on the Polish peasants who immigrated to the United States. The researchers collected letters sent between Poland and the United States during the period 1901 to 1914 as a major source in their investigation of the problems that arose when ethnic communities immigrate. The letters permitted the investigators to examine, among other things,

---

43. Edwin H. Sutherland, *The Professional Thief* (Chicago: University of Chicago Press, 1988), p. v.
44. Bill Read, *The Days of Dylan Thomas* (New York: McGraw-Hill, 1964).

---

**Unobtrusive Measures Used in Secondary Data Analysis**

- *Physical Evidence:* Signs of wear on objects *(erosion measures)* or materials deposited by a population *(accretion measures).*
- *Simple Observations:* Observations made without interacting in any way with the people being observed. Types of simple observations include exterior body and physical signs, expressive movements, physical location, and language behavior.
- *Archival Records:* Data collected from sources such as actuarial records, political and judicial records, government documents, the mass media, and private records.

---

the writers' personalities and the kinds of interactions carried on with their correspondents in the old country.[45]

---

# Content Analysis

Investigators can systematically analyze the data obtained from archival records, documents, and the mass media. Letters, diaries, newspaper articles, minutes of meetings, live reportage (as in the example from the 1992 Winter Olympics cited above), films, and TV and radio shows can all be analyzed using content analysis, which is a method of data analysis as well as a method of observation. Instead of observing people's behavior directly or asking them about it, the researcher obtains copies of the communications that people have produced (when available) and asks questions about these records. The content of the communication serves as the basis of inference. For example, in *Megatrends,* John Naisbitt analyzed the economic, social, and political currents in the United States as a basis for his forecasts of new trends and directions.[46] The study involved a content analysis of more than 2 million articles about local events published in local newspapers throughout the country during a 12-year period. Among other findings, Naisbitt reported that there are five states (California, Florida, Washington, Colorado, and Connecticut) in which most social innovation occurs.

Broadly defined, **content analysis** is "any technique for making inferences by systematically and objectively identifying specified characteristics of messages."[47] Researchers guarantee objectivity by carrying out their analyses accord-

45. William I. Thomas and Florian Znaniecki, *The Polish Peasant in Europe and America* (Champaign: University of Illinois Press, 1984).

46. John Naisbitt, *Megatrends: Ten New Directions Transforming Our Lives* (New York: Warner Books, 1984).

47. Ole R. Holsti, "Content Analysis," in *The Handbook of Social Psychology,* ed. Gardner Lindzey and Elliot Aronson (Reading, Mass.: Addison-Wesley, 1968), p. 601. The following discussion is based on this work.

ing to explicit rules that enable different investigators to obtain the same results from the same messages or documents. That is, in a systematic content analysis, the "inclusion or exclusion of content is done according to consistently applied criteria of selection; this requirement eliminates analyses in which only materials supporting the investigator's hypotheses are examined."[48]

## Applications of Content Analysis

Although content analysis is always performed on a message, researchers may also use it to answer questions about other elements of communication. Harold Lasswell formulated the basic question that can be raised by researchers: "Who says what, to whom, how, and with what effect?"[49] More explicitly, a researcher may analyze messages to test hypotheses about characteristics of the text, what inspired the message, or the effects of the communication. These three aspects differ with respect to the questions researchers ask of the data, the dimension of communication they analyze, and the research design they employ.

Content analysis is most frequently applied in describing the attributes of the message. For example, early research on revolution and the development of international relations involved a survey of political symbols. The investigators constructed research designs enabling them to test hypotheses on "world revolution" by identifying trends in the use of symbols that express the major goals and values of modern politics. In one study researchers analyzed editorials from ten prestigious newspapers in the United States, England, France, Germany, and the Soviet Union for the period 1890 to 1949. Editorials appearing on the first and the fifteenth day of each month were coded for the presence of 416 key symbols. These symbols included 206 geographic terms, such as names of countries and international organizations, and 210 ideological references, such as *equality, democracy,* and *communism.* When a symbol appeared, the coders scored it as present and recorded the expressed attitudes toward it in one of three categories: approval, disapproval, or neutrality. Researchers used the data collected from 19,553 editorials to trace changing foci of attention and attitude.[50]

Content analysis need not, however, be used only in regard to verbal data. Philip White and James Gillett analyzed 916 advertisements in *Flex,* a popular bodybuilding magazine, in a study designed to decode the basic themes communicated. The themes White and Gillett discerned were: positioning the reader as inferior (43% of the content), promises of transformation (64.5%), and the muscular body as a sign of hegemonic masculinity (70.6%). They then applied cultural and ideological models to explain the results. They concluded that these ads lend legitimacy to the act of substituting the body for reality and emotions, and that

48. Ibid., p. 598.

49. Harold D. Lasswell, "Detection: Propaganda Detection and the Courts," in Harold D. Lasswell et al., *The Language of Politics: Studies in Quantitative Semantics* (Cambridge, Mass.: MIT Press, 1965), p. 12.

50. Ithiel de Sola Pool, *Symbols of Democracy* (Westport, Conn.: Greenwood Press, 1981). Originally published 1952.

for readers of the magazine, male muscularity served as a symbol of male superiority and a compensation for diminished privileges in other areas of life. These processes in turn supported a gender ideology in which biological attributes provided a basis for gender differences in the sociocultural and economic realms.[51]

The second application of content analysis—who says what and why and to whom—is that in which a text is analyzed in order to make inferences about the sender of the message and about the causes or antecedents. A well-known attempt to determine the sender's identity is the Frederick Mosteller and David Wallace study of the authorship of the *Federalist Papers,* Nos. 49–58, 62, and 63. The authors started with four sets of papers: those known to have been written by Madison, those thought to have been written by Madison or by Hamilton, and those thought to have been written by both. After examining the texts of the acknowledged set of papers, the investigators were able to select words that were used selectively by the two authors. For example, Hamilton tended to use the word *enough,* whereas Madison did not. Mosteller and Wallace then used these key differentiating words in combination with other terms to attribute the authorship of the disputed papers. The data strongly supported the claim that Madison wrote them.[52] This finding helped in resolving certain historical questions about the intellectual foundations of the Constitution.

Content analysis has also been used to infer elements of culture and cultural change. David McClelland tested his "need for achievement" (i.e., n-Achievement) theory by analyzing the content of literature in different cultures. In McClelland's view, an individual with high n-Achievement is someone who wants to succeed, who is nonconforming, and who enjoys tasks that involve elements of risk; an n-Achievement score is thus "a sum of the number of instances of achievement 'ideas' or images" appearing in a culture's literary production. McClelland's hypothesis was that "a society with a relatively high percentage of individuals with high n-Achievement should contain a strong entrepreneurial class which will tend to be active and successful particularly in business enterprises so that the society will grow in power and influence." He tested this hypothesis by scoring samples of literature from different periods of Greek civilization.[53]

In the third major application of content analysis, researchers make inferences about the effects of messages on recipients. The researcher determines the effects of A's messages on B by analyzing the content of B's messages. Alternatively, an investigator can study the effects of communication by examining other aspects of the recipient's behavior. In sum, content analysis helps to delineate the relevant independent variables that are related to the recipient's behavior in the process of communication.

51. Philip G. White and James Gillett, "Reading the Muscular Body, A Critical Decoding of Advertisements in Flex Magazine," *Sociology of Sport Journal,* 11(1994), pp. 18–39.

52. Frederick Mosteller and David L. Wallace, *Inference and Disputed Authorship: The Federalist* (Reading, Mass.: Addison-Wesley, 1964).

53. David C. McClelland, "The Use of Measures of Human Motivation in the Study of Society," in *Motives in Fantasy, Action and Society,* ed. John W. Atkinson (New York: Van Nostrand, 1966), p. 518.

---

### Three Applications of Content Analysis

- To describe the attributes of the message.
- To make inferences about the sender of the message and about its causes or antecedents.
- To make inferences about the effects of messages on recipients.

---

## Units and Categories

Content analysis involves the interaction of two processes: *specification* of the characteristics of the content that researchers are to measure and *application of the rules* researchers must use for identifying and recording the characteristics appearing in the texts to be analyzed. The categories into which researchers code content vary with the nature of the data and the research purpose. Before discussing general procedures for constructing categories, we will specify the recording units used in research and distinguish between recording units and context units. The **recording unit** is the smallest body of content in which the appearance of a reference is noted (a reference is a single occurrence of the content element). The **context unit** is the largest body of content that may be examined when characterizing a recording unit. For example, the recording unit may be a single term, but in order to decide whether the term is treated favorably, the researcher has to consider the entire sentence in which the term appears (the context unit). Thus the whole sentence is taken into account when the researcher records (and subsequently codes) the term.

Five major recording units have been used in content analysis research: *words* or *terms, themes, characters, paragraphs,* and *items.* The word is the smallest unit generally applied in research. When the recoding unit is a word, the analysis yields a list of frequencies of these words or terms. For many research purposes, the theme is a useful recording unit, particularly in the study of propaganda, attitudes, images, and values. In its simplest form, a theme is a simple sentence, that is, a subject and a predicate. Because themes can be found in clauses, paragraphs, and illustrations in most texts, researchers specify which of these the coder will search when using the theme as a recording unit. For example, a coder may consider only the primary theme in each paragraph or count every theme in the text.

In some studies, the character is employed as the recording unit. In these cases, the researcher counts the number of persons appearing in the text rather than the number of words or themes. This choice permits examination of the personality traits of individuals appearing in various texts.

The paragraph is infrequently used as a recording unit because of its complexity. Coders have difficulty in classifying and coding the numerous and varied elements covered in a single paragraph.

The *item* is the whole unit the producer of a message employs. The item may be an entire book, an article, a speech, or the like. Analysis by the entire item is appropriate whenever the variations within the item are small and insignificant. For example, news stories can often be classified by subject matter such as crime, labor, or sports.

Eventually, recording units are classified and coded into *categories*. Category construction, as Bernard Berelson points out, is the most crucial aspect of content analysis:

> Content analysis stands or falls by its categories. Particular studies have been productive to the extent that the categories were clearly formulated and well adapted to the problem and to the content. Content analysis studies done on a hit or miss basis, without clearly formulated problems for investigation and with vaguely drawn or poorly articulated categories, are almost certain to be of indifferent or low quality as research productions. . . . Since the categories contain the substance of the investigation, a content analysis can be no better than its system of categories.[54]

Among the types of categories employed frequently in content analysis research are the following:[55]

*"What Is Said" Categories*

SUBJECT MATTER. What is the communication about?
DIRECTION. How is the subject matter treated (for example, favorably or unfavorably)?
STANDARD. What is the basis on which the classification is made?
VALUES. What values, goals, or desires are revealed?
METHODS. What methods are used to achieve goals?
TRAITS. What are the characteristics used in describing people?
ACTOR. Who is presented as undertaking certain acts?
AUTHORITY. In whose name are statements made?
ORIGIN. Where does the communication originate?
LOCATION. Where does the action take place?
CONFLICT. What are the sources and levels of conflict?
ENDINGS. Are conflicts resolved happily, ambiguously, or tragically?
TIME. When does the action take place?

*"How It Is Said" Categories*

FORM OR TYPE OF COMMUNICATION. What is the medium of communication (radio, newspaper, speech, television, etc.)?
FORM OF STATEMENT. What is the grammatical or syntactical form of the communication?
DEVICE. What is the rhetorical or propagandistic method used?

Categories must relate to the research purpose, and must be exhaustive and mutually exclusive. *Exhaustiveness* ensures that every recording unit relevant to the study can be classified. *Mutual exclusivity* means that no recording unit can be included in more than one given category within the system (see Chapter 14).

---

54. Bernard Berelson, *Content Analysis in Communication Research* (New York: Hafner, 1971), p. 147.
55. Holsti, "Content Analysis."

The researcher also has to explicitly specify the criteria that determine which re-cording units fall into each category. This enables replication, an essential require-ment of objective and systematic content analysis.

Most content analysis research is quantitative in one form or another. In order to perform quantification, researchers employ one of the following four systems of enumeration:

1. A *time-space system* based on measures of space (for example, column inches) or units of time (for example, minutes devoted to a news item on the radio) to describe the relative emphases of different categories in the analyzed material.
2. An *appearance system* in which coders search the material for appearances of certain attributes. The size of the context unit determines the frequency with which repeated recording units occurring in close proximity to each other are counted separately.
3. A *frequency system* in which every occurrence of a given attribute is recorded.
4. An *intensity system,* generally employed in studies dealing with attitudes and values.

Methods of quantifying for *intensity* are based on the construction of scales (see Chapter 18). For example, using the paired-comparison technique developed by Thurstone, raters decide which of a possible pair of intensity indicators ranks higher on a scale of attitudes. The judgments are then used to construct categories into which recording units are placed.[56]

---

## Summary

---

**1.** Secondary data analysis is performed on data collected by others. Sec-ondary data may be the only source available to study certain research problems. It may also be used for comparative purposes. There are several methodological advantages to using secondary analysis: it provides an opportunity for replication, it permits longitudinal research designs, it may improve the measurement of cer-tain variables, and it often allows for an increased sample size. Finally, secondary data are considerably less expensive to obtain than are primary data.

**2.** A widely used source of secondary data is the census data collected by governments for administrative and public policy purposes. Census data are used by researchers to investigate, among other things, the structure of households, neighborhood and housing characteristics, and changes in family composition. Printed statistical reports are the primary source of census data and are convenient

---

56. The most recent development in content analysis is the programming of computers to process the variety of operations involved in textual analysis. It is beyond the scope of this book to survey these developments, but a good start would be Robert P. Weber, *Basic Content Analysis* (Thousand Oaks, Calif.: Sage, 1990).

and readily available. The Bureau of the Census provides census data on computer tapes for users needing census statistics in greater detail or for smaller geographic and statistical units than are available in the printed reports. The Bureau is also beginning to make such data available on CD-ROMs.

   **3.** Unobtrusive measures are another source of data that distances the investigator from the population being researched. With unobtrusive measures, subjects are not aware they are being researched, and there is little danger that the act of measurement itself will introduce a change in behavior or elicit role playing that might bias the data. We discussed three general types of unobtrusive measures: physical traces, simple observation, and archival records.

   **4.** Individuals leave physical traces without any awareness that they will be used by researchers. The two broad classes of physical traces are erosion measures and accretion measures. Erosion measures, the signs of wear left on objects, provide evidence of a population's activity. Accretion measures constitute the materials deposited by a population.

   **5.** Simple observation occurs in situations in which the observer has no control over the behavior in question and remains unobserved during the research. There are four types of simple observation: observation of exterior body and physical signs, analysis of expressive movement, physical location analysis, and observation of language behavior.

   **6.** Another unobtrusive measure is the analysis of public and private archival records. These data are collected from diverse sources, such as actuarial records, political and judicial records, governmental documents, the mass media, and private records, including autobiographies, diaries, and letters. A major problem with private records is establishing their authenticity; researchers must determine that the events recorded have not been consciously or unconsciously misrepresented by the author.

   **7.** Content analysis permits researchers to systematically analyze data obtained from archival records and documents. Instead of directly observing people's behavior or asking them about it, the investigator uses the communications that people have produced and asks questions about these messages. The content analysis procedure involves the interaction of two processes: researchers specify the content characteristics to be analyzed and apply rules for identifying and recording these characteristics when they appear in the materials being analyzed. Obviously, the categories into which content is coded vary with the nature of the research problem and the data.

---

## Key Terms for Review

---

accretion measures (p. 316)
actuarial records (p. 318)
authenticity (p. 321)
census block (p. 311)

Census Designated Places (CDP)
   (p. 311)
census tract (p. 311)
complete count census (p. 310)

content analysis (p. 324)
context unit (p. 327)
erosion measures (p. 316)
Metropolitan Statistical Areas (MSA)
   (p. 311)

physical location analysis (p. 317)
recording unit (p. 327)
simple observation (p. 316)
unobtrusive measures (p. 315)

## Study Questions

1. What are the advantages of secondary data analysis?
2. Propose a research problem and specify how to obtain the secondary data relevant to your hypothesis.
3. Define the main types of census data and indicate the research purposes most appropriate for their use.
4. Explain how the methodology of simple observation differs from experimental observation.
5. Discuss the major methodological issues in content analysis and how you would go about resolving them.

## Additional Readings

Bertaux, Daniel, ed. *Biography and Society: The Life History Approach in the Social Sciences.* Newbury Park, Calif.: Sage, 1981.

Bertaux, Daniel and Paul Thompson. *International Handbook of Oral History and Life Stories,* Vol. 2. New York: Oxford University Press, 1993.

Bloch, Marc. *The Historian's Craft.* New York: McGraw-Hill, 1964.

Bouchard, J. T. "Unobtrusive Measures: An Inventory of Uses," *Sociological Methods and Research,* 4 (1976): 267–300.

Denzin, Norman K. *Interpretive Biography.* Thousand Oaks, Calif.: Sage, 1989.

Felson, M. "Unobtrusive Indicators of Cultural Change: Neckties, Girdles, Marijuana, Garbage, Magazines, and Urban Sprawl," *American Behavioral Scientist,* 26 (1983): 534–542.

Hakim, Catherine. *Secondary Analysis in Social Research: A Guide to Data Sources and Methods with Examples.* Boston: Allen & Unwin, 1982.

Hakim, Catherine. *Research Design: Strategies and Choices in the Design of Social Research.* New York: Toutledge, Chapman & Hall, 1987.

Jacob, Herbert. *Using Published Data: Errors and Remedies.* Thousand Oaks, Calif.: Sage, 1984.

Krippendorff, Klaus. *Content Analysis: An Introduction to Its Methodology.* Thousand Oaks, Calif.: Sage, 1980.

Stewart, David W., and Michael A. Kamins. *Secondary Research: Information Sources and Methods.* 2d ed. Thousand Oaks, Calif.: Sage, 1993.

Weber, Robert P. *Basic Content Analysis.* Thousand Oaks, Calif.: Sage, 1990.

# CHAPTER 14
# Data Preparation and Analysis

**Coding Schemes**
Rules of Coding
**Codebook Construction**
Coding Reliability and Data Entry Devices
Coding Reliability
Coding Devices
Editing and Cleaning the Data
**Using Computers in Social Science Research**
Types of Computers
Linkages through Communication Networks

It took the Census Bureau almost seven years to hand tally and tabulate the data collected for the 10th census, the census of 1880. By the time this work was completed ten years later, the information was almost too obsolete to be used for apportioning taxes and political representation. It was obvious that the Census Bureau had to develop new techniques to allow for a more timely counting of the American population. Herman Hollerith, an employee of the bureau, invented an electric tabulating machine that, in 1890—the 11th decennial census—permitted the data to be tabulated in two and a half years. Hollerith's machine "tallied items by causing an electrical current to trigger simple clock-like counting devices. When an electrical current flowed through a hole punched into non-conducting paper strips, a counter was activated by an electromagnet."[1]

As the Census Bureau prepares for the upcoming 22nd census to be conducted in the year 2000, Hollerith's electric tabulating machines seem like an ancient relic from the past. For instance, while Hollerith's machine processed 10,000 to 20,000 data cards per day during the 1890 census, the Census Bureau's mainframe computers currently can tabulate one million data items per minute.

A S THIS STORY ILLUSTRATES, METHODS OF DATA PREPARAtion and analysis have improved substantially since the days of the 1890 census. In this chapter, we examine common contemporary methods of preparing and coding data. We discuss deductive coding—in which researchers derive codes from theory—as well as inductive coding—in which researchers identify categories from data—and provide rules for coding and codebook construction. We address the issue of coding reliability and discuss methods researchers can use to increase reliability. Finally, we describe various coding devices and the use of computers in storing, processing, accessing, and analyzing data sets.

Today, data collected for analysis is almost always coded, stored, retrieved, and analyzed using computerized systems. Whether you are comfortable using a personal computer, minicomputer, or mainframe, the logic of the data handling and management is similar. The purpose of this chapter is to acquaint students with common methods of preparing data for coding and codebook construction. When researchers assign numeric codes to their data, they increase their ability to use computers to retrieve and analyze data.

# Coding Schemes

As you learned in Chapter 6, measurement consists of devising a system for assigning numbers to observations. These assignments may be purely arbitrary (as they are for nominal-level variables), or they may reflect the ranking of ordinal or

1. George E. Biles, Alfred A. Bolton, and Bernadette DiRe, "Herman Hollerith: Inventor, Manager, Entrepreneur—A Centennial Remembrance." *The Journal of Management,* 15 (1989): 603–615.

interval variables. The number assigned to an observation is called a **code.** This code should be consistent across cases or units of analysis when the same condition exists. For example, if a code of 1 means "female," the variable associated with gender should be coded as 1 for each female. Information on what a code means should be listed in a codebook that accompanies the data set. This section describes the process by which researchers assign codes to observations.

Researchers can also use codes to group various classifications of a concept. Suppose that an investigator has gathered information on the occupations of several hundred individuals. The following are examples of the occupations listed:

| | |
|---|---|
| *Lawyer* | *Practical nurse* |
| *Barber* | *Migrant farm laborer* |
| *Carpenter* | *Executive* |
| *Broker* | *Engineer* |
| *Elevator operator* | *Electrician* |
| *Veterinarian* | *Advertising agent* |

Before these data can be analyzed, the researcher needs to organize the occupations into categories. The following is one acceptable way to classify occupations into categories:

1. *Professional and managerial:* lawyer, veterinarian, executive, engineer.
2. *Technical and sales:* advertising agent, broker.
3. *Service and skilled labor:* barber, elevator operator, practical nurse, electrician, carpenter.
4. *Unskilled labor:* migrant farm worker.

This system categorizes occupations according to the level of income, prestige, and education that they have in common, and permits the researcher to use four well-defined categories in his or her analysis rather than several dozen specific occupations. Systems of categories such as this one, used to classify responses or acts that relate to a single item or variable, are referred to as **coding schemes.** The principles involved in constructing such schemes are discussed in the following sections.

## Rules of Coding

Since coding is the process by which responses are classified into meaningful categories, the initial rule of coding is that the numbers assigned must make intuitive sense. For example, higher scores on a variable should be assigned higher codes than lower scores. This is most easily demonstrated with interval-level variables. A person who is older than another should receive a higher code on age. Intuitively, a 28-year-old person would receive an age code of 28. A person who is 46 years old should receive a code higher than the one for the 28-year-old— probably 46 if coded in years. Even if age categories are grouped ordinally, a higher age should be associated with a higher grouping code. That makes intuitive sense.

However, for some variables (nominal ones), by definition there is no intuitively pleasing rationale for assigning numbers. Someone with a gender of 2 ("female") does not have more gender than one with 1 ("male"). Moreover, it would not make any difference whether you assigned the numbers 6 and 4, respectively, or even 4 and 6. However, in order to maintain the reliability of your coding, you would probably want to confine coding numbers to those starting with 0 or 1 and increasing by 1 over each category. Sequentially numbering the categories starting at 0 or 1 helps to minimize the risk of miscoding (see "Editing and Cleaning the Data" later on).

***Theory and Deductive Coding.***    A researcher's intuition is one of several factors involved in coding decisions; theory, mutual exclusivity, exhaustiveness, and detail must also be considered. Researchers who engage in quantitative analysis generally test hypotheses derived from theory, and the coding system they use should be linked to the theory they hope to support or falsify. An examination of the theory will provide the researcher with an idea of the types of responses they may expect from respondents. Many issues are multidimensional and require a separate category for each dimension. For example, a researcher interested in examining "liberalism" would learn from theory that this concept is multidimensional. A person who is a social liberal (e.g., one who believes in a woman's right to birth choice) may not be a fiscal liberal (e.g., the same person does not believe that the government should fund contraception). In this case, a high score on social liberalism does not correlate with a high score on fiscal liberalism. The researcher would have to provide categories for both social and fiscal liberalism.

The actual categories the researcher develops must be mutually exclusive and exhaustive. That is, each response should clearly fall into only one category (mutually exclusive), and every response must fall into a category (exhaustive). Researchers must also ensure that the categories they choose are not so broad that important differences are obscured (detail).

***Mutual Exclusivity.***    Under the rule of **mutual exclusivity,** the coding categories for each variable must be designed so that each case or unit of analysis can be coded into one and only one category of the variable. For example, consider the following categories designed to determine the living arrangements of students:

(1) live in dormitory
(2) live with parent(s)
(3) live off campus
(4) live with spouse

These categories are not mutually exclusive because students who live with their parent(s) most likely also live off campus, and students who live with a spouse might live in either a dormitory or off campus. Respondents could not be sure which category they should mark, and people in the same living arrangement might choose different categories. The purpose of the research and the theory from which the research question is derived can clarify the categories we choose. If we are interested in learning whether students in supervised, semi-supervised, and un-supervised living arrangements differ in academic performance, we might use these categories:

(1) live with parent(s) (supervised)
(2) live in dormitory (semi-supervised)
(3) live off campus either alone, with friends, or with spouse (unsupervised).

*Exhaustiveness.* The rule of **exhaustiveness** dictates that the enumeration of categories is sufficient to exhaust all the relevant categories expected of respondents—each and every response or behavior can be classified without a substantial number being classified as "other." Theory and knowledge about the expected sample can help the researcher to determine exhaustiveness. An example of a lack of exhaustiveness is the common classification of marital—relational status into four categories only: "married," "single," "divorced," and "widowed." Since respondents who are "living together" but not legally married would not fit into the coding scheme, the requirement of exhaustiveness is violated. If the sample included only junior high school students, not only would the original coding scheme be exhaustive, but it would also be irrelevant (the variable would be a constant) since virtually all junior high school students are unmarried.

*Detail.* The **detail** of categories in a coding scheme depends on the research question, but some general guidelines exist. First, when in doubt, add another category. You can always collapse categories to generalize responses (see Appendix A for examples of how to do this with the statistical computer package SPSS); you cannot, however, disaggregate responses coded to a more general level. Second, the theory and your knowledge of the subject matter and sample should all guide the level of detail of the categories. It would make no sense to ask medical doctors to report their incomes in the categories under $5,000, $5,000 to $10,000, $10,000 to $15,000, $15,000 to $20,000, and $20,000 and above, whereas those distinctions would be appropriate when surveying people living in poverty.

**Deductive coding** allows researchers to use theory to construct response categories before they administer the instrument to respondents. Researchers using deductive coding often pretest the instrument on a small sample of the population of interest so they can modify the categories suggested by theory to fit the specific population. Closed-ended questions are an example of precoding in which responses are directly classified into categories.

*Inductive Coding.* When a study is exploratory or when there is little theory informing the researcher about the kind of responses to expect, **inductive coding** may be appropriate. In inductive coding, the researcher designs the coding scheme on the basis of a representative sample of responses to questions (particularly open-ended questions), data from documents, or data collected through participant observation (see Chapter 12). Once the researcher has identified a coding scheme, it is applied to the remainder of the data set. Consider the responses to the following question, designed to determine women's reactions to being abused by a husband or a live-in partner.[2]

> In general, if a man physically abuses his wife or live-in partner, what do you think the woman should do?
>
> 1. She should stay and try to work out the problem.
> 2. She should leave the house or apartment.
> 3. She should call a social service agency for advice.
> 4. She should call the police.
> 5. She should obtain a temporary restraining order against the abuser.
> 6. She should call a friend or relative for help.
> 7. Other (specify) _____
> 8. Don't know/refused to answer.
> 9. Missing.

In an inductive coding scheme, the responses mentioned most frequently are included in the coding scheme used to analyze the data. In the preceding example, values 1 through 6 were mentioned frequently enough to merit their own categories. Values 7 through 9 were added once the inductive approach generated the first categories. In the final coding scheme, the researcher will use the "other" category for less frequently mentioned responses.

Categories are not always easily identified, and a comprehensive coding scheme can take a long time to construct. The researchers' time is spent switching back and forth between the raw data and the evolving scheme until the categories are applicable to and tied in with the general purpose of the study. Paul Lazarsfeld and Alan Barton, examining some general principles of coding, illustrate this process by using some of the coding schemes constructed in the classic study *The American Soldier*.[3] In an attempt to determine which factors offset combat stress, the researchers who were investigating the American soldier drew up a preliminary list of categories on the basis of many responses:

1. Coercive formal authority.
2. Leadership practices (e.g., encouragement).
3. Informal group:
   a. Affectional support.
   b. Code of behavior.
   c. Provision of realistic security and power.
4. Convictions about the war and the enemy.
5. Desire to complete the job by winning war, to go home.
6. Prayer and personal philosophies.

2. Adapted from *Spouse Abuse in Texas: A Study of Women's Attitudes and Experiences* (Huntsville, Texas: Criminal Justice Center, 1983).
3. Paul F. Lazarsfeld and Alan Barton, "Qualitative Measurement in the Social Sciences: Classification, Typologies, and Indices," in *The Policy Sciences*, ed. Daniel Lerner and Harold D. Lasswell (Stanford, Calif.: Stanford University Press, 1951), p. 160, and Samuel A. Stouffer, *The American Soldier* (New York: Wiley, 1965).

These preliminary coding schemes enabled the investigators in this study to classify the raw data and substantially reduce the number of responses to be analyzed. The investigators introduced a further modification after they noted that formal sanctions are often more effective when channeled through informal group sanctions and internal sanctions. Conversely, the norms of the informal groups are influenced by formal sanctions as well as by individual conscience. On this basis, the researchers reanalyzed the responses and obtained additional information to produce a modified coding scheme (Table 14.1).

The following responses conform to the modified categories found in Table 14.1:

(a) I fight because I'll be punished if I quit.

(b) I fight because it's my duty to my country, the army, the government; it would be wrong for me to quit.

(c) I fight because I'll lose the respect of my buddies if I quit.

(d) I fight because it would be wrong to let my buddies down.

(e) You have to look out for your buddies even if it means violating orders, or they won't look out for you.

(f) You have to look out for your buddies even if it means violating orders because it would be wrong to leave them behind.

(g) I am fighting because I believe in democracy and hate fascism.

The chief advantages of the inductive approach are its flexibility and its richness, which enable the researcher to generate explanations from the findings. Moreover, it allows researchers to apply a variety of coding schemes to the same observation, and it often suggests new categories as well. The shortcoming of this

**Table 14.1**

How Norms Bear on Individual Behavior in Combat

| Underlying Source of Norms | Channels |
|---|---|
| Norms of formal authorities | *Direct:*<br>(a) Formal sanctions<br>(b) Internal sanctions<br><br>*Via group norms:*<br>(c) Informal group sanctions<br>(d) Internal sanctions |
| Norms of informal groups | (e) Formal group sanctions<br>(f) Internal sanctions |
| Individual norms | (g) Internal sanctions |

From Paul F. Lazarsfeld and Alan Barton, "Qualitative Measurement in the Social Sciences: Classification, Typologies, and Indices," in *The Policy Sciences*, ed. Daniel Lerner and Harold D. Lasswell (Stanford, Calif.: Stanford University Press, 1951), p. 161. Reprinted with permission.

---

### Rules of Coding

- Code numbers should make intuitive sense for variables that can be rank ordered—for example, higher scores should be assigned higher code numbers.
- In deductive coding, categories should be linked to the theory from which the research hypothesis was derived. Deductive coding is most common with quantitative research. Qualitative researchers usually design the coding scheme inductively from the data in their effort to develop grounded theory.
- The coding categories must be mutually exclusive—each unit of analysis should fit into one and only one category.
- The coding scheme must be exhaustive—every response must fit into a category with few responses being classified as "other."
- Categories must be specific enough to capture differences using the smallest possible number of categories—the criterion of detail.

---

method is that researchers may be bogged down by the mass of details as they try to explain the data. Sometimes too little context is preserved for the coder to determine which details are trivial and can therefore be eliminated.

---

# Codebook Construction

Once you have developed a coding scheme for each of the variables used in a research project, you should compile this information in a **codebook.** Codebooks vary in their detail; however, all good codebooks contain information regarding each variable's name or number, the coding scheme, and codes for missing data. The codebook serves as a guide for the coders who will translate the raw data onto an input device for later use in computerized statistical analysis. It is also a reference for the principal researcher and any other researchers who wish to use the data set. For research involving the use of surveys, the actual survey question is often included in the codebook. A subset of a codebook used in the Cleveland Poverty Survey is reproduced in Exhibit 14.1.

Note that each variable in Exhibit 14.1 is identified by its name (e.g., Q1), brief question content, the coding scheme employed (values), column numbers, which values stand for a missing value, and any other special coding rules employed on a variable-by-variable basis. Statistics computer programs arrange data in spreadsheet form. The variables are arrayed in the columns and the cases in the rows. Each column number in Exhibit 14.1 tells any researcher interested in using the data set which columns contain the values for specific variables. From the information contained in the codebook, any researcher should be able to reconstruct the data set.

**Exhibit 14.1**

A Codebook Format: Cleveland Poverty Survey

| Variable Name | | Column Numbers |
|---|---|---|
| IDNUMBER | Interviewee identification number<br>Code Actual Number<br>(001–528) | 1–3 |
| Q1 | Highest Grade Completed<br>1 = 1–8<br>2 = 9–11<br>3 = 12<br>4 = 13–15<br>5 = 16<br>6 = 17+<br>.<br>.<br>. | 4 |
| Q4 | Gender<br>1 = Male<br>2 = Female | 7 |
| Q5 | Weekly Take-Home Pay Current/Last Job<br>Code in Actual Dollars | 8–11 |
| Q6 | Hours Worked per Week Current/Last Job<br>Code in Actual Hours | 12–13 |
| Q7 | General Health Condition<br>1 = Excellent<br>2 = Very Good<br>3 = Good<br>4 = Fair<br>5 = Poor<br>9 = DK/NA | 14 |
| Q8 | Good Education Way to Get Ahead<br>1 = Strongly Agree<br>2 = Agree<br>3 = Somewhat Agree<br>4 = Somewhat Disagree<br>5 = Disagree<br>6 = Disagree Strongly<br>9 = DK/NA | 15 |
| Q9 | Reading Ability<br>1 = Excellent<br>2 = Good<br>3 = Fair<br>4 = Poor<br>9 = DK/NA | 16 |

## Coding Reliability and Data Entry Devices

Once the researcher has constructed the codebook, the data need to be "coded" or transferred to a form from which someone can enter them into a statistical computer program for storage and analysis. For instance, someone must translate a circled number on a questionnaire to the proper column or "field" represented by the variable (and defined in the codebook). The coder may be the researcher himself or herself or may be a hired or student research assistant. Raw data can be coded in a number of ways to facilitate efficient computer entry. After dealing with human coder reliability, we shall consider reliability and the use of transfer sheets, edge coding, optical scanning, and direct data entry.

## Coding Reliability

Studies with a well-constructed codebook; precoded, closed-ended questions; and proper coder training are prone to fewer problems with coder reliability than other studies, all things being equal, because coders do not have to exercise their own judgment in deciding what code to give a response. One of the biggest problems in these studies is making sure that the coders place the code in the correct column. It is standard practice to recheck or verify a sample of each coder's work to ensure that they have not become lax. The coding devices we will discuss demonstrate the trade-offs for coder reliability based on choice of device.

Coders are required to exercise more judgment in classifying responses when they are coding open-ended questions or other nonstructured material. When the rules for classifying responses do not clearly apply to a specific response, different coders may classify the same response differently. In such instances, the coding process becomes unreliable, a problem that is just as serious as the unreliability of interviewers or observers. Indeed, very often the coding phase of data analysis contributes the largest component of error. To increase coding reliability, researchers need to keep the schemes as simple as possible and train coders thoroughly. The simplest solution is to compare the codings of two or more coders and resolve all differences by letting them decide on problematic items. An example of instructions to coders to ensure reliability is presented in Exhibit 14.2.

The instructions in Exhibit 14.2 are designed to address any questions that may arise as coders prepare data to be keyed into the computer. When coders place the code directly on the measuring instrument, it is helpful to use a red pencil to differentiate the code from any other markings on the instrument. Red pencil can be erased to correct coding errors. Note that green marks are used to differentiate field corrections from either interviewer or coder markings. It is important that coders never erase any interviewer marks on the instrument so that supervisors can check the accuracy of the coding. When coders have difficulty interpreting a response, they may use a flag to call the entry to the supervisor's attention so a judgment can be made about the proper code to use.

In some cases a code number cannot be assigned to a response. In Exhibit 14.2, coders are asked to list on a separate form all of the verbatim responses to questions for which there are no specified code numbers. For example, researchers in a study may be interested in knowing the particular responses people classify as "other" and may state the question as "other, please specify." If the coder simply places a code number on the form, the information in which the researcher is interested is lost.

Coders must know what code to use for different types of nonresponse. In Exhibit 14.2 nonresponses may take three different forms: 1) the respondent may refuse to answer the question, 2) the question may not be applicable to the respondent, or 3) the respondent may not know the answer to the question. The coding instructions clearly indicate the code number(s) or letter the coders should record.

---

### Exhibit 14.2
### General Coding Instructions

---

A. Coding must be done in red *pencil.*

B. Never erase any interviewer-circled codes or comments. If the questionnaire must be corrected, draw a line through the code circled in error. Do not make it impossible to read what was done originally. Please note that green marks are field department corrections.

C. Every column must have a code, and no column may contain more than one clearly circled code.

D. For those questions noted *FLAG:* this instruction applies to questions where special coding problems have been anticipated. Coders will be provided with a supply of little clips (flags) to attach to the page where the problem occurs. Coders may also flag all other areas in the questionnaire where information is incomplete or unclear and requires the supervisor's attention.

E. For those questions noted *LIST:* record on an "OTHER" list form the questionnaire identification and all verbatim comments relating to the response to be listed. A separate list should be kept for each question. If, however, a question has more than one listed code, keep a separate list for each code. Record at the top of each form the study number, the question number, the deck and column number, and the listed code. In most surveys, all "Other (SPECIFY)" codes are listed.

F. The "no answer" (NA) and "refusal" code for this questionnaire is '9' in a one-column field, '99' in a two-column field, etc. NA is coded when the respondent does not give an answer, when the interviewer fails to ask a question or to record the answer, when the written information is contradictory or too vague to code, and when the coder needs to supply a code in order to resolve a tricky skip pattern. NA is allowed for every question except those specifically excepted in the codebook, such as race and sex.

G. The "not applicable" (NAP) code is "R," which means "reject" or "blank" to our keypunchers. NAP is coded when a question was not supposed to have been asked (i.e., because of directions to skip it).

---

**Exhibt 14.2** *(continued)*

---

H. If "don't know" (DK) is not a preprinted code, then DK is coded '8' in a one-column field, '98' in a two-column field, '998' in a three-column field, etc. If DK has been listed along with other responses in one question, edit out (or do not code) the DK response.

From the National Opinion Research Center, University of Chicago, *General Social Survey, 1972–1989: Cumulative Codebook* (Storrs, Conn.: Roper Center for Public Opinion Research, 1989).

---

Discrepancies can occur in the way coders and respondents interpret the meaning of a given response. This problem is discussed in the literature much less frequently, but was addressed by Kenneth Kammeyer and Julius Ross in a study that attempted to assess whether respondent and coder would agree on the meaning of a response.[4]

In other words, how would the research participants themselves code their answers within the set of categories provided by the researcher? If the research participants who provide the responses could also serve as coders, would their code differ from that of other coders, or would the research participants code their own responses as they are coded by others? Kammeyer and Ross asked 64 college students to complete a questionnaire that included fixed-alternative questions as well as open-ended ones. Later on, every research participant independently coded the questionnaires of several other participants as well as his or her own. The researchers then compared each participant's coding of his or her own response with the way that response was coded by others. The comparison revealed that coders often interpreted responses differently than the research participant, which resulted in a misrepresentation of the research participant's actual attitudes. The direction of the deviation was determined by the content of the item. The less structured the item, the larger the discrepancy between the respondent's interpretation and that of a coder. These findings raise some serious doubts regarding the process of coding nonstructured material. It is clear that such bias might distort the findings about the relationships between the variables the researcher is investigating.

## Coding Devices

*Transfer Sheets.*    Years ago, all data were keypunched onto computer cards and read into the computer. Coders used *transfer sheets,* which were paper representations of the keypunch card, to record data in the columns specified by the codebook, and keypunchers then transferred the data to the cards. Although such cards are no longer used, researchers may still use a version of the transfer sheet when dealing with complex questionnaires or when gathering data from a number of sources.

---

4. Kenneth C. W. Kammeyer and Julius A. Roth, "Coding Response to Open-ended Questions," in *Sociological Methodology,* ed. Herbert L. Costner (San Francisco: Jossey-Bass, 1971).

Coders can use spreadsheet forms to organize cases in the rows and values of the variables across the columns. Most statistical programs require that data be arranged in this manner, and data entry personnel can quickly key in each line from the spreadsheet. However, the use of any kind of transfer sheet requires multiple handling of the data, which increases the possibility of miscodings and threatens reliability.

*Edge Coding.*    The use of **edge coding** is one way researchers have eliminated the need for transfer sheets. In this method, coders transfer questionnaire information directly onto spaces at the outside edge of the instrument. Note that in Figure 14.1 the column numbers associated with each variable are indicated on the right edge of the form, labeled "for project use only." When the instrument has been edge coded, a data entry worker can key the information from the edge directly to the data storage device. Reliability is enhanced because the coders' eyes do not have to leave the instrument, and they do not have to keep close track of column positions, as is the case with transfer sheets.

*Optical Scanning.*    Coders may also transfer data onto optical scanning sheets like the ones often used in computer-graded multiple-choice examinations. Scanning machines read black pencil marks and produce the data files automatically. This method enhances reliability since it eliminates keying errors associated with manual data entry. However, poorly designed scanner sheets may affect the coder's ability to keep track of item numbers.

Since the use of **optical scanning** is so common and the procedure for filling out the scanning sheets is simple, respondents may be asked to record their re sponses directly onto the scanning sheets. Scanning sheets should be designed specifically for the instrument to increase the ease and accuracy with which the respondents can complete the survey.

*Direct Data Entry.*    Perhaps the most important innovations in coding have come from **direct data entry.** There are two forms of direct data coding: coding from a questionnaire and coding by telephone interview. Both forms are based on computer programs that display each questionnaire item on a screen and prompt the coder or interviewer to key in the response to the question displayed.

Material coded from questionnaires must be edited to ensure that missing responses have a designated code for the input. The coder then keys in the response. When a case is completed, the computer program adds the information directly into the raw data file. Again, this method reduces the number of data handlers, which enhances reliability.

Computer-assisted telephone interviewing (CATI) is a highly sophisticated system that greatly reduces miscoding. Interviewers read questionnaire items directly to respondents from the computer screen and input responses as they are given. If the coder keys in an inappropriate code (a value that is not designated for the particular variable), the coder is prompted to give a "real" value. CATI also automatically skips questions or jumps to others as a result of filter questions, and interviewers do not have to flip through screens to access the appropriate next

## Figure 14.1
### An Edge-Coded Questionnaire

|  |  | FOR PROJECT USE ONLY |
|---|---|---|

**THE UNIVERSITY OF WISCONSIN—MILWAUKEE**
College of Letters and Science
Department of Political Science

№  2183

# Civil Libertarian Project

**INSTRUCTIONS:** For each of the following questions please mark the answer that comes closest to the way you feel about the issue. There are no "right" or "wrong" answers — please answer the questions as honestly as possible. Answer each of the questions in the order in which it appears. If you wish to make additional comments on any of the specific questions or on the issues in general, use the space at the end of the questionnaire. Your opinions are extremely important for understanding these complex civil liberty issues — we greatly appreciate your cooperation!

We would like to begin with a few questions about your relationship with the American Civil Liberties Union (ACLU).      6 _1_

1a. About how many years have you been a member of ACLU? _____ years.      7 _ 8 _

1b. Why did you join the ACLU? That is, was there any particular cause that the ACLU was supporting or defending that prompted you to join the organization?
☐ Specific cause(s) – – → Which cause(s) _____
☐ No specific cause
☐ Don't remember      9 _

1c. Have you been very active in the affairs of the ACLU? For instance, have you done any of the following in the last five years?

|  | Yes | No | Don't Remember |  |
|---|---|---|---|---|
| a. made financial contributions (beyond membership dues) | ☐ | ☐ | ☐ | 10 __ |
| b. written letters to ACLU leaders | ☐ | ☐ | ☐ | 11 __ |
| c. served in a leadership role | ☐ | ☐ | ☐ | 12 __ |
| d. attended local meetings of ACLU | ☐ | ☐ | ☐ | 13 __ |
| e. read ACLU newsletters and literature | ☐ | ☐ | ☐ | 14 __ |
| f. written letters to public officials at the urging of ACLU | ☐ | ☐ | ☐ | 15 __ |
| g. attended an ACLU party or benefit | ☐ | ☐ | ☐ | 16 __ |
| h. done volunteer work for ACLU (e.g., office assistance, phone calling, etc.) | ☐ | ☐ | ☐ | 17 __ |
| i. participated in a court case or public hearing at the urging of ACLU | ☐ | ☐ | ☐ | 18 __ |

1d. The ACLU publishes a number of specialized newsletters and magazines that not all of the members receive. We would like to know if you have received any of these publications and, if so, how frequently you found the time to read them. For each of the following please check the most appropriate box.

|  | I have not received this publication | I received the publication and usually read it | I received the publication but rarely had time to read it | Don't Know |  |
|---|---|---|---|---|---|
| a. Civil Liberties Review | ☐ | ☐ | ☐ | ( ) | 19 __ |
| b. Children's Rights Report | ☐ | ☐ | ☐ | ( ) | 20 __ |
| c. First Principles | ☐ | ☐ | ☐ | ( ) | 21 __ |
| d. Notes from the Women's Rights Project | ☐ | ☐ | ☐ | ( ) | 22 __ |
| e. Civil Liberties Alert | ☐ | ☐ | ☐ | ( ) | 23 __ |
| f. The Privacy Report | ☐ | ☐ | ☐ | ( ) | 24 __ |
| g. Civil Liberties | ☐ | ☐ | ☐ | ( ) | 25 __ |

1e. Over the course of your membership, how satisfied have you been, in general, with the positions ACLU has taken on major issues?
☐ always in agreement       ☐ usually in disagreement       ☐ don't know      26 __
☐ usually in agreement       ☐ always in disagreement

2a. There are always some people whose ideas are considered bad or dangerous by other people. For instance, somebody who is against all churches and religion.

|  | Yes | No | No Opinion |  |
|---|---|---|---|---|
| a. If such a person wanted to make a speech in your community against churches and religion, should he/she be allowed to speak or not? | ☐ | ☐ | ☐ | 27 __ |
| b. Should such a person be allowed to organize a march against churches and religion in your community? | ☐ | ☐ | ☐ | 28 __ |
| c. Should such a person be allowed to teach in a college or university, or not? | ☐ | ☐ | ☐ | 29 __ |
| d. If some people in your community suggested that a book he/she wrote against churches and religion should be taken out of your public library, would you favor removing the book, or not? | ☐ | ☐ | ☐ | 30 __ |

Source: Reprinted by permission of Greenwood Publishing Group, Inc., Westport, CT, from *Civil Liberties and the Nazis* by James L. Gibson and Richard D. Bingham. Copyright © 1985, Praeger Publishers, New York, NY.

item. Therefore, not only does the program increase coder reliability, but it also ensures that respondents do not answer inappropriate questions. Because improvements in CATI technology have resulted in high response rates, ease of implementation and use, and increased reliability of data collection and coding, CATI has sharply reduced the use of mail surveys.

## Editing and Cleaning the Data

Editing and cleaning the data are important steps in data processing that should always precede analysis of the collected information. **Data editing** occurs both during and after the coding phase. Coders perform some editing by checking for errors and omissions and by making sure that all interview schedules have been completed as required. Most of the editing, however, especially in large-scale surveys, is performed by a supervisor who reviews each completed questionnaire to evaluate the interviews' reliability and check for inconsistencies in responses. For example, the National Opinion Research Center, which conducts the General Social Survey, instructs supervisors to check that all filter (contingency) questions have been correctly marked so that the data will fit into the correct skip (or "go to") pattern. If more than one response is given to the filter question or if the filter question was left blank, the supervisor will determine what the code should be.

**Data cleaning** is the proofreading of the data to catch and correct errors and inconsistent codes. Computers perform most of the data cleaning for large-scale efforts using software designed to test for logical consistency set up in the coding specification.[5] Though many questions are answered and coded independently, others are interconnected and must be internally consistent. For example, if a respondent has no children, all questions relating to children must be coded NA ("no answer") or left blank. Similarly, an error is indicated if a respondent reporting her age as 5 years old also responds that she has two children.

Another function of data cleaning is checking for wild codes. For example, the question "Do you believe there is a life after death?" may have legitimate codes of 1 for "yes," 2 for "no," 8 for "undecided," and 9 for "no answer." Any code other than these four would be considered illegitimate. The simplest procedure to check for wild codes is to generate a frequency distribution (discussed in Chapter 15) for each variable. This method of data cleaning is also outlined in Appendix A.

# Using Computers in Social Science Research

By now everyone is affected by and familiar with the use of computers in many facets of life, and computers have been used in social science research for decades. Computer technology has changed drastically over time, but the rationale for the

---

5. For example, Winona Ailkins, *EDIT: The NORC Cleaning Program: A Program to Develop Sequential Files* (Chicago: National Opinion Research Center, 1975).

use of computers in research has remained the same across the years. Computers are simply tools that help us to store, process, access, and analyze data sets more quickly and easily. Once we understand the research methods and statistics discussed in this book, we can let a computer calculate the statistics and provide printouts of the results. However, it is up to the researcher to supply correct and reliable data, choose statistics that are appropriate for the level of data, and interpret the results properly.

## Types of Computers

Researchers use three basic kinds of computers to analyze social science data: mainframes, minicomputers, and personal computers (PCs). **Mainframe computers** are large central-site computers that simultaneously handle the computing needs of many users. Users tend to "time-share" the capacity of the central processing unit so that the greatest number of users can access the computer at any given time. Mainframe sites also tend to have the capacity for reading magnetic data tapes sent by data repositories to members or clients. The Interuniversity Consortium for Political and Social Research at the University of Michigan is the largest repository for social science data. Besides storing academic research, it holds the data sets from national opinion firms like Roper, Harris, and the National Opinion Research Center (NORC), which form the basis for many research projects. Because mainframes also support the major statistical packages used to analyze social science data, individual researchers and students do not have to purchase multiple software packages.

Minicomputers also support software packages, which can be accessed by multiple users, but a minicomputer cannot accommodate as many users as a typical mainframe. Dedicated terminals and networked personal computers (PCs) access the programs and data files in a miniature version of the time-share model.

In response to the increasing affordability and use of personal computers, the major statistical software manufacturers have developed PC versions of the mainframe software researchers have used for years. For example, the Statistical Package for the Social Sciences (SPSS) (described in Appendix A) has a PC version. Manufacturers have also developed and marketed statistical packages designed specifically for use on personal computers. Since data can be transferred between most of the statistical packages, researchers using PCs can choose to purchase the package with which they are most familiar or that they can best afford.

The major difference between the PC and the other computers is that the PC is self-contained. Most professional PC versions of major statistical packages require no more than a hard disk and a math coprocessor to perform efficiently. While it is not necessary for the PC to be linked to a mainframe or a minicomputer, there are advantages to using communication networks.

## Linkages through Communication Networks

Not long ago, researchers either had to choose a medium (mainframe, mini, PC) by which they would do their computing or learn how to use a variety of systems. Modems were developed to allow people to use regular telephone lines to access mainframe or minicomputers from terminals located at remote sites. In the early days of modems, data transmission required a dedicated line. Today "voice over data" telephone lines allow people to use a single line to simultaneously transmit or receive data and converse on the phone. Modems for these types of lines are often within the telephone itself.

Remote terminals are no longer required for communication with mainframe or minicomputers. All that is required for any kind of computer to link with another is compatible communication software and modem speed. Today's researchers can easily "upload" information from a PC to the mainframe or "download" information from the mainframe to a PC.

Since the 1970s, local area networks (LANs) have been used to link work-stations through a central computer system. Network partners share a common line of transmission, and only one computer in a network can transmit data on the network at a time. The slow transmission speed in early LANs often caused the network to get bogged down and stall. Newer technologies have speeded transmissions and reduced congestion in networks. Multimedia networks in the 1990s combine voice, data, and video transmissions and have influenced the way social scientists compute and communicate their findings.

A final way to link computers is through software programs. Statistical output generated by one program can be read into a word processing program from which reports and manuscripts can be generated. Some older software programs require that data be converted to a generic format before it can be transferred to another program, and sometimes layout information is lost in the conversion. Many of the major software manufacturers today are marketing *software suites* that consist of a number of different programs designed for specific purposes. The data from any program in the suite can be read directly into any other program in the suite. Since no conversion is necessary, layout information remains intact.

---

## Summary

---

**1.** Data processing is a link between data collection and data analysis whereby observations are transformed into codes that are amenable to analysis. At the first stage of data processing, researchers classify numerous individual observations into a smaller number of categories to simplify the description and analysis of the data. Such systems are referred to as coding schemes.

**2.** Coding schemes must be linked to theory and the problem under study, which dictates the categories to be included. Other requirements of a coding scheme are that it be both exhaustive and mutually exclusive so that all observations can be classified and each observation falls into only one category. Researchers use coding schemes to translate data into a format that allows computer processing. The translation is usually guided by a codebook, which presents the schemes with their assigned values together with coding instructions.

**3.** A variety of coding devices may be used to organize the raw data. These include transfer sheets, edge coding, optical scanning, and direct data entry. The choice of method depends on the format of the research and the technology available to the researcher. Each method has implications for coding reliability. In general, the fewer times the data is transferred, the greater the reliability. Computer-assisted telephone interviewing (CATI) provides high reliability because responses are recorded directly into the computer as the questions are asked.

**4.** Social scientists have been using computers to organize the research process for many years. Technology is rapidly changing in this area, and students may be exposed to mainframe computers, minicomputers, and personal computers in the same class. Software compatibility and communications networking are important technological developments in computing.

---

## Key Terms for Review

---

code (p. 335)

codebook (p. 340)

coding scheme (p. 335)

data cleaning (p. 347)

data editing (p. 347)

deductive coding (p. 337)

detail (p. 337)

direct data entry (p. 345)

edge coding (p. 345)

exhaustiveness (p. 337)

inductive coding (p. 337)

mainframe computer (p. 348)

mutual exclusivity (p. 336)

optical scanning (p. 345)

---

## Study Questions

---

1. Discuss the differences between inductive and deductive coding schemes.
2. What are the main criteria of coding schemes?
3. Describe the steps involved in determining coding reliability.
4. What are the different types of data processing?

---

## Computer Exercise

---

By using a spreadsheet or by inputting data directly into an SPSS runstream (e.g., using REVIEW in SPSS/PC+ or the NEWDATA window), set up the following hypothetical data set on cities:

| IDNUMBER | STATE | FORM | POPULATION | BUDGET/1000S |
|----------|-------|------|-----------|--------------|
| 001 | WI | manager | 68000 | 2685 |
| 002 | WI | mayor | 42860 | 3489 |
| 003 | WI | mayor | 285000 | 42330 |
| 004 | OH | mayor | 573803 | 88677 |
| 005 | OH | mayor | 29386 | 1483 |
| 006 | OH | manager | 88421 | 7456 |
| 007 | CA | manager | 436798 | 72698 |
| 008 | CA | manager | 55390 | 6331 |
| 009 | CA | manager | 125800 | 55896 |
| 010 | CA | mayor | 3134388 | 90444 |

Assign numerical codes for STATE and FORM. Use VARIABLE LABELS and VALUE LABELS to further specify your system file. Run FREQUENCIES on all variables and clean the dataset, checking for coding errors. (See Appendix A, pp. 504–514)

---

## Additional Readings

---

Bryman, Alan, and Duncan Cramer. *Quantitative Data Analysis for Social Scientists*. New York: Routledge, 1990.

Cozby, Paul C. *Using Computers in the Behavioral Sciences*. Mountain View, Calif.: Mayfield, 1986.

Dey, Ian. *Qualitative Data Analysis: A User Friendly Guide for Social Scientists*. New York: Routledge, 1993.

Flaherty, Douglas. *Humanizing the Computer*. Belmont, Calif.: Wadsworth, 1986.

Leff, S. Lawrence. *Data Processing: The Easy Way*. New York: Barron's, 1984.

Lefkowitz, Jerry M. *Introduction to Statistical Computer Packages*. North Scituate, Mass.: Duxbury Press, 1985.

Shermis, Mark D. *Using Microcomputers in Social Science Research*. Boston: Allyn and Bacon, 1991.

# CHAPTER 15

# The Univariate Distribution

**The Role of Statistics**

**Frequency Distributions**
Frequency Distributions with Interval Variables
Percentage Distributions

**Using Graphs to Describe Distributions**
The Pie Chart
The Bar Chart
The Histogram

**Measures of Central Tendency**
Mode
Median
Other Measures of Location
Arithmetic Mean
Comparison of the Mode, the Median, and the Mean

**Basic Measures of Dispersion**
Measure of Qualitative Variation
Range and Interquartile Range

**Measures of Dispersion Based on the Mean**
Variance and Standard Deviation
Variance and Standard Deviation for Grouped Data
Standard Deviation: Advantages and Applications
Coefficient of Variation

**Types of Frequency Distributions**
Normal Curve
Standard Scores

How does economic change in a society shape women's lives? Following World War II, as the result of a joint effort between the governments of Puerto Rico and the United States, Puerto Rico was industrialized. The transformation from an agricultural to a low-wage service and manufacturing economy increased the demand for women's labor while decreasing the demand for men. Recently, researchers Barbara Zsembik and Chuck Peek examined possible reasons why married Puerto Rican women increasingly return to the paid work force within 12 months of the birth of their first child.[1] They noted that since 1950, Puerto Rican women have increased their investment in formal education and training, which has resulted in higher costs for women who leave the work force to raise children.

To determine whether the investments in the form of education differ between men and women, the researchers compared the average educational level of men and women by computing the mean years of formal education for each. They found that, on the average, women completed 11.74 years of formal schooling, and men completed 11.84 years of school; thus Puerto Rican men and women appear to invest equally in education. To determine whether these nearly equal means were the result of similar distributions, the researchers computed the standard deviations—which show how widely scores are dispersed from the mean—for the distributions. The standard deviation was 3.69 for women and 3.71 for men, showing that the distributions were also similar.

I IN THIS CHAPTER, WE EXPLAIN THE MAIN CHARACTERISTICS OF single variable, or univariate, distributions. First we define and describe frequency distributions, which researchers use to organize their data for statistical analysis. Then we focus on measures of central tendency and measures of dispersion, which can be used to describe distributions. Finally, we deal with the general form of distributions, emphasizing the normal curve.

Since the 1950s, all social science disciplines have experienced a rapid increase in the use of statistics, and they have become essential to the field. Without statistics, we could not see the patterns and regularities in the phenomena we study. We need statistical methods to organize data, to display information in a meaningful manner, and to describe and interpret the observations in terms that will help us evaluate our hypotheses.

The word *statistics* has a dual meaning. Although it is used to refer to numbers—per capita income, batting averages, and the like—it is also a field of study. We refer to the latter usage in our discussion, which will cover some of the basic applications of statistics in the social sciences.

1. Barbara A. Zsembik and Chuck W. Peek, "The Effect of Economic Restructuring on Puerto Rican Women's Labor Force Participation in the Formal Sector," *Gender & Society*, Vol. 8, No. 4 (1994): 525–540.

# The Role of Statistics

The field of statistics involves methods for describing and analyzing data and for making decisions or inferences about phenomena represented by the data. Methods in the first category are referred to as *descriptive statistics;* methods in the second category are called *inferential statistics.*

**Descriptive statistics** enable the researcher to summarize and organize data in an effective and meaningful way. They provide tools for describing collections of statistical observations and reducing information to an understandable form.

**Inferential statistics** allow the researcher to make decisions or inferences by interpreting data patterns. Researchers use inferential statistics to determine whether an expected pattern designated by the theory and hypotheses is actually found in the observations. We might hypothesize, for example, that blue-collar workers are politically more conservative than professionals. To decide whether this hypothesis is true, we might survey blue-collar workers and professionals, asking them about their political views. We would then use descriptive statistics to make comparisons between these groups, and we would employ inferential statistics to determine whether the differences between the groups support our expectations.

Both descriptive and inferential statistics help social scientists develop explanations for complex social phenomena that deal with relationships between variables. Statistics provides the tools to analyze, represent, and interpret those relationships.

# Frequency Distributions

After data have been coded and prepared for automatic processing, they are ready for analysis. The researcher's first task is to construct frequency distributions to examine the pattern of response to each of the independent and dependent variables under investigation. (In the following discussion, *responses, answers, observations, cases, acts,* and *behavior* are used interchangeably.) A frequency distribution of a single variable, known as a *univariate frequency distribution,* is a table that shows the frequency of observations in each category of a variable. For example, to examine the pattern of response to the variable "religious affiliation," a researcher would describe the number of respondents who claimed they were Protestants, Catholics, Jews, Muslims, and so on.

To construct a **frequency distribution,** the researcher simply lists the categories of the variable and counts the number of observations in each. Table 15.1 is an example of the standard form of a univariate frequency distribution. The table has five rows, the first four being the categories of the variable, which appear in the left-hand column, and the right-hand column shows the number of observations in each category. This number is called a *frequency,* and is usually denoted by the

**Table 15.1**
General Form of a Univariate Frequency Distribution

| Category | Frequency ($f$) |
|----------|-----------------|
| I | $f$ |
| II | $f$ |
| III | $f$ |
| IV | $f$ |
| Total | $N$ |

letter $f$. The last row (marked $N$) is the total of all frequencies appearing in the table. When the categories are mutually exclusive so that each observation is classified only once, the total number of frequencies is equal to the total number of observations in the sample.

The order in which the researcher lists the categories of the variable in the frequency distribution is determined by the level at which the data were measured. As we discussed in Chapter 7, there are four levels of data measurement—nominal, ordinal, interval, and ratio. At all levels the categories must be both exhaustive and mutually exclusive. At the nominal level the categories are simply names, which do not imply any kind of ranking. Gender, ethnicity, and religious preference are examples of nominal variables. The categories of ordinal level variables may be ranked from highest to lowest or vice versa, but the categories do not reflect how much greater or smaller one level is in comparison to another. At the interval and ratio levels, the categories of the variable reflect both the rank of the categories and the magnitude of the difference between categories. The only difference between interval and ratio level variables is that ratio variables have a true zero point, which allows researchers to say, for example, that one category is twice as great as another.

With nominal variables, the researcher may list the categories in any order. Thus for the variable "gender," either category—"male" or "female"—may be listed first. However, because the categories of ordinal variables represent different rankings, they must be arranged in increasing or decreasing order. Consider the frequency distribution in Table 15.2, from a government study that examined child abuse. The variable "child abuse" is listed by type of abuse—"physical," "sexual," or "neglect."

## Frequency Distributions with Interval Variables

When a researcher is summarizing interval variables in frequency distributions, he or she must first decide on the number of categories to use and the cutting points between them. Because interval variables are ordinarily continuous, the classification into distinct categories may be quite arbitrary. For example, age may be classified into one-year, two-year, or five-year groups. Similarly, income can be classified in a number of ways.

**Table 15.2**
Distribution of Child Abuse, 1992

| Category | f |
|---|---|
| Physical abuse | 212,281 |
| Sexual abuse | 129,982 |
| Neglect | 449,442 |
| Total | 791,705 |

Adapted from: Alison Landes, Jacquelyn Quiram and Nancy R. Jacobs (eds.), *Child Abuse: Betraying a Trust.* (Wyle, Texas: Information Plus, 1995), p. 33.

The intervals are usually of equal width, but the width depends on both the number of observations to be classified and the research purpose. The larger the number of observations, the wider the intervals become. However, wider categories also result in greater loss of detailed information. A general guideline to follow is that the intervals should not be so wide that two measurements included in it have a difference between them that is considered important. For example, if a researcher is studying cognitive development and an age difference of one year is not of special significance but a difference of two years is especially important, he or she could choose the intervals 1–2, 3–4, 5–6. The intervals and their frequency for a hypothetical population are presented in the first two columns of Table 15.3.

The two right columns of Table 15.3 show the real limits and midpoints of the intervals. Researchers use real limits to show that the variable is continuous —a requirement for certain graphic and statistical techniques. The midpoints provide a single number to describe each interval that the researcher can use in statistical calculations. The *real limits* express the interval boundaries that extend one-half of one year on either side of the interval. The interval width, expressed as *w*, is the difference between the real limits of the interval:

$$w = U - L$$

where $U$ is the upper real limit, and $L$ is the lower real limit. For the last interval of Table 15.3, the width is

$$2 = 8.5 - 6.5$$

**Table 15.3**
A Frequency Distribution of Family Size

| Age in Years | f | Real Limits | Interval Midpoint (x) |
|---|---|---|---|
| 1–2 | 6 | .5–2.5 | 1.5 |
| 3–4 | 4 | 2.5–4.5 | 3.5 |
| 5–6 | 10 | 4.5–6.5 | 5.5 |
| 7–8 | 3 | 6.5–8.5 | 7.5 |

The midpoint of each interval, symbolized by $x$, is a single value, representing the interval. It is obtained by adding half the interval width to the lower real limit of a class.

$$x = L + \frac{w}{2}$$

Thus for the second class interval of Table 15.3, the midpoint is

$$x = 2.5 + \frac{2}{2} = 3.5$$

## Percentage Distributions

Summarizing the data by constructing frequency distributions of single variables is only the first step in data analysis. Next the researcher must convert the frequencies into measures that can be interpreted meaningfully. An absolute frequency is meaningless in itself; it must be compared with other frequencies. For instance, an investigator can assess the significance of 2,000 registered Democrats in one community only in relation to the number of all registered voters, to the number of registered Republicans, or to the number of registered Democrats in other communities.

To facilitate comparisons, researchers convert frequencies to *proportions* or *percentages*. You obtain a proportion by dividing the frequency of a category by the total number of responses in the distribution. When multiplied by 100, a proportion becomes a percentage. Proportions are usually expressed as $f/N$ and percentages as $f/N \times 100$. Both proportions and percentages reflect the relative weight of a specific category in the distribution. For example, the relative weight of physical child abuse in Table 15.2 is expressed by the proportion $212,281/791,705 = .268$ or by the percentage $212,281/791,705 \times 100 = 26.8$ percent. These figures indicate that about one out of every two cases of child abuse involves physical abuse.

Proportions and percentages permit the researcher to compare two or more frequency distributions. Note, for instance, the social-class distributions of black and white respondents to the 1988–1991 General Social Survey (GSS), which are displayed in Tables 15.4 and 15.5. (For more information on the General Social

**Table 15.4**
Social-Class Distribution: White Population
(in Absolute Frequencies and Percentages)

| Social Class | $f$ | Percent |
|---|---|---|
| Upper class | 25 | 5 |
| Middle class | 221 | 48 |
| Working class | 201 | 43 |
| Lower class | 16 | 4 |
| Total ($N$) | 463 | 100 |

Source: General Social Survey, 1988–1991.

**Table 15.5**
Social-Class Distribution: Black Population
(in Absolute Frequencies and Percentages)

| Social Class | f | Percent |
|---|---|---|
| Upper class | 14 | 7 |
| Middle class | 82 | 39 |
| Working class | 93 | 44 |
| Lower class | 22 | 10 |
| Total (N) | 211 | 100 |

Source: General Social Survey, 1988–1991.

Survey, see Appendix A) Although there are more working class white re-spondents than black respondents (201 versus 93), a straightforward comparison of the absolute frequencies is misleading since the total number of responses (N) is different in each population. To assess the relative weight of the classes within each distribution, you need to convert the frequencies to percentages. The per-centages reveal that the impression gained from the absolute frequencies was indeed misleading. The working class constitutes nearly equal parts of both the black and white populations—43 percent of the white population and 44 percent of the black population. The new figures make it easier to compare the two fre-quency distributions.

# Using Graphs to Describe Distributions

Frequency distributions provide researchers with a way to communicate infor-mation about their data to other social scientists and, in some cases, to the public. However, some people find it difficult to read and understand numerical tables. Graphs provide researchers with an alternative method of displaying the infor-mation organized in frequency distributions. By using graphs to create a visual impression of the data, researchers can often communicate information more effectively. Three of the graphs researchers most commonly use are the pie chart, the bar chart, and the histogram. Both the pie chart and the bar chart can be used to present data measured at the nominal and ordinal levels. Researchers use the histogram to display data measured at interval or ratio levels.

## The Pie Chart

The pie chart shows differences in frequencies or percentages among categories of nominal or ordinal variables by displaying the categories as segments of a circle. The segments are either differently shaded or differently patterned to differentiate among them, and they sum to either 100 percent or the total frequencies. While one pie chart can be used to represent a single distribution, researchers often use

**360**   DATA PROCESSING AND ANALYSIS

two or more pies to compare distributions. When you want to highlight some aspect of the data, you can move or "cut" one or more segments out from the others to call attention to that aspect.

Table 15.6 displays percentage distributions of opinions of government spending on child care for poor children and for all children whose parents work. The data in Table 15.6 show that people are more willing to support government spending on child care for poor children (16% favor much more spending and 45% favor more spending) than they are for all children whose parents work (11% favor much more spending and only 26% favor more spending).

The pie charts shown in Figure 15.1 display the same information presented in Table 15.6. Notice that the slices displaying support for "much more" and "more" spending have been "cut" from the pie to emphasize the difference in support for more child-care spending between the two groups. The pie charts allow you to immediately see differences between the groups without going through the process of analyzing the percentage distribution.

## The Bar Chart

Like the pie chart, the bar chart provides researchers with a tool for displaying nominal or ordinal data. Unlike the pie chart, two or more distributions may be presented on a single bar chart. Bar charts are constructed by labeling the categories of the variable along the horizontal axis and drawing rectangles of equal width for each category. The height of each rectangle is proportional to the frequency or percentage of the category. Bar charts may be displayed either horizontally or vertically. Figure 15.2 on page 362 is a vertical bar chart. A horizontal bar chart is constructed in the same manner except that the categories of the variable are arrayed on the vertical axis and the rectangles are drawn horizontally.

Table 15.7 shows percentage distributions of attitudes toward government spending for social security and welfare. The distribution for the variable social

**Table 15.6**
Opinion of Government Spending on Child Care

| Government Should Spend | Poor Children | Children with Working Parents |
|---|---|---|
| Much more | 16% | 11% |
| More | 45% | 26% |
| No change | 33% | 39% |
| Less | 5% | 16% |
| Much less | 1% | 8% |
| Total | 100% | 100% |

Source: General Social Survey, 1991.

**Figure 15.1**

Opinion of Government Spending on Child Care
for Poor Children and All Children with Working Parents

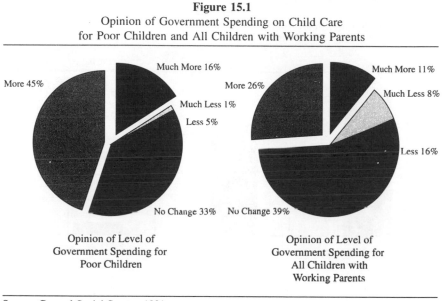

Much More 16%

More 45%

Much Less 1%

Less 5%

No Change 33%

Opinion of Level of
Government Spending for
Poor Children

Much More 11%

More 26%

Much Less 8%

Less 16%

No Change 39%

Opinion of Level of
Government Spending for
All Children with
Working Parents

Source: General Social Survey, 1991.

**Table 15.7**

Attitude toward Government Spending
on Social Security and Welfare

| Government Spends | Social Security | Welfare |
|---|---|---|
| Too little | 54.7% | 23.5% |
| About right | 41.0% | 36.9% |
| Too much | 4.3% | 39.6% |
| Total | 100% | 100% |

Source: General Social Survey, 1991.

security shows that most respondents favor government spending on this form of assistance (only 4.3% feel government spends too much). The distribution for welfare shows that respondents are more divided in their attitudes, but many people would support welfare cuts (39.6% feel government spends too much).

The bar chart presented in Figure 15.2 shows the opposing trends in attitudes toward government spending and welfare. The contiguous pairs of rectangles represent the two variables—social security and welfare. Notice that the rectangles representing each variable are differently shaded to facilitate comparisons, and each category of the variable "attitude toward spending" contains a pair of rectangles.

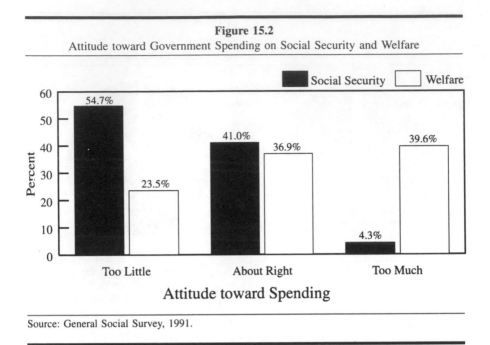

**Figure 15.2**
Attitude toward Government Spending on Social Security and Welfare

Source: General Social Survey, 1991.

## The Histogram

Researchers use the histogram to display frequency distributions of interval or ratio level data. The histogram looks like a bar graph with no spaces between the rectangles. The rectangles are constructed contiguously to show that the variable is continuous, and intervals, rather than discrete categories, are displayed across the horizontal axis. The heights of the rectangles in the histogram reflect the percent or frequency of the interval. Unlike the bar chart, the histogram cannot be used to display information for more than one variable. Table 15.8 and Figure 15.3 show the distribution of AIDS deaths by age from 1982 through 1991.

**Table 15.8**
Distribution of AIDS Deaths by Age: 1982 through 1991

| Age | Percent of AIDS Deaths |
| --- | --- |
| Under 13 | 1% |
| 13–29 | 19% |
| 30–39 | 45% |
| 40–49 | 23% |
| 50–59 | 8% |
| 60 and over | 4% |
| Total | 100% |

Source: Statistical Abstracts, 1992.

**Figure 15.3**
Distribution of AIDS Deaths by Age: 1982 through 1991

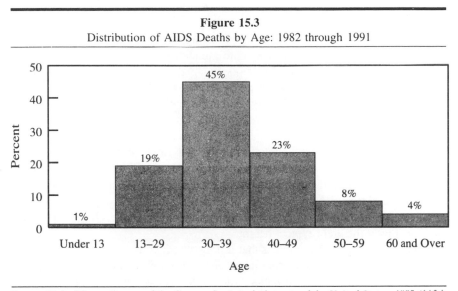

Source: United States Bureau of the Census, *Statistical Abstracts of the United States: 1992* (112th edition). Washington, D.C., 1992.

# Measures of Central Tendency

When only a short summary of the data is required, the entire distribution need not be presented. While you could use a frequency distribution to describe the educational level of Americans, your table could be rather cumbersome. Instead, you could point out that most Americans are high school graduates or that the average level of education in the United States is 12 years.

In most distributions, the observations tend to cluster around a central value. For instance, an income distribution can be characterized by the most common income or an average income. Similarly, attitude distributions cluster around a certain range. This property allows researchers to represent a distribution using a single value rather than a large table and makes it easier for them to compare different distributions. For example, you could compare the average income in the United States with the average income in England or contrast the average intelligence scores of Russian students with those of American students.

Statistical measures that reflect a "typical" or an "average" characteristic of a frequency distribution are referred to as *measures of central tendency*. The three measures social scientists most commonly use are the mode, the median, and the arithmetic mean.

## Mode

The **mode** is the category or observation that appears most frequently in the distribution. It is used as a measure of central tendency mostly with distributions of nominal variables. You identify the mode by singling out the category containing the largest number of responses. For example, consider the distribution of religious groups presented in Table 15.9. The distribution includes five categories; the first, the Protestant group, is the most predominant. This category is thus the mode of the distribution.

Most distributions are unimodal; that is, they include only one category in which the most cases are concentrated. At times, however, the distribution is bimodal: it has two such maximum points. Such a pattern usually exists in distributions that combine two populations. For instance, the distribution of the heights of adults is bimodal; it comprises both men and women, and each gender is characterized by a different typical height.

The advantage of the mode is that it is easy to identify by inspecting the frequency distribution, and therefore it can be used as a first and quick indicator of the central tendency in a distribution. Although it is easy to determine the mode, it is a sensitive indicator. Its position can shift if the researcher changes the way the distribution is divided into categories. Therefore, it is not a very stable measure of central tendency.

## Median

The **median** is a positional measure that divides the distribution into two equal parts. It is defined as the observation that is located halfway between the smallest and the largest observations in the distribution. For example, in the series 1, 3, 4, 6, 7, the median is 4. The median can only be calculated for observations that are ranked according to size, and thus it is suitable for use with variables measured at or above the ordinal level.

A researcher can obtain the median of ungrouped data by identifying the middle observation. For an odd number of cases, it is the observation $(N + 1)/2$, where $N$ is the total number of cases. Consider the following set of nine observations:

**Table 15.9**
Frequency Distribution of Religious Groups

| Religious Group | $f$ |
| --- | --- |
| Protestant | 62 |
| Catholic | 52 |
| Jewish | 10 |
| Muslim | 12 |
| Buddhist | 2 |
| Total ($N$) | 138 |

6, 9, 11, 12, 16, 18, 21, 24, 30
↑
Median

The fifth observation $[(9 + 1)/2]$ divides the distribution in half; the median is therefore the value of the fifth observation, 16. With an even number of observations, the median is located halfway between the two middle observations and is calculated as an average of the observations $N/2$ and $N/2 + 1$. For example, in the following set of observations

1, 3, 4, 5, 6, 7, 8, 9
↑
Median

the median is the average of the fourth $(8/2)$ and the fifth $(8/2 + 1)$ observations: $(5 + 6)/2 = 5.5$.

For grouped data, the researcher locates the median by interpolating within the interval containing the middle observation. The formula for finding the median is

$$Md = L + \left[\frac{N(.5) - cf_{below}}{f}\right]w \qquad (15.1)$$

where $Md$ = the median

$L$ = the lower limit of the interval containing the median

$cf_{below}$ = the cumulative sum of the frequencies below the interval containing the median

$f$ = the frequency of the interval containing the median

$w$ = the width of the interval containing the median

$N$ = the total number of cases

To illustrate the computation of the median, we will consider the distribution in Table 15.10. The table shows the age distribution of 134 persons, divided into eight 10-year age groups. Because there are 134 observations $(N = 134)$, the median has the value of the sixty-seventh observation $[134(.5) = 67]$. The cumulative frequency column shows that there are 60 observations preceding the interval 41–50. The interval 41–50 contains 25 more observations. Hence the sixty-seventh observation is located within that interval. In order to find the median, then, it is necessary to find the exact age corresponding to the seventh case in this interval. These seven cases constitute $7/25 = 28$ percent of the cases in the interval. As the width of the interval is 10, we must add 28 percent of $10 = 2.8$ years to the lower limit of the interval containing the median. The median is therefore $40.5 + 2.8 = 43.3$. These steps can be summarized by employing Equation (15.1):

$$Md = 40.5 + \left[\frac{134(.5) - 60}{25}\right]10 = 40.5 + \left(\frac{7}{25}\right)10 = 40.5 + 2.8 = 43.3$$

Often, researchers are more interested in locating the interval in which the median is located than in finding a specific number within the interval. When this

**Table 15.10**
Age Distribution of 134 Cases (Hypothetical)

| Age | Real Class Limits | f | Cumulative Frequency (cf) | Cumulative Percentage (c%) |
|---|---|---|---|---|
| 1–10 | 0.5–10.5 | 10 | 10 | 7% |
| 11–20 | 10.5–20.5 | 12 | 22 | 16% |
| 21–30 | 20.5–30.5 | 17 | 39 | 29% |
| 31–40 | 30.5–40.5 | 21 | 60 | 45% |
| 41–50 | 40.5–50.5 | 25 | 85 | 63% |
| 51–60 | 50.5–60.5 | 20 | 105 | 78% |
| 61–70 | 60.5–70.5 | 18 | 123 | 92% |
| 71–80 | 70.5–80.5 | 11 | 134 | 100% |
| N | | 134 | 134 | |

is the case, they can use cumulative percentages to locate the median interval. Table 15.10 includes a cumulative percentage column. To determine the median interval, we must locate the interval containing the cumulative percentage of 50%. The age interval 31–40 has a cumulative percentage of 45% and the age interval 41–50 has a cumulative percentage of 63%, thus the age interval of 41–50 must contain the 50% cumulative percentage.

Table 15.11, which describes the educational level of 12 groups, provides an example of the application of the median. The investigators compared the median education of each group. The medians reflect the educational characteristics of 12 different populations, each represented by a single value. For instance, 50 percent of the white rural males completed at least 12.3 years of education; such extended schooling was enjoyed by a smaller ratio of the equivalent black population, whose median was only 8.9 years.

**Table 15.11**
Median Years of Schooling

| | White | Black |
|---|---|---|
| *Males:* | | |
| Residents of city center | 12.1 | 8.7 |
| Residents of suburbs | 12.1 | 9.7 |
| Residents of rural areas | 12.3 | 8.9 |
| *Females:* | | |
| Residents of city center | 12.1 | 10.5 |
| Residents of suburbs | 12.3 | 10.7 |
| Residents of rural areas | 11.8 | 8.0 |

## Other Measures of Location

At times it is useful to identify values that divide the distribution into not just two but three, four, or ten groups. For example, the admissions office of a university that has decided to accept one-fourth of its applicants will be interested in finding the 25 percent with the highest scores on the entrance examinations. The median, then, is a special case of a more general set of measures of location called *percentiles*. The *n*th percentile is a number such that *n* percent of the scores fall below it and $(100 - n)$ percent fall above it. The median is the $n = 50$th percentile; that is, it is a number that is larger than 50 percent of the measurements and smaller than the other 50 percent. The university admissions office needs to locate the seventy-fifth percentile, also called the upper quartile $(Q_3)$, which is the point above which 25 percent of the scores lie.

Equation (15.1) can be adjusted to find positional values such as the seventy-fifth percentile, the twenty-fifth percentile (also called the lower quartile, or $Q_1$), or the tenth percentile $(D_1)$. To adjust the equation, substitute the required proportion by which the number of cases are multiplied, then locate the interval containing the result of the calculation. Equations (15.2) to (15.4) define $Q_1$, $Q_3$, and $D_1$.

$$Q_1 = L + \left[ \frac{N(.25) - cf_{\text{below}}}{f} \right] w \qquad (15.2)$$

$$Q_3 = L + \left[ \frac{N(.75) - cf_{\text{below}}}{f} \right] w \qquad (15.3)$$

$$D_1 = L + \left[ \frac{N(.10) - cf_{\text{below}}}{f} \right] w \qquad (15.4)$$

In the following calculation, we employ the data contained in Table 15.10 to find the tenth percentile.

$$D_1 = 10.5 + \left[ \frac{134(.10) - 10}{12} \right] 10 = 10.5 + \left( \frac{3.4}{12} \right) 10 = 10.5 + 2.8 = 13.3$$

## Arithmetic Mean

The **arithmetic mean** is the most frequently used measure of central tendency. Although the mode and the median are both considered to be averages, the mean is what most people commonly consider to be the average. When we talk about such things as the average score on a test or the average height of a professional basketball player, we are usually talking about the mean. The mean is suitable for representing distributions measured on an interval level and lends itself to mathematical calculations; it also serves as a basis for other statistical measures. The arithmetic mean is defined as the sum total of all observations divided by their number.

In symbolic notations, the mean is defined as

$$\overline{X} = \frac{\Sigma X}{N} \tag{15.5}$$

where $\overline{X}$ = the arithmetic mean

$\Sigma X$ = the sum of total observations

$N$ = the number of observations

According to this equation, the mean ($\overline{X}$) of the series 6, 7, 12, 11, 10, 3, 4, 1, is 54/8 = 6.75.

When you are computing the mean from a frequency distribution, it is not necessary to add up all the individual observations. Instead, you can give each category its proper weight by multiplying it by its frequency, and the following equation can be used:

$$\overline{X} = \frac{\Sigma fX}{N} \tag{15.6}$$

where $\Sigma fX$ = the sum total of all categories multiplied by their respective frequencies.

Table 15.12 presents data on the amount of schooling received by 34 individuals. The mean education of this group can be calculated by using Equation (15.6). To calculate the value of $\Sigma fX$ (column 3), we have multiplied each category (column 1) by its frequency (column 2), and added up the products. The mean number of years of schooling is therefore

$$\overline{X} = \frac{278}{34} = 8.18$$

Equation (15.6) can be easily applied to grouped frequency distributions, where the midpoint of the interval is taken to represent $x$. For example, in the calculation of the mean family size for the group of respondents presented in Table 15.13, only the midpoint of each interval is entered in the calculations:

$$\overline{X} = \frac{51}{18} = 2.83$$

**Table 15.12**
Distribution of Years of Study

| (1) Years of Study | (2) f | (3) fX |
|---|---|---|
| 2 | 3 | 6 |
| 3 | 2 | 6 |
| 6 | 5 | 30 |
| 8 | 10 | 80 |
| 10 | 8 | 80 |
| 12 | 4 | 48 |
| 14 | 2 | 28 |
| Total | N = 34 | $\Sigma fX$ = 278 |

**Table 15.13**
Family Size for a Group of Respondents

| Family Size | Midpoint | f | fX |
|---|---|---|---|
| 0–2 | 1 | 10 | 10 |
| 3–5 | 4 | 5 | 20 |
| 6–8 | 7 | 3 | 21 |
| Total | | N = 18 | ΣfX = 51 |

Unlike the mode and the median, the arithmetic mean takes into account all the values in the distribution, making it especially sensitive to extreme values. For example, if one person in a group of ten earns $60,000 annually and each of the others earns $5,000, the mean income of the group would be $10,500, which is not a good representation of the distribution. The mean will thus be a misleading measure of central tendency whenever there are some observations with extremely high or low values.

Exhibit 15.1 illustrates the procedure for finding the three measures of central tendency.

**Exhibit 15.1**
Finding the Three Averages

**Mode** = the most frequent category = 9

Each * represents one observation
Total cases = 39

```
                                9
                        8       *
                        *       *
                6       *       *
                *       *       *       5
        4       *       *       *       *
        *       *       *       *       *       3
2       *       *       *       *       *       *
*       *       *       *       *       *       *       1       1
*       *       *       *       *       *       *       *       *
```
```
5       6       7       8       9       10      11      12      13
                        (value of the variable)
```

**Median** = the midpoint = $(N + 1) \div 2$
= $(39 + 1) \div 2 = 20$

5 5 6 6 6 6 7 7 7 7 7 7 8 8 8 8 8 8 8 9 9 9 9 9 9 9 9 9 10 10 10 10 10 11 11 11 11 12 13
                        ↑
                  Midpoint = the 20th case = 8

---

**Exhibit 15.1** *(continued)*

---

**Mean** = the arithmetic average =

$$
\begin{aligned}
5 \times 2 &= \phantom{0}10 \\
6 \times 4 &= \phantom{0}24 \\
7 \times 6 &= \phantom{0}42 \\
8 \times 8 &= \phantom{0}64 \\
9 \times 9 &= \phantom{0}81 \\
10 \times 5 &= \phantom{0}50 \\
11 \times 3 &= \phantom{0}33 \\
12 \times 1 &= \phantom{0}12 \\
13 \times 1 &= \phantom{0}\underline{13}
\end{aligned}
$$

$$
\underset{\text{(Total)}}{329} \div \underset{\text{(Cases)}}{39} = \underset{\text{(Mean)}}{8.44}
$$

---

## Comparison of the Mode, the Median, and the Mean

All three measures of central tendency can be used to represent univariate distributions. However, each has its own characteristics, which both prescribe and limit its use. The mode indicates the point in the distribution with the highest density, the median is the distribution's midpoint, and the arithmetic mean is an average of all the values in the distribution. Accordingly, these measures cannot be applied mechanically. How, then, does a researcher know when it is appropriate to use a

---

### The Three Measures of Central Tendency

- *Mode:* The category or observation that appears most frequently in the distribution. Researchers find the mode by locating the category with the largest number of responses.
- *Median:* The observation, category, or interval that divides the distribution into two equal parts. To find the median for ungrouped data with an uneven number of scores, the researcher lists the observations in increasing order and locates the middle score. If the number of scores is even, the median is located between the middle two scores. To find the median for grouped data, use Equation (15.1). The median is one example of a group of measures called percentiles. Equation (15.1) can be adapted to find any percentile; Equations (15.2), (15.3), and (15.4) show some of these adaptations.
- *Arithmetic Mean:* The mean is equal to the sum of all of the observations divided by the total number of observations. The formula for finding the mean of ungrouped data can be found in Equation (15.5), and the formula for finding the mean of grouped data can be found in Equation (15.6)

certain measure? There is no simple answer to the question; it depends on the objective of the study. For example, if the researcher is investigating the average level of income of a group in order to establish how much each person would receive if all incomes were distributed equally, the mean would be most pertinent, as it reflects the highest as well as the lowest income. If, by contrast, an administrator needs the information to estimate the eligibility of the group to receive financial aid, the mode would be appropriate, for it shows the most typical income and is unaffected by extreme values.

A researcher must also consider the level of measurement of the variable being analyzed when deciding which measure of central tendency to apply. The mode can be used at any level of measurement, but it is the only appropriate measure of central tendency for nominal variables such as party affiliation. The median can be applied to ordinal level variables such as political attitudes, but it may also be used to describe variables measured at a higher level. The arithmetic mean may be used with interval or ratio variables such as income and age.

---

# Basic Measures of Dispersion

Measures of central tendency identify the most representative value of the distribution and provide researchers with a way to summarize their data; however, they do not always tell researchers all they need to know about the distribution. For example, consider the following two distributions:

    1)   8, 8, 9, 9, 9, 10, 10, 10, 10, 10, 11, 11, 11, 12, 12
    2)   4, 5, 6, 7, 8, 9, 10, 10, 10, 11, 12, 13, 14, 15, 16

In both groups the mean, median, and mode are 10, and we can summarize the distributions using one of these central values. However, this single summarizing measure may give the impression that the two distributions are the same when they clearly are not. In the first distribution, the numbers tend to cluster around the central value; in the second distribution, they are more widely dispersed. A complete description of any distribution requires that we measure the extent of dispersion about the central value. (In the following discussion, the terms *dispersion, scatter,* and *variation* are used interchangeably.) The actual observations are distributed among many values, and the extent of their spread varies from one distribution to another. For example, two classes may have the same average grade; however, one class may include some excellent students as well as some very poor ones, whereas all the students in the other class may be of average ability. Similarly, income distributions with an identical mean may present different patterns of dispersion. In some distributions, most incomes are clustered around the mean; in others, the incomes are widely dispersed. Researchers obtain a description of the extent of dispersions about the central value by using measures designated as measures of dispersion. We shall discuss the measure of qualitative variation, the range, the mean deviation, the variance, the standard deviation, and the coefficient of variation.

## Measure of Qualitative Variation

Researchers can assess the extent of dispersion in nominal distributions by means of an index of heterogeneity designated as the **measure of qualitative variation.** This index reflects the number of differences among the categories of the distribution and is based on the number of categories and their respective frequencies. In general, the larger the number of categories and the greater the overall differences among them, the greater the degree of variation. Likewise, the smaller the number of categories and their differences, the smaller the variation within the distribution. Consider the racial/ethnic composition of two states—New Mexico and Vermont. The population in Vermont is composed mainly, although not exclusively, of whites. In New Mexico, only about half of the population is white. The remainder of the population is composed largely of Hispanics and, to a lesser degree, American Indians, but other racial/ethnic groups are also represented. The amount of variation depends on the racial/ethnic composition of the state. When most people belong to a single racial/ethnic group, the number of racial differences among the members of the state will be relatively small. Conversely, when most members are divided among several racial/ethnic groups, the number of differences will be large. In Vermont variation is small, and in New Mexico it is large. The measure of qualitative variation is based on the ratio of the total number of differences in the distribution to the maximum number of possible differences within the same distribution.

*Calculating the Total Number of Differences.*   To find the total number of differences in the distribution, a researcher would count and sum the differences between each category and every other category. For instance, in a group of 50 whites and 50 blacks, there would be $50 \times 50 = 2{,}500$ racial differences. Similarly, with 70 whites and 30 blacks, you would count $70 \times 30 = 2{,}100$ differences, and with 100 whites and no blacks, there would be $0 \times 100 = 0$ racial differences.

The procedure for calculating the total number of differences can be expressed in the following equation:

$$\text{Total observed differences} = \Sigma f_i f_j, \; i \neq j \tag{15.7}$$

where $f_i$ = frequency of category $i$

$f_j$ = frequency of category $j$

For example, in a group of 20 Catholics, 30 Jews, and 10 Muslims, there would be $(20 \times 30) + (20 \times 10) + (30 \times 10) = 1{,}100$ religious differences.

*Calculating the Maximum Possible Differences.*   Because each distribution has a different number of categories and frequencies, the total of observed differences is meaningful only in relation to the maximum possible number of differences. By relating the observed differences to the maximum possible differences, the researcher can control for these factors. The maximum number of differences occurs when each category in the distribution has an identical frequency. Thus the maximum number of frequencies is computed by finding the number of differences that would be observed if all frequencies were equal. Symbolically,

$$\text{Maximum possible differences} = \frac{n(n-1)}{2}\left(\frac{F}{n}\right)^2 \qquad (15.8)$$

where $n$ = the number of categories in the distribution

$\quad F$ = total frequency

For the sample with 20 Catholics, 30 Jews, and 10 Muslims, the maximum possible differences are

$$\left(\frac{3 \times 2}{2}\right)\left(\frac{60}{3}\right)^2 = 1,200$$

The measure of qualitative variation is the ratio between the total observed differences and the maximum possible differences. In other words,

$$\text{Measure of qualitative variation} = \frac{\text{Total observed differences}}{\text{Maximum possible differences}}$$

Symbolically, the measure is expressed in the following equation:

$$\text{Measure of qualitative variation} = \frac{\sum f_i f_j}{\dfrac{n(n-1)}{2}\left(\dfrac{F}{n}\right)^2} \qquad (15.9)$$

The measure of variation for our example is thus

$$\text{Measure of qualitative variation} = \frac{1,100}{1,200} = .92$$

The measure of qualitative variation varies between zero and one. Zero indicates the absence of any variation, and one reflects maximum variation. The measure will be zero whenever the total observed differences are zero. It will take the value of one when the number of observed differences is equal to the maximum possible differences.

At the beginning of this section we asked you to consider the racial/ethnic composition of two states—New Mexico and Vermont—and stated that the amount of racial/ethnic variation was large in New Mexico and small in Vermont. We can use the index of qualitative variation to compare the amount of diversity in the two states. Table 15.14 shows the population by race and ethnicity and the measure of qualitative variation (IQV) for 17 states. The table is arranged in order of decreasing diversity. You can see that there is wide variation in racial/ethnic diversity in the United States. New Mexico, with an IQV of .70, is the most diverse state; Vermont, with an IQV of only .04, is the most homogeneous state.

## Table 15.14
### Population by Race and Ethnicity and IQVs for 17 States

| State | White | Black | Am. Indian, Eskimo, or Aleut | Asian or Pacific Islander | Other | Hispanic | IQV |
|---|---|---|---|---|---|---|---|
| New Mexico | 764,164 | 27,642 | 128,068 | 12,587 | 3,384 | 579,224 | 0.70 |
| Texas | 10,291,680 | 1,976,360 | 52,803 | 303,825 | 21,937 | 4,339,905 | 0.66 |
| Mississippi | 1,624,198 | 911,891 | 8,316 | 12,543 | 337 | 15,931 | 0.57 |
| Florida | 9,475,326 | 1,701,103 | 32,910 | 146,159 | 8,285 | 1,574,143 | 0.52 |
| New Jersey | 5,718,966 | 984,845 | 12,490 | 264,341 | 9,685 | 739,861 | 0.51 |
| Alaska | 406,722 | 21,799 | 84,594 | 18,730 | 395 | 17,803 | 0.48 |
| Delaware | 528,092 | 111,011 | 1,938 | 8,854 | 453 | 15,820 | 0.43 |
| Colorado | 2,658,945 | 128,057 | 22,068 | 56,773 | 4,249 | 424,302 | 0.39 |
| Arkansas | 1,933,082 | 372,762 | 12,393 | 12,144 | 468 | 19,876 | 0.35 |
| Missouri | 4,448,465 | 545,527 | 18,873 | 40,087 | 2,419 | 61,702 | 0.28 |
| Pennsylvania | 10,422,058 | 1,072,459 | 13,505 | 134,056 | 7,303 | 232,262 | 0.26 |
| Rhode Island | 896,109 | 34,283 | 3,629 | 17,584 | 6,107 | 45,752 | 0.23 |
| Kentucky | 3,378,022 | 261,360 | 5,518 | 17,201 | 1,211 | 21,984 | 0.19 |
| Utah | 1,571,254 | 10,868 | 22,748 | 32,490 | 893 | 84,597 | 0.18 |
| Minnesota | 4,101,266 | 93,040 | 48,251 | 76,229 | 2,429 | 53,884 | 0.14 |
| West Virginia | 1,718,896 | 55,986 | 2,363 | 7,252 | 491 | 8,489 | 0.10 |
| Vermont | 552,184 | 1,868 | 1,651 | 3,159 | 235 | 3,661 | 0.04 |

Source: 1990 Census of the Population: General Population Characteristics. Distributed by the U.S. Department of Commerce Economic and Statistics Administration, Bureau of the Census, CP-1-1 through CP-1-512.

## Range and Interquartile Range

The **range** measures the distance between the highest and lowest values of the distribution. For example, in the following set of observations

$$4, 6, 8, 9, 17$$

the range is the difference between 17 and 4; that is, 13 ($17 - 4 = 13$). To calculate the range, the observations must be ranked according to size; thus the range can be applied in cases where the distribution is at least on an ordinal level of measurement. The range has a special significance when a dearth of information produces a distorted picture of reality. For instance, suppose that two factories with annual average wages of $15,000 have different pay ranges: one has a range of $2,000, and the other has a range of $9,000. Without the additional information supplied by the range, a comparison of the averages would give you the impression that the wage scales in both factories were identical. Although the range is a useful device for gaining a quick impression of the data, it is a crude measure of dispersion because it takes into account only the two extreme values of the distribution. Thus it is sensitive to changes in a single score.

An alternative to the range is the **interquartile range,** which is the difference between the lower and upper quartiles ($Q_1$ and $Q_3$). Because it measures the spread of the middle half of the distribution, it is less affected by extreme observations. The lower and upper quartiles will vary less from distribution to distribution than the most extreme observations. To illustrate the interquartile range, consider the data presented earlier in Table 15.10. The lower quartile ($Q_1$) for these data is 27.76, and the upper quartile ($Q_3$) is 58.75. These values were calculated with Equations (15.2) and (15.3). The interquartile range is thus $58.75 - 27.76 = 30.99$. The range can also be calculated for other measures of location. For example, you can calculate the range between the tenth and ninetieth percentiles to measure the dispersion of the middle 80 percent of the observations.

*Limitations.*     The major drawback of the range and the interquartile range is that because they are based on only two values, they reflect only the dispersion in some defined section of the distribution. In order to get a more accurate picture of the distribution, some measure must be devised that will reflect the aggregate dispersion in the distribution. However, to measure aggregate dispersion it is necessary to establish the deviation of all the values in the distribution from some criterion. In other words, the researcher must decide on some norm that will permit him or her to determine which value is higher or lower than expected. For example, the evaluation of income as "high" or "low" is meaningful only in relation to some fixed criterion. Income evaluated as high in India would be considered low in the United States.

A researcher can choose any of the measures of central tendency as a norm. It is possible to measure deviations from the mode, the median, or the arithmetic mean; however, the mean is the most widely employed.

# Measures of Dispersion Based on the Mean

The simplest way to obtain a measure of deviation is to calculate the average deviation from the arithmetic mean:

$$\text{Average deviation} = \frac{\sum(X - \overline{X})}{N}$$

where $X$ = each individual observation

$\overline{X}$ = the arithmetic mean

$N$ = the total number of observations

However, the sum of the deviations from the mean is always equal to zero;[2] thus the average deviation will be zero, for its numerator will always be zero. To compensate for this property of the mean, we square each deviation to calculate standard deviation—the measure of dispersion most commonly applied to interval level data.

## Variance and Standard Deviation

Whenever possible, researchers will choose to use variance and standard deviation as measures of dispersion because they can be used in more advanced statistical calculations. Variance and standard deviation are calculated by squaring and summing the deviations then dividing the sum by the total number of observations. The definitional formula for the **variance** is[3]

$$s^2 = \frac{\sum(X - \overline{X})^2}{N} \tag{15.10}$$

where $s^2$ = variance. In other words, the arithmetic mean is subtracted from each score; the differences are then squared, summed, and divided by the total number of observations. The numerical example in Table 15.15 illustrates the various steps involved in the computation of the variance. Applying Equation (15.10) to the data, we get

$$s^2 = \frac{200}{5} = 40$$

To calculate variance, researchers use a computational formula instead of the definitional formula. In the computational formula of the variance, the squared

2. For example, the mean of the numbers 2, 4, 6, and 8 is 5. If we subtract 5 from each of these numbers we get −3, −1, 1, and 3. The total of these differences—(−3) + (−1) + 1 + 3—is equal to zero.

3. The formulas for standard deviation and variance in this chapter are population formulas. When researchers calculate standard deviation and variance for samples of the population, they use $(N - 1)$ in the denominator rather than $N$.

mean is subtracted from the squared sum of all scores divided by the number of observations; that is,

$$s^2 = \frac{\sum X^2}{N} - (\bar{X})^2 \tag{15.11}$$

When we apply Equation (15.11) to the same data in Table 15.15, we get the following result:

$$s^2 = \frac{605}{5} - (9)^2 = 121 - 81 = 40$$

The variance expresses the average dispersion in the distribution not in the original units of measurement but in squared units. We can bypass this problem, however, by taking the square root of the variance, thereby transforming the variance into the standard deviation. The **standard deviation** is a measure expressing dispersion in the original units of measurement. Symbolically, the standard deviation is expressed in Equations (15.12) and (15.13), which correspond to Equations (15.10) and (15.11), respectively:

$$s = \sqrt{\frac{\sum (X - \bar{X})^2}{N}} \tag{15.12}$$

$$s = \sqrt{\frac{\sum X^2}{N} - (\bar{X})^2} \tag{15.13}$$

where $s$ = standard deviation. For our earlier example, the value of the standard deviation, using Equation (15.12), is

$$s = \sqrt{\frac{200}{5}} = \sqrt{40} = 6.3$$

The data in Table 15.15 are displayed in an ungrouped frequency distribution with a single frequency for each value of $X$. When data are arranged in an un-

**Table 15.15**
Computation of the Variance

| $X$ | $X - \bar{X}$ | $(X - \bar{X})^2$ | $X^2$ |
|---|---|---|---|
| 3 | −6 | 36 | 9 |
| 4 | −5 | 25 | 16 |
| 6 | −3 | 9 | 36 |
| 12 | 3 | 9 | 144 |
| 20 | 11 | 121 | 400 |
| Total | | 200 | 605 |

$\bar{X} = 9$

grouped frequency distribution and there are multiple frequencies for any or all values of $X$, we can use the following modified definitional formula to calculate variance:

$$s^2 = \frac{\sum f(X - \bar{X})^2}{N}$$

This modified computational formula is easier to use:

$$s^2 = \frac{\sum fY^2}{N} - \left(\frac{\sum fY}{N}\right)^2$$

## Variance and Standard Deviation for Grouped Data

If data are grouped, as they often are, researchers need to employ a different procedure for computing the variance and the standard deviation. Equation (15.14) provides the formula for computing the variance of grouped data where the interval's midpoint is represented by $X$ and $f$ stands for the corresponding frequencies:

$$s^2 = \frac{\sum fX^2 - \frac{(\sum fX)^2}{N}}{N} \tag{15.14}$$

This formula is applied to the data of Table 15.16:

$$s^2 = \frac{1,094 - \frac{(136)^2}{20}}{20} = \frac{1,094 - \frac{18,496}{20}}{20}$$

$$= \frac{1,094 - 924.8}{20} = \frac{169.20}{20} = 8.46$$

We can now obtain the standard deviation by simply taking the square root of 8.46. Thus

$$s = \sqrt{8.46} = 2.91$$

**Table 15.16**
Age Distribution of 20 Respondents

| Age | Midpoint X | f | $X^2$ | $fX^2$ | $fX$ |
|---|---|---|---|---|---|
| 1–3 | 2 | 4 | 4 | 16 | 8 |
| 4–6 | 5 | 3 | 25 | 75 | 15 |
| 7–9 | 8 | 10 | 64 | 640 | 80 |
| 10–12 | 11 | 3 | 121 | 363 | 33 |
| Total | | 20 | | $\sum fX^2 = 1094$ | $\sum fX = 136$ |

## Standard Deviation: Advantages and Applications

The standard deviation has various advantages over other measures of dispersion. First, it is more stable from sample to sample (on sampling, see Chapter 8). Second, it has some important mathematical properties that enable the researcher to obtain the standard deviation for two or more groups combined. Furthermore, its mathematical properties make it a useful measure in more advanced statistical work, especially in the area of statistical inferences (discussed in Chapters 8 and 19).

The application of standard deviation as a research device is illustrated in the following example. Table 15.17 compares differences in feelings of life satisfaction among people who live in several countries, using the mean and standard deviation of the variable "life satisfaction" in each country. The mean scores are almost identical, implying that satisfaction with life is similar in the four countries. However, there are differences in the standard deviations of each country. The relatively low standard deviations in England, Germany, and the United States indicate that these countries are homogeneous as far as satisfaction is concerned; that is, people have a satisfaction score that is close to their group's mean score. In Italy, however, the dispersion is greater, suggesting that the degree of satisfaction reflected by the mean is not common to all the Italians in the group studied.

## Coefficient of Variation

In instances where the distributions the researcher is comparing have very different means, he or she cannot compare the absolute magnitudes of the standard deviations. A standard deviation of 2, for instance, would convey a different meaning in relation to a mean of 6 than to a mean of 60. Therefore, the researcher needs to calculate the degree of dispersion relative to the mean of the distribution. This principle is reflected in the **coefficient of variation,** which reflects relative variation. Symbolically, the coefficient of variation is defined as follows:

$$V = \frac{s}{\overline{X}} \qquad (15.15)$$

where $V$ = the coefficient of variation

$s$ = the standard deviation

$\overline{X}$ = the arithmetic mean

**Table 15.17**

Mean and Standard Deviation on an Index of Life Satisfaction in Four Western Nations (Hypothetical Data)

|  | England | Germany | Italy | United States |
|---|---|---|---|---|
| Mean | 6.7 | 6.7 | 6.6 | 6.5 |
| Standard deviation | 1.0 | 1.2 | 3.2 | 1.3 |

**Table 15.18**
Attitudes toward Federal Support for Abortion in Four States
(Hypothetical Data)

|  | Wisconsin | Illinois | Alabama | Massachusetts |
|---|---|---|---|---|
| Mean | 5.48 | 4.82 | 3.67 | 5.82 |
| Standard deviation | 2.9 | 2.9 | 2.8 | 2.7 |

Table 15.18 on attitudes toward federal support for abortion presents the means and standard deviations of the distributions in four states. In absolute magnitudes, there are no significant differences among the standard deviations in the four states. However, there are substantial differences between the means, indicating varying degrees of support for abortion in each state. In Alabama, for example, the mean is much lower than in the other states, but the degree of dispersion is almost identical. Assuming that we have measured attitudes on a scale from 1 to 10, with 1 indicating strong opposition to federal support for abortion and 10 indicating strong support, it seems, intuitively, that a deviation of 2.8 has a greater significance in relation to a mean of 3.67 than to a mean of 4.82 or 5.48 because a mean of 3.67 is more extreme than a mean of either 4.82 or 5.48. To correct for

## Measures of Dispersion

- *Measure of Qualitative Variation:* An index that indicates the heterogeneity or homogeneity of a population. It is determined by comparing the total observed differences in a distribution to the maximum possible number of differences and is calculated using Equations (15.7), (15.8), and (15.9).
- *Range:* The distance between the highest and the lowest values of the distribution. The range can provide misleading information to researchers because it takes into account only the two extreme scores in a distribution.
- *Interquartile Range:* The difference between the lower quartile (25th percentile) and the upper quartile (75th percentile). Because it measures the spread of the middle half of the distribution, the interquartile range is not affected by extreme scores.
- *Variance:* Variance is the average of the squared deviations from the mean. It can be calculated using either the definitional formula or the simpler computational formula. These formulas have several variations. The choice of the proper formula is determined by whether the researcher is using a grouped or an ungrouped frequency distribution and if there are multiple frequencies for any value of the variable. Equations (15.10), (15.11), and (15.14) show formulas for variance.
- *Standard Deviation:* Standard deviation is equal to the square root of the variance. Unlike variance, the standard deviation expresses dispersion in the original units of measurement. Standard deviation can be calculated using Equations (15.12) and (15.13), or can be determined by taking the square root of the variance.

**Table 15.19**
Means of Attitudes toward Federal Support for Abortion and Coefficient of Variation
in Four States (Hypothetical Data)

|  | Wisconsin | Illinois | Alabama | Massachusetts |
|---|---|---|---|---|
| Mean | 5.48 | 4.82 | 3.67 | 5.82 |
| Coefficient of variation | .53 | .60 | .76 | .46 |

these discrepancies, the standard deviations were converted into coefficients of
variation. The results are displayed in Table 15.19. Note that, indeed, the relative
deviation from the mean is higher in Alabama than in other states, reflecting the
lower degree of homogeneity of attitudes toward abortion.

## Types of Frequency Distributions

Our discussion of univariate distributions has so far been limited to measures that
allow researchers to describe their data in terms of central tendencies and dispersion. The next step in describing a distribution is to identify its general form. Distributions may have distinctive forms with few low scores and many high scores, with
many scores concentrated in the middle of the distribution, or with many low
scores and few high scores. The simplest way to describe a distribution is by a
visual representation. Examples of different forms are presented in Figure 15.4.

The values of the variable are represented along the baseline, and the area
under the curve represents the frequencies. For example, in distribution *a*, the frequency of the interval 25–35 is represented by the area under the curve in that
interval. The distribution in Figure 15.4*a* is symmetrical; that is, the frequencies
at the right and left tails of the distribution are identical, so if the distribution is
divided into two halves, each will be the mirror image of the other. This usually
means that most of the observations are concentrated at the middle of the distri-

**Figure 15.4**
Types of Frequency Distributions

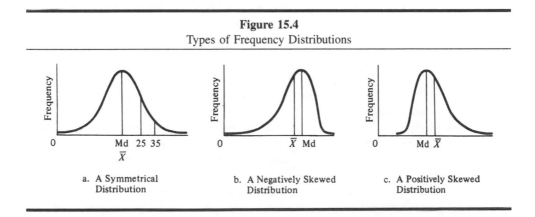

a. A Symmetrical
Distribution

b. A Negatively Skewed
Distribution

c. A Positively Skewed
Distribution

bution and that there are few observations with very high or very low scores. Male height is an example of a symmetrical distribution. Few men are very short or very tall; most are of medium height. Many other variables tend to be distributed symmetrically, and this form of distribution plays an important role in the field of statistical inference.

In nonsymmetrical or skewed distributions, there are more extreme cases in one direction of the distribution than in the other. A nonsymmetrical distribution in which there are more extremely low scores is referred to as a *negatively skewed distribution* (Figure 15.4*b*). When there are more extremely high scores, the distribution is *positively skewed* (Figure 15.4*c*). Most income distributions are positively skewed, with few families having extremely high incomes.

Skewness can also be identified according to the positions of the measures of central tendency. In symmetrical distributions, the mean will coincide with the median and the mode; in skewed distributions, there will be discrepancies between these measures. In a negatively skewed distribution, the mean will be pulled in the direction of the lower scores; in a positively skewed distribution, it will be located closer to the high scores. This property of skewed distributions makes the choice of a measure of central tendency a critical issue. Since the mean is pulled in the direction of the extreme scores, it loses its typicality and hence its usefulness as a representative measure. In such instances, it might be advisable to employ the median or the mode instead.

## Normal Curve

One type of symmetrical distribution, called the normal curve, has great significance in the field of statistics. A normal curve is shown in Figure 15.5. Its principal properties are as follows:

1. It is symmetrical and bell-shaped.
2. The mode, the median, and the mean coincide at the center of the distribution.
3. The curve is based on an infinite number of observations.
4. A single mathematical formula describes how frequencies are related to the values of the variable.

The fifth property of the normal curve is its most distinct characteristic: *in any normal distribution, a fixed proportion of the observations lies between the mean and fixed units of standard deviations.* The proportions can be seen in Figure 15.5. The mean of the distribution divides it exactly in half; 34.13 percent of the observations fall between the mean and one standard deviation to the right of the mean; the same proportion fall between the mean and one standard deviation to the left of the mean. The plus signs indicate standard deviations above the mean; the minus signs, standard deviations below the mean. Thus 68.26 percent of all observations fall between $\bar{X} \pm 1s$; 95.46 of all the observations fall between $\bar{x} \pm 2s$; and 99.73 percent of all the observations fall between $\bar{x} \pm 3s$.

**Figure 15.5**
Proportions under the Normal Curve

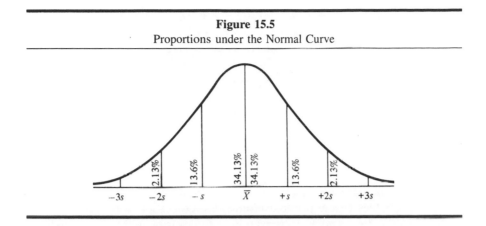

In any univariate distribution that is normally distributed, the proportion of observations included within fixed distances of the mean can be determined. For example, in a distribution of intelligence quotients with a mean of 110 and a standard deviation of 10, 68.26 percent of all subjects will have an IQ of 110 ± 1$s$—that is, between 100 and 120—and 95.46 percent will have a score that is not below 90 and does not exceed 130.

## Standard Scores

Researchers can use the normal curve to evaluate the proportion of observations included within a desired interval, but the raw scores must be converted to standard deviation units to use the table, which reports areas under the normal curve. When raw scores have been converted to standard scores, a single table can be used to evaluate any distribution regardless of the scale on which the data were measured, and distributions measured on different scales can be directly compared. If, for instance, we want to find the proportion of cases that have an IQ between 110 and 130, we must determine how many standard deviations away from the mean the score of 130 is located. Observations are converted into standard deviation units by means of Equation (15.16):

$$Z = \frac{X - \overline{X}}{s} \tag{15.16}$$

where $Z$ = number of standard deviation units

$X$ = any observation

$\overline{X}$ = the arithmetic mean

$s$ = the standard deviation

Z, sometimes referred to as a **standard score,** expresses the distance between a specific observation ($X$) and the mean in terms of standard deviation units.

A Z of 2 means that the distance between the mean of the distribution and $X$ is two standard deviations. For example, in a distribution with a mean of 40 and a standard deviation of 5, the score of 50 is expressed as follows:

$$Z = \frac{50 - 40}{5} = \frac{10}{5} = 2$$

The score of 50 lies two standard deviations above the mean. Similarly, 30 is two standard deviations below the mean:

$$Z = \frac{30 - 40}{5} = \frac{-10}{5} = -2$$

Special tables have been constructed for the standard form of the normal curve. These tables enable you to determine the proportion of observations that lie between the mean and any observation in the distribution. (See Appendix E for an example of such a table.) The table shows proportions for various Z values. The first two digits of Z are listed in the left-hand column; the third digit is shown across the top. Thus, for example, the proportion included between the mean and a Z of 1 is .3413, or 34.13 percent; the value of a Z of 1.65 is .4505. The table shows only half of the curve's proportions because the curve is symmetrical. Thus the distance between the mean and a Z of – 1.0 is identical to the area between the mean and a Z of 1.0. To use the table, find the appropriate Z score for any particular observation by applying Equation (15.16), and then consult Appendix E.

To illustrate the use of the standard normal table, suppose that the distribution of income in a particular community is normal, its mean income is $15,000, and the standard deviation is $2,000. We want to determine what proportion of the people in this community have an income between $11,000 and $15,000. First, we convert $11,000 into standard deviation units:

$$Z = \frac{11,000 - 15,000}{2,000} = -2$$

Next, we consult Appendix E to determine that .4773 of all observations are included between the mean and a Z of 2. In other words, 47.73 percent of all people in the community earn between $11,000 and $15,000 a year. This is shown in Figure 15.6.

What proportion of the community earns between $16,000 and $20,000? We determine this by converting both figures into standard scores:

$$Z_1 = \frac{16,000 - 15,000}{2,000} = 0.5$$

$$Z_2 = \frac{20,000 - 15,000}{2,000} = 2.5$$

Appendix E indicates that .4938 is included between the mean and 2.5 standard deviation units and .1915 between the mean and 0.5 units. Therefore, the area included between $16,000 and $20,000 is .4938 – .1915 = .3023 (30.23 percent). This is shown in Figure 15.7.

**Figure 15.6**
Proportion of Population Earning between $11,000 and $15,000

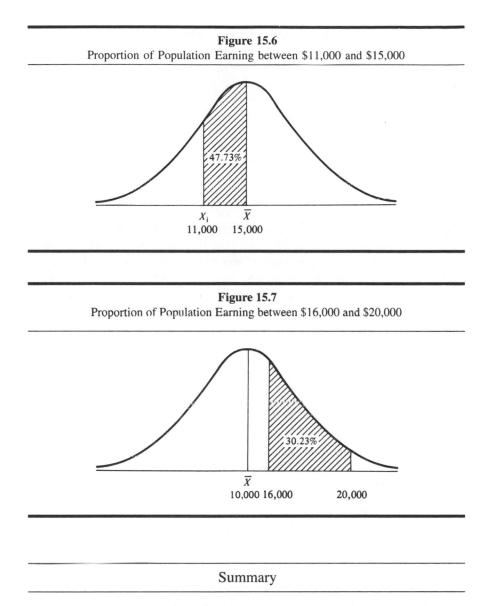

**Figure 15.7**
Proportion of Population Earning between $16,000 and $20,000

## Summary

**1.** During the preliminary stage of analysis, researchers use quite ordinary methods designed to provide a straightforward description of the data. Once coded, each item is summarized in some tabular form, and measures such as averages and percentages are calculated to describe its main characteristics. Researchers usually begin the analysis by showing how the respondents are distributed on all the items of the investigation. A distribution might show, for instance, that 20 of the 80 respondents included in a sample are males and the rest are females; that 46 are Democrats, 20 are Republicans, and 14 do not identify with either party. Such listings of the number of observations that fall into each of several categories are termed *frequency distributions.* Frequencies are often converted into proportions or percentages; these are helpful in assessing the weight of a single category in relation to other categories of the distribution or in relation to other distributions.

**2.** Often it is useful to obtain some average value that is representative of the distribution. For example, a researcher may need to answer such questions as "What is the most typical political orientation of this group of respondents?" or "What is their average income?" These questions can be answered by using measures of central tendency. The three most commonly used statistical measures of central tendency are the mode, the median, and the arithmetic mean.

**3.** Measures of central tendency can be misleading if they are not accompanied by measures that describe the amount of dispersion in the distribution. Whereas the measures of central tendency reflect the most typical or average characteristics of the group, the measures of dispersion indicate how many members of the group deviate from it and the extent of the deviation. A small deviation denotes that most responses are clustered around the measure of central tendency; a large deviation indicates that the measure of central tendency is a poor representation of the distribution.

**4.** One of the important steps in examining a distribution is to identify its general form. Certain forms are characteristic of different empirical phenomena. For instance, many income distributions have few extremely high incomes; most incomes are concentrated in the middle or lower ranges. Such distributions are skewed toward the higher values. In contrast, intelligence distributions are typically symmetrical; most scores are concentrated in the middle range, with very few extremely high or extremely low scores.

---

## Key Terms for Review

---

arithmetic mean (p. 367)
coefficient of variation (p. 379)
descriptive statistics (p. 355)
frequency distribution (p. 355)
inferential statistics (p. 355)
interquartile range (p. 375)
measure of qualitative variation
    (p. 372)

median (p. 364)
mode (p. 364)
normal curve (p. 382)
range (p. 375)
skewed distribution (p. 382)
standard deviation (p. 377)
standard score (p. 383)
variance (p. 376)

---

## Study Questions

---

1. The following table describes the employment status of women in two communities. What conclusions can be drawn from the absolute numbers? From the percentages?

|              | Community A |        | Community B |        |
| ------------ | ----------- | ------ | ----------- | ------ |
| *In labor force:* |        |        |             |        |
| Professional | 20,000      | 4%     | 20,000      | 10%    |
| Skilled      | 45,000      | 9%     | 24,000      | 12%    |
| Semiskilled  | 70,000      | 14%    | 28,000      | 14%    |
| Unskilled    | 170,000     | 34%    | 28,000      | 14%    |
| *Not in labor force:* | 195,000 | 39% | 100,000     | 50%    |
| Total        | 500,000     | 100%   | 200,000     | 100%   |

2. Give two examples of problems in which (a) the mean is the best measure of central tendency; (b) the mode is the best measure of central tendency; (c) the median is the best measure of central tendency.
3. Give the mean, median, and mode of the following distribution:

$$22, 41, 43, 56, 33, 22, 20, 37$$

4. The following is the income distribution of a group of workers:

| Income   | Frequency |
| -------- | --------- |
| $18,000  | 6         |
| 22,000   | 3         |
| 27,500   | 3         |
| 30,000   | 2         |
| 75,000   | 1         |
|          | N = 15    |

   a. Which measure of central tendency would you use to represent the income of this group?

   b. Compute the measure of central tendency you would use.

5. On the curve shown here, what would be the approximate position of the mean? The median? The mode? Define the curve with respect to skewness.

6. Suppose that you obtain a set of scores of attitudes toward legal abortion from a group of respondents and that the standard deviation of this set of scores is zero. What does this imply about the group?
7. Attitudes toward authority often can be treated as an interval variable. Suppose that this variable is normally distributed with a mean score of 60 and a standard deviation of 10.

   a. What proportion of cases have scores between 60 and 63?

   b. What proportion have scores of less than 48?

   c. What proportion score between 72 and 83? Between 52 and 55?

## Computer Exercises

1. Using the GSS file that accompanies this text, or a dataset of your own, generate univariate FREQUENCIES for one nominal, one ordinal, and one interval level variable. Also generate only those measures of central tendency and dispersion that are appropriate for each variable's level.
2. Calculate the statistics from question 1 by hand to check your results with those from the output.
3. Generate a bar chart for the nominal and ordinal variables.

(See Appendix A, p. 514)

## Additional Readings

Agresti, Alan, and Barbara Finlay. *Statistical Methods for the Social Sciences.* San Francisco: Dellen, 1986.

Knoke, David, and George W. Bohrnstedt. *Basic Social Statistics.* Itasca, Ill.: Peacock, 1991.

Healey, Joseph F. *Statistics: A Tool for Social Research.* Belmont, Calif.: Wadsworth, 1993.

Hickey, Anthony A. *An Introduction to Statistical Techniques for Social Research.* New York: Random House, 1990.

Vernoy, Mark W., and Judith A. Vernoy. *Behavioral Statistics in Action.* Belmont, Calif.: Wadsworth, 1992.

# CHAPTER 16

# Bivariate Analysis

**The Concept of Relationship**
How to Construct a Bivariate Table
Principle of Covariation: An Example
Percentaging Bivariate Tables
Median and Mean as Covariation Measures

**Measurement of Relationship**
Proportional Reduction of Error

**Nominal Measures of Relationship**
Lambda, the Guttman Coefficient of Predictability

**Ordinal Measures of Relationship**
The Pair Concept
Types of Pairs
Gamma
Kendall's Tau-*b*

**Interval Measures of Relationship**
Prediction Rules
Linear Regression
Criterion of Least squares
Errors of Prediction
Pearson's Product-Moment Correlation Coefficient (*r*)

Fantasies about sex are as old as humankind, but the facts about what Americans do in bed, with whom, and how often have been studied systematically only during the last half-century. In 1992, a team of researchers from the University of Chicago released the results of a comprehensive survey of nearly 3,500 Americans, ages 18 to 59. Their findings, published in a book titled *Sex in America: A Definitive Survey* include among others, the observation that the majority of Americans are largely monogamous; seventy-one percent have one sexual partner a year, and an average of three sexual partners since age 18. The study also confirms that teenagers do have sex earlier now; about half of all adolescents have their first sexual experience by the time they are 17 years old.[1]

The study *Sex in America* is significant not only because it describes patterns of sexual behavior in America, but also because it focuses on how sexual behavior varies by gender, race, or religion. For example, the study confirms that men think about sex more than women and that men and women have a different view about what constitutes consent. Sexual practice also varies by religious affiliation; Roman Catholics are the most likely to be virgins and Jews have the most sexual partners.

The examination of differences in sexual behavior between men and women, or between Roman Catholics and Jews, is what social scientists call bivariate analysis. Bivariate analysis allows us to examine the relationship between two variables. For example, the researchers of *Sex in America* analyzed the bivariate relation between gender and sexual practice by comparing the sexual practices of men and women. They also analyzed the relationship between religious affiliation and sexual practice by comparing the differences in the sexual practices of Roman Catholics and Jews (as well as other religious groups).

I N THIS CHAPTER, WE EXPLORE THE CONCEPT OF RELATIONSHIPS between two variables and examine different methods for measuring bivariate relationships. In the first section we discuss the concept of bivariate relationship; the second section describes nominal measures of relationship; the third section deals with ordinal measures of relationship; and the last section presents interval measures of relationship.

---

# The Concept of Relationship

Each of us knows what relationships are. We know that in the world around us, things go together. We observe that as children grow, their weight increases; that cities tend to be more polluted than rural areas; and that women earn less money than men. Each of these observations is a statement of a relationship: between age and weight, between degree of urbanization and pollution, and between gender and earnings.

1. Robert T. Michael et al., *Sex in America: A Definitive Survey* (New York: Little, Brown, 1994).

To say that cities tend to be more polluted than rural areas is to describe a relationship between urbanization and pollution. This statement can be made only if we can show that the level of pollution in the more urbanized cities is higher than the level of pollution in the less urbanized rural areas. In other words, to state a relationship between $X$ and $Y$ is to say that certain categories of the variable $X$ go with certain categories of the variable $Y$. This principle of *covariation* is basic to the notion of association and relation.

As a first step in examining a relationship between two variables, researchers usually construct a bivariate table.

## How to Construct a Bivariate Table

In a bivariate table, two variables are cross-classified. Such a table consists of rows and columns; the categories of one variable are labels for the rows, and the categories of the second variable are labels for the columns. Usually, the independent variable is the column variable (listed across the top), and the dependent variable is the row variable (listed at the left side of the table). Exhibit 16.1 is an illustration of how a bivariate table is constructed. Sixteen individuals are first listed by their gender and their job satisfaction scores. Then these observations are tallied and classified by their joint position on gender and job satisfaction into the appropriate cells in Table 16.1. The table is a 3 × 2 table because it has three rows and two columns, each representing a category of either the variable "gender" or the variable "job satisfaction." The fourth row represents the column totals; the third column, the row totals.

---

**Exhibit 16.1**
Constructing a Bivariate Table

---

| Gender | Job Satisfaction |
|---|---|
| Male = M | High = H |
| Female = F | Medium = M |
|  | Low = L |

| ID Number | Gender | Job Satisfaction |
|---|---|---|
| 1 | M | H |
| 2 | M | H |
| 3 | F | H |
| 4 | M | M |
| 5 | F | L |
| 6 | F | L |
| 7 | F | L |
| 8 | M | M |
| 9 | M | H |
| 10 | F | M |
| 11 | M | H |

**Exhibit 16.1** *(continued)*

| | | |
|---|---|---|
| 12 | M | H |
| 13 | M | L |
| 14 | F | M |
| 15 | F | L |
| 16 | F | H |

**Table 16.1**
Job Satisfaction by Gender

| Job Satisfaction | Gender | | Row Totals |
|---|---|---|---|
| | Male | Female | |
| High | 5 | 2 | 7 |
| Medium | 2 | 2 | 4 |
| Low | 1 | 4 | 5 |
| Column Totals | 8 | 8 | 16 |

## Principle of Covariation: An Example

The principle of covariation is demonstrated in Tables 16.2, 16.3, and 16.4. These tables summarize hypothetical information on two variables: religious denomination and social class. Table 16.2 illustrates a pattern of perfect covariation of the variables: all the Catholics are classified into the low social-class category, all Jews belong to the middle class, and the Protestants occupy the high social-class category. The two variables covary because specific categories of the variable "religious denomination" go with specific categories of the variable "social class."

The same pattern recurs in Table 16.3, but to a lesser extent because not all members of a given religious denomination belong to the same class. Yet it can still be said that most members of a particular religion belong to a particular social stratum.

When variables are not related, we say that they are independent of each other; that is, they do not "go together." Table 16.4 illustrates this situation. There is no clear pattern for any of the religious groups in the table. Catholics can be in the upper, middle, and lower classes; the same goes for Jews and Protestants. In other

**Table 16.2**
Social Class by Religious Denomination (Perfect Covariation)

| Social Class | Religious Denomination | | | Total |
|---|---|---|---|---|
| | Catholic | Jewish | Protestant | |
| Upper | 0 | 0 | 8 | 8 |
| Middle | 0 | 8 | 0 | 8 |
| Lower | 8 | 0 | 0 | 8 |
| Total | 8 | 8 | 8 | 24 |

**Table 16.3**

Social Class by Religious Denomination (Moderate Covariation)

| Social Class | Religious Denomination | | | Total |
|---|---|---|---|---|
| | Catholic | Jewish | Protestant | |
| Upper | 0 | 2 | 6 | 8 |
| Middle | 1 | 6 | 1 | 8 |
| Lower | 7 | 0 | 1 | 8 |
| Total | 8 | 8 | 8 | 24 |

**Table 16.4**

Social Class by Religious Denomination (Near-Zero Covariation)

| Social Class | Religious Denomination | | | Total |
|---|---|---|---|---|
| | Catholic | Jewish | Protestant | |
| Upper | 2 | 3 | 3 | 8 |
| Middle | 3 | 2 | 3 | 8 |
| Lower | 3 | 3 | 2 | 8 |
| Total | 8 | 8 | 8 | 24 |

words, you cannot say anything about a person's socioeconomic status on the basis of the person's religion.

Tables 16.2, 16.3, and 16.4 are examples of bivariate distributions arranged in tabular form. The bivariate distribution consists of the categories of two variables and their joint frequencies. Its components are displayed in the bivariate tables of our example. Each table has two dimensions, one per variable. The variables are divided into a number of categories; for example, the variable "social class" has been divided into the categories "upper," "middle," and "lower" and the variable "religious denomination" into "Catholic," "Jewish," and "Protestant." The cells of the table constitute an intersection between two categories, each of one variable. The frequencies in each cell are of observations that have two traits in common. For example, Table 16.4 shows two Catholics from the upper class, three from the middle class, and three from the lower class. The Jews have three members of the upper class, two members in the middle class, and three in the lower class; finally, there are three Protestants in the upper class, three in the middle class, and two in the lower class.

The bivariate table can also be visualized as a series of univariate distributions.[2] By splitting each table down its columns and taking each column separately, we will have divided each bivariate distribution into three univariate distributions, representing the class standing of Protestants, Catholics, and Jews. When we compare the three univariate distributions derived from, say, Table 16.3, we can see that

2. Theodore R. Anderson and Morris Zelditch, Jr., *A Basic Course in Statistics* (Fort Worth: Holt, Rinehart and Winston, 1968), Chapter 6.

each distribution differs from the others in its pattern of dispersion. In the Protestant distribution, most of the respondents tend to cluster at the upper extremity of the distribution, the Jews are clustered in the center, and the Catholics tend toward the lower section. This tendency is even more pronounced in Table 16.2; it becomes absolute (that is, all Protestants are upper-class, and so on). In Table 16.4, by contrast, there is practically no difference among the three distributions, the dispersion being identical in each. Thus a researcher can determine the amount of covariation in a bivariate table by comparing the univariate distributions that constitute the table. The larger the difference, the higher the degree of covariation of the two variables.

## Percentaging Bivariate Tables

A useful way of summarizing a bivariate table and comparing its univariate distributions to assess relationship is by expressing its frequencies as percentages. Percentaging tables is appropriate whenever the variables are nominal, but researchers usually use percentages even when the variables being analyzed are ordinal or interval. In Table 16.5, gender and marital status among public officials have been cross-tabulated to examine the hypothesis that the private life situation of women in elective office differs from that of their male counterparts. The table has been set up in the conventional way: "gender" (the independent variable) is at the top of the table, and "marital status" (the dependent variable) is on the left-hand side. Each gender group can be visualized as a univariate distribution, and its frequencies can be transformed into percentages by using the total number of cases in each distribution as a base for percentaging (that is, 72 women and 66 men each represent 100 percent). The percentages are presented in Table 16.6. The researcher's next step is to compare the univariate distributions to determine the extent of correlation between gender and marital status among public officials. Whereas the computation of percentages goes down the columns, the comparison cuts across the rows. The proportion of women who are married is compared with the proportion of married men (68.1 percent and 89.4 percent, respectively). Table 16.6

**Table 16.5**
Distribution of Marital Status by Gender among Public Officials

| Marital Status | Gender | |
|---|---|---|
|  | Women | Men |
| Married | 49 | 59 |
| Single, never married | 2 | 2 |
| Divorced, separated | 10 | 5 |
| Widowed | 11 | — |
| Total | 72 | 66 |

Source: Susan J. Carroll, "The Personal Is Political: The Intersection of Private Lives and Public Roles among Women and Men in Elective and Appointive Office," *Women and Politics*, Vol. 9, 2 (1989).

**Table 16.6**
Distribution of Marital Status by Gender among Public Officials
(in Percentages)

| | Gender | |
| --- | --- | --- |
| Marital Status | Women | Men |
| Married | 68.1% | 89.4% |
| Single, never married | 2.8 | 3.0 |
| Divorced, separated | 13.9 | 7.6 |
| Widowed | 15.3 | — |
| Total | 100.0 | 100.0 |
| | (N = 72) | (N = 66) |

displays a clear pattern of correlation: gender is associated with marital status among public officials. The two univariate distributions differ in their pattern of distribution: women in public office are less likely than their male counterparts to be married and more likely to be divorced or widowed. This relation between gender and marital status among public officials is also depicted in Figure 16.1

**Figure 16.1**
Marital Status by Gender among Public Officials

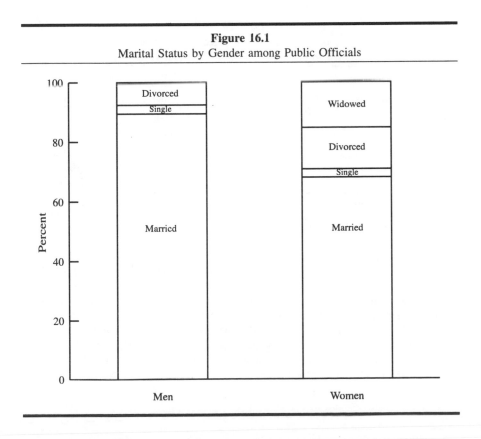

Whenever one variable is considered the independent variable and the other the dependent one, the percentages should be computed in the direction of the independent variable. If gender were considered a dependent variable and marital status the independent variable (which seems unlikely in this example), percentages would be computed across the rows instead of along the columns.

For further details on reading tables, see Exhibit 16.2 and Appendix A.

---

### Exhibit 16.2
### The Principles of Table Reading

---

Social scientists use statistical tables extensively as a way of presenting research results. The following discussion is a quick guide to reading tables.

1. *Look for the title.* The title describes the information that is contained in the table. In Table 16.7, the title tells about differences in abortion attitudes between men and women.

2. *Examine the source.* As in Table 16.7, the source of the data is usually written at the bottom of the table. Identifying the source will help you to assess the reliability of the information as well as to find the original data in case you need further information.

### Table 16.7
Abortion Attitudes for Men and Women
(compiled from the General Social Survey, 1988–1991)

| Abortion Attitudes | Gender | | Totals |
|---|---|---|---|
| | Men | Women | |
| Pro-life | 41% | 37% | 39% |
| Situationalist | 53 | 54 | 53 |
| Pro-choice | 6 | 9 | 8 |
| Totals | 100% | 100% | 100% |
| | (N=1,300) | (N=1,600) | (N=2,900) |

Adapted from Elizabeth Addel Cook, Ted G. Jelen, and Clyde Wilcox, "The Social Bases of Abortion Attitudes," Chapter 2 in *Between Two Absolutes: Public Opinions and the Politics of Abortion* (Boulder, Colo.: Westview Press, 1992).

3. *Determine in which direction the percentages have been computed.* This step is crucial and should be done carefully. It is important to examine whether the percentages have been computed down the columns, across the rows, or on the basis of the whole table. Or is the table an abbreviated one, in which the percentages, as presented, do not add up to 100 percent? Determine the direction by examining where "100%" or the figure for total cases has been inserted. In Table 16.7, the percentages have been computed down the column. By contrast, in Table 16.8, the percentages have been computed in the opposite direction, across the rows. Figures 16.2a and 16.2b are simple bar charts illustrating the two methods of calculating percentages as depicted in Tables 16.7 and 16.8.

**Table 16.8**
Level of Education in Relation to Social Class

| Social Class | Did Not Finish High School | Graduated from High School but Did Not Enter College | Entered College but Did Not Finish | Completed a Four-Year College Program | Total |
|---|---|---|---|---|---|
| Upper and upper middle | 5% | 15% | 10% | 70% | 100% (N = 600) |
| Lower middle | 3% | 12% | 36% | 49% | 100% (N = 420) |
| Working | 16% | 23% | 41% | 20% | 100% (N = 510) |

**Figure 16.2**
Bar Charts Comparing Column and Row Percents Shown in Tables 16.7 and 16.8

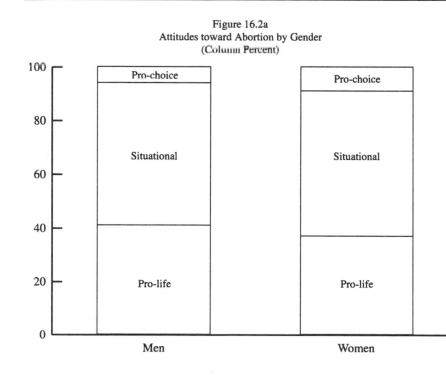

Figure 16.2a
Attitudes toward Abortion by Gender
(Column Percent)

## Exhibit 16.2 *(continued)*

Figure 16.2b
Education in Relation to Social Class
(Row Percent)

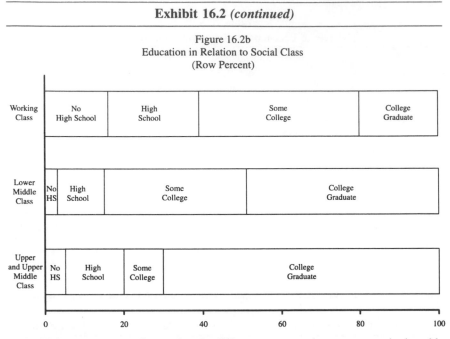

4. *Make comparisons.* Comparing the differences among the percentages in the table is a quick method for assessing the extent of a relationship between the variables. You should always make comparisons in the direction opposite to the one in which the percentages have been computed. If the percentages have been computed down the column, as in Table 16.7, then we compare percentages across the rows. The percentage of men who are pro-life is compared to the percentage of women who are pro-life (41 percent to 37 percent). We can also compare the percentage of men and women who are situationalist (53 percent and 54 percent) or pro-choice (6 percent with 9 percent). By making these comparisons, we determine that there are virtually no gender differences in abortion attitudes. Both men and women are equally likely to support or oppose abortions.

In Table 16.8, because the percentages have been calculated across the rows, we compare up or down the columns. For instance we can compare the percentage of working-class, lower-middle class, and upper-middle class respondents who completed a four year college (20 percent, 49 percent and 70 percent). Similar comparisons can be made for other levels of education. Based on these comparisons we can say that level of education is associated with social class.

### Table 16.9
Gender and the Percentage of People Who Report Some Same-Sex
Desires or Experiences

| Gender | Percentage of Each Group Who Reported Same-Sex Desires |
|---|---|
| Men | 10.1 ($N = 1,700$) |
| Women | 8.6 ($N = 1,650$) |

Adapted from *New York Times,* "So, Now We Know What Americans Do in Bed. So?" October 9, 1994, p. 3.

Often, for the sake of simplicity, a researcher will present only part of the table. Table 16.9 is an example. It is based on the survey *Sex in America* reported earlier. The table compares the same-sex experiences of men and women. It is important to observe that the two percentages in this table do not add up to 100 percent and that they are to be compared directly. They represent the different proportion of individuals in the two categories of the independent variable (gender) who belong to one response category of the dependent variable (having same sex experience or desire).

Based on Roberta G. Simmons, "Basic Principles of Table Reading," in Morris Rosenberg, *The Logic of Survey Analysis* (New York: Basic Books, 1968), pp. 251–258.

## Median and Mean as Covariation Measures

When the variables of a bivariate distribution are ordinal, the researcher can use the medians of the various univariate distributions as measures of covariation, as the survey data in Table 16.10 illustrate. Some 307 individuals were classified according to religion and their evaluation of the quality of community life. The dependent variable "quality of community life" is on the left-hand side, and each religious group is assumed to be a univariate distribution. The variable "quality of community life" is ranked from 1 (excellent) to 4 (somewhat poor). The appropriate summary measure for ordinal data is the median, which can be used to summarize each of the three distributions—Catholic, Jewish, and Protestant. By examining the cumulative percentages for each distribution and identifying the category associated with the cumulative percentage closest to 50%, we can see that, for Catholics, the median is 2; among Jews, it is 1; and among Protestants, it is 2. Thus the data from this survey indicate that Jews consider the quality of their community life to be better than Catholics or Protestants do. These differences indicate a relationship or covariation between religion and quality of community life.

**Table 16.10**
Quality of Community Life by Religion

| Quality of Community Life | Catholic | | Jewish | | Protestant | |
|---|---|---|---|---|---|---|
| | Percent | Cumulative Percent | Percent | Cumulative Percent | Percent | Cumulative Percent |
| 1 Excellent | 20 | 20 | 67 | 67 | 22 | 22 |
| 2 Good | 55 | 75 | 17 | 84 | 43 | 65 |
| 3 Average | 22 | 97 | 16 | 100 | 29 | 94 |
| 4 Somewhat poor | 3 | 100 | — | — | 6 | 100 |
| Total | 100 | | 100 | | 100 | |
| | (N=151) | | (N=6) | | (N=150) | |

Source: *Social and Political Survey: Winter 1989*. Social Science Research Facility, University of Wisconsin, Milwaukee (unpublished).

**Table 16.11**

Intelligence Test Scores by Age (Hypothetical Data)

| IQ Test Scores | Age | | | | |
|---|---|---|---|---|---|
| | 6–10 | 11–15 | 16–20 | 21–25 | Total |
| 0–4 | 10 | 6 | 4 | 1 | 21 |
| 5–9 | 8 | 10 | 3 | 2 | 23 |
| 10–14 | 6 | 7 | 8 | 8 | 29 |
| 15–19 | 4 | 3 | 3 | 10 | 20 |
| Total | 28 | 26 | 18 | 21 | 93 |

**Table 16.12**

Mean IQ Test Scores in Four Age Groups

| Age Group | Mean |
|---|---|
| 6–10 | 7.7 |
| 11–15 | 8.3 |
| 16–20 | 9.8 |
| 21–25 | 13.4 |

With interval variables, the researcher can use the arithmetic mean as a comparative measure. Table 16.11 is a bivariate distribution of intelligence test scores by age. Each age group can be visualized as a distribution and summarized by the arithmetic mean. Table 16.12 presents the arithmetic means of the distribution. Each pair of means can be compared. Note that average scores rise with age, a fact that permits us to deduce that the variables "age" and "intelligence" covary.

# Measurement of Relationship

So far, we have assessed the extent of covariation of two variables by comparing the univariate distributions that constitute the bivariate table. However, there are various statistical techniques that allow the researcher to assess the extent to which two variables are associated by a single summarizing measure. Such measures of relationship, often referred to as **correlation coefficients,** reflect the strength and the direction of association between the variables and the degree to which one variable can be predicted from the other.

The notion of prediction is inherent in the concept of covariation. When two variables covary, it is possible to use one to predict the other; when they do not, information about one will not enable us to predict the other. Consider Tables 16.2, 16.3, and 16.4 again; assume that no information is available about the religious denomination of the 24 persons and that we are forced to guess the social status of each one. Generally, our best guess would be the most frequent category. However, since in all three tables the frequencies of all the categories are identical, we could arbitrarily select any category. Suppose that we choose the middle class as the best guess for each person. Since only eight cases in each table do in fact belong to the middle class, we will make 16 errors out of 24 guesses in each of the three tables.

Religious denomination can be used to predict social class only if it is likely to reduce the number of errors in prediction. Suppose we predict that all Protestants are upper-class, all Jews are middle-class, and all Catholics are lower-class. In Table 16.2, this prediction is accurate in each of the 24 cases; in Table 16.3, there are 5 errors; in Table 16.4, there are 16 errors.

As Exhibit 16.3 demonstrates, we can calculate the advantage of employing religious denomination to predict social class by subtracting the new number of errors from the previous total. In Table 16.2, the advantage is absolute because the reduction in the number of errors is the greatest ($16 - 0 = 16$). In Table 16.3, we

---

**Exhibit 16.3**
Covariation and Prediction

---

Number of errors if we predict that each person is middle class: 16.

■ For Table 16.2: *Perfect Covariation*

| *Upper Class* | *Prediction* | |
|---|---|---|
| P P P P P P P P | All Protestants are upper class | |
| | Number of errors: | 0 |
| *Middle Class* | | |
| J J J J J J J J | All Jews are middle class | |
| | Number of errors: | 0 |
| *Lower Class* | | |
| C C C C C C C C | All Catholics are lower class | |
| | Number of errors: | 0 |
| | TOTAL NUMBER OF ERRORS: | 0 |

■ For Table 16.3: *Moderate Covariation*

| *Upper Class* | *Prediction* | |
|---|---|---|
| J J P P P P P P | All Protestants are upper class | |
| | Number of errors: | 2 |
| *Middle Class* | | |
| C J J J J J J P | All Jews are middle class | |
| | Number of errors: | 2 |
| *Lower Class* | | |
| C C C C C C C P | All Catholics are lower class | |
| | Number of errors: | 1 |
| | TOTAL NUMBER OF ERRORS: | 5 |

---

**Exhibit 16.3** *(continued)*

---

■ For Table 16.4: *Near-Zero Covariation*

| *Upper Class* | *Prediction* | |
| C C J J J P P P | All Protestants are upper class | |
| | Number of errors: | 5 |
| *Middle Class* | | |
| C C C J J P P P | All Jews are middle class | |
| | Number of errors: | 6 |
| *Lower Class* | | |
| C C C J J J P P | All Catholics are lower class | |
| | Number of errors: | 5 |
| | TOTAL NUMBER OF ERRORS: | 16 |

---

gain a considerable advantage as well since the number of errors is reduced by 11 ($16 - 5 = 11$). In Table 16.4, there is no change in the number of errors, despite the employment of religious denomination ($16 - 16 = 0$). The number of errors in this case is the same as if we had predicted that each person is middle class.

## Proportional Reduction of Error

We can assess the strength of the association between social class and religious denomination by calculating the proportional reduction in prediction error when using one variable to predict another. The **proportional reduction of error** is defined as follows:[3]

$$\frac{b - a}{b} \tag{16.1}$$

where $b$ = the original number of errors (before employing the independent variable as a predictor)

$a$ = the new number of errors (after employing the independent variable as a predictor)

The proportion varies between 0 and 1 and is expressed as a percentage, with 0 indicating that there is no reduction in prediction error (0 percent) and 1, that there is a 100 percent reduction in prediction error.

Using Equation (16.1), you can calculate the proportional reduction in errors of prediction from Tables 16.2, 16.3, and 16.4.

$$\text{For Table 16.2: } \frac{16 - 0}{16} = \frac{16}{16} = 1$$

$$\text{For Table 16.3: } \frac{16 - 5}{16} = \frac{11}{16} = .69$$

---

3. Mueller et al., *Statistical Reasoning in Sociology*, p. 248.

$$\text{For Table 16.4: } \frac{16 - 16}{16} = \frac{0}{16} = 0$$

The proportional reduction of error is absolute in Table 16.2, as reflected in the magnitude of the coefficient of 1 (100 percent reduction of error), expressing a perfect relationship between the variables "religious denomination" and "social status." In Table 16.3, the number of errors has been reduced by almost 70 percent by employing religious denomination as a predictor. This is expressed by the coefficient of .69. In Table 16.4, however, there is no advantage in using religious denomination. The coefficient of 0 expresses the absence of any association between the two variables.

Any measure of association can be developed using similar logic, provided that it is based on two kinds of rules:

1. A rule that allows the researcher to predict the dependent variable (e.g., social class) on the basis of an independent variable (e.g.,religious denomination).
2. A rule that allows the prediction of the dependent variable independently of an independent variable.[4]

On this basis, any measure of association can be defined as in Equation (16.2):

$$\frac{\text{error by rule 2} - \text{error by rule 1}}{\text{error by rule 2}} \tag{16.2}$$

We will analyze most of the measures of relationship introduced in this chapter according to this definition. We shall discuss lambda, which measures the relation between nominal variables; gamma and Kendall's tau-*b*, which are ordinal coefficients; and Pearson's *r*, an interval measure of relation.

---

# Nominal Measures of Relationship

## Lambda, the Guttman Coefficient of Predictability

The correlation **lambda** ($\lambda$), also known as the **Guttman coefficient of predictability,** is suitable for calculating relationships between nominal variables.[5] Suppose that we are interested in predicting the party identification of nonsouthern whites in a local election in 1996. One possibility is to use party identification during 1996, thereby making use of prediction rule 2. The univariate distribution of party identification is presented in Table 16.13.

The most effective way of guessing the party identification of each of these 300 voters, on the basis of the distribution from 1996 (given earlier), is to use a

4. Herbert L. Costner, "Criteria for Measures of Association," *American Sociological Review,* 30 (1965): 344.
5. Louis Guttman, "An Outline of the Statistical Theory of Prediction," in *The Prediction of Personal Adjustment,* ed. Paul Horst (New York: Social Science Research Council, 1941).

**Table 16.13**
1996 Party Identification among Nonsouthern Whites
(Hypothetical Data)

| Party Identification | $f$ |
|---|---|
| Democrat | 126 |
| Independent | 78 |
| Republican | 96 |
| Total | 300 |

measure of central tendency that will yield the smallest number of errors in prediction. Because party identification is a nominal variable, the mode is the most appropriate measure to use. Since Democrats are in the most frequent category ($f$ = 126), the best guess is that each voter is identified with the Democratic party, for the number of errors will not exceed 174 (78 independents and 96 Republicans). Any other guess would magnify the number of errors. When guessing voters' party identification on the basis of the dependent variable alone, you should choose the most frequent category. According to this prediction (rule 2), the number of errors is 174 out of 300 guesses, that is, 58 percent.

The percentage of error might be reduced if another variable, "1992 party identification," is used as a predictor. Information is available on each of the 300 voters regarding their party identification in 1992. On this basis, we can construct a bivariate table (Table 16.14) where all voters are classified according to two variables: their party identification in 1992 and in 1996. With this additional information, we can predict the party identification of nonsouthern whites prior to the elections of 1996 on the basis of their 1992 party identification. First, take those who declared themselves Democratic in 1992; there were 108 respondents, 93 of whom gave the same identification in 1996. As this is the most frequent category, we assume that anyone who identified with the Democratic party in 1992 did so again in 1996. By making this assumption, however, we make 15 errors of predictions because 15 of the 108 identified themselves otherwise in 1996.

**Table 16.14**
1992 and 1996 Party Identification among Nonsouthern Whites
(Hypothetical Data)

| Party Identification, 1996 | Party Identification, 1992 | | | Total |
|---|---|---|---|---|
| | Democrat | Independent | Republican | |
| Democrat | 93 | 27 | 6 | 126 |
| Independent | 15 | 48 | 15 | 78 |
| Republican | — | 15 | 81 | 96 |
| Total | 108 | 90 | 102 | 300 |

Ninety voters identified themselves as independents in 1992; 48 of them did so again in 1996. We can therefore assume that whoever identified themselves as independents in 1992 did so in 1996 as well. With this assumption, the number of errors is 27 + 15 = 42, the number who did not identify themselves as independents. Finally, for the 102 who identified with the Republicans in 1992, if it is assumed that their preference patterns did not change in 1996, 15 + 6 = 21 errors are made.

The total number of errors made by using rule 1 is 15 + 42 + 21 = 78 errors out of 300 predictions, or 26 percent. Using an independent variable as a predictor leads to a decrease in the error of prediction, as expressed in the magnitude of the correlation, which can now be calculated:

$$\text{Error stemming from rule } 2 = 174$$

$$\text{Error stemming from rule } 1 = 78$$

$$\lambda = \frac{174 - 78}{174} = .55$$

Thus we eliminate 55 percent of the errors of prediction concerning party identification in 1996 by using the identification pattern during the 1992 elections.

Lambda is an asymmetrical coefficient, as it reflects relationships between variables in one direction only. In practice, it is often represented as $\lambda_a$, $a$ indicating that it is asymmetrical. The coefficient .55 expresses the relationship between party identification in 1992 and 1996, with that of 1992 serving as an independent variable. The correlation coefficient can also be calculated in the opposite direction, with 1996 serving as the independent variable and 1992 as the dependent variable. The method of calculation is identical: we compute the number of errors made when estimating 1992 identification patterns without reference to 1996 data and then calculate the advantage obtained by gauging the 1992 data from those of 1996. Thus, when switching the order of the variables, lambda would be:

$$\lambda = \frac{193 - 78}{193} = .60$$

Notice that lambda calculated in the opposite way results in a different answer. By using 1996 data to predict 1992 party identification we have reduced 60 percent of the errors of prediction.

***Alternative Procedure for Computing Lambda.***    Lambda can also be computed by a slightly simpler procedure using Formula (16.3).[6]

$$\lambda_a = \frac{\Sigma f_i - F_d}{N - F_d} \tag{16.3}$$

6. Linton C. Freeman, *Elementary Applied Statistics* (New York: Wiley, 1965), p. 74.

where $f_i$ = the modal frequency within each category of the independent variable

$F_d$ = the modal frequency in the marginal totals of the dependent variable

$N$ = the total number of cases

We can now repeat our calculation of the correlation between the data from 1992 and those from 1996, with the 1992 party identification serving as an independent variable.

$$\Sigma f_i = 93 + 48 + 81 = 222$$

$$F_d = 126$$

$$N = 300$$

$$\lambda_a = \frac{222 - 126}{300 - 126} = \frac{96}{174} = .55$$

To summarize, the magnitude of lambda expresses the proportional reduction in error of estimate when switching from rule 2 to rule 1. The strength of the association between the two variables reflects the improvement in prediction we can attain with the aid of a second variable. Lambda may range from zero to one; zero indicates that there is nothing to be gained by shifting from one prediction rule to another, whereas one reflects a situation where by using an independent variable we can predict the dependent variable without any error at all.

***Limitations of Lambda.*** Lambda has a limitation in situations where the modal frequencies of the independent variable are all concentrated in one category of the dependent variable. In such a case, lambda will always be zero, even in instances where the two variables are in fact related. For example, in the bivariate distribution presented in Table 16.15, we can see that place of residence is associated with self-esteem. More residents of rural areas (75 percent) have high self-esteem than residents of cities (66 percent). However, because the sum of all modal frequencies of the variable "place of residence" ($\Sigma f_i = 300 + 200$) is equal to the modal frequency of the marginal totals of the variable "self-esteem" ($F_d = 500$), lambda will take on the value of zero. Such a pattern of distribution is likely to occur when the marginal totals of the dependent variable are extremely uneven. Lambda would then be inappropriate.

**Table 16.15**
Place of Residence and Self-Esteem

| Self-Esteem | Place of Residence | | Total |
|---|---|---|---|
| | Rural Areas | Urban Areas | |
| High | 300 | 200 | 500 |
| Low | 100 | 100 | 200 |
| Total | 400 | 300 | 700 |

# Ordinal Measures of Relationship

When both variables of a bivariate distribution are ordinal, the construction of a measure of relationship is based on the principal property of the ordinal scale. Researchers use the ordinal scale to rank observations in relation to the variables being measured. With a single variable, researchers are generally interested in evaluating the relative position of the observations on the variable. For example, professions can be ranked according to the amount of prestige they command, and students can be ranked according to their relative degree of political tolerance. The same principle can be applied with two variables. Here the researcher is interested in examining whether the ranking of observations on each of the variables is identical, similar, or different. The investigator compares every two observations and notes whether one that is ranked higher on one variable is also ranked higher with regard to the other variable. For instance, we can examine whether the ranking of professions by their prestige in the 1950s resembles their ranking in the 1990s or whether persons with a conservative orientation on foreign affairs show a similar tendency on domestic issues.

When observations display the same order on both variables, the relationship is said to be positive; when the order is inverse, so that the observation ranking highest on one variable is the lowest on the second variable, the relationship is negative. When there is no clear pattern in the relative position of the observations on both variables, the variables are said to be independent. Consider the following example: If all military personnel with high rank are also more liberal on political issues than lower-ranking officers, one may say that military rank and political liberalism are positively related. If, however, the high-ranking officers are less liberal, the association is negative. If some high officers are liberal and others are not, rank and liberalism are independent of each other.

## The Pair Concept

Most ordinal measures of relationship are based on the *pair* as a unit of analysis and the relative ranking of the two parts of the pair on both variables.

Suppose that six officers are classified according to their military rank and degree of liberalism. The observations are presented in Table 16.16.

For the purpose of illustration we have assigned names to each of the officers in Table 16.16. Their names are presented in Table 16.17.

In Table 16.18 we pair these six people and describe their rank order on the variables military rank and liberalism.* The first column lists the name of each member of a pair; the second column designates their cell number, and the third

---

* We have not listed the pairs that can be created within each cell (e.g. John and Ruth) because such pairs share the same rank on both variables and are therefore not relevant to the discussion of the ordinal measures presented in this chapter.

**Table 16.16**
Liberalism by Military Rank (Hypothetical Data)

| Liberalism (Y) | Military Rank (X) | | Total |
| | Column 1 Low | Column 2 High | |
|---|---|---|---|
| Row 1    Low | $2_{(11)}$ | $1_{(12)}$ | 3 |
| Row 2    High | $1_{(21)}$ | $2_{(22)}$ | 3 |
| Total | 3 | 3 | 6 |

The numbers in parentheses designate the cell numbers, with row numbers designated first and column numbers second. For example, (11) indicates cell 11 corresponding to the frequency with column 1 (low rank) and row 1 (low liberalism).

**Table 16.17**
Liberalism by Military Rank for Six Officers

| Liberalism (Y) | Military Rank (X) | | Total |
| | Low | High | |
|---|---|---|---|
| Low | John, $Ruth_{(11)}$ | $Susan_{(12)}$ | 3 |
| High | $Alice_{(21)}$ | Jim, $Glenn_{(22)}$ | 3 |
| Total | 3 | 3 | 6 |

and fourth columns, their rank and degree of liberalism. The last column describes the relative position of the pair on the two variables.

For instance, John from cell 11, and Susan from cell 12, are designated as tied on $Y$ (liberalism). They have different rank but share the same political views. Pairs tied on $Y$ are officers of different ranks sharing the same political views; pairs tied on $X$ (for instance, John and Alice) are officers of the same rank but of different political views; pairs designated as "same" are officers who have the same relative position on both variables, so the officer with the higher rank would be the more liberal as well. Pairs designated as "inverse" have a different relative position on both variables, so the officer with the higher rank would be the less liberal of the pair.

## Types of Pairs

From Table 16.18, the following groups of pairs can be distinguished:

1. Pairs that display the same order on both $X$ and $Y$; they will be denoted as $Ns$.
2. Pairs that display an inverse order on $X$ and $Y$; they will be denoted as $Nd$.
3. Pairs tied on $X$, denoted as $Tx$.
4. Pairs tied on $Y$, denoted as $Ty$.

**Table 16.18**
Relative Position of Officers in Military Rank and Liberalism

| Person | From Cell | Military Rank of Officer (X) | Degree of Liberalism (Y) | Order |
|---|---|---|---|---|
| John | 11 | L | L | Tie on Y |
| Susan | 12 | H | L | |
| | | | | |
| Ruth | 11 | L | L | Tie on Y |
| Susan | 12 | H | L | |
| | | | | |
| John | 11 | L | L | Tie on X |
| Alice | 21 | L | H | |
| | | | | |
| Ruth | 11 | L | L | Tie on X |
| Alice | 21 | L | H | |
| | | | | |
| John | 11 | L | L | Same |
| Jim | 22 | H | H | |
| | | | | |
| Ruth | 11 | L | L | Same |
| Jim | 22 | H | H | |
| | | | | |
| John | 11 | L | L | Same |
| Glenn | 22 | H | H | |
| | | | | |
| Ruth | 11 | L | L | Same |
| Glenn | 22 | H | H | |
| | | | | |
| Susan | 12 | H | L | Inverse |
| Alice | 21 | L | H | |
| | | | | |
| Susan | 12 | H | L | Tie on X |
| Jim | 22 | H | H | |
| | | | | |
| Susan | 12 | H | L | Tie on X |
| Glenn | 22 | H | H | |
| | | | | |
| Alice | 21 | L | H | Tie on Y |
| Jim | 22 | H | H | |
| | | | | |
| Alice | 21 | L | H | Tie on Y |
| Glenn | 22 | H | H | |

1. To find $N_s$ in the general bivariate table, multiply the frequency in every cell by the total of all the frequencies in the cells below it and to its right, and add up the products. In Table 16.16, the number of pairs displaying the same ranking on both variables is $2 \times 2 = 4$.

2. To calculate $N_d$ in the general bivariate table, multiply the frequency in each cell by the total of all the frequencies in the cells below it and to its left, and

add up the products. In Table 16.16, the number of pairs displaying different rankings on the two variables is $1 \times 1 = 1$.

3. To find the number of pairs tied on $X$ ($Tx$), multiply the frequency in every cell by the total of all the frequencies in the cells in that column, and add up the products. The number of pairs tied on $X$ is $(2 \times 1) + (1 \times 2) = 4$.

4. To find the number of pairs tied on $Y$ ($Ty$), multiply the frequency in each cell by the sum of the frequencies in the cells in that row, and add up the products. The number of pairs tied on $Y$ in Table 16.16 is $(2 \times 1) + (1 \times 2) = 4$.

## Gamma

**Gamma** ($\gamma$ or **G**), a coefficient used for measuring the association between ordinal variables, was developed by Leo Goodman and William Kruskal.[7] It is a symmetrical statistic, based on the number of same-order pairs ($Ns$) and the number of different-order pairs ($Nd$). Tied pairs play no part in the definition of gamma.

The coefficient is defined by Formula (16.4):[8]

$$\gamma = \frac{0.5(Ns + Nd) - Minimum\ (Ns,Nd)}{0.5(Ns + Nd)} \qquad (16.4)$$

To illustrate the calculation of gamma, consider the data presented in Table 16.19 on class standing and political tolerance of students. The researchers collected data to examine the hypothesis that students tend to become politically more liberal as their class standing increases. They assumed that if these two variables are associated, it will be possible to predict students' political tolerance on the basis of their class standing with a minimum of error.

First, we need to count the number of pairs that can be constructed from 1,032 observations. With tied pairs excluded, the overall number of pairs that can be constructed from a bivariate table is $Ns + Nd$. $Ns$ and $Nd$ are calculated according to the definitions presented on page 000.

$$
\begin{aligned}
Ns = {}& 30(75 + 51 + 79 + 59 + 79 + 63 + 120 + 151 + 45 + 34) \\
& + 66(51 + 59 + 63 + 151 + 34) \\
& + 30(79 + 59 + 79 + 63 + 120 + 151 + 45 + 34) \\
& + 75(59 + 63 + 151 + 34) \\
& + 34(79 + 63 + 120 + 151 + 45 + 34) \\
& + 79(63 + 151 + 34) + 33(120 + 151 + 45 + 34) \\
& + 79(151 + 34) + 40(45 + 34) + 120(34) \\
= {}& 157{,}958 \\
Nd = {}& 15(120 + 151 + 79 + 63 + 79 + 59 + 75 + 51 + 66 + 28) \\
& + 45(151 + 63 + 59 + 51 + 28) \\
& + 40(79 + 63 + 79 + 59 + 75 + 51 + 66 + 28) \\
& + 120(63 + 59 + 51 + 28) \\
& + 33(79 + 59 + 75 + 51 + 66 + 28)
\end{aligned}
$$

7. Leo A. Goodman and William H. Kruskal, "Measure of Association for Cross Classification," *Journal of the American Statistical Association,* 49 (1954): 732–764.

8. Mueller et al., *Statistical Reasoning in Sociology,* p. 282.

## Table 16.19
Political Tolerance of College Students by Class Standing

| | Class Standing | | | | | | |
| | Fresh-man | Sopho-more | Junior | Senior | Graduate Student (Full-Time) | Graduate Student (Part-Time) | Total |
|---|---|---|---|---|---|---|---|
| Less tolerant | 30 | 30 | 34 | 33 | 40 | 15 | 182 |
| Somewhat tolerant | 66 | 75 | 79 | 79 | 120 | 45 | 464 |
| More tolerant | 28 | 51 | 59 | 63 | 151 | 34 | 386 |
| Total | 124 | 156 | 172 | 175 | 311 | 94 | 1,032 |

$$+ \ 79(59 + 51 + 28) + 34(75 + 51 + 66 + 28) + 79(51 + 28)$$
$$+ \ 30(66 + 28) + 75(28)$$
$$= 112,882$$

The total number of pairs (tied pairs excluded) is $Ns + Nd = 157,958 + 112,882 = 270,840$.

Next we determine the relative political tolerance of the students on the basis of the dependent variable alone—rule 2. To find the relative position of each of the 270,840 pairs, we use a random system. For example, we can label members of each pair as heads or tails and by flipping a coin decide which member is more tolerant. If this process is repeated for each pair, we can expect that in the long run, 50 percent of the guesses about the relative position of the students will be accurate, whereas the other 50 percent will be erroneous. Hence prediction rule 2 will produce $(Ns + Nd)/2 = 135,420$ errors.

Prediction rule 1 states that if there are more pairs displaying the same order $(Ns)$, this order will be predicted for all other pairs as well. In that case, the number of errors will be $Nd$, that is, the number of pairs whose ranking is different on the two variables. In the same way, should the number of inverted pairs $(Nd)$ be greater, this order would be predicted for all remaining pairs, and the number of errors will equal $Ns$.

The calculations based on the information in Table 16.19 indicate that the number of pairs with the same ranking is greater than the number whose ranking is inverted $(Ns > Nd)$. Hence we predict the relative position of political tolerance for each pair on the basis of its members' class standing, meaning that the student with the greater seniority exhibits greater tolerance. If Mary is a sophomore and John is a freshman, Mary will be more tolerant than John. As not all pairs display the same order, the number of errors made by such a prediction rule is $Nd = 112,882$.

We can now formulate the relationship between class standing and political tolerance, using the general formula for measures of association:

$$\frac{b - a}{b}$$

where $b = (Ns + Nd)/2$ and $a = (Ns, Nd)_{min}$. Accordingly,

$$\gamma = \frac{\dfrac{(Ns + Nd)}{2} - Nd}{\dfrac{(Ns + Nd)}{2}} = \frac{135,420 - 112,882}{135,420} = \frac{22,538}{135,420} = .17$$

A value of .17 for $\gamma$ reflects the advantage we gain by using the variable "class standing" in predicting political tolerance. By using this variable, we eliminate 17 percent of the total number of errors.

**Another Formula for Gamma.**     Gamma can also be calculated by using Formula (16.5):

$$\gamma = \frac{Ns - Nd}{Ns + Nd} \qquad (16.5)$$

This formula reflects the relative predominance of same-order or different-order pairs. When same-order pairs predominate, the coefficient is positive; when different-order pairs predominate, it is negative. Gamma can vary from 0 to ± 1. When all the pairs are same order pairs ($Nd=0$), gamma equals 1.0.

$$\gamma = \frac{Ns - 0}{Ns + 0} = \frac{Ns}{Ns} = 1.0$$

When all the pairs are different order pairs ($Ns=0$), gamma equals −1.

$$\gamma = \frac{0 - Nd}{0 + Nd} = \frac{-Nd}{Nd} = -1.0$$

A coefficient of ±1.0 indicates that the dependent variable can be predicted on the basis of the independent variable without any error.

When the number of different-order pairs is equal to the number of same order pairs, gamma is zero:

$$\gamma = \frac{Ns - Nd}{Ns + Nd} = \frac{0}{Ns + Nd} = 0$$

A gamma of zero reflects that there is nothing to be gained by using the independent variable to predict the dependent variable.

**Limitations of Gamma.**     The main weakness of gamma as a measure of ordinal association is the exclusion of tied pairs from its computation. Hence it will reach a value of ±1 even under conditions of less than perfect association. For example, a perfect relationship was described early in the chapter as in the following table:

| | |
|---|---|
| 50 | 0 |
| 0 | 50 |

$$\gamma = 1$$

However, because gamma is based on untied pairs only, it becomes 1 under the following conditions as well:

| | |
|---|---|
| 50 | 50 |
| 0 | 50 |

$$\gamma = 1$$

In general, when a large proportion of the observations are concentrated in only few categories, there will be many tied pairs, and gamma will be based on the smaller proportion of untied pairs.

## Kendall's Tau-*b*

When there are many tied pairs, researchers use a different measure that handles the problem of ties. It is **Kendall's tau-*b*,** defined as follows:

$$\tau b = \frac{Ns - Nd}{\sqrt{(Ns + Nd + Ty)\,(Ns + Nd + Tx)}} \tag{16.6}$$

Tau-*b* varies from $-1$ to $+1$ and is a symmetrical coefficient. It has the same numerator as gamma but has a correction factor for ties in its denominator (*Ty* and *Tx*). For example, for the following bivariate distribution

$$X$$

| | | | |
|---|---|---|---|
| | 30 | 70 | 100 |
| *Y* | 30 | 20 | 50 |
| | 60 | 90 | 150 |

we get

$$Ns = 600 \qquad Ty = 2{,}700$$
$$Nd = 2{,}100 \qquad Tx = 2{,}300$$

Therefore,

$$\tau b = \frac{600 - 2{,}100}{\sqrt{(600 + 2{,}100 + 2{,}700)\,(600 + 2{,}100 + 2{,}300)}} = \frac{-1{,}500}{5{,}196} = -.29$$

Note that under the same conditions, gamma gives a considerably higher figure than tau-*b*:

$$\gamma = \frac{600 - 2{,}100}{600 + 2{,}100} = \frac{-1{,}500}{2{,}700} = -.56$$

Gamma will always exceed tau-*b* when there are tied pairs. With no ties, its value will be identical with tau-*b*.

# Interval Measures of Relationship

At lower levels of measurement, a researcher's ability to make predictions is restricted, even when the variables he or she is considering are associated. At most, researchers can point out an interdependence of certain categories or properties, such as the fact that Catholics tend to vote Democratic, or they can expect the same relative position of observations on two variables, for instance, that military rank is associated with liberalism. However, predictions of this type are imprecise, and there is frequently a need for more accurate predictive statements, as, for example, when an investigator wishes to predict individuals' future income on the basis of their level of education or a country's GNP per capita from it's level of industrilization.

## Prediction Rules

When the variables they are analyzing are at least interval, researchers can be more precise in describing the nature and the form of the relationship.

Most relationships between interval variables can be formulated in terms of a linear function rule. A function is said to be linear when pairs of $(X, Y)$ values fall exactly into a function that can be plotted as a straight line. All such functions have rules of the form $Y = a + bX$, where $a$ and $b$ are constant numbers.

For example, there is a perfect linear relationship between the distance and the time that a car travels at a fixed speed (Table 16.20). If its speed is 60 miles per hour, it will go 60 miles in one hour, or $X$ miles in $Y$ time. The linear function expresses the relationship between the time and the distance that the car travels. Such a function takes the form of $Y = 1X$, reflecting the fact that a change of one unit of distance (miles) will bring about a change of one unit of time (minutes). The constant 1 preceding $X$ in the formula is $b$, called the slope, expressing the number of units of change in $Y$ accompanying one unit of change in $X$.

**Table 16.20**
Distance by Time

| $X$ (Miles) | $Y$ (Time in Minutes) |
|:-----------:|:---------------------:|
| 1 | 1 |
| 3 | 3 |
| 5 | 5 |
| 10 | 10 |
| 15 | 15 |

## Linear Regression

The method of specifying the nature of a relationship between two interval variables using a linear function is referred to as *regression analysis*. Scientists use regression to find some algebraic expression by which to represent the functional relationship between the variables. The equation $Y = a + bX$ is a linear regression equation, meaning that the function describing the relation between $X$ and $Y$ is that of a straight line. Ordinarily, researchers display the observations of $X$ and $Y$—and the **regression line** connecting them—in the form of a graph. The variables $X$ and $Y$ are represented by two intersecting axes. Each observation is entered as a dot at the point where the $X$ and $Y$ scores intersect. In Figure 16.3, we have entered the observations from Table 16.20 to illustrate the graphical presentation of bivariate observations and the functional form that describes their interrelationship. The independent variable, $X$, is placed on the horizontal axis; $Y$, the dependent variable, is placed on the vertical axis; and each observation is plotted at the intersection of the two axes. For example, the last observation of Table 16.20 is plotted at the intersection of the two axes on the score 15, to represent its score of 15 on the two variables.

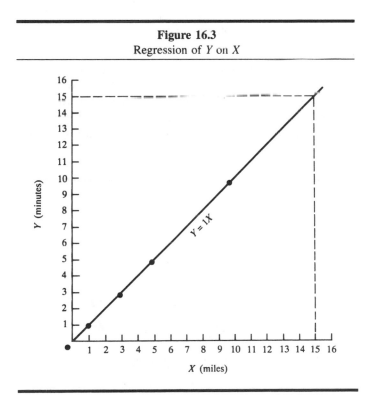

**Figure 16.3**
Regression of $Y$ on $X$

The regression line does not always pass through the intersection of the $X$ and $Y$ axes. When a straight line intersects the $Y$ axis, another constant needs to be introduced into the linear regression equation. This constant is symbolized by the letter $a$ and is called the $Y$ intercept. The intercept reflects the value of $Y$ when $X$ is zero. Each of the three regression lines in Figure 16.4 has different values for $a$ and $b$. The three different values of $a$ (6, 1, 2) are reflected in the three different intersections of the lines. The different values of $b$ (−3, .5, 3) reflect the steepness of the slopes. The higher the value of $b$, the steeper the slope. Finally, the sign of $b$ expresses the direction of the relationship between $X$ and $Y$: when $b$ is positive, an increase in $X$ is accompanied by an increase in $Y$ (Figure 16.4$b$ and 16.4$c$); when $b$ is negative, $Y$ decreases as $X$ increases (Figure 16.4$a$).

Most relationships in the social sciences can be fairly well expressed by the linear function. For example, the equation $Y = 5,000 + 1,000X$ could express the relation between income and education; $a$ would stand for the initial yearly salary ($\$5,000$) for individuals who had no education at all and $b$ for an increment of $\$1,000$ for each additional year of education. Using this prediction rule, we could expect individuals having ten years of schooling to make $\$15,000$ [$Y = 5,000 + 1,000(10)$].

## Criterion of Least Squares

The regression equation, however, is only a prediction rule; thus there are discrepancies between actual observations and the ones predicted. The goal is to construct an equation in which the deviations, or **error of prediction,** will be at a minimum. If the researcher adopts a specific criterion in determining $a$ and $b$ of the linear equation, it is possible to create a function that will minimize the variance around the regression line. This is the **criterion of least squares,** which minimizes

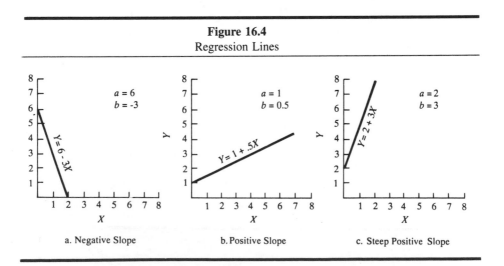

**Figure 16.4**
Regression Lines

a. Negative Slope          b. Positive Slope          c. Steep Positive Slope

the sum of the squared differences between the observed $Y$'s and the $Y$'s predicted with the regression equation. This prediction equation is

$$\hat{Y} = a + bX \tag{16.7}$$

where $\hat{Y}$ denotes predicted scores of the variable $Y$.

According to the least squares criterion, $a$ and $b$ can be calculated by the following formulas:

$$b = \frac{\sum (X - \bar{X})(Y - \bar{Y})}{\sum (X - \bar{X})^2} \tag{16.8}$$

$$a = \frac{\sum Y - b \sum X}{N} = \bar{Y} - b\bar{X} \tag{16.9}$$

A more convenient formula for computing $b$ is

$$b = \frac{N \sum XY - (\sum X)(\sum Y)}{N \sum X^2 - (\sum X)^2} \tag{16.10}$$

***An Illustration.*** As an illustration of how to construct a precise prediction rule for interval variables, consider the series of observations in Table 16.21 on the number of robberies (per 100,000 population) and the percentage of the urban population living in metropolitan areas. These observations on ten states are presented in order to explore the relationship between the degree of urbanization and

**Table 16.21**
Robbery Rate and Percentage of Urban Population in Metropolitan Areas, 1986

| State | Percentage of Urban Population ($X$) | Robberies per 100,000 Population ($Y$) | $XY$ | $X^2$ | $Y^2$ |
|---|---|---|---|---|---|
| Massachusetts | 91 | 193 | 17,563 | 8,281 | 37,249 |
| Wisconsin | 67 | 73 | 4,891 | 4,489 | 5,329 |
| South Dakota | 28 | 16 | 448 | 784 | 256 |
| Virginia | 72 | 106 | 7,632 | 5,184 | 11,236 |
| South Carolina | 60 | 99 | 5,940 | 3,600 | 9,801 |
| Texas | 81 | 240 | 19,440 | 6,561 | 57,600 |
| Arizona | 75 | 169 | 12,675 | 5,625 | 28,561 |
| California | 96 | 343 | 32,928 | 9,216 | 117,649 |
| Arkansas | 44 | 88 | 3,872 | 1,936 | 7,744 |
| Hawaii | 77 | 106 | 8,162 | 5,929 | 11,236 |
| Total | 691 | 1,433 | 113,551 | 51,605 | 286,661 |

Source: United States Bureau of the Census, *Statistical Abstracts of the United States: 1988* (108th edition). Washington, D.C., 1988.

the crime rate. The variable to be predicted (the dependent variable) is "robberies per 100,000 population," and the independent variable is "percentage of urban population."

To predict the number of robberies in any state, without any additional information, we will choose a value that will produce the smallest possible number of errors as an estimate for each state in the distribution. The arithmetic mean is the best guess for each interval distribution because the mean of its squared distribution is lower than for any other value. The average robbery rate for 100,000 population, according to the data, is

$$\bar{Y} = \frac{\Sigma Y}{N} = \frac{1,433}{10} = 143.3$$

To assess the prediction error, we subtract each observation from the mean (to calculate the deviations), and square the deviations. We then select the sum of the squared deviations, referred to as total variation about $\bar{Y}$, as an estimate of error of prediction—rule 2—because it produces the minimum amount of errors. The total variation about $\bar{Y}$ is defined as in Equation (16.11):

$$\text{Total variation} = \Sigma (Y - \bar{Y})^2 \qquad (16.11)$$

Our next step is to reduce the errors of prediction of number of robberies by employing a second variable, "percentage of urban," as a predictor. We accomplish this by constructing a prediction rule in the form of a regression equation that will best describe the relationship between these two variables and that will allow us to predict the number of robberies in any state on the basis of percentage of urban population with a minimum of error.

The observations in Table 16.21 can be displayed in a scatter diagram, which is a graphic device providing a first approximation of the relationship between the two variables (Figure 16.5). Each pair of letters (representing the abbreviation for each state) represents an observation that has a fixed $X$ and $Y$ characteristic. For example, point WI represents Wisconsin with 73 robberies per 100,000 population and 67 percent of its population in metropolitan areas. After we have plotted all points, we draw a line that best approximates the trend displayed by the points. Obviously, we could draw several such lines among the points, but only one—the line of least squares—comes as close as possible to all the individual observations. Before drawing this line, we need to calculate the constants $a$ and $b$:

$$b = \frac{10(113,551) - (691)(1,433)}{10(51,605) - (691)^2} = 3.76$$

$$a = 143.3 - 3.76(69.1) = -117.0$$

The resulting linear equation is therefore:

$$\hat{Y} = -117.0 + 3.76X$$

We can now draw the estimated regression line and apply it to predict the robbery rate for every level of urban population. For example, if 50 percent of a state's population were in metropolitan areas, its predicted robbery rate per 100,000 population would be

$$\hat{Y} = 117.0 + 3.76(50) = 71.0$$

## Errors of Prediction

As you can see from Figure 16.5, most of the observations are spread around the regression line. These deviations of the actual observations from the predicted ones represent the errors produced when we use the prediction rule specified for predicting the robbery rate based on the percentage of urban population (rule 1).

We can estimate the error involved in predicting robberies based on the percentage of urban population by measuring the deviations of the actual observations from the regression line. First we subtract the predicted robbery rate for each state from the actual observations recorded in Table 16.21. In Texas, for example, the predicted robbery rate per 100,000 population according to the prediction rule is $\hat{Y} = -117.0 + 3.76(81) = 187.56$. The actual robbery rate for Texas is 240; the error of prediction, therefore, is $240 - 187.56 = 52.44$.

The sum of the squared errors of prediction is the variation unexplained by the independent variable. It is defined in Formula (16.12):

$$\text{Unexplained variation} = \sum (Y_i - \hat{Y})^2 \qquad (16.12)$$

where $Y_i$ = actual observations and $\hat{Y}$ = predicted observations.

Another measure of error that is widely used is the *standard error of estimate* $(Sy.x)$. It is based on the *unexplained variation* around the regression line and is defined as follows:

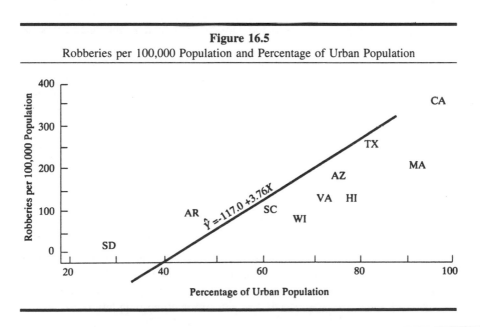

**Figure 16.5**
Robberies per 100,000 Population and Percentage of Urban Population

$$Sy.x = \sqrt{\frac{\sum (Y_i - \hat{Y})^2}{N}} \qquad (16.13)$$

The standard error of estimate closely parallels the standard deviation, discussed in Chapter 15.

## Pearson's Product-Moment Correlation Coefficient (r)

There are two measures of variability for $Y$. The first, the total variation about $\bar{Y}$, is the error obtained when we predict $Y$ with no prior knowledge of $X$—rule 2. (Rule 2 is the total variation about $\bar{Y}$.) The second, the unexplained variation, as defined by Equation (16.12), is the error obtained when using linear regression as the prediction rule—rule 1.

These two estimates of error permit us to construct an interval measure of association that reflects a proportional reduction in error when one shifts from rule 2, the mean, to rule 1, the linear regression equation, to evaluate $Y$. This measure, $r^2$, is defined in Equation (16.14):

$$r^2 = \frac{\text{total variation} - \text{unexplained variation}}{\text{total variation}} \qquad (16.14)$$

The unexplained variation is subtracted from the original error of prediction to evaluate the proportional reduction in error. The proportional reduction in error is reflected by $r^2$ when $X$ is used to predict $Y$.

An unexplained variation of zero means that the regression equation eliminated all errors in predicting $Y$, and $r^2$ then equals one, meaning that any variation in $Y$ can be explained by $X$. Conversely, when the unexplained variation is identical to the total variation, $r^2$ is zero, indicating complete independence between $X$ and $Y$.

Conventionally, the square root of $r^2$, $r$, designated *Pearson's product-moment correlation coefficient* or **Pearson's r**, rather than $r^2$, is used as a coefficient of correlation. Pearson's $r$ ranges from $-1.0$ to $+1.0$, where a negative coefficient indicates inverse relations between the variables. A simple formula for computing $r$ is

$$r = \frac{N\sum XY - (\sum X)(\sum Y)}{\sqrt{[N\sum X^2 - (\sum X)^2][N\sum Y^2 - (\sum Y)^2]}} \qquad (16.15)$$

For our example the correlation coefficient will be:

$$r = \frac{10(113,551) - (691)(1,433)}{\sqrt{[10(51,605) - (691)^2][10(286,661) - (1,433)^2]}} = .82$$

Thus $r^2$ is $.82^2 = .67$, which indicates a proportional reduction of error of 67 percent when percent of urban population is used to predict robberies per 100,000 population. Another way to express this is to say that 67 percent of the variance in robbery rate is accounted for by the percent of urban population.

## Measures of Relationships

Measures of relationships indicate the proportional reduction in error of estimate when the dependent variable is predicted on the basis of the independent variable (rule 1) instead of independently of the independent variable (rule 2).

- *Lambda* ($\lambda$): Lambda is used for nominal variables and is calculated using formulas (16.2) or (16.3).
- *Gamma* ($\gamma$): Gamma is used for measuring the association between ordinal variables, and is calculated using formulas (16.4) or (16.5).
- *Kendall's tau*-b: Tau-*b* is used for measuring the association between ordinal variables when there are many tied pairs. It is calculated using formula (16.6).
- *Linear regression:* A method of specifying a relationship between two interval variables using a linear function of the form $\hat{Y} = a + bx$.
- *Pearson's* r: Pearson's *r* is used for measuring the association between interval variables, which can be plotted on a graph. It is calculated using formula (16.15).
- *Criterion of Least Squares:* A method of selecting a regression equation that minimizes the sum of the square differences between the observed and the predicted *Y*'s.

The size of $r^2$ or $r$ is determined by the spread of the actual observations around the regression line. Thus if all the observations are on the line, $r$ will be 1.0; if they are randomly scattered, $r$ will approximate zero. Figure 16.6 illustrates a hypothetical strong positive relationship, a weak positive relationship, and no relationship. However, when $r$ or $r^2$ approximates or equals zero, you should not rush to the conclusion that the variables are not related. The relationship may be curvilinear—that is, it may not be described by a straight line—so that a coefficient based on the linear model would not give a correct picture of the statistical rela-

**Figure 16.6**
Recognizing Trends from Scatter Diagrams

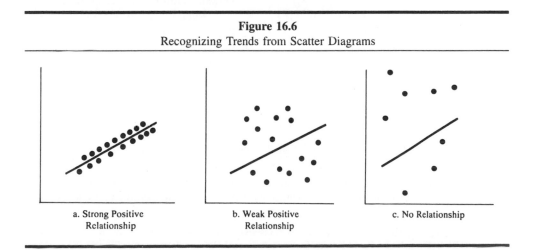

| a. Strong Positive Relationship | b. Weak Positive Relationship | c. No Relationship |

tionship. In general, careful scrutiny of the scatter diagram will indicate the extent to which the observations display a linear or a curvilinear trend or none at all.[9]

## Summary

**1.** This chapter focused on the nature of relationships between two variables and on the construction of measures of relationship. Variables that are related vary together: specific categories of one variable "go together" with specific categories of the second or there is some correspondence in the relative position of the two variables.

**2.** Researchers can assess a relationship between two variables by comparing the univariate distributions that constitute the bivariate table, using summary measures such as the median or the mean. Alternatively, they can describe associations by special measures of relationships that reflect the relative utility of using one variable to predict another.

**3.** Measures of relationship usually correspond to the variables' level of measurement. Nominal relations can be assessed by lambda. Either gamma or Kendall's tau-$b$ is used to calculate relations between ordinal variables.

**4.** It is sometimes possible to describe the relationship between interval variables by employing specific functions that permit exact predictions. The linear regression equation is such a function. Pearson's $r$ is an interval measure of relationship that reflects the proportional reduction of error when one shifts from the mean as a prediction rule to the linear regression equation.

## Key Terms for Review

correlation coefficient (p. 400)
criterion of least squares (p. 416)
error of prediction (p. 416)
gamma (p. 410)
Kendall's tau-$b$ (p. 413)

lambda (Guttman coefficient of
    predictability) (p. 403)
Pearson's $r$ (p. 420)
proportional reduction of error (p. 402)
regression line (p. 415)

## Study Questions

1. Discuss the concept of relationship between variables in terms of the proportional reduction of error.
2. Give an example of a bivariate nominal distribution for which lambda is not suitable as a measure of relationship. What measure would you use instead?

9. It is beyond the scope of this text to discuss curvilinear relations. For further discussion, see George W. Bohrnstedt and David Knoke, *Statistics for Social Data Analysis* (Itasca, Ill.: Peacock, 1988).

3. The following is a bivariate distribution of alienation by social status. By making a percentage comparison assess the following hypothesis: as status increases, the degree of alienation decreases. What other measures of relationships can you use to test this hypothesis?

| Alienation | Social Status | | | |
|---|---|---|---|---|
| | Low | Medium | High | Total |
| High | 93 | 41 | 10 | 144 |
| Medium | 77 | 78 | 46 | 201 |
| Low | 68 | 128 | 140 | 336 |
| Total | 238 | 247 | 196 | 681 |

4. Construct a 2 × 2 table based on 200 respondents of whom 69 percent are Democrats and 58 percent are for legalizing marijuana. Of the Democrats, 56 percent are for legalizing marijuana. With attitudes toward the legalization of marijuana as the dependent variable, compute lambda. Discuss the relationship between the two variables.

5. Suppose that the correlation $r = .28$ exists between social class and college intentions. Analyze the meaning of this correlation.

6. Social scientists have been attempting to identify social variables that may be associated with economic variables. Use the following data to investigate the relationship between unemployment rates and other variables. Discuss the relationship between each of the independent variables and unemployment. Base your discussion on the following measures: $b$, $r$, $r^2$.

| Country | Unemployment Rate | Political Stability | Level of Economic Development | Rate of Urbanization |
|---|---|---|---|---|
| United States | 4.2 | 8.0 | 2.34 | 1.8 |
| New Zealand | 4.0 | 8.6 | 1.71 | .8 |
| Norway | 3.1 | 8.6 | 1.41 | 1.2 |
| Finland | 3.6 | 8.1 | .83 | .7 |
| Uruguay | 6.2 | 3.2 | .46 | .9 |
| Israel | 4.8 | 8.1 | .40 | .9 |
| Taiwan | 5.8 | 7.2 | .80 | .6 |
| Ghana | 8.1 | 5.0 | .02 | .2 |
| England | 8.2 | 2.6 | 1.46 | 1.1 |
| Greece | 8.8 | 2.1 | .09 | .9 |

# Computer Exercises

1. Using the GSS file that accompanies this text, or a dataset of your own, use CROSSTABS to show the association between two nominal variables and then two ordinal variables. Choose one cell from each table and interpret in words

the row and column percentages. For example, 70 percent of females favor busing to support desegregation (hypothetical).
2. Generate the appropriate measures of association for the tables constructed for question 1. What is the strength of the relationships you find?
3. Select two interval level variables from the GSS set and generate a Pearson's *r* using the procedure CORRELATIONS. How strong is the relationship?

(See Appendix A, pp. 518–522)

---

## Additional Readings

---

Achen, Christopher H. *Interpreting and Using Regression.* Newbury Park, Calif.: Sage, 1982.

Healey, Joseph F. *Statistics: A Tool for Social Research.* Belmont, Calif.: Wadsworth, 1993.

Knoke, David, and George W. Bohrnstedt. *Basic Social Statistics.* Itasca, Ill.: Peacock, 1991.

Levin, Jack, and James Allan Fox. *Elementary Statistics in Social Research,* 6th ed. New York: HarperCollins, 1994.

Lewis-Beck, Michael S. *Applied Regression.* Newbury Park, Calif.: Sage, 1980.

Vernoy, Mark W., and Judith A. Vernoy. *Behavioral Statistics in Action.* Belmont, Calif.: Wadsworth, 1992.

# CHAPTER 17

# Control, Elaboration, and Multivariate Analysis

Does social class standing affect men's participation in household tasks in dual-earner families in the United States? Guided by Marxian theory, Wright et al. hypothesized that this was the case.[1] Using bivariate techniques, they found that class had a marginal effect on the division of labor in dual-earner homes. The researchers then questioned whether other variables might affect men's household work. Using multivariate techniques, they examined the relative effects of eight variables: class, wife's educational level, wife's hours of paid work, wife's contribution to total family income, total family income, respondent's gender ideology (what they perceived to be proper roles for men and women), age, and whether there were children under age 16 in the household. When the researchers controlled for these other variables, they found that the original small class effects disappeared. Only the number of hours the wife spent on paid work and the respondent's age had strong effects on how much of the household work was performed by husbands; gender ideology had a weak effect.

If the researchers in this study had used only bivariate techniques to examine the relationship between class and men's work in the home, they might have erroneously concluded that class has at least some effect. Multivariate techniques allowed them to control for the effects of other variables, and they avoided making an erroneous conclusion.

T HIS CHAPTER FOCUSES ON THE METHODS RESEARCHERS USE to analyze more than two variables. The analysis of more than two variables serves three major functions in empirical research: control, elaboration, and prediction. The first function substitutes for the mechanism of experimental control when it is lacking. The second function clarifies bivariate relationships by introducing intervening or conditional variables. The third function is served by analyzing two or more independent variables to account for the variation in the dependent variable. This chapter discusses ways in which a third variable may enter into empirical research. First, we consider the strategy of controlling for a third variable through elaboration. Then we examine multivariate counterparts to the bivariate measures of relations. Finally, we examine the techniques of causal modeling and path analysis.

The examination of a bivariate relationship is but the first step in data analysis. In the next step, researchers evaluate the substantive implications of their findings and draw causal inferences. In other words, after researchers establish covariation and its direction using a bivariate measure, they interpret the findings and assess the causal priorities of the investigated variables by introducing other variables into the analysis. Suppose that you find a relationship between parents' age and

1. Erik Olin Wright, Karen Shire, Shu-Ling Hwang, Maureen Dolan, and Janeen Baxter, "The Non-Effects of Class on the Gender Division of Labor in the Home: A Comparative Study of Sweden and the United States," *Gender & Society,* Vol. 6 No. 2 (1992): 252–282.

child-rearing practices, that is, that older parents tend to be more restrictive than younger parents with their children. What interpretation can you give to this finding? You may claim that the variables are causally related and that increasing age of parents is associated with a shift from permissive toward restrictive attitudes. However, it is possible that a difference in child-rearing practices is due not to a difference in age but rather to a difference in orientation: older parents were exposed to an orientation stressing restriction, whereas younger parents behave according to a more liberal orientation advocating more permissive practices. In other words, the relationship between parents' age and child-rearing practices may be due to the fact that the variables "age" and "child-rearing practices" are both associated with a third variable, "orientation."

An observed correlation between two or more variables does not, of itself, permit the investigator to make causal interpretations. A bivariate relationship may be the product of chance, or it may exist because the variables are related to a third, unrevealed variable. Furthermore, the phenomenon under investigation can often be explained by more than a single independent variable. In any case, the introduction of additional variables serves the purpose of clarifying and elaborating the original relationship.

---

# Control

An association between two variables is not a sufficient basis for an inference that the two are causally related. Other variables must be ruled out as alternative explanations. For example, a relationship between height and income can probably be accounted for by the variable "age." Age is related to both income and height, and this joint relationship produces a statistical relationship that has no causal significance. The original relation between height and income is said to be a **spurious relation.** Spuriousness is a concept that applies to situations where an extraneous variable produces a "fake" relation between the independent and dependent variables. It is essential that an investigation uncover the extraneous factors contaminating the data in this way. Thus in validating bivariate associations, an important step is to rule out the largest possible number of variables that might conceivably explain the original association. Researchers rule out variables through the process of *control,* a basic principle in all research designs.

In experimental designs, control is accomplished by randomly assigning research participants to experimental and control groups. The logic of controlled experimentation assures the researcher that all extraneous variables have been controlled for and that the two groups differ only with regard to their exposure to the independent variable. However, as we have seen in earlier chapters, social scientists find it difficult to manipulate social groups and to apply experimental treatment prior to observations. Consequently, they lack control over numerous factors that throw doubt on any association between independent and dependent variables employed in the investigation.

In quasi-experimental designs, statistical techniques substitute for the experimental method of control. Researchers employ these techniques during data analysis rather than at the data collection stage. There are three methods of statistical control. The first entails subgroup comparisons using the technique of cross-tabulation. The second technique, partial correlation, employs mathematical procedures to readjust the value of a bivariate correlation coefficient. The third method is multiple regression, which enables us to estimate the effect of an independent variable on the dependent variable while controlling for the effect of other variables.

---

# Methods of Control

## Cross-Tabulation as a Control Operation

We can compare the **cross-tabulation** method of control to the procedure of matching employed in experiments. In both techniques, the investigator attempts to equate the groups examined with respect to variables that may bias the results. In experiments, researchers equate research participants prior to their exposure to the independent variable by identifying pairs of participants that are identical with respect to the controlled factors and physically allocating one member of each pair to the experimental group and one member to the control group. With cross-tabulation, investigators allocate research participants to the respective groups only during the analysis stage. Whereas matching is a physical control mechanism, cross-tabulation is a statistical operation.

Cross-tabulation involves the division of the sample into subgroups according to the categories of the controlled variable (called the **control variable**). The researcher then reassesses the original bivariate relation within each subgroup. By dividing the sample into subgroups, the researcher removes the biasing inequality by computing a measure of relationship for groups that are internally homogeneous with respect to the biasing factor.

Generally, only variables that are associated with both the independent variable and the dependent variable can potentially bias the results. Thus the researcher selects as control variables only variables that show an association with the independent and dependent variables under investigation.

*An Illustration.* The following example illustrates the steps involved in controlling for a third variable through cross-tabulation. Suppose we select a sample of 900 respondents to test the hypothesis that people from urban areas are politically more liberal than rural dwellers. The data obtained are presented in Table 17.1 and illustrated in Figure 17.1. We observe that 50 percent of urban residents are liberal, compared to only 28 percent of the respondents from rural areas. Thus we may conclude that political liberalism is associated with place of residence. The question is whether this association is direct (in which case the hypothesis may be supported) or is based on a spurious relation with another variable. One such additional variable might be education, which is associated with both place

**Table 17.1**
Political Liberalism by Urban-Rural Location

| Political Liberalism | Urban Area | Rural Area |
|---|---|---|
| High | 50%<br>(200) | 28%<br>(140) |
| Low | 50%<br>(200) | 72%<br>(360) |
| Total | 100%<br>(400) | 100%<br>(500) |

**Figure 17.1**
Liberalism by Urban-Rural Location

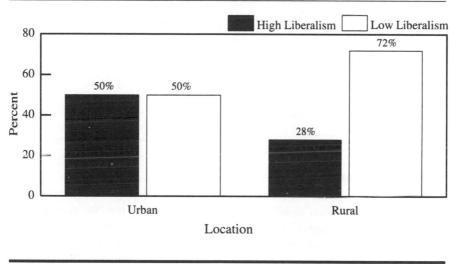

of residence and political liberalism, as reflected in the hypothetical bivariate distributions of Tables 17.2 and 17.3, which are illustrated in Figure 17.2.

## Partial Tables

To control for education, we divide the 900 persons into two groups according to level of education (high, low). Within each group, urban-rural location is cross-tabulated with political liberalism. We then estimate the original bivariate association in each of the subgroups. The controlled data are summarized in Table 17.4 and illustrated in Figure 17.3 (see p. 432).

The resulting two bivariate tables of Table 17.4 are referred to as **partial tables** because each one reflects only part of the total association. Each pair of parallel cells in the two partial tables adds up to the corresponding cell in the

**Table 17.2**
Education by Urban-Rural Location

| Education | Urban Area | Rural Area |
|---|---|---|
| High | 75% | 20% |
| | (300) | (100) |
| Low | 25% | 80% |
| | (100) | (400) |
| Total | 100% | 100% |
| | (400) | (500) |

**Table 17.3**
Political Liberalism by Education

| Political Liberalism | Education | |
|---|---|---|
| | High | Low |
| High | 60% | 20% |
| | (240) | (100) |
| Low | 40% | 80% |
| | (160) | (400) |
| Total | 100% | 100% |
| | (400) | (500) |

original table (Table 17.1). For example, the 180 highly educated respondents who come from urban areas and are liberals plus the 20 respondents who are urban liberals with a low level of education together constitute the 200 urban, liberal respondents in the original bivariate table.

To assess the partial association, we compute a measure of relationship for each of the control groups and compare it with the original result, selecting appropriate measures in the same way as for regular bivariate distributions. We can use difference of percentages, gamma, or Pearson's $r$, depending on the level of measurement.

The value of the partial association can be either identical or almost identical to the original association, it can vanish, or it can change. For the examination of spurious relationships, only the first two possibilities are relevant. When the partial association is identical or almost identical to the original association, we can conclude that the control variable does not account for the original relation and that the relation is direct. If it vanishes, the original association is said to be spurious. (A third variable may intervene between the dependent and independent variables, in which case the partial association will also vanish or approximate zero. We will consider an example of this situation shortly.)

If the partial association does not vanish but is different from the original association or if it is different in each of the partial tables, the independent and dependent variables are said to *interact*. We will return to interaction later.

**Figure 17.2**
The Relationship between Liberalism, Urban-Rural Location, and Education

Figure 17.2a
Education by Urban-Rural Location

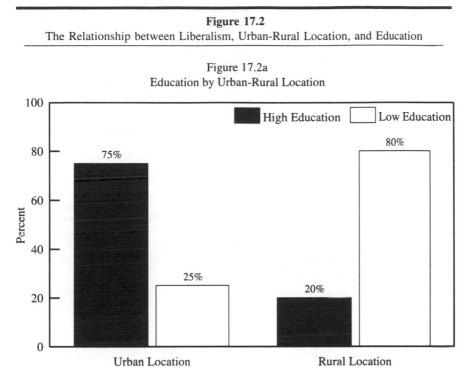

Figure 17.2b
Political Liberalism by Education

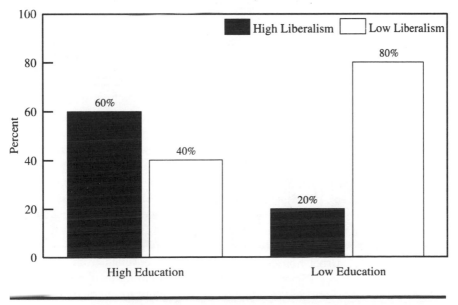

**Table 17.4**
Political Liberalism by Urban-Rural Location, Controlling for Education
(Spurious Relationship)

| Political Liberalism | High Education | | Low Education | |
|---|---|---|---|---|
| | Urban Area | Rural Area | Urban Area | Rural Area |
| High | 60% | 60% | 20% | 20% |
| | (180) | (60) | (20) | (80) |
| Low | 40% | 40% | 80% | 80% |
| | (120) | (40) | (80) | (320) |
| Total | 100% | 100% | 100% | 100% |
| | (300) | (100) | (100) | (400) |

***Spurious Original Association.***   In the example of Table 17.4, a percentage comparison shows that education completely accounts for the relation between residence and liberalism, for there is no difference between rural and urban residents in their degree of liberalism within either of the two education groups. Sixty percent of the highly educated rural residents, like 60 percent of the highly educated urban residents, are politically liberal. Within the low-education group, 20 percent are liberal wherever they reside. The overall association between the

**Figure 17.3**
Political Liberalism by Location, Controlling for Education (Spurious Relationship)

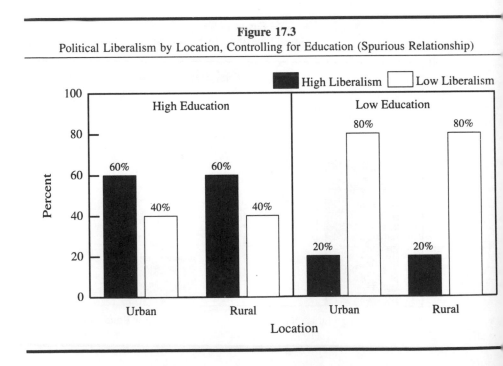

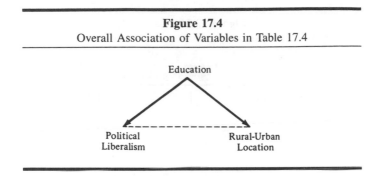

**Figure 17.4**
Overall Association of Variables in Table 17.4

independent and dependent variables is completely accounted for by the association of each with education, as is illustrated in the bar graph shown in Figure 17.3. This pattern can also be represented by the drawing shown in Figure 17.4.

Education determines both political liberalism and place of residence. That is, people who are educated tend to live in cities and are generally politically liberal. There is no inherent link between political liberalism and place of residence, and the association between them is spurious.

*Direct Original Association.*    The control of a third variable may lead to entirely different results, however. In the hypothetical example of Table 17.5, the original bivariate association remains unchanged by educational level. In the total sample, as well as in each educational group, a percentage comparison shows that 50 percent of urban residents are liberal, compared with 28 percent of rural residents. The bar graph presented in Figure 17.5 clearly shows that the overall relationship between the two original variables is not accounted for by the control variable. The investigator can be confident that education is an irrelevant factor with respect to this particular association and that the association between the two original variables is direct.

**Table 17.5**
Political Liberalism by Urban-Rural Location, Controlling for Education
(Nonspurious Relationship)

| Political Liberalism | High Education | | Low Education | |
|---|---|---|---|---|
| | Urban Area | Rural Area | Urban Area | Rural Area |
| High | 50% | 28% | 50% | 28% |
| | (50) | (35) | (150) | (105) |
| Low | 50% | 72% | 50% | 72% |
| | (50) | (90) | (150) | (270) |
| Total | 100% | 100% | 100% | 100% |
| | (100) | (125) | (300) | (375) |

**Figure 17.5**

Political Liberalism by Location, Controlling for Education (Nonspurious Relationship)

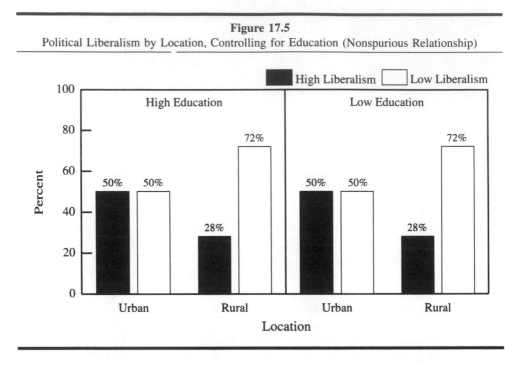

In practice, the results are not as clear-cut as presented here. It is very rare for associations either to vanish or to remain identical with the original results. Often the partial tables show a clear decrease in the size of the original relationship; at times the reduction is slight. This is because of the numerous factors that can account for a bivariate association. In our example, other variables such as income, party identification, or religious affiliation might conceivably explain the relationship between urban-rural location and political liberalism. Statisticians refer to this characteristic of variables as "block-booking,"[2] a term that reflects the multidimensionality of human beings and of their social interaction. When researchers compare people in terms of social class, they consider only one dimension of human experience. People may differ thoroughly from each other in a great many things, and all these other factors may enter into the phenomenon to be explained. The block-booked factors become our control variables; but when we control for only one or some of them, the rest may still explain the remaining residual in the dependent variable.

The procedure, then, is to hold constant all other variables that may be relevant to the subject of investigation. The selection of these variables is a logical and theoretical operation, the only statistical guideline being the requirement that the potential control factor be related to both the independent and dependent variables.

2. Morris Rosenberg, *The Logic of Survey Analysis* (New York: Basic Books, 1968), pp. 26–28.

Of course, a researcher can never be completely sure that he or she has introduced all relevant variables into the analysis. However, the greater the number of relevant factors controlled for, the greater the confidence that the relationship is not spurious.

# Elaboration

The mechanism of control is designed to uncover factors that might invalidate the original bivariate association. In that case, the investigators are likely to turn to other factors that they can employ as independent variables and then repeat the process of validating the relationship. However, if the relationship observed is non-spurious, researchers can proceed to a more advanced stage of analysis and elaborate the bivariate association. **Elaboration** usually involves the introduction of other variables to determine the links between the independent and dependent variables or to specify the conditions under which the association takes place.

Some concrete examples will help us illustrate the meaning of elaboration. In the past decade, social scientists have paid close attention to the effect of early childbearing on the life chances of adolescent parents. Investigators have discovered that early childbearers are more likely to experience economic hardship and family disruption in later life than later childbearers.[3] Early childbearing appears to be linked to dropping out of school, particularly for adolescent mothers. Low educational attainment in turn makes it more difficult for teenage mothers to find stable and remunerative employment. We can represent these relationships schematically as follows:

Early childbearing → low educational attainment → economic disadvantage

In this scheme, low educational attainment provides a link between early child-bearing and economic disadvantage. It is an **intervening variable** between the independent variable (early childbearing) and the dependent variable (economic disadvantage).

Although low educational attainment accounts for the economic disadvantage of many teenage mothers, the life chances of these women vary enormously. For instance, a recent study found that one-fourth of early childbearers were on welfare while another fourth were relatively comfortable economically with a family income of more than $25,000 a year.[4] To account for these differences, researchers controlled for a number of variables. One of these variables was race. They discovered that white mothers were more likely to attain a higher economic level than black mothers. In this example, the original bivariate association between early childbearing and economic disadvantage is pronounced only among one subgroup,

3. Frank F. Furstenberg, Jr., J. Brooks-Gunn, and S. Philip Morgan, *Adolescent Mothers in Later Life* (Cambridge: Cambridge University Press, 1987).

4. Ibid., p. 48.

black mothers. The control variable, race, is thus said to be a **conditional variable,** and the pattern is called **interaction.** Schematically, this pattern may be represented as follows:

$$\text{Early childbearing} \begin{cases} \text{black} \longrightarrow \text{economic disadvantage} \\ \\ \text{white} \longrightarrow \text{no economic disadvantage} \end{cases}$$

We shall examine empirical examples of both intervening variables and interaction.

## Intervening Variables

Let us return to the first case, in which the controlled variable is said to intervene between the independent and dependent variables. Table 17.6 shows the relationship between childbearing and economic status. The data demonstrate that these two variables are associated: early childbearers are more likely to have low economic status. The investigators hypothesized that these differences could be explained by the variable "educational attainment." That is, early childbearing affects economic status indirectly through educational attainment because young mothers are more likely to drop out of school than nonmothers.

As a means of testing this hypothesis, the investigators held educational attainment constant and reexamined the original relationship. If, as suggested, childbearing has only an indirect influence on economic status, then when the intermediate link is controlled for, the association between childbearing and economic status should disappear. The results in Table 17.7 confirm the hypothesis: there are no differences in economic status between mothers and nonmothers when the level of educational attainment is the same. The original relationship vanishes when educational attainment is controlled for.

In order to infer that a control variable links the independent and dependent variables, the researcher must demonstrate that the control variable is associated with both the independent and dependent variables and that when controlled for, the original relationship vanishes (or diminishes considerably) in all categories of the control variable. You may be exclaiming that these were the identical condi-

**Table 17.6**
Childbearing and Economic Status (Hypothetical Data)

| Economic Status | Early Childbearing | | Total |
| --- | --- | --- | --- |
| | Yes | No | |
| Low | 54% | 33% | |
| | (869) | (653) | (1,522) |
| High | 46% | 67% | |
| | (731) | (1,347) | (2,078) |
| Total | 100% | 100% | |
| | (1,600) | (2,000) | (3,600) |

**Table 17.7**
Childbearing and Economic Status by Educational Attainment
(Hypothetical Data)

| Economic Status | High Educational Attainment Early Childbearing | | Low Educational Attainment Early Childbearing | | Total |
|---|---|---|---|---|---|
| | Yes | No | Yes | No | Total |
| Low | 18% | 18% | 64% | 65% | |
| | (90) | (216) | (704) | (512) | (1,522) |
| High | 82% | 82% | 36% | 36% | |
| | (410) | (984) | (396) | (288) | (2,078) |
| Total | 100% | 100% | 100% | 100% | |
| | (500) | (1,200) | (1,100) | (800) | (3,600) |

tions required for declaring the relationship spurious, and we can confirm that this is indeed true. The statistical tests in both cases are identical, but the interpretation is significantly different. With a spurious interpretation, the statistical results invalidate a hypothesis about the relationship between the independent and dependent variable; an intervening interpretation, by contrast, clarifies and explains such a relationship. How, then, can we distinguish between the two?

Morris Rosenberg maintains that the difference is a theoretical issue rather than a statistical one and that it lies in the assumed causal relationship among the variables,[5] With a spurious interpretation, it is assumed that there is no causal relation between the independent and dependent variables; in the case of an intervening variable, the two are indirectly related through an intermediate link, the control variable.

## Interaction

For the second type of elaboration, interaction, the researcher specifies the conditions or contingencies necessary for the relationship to occur. We will illustrate the meaning of interaction using the example of childbearing, economic status, and race. The bivariate association between childbearing and economic status already presented in Table 17.6 demonstrated that these two variables are associated. To gain further insight, a researcher might control for race. The results are presented in Table 17.8.

The results clearly demonstrate an interactive relationship since the relationship between childbearing and economic status is different for white and black women; whereas for black women, early childbearing has a considerable impact on economic status (66 percent of the early childbearers have a low economic status compared to only 31 percent of women who are not early childbearers);

5. Rosenberg, *Logic of Survey Analysis*, pp. 54–66.

**Table 17.8**

Childbearing and Economic Status by Race (Hypothetical Data)

| Economic Status | Black Early Childbearing | | White Early Childbearing | | Total |
|---|---|---|---|---|---|
| | Yes | No | Yes | No | |
| Low | 66% | 31% | 36% | 38% | |
| | (594) | (372) | (252) | (304) | (1,522) |
| High | 34% | 69% | 64% | 62% | |
| | (306) | (828) | (448) | (496) | (2,078) |
| Total | 100% | 100% | 100% | 100% | |
| | (900) | (1,200) | (700) | (800) | (3,600) |

among white women, there is no relationship between these two variables. For white women, a little over one-third in both groups (36 percent and 38 percent) are in the low-status group. Based on these results, it may be concluded that early childbearing and race interact in their effect on economic status; that is, the relationship between the independent and dependent variables is conditioned by race. One possible interpretation is that early childbearing has economic consequences only for women who are already disadvantaged.

Conditional relationships such as this one are quite common in social science research and can be inferred whenever the relative size or direction of the original bivariate relationship is more pronounced in one category of the control variable than in another. The presence of such differences between subgroups reflects the nature of social reality, where each variable can be broken down into various components. Indeed, many conditional factors are associated with almost any two-variable relationships. This social complexity makes the analysis of interaction one of the most important aspects of statistical analysis.

*Interest and Concern as a Condition.*    Herbert Hyman analyzed the various factors that are generally considered conditions for most bivariate association and classified them into three major groups.[6] The first class consists of variables that specify relationships in terms of interest and concern. In many situations, interest and concern specify the conditions under which the effectiveness of an independent variable is more or less pronounced. People tend to differ in their interests, which in turn affect their attitudes and behavior patterns. Thus social stimuli are likely to have differential effects on them, and the identification of these differing patterns may prove to be essential to the social scientist. For instance, consider Morris Rosenberg's finding that self-esteem is associated with intensity of political discussion.[7] Adolescents with low self-esteem, who are more self-conscious, tend

6. Herbert H. Hyman, *Survey Design and Analysis* (New York: Free Press, 1955), pp. 295–311.
7. Morris Rosenberg, "Self-esteem and Concern with Public Affairs," *Public Opinion Quarterly,* 26 (1962): 201–211.

to avoid expressing their political views. Taking into account the level of political interest, Rosenberg observed that the relationship holds only among those who are interested in politics. Those who are not interested in politics also do not discuss politics, even though they might have a high degree of self-esteem. Thus the use of the conditional factor helps to clarify the original findings.

*Time and Place as a Condition.*      The second class of factors specifies associations in terms of time and place. A relationship between two variables can vary according to the time and place at which it is studied. In studies in comparative politics, researchers typically introduce "place" as a control variable. The effect of class, gender, and race on voting, for example, differs from one country to another.

Specification by time is meaningful too. Often a relationship that holds at one time will be dismissed or changed at another time. For example, a growing body of research has documented a gender difference in support of women in politics, with women more likely than men to reject stereotypical notions that "politics is for men."[8] In a number of studies comparing the effect of gender on attitudes toward women in politics over time, researchers have hypothesized that time will reduce gender differences because of the presence of more female political role models. Research into the general process of development and socialization offers another example. The family is known to affect various behavioral patterns in children. This effect is pronounced, especially at the early stages, when the child is more exposed and more vulnerable to his or her family. At later stages, however, other aspects of socialization play an important role, and the family's influence diminishes. Thus a relationship between family characteristics and behavioral orientations would not stay constant if a researcher examined them at different times.

---

### Types of Elaboration

- *Intervening Variables:* Variables that link the independent and dependent variables and explain the relationship between them. In order to conclude that a variable links the independent and dependent variables, the researcher must show that the control variable is associated with both the independent and dependent variables and that when controlled for, the original relationship decreases significantly, or disappears, in all categories of the control variable.
- *Interaction:* To demonstrate interaction, the researcher must determine the conditions or contingencies necessary for the relationship to occur. Researchers can infer conditional relationships whenever the relative size or direction of the original bivariate relationship is more pronounced in one category of the control variable than in another.

---

8. Diane Gillespie and Cassie Spohn, "Adolescents Attitudes toward Women in Politics: A Follow-up Study," *Women and Politics,* 10 (1990): 1–16.

*Background Characteristics as a Condition.*    Background characteristics of the units of analysis are the last class of factors. Often associations are likely to differ for persons or groups that do not share the same characteristics. Thus the relation between class position and voting behavior is different for men and for women, and the effect of teachers' encouragement on self-esteem is not identical for black and white children. Background characteristics are perhaps the most common among the types of conditions employed in the social sciences. In fact, some researchers employ such control variables as "social class," "level of education," "gender," and "age" almost automatically, reexamining all relationships obtained.

## Partial Correlation as a Control Operation

The cross-tabulation control operation is quite popular in empirical research, and it is applied to all levels of measurement. However, it has a drawback that limits its use when the number of cases is relatively small. In order to use the cross-tabulation method of control, the researcher must subdivide the sample into progressively smaller subgroups, according to the number of categories of the controlled factor. Subdividing the sample reduces the number of cases that serve as a basis for computing the coefficient, and a small sample size calls into question the validity and reliability of the findings. This problem is particularly acute when several variables are controlled simultaneously.

A second method of control, not limited by the number of cases, is the **partial correlation.** This method, a mathematical adjustment of the bivariate correlation, is designed to cancel out the effect of the control variable on the independent and dependent variables. The logic underlying the calculation of this measure of association is similar to that of cross-tabulation. The original association between the independent and dependent variables is reassessed to determine whether it reflects a direct association, independent of the variables' association to a third extraneous factor.

The formula for calculating partial correlation coefficients employs certain notational conventions with which you must be familiar. The independent variable is designated as $X_1$, the dependent variable as $X_2$, and the control variable as $X_3$. Additional control variables are designated as $X_4, X_5, X_6$, and so forth. The symbol $r$ is a shorthand notation for the correlation coefficient, and researchers use the $X$ subscripts to show which correlation they are describing. For example, $r_{12}$ denotes the correlation between the independent variable ($X_1$) and the dependent variable ($X_2$). The correlations between the control variable ($X_3$) and the independent and dependent variables are shown as $r_{31}$ and $r_{32}$ respectively.

Suppose that a correlation of $r_{12} = .60$ is found between self-esteem ($X_1$) and educational expectation ($X_2$). To test the nature of this association, the researcher can introduce an additional variable such as social class ($X_3$), which is related to both self-esteem ($r_{31} = .30$) and educational expectation ($r_{32} = .40$). The researcher can use partial correlation to obtain a measure of association with the effect of social class removed. The formula for calculating the partial correlation coefficient is

$$r_{12.3} = \frac{r_{12} - (r_{31})(r_{32})}{\sqrt{1 - (r_{31})^2}\sqrt{1 - (r_{32})^2}} \qquad (17.1)$$

where $X_1$ = independent variable (in our example, self-esteem)

$X_2$ = dependent variable (educational expectation)

$X_3$ = control variable (social class)

The symbol to the right of the dot indicates the variable to be controlled. Thus $r_{12.3}$ is the correlation between variables $X_1$ and $X_2$ controlling for variable $X_3$. Similarly, a partial coefficient between variables $X_1$ and $X_3$ controlling for $X_2$ would be denoted $r_{13.2}$. A partial with one control is referred to as a *first-order partial* to distinguish it from a bivariate correlation, often denoted as a *zero-order correlation*. A partial with two controls is referred to as a *second-order partial*, and so on. When more than one variable is controlled for simultaneously, their numbers are added to the right of the dot. Thus controlling for variables $X_3$ and $X_4$ would be expressed as $r_{12.34}$.

We can now calculate the partial correlation for self-esteem and educational expectation:

$$r_{12.3} = \frac{.60 - (.30)(.40)}{\sqrt{1 - (.30)^2}\sqrt{1 - (.40)^2}} = \frac{.48}{\sqrt{.7644}} = \frac{.48}{.87} = .55$$

When the partial correlation is squared, the result reflects the proportion of variation left unexplained by the control variable and explained by the independent variable. Thus about 30 percent [$(.55)^2 \times 100$] of the variation in educational expectation was explained by self-esteem after removing the effect of social class.

In contrast to the cross-tabulation method of control, the partial correlation yields a single summarizing measure that reflects the degree of correlation between two variables while controlling for a third. Thus the partial correlation does not reflect variation in the partial associations in different categories of the controlled variable because it averages out the different partials. This property of the measure is its main disadvantage, as it might obscure otherwise essential information. In cases where the investigator suspects that there are significant differences between the partials of the various subgroups, it is advisable to use the cross-tabulation technique instead.

## Multiple Regression as a Control Operation

Another method that allows us to assess the relationship between two variables while controlling for the effect of others is **multiple regression**. Multiple regression is a simple extension of bivariate regression, which was discussed in Chapter 16. A multiple regression equation, shown in Equation (17.2), describes the extent of linear relationships between the dependent variable and a number of other independent (or control) variables:

$$\hat{Y} = a + b_1 X_1 + b_2 X_2 \qquad (17.2)$$

where $\hat{Y}$ is the dependent variable and $X_1$ and $X_2$ are the independent variables. Designated as partial regression coefficients, $b_1$ and $b_2$ are the slope of the regression line for each independent variable, controlling for the other. Thus $b_1$ reflects the amount of change in $Y$ associated with a given change in $X_1$, holding $X_2$ constant; $b_2$ is the amount of change in $Y$ associated with a given change in $X_2$, holding $X_1$ constant; and $a$ is the intercept point on the $Y$ axis for both $X_1$ and $X_2$.

As with bivariate regression, the constants of the multiple linear regression equation are estimated so as to minimize the average squared error in prediction. This is accomplished by using the least squares criterion to obtain the best fit to the data. The least squares estimates of $a$, $b_1$, and $b_2$ are shown in Equations (17.3), (17.4), and (17.5):

$$b_1 = \left(\frac{s_Y}{s_1}\right)\frac{r_{y1} - r_{y2}r_{12}}{1 - (r_{12})^2} \tag{17.3}$$

$$b_2 = \left(\frac{s_Y}{s_2}\right)\frac{r_{y2} - r_{y2}r_{12}}{1 - (r_{12})^2} \tag{17.4}$$

$$a = \bar{Y} - b_1\bar{X}_1 - b_2\bar{X}_2 \tag{17.5}$$

We will illustrate the computation of the multiple regression constants using Equations (17.3), (17.4), and (17.5) by attempting to estimate the effects of self-esteem and education on political liberalism.

We have designated liberalism as $Y$, education as $X_1$, and self-esteem as $X_2$. Liberalism has been measured on a scale from 1 to 10 and self-esteem has been measured on a scale from 1 to 9, with higher numbers indicating higher levels of each of these variables. Education is measured in years of school. The following are the hypothetical means, standard deviations, and bivariate correlation coefficients for these variables:

$$\bar{Y} = 6.5 \qquad s_Y = 3 \qquad r_{y1} = .86 \text{ (liberalism by education)}$$
$$\bar{X}_1 = 8.9 \qquad s_1 = 4.1 \qquad r_{y2} = .70 \text{ (liberalism by self-esteem)}$$
$$\bar{X}_2 = 5.8 \qquad s_2 = 2.2 \qquad r_{12} = .75 \text{ (education by self-esteem)}$$

For this problem, $b_1$ stands for the effect of education on liberalism controlling for self-esteem and $b_2$ for the effect of self-esteem on liberalism controlling for education.

Substituting the data into the formulas for $b_1$ and $b_2$, we have

$$b_1 = \left(\frac{3}{4.1}\right)\frac{.86 - (.70)(.75)}{1 - (.75)^2} = .56$$

$$b_2 = \left(\frac{3}{2.2}\right)\frac{.70 - (.86)(.75)}{1 - (.75)^2} = .17$$

The intercept for the multiple regression equation is

$$a = 6.5 - (.56)(8.9) - (.17)(5.8) = .53$$

With the obtained values of $b_1$, $b_2$, and $a$, the complete multiple regression equation for predicting liberalism on the basis of education and self-esteem would therefore be

$$\hat{Y} = .53 + .56X_1 + .17X_2$$

It indicates the extent of political liberalism that would be expected, on the average, with a given level of education and a given level of self-esteem. For example, for a person with ten years of schooling and a self-esteem score of 8, the expected level of liberalism would be

$$\hat{Y} = .53 + (.56)(10) + (.17)(8) = 7.49$$

As the $b$ coefficients reflect the net effect of each variable, we can compare them in order to denote the relative importance of the independent variables. However, since each variable is measured on a different scale in different units, $b$ *must be standardized to be comparable.* The standardized equivalent of the $b$ coefficient is called the *beta weight* or *beta coefficient*; it is symbolized as $\beta$. We obtain the beta weights by multiplying $b$ by the ratio of the standard deviation of the independent variable to the standard deviation of the dependent variable. Thus $\beta_1$ and $\beta_2$ would be expressed as follows:

$$\beta_1 = \left(\frac{s_1}{s_Y}\right)b_1$$

$$\beta_2 = \left(\frac{s_2}{s_Y}\right)b_2$$

For our example, we get

$$\beta_1 = \left(\frac{4.1}{3}\right)(.56) = .765$$

$$\beta_2 = \left(\frac{2.2}{3}\right)(.17) = .125$$

The intercept for a standardized regression equation is zero. Therefore, we have

$$\hat{Y}_z = X_{1z} + X_{2z}$$

The subscript $z$ indicates that the variables have been standardized.

The standardized regression equation shows that for every increase of one standard deviation in education, political liberalism increases by .765 standard deviations, and with an increase of one standard deviation in self-esteem, liberalism increases by .125 standard deviations. One main advantage to using the standardized regression equation is that it translates the variables to a uniform scale that lets us easily compare the relative strength of education and self-esteem in their effect on liberalism. It is evident that education contributes more to liberalism (.765) than does self-esteem (.125).

**Three Methods of Statistical Control**

- *Cross-tabulation:* When researchers use cross-tabulation as a method of control, they divide the original sample into subgroups according to the categories of the control variable and reassess the original bivariate relation within each subgroup. The researcher must select as control variables only those associated with the independent and dependent variables under investigation. The resulting partial tables are analyzed to determine whether the relation is spurious, direct, caused by an intervening variable, or is the result of an interaction. Cross-tabulation allows researchers to clarify relationships between variables measured at nominal and ordinal levels and can also be used with interval level data.
- *Partial Correlation:* Partial correlation can only be used with interval level data. Researchers use partial correlation to mathematically adjust the bivariate correlation to cancel out the effect of the control variable on the independent and dependent variable, and the result reflects only the direct association between the independent and dependent variables. A partial with one control is called a first-order partial, one with two controls is called a second-order partial, and so forth. The squared partial correlation reflects the proportion of variation left unexplained by the control variable and explained by the independent variable. The partial correlation is calculated using Formula (17.1).
- *Multiple Regression:* A multiple regression equation describes the extent of linear relationships between the dependent variable and a number of independent or control variables. Researchers use Equations (17.2), (17.3), (17.4), and (17.5) to determine the extent of these relationships. Before we can compare the relative importance of independent variables measured on different scales and/or in different units, the effects of the variables, or *b* coefficients, must be standardized. To do this researchers calculate what is called the beta weight or beta coefficient—symbolized as $\beta$.

Just as the partial correlation coefficient measures the effect of one independent variable on the dependent variable while controlling for another, the multiple regression coefficient measures the amount of change in the dependent variable with one unit change in the independent variable while controlling for all other variables in the equation.

In fact, beta weights and partial correlation coefficients are directly comparable, are usually similar in size, and always have the same sign indicating the direction of the relationship.

# Multivariate Analysis: Multiple Relationships

Up to this point, we have considered only situations in which one independent variable is said to determine the dependent variable being studied. However, in the social world, we rarely find that only one variable is relevant to what is to be explained. Often numerous variables are directly associated with the dependent variable. Population change, for example, is explained by four variables: "birth rate," "death rate," "immigration rate," and "emigration rate." Similarly, differences in support for legal abortion are often explained by differences in "religion," "gender," and "age." Thus there are often several independent variables, each of which may contribute to our ability to predict the dependent variable.

In a typical research problem, say, in which a researcher is attempting to explain differences in voting behavior, he or she would use a number of independent variables, for example, "social class," "religion," "gender," and "political attitudes." The researcher would attempt to look at the effects of each independent variable while controlling for the effects of others, as well as at the combined effect of all the independent variables on voting.

The technique of multiple regression introduced earlier in this chapter is most appropriate for problems involving two or more independent variables. We have seen that the standardized regression coefficient—the beta weights—allows us to assess the independent effect of each variable in the regression equation on the dependent variable.

To examine the *combined* effect of all the independent variables, we compute a measure called the *coefficient of determination,* denoted $R^2$.

Just as with simple bivariate regression, in multiple regression we need to estimate how well the regression rule fits the actual data. In simple regression, the fit (or the relative reduction of error) was measured using $r^2$, which is defined as the ratio of the variation explained to the total variation in the dependent variable. Similarly, when the prediction is based on several variables, an estimate of the relative reduction of error is based on the ratio of the variation explained with several variables simultaneously to the total variation. This measure, $R^2$, designates the percentage of the variation explained by all the independent variables in the multiple regression equation. The square root of $R^2$ indicates the correlation between all independent variables taken together with the dependent variable; it is thus the *coefficient of multiple correlation.*

For the three-variable case, the two formulas for $R^2$ are as follows:

$$R^2_{y.12} = \frac{r^2_{y1} + r^2_{y2} - 2r_{y1}r_{y2}r_{12}}{1 - (r_{12})^2} \tag{17.6}$$

or

$$R^2_{y.12} = \beta_1 r_{y1} + \beta_2 r_{y2} \tag{17.7}$$

As an example, let us calculate the percentage of variation in political liberalism ($Y$) using education ($X_1$) and self-esteem ($X_2$) as predictors. We will use the data we presented in our discussion of multiple regression on pages 000–000, and Equation (17.7) to calculate $R^2$.

$$r^2_{y.12} = (.765)(.86) + (.125)(.70) = .745$$

This means that almost 75 percent of the variation in political liberalism is accounted for by the combined effects of education and self-esteem.

# Causal Models and Path Analysis

So far our discussion has focused on methods of control that provide an interpretation of the relation between two variables. We indicated that a direct relationship is one that does not prove to be spurious. This is determined by the time sequence of the variables and the relative size of the partial associations.

Paul Lazarsfeld had suggested that these two elements—the size of the partials relative to the original bivariate associations and the assumed time order between the variables—are the kind of evidence required for inferring causation:

> We can suggest a clear-cut definition of the causal relation between two attributes. If we have a relationship between $X$ and $Y$, and if for any antecedent test factor $c$ the partial relationship between $X$ and $Y$ does not disappear, then the original relationship should be called a causal one.[9]

Although we can never directly demonstrate causality from correlational data, it is possible for us to make causal inferences concerning the adequacy of specific causal models.

Statistical methods that enable us to draw causal inferences involve a finite set of explicitly defined variables, assumptions about how these variables are interrelated causally, and assumptions about the effect of outside variables on the variables included in the model.[10]

## Some Examples of Causal Diagrams

Hypothetically, there could be six causal connections between three variables $X_1$, $X_2$, and $X_3$, as follows:

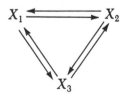

In the diagram, the causal order between two variables is represented by a single-headed arrow, with the head pointing to the effect and the tail to the cause. A simplifying assumption[11] rules out two-way causation either directly in the form $X_1 \longleftrightarrow X_2$ or indirectly as in

9. Paul F. Lazarsfeld, "The Algebra of Dichotomous Systems," in *Studies in Items Analysis and Prediction*, ed. Herbert Solomon (Stanford, Calif.: Stanford University Press, 1959), p. 146.

10. Herbert A. Simon, *Models of Man: Social and Rational* (New York: Wiley, 1957).

11. Hubert M. Blalock, Jr., *Causal Inference in Nonexperimental Research* (Chapel Hill: University of North Carolina Press, 1964).

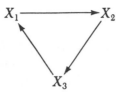

Furthermore, under this assumption a dependent variable cannot cause any of the variables preceding it in the causal sequence. Thus in a causal system where $X_1$ is the independent variable, $X_2$ the intervening variable, and $X_3$ the dependent variable, $X_2$ cannot cause $X_1$, and $X_3$ cannot cause $X_2$ or $X_1$.

With these assumptions, we can construct some possible models explaining relations between $X_1$, $X_2$, and $X_3$; some examples are presented in Figure 17.6.

These diagrams display direct relations, indirect relations, and no effect between the variables. Diagram *a* shows a direct effect of $X_1$ on $X_2$, a direct effect of $X_2$ on $X_3$, and an indirect effect of $X_1$ on $X_3$ through $X_2$. Similarly, in diagram *b*, $X_1$ and $X_2$ affect $X_3$ directly and $X_1$ has no effect on $X_2$.

To illustrate how some of these ideas are applied, let us look at the following example of research on voting behavior and its determinants. It is hypothesized that voting behavior ($X_4$) is directly determined by party identification ($X_1$), candidate evaluation ($X_2$), and perception of campaign issues ($X_3$) and that candidate evaluation and campaign issues are directly determined by party identification. Furthermore, party identification influences voting behavior indirectly,

**Figure 17.6**
Models for Three Variables

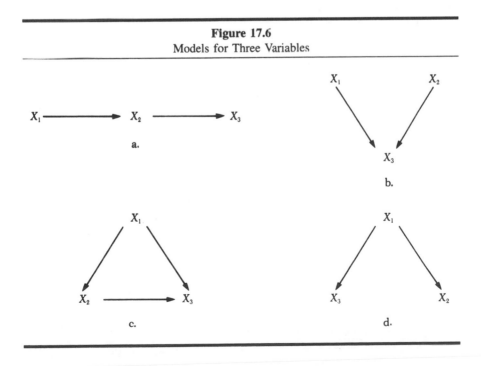

through candidate evaluation and campaign issues. These ideas are presented in Figure 17.7.

The variables *U, V,* and *W* are called *residual variables;* the arrows between them and each of the dependent variables in the model express the fact that variation in the dependent variables is not solely accounted for by variables in the model. Thus *W,* for example, would represent variation in voting behavior not accounted for by party identification, candidate evaluation, or perceptions of campaign issues.

## Path Analysis

**Path analysis** is a technique that uses both bivariate and multiple linear regression techniques to test the causal relations among the variables specified in the model. It involves three major steps:

1. The researcher draws a path diagram based on a theory or a set of hypotheses.
2. The researcher then calculates path coefficients (direct effects) using regression techniques.
3. Finally, the researcher determines indirect effects.

Our illustration on voting behavior on pages 428–435 provides an example of the first step of path analysis. Therefore, we will start with a discussion of step 2. You will notice that Figure 17.7 includes a set of coefficients identified as $P_{ij}$, $i$ being the dependent variable and $j$ the independent variable. These values are called **path coefficients.** For example, $P_{31}$ is the path coefficient connecting $X_1$ with $X_3$, with $X_3$ being determined by $X_1$. Similarly, $P_{4w}$ is the path coefficient linking $X_4$ with the residual variable $W$.

---

**Figure 17.7**
A Path Diagram of Voting Behavior

---

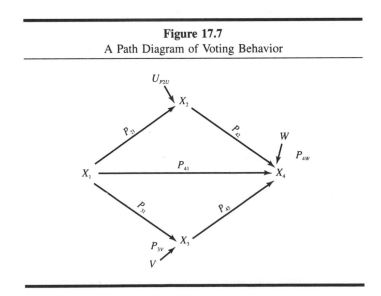

To estimate the path coefficients, we first write a set of regression equations that represent the structure of the model. We should have as many equations as we have dependent variables. Thus to represent the model of Figure 17.7, we have

$$X_2 = P_{21}X_1 + P_{2u}U$$
$$X_3 = P_{31}X_1 + P_{3v}V$$
$$X_4 = P_{41}X_1 + P_{42}X_2 + P_{43}X_3 + P_{4w}W$$

You will notice that each equation includes as many terms as there are arrows leading to the dependent variable. Thus $X_4$ has four arrows, each representing a determining factor: $X_1$, $X_2$, $X_3$, and $W$.

To obtain estimates of the path coefficients, we simply regress each dependent variable on the independent variables in the equation. To estimate $P_{21}$, we regress $X_2$ on $X_1$. For $P_{31}$, we regress $X_3$ on $X_1$, and for $P_{41}$, $P_{42}$, and $P_{43}$, we regress $X_4$ on $X_1$, $X_2$, and $X_3$. The path coefficients are simply the beta weights for each equation; that is,

$$P_{21} = \beta_{21} \qquad P_{42} = \beta_{42}$$
$$P_{31} = \beta_{31} \qquad P_{43} = \beta_{43}$$
$$P_{41} = \beta_{41}$$

The residual path coefficient ($P_{2u}$, $P_{3v}$, $P_{4w}$) is the square root of the unexplained variation in the dependent variable under analysis. For the model presented in Figure 17.7, the residual paths are

$$P_{2u} = \sqrt{1 - R^2_{2.1}}$$

$$P_{3v} = \sqrt{1 - R^2_{3.1}}$$

$$P_{4w} = \sqrt{1 - R^2_{4.123}}$$

By estimating the path coefficient, we obtain an assessment of the direct effects on all variables in the model. Thus $P_{21}$ expresses the direct effect of $X_1$ on $X_2$; $P_{31}$, the direct effect of $X_1$ on $X_3$; $P_{41}$, the direct effect of $X_1$ on $X_4$; and so on. However, as can be observed in Figure 17.7, $X_1$ affects $X_4$ indirectly as well, through $X_2$ and $X_3$.

To estimate the **indirect effects,** we multiply the path coefficients of paths connecting two variables via intervening variables. Thus for Figure 17.7, the indirect effect of $X_1$ on $X_4$ via $X_2$ would be expressed by $P_{21} P_{42}$, and the indirect effect of $X_1$ on $X_4$ via $X_3$ would be $P_{31} P_{43}$.

One interesting application of path analysis[12] is the Tompkins welfare expenditures model in the American states. Drawing on the theoretical literature, Gary L. Tompkins has constructed a path model that includes six variables: indus-

12. David Nachmias, *Public Policy Evaluation* (New York: St. Martin's Press, 1979).

**Figure 17.8**

A Path Diagram with Path Coefficients and Residual Paths for Welfare
Expenditures in the United States

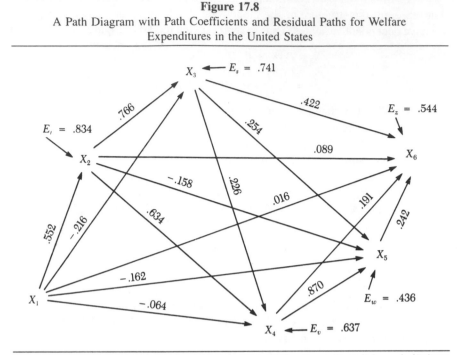

Adapted from Gary L. Tompkins, "A Causal Model of State Welfare Expenditures," *Journal of Politics,*
37 (1975): 406.

trialization ($X_1$), income ($X_2$), ethnicity ($X_3$), interparty competition ($X_4$), voter
turnout ($X_5$), and welfare expenditures ($X_6$).[13] Given the assumption of one-way
causation, there are 15 possible path arrows between the six variables, as illustrated
in Figure 17.8. The values for the path coefficients and those for the residual paths
are also reported in this figure. Although this path model accurately reflects the
empirical relationships among the six variables, Tompkins has developed a simplified model, which he obtained by eliminating weak path coefficients (coefficients with an absolute value less than .200) and then recalculating the various
estimates. By eliminating six weak path coefficients, Tompkins developed the
more economical but nonetheless powerful model shown in Figure 17.9. Now
it is possible to assess the direct and indirect effects of the variables on welfare
expenditures.

Thus, for example, ethnicity ($X_3$) exerts a strong direct effect on the level of
welfare expenditure ($P_{63} = .499$) and a relatively moderate indirect effect via interparty competition: $P_{64}P_{43} = .102$. Income exerts no direct effect on welfare expen-

13. Gary L. Tompkins, "A Causal Model of State Welfare Expenditures," *Journal of Politics,* 37
(1975): 392–416.

**Figure 17.9**

A Modified Path Diagram with Path Coefficients and Residual Paths for Welfare
Expenditures in the United States

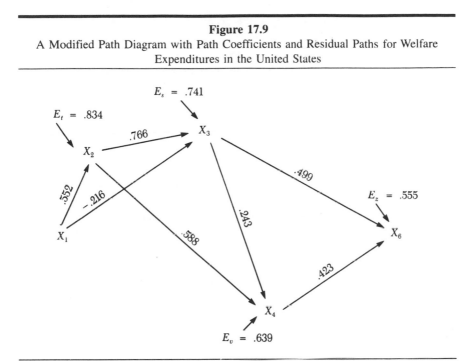

Adapted from Gary L. Tompkins, "A Causal Model of State Welfare Expenditures," *Journal of Politics*,
37 (1975): 409.

ditures. However, income has a strong indirect effect via ethnicity and interparty
competition: $(P_{63}P_{32}) + P_{64} [P_{42} + (P_{43}P_{32})]$ $(.499 \times .766) + .423 [.588 + (.243 \times .766)] = .710$.

## Summary

**1.** Multivariate analysis has three basic functions: control, interpretation, and
prediction. Statistical control is a substitute for experimental control and is accomplished through cross-tabulation, partial correlation, or multiple regression.
With cross-tabulation, the researcher attempts to equate groups exposed to the
independent variable with those not exposed in all relevant matters. The selection of relevant control variables is based on theoretical as well as statistical considerations. The control variable must be associated with both the independent and
dependent variables. When they use the partial correlation method, researchers statistically adjust the bivariate correlation to cancel out the effect of the control variable on the independent and dependent variables. Multiple regression
estimates the effect of one variable on another while controlling for the effect
of others.

**2.** When the mechanism of control is applied to a bivariate association, it can either cancel out the original relationship or have no effect on it. In the first case, the association is either spurious or mediated by the control variable; in the second case, the association is considered direct and is subject to further analysis. Whereas an interpretation of spuriousness invalidates a bivariate association, an intervening interpretation clarifies it and explains how the independent and dependent variables are related. A second class of interpretation specifies the conditions under which the association holds. These conditions can be interest and concern, time and place, and specific qualifications or characteristics.

**3.** Multiple regression and correlation comprise a technique for assessing the simultaneous effect of several independent variables on the dependent variable under study. In multiple regression, the researcher estimates a prediction rule that evaluates the extent of change produced in the dependent variable by an independent variable, holding other relevant independent variables constant. The multiple correlation estimates the degree of fit of the prediction equation with the empirical data. $R^2$, the multiple correlation coefficient, measures the amount of variance in the dependent variable explained by the independent variables employed.

**4.** Path analysis is a multivariate technique based on linear regression analysis that makes it possible for researchers to test causal relations among a set of variables. Researchers employing path analysis draw diagrams founded in theory and then determine direct and indirect effects of variables.

---

## Key Terms for Review

---

conditional variable (p. 436)
control variable (p. 428)
cross-tabulation (p. 428)
elaboration (p. 435)
indirect effect (p. 449)
interaction (p. 436)
intervening variable (p. 435)

multiple regression (p. 441)
partial correlation (p. 440)
partial tables (p. 429)
path analysis (p. 448)
path coefficient (p. 448)
spurious relation (p. 427)

---

## Study Questions

---

1. The first table below shows the relationship between religion and life satisfaction. The second table shows the relationship between religion and life satisfaction when a third variable is held constant.
   a. Examine the relationship between the independent and dependent variables in the two tables by making a percentage comparison.
   b. Define the control variable. How does it affect the original relationship?

Life Satisfaction by Religion

|  | Religion | |
|---|---|---|
|  | Protestant | Catholic |
| Satisfied | 256 | 126 |
| Not satisfied | 258 | 139 |
| Total | 514 | 265 |

Life Satisfaction by Religion Controlling for a Third Variable

|  | Education | | | | | |
|---|---|---|---|---|---|---|
|  | High | | Medium | | Low | |
|  | Prot-estant | Cath-olic | Prot-estant | Cath-olic | Prot-estant | Cath-olic |
| Satisfied | 89 | 13 | 116 | 35 | 51 | 78 |
| Not satisfied | 104 | 20 | 124 | 59 | 30 | 60 |
| Total | 193 | 33 | 240 | 94 | 81 | 138 |

2. The accompanying table shows the relationship between voting and social class, controlling for gender.
   a. Examine and describe (by making a percentage comparison) the relationship between the independent and dependent variables in the partial tables.
   b. Reconstruct the bivariate table showing the relationship between gender and social class.
   c. Reconstruct the bivariate table showing the relationship between gender and voting.
   d. Reconstruct the bivariate table showing the relationship between voting and social class.

Voting by Social Class Controlling for Sex

|  | Male | | | Female | | |
|---|---|---|---|---|---|---|
|  | Upper Class | Lower Class | Total | Upper Class | Lower Class | Total |
| Democratic | 55 | 45 | 100 | 115 | 285 | 400 |
| Republican | 545 | 355 | 900 | 285 | 615 | 900 |
| Total | 600 | 400 | 1,000 | 400 | 900 | 1,300 |

3. Using the data from question 6 in Chapter 16:
   a. Obtain the partial correlation between unemployment and political stability controlling for economic development.
   b. Obtain the partial correlation between unemployment and economic development controlling for political stability.

c. Obtain the multiple regression equation using political stability and level of economic development as independent variables and unemployment rate as the dependent variable. Evaluate the relative effect of each independent variable on unemployment by comparing the beta weights.
d. What percentage of the variance in unemployment is explained by the two independent variables taken together?

## Computer Exercises

1. Using the GSS file that accompanies this text, or a dataset of your own, construct a cross-tabulation table using a third variable as a control. Does the original relationship change with the introduction of the third variable? If so, how? (See Appendix A, pp. 519–522.)
2. Using interval level variables, generate a PARTIAL CORR and interpret the results. Do you find evidence of a spurious relationship? Why or why not? (See Appendix A, pp. 522–524.)
3. Identify an interval level dependent variable whose variance you wish to explain. Choose at least three other interval level independent variables and generate a REGRESSION. Interpret the impact of each independent variable on the level of the dependent variable. (See Appendix A, pp. 524–530.)

## Additional Readings

Achen, Christopher H. *Interpreting and Using Regression.* Newbury Park, Calif.: Sage, 1982.
Black, Thomas R. *Evaluating Social Science Research.* Thousand Oaks, Calif., Sage, 1993.
Blalock, Hubert M., Jr., ed. *Causal Models in the Social Sciences.* 2d ed. Hawthorne, N.Y.: Aldine, 1985.
Duncan, O. D. "Path Analysis: Sociological Examples," *American Journal of Sociology,* 72: (1966): 1–16.
Edwards, Allen L. *Multiple Regression and the Analysis of Variance and Covariance.* 2d ed. New York: Freeman, 1985.
Healey, Joseph F. *Statistics: A Tool For Social Research.* 3d ed. Belmont, Calif.: Wadsworth, 1993.
Johnson, Richard A., and Dean W. Wichern. *Applied Multivariate Statistical Analysis.* Englewood Cliffs, N.J.: Prentice-Hall, 1982.
Lewis-Beck, Michael S. *Applied Regression: An Introduction.* Newbury Park, Calif.: Sage, 1982.

# CHAPTER 18

# Index Construction and Scaling Methods

**Index Construction**

    Defining the Purpose of the Index

    Selecting and Collecting Data

    Selecting the Base of Comparison

    Methods of Aggregation and Weighting

    Index Construction: Examples

    Attitude Indexes

**Scaling Methods**

    Likert Scales

    Other Composite Measures

    Guttman Scaling

    Guttman Scale Application: An Example

    Factor Analysis

"How are we doing?" People interested in answering that question tend to refer to a number of "thermometers" such as the Consumer Price Index, which measures the ups and downs of inflation, or the FBI Uniform Crime Report, which serves as a measure of social order. One group of concerned social scientists, centered at the Fordham Institute for Innovation in Social Policy in Tarrytown, New York, has developed a measure of how well the nation is confronting social issues. Its report, "The Index of Social Health," analyzes the progress made in solving social problems. The institute's researchers keep track of changes in 16 socioeconomic indicators, including teenage suicide, high school dropout rates, and out-of-pocket health costs for the elderly. They then calculate a single figure, ranging from 0 to 100. The higher the figure, the healthier the nation.

In their 1992 report, 9 of the 16 indicators either stayed the same or declined; the rise in the other 7 was sufficient to raise the total index—a sign that total social health is increasing. Dr. Marc L. Miringoff, the institute's director and author of this report, notes that the index often rises during presidential election years, a response, he believes, to the increase in funding typical of those periods.[1] How social scientists construct such indexes, and why they do so, are the major topics discussed in this chapter.

I N CHAPTER 7, WE DEFINED MEASUREMENT AS A PROCEDURE IN which the researcher assigns symbols or numbers to empirical properties according to rules. We also discussed the structure of measurement, the idea of isomorphism, the four levels of measurement, and techniques for assessing validity and reliability. In this chapter, we will present the more advanced topics of index construction and scaling.

We first discuss the logic of index construction and present several techniques for constructing indexes. Next, we discuss the Likert scaling technique, which measures attitudes on the ordinal and the interval levels of measurement. Then we present and illustrate Guttman scaling, or scalogram analysis, as a method for scaling. The Guttman technique can be applied to nominal and ordinal levels of analysis.

Indexes and scales are measuring instruments. They are designed to more reliably represent the complexities inherent in human behavior. Indeed, concepts such as power, equity, freedom, intelligence, and bureaucracy are extremely difficult to measure because, among other things, they are composites of several empirical properties. Indexes and scales are means of measuring such complex phenomena.

In most cases, indexes and scales are composite measures, constructed by combining two or more variables, which are employed as indicators. These are tech-

1. "Social Health is Improving, A Study Says," *New York Times*, 24 October 1994, p. A15.

nically referred to as **items.** For example, socioeconomic status is a common index constructed by combining three indicators: income, education, and occupation.

Social scientists employ scales and indexes for several reasons. First, they enable researchers to represent several variables by a single score that reduces the difficulties of dealing with complex data. Second, scales and indexes provide quantitative measures that are amenable to more precise statistical manipulation. Finally, indexes and scales increase the reliability of measurement. A score on a scale or an index is considered a more reliable indicator of the property being measured than is a measure based on a response to a single question or item. Exam grades provide a familiar example. Few students would like to have an exam grade determined solely by their answer to a single multiple-choice or true-false question. In the first place, the total universe of course material is not likely to be covered. Second, if a student misinterprets or makes a mistake on any one question, that one error could lead the professor to the wrong conclusion about the student's knowledge of the topic. If there are a larger number of questions on the test, the grade would be more accurate. Following this line of argument, we see that researchers use multiple-item scales and indexes to increase the reliability of the measurement and to obtain greater precision.

Scales differ from indexes by their greater rigor. Whereas researchers construct indexes by the simple accumulation of scores, they pay greater attention to tests of validity and reliability when they construct scales. Moreover, most scales involve the underlying principle of **unidimensionality.** According to this principle, the items comprising a scale reflect a single dimension, and can be placed on a continuum presumed to apply to one and only one concept.

Unidimensionality does, however, prevent variety in scaling purposes and specific techniques. The item analyses used in some scaling techniques are employed to identify questions or items that do not belong in the set. Other scaling techniques permit us to rank items by level of difficulty or intensity. In addition, some scaling methods produce interval-level scales, thereby avoiding the limitations imposed by nominal or ordinal data.

Before constructing a new scale, it is important to make a survey of the literature to ascertain if an appropriate scale is already available. The works listed in the additional readings at the end of this chapter constitute a comprehensive source of information on scales available in the social sciences.

---

# Index Construction

The combination of two or more items or indicators yields a composite measure, usually referred to as an **index.** For example, the consumer price index (CPI) is a composite measure of changes in retail prices. The retail prices that make up the index are comprised of eight major groups: food, housing, apparel, transportation, medical care, personal care, reading and recreation, and other goods and services. The approximately 400 commodities and services included in the CPI were selected because they were considered to be representative of the price trends displayed by the subgroups of related items. These include the cost of diverse commodities and services, such as rice, gasoline, haircuts, men's work gloves, women's wool suits, rent, and interest on mortgages. The Department of Labor collects data on prices of these 400 commodities and services in 50 urban areas. These areas have been selected as representative of the urban characteristics, such as city size, climate, population density, and income level, that affect the way in which families spend their money. Within each city, price quotations are recorded in the shops where families of wage and salaried workers typically purchase goods and services. For each item, the prices reported by the various sources are combined and weighted to ascertain average price changes for the city. The Department of Labor prepares index figures monthly for the country as a whole and for each of five major cities, and quarterly for other cities.[2]

Four major problems are involved in constructing indexes: defining the purpose for which the index is being compiled, selecting sources of data, selecting the base for comparison, and selecting methods of aggregation and weighting.

## Defining the Purpose of the Index

Two questions are essential to the process of index construction: what are we attempting to measure, and how are we going to use the measure? Logically speaking, if $A$ is an index of $X$, $A$ may still be only one of several indexes of $X$. Thus some kind of supporting evidence is needed to make the case that the values of $A$ correspond to the values of $X$ in a more precise and valid way than do other indexes. Most often, $X$ is a broad concept, such as public welfare or political participation. Such concepts consist of a complex combination of phenomena, subject to differing interpretations. Accordingly, no single indicator will cover all the dimensions of a concept, and a number of indicators have to be selected. Each indicator in turn serves a specific purpose that must be set forth and explained prior to construction of the index.

## Selecting and Collecting Data

Researchers can employ either obtrusive or unobtrusive methods of data collection (or both) to construct indexes. They decide which source of data to use depending on the purpose of the index and on the research design employed. In all cases, the investigator must ascertain that the data pertain strictly to the phenomenon being measured. This decision involves the issues of validity and reliability discussed in Chapter 7.

---

2. The following discussion is based on U.S. Bureau of Labor Statistics, *The Consumer Price Index: A Short Description of the Index as Revised* (Washington, D.C.: U.S. Government Printing Office, 1964), and William H. Wallace, *Measuring Price Changes: A Study of Price Indexes* (Richmond, Va.: Federal Reserve Bank of Richmond, 1970).

## ·Selecting the Base of Comparison

For purposes of comparison, indexes are expressed in the form of a proportion, a percentage, or a ratio. Each of these measures can be calculated either in terms of the actual data collected or reported, or in terms of another year's data, which is used as a numerical base for adjusting noncomparable figures in order to enable their comparison. A *proportion* is defined as the frequency of observations in any given category ($f_i$) divided by the total number of observations ($N$), or $f_i/N$. A proportion may range from zero to one. A proportion becomes a percentage when multiplied by 100 ($f_i/N \times 100$), and a *percentage,* by definition, may range from zero to 100. A *ratio* is a fraction that expresses the relative magnitude of any two sets of frequencies. To find the ratio between two frequencies, take the first frequency and divide by the second. For example, if a group consisted of 500 females and 250 males, the ratio of females to males is found by dividing 500 by 250, or 2/1.

Table 18.1 illustrates the use of these measures. It reports the frequencies, proportions, and percentages of selected criminal offenses in a New Jersey city by the sources of the official data.[3] The first, crime in New Jersey (CNJ), is compiled annually by the office of the state attorney general. The other data were compiled from the municipal court dockets (MCD) in the city.

An examination of the table reveals serious ambiguities in the crime data. First, there are differences in the amounts of officially recognized crimes: CNJ reports more offenses than court dockets do. This is consistent with the fact that court dockets report information from a higher jurisdiction than CNJ—CNJ reports offenses that are known to police, whereas court dockets report cases in which offenders have been identified, arrested, and booked on official complaints. Given that many offenses occur for which offenders are not apprehended, we

**Table 18.1**
Selected Offenses and Source of Information

| Selected Offenses | CNJ | | | MCD | | |
|---|---|---|---|---|---|---|
| | $f$ | Proportion | % | $f$ | Proportion | % |
| Armed robbery | 23 | .04 | 4.0 | 0 | .00 | .0 |
| Robbery | 17 | .03 | 3.0 | 5 | .01 | 1.0 |
| Atrocious assault | 13 | .02 | 2.0 | 2 | .007 | .7 |
| Simple assault | 223 | .40 | 40.0 | 250 | .89 | 89.0 |
| Break and entry | 206 | .37 | 37.0 | 1 | .003 | .3 |
| Larceny | 78 | .14 | 14.0 | 24 | .09 | 9.0 |
| Total | 560 | 1.00 | 100.0 | 282 | 1.00 | 100.0 |

3. The frequencies are reported in W. Boyd Littrell, "The Problem of Jurisdiction and Official Statistics of Crime," in *Current Issues of Social Policy,* ed. W. Boyd Littrell and Gideon Sjoberg (Newbury Park, Calif.: Sage, 1976), p. 236.

would expect attrition of cases as they move upward through the levels of each jurisdiction. Second, the data for the "simple assault" category are highly problematic because it appears that municipal courts heard more cases of specific offenses than were known to the police in a city where the courts and the police share the same jurisdiction. Such a situation is quite improbable. This example suggests that were an index based on these data, it would be misleading.

*Shifting the Base.*   In order to make meaningful comparisons of different indexes, or of the same index during different years or between regions, we are often required to "shift the base" of the index. When we *shift a base,* we are essentially converting the data, or standardizing it, in a way to make them comparable. This procedure is often methodologically necessary because only by converting, or basing, our data on a uniform measure can social scientists analyze trends or changes in the phenomena being studied. For example, we might shift the base of an index number series from one year to another. Uniformity would be achieved by setting the values for that year at 100. As we shall see, the Cost of Living Index employs such a procedure. It uses the prices for a selected year as the base for comparing prices for the next five or ten years.

In the following example (see Table 18.2), we will be converting the values of the old index of small business startups based on 1990 data into a new index of startups, one based on 1986 data. We do so because we have hypothesized that the interest rate for small-business loans in an earlier year, 1986, may have had greater impact on startups in the sector under study than did similar changes in the later year, 1990. To obtain the new index (values based on 1986 data) for 1990, we divide the original figure (based on 1990 data) for 1986 by 70 and then multiply by 100. This results in $(70/70) \times 100 = 100$. The new value for 1987 equals $(80/70) \times 100 = 114.3$, and so forth, until all the original figures have been converted into the new series.

**Table 18.2**
Changing the Base of an Index Number

| Year | Values of Old Index (1990=100) | Values of New Index (1986=100) |
|------|------|------|
| 1986 | 70 | 100.0 |
| 1987 | 80 | 114.3 |
| 1988 | 60 | 85.7 |
| 1989 | 95 | 135.7 |
| 1990 | 100 | 142.9 |
| 1991 | 115 | 164.3 |
| 1992 | 120 | 171.4 |
| 1993 | 118 | 168.6 |
| 1994 | 105 | 150.0 |

## Methods of Aggregation and Weighting

A common method for constructing indexes is by computing aggregate values. The aggregates can be either simple or weighted, depending on the purpose of the index.

*Simple Aggregates.*    Table 18.3 illustrates the construction of a simple aggregative price index. The prices of each commodity $(C_i)$ in any given year are added to give the index for that year. As noted earlier, it is convenient to designate some year as a base, which is set equal to 100. In this example, all the indexes are expressed in the last row as a percentage of the 1990 figure, obtained by dividing each of the numbers by the value in the base period ($20.13) and multiplying by 100. Symbolically,

$$PI = \Sigma p_n / \Sigma p_o \times 100 \qquad (18.1)$$

where $PI$ = price index

$p$ = the price of an individual commodity

$o$ = the base period at which price changes are measured

$n$ = the given period that is being compared with the base

The formula for a particular year (for instance 1994, with 1990 being the base) is

$$PI_{90,94} = \Sigma p_{94} / \Sigma p_{90} \times 100 \qquad (18.2)$$

Thus,

$$PI_{90,94} = \frac{6.10 + 7.18 + 7.90 + 6.80}{3.21 + 5.40 + 6.62 + 4.90} \times 100$$

$$= \frac{27.98}{20.13} \times 100 = 139.00$$

*Weighted Aggregates.*    Simple aggregates may conceal the relative influence of each indicator of an index. To prevent such misrepresentation, **weighted**

**Table 18.3**
Construction of Simple Aggregative Index Numbers
(Hypothetical Unit Prices)

| Commodities | 1990 | 1991 | 1992 | 1993 | 1994 |
|---|---|---|---|---|---|
| $C_1$ | $3.21 | $4.14 | $4.90 | $5.80 | $6.10 |
| $C_2$ | 5.40 | 5.60 | 5.10 | 6.40 | 7.18 |
| $C_3$ | 6.62 | 8.10 | 9.00 | 8.35 | 7.90 |
| $C_4$ | 4.90 | 5.40 | 5.10 | 7.25 | 6.80 |
| Aggregate Value | $20.13 | $23.24 | $24.10 | $27.80 | $27.98 |
| Index | 100.00 | 115.45 | 119.72 | 138.10 | 139.00 |

**aggregates** are often used. To construct a weighted aggregative price index for the data in Table 18.3, list the quantities of the specified commodities and calculate them to determine what this aggregate of goods is worth each year at current prices. This means that each unit price is multiplied by the number of units, and the resulting values are summed for each period. Symbolically,

$$PI = \Sigma p_n q / \Sigma poq \times 100 \qquad (18.3)$$

where $q$ represents the quantity of the commodity marketed, produced, or consumed, that is, the quantity weight, or multiplier. The procedure, using the quantities in 1990 as multipliers, is illustrated in Table 18.4. Because the total value changes while the components of the aggregate do not, these changes must be due to price changes. Thus, the aggregative price index measures the changing value of a fixed aggregate of goods.

## Index Construction: Examples

Let us first look at a simple index developed to evaluate statistics textbooks used in the social sciences according to students' instructional needs.[4] The index, the Statistics Textbook Anxiety Rating Test (START), uses seven factors keyed to aspects of statistics textbooks. These factors are related to deficiencies in students' math backgrounds and the corresponding anxieties they arouse:

1. Reviews basic algebraic operations.
2. Contains a section on notations.
3. Includes exercise answers.
4. Explains exercise answers.
5. Does not use definitional formulas.
6. Uses relevant examples.
7. Explicitly addresses student statistics or math anxiety.

**Table 18.4**
Construction of Aggregative Index Weighted by Consumption in 1990

| Commod-ities | Consump-tion | Value of 1990 Quantity at Price of Specified Year | | | | |
| --- | --- | --- | --- | --- | --- | --- |
| | | 1990 | 1991 | 1992 | 1993 | 1994 |
| $C_1$ | 800 | $ 2,568 | $ 3,312 | $ 3,920 | $ 4,640 | $ 4,880 |
| $C_2$ | 300 | 1,620 | 1,680 | 1,530 | 1,920 | 2,154 |
| $C_3$ | 450 | 2,979 | 3,645 | 4,050 | 3,758 | 3,555 |
| $C_4$ | 600 | 2,940 | 3,240 | 3,060 | 4,350 | 4,080 |
| Aggregate value | | $10,107 | $11,877 | $12,560 | $14,668 | $14,669 |
| Index | | 100.0 | 117.5 | 124.3 | 145.1 | 145.1 |

4. Steven P. Schacht, "Statistics Textbooks: Pedagogical Tools or Impediments to Learning?" *Teaching Sociology,* 18 (1990): 390–396.

The index works as follows: textbooks are given a score on each factor—1 if the book meets the criterion, 0 if it does not. Summing all the scores yields a composite score ranging from 0 to 7. When the index was used to evaluate 12 popular textbooks, the scores ranged from 0 to 4.

Another example is the Sellin and Wolfgang Index of Delinquency. In order to evaluate crime control policies, policymakers require at least three major types of information: data on the incidence of crimes, data on the response of the criminal justice system, and data on sociodemographic characteristics. With respect to the incidence of crimes, a major problem is that offenses vary in nature and magnitude. Some result in death, others inflict losses of property, and still others merely cause inconvenience. A traditional way of comparing, say, one year's crime with another has been simply to count offenses, disregarding the differences in their character. Given the variety of crimes and their varying degrees of seriousness, such unweighted indexes are misleading. A police report that shows an overall decrease or increase in the total number of offenses committed may be misleading if there are significant changes in the type of offenses committed. For example, a small decline in auto theft but a large increase in armed robbery would lead to a decline in an unweighted crime index because reported auto thefts are usually much greater in absolute numbers than reported armed robberies.

In a pioneering attempt to tackle this problem in the area of delinquency, Thorsten Sellin and Marvin Wolfgang developed their weighting system by distributing 141 carefully prepared accounts of different crimes to three samples of police officers, juvenile court judges, and college students.[5] The accounts of the different crimes included combinations of circumstances, such as death or hospitalization of the victim, type of weapon, and value of property stolen, damaged, or destroyed; for example, "The offender robs a person at gunpoint," "The victim struggles and is shot to death," "The offender forces open a cash register in a department store and steals five dollars," "The offender smokes marijuana." Members of the samples were asked to rate each of these on a "category scale" and a "magnitude estimating scale." The researchers used their ratings to construct the weighting system. For example, a crime with the following "attributes" would be given the following number of points:

| | |
|---|---|
| A house is forcibly entered. | 1 |
| A person is murdered. | 26 |
| The spouse receives a minor injury. | 1 |
| Between $251 and $2,000 is taken. | 2 |
| Total score | 30 |

With such an index, policymakers and researchers can make meaningful comparisons over time and between different communities, as they take into account the seriousness of the crimes committed in addition to the frequencies of such crimes.

5. Thorsten Sellin and Marvin E. Wolfgang, *The Measurement of Delinquency* (New York: Wiley, 1964).

## Attitude Indexes

To construct *attitude indexes,* researchers prepare a set of questions, selected on an a priori basis. Numerical values (e.g., 0 to 4 or 1 to 5) are assigned arbitrarily to the item or question responses, and these values are added to obtain total scores. Investigators then interpret the scores as indicators of the attitudes of the respondents. Consider the following five statements designed to measure alienation:

1. Sometimes I have the feeling that other people are using me.
   ☐ Strongly agree       ☐ Disagree
   ☐ Agree                ☐ Strongly disagree
   ☐ Neither agree nor disagree
2. We are just so many cogs in the machinery of life.
   ☐ Strongly agree       ☐ Disagree
   ☐ Agree                ☐ Strongly disagree
   ☐ Neither agree nor disagree
3. The future looks very dismal.
   ☐ Strongly agree       ☐ Disagree
   ☐ Agree                ☐ Strongly disagree
   ☐ Neither agree nor disagree
4. More and more, I feel helpless in the face of what's happening in the world today.
   ☐ Strongly agree       ☐ Disagree
   ☐ Agree                ☐ Strongly disagree
   ☐ Neither agree nor disagree
5. People like me have no influence in society.
   ☐ Strongly agree       ☐ Disagree
   ☐ Agree                ☐ Strongly disagree
   ☐ Neither agree nor disagree

Suppose that we arbitrarily assign response scores in the following way: Strongly agree = 4; Agree = 3; Neither = 2; Disagree = 1; and Strongly disagree = 0. A respondent who answers "Strongly agree" to all five statements will have a total score of 20, indicating a high degree of alienation; a respondent who answers "Strongly disagree" to all five statements will have a total score of 0, indicating that that person is not alienated at all. In reality, most respondents will obtain scores between these two extremes. The researcher will then work out a system that classifies respondents according to their degree of alienation on the basis of their total scores. For example, respondents who score 0 to 6 are not alienated, respondents who score from 7 to 13 are somewhat alienated, and those who score between 14 and 20 are most alienated.

This index is sometimes termed an *arbitrary scale* because nothing about the procedure guarantees that any one statement or item taps the same attitude as the other items. Is item 3 tapping the same aspect of alienation as item 5? Does item 4 correspond to the remaining items? Will another researcher who uses the index get the same findings? That is, is the index reliable? We will address these cardinal questions in our discussion of scaling methods.

---

# Scaling Methods

## Likert Scales

Likert scaling is a method designed to measure attitudes. To construct a **Likert scale,** researchers usually follow six steps—they (1) compile possible scale items, (2) administer these items to a random sample of respondents, (3) compute a total score for each respondent, (4) determine the *discriminative power* of items, (5) select the scale items, and (6) test reliability.

*Compiling Possible Scale Items.*    In the first step, the researcher compiles a series of items that express a wide range of attitudes, from extremely positive to extremely negative. Each item requires the respondent to check one of the offered five fixed-alternative expressions such as "strongly agree," "agree," "neither agree nor disagree," "disagree," and "strongly disagree," comprising a continuum of responses. (Occasionally, three, four, six, or seven fixed-alternative expressions are used. Optional expressions include "almost always," "frequently," "occasionally," "rarely," and "almost never".) In this five-point continuum, values of 1, 2, 3, 4, 5 or 5, 4, 3, 2, 1 are assigned. These values express the relative weights and their direction, determined by the favorableness or unfavorableness of the item.

In a classic example of the Likert method, Wayne Kirchner developed a 24-item scale to measure attitudes toward employment of older people. The following four items illustrate the scoring technique.[6]

1. Most companies are unfair to older employees.
   - ☐ Strongly agree      ☐ Disagree
   - ☐ Agree               ☐ Strongly disagree
   - ☐ Uncertain
2. I think that older employees make better employees.
   - ☐ Strongly agree      ☐ Disagree
   - ☐ Agree               ☐ Strongly disagree
   - ☐ Uncertain
3. In a case where two people can do a job about equally well, I'd pick the older person for the job.
   - ☐ Strongly agree      ☐ Disagree
   - ☐ Agree               ☐ Strongly disagree
   - ☐ Uncertain

---

6. Wayne K. Kirchner, "The Attitudes of Special Groups toward the Employment of Older Persons," *Journal of Gerontology,* 12 (1957): 216–220.

4. I think older employees have as much ability to learn new methods as other employees.
   ☐ Strongly agree     ☐ Disagree
   ☐ Agree              ☐ Strongly disagree
   ☐ Uncertain

Kirchner scored this scale by assigning higher weights to responses to positive items (acceptance of hiring older persons) as follows: Strongly agree, 5; Agree, 4; Uncertain, 3; Disagree, 2; Strongly disagree, 1. If he had included negative items (that is, items indicating rejection of employment of older persons) in the scale, their weights would have been reversed.

*Administering All Items.*   In the second step, a large number of respondents, selected randomly from the population to be measured, are asked to indicate their attitudes on the list of items.

*Computing a Total Score.*   In this step, the researcher calculates a total score for each respondent by summing the value of all items checked. Suppose that a respondent checked "Strongly agree" in item 1 (score 5), "Uncertain" in item 2 (score 3), "Agree" in item 3 (score 4), and "Disagree" in item 4 (score 2). This person's total score is $5 + 3 + 4 + 2 = 14$.

*Determining the Discriminative Power.*   In the fourth step, the researcher has to determine a basis for the selection of items for the final scale. Regardless of the method employed, the objective is to find items that consistently distinguish those who are high on the attitude continuum from those who are low. This can be done by applying either the *internal consistency method*—that is, by correlating each item with the total score and retaining those with the highest correlations—or with *item analysis*. Both methods yield an internally consistent scale. With item analysis, the researcher subjects each item to a measurement of its ability to differentiate the highs (clearly positive attitudes) from the lows (clearly negative attitudes). This measure is called the **discriminative power (DP)** of the item. In calculating the *DP,* we add the scored items for each respondent and place the scores in an array, usually from lowest to highest. Next we compare the range above the upper quartile ($Q_1$) with that below the lower quartile ($Q_3$), and calculate the *DP* as the difference between the weighted means of the scores above $Q_1$ and of those that fall below $Q_3$, as illustrated in Table 18.5.

*Selecting the Scale Items.*   The *DP* value is computed for each of the possible scale items, and those items with the highest *DP* values are selected. These are the items that best discriminate among individuals expressing differing attitudes toward the measured attitude.

*Testing Reliability.*   The reliability of the scale can be tested in much the same manner as with other measuring procedures. For example, we can select

**Table 18.5**
Table for Computing the *DP* for One Item

| Group | Number in Group | 1 | 2 | 3 | 4 | 5 | Weighted Total* | Weighted Mean† | *DP* $(Q_1 - Q_3)$ |
|---|---|---|---|---|---|---|---|---|---|
| High (top 25%) | 9 | 0 | 1 | 2 | 3 | 3 | 35 | 3.89 | |
| | | | | | | | | | 2.00 |
| Low (bottom 25%) | 9 | 1 | 8 | 0 | 0 | 0 | 17 | 1.89 | |

*Weighted total = score × number who check that score
†Weighted mean = $\dfrac{\text{weighted total}}{\text{number in group}}$

enough items for two scales (at least 100) and divide them into two sets, constituting two scales. We can then employ the split-half reliability test (see Chapter 7).

## Other Composite Measures

Social scientists have developed various scaling procedures that incorporate a number of features from Likert scaling techniques. These procedures almost always include the steps described above, that is, the initial compilation of possible scale items, administering the items to a large number of respondents, and some methods for selecting the set of items to be included in the final scale. The most common format for the items is a rating scale on which respondents are asked to make a judgment in terms of sets of ordered categories.

Most statistical computer programs today include procedures and statistics that make it easier to select items for scales and evaluate how well the various items measure the underlying phenomena.

One of the simplest statistics used to examine items is the bivariate correlation (Pearson's *r*), which links each item with the whole scale. In general, items strongly associated with other items will show higher overall correlations with the total scale. Examining the bivariate correlation helps researchers to decide which items to include in the scale and which items to discard. Another helpful statistic is *Cronbach's alpha,* which is an estimate of the average of all possible split-half reliability coefficients. (For a discussion of reliability, see Chapter 7.) The alpha measures the extent to which the individual items comprising the scale "hang together."[7] A high alpha (.70 is an acceptable level) indicates that the items in the scale are "tightly connected."

## Guttman Scaling

The **Guttman scale,** first developed by Louis Guttman in the early 1940s, was designed to incorporate an empirical test of the unidimensionality of a set of items within the scale-construction process. Guttman suggested that if the items com-

---

7. See William Sims Bainbridge, *Survey Research: A Computer-assisted Introduction* (Belmont, Calif.: Wadsworth, 1989).

prising the scale tap the same attitudinal dimension, they can be arranged on a continuum that indicates varying degrees of one underlying dimension. More explicitly, Guttman scales are unidimensional and cumulative. The cumulative characteristic implies that a researcher can order the items by degree of difficulty and that respondents who reply positively to a difficult item will also respond positively to less difficult items. If we take an example from the physical world, we know that if an object is four feet long, it is longer than one foot and longer than two or three feet. In the social world, we know that if an executive director of a corporation would allow his daughter to marry an electrician, he would also agree to an electrician belonging to his social club. Similarly, if he did not object to this person as a member of his club, he would not mind having him as a neighbor. Table 18.6 illustrates the scale that would result from administering these three items to a group of respondents. This scale is unidimensional as well as cumulative—the items can be ranked on a single underlying dimension, such as social acceptability; the scale is cumulative in that none of the respondents have given totally mixed responses to the questions in the order in which they were presented to them. Thus information on the position of any respondent's last positive response allows the researcher to predict all of the responses to the scale items following the selected item.

In practice, a perfect Guttman scale is rarely obtained. In most cases, inconsistencies are present. Consequently, it is necessary to establish a criterion for evaluating the unidimensional and cumulative assumptions. For this purpose, Guttman developed the **coefficient of reproducibility ($CR$).** This scale, which measures the degree of conformity to a perfect scalable pattern as a way of ascertaining the validity of the scale, will be discussed below.

*Selecting Scale Items.* In discussing the considerations involved in discovering and selecting items for a Guttman scale, Raymond L. Gorden lists three conditions that must be met, in the following order:[8]

---

**Table 18.6**
A Hypothetical Perfect Guttman Scale

| | Items in the Scale | | | |
|---|---|---|---|---|
| Respondent | Item 1:<br>Admit to close<br>kinship by marriage | Item 2:<br>Admit to the<br>same social club | Item 3:<br>Admit as a<br>neighbor | Total<br>Score |
| A | + | + | + | 3 |
| B | − | + | + | 2 |
| C | − | − | + | 1 |
| D | − | − | − | 0 |

+ indicates agreement with the statement; − indicates disagreement.

---

8. Raymond L. Gorden, *Unidimensional Scaling of Social Variables* (New York: Macmillan, 1977), p. 46.

1. There must actually be an attitude toward the object (class of objects, events, or ideas) in the minds of the people in the population to be sampled and tested.
2. A set of statements about the object must be found that has meaning to the members of the sample and elicits from them a response that is a valid indicator of that attitude.
3. The items in this set of statements or questions must represent different degrees along a single dimension.

Researchers can select attitude scale items by a variety of methods from all available sources: newspapers, books, scholarly articles, and their own knowledge of the phenomenon. Interviewing experts as well as a subgroup of respondents will also help in securing good items. After a large set of potential items is compiled, the investigator selects a preliminary set of items. Items should be selected that clearly relate to the attitude being measured and cover the total continuum from strongly favorable to strongly unfavorable statements. Two to seven response categories may be constructed for each statement. The most common formats are Likert-type items with five-point scales, as in the following example:

Please indicate how much you agree or disagree with the following statement: Nowadays a person has to live pretty much for today and let tomorrow take care of itself.
  ☐ Strongly agree      ☐ Disagree
  ☐ Agree               ☐ Strongly disagree
  ☐ Neither agree nor disagree

After selecting the items the researcher usually includes them in a questionnaire that he or she administers to a sample of the target population. Before the answers to the questionnaire are scored, items are arranged so that higher numbers will consistently stand for either the most positive or most negative feelings. Items that do not correspond to this pattern should be rearranged.

***Calculating the Coefficient of Reproducibility.***    The coefficient of reproducibility is defined as the extent to which the total response pattern on a set of items can be reproduced even if only the total score is known. This depends on the extent to which the pattern of responses conforms to a perfectly scalable pattern, demonstrated in Table 18.6. When the obtained coefficient of reproducibility is below the required .90 criterion, the scale needs to be refined until the coefficient of reproducibility reaches the desired level. The *CR* is calculated as follows:

$$CR = 1 - \frac{\Sigma_e}{Nr} \qquad (18.4)$$

where $CR$ = the coefficient of reproducibility
  $\Sigma_e$ = the total number of inconsistencies
  $Nr$ = the total number of responses (number of cases × number of items)

A *CR* of .90 is the minimum standard for accepting a scale as unidimensional.

## Guttman Scale Application: An Example

After the researcher has developed and refined a Guttman scale, he or she can present the results to describe the distribution of the variable measured, as well as relate the scale to other variables in the study. An example of the development and application of a Guttman scale is Jules J. Wanderer's study on the severity of riots in American cities.[9] This study is a particularly interesting application of the Guttman scaling technique because it is based on behavioral indicators rather than on attitudes. The investigator analyzed 75 riots and criminal disorders reported to have taken place during the summer of 1967. The information Wanderer used in the construction of the scale was provided by the mayors' offices at the request of a U.S. Senate subcommittee. The scale includes the following items of riot severity: killing, calling up of the National Guard, calling up of the state police, sniping, looting, interference with firefighters, and vandalism. These items are ordered either from most to least severe or from least to most frequently reported. The coefficient of reproducibility of this Guttman scale of riot severity is .92. Table 18.7 presents the scale and the distribution of the cities along the scale. Cities are organized into eight scale types according to the degree of severity, with 8 indicating the least severe and 1 the most severe riot activity.

At the second stage of the analysis, Wanderer treated riot severity, as measured by the Guttman scale, as a dependent variable and examined a set of independent variables in terms of their relationship to riot severity. For example, he found a relationship between the percentage increase of nonwhites participating and riot severity as measured by the scale; that is, once a riot takes place, the greater the percentage of nonwhites rioting, the greater the severity of the riot.

### Table 18.7
#### A Guttman Scale of Riot Severity

| Scale Type | Percent of Cities (n = 75) | Items Reported |
|---|---|---|
| 8 | 4 | No scale items |
| 7 | 19 | "Vandalism" |
| 6 | 13 | All of the above and "interference with firefighters" |
| 5 | 16 | All of the above and "looting" |
| 4 | 13 | All of the above and "sniping" |
| 3 | 7 | All of the above and "called state police" |
| 2 | 17 | All of the above and "called National Guard" |
| 1 | 11 | All of the above and "law officer or civilian killed" |
| Total | 100 | |

Based on Jules J. Wanderer, "An Index of Riot Severity and Some Correlates," *American Journal of Sociology,* 74 (1969): 503.

9. Jules J. Wanderer, "An Index of Riot Severity and Some Correlates," *American Journal of Sociology,* 74 (1969): 503.

The Guttman scale of riot severity developed in this study suggests that the events that constitute riots and civil criminal disorders are neither erratic nor randomly generated. On the contrary, by employing a Guttman scale, a researcher can predict the sequence of events that will take place for each level of riot severity.

## Factor Analysis

**Factor analysis** is a statistical technique for classifying a large number of inter-related variables into a limited number of dimensions or factors. It is a useful method for constructing multiple-item scales, where each scale represents a dimension of a highly abstract construct. Take, for example, community satisfaction. Many questions or items can be used to describe community satisfaction: satisfaction with public schools, shopping facilities, garbage collection, the local churches, the friendliness of the neighborhood, and so forth. However, the researcher can simplify the measurement of community satisfaction by identifying a number of underlying dimensions of community satisfaction.

Some studies dealing with community satisfaction have indeed adopted this approach. Researchers divided community or neighborhood satisfaction into the following subconcepts: (1) satisfaction with service delivery, (2) satisfaction with community organization, (3) satisfaction with neighborhood quality, and (4) satisfaction with cultural amenities. The relationship between the subconcepts and community satisfaction could then be expressed as follows:

community satisfaction = $S$ (service delivery) + $S$ (community organization) + $S$ (neighborhood quality) + $S$ (cultural amenities)

where $S$ = satisfaction.

In this formulation, community satisfaction is a construct represented by a few basic factors. In factor analysis, the factors are not directly observed; rather, they are defined by a group of variables or items that are components of the abstract factors. The research actually begins by selecting a large number of items to define each of the factors. These are the items administered to the respondents via questionnaires during the course of the study.

In the first stage of factor analysis, the researcher computes bivariate correlations (Pearson's $r$) between all the items. He or she then places the correlations into a matrix format. The correlation matrix is then used as input in the factor analysis procedure. The extraction of factors is based on the identification of common variation between a set of items. The method assumes that variables or items representing a single dimension will be highly correlated with that dimension.

By this we mean that the correlation between an item and a factor is represented by a **factor loading.** A factor loading is similar to a correlation coefficient; it varies between zero and one and can be interpreted in the same way. Table 18.8 presents the factor loadings of 14 items expressing community satisfaction on four factors. The items with the highest loading on each factor are underlined; these items are taken as the best indicators for these factors. Among the 14 items, only

**Table 18.8**

Factor Loadings of Community Satisfaction Items

| Item Description | Factor 1 | Factor 2 | Factor 3 | Factor 4 |
|---|---|---|---|---|
| 1. Neighborliness | .12361 | .03216 | .76182 | .32101 |
| 2. Parks and playgrounds | .62375 | .33610 | .32101 | .02120 |
| 3. Public schools | .74519 | .34510 | .12102 | .01320 |
| 4. Shopping facilities | .32100 | .06121 | .68123 | .12356 |
| 5. Police protection | .90987 | .12618 | .21361 | .01320 |
| 6. Local churches | .21032 | .75847 | .21362 | .11620 |
| 7. Church groups and organization in the community | .01362 | .83210 | .01231 | .11632 |
| 8. Community entertainment and recreational opportunities | .25617 | .01320 | .12341 | .75642 |
| 9. Cultural activities | .16320 | .12310 | .32134 | .82316 |
| 10. Quality of air | .02313 | .11621 | .83612 | .32131 |
| 11. Noise level | .26154 | .21320 | .78672 | .21368 |
| 12. Overcrowding | .24321 | .02151 | .91638 | .02016 |
| 13. Racial problems | .08091 | .11320 | .82316 | .16342 |
| 14. Neighborhood pride | .18642 | .11218 | .71321 | .18321 |
| Percentage of variance | 18.2 | 5.6 | 40.1 | 2.4 |

three have a high loading on factor 1. These items all refer to satisfaction with services; thus we can identify factor 1 as representing the dimension of *service delivery.* Similarly, factor 2 represents satisfaction with *community organization;* factor 3, *quality of life;* and factor 4, *cultural amenities.* Loadings of .30 or below are generally considered too weak to represent a factor. Examination of the results reveals that although all items displayed loadings on each of the factors, most item loadings are too weak to be considered as good indicators of the dimensions investigated.

The extent to which each factor is explained by the items' loadings is reflected in the percentage of explained variance. Generally, factors with the highest percentage of explained variance provide the most parsimonious representation of the items. That is, the researcher can employ this factor fairly exclusively to represent the dimension studied. The table reveals that the most parsimonious factor is quality of life (40.1 percent) and the least parsimonious is cultural amenities (2.4 percent).

In the final step of factor analysis, the researcher develops a composite scale for each factor. For each observation or item, a factor score (scale score) is cal-

**Table 18.9**
Standardized Factor Score Coefficients

| Item | Coefficient |
|------|-------------|
| 1    | .6812       |
| 10   | .7234       |
| 11   | .6916       |
| 12   | .8162       |
| 13   | .8110       |
| 14   | .6910       |

culated. A factor score is a case's score on a factor. It is obtained by using yet another type of coefficient, a **factor score coefficient.** To construct a case's factor score, we multiply the factor score coefficients for each variable by the standardized values of the variable obtained for that case. For example, Table 18.9 represents the factor score coefficients for the items loading on factor 3. We may construct a case's factor score $f_3$, a composite scale representing factor 3, as follows:

$$f_3 = .6812Z_1 + .7234Z_{10} + .6916Z_{11} + .8162Z_{12} + .8110Z_{13} + .6910Z_{14}$$

$Z_1$ through $Z_{14}$ represent the standardized values of items 1 through 14 for that case.

In conclusion, factor analysis is an efficient method for reorganizing the items a researcher is investigating into conceptually more precise groups of variables.

## Summary

**1.** An index is a composite measure of two or more indicators or items. The consumer price index (CPI), which is a composite measure of changes in retail prices, may be the best-known of frequently used indexes. Four major problems are involved in constructing indexes: defining the purpose for which the index is being compiled, selecting the sources of data, selecting the base for comparison, and selecting the methods of aggregation and weighting.

**2.** Scaling is a method of measuring the amount of a property possessed by a class of objects or events. It is most often associated with the measurement of attitudes. Attitude scales consist of a number of attitude statements with which the respondent is asked to agree or disagree. Scaling techniques are utilized to select the order of statements along some continuum. They transform a series of qualitative facts into a quantitative series. All the scales discussed in this chapter are either assumed to be unidimensional or can be tested for unidimensionality. This means that the items comprising the scale can be arranged on a continuum, which is presumed to reflect one and only one concept.

**3.** One technique for scale construction is the Likert scale. Likert scaling requires the researcher to compile possible scale items, administer them to a random sample of respondents, compute a total score for each respondent, determine the discriminative power of each item, and select the final scale items.

**4.** Another method of scaling is the Guttman scaling technique. This method was designed to incorporate an empirical test of the unidimensionality of a set of items within the scale construction process. A Guttman scale is unidimensional— items are ranked on a single underlying dimension—as well as cumulative, in that information on the position of any respondent's last positive response allows the researcher to predict all of that person's responses to the other items. To measure the degree of conformity to a perfect scalable pattern, Guttman developed the coefficient of reproducibility (*CR*). A coefficient of reproducibility of .90 is the conventional minimum standard for accepting a scale as unidimensional.

**5.** Factor analysis is a statistical technique for classifying a large number of interrelated variables into a smaller number of dimensions or factors. It is a useful method for the construction of multiple-item scales, where each scale represents a dimension in a more abstract construct.

---

## Key Terms for Review

---

coefficient of reproducibility (CR)
  (p. 468)
discriminative power (*DP*) (p. 466)
factor analysis (p. 471)
factor loading (p. 471)
factor score coefficient (p. 473)

Guttman scale (p. 467)
index (p. 457)
item (p. 457)
Likert scale (p. 465)
unidimensionality (p. 457)
weighted aggregate (p. 462)

---

## Study Questions

---

1. What is the difference between a scale and an index? Can you identify commonly used examples of each?
2. Why do social scientists use scales and indexes in their research?
3. Develop an index to measure "popularity" among college students. Use about ten subjects to obtain the data for your scale. Use a method of aggregation with items of the type "How many times . . . ?" "How often . . . ?" "How many . . . ?" Consider and incorporate weighting when appropriate. Discuss the problems of validity and reliability as they apply to your index. On the basis of your results, submit a revised index of popularity.
4. Based on the results to question 3, suggest how the index can be converted into a scale.
5. When would factor analysis be preferable to scaling? State your methodological as well as theoretical considerations.

## Computer Exercises

1. Using the GSS file, or a dataset of your own, construct a scale (e.g., using COMPUTEs) that makes sense to you. Generate the FREQUENCIES of your scale and determine if it has a normal distribution. (See Appendix A, pp. 514–515.)
2. Using the RELIABILITY procedure, evaluate the reliability of your scale. (See Appendix A, pp. 515–518.)

## Additional Readings

Beere, Carole A. *Gender Roles: A Handbook of Tests and Measures.* Westport, Conn.: Greenwood Press, 1990.

Bohrnstedt, George W., and Edgar F. Borgatta, eds. *Social Measurement: Current Issues.* Newbury Park, Calif.: Sage, 1981.

Brodsky, Stanley L., and H. O'Neal Smitherman. *Handbook of Scales for Research in Crime and Delinquency.* New York: Plenum Press, 1983.

Dawes, R. H., and T. W. Smith. "Attitude and Opinion Measurement." In *The Handbook of Social Psychology.* 3d ed., ed. Gardner Lindzey and Elliot Aronson. Hillsdale, N.J.: Erlbaum, 1985, pp. 507–566.

Kim, Jae-On, and Charles W. Mueller. *Introduction to Factor Analysis.* Newbury Park, Calif.: Sage, 1978.

Lodge, Milton. *Magnitude Scaling.* Newbury Park, Calif.: Sage, 1981.

Long, J. Scott. *Confirmatory Factor Analysis.* Newbury Park, Calif.: Sage, 1983.

Maranell, Gary M., ed. *Scaling: A Sourcebook for Behavioral Scientists.* 4th ed. Hawthorne, N.Y.: Aldine, 1974.

Miller, Delbert C. *Handbook of Research Design and Social Measurement.* 5th ed. Thousand Oaks, Calif.: Sage, 1991.

Robinson, John P., Jerrold G. Rusk, and Kendra B. Head. *Measures of Political Attitudes.* Ann Arbor: Institute for Social Research, University of Michigan, 1968.

Robinson, John P., and Philip R. Shaver. *Measures of Social Psychological Attitudes.* Rev. ed. Ann Arbor: Institute for Social Research, University of Michigan, 1973.

Shye, Samuel, ed. *Theory Construction and Data Analysis in the Behavioral Sciences.* San Francisco: Jossey-Bass, 1978.

Sullivan, John L., and Stanley Feldman. *Multiple Indicators: An Introduction.* Newbury Park, Calif.: Sage, 1979.

Touliatos, John, Barry F. Perlmutter, and Murray A. Straus. *Handbook of Family Measurement Techniques.* Thousand Oaks, Calif.: Sage, 1989.

# CHAPTER 19
# Inferences

Throughout the history of the United States, white men have enjoyed higher occupational prestige than women and members of racial/ethnic minorities. Researchers in numerous studies have examined the individual effects of race/ethnicity and gender on occupational prestige, but few have investigated the interactive effects of these variables. Two researchers, however, *have* studied these effects. Wu Xu and Ann Leffler drew a sample of occupations from 1980 census data, which they used to assess the relative effects of race/ethnicity and gender on occupational prestige.[1] They compared prestige across four racial/ethnic groups (white, black, Asian-American, and Hispanic), between genders, and between genders within each racial/ethnic group. They found that race has a stronger effect than gender on occupational prestige, but gender affects prestige differently in different racial groups. Their study showed that whites and Asian-Americans of both genders enjoy higher occupational prestige than blacks and Hispanics. Within groups they found that white and Asian-American women enjoy less occupational prestige than their male counterparts, but gender has a much stronger effect among Asian-Americans than among whites. They found that black and Hispanic women have more occupational prestige than men; however, the gender difference among Hispanics is very small. In the four groups, gender most affects the occupational prestige of Asian-Americans and least affects Hispanics.

The researchers in this study used hypothesis testing to support their theory that both race and gender influence occupational prestige. Using statistical techniques, they were able to make inferences about the entire population of the United States from their findings about a sample of the population.

I N THIS CHAPTER, WE DESCRIBE THE STRATEGY OF HYPOTHESIS testing by focusing on concepts such as the sampling distribution, Type I and Type II errors, and the level of significance. We then consider several methods of testing hypotheses about the relationship between two variables: difference between means, Pearson's $r$, the Mann-Whitney test, and the chi-square test.

In Chapter 8, we introduced the general idea of inferential statistics, which deal with the problem of evaluating population characteristics when only the sample evidence is given. We demonstrated that sample statistics may give good estimates of particular population parameters but that virtually any estimate will deviate from the true value owing to sampling fluctuations. The process of statistical inference enables investigators to evaluate the accuracy of their estimates.

Researchers also use inferential statistics to assess the probability of specific sample results under assumed population conditions. This type of inferential sta-

---

1. Wu Xu and Ann Leffler, "Gender and Race Effects on Occupational Prestige, Segregation, and Earnings," *Gender & Society,* Vol. 6, No. 3 (1992): 376–391.

tistics is called *hypothesis testing* and will occupy us throughout this chapter. With estimation, a researcher selects a sample to evaluate the population parameter; when a researcher tests hypotheses, by contrast, he or she makes assumptions about the population parameter in advance, and the sample then provides the test of these assumptions. With estimation, the sample provides information about single population parameters such as the mean income or the variance of education; with hypothesis testing, a researcher is usually making an inference about relationships among variables—for example, the relationship between education and income or between occupation and particular political attitudes.

# The Strategy of Testing Hypotheses

The first step in testing a hypothesis is to formulate it in statistical terms. We have already discussed how to draw a hypothesis from a theory or how to formulate a research problem as a hypothesis. However, in order to test the hypothesis, a researcher must formulate it in terms that can be analyzed with statistical tools. For example, if the purpose of the investigation is to establish that educated individuals have higher incomes than noneducated individuals, the statistical hypothesis might be that there is a positive correlation between education and income or that the mean income of a highly educated group will be larger than the mean income of a group with a lower level of education. In both cases, the researcher formulates the statistical hypothesis in terms of descriptive statistics (such as a correlation or a mean) and specifies a set of conditions about these statistics (such as a positive correlation or a difference between the means).

The statistical hypothesis always applies to the population of interest. If the researcher could test the population directly, no inferences would be necessary, and any difference between the means (or a positive correlation of any size) would support the hypothesis. However, sample results are subject to sampling fluctuations, which could also account for the difference between the means or the positive coefficient. Thus a result that supports the hypothesis may imply either that the hypothesis is true or that it is false, with the results being due to chance factors. Conversely, if the sample results deviate from the expected population value, the deviation could mean either that the hypothesis is false or that it is true, with the difference between the expected and obtained values being due to chance. Table 19.1 illustrates these four possibilities.

Whether a sample result matches or deviates from expectation, either case can imply that the hypothesis is either *true or false*. Therefore, sample results cannot be interpreted directly; researchers need a decision rule to enable them to reject or retain a hypothesis about the population on the basis of sample results. The procedure of statistical inference enables the researcher to determine whether a particular sample result falls within a range that can occur by an acceptable level of chance. This procedure involves the following steps, which we will discuss in some detail:

**Table 19.1**
Alternative Interpretations of Sample Results

| Hypothesis Status | Sample Results | |
| --- | --- | --- |
| | According to Expectation | Deviation from Expectation |
| True | Results validate hypothesis | Results due to sampling fluctuation |
| False | Results due to sampling fluctuation | Results validate hypothesis |

1. Formulate a null hypothesis and a research hypothesis.
2. Choose a sampling distribution and a statistical test according to the null hypothesis.
3. Specify a significance level ($\alpha$), and define the region of rejection.
4. Compute the statistical test, and reject or retain the null hypothesis accordingly.

# Null and Research Hypotheses

Two statistical hypotheses are involved in hypothesis testing. The first is the **research hypothesis,** which is usually symbolized by $H_1$. The second, symbolized by $H_0$, is the **null hypothesis;** $H_0$ is determined by $H_1$, which is really what you want to know; $H_0$ is the antithesis of $H_1$.

Suppose that the research hypothesis states that Catholics have larger families than Protestants. With the mean score for the size of family in the Catholic population designated as $\mu_1$ and in the Protestant population as $\mu_2$, the research hypothesis would be

$$H_1: \mu_1 > \mu_2$$

The null hypothesis would be

$$H_0: \mu_1 = \mu_2$$

The null hypothesis can be expressed in several ways. However, it is usually an expression of no difference or no relationship between the variables. Researchers express both the null hypothesis and the research hypothesis in terms of the population parameters, not in terms of the sample statistics. The null hypothesis is the one that the researcher tests directly; the research hypothesis is supported when the null hypothesis is rejected as being unlikely.

The need for two hypotheses arises out of a logical necessity: the null hypothesis is based on negative inference in order to avoid the *fallacy of affirming the consequent*—that is, researchers must eliminate false hypotheses rather than accept true ones. For instance, suppose that theory A implies empirical observation B. When B is false, one knows that A must also be false. But when B is true, A cannot be accepted as true, because B can be an empirical implication of several other theories that are not necessarily A. Therefore, if a researcher accepts A as true, he or she would be committing the fallacy of affirming the consequent.

Durkheim's theory of suicide may serve as an illustration. One of its propositions (A) is that people in individualistic situations are more likely to commit suicide. The empirical observation (B) derived from this proposition is that the suicide rate will be higher among single than married individuals. If B proves to be false (if there is no difference in the suicide rates of married and single persons), theory A is false. But what if B is true? A cannot be accepted as true; there are many other explanations for B that are not necessarily A. For instance, the higher suicide rate of single persons might be explained not by individualism but rather by excessive drinking, which may lead to depression and to suicide. Thus observation B might imply that $A_1$, another theory, is true.

Usually, many alternative theories might explain the same observations; the researcher has to select the most credible one. The credibility of a theory can be established only by the elimination of all alternative theories:

> For any given observation which is an implication of A, say $B_1$, there will be *some of* the possible alternative theories which will imply not-$B_1$. If we then demonstrate $B_1$, these alternative theories are falsified. This leaves us with *fewer alternative possible theories to our own.*[2]

---

# Sampling Distribution

Having formulated a specific null hypothesis, the investigator proceeds to test it against the sample results. For instance, if the hypothesis states that there is no difference between the means of two populations ($\mu_1 = \mu_2$), the procedure would be to draw a random sample from each population, compare the two sample means ($\bar{X}_1$ and $\bar{X}_2$), and make an inference from the samples to the populations. However, the sample result is subject to sampling error; therefore, it does not always reflect the true population value. If samples of the same size are drawn from the population, each sample will usually produce a different result.

To determine the accuracy of the sample statistic, the researcher has to compare it to a statistical model that gives the probability of observing such a result. Such a statistical model is called a **sampling distribution.** A sampling distribution of a statistic is obtained by drawing a large number of random samples of the same size from the defined population, computing the statistic for each sample, and plotting the frequency distribution of the statistic. In Chapter 8, we saw an example

---

2. Arthur L. Stinchcombe, *Constructing Social Theories* (Orlando, Fla.: Harcourt Brace Jovanovich, 1968), p. 20.

of such a distribution: the sampling distribution of the mean. It is possible to construct a sampling distribution of any other statistic, for example, of the variance ($s^2$), of the standard deviation ($s$), of the difference between means ($\overline{X}_1$ and $\overline{X}_2$), or of proportions ($p$).

As an illustration, let us go back to Durkheim's theory of suicide. The hypothesis to be tested is that single people have a relatively higher suicide rate than the general population. One way of evaluating the proportion of suicide among single people is comparing the number of suicides in this group to the average proportion in the population at large. Suppose that the records of health centers indicate that the national suicide rate in the adult population is 20 out of every 100, or .20. The research hypothesis would then imply that the rate of suicide among single people is higher than .20. Thus

$H_1$: The proportion of suicides among single people > .20

The null hypothesis would state that the proportion of suicides among single people is the same as the national average:

$H_0$: The proportion of suicides among singles = .20

Suppose we draw a sample of 100 from the health centers' records for single people, and we find that the rate of suicide is .30. Is this result sufficiently larger than .20 to justify the rejection of the null hypothesis? To assess the likelihood of obtaining a rate of .30 under the assumption of the null hypothesis, we compare the rate to a distribution of suicide rates of the entire adult population. Let us assume that 1,000 random samples of 100 each are drawn from the health centers' records for all adults and that the suicide rate is computed for each sample. Table 19.2 presents the obtained hypothetical sampling distribution.[3] This sampling distribution may serve as a statistical model for assessing the likelihood of observing a suicide rate of .30 among single people if their rate were equivalent to that of the adult population. The probability of observing any particular result can be determined by dividing its frequency in the distribution by the total number of samples.

The probabilities we would obtain are displayed in the third column of Table 19.2. For example, the suicide rate of .38–.39 occurred five times; therefore, the probability that any sample of size $n = 100$ will have this suicide rate is 5/1,000 or .005; that is, we would expect to obtain such a result in approximately .5 percent of the samples of 100 drawn from the population. Similarly, the probability of obtaining a rate of .30–.31 is .015, or 1.5 percent. The probability of obtaining a rate of .30 or more is equal to the sum of the probabilities of .30–.31, .32–.33, .34–.35, .36–.37, .38–.39, and .40 or more; that is, .015 + .010 + .010 + .010 + .005 + .000 = .050. Thus we would expect 5 percent of all samples of 100 drawn from this population to have a suicide rate of .30 or more.

---

3. Such a distribution is often called an *experimental sampling distribution* because it is obtained from observed data.

**Table 19.2**

Hypothetical Sampling Distribution of Suicide Rates for All Adults
for 1,000 Random Samples ($n = 100$)

| Suicide Rate | Number of Samples ($f$) | Proportion of Samples ($p = f/n$) |
|---|---|---|
| .40 or more | 0 | .000 |
| .38–.39 | 5 | .005 |
| .36–.37 | 10 | .010 |
| .34–.35 | 10 | .010 |
| .32–.33 | 10 | .010 |
| .30–.31 | 15 | .015 |
| .28–.29 | 50 | .050 |
| .26–.27 | 50 | .050 |
| .24–.25 | 50 | .050 |
| .22–.23 | 150 | .150 |
| .20–.21 | 200 | .200 |
| .18–.19 | 150 | .150 |
| .16–.17 | 100 | .100 |
| .14–.15 | 100 | .100 |
| .12–.13 | 50 | .050 |
| .10–.11 | 15 | .015 |
| .08–.09 | 10 | .010 |
| .06–.07 | 10 | .010 |
| .04–.05 | 10 | .010 |
| .02–.03 | 5 | .005 |
| .01 or less | 0 | .000 |
| Total | 1,000 | 1.000 |

# Level of Significance and Region of Rejection

After we have constructed the sampling distribution, we can evaluate the
likelihood of the result of .30 (given the assumption of the null hypothesis). The
decision as to what result is sufficiently unlikely to justify the rejection of the null
hypothesis is quite arbitrary. We can select any set of extreme results as a basis
for rejecting the null hypothesis. The range of these results is designated as the
**region of rejection.** The sum of the probabilities of the results included in the
region of rejection is denoted as the **level of significance,** or $\alpha$. It is customary
to set the level of significance at .05 or .01, which means that the null hypothesis
is to be rejected if the sample outcome is among the results that would have
occurred by chance no more than 5 percent or 1 percent of the time.

Figure 19.1 graphically represents the sampling distribution of Table 19.2 and the region of rejection with $\alpha = .05$. The region of rejection includes all the suicide rates of .30 and above. As we have seen, the sum of the probabilities of these results is equal to the level of significance, .05.

The sample result of .30 that we obtained falls within the region of rejection; thus the null hypothesis can be rejected at the .05 level of significance. The rejection of the null hypothesis lends support to the research hypothesis that the suicide rate of single people is higher than the rate in the general adult population.

**Figure 19.1**

Sampling Distribution of Suicide Rates for 1,000 Samples ($n = 100$)

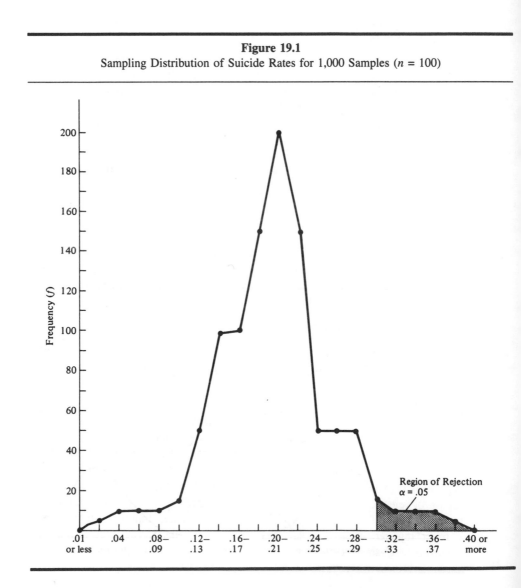

## One-Tailed and Two-Tailed Tests

In the preceding example, we selected the set of extreme results from the right tail of the sampling distribution. However, extreme sample outcomes are also located at the left-hand tail. In Table 19.2, the probability of a suicide rate of .11 and below is equal to the probability of obtaining a rate of .30 and above; in both cases, it is .05.

A statistical test may be *one-tailed* or *two-tailed*. In a **two-tailed test,** the region of rejection is located at both the left and right tails. In a **one-tailed test,** extreme results leading to rejection of the null hypothesis can be located at either tail.

The decision to locate the region of rejection in one or two tails will depend on whether $H_1$ implies a specific direction to the predicted results and whether it specifies large or small values. When $H_1$ predicts larger values, the region of rejection will be located at the right tail of the sampling distribution (as in the example of suicide). When $H_1$ implies lower values, the left tail is selected as the region of rejection. For instance, suppose that the research hypothesis had implied that single people have a lower suicide rate than the general adult population; that is,

$H_1$: The proportion of suicide in single population < .20

The results considered unlikely under this hypothesis are at the left tail of the distribution. At the .05 level of significance, the critical region will consist of the following rates: .10–.11, .08–.09, .06–.07, .04–.05, .02–.03, .01 or less. The sum of the probabilities of these results is .015 + .010 + .010 + .010 + .005 + .000 = .050. Figure 19.2 presents the right-tailed and left-tailed alternatives.

There are occasions when we cannot accurately predict the direction of the research hypothesis. For example, suppose we suspect that single persons have a different suicide rate but are unable to specify the direction of the difference. We would express the research hypothesis as

$H_1$: The proportion of single persons' suicide ≠ 20

When we cannot accurately specify the direction of $H_1$, we reject $H_0$ whenever we obtain extreme values in either direction. In such a case, the statistical test is

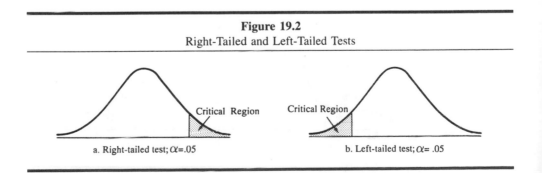

**Figure 19.2**
Right-Tailed and Left-Tailed Tests

Critical Region

Critical Region

a. Right-tailed test; $\alpha$=.05          b. Left-tailed test; $\alpha$= .05

designated as a two-tailed test, and the level of significance is divided in two. Thus a .05 level of significance would mean that $H_0$ will be rejected if the sample outcome falls among the lowest 2.5 percent or the highest 2.5 percent of the sampling distribution. This alternative is diagrammed in Figure 19.3.

Let us select the .05 level of significance and make use of a two-tailed test in the suicide example. The critical region will consist of the alternatives .34–.35, .36–.37, .38–.39, .40 or more (.010 + .010 + .005 + .000 = .025) and .06–.07, .04–.05, .02–.03, .01 or less (.010 + .010 + .005 + .000 = .025). With a two-tailed test, a sample result of .30 is not in the region of rejection; thus the null hypothesis would not have been rejected in this case.

## Type I and Type II Errors

Because the entire population is not measured directly in statistical hypothesis testing, the statistical test can never prove if the null hypothesis is true or false. The only evidence it provides is whether the sample result is sufficiently likely or unlikely to justify the decision to retain or to reject the null hypothesis.

The null hypothesis can be either true or false, and in both cases it can be rejected or retained. If it is true and is rejected nonetheless, the decision is in error. The error is the *rejection of a true hypothesis*—a **Type I error.** If the null hypothesis is false but is retained, the error committed is the *acceptance of a false hypothesis;* this error is designated as a **Type 11 error.** These four alternatives are presented schematically in Table 19.3.

The probability of rejecting a true hypothesis—a Type I error—is defined as the *level of significance.* Thus in the long run, an investigator employing the .05 level of significance will falsely reject 5 percent of the true hypotheses tested. Naturally, researchers are interested in minimizing the error of rejecting a true hypothesis, which they can do by making the level of significance as low as possible. However, Type I errors and Type II errors are inversely related: a decrease in the

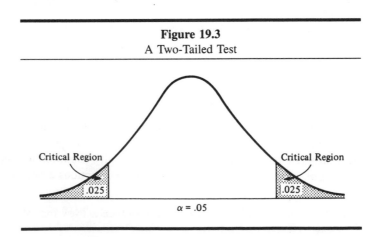

**Figure 19.3**
A Two-Tailed Test

Critical Region            Critical Region

.025            .025

$\alpha = .05$

**Table 19.3**
Alternative Decisions in Hypothesis Testing

| Decision | Null Hypothesis Is True | Null Hypothesis Is False |
| --- | --- | --- |
| Reject hypothesis | Type I error | No error |
| Accept hypothesis | No error | Type II error |

probability of rejecting a true hypothesis leads to an increase in the probability of retaining a false one. Under these conditions, the selection of $\alpha$ is determined by (1) the type of problem one is investigating and (2) the consequences of rejecting a true hypothesis or retaining a false one. If, for example, the researcher is investigating the effect of an experimental teaching method on the achievement of disadvantaged children and the results of the study will determine whether the teaching method is implemented throughout the school system, he or she should carefully consider the consequences of making a mistake. Suppose that the null hypothesis states that the new teaching method has negative effects. If the researcher rejected the null hypothesis when it was actually true, the consequences could be very severe; hundreds of thousands of disadvantaged children would be harmed. If, conversely, it is not rejected when it is actually false, the school system could postpone implementation of the new method until further evidence became available. Therefore, in this case it would be preferable to minimize $\alpha$ because the implications of rejecting a true hypothesis are more severe than those of retaining a false one.

When a study does not have practical implications, the selection of $\alpha$ will be arbitrary, but the choice will usually be governed by accepted conventions. The significance levels commonly used in social science research are .001, .01, and .05.

# Parametric and Nonparametric Tests of Significance

The tests of significance that are most common in social science research are divided into two major groups: parametric tests and nonparametric tests. A **parametric test** is a statistical test based on several assumptions about the parameters of the population from which the sample was drawn. Among the most important ones are the assumptions that (1) the observations must be drawn from a normally distributed population and (2) the variables are measured on at least an interval scale.[4] The results of a parametric test are meaningful only insofar as these assumptions are valid.

A **nonparametric test** neither specifies the normality condition nor requires an interval level of measurement. There are certain assumptions associated with

4. Sidney N. Siegel, *Nonparametric Statistics for the Behavioral Sciences* (New York: McGraw-Hill, 1956), pp. 2–3.

most nonparametric tests; however, they are weaker and fewer than those associated with parametric tests.

In practice, researchers do not need to go through the laborious procedure of constructing a sampling distribution. In many instances, sampling distributions have been constructed by previous researchers and are known in advance. Moreover, distributions exist that can be used as approximations of certain sampling distributions. For example, the sampling distribution of the mean closely approximates the normal curve distribution; therefore, researchers can use the normal curve distribution in testing hypotheses about means.

In the discussion of specific tests that follows, we will refer to existing sampling distributions that have been constructed in advance or that approximate the desired distribution. The sampling distributions employed in this section are provided in Appendixes E through I.

## Selected Parametric Tests

*Difference between Means.*    Many hypotheses in empirical research involve a comparison between populations. For example, to assess the relationship between social class and voting, a researcher could compare different social classes with respect to their voting patterns. Similarly, in comparing Asian-Americans and Hispanic-Americans with respect to achievement, a researcher is relating ethnicity to achievement.

When the dependent variable we are investigating is measured on an interval scale, we can compare means in order to reflect the amount of relationship between two variables (see Chapter 16). To assess the significance of a difference between means, we use the **difference-between-means test.**

To illustrate the testing of hypotheses about the difference between means, data are presented in Table 19.4 that show scores on attitudes on gender issues for two samples: evangelical and nonevangelical women. A higher mean score indicates a more feminist attitude on gender issues. According to the literature, evangelicals are less likely to take feminist positions than nonevangelicals.[5] This would lead to the following research hypothesis: $H_1: \mu_1 > \mu_2$ where $\mu_1$ is the mean score of the population of nonevangelical women and $\mu_2$ the mean score of evangelical women. The null hypothesis could state that there is no difference in the mean score of the two populations; that is, $H_0: \mu_1 = \mu_2$.

The data reveal a difference between the two sample means of 2.50 (6.10 − 3.60). Although this difference is in the expected direction, we need to determine its probability of occurrence under the assumption of the null hypothesis. If such a difference is unlikely to occur, assuming that the population means are identical, we must reject the null hypothesis.

The sampling distribution we select for testing the difference between means depends on the sample size. When each sample is larger than 30 ($n > 30$), the

5. Clyde Wilcox and Elizabeth Adell Cook, "Evangelical Women and Feminism: Some Additional Evidence," *Women and Politics,* 9 (1989): 27–49.

**Table 19.4**

Mean Scores of Attitudes on Gender Issues for Evangelical
Women and Others (Hypothetical Data)

|  | Evangelicals | Others |
|---|---|---|
| $n$ | 126 | 101 |
| $\overline{X}$ | 3.60 | 6.10 |
| $s$ | 3.04 | 4.52 |

sampling distribution of the difference between means approaches normality, and thus we can use the normal curve (Appendix E) as the statistical model. The procedure is similar to the one employed in estimating population means (see Chapter 8). We can translate the difference between the means to standard Z scores and then determine its probability of occurrence according to the normal curve distribution. For a two-tailed test, using the .05 level of significance, the critical region expressed in Z scores includes all the positive scores of 1.96 and above or all the negative scores of −1.96 and below, whose likelihood of occurrence is .025. For a one-tailed test, the critical region contains all scores of 1.65 and above or −1.65 and below. Similarly, for the .01 level of significance, Z is ±2.58 and ±2.33, respectively.

To test the null hypothesis on difference in attitudes on gender issues, we can select a right-tailed test because $H_1$ is a directional hypothesis implying larger values. The level of significance selected will be .01; any value larger than 2.33 will lead to rejection of the null hypothesis.

To determine the significance of the difference between the means using the normal curve, we must first convert the difference to standard scores. This conversion can be accomplished using a test statistic denoted as $t$, which is defined in Formula (19.1):

$$t = \frac{(\overline{X}_1 - \overline{X}_2) - (\mu_1 - \mu_2)}{\hat{\sigma}_{\overline{x}1 - \overline{x}2}} \tag{19.1}$$

where $\overline{X}_1 - \overline{X}_2$ = the difference between the sample means

$\mu_1 - \mu_2$ = the means of the sampling distribution of the difference between means

$\hat{\sigma}_{\overline{x}1 - \overline{x}2}$ = an estimate of the standard error[6] of the sampling distribution of the difference between the means

Like Z, $t$ measures deviations from the means in terms of standard deviation units; $\overline{X}_1 - \overline{X}_2$ replaces $X$, $\mu_1 - \mu_2$ replaces $\overline{X}$, and $\hat{\sigma}$ replaces $s$. We cannot calculate Z, however, when the variances of the two populations ($\sigma_1^2$ and $\sigma_2^2$) are unknown. That is, $t$ substitutes for Z whenever sample variances ($s_1^2$ and $s_2^2$) are used as estimates of the populations' parameters. Because the populations' variances are

---

6. The standard error is the standard deviation of the sampling distribution; see Chapter 8 for a discussion of this concept.

almost never available, for all practical purposes, the $t$ statistic is used to transform mean differences to standard scores. The $t$ is normally distributed when $n > 30$; thus the normal distribution can be employed whenever each sample size is greater than 30. However, when $n \leqq 30$, the normal approximation is not appropriate, and the sampling distribution of $t$ must be used.

We can obtain the estimate of the standard error ($\hat{\sigma}_{\bar{x}1-\bar{x}2}$) by two methods. The first assumes that the two population variances are equal—for instance, $\sigma_1^2 = \sigma_2^2$—and thus the variances of the two samples are combined into a single estimate of $\sigma_1^2$ or $\sigma_2^2$. The standard error under these conditions is as follows:

$$\hat{\sigma}_{\bar{x}1 - \bar{x}2} = \sqrt{\frac{n_1 s_1^2 + n_2 s_2^2}{n_1 + n_2 - 2}} \sqrt{\frac{n_1 + n_2}{n_1 n_2}} \tag{19.2}$$

where $n_1$ and $n_2$ are the sample sizes of sample 1 and sample 2, respectively, and $s_1^2$ and $s_2^2$ are the variances of sample 1 and sample 2.

When there is no basis for assuming that the population variances are identical, it is not possible to pool the sample variance. In this instance, we would estimate the two variances separately, and the obtained formula for the standard error is

$$\hat{\sigma}_{\bar{x}1 - \bar{x}2} = \sqrt{\frac{s_1^2}{n_1 - 1} + \frac{s_2^2}{n_2 - 1}} \tag{19.3}$$

To calculate $t$ for the data summarized in Table 19.4, we assume that $\sigma_1^2 = \sigma_2^2$ and calculate the pooled estimate of the standard error:

$$\hat{\sigma}_{\bar{x}1 - \bar{x}2} = \sqrt{\frac{(101)(4.52)^2 + 126(3.04)^2}{101 + 126 - 2}} \sqrt{\frac{101 + 126}{(101)(126)}} = .50$$

Because under the null hypothesis it has been assumed that $\mu_1 = \mu_2$, the definition of $t$ reduces to

$$t = \frac{\overline{X}_1 - \overline{X}_2}{\hat{\sigma}_{\bar{x}1 - \bar{x}2}} \tag{19.4}$$

We obtain the following result for our example:

$$t = \frac{6.1 - 3.6}{.50} = \frac{2.5}{.50} = 5$$

Referring to the normal curve table (Appendix E), we observe that the value of $t$ is in fact greater than the value needed for rejection (2.33) at the .01 level of significance. In other words, the difference between the sample mean of evangelical women and that of nonevangelical women students is not likely to be due to sampling error. Accordingly, we reject $H_0$ and conclude that the difference between the samples reflects different attitudes toward gender issues.

***The t Distribution.***   When either or both of the sample sizes are less than 30, the normal curve does not approximate the sampling distribution of the difference between means. As a result, using the normal curve to determine the probability of $H_0$ will yield inaccurate conclusions, and the sampling distribution of $t$ has to be used instead. The $t$ is actually a family of curves, each determined by the sample size. Thus for a sample size of 7, $t$ has a different distribution from that for a sample size of 10. The sampling distribution of $t$ is reproduced in Appendix F. The values in this table are given in terms of the significance level (one tail and two tails) and the degrees of freedom.

***Degrees of Freedom.***   The concept of **degrees of freedom** (*df*) is a basic one that researchers use in several statistical tests, including the *t* **test,** which can be used when the normal curve does not apply. When we use the normal curve, our calculations are based on the total sample size ($N$) and the shape of the curve is always the same. When we use other distributions to test hypotheses, we must adjust the sample size to reflect restrictions placed on our choice of cases to be included in the sample because the shape of the distribution changes depending on how many cases can be freely chosen to be in the sample. *Degrees of freedom* refers to the number of free choices you can make in repeated random samples that constitute a sampling distribution and reflects the adjustment to the sample size. To determine degrees of freedom, you must know the sample size and whether there are any restrictions that limit your choice of observations to be included in the sample, because we calculate degrees of freedom by subtracting the number of restrictions on our choices from the total sample size.

For example, suppose you are asked to choose any two numbers from a group of numbers ranging from 0 to 10. The sample size in this case is two, there are no restrictions on the numbers you can choose, and the degrees of freedom is 2 (2 cases − 0 restrictions = 2 *df*). Now suppose that you are asked to choose two numbers from the same group that sum to 10. We have now placed a restriction on the number of free choices you can make. You can choose one number freely, but you have no choice about the value of the second number. If you choose 10 as the first number, the second number must be 0, and the degrees of freedom is 1 (2 cases − 1 restriction = 1 *df*). The number of degrees of freedom of the *t* distribution is limited by the fact that for each sample, the population variance has to be estimated, so there are only $n - 1$ quantities that are free to vary in each sample (1 restriction has been applied to each sample). When we use the *t* distribution to test a hypothesis about a difference between two samples, we determine the total degrees of freedom by summing the degrees of freedom for the two samples and *df* is equivalent to $(n_1 - 1) + (n_2 - 1) = n_1 + n_2 - 2$.

To illustrate the use of the *t* table, we shall test the hypothesis that students' achievement is associated with their assignment to tracks in a secondary school. The data are summarized in Table 19.5. The investigators hypothesized that achievement and track assignment were related so that a college preparatory track had more students who were high achievers than a noncollege track. The null

**Table 19.5**
Mean Achievement of Students in College Preparatory and
Noncollege Tracks

|  | College Preparatory Track | Noncollege Track |
|---|---|---|
| $n$ | 13 | 6 |
| $\bar{X}$ | 48.3 | 20.5 |
| $s$ | 23.6 | 12.2 |

hypothesis to be tested is that the means of the two populations are identical, whereas the research hypothesis states that the mean achievement of the college preparatory track ($\mu_1$) is higher than that of the noncollege track ($\mu_2$):

$$H_0: \mu_1 = \mu_2$$
$$H_1: \mu_1 > \mu_2$$

We can follow the same procedure in calculating the standard error and the $t$ ratio, using Equations (19.2) and (19.4):

$$\hat{\sigma}_{\bar{x}-\bar{x}2} = \sqrt{\frac{13(23.6)^2 + 6(12.2)^2}{13 + 6 - 2}}\sqrt{\frac{13+6}{(13)(6)}} = 10.8$$

$$t = \frac{48.3 - 20.5}{10.8} = \frac{27.8}{10.8} = 2.574$$

The obtained $t$ can now be compared with the appropriate value in the sampling distribution of $t$. The number of degrees of freedom for sample sizes of 13 and 6 is 17 (13 + 6 − 2). At the .01 level of significance with a one-tailed test (right tail), the $t$ for which $H_0$ will be rejected is 2.567. A $t$ larger than 2.567 is unlikely to occur if $H_0$ is true. As 2.574 is larger than 2.567, the null hypothesis is rejected, and the investigator can conclude that the difference in achievement between the two tracks is statistically significant.

*A Significance Test for Pearson's* **r.**    The correlation coefficient Pearson's $r$—like $\bar{X}$, $Md$, or $b$—is a statistic obtained from sample data; as such, it is just an estimate of a population parameter. Pearson's $r$ corresponds to the population correlation denoted as $\rho$ or rho. As with other sample statistics, $r$ is subject to sampling fluctuations; the test of its statistical significance is an assessment of the likelihood that the obtained correlation is due to sampling error. For example, a researcher may test the hypothesis that liberalism is correlated with income and draw a random sample of 24, obtaining an $r$ of .30. It is probable that in the population these two variables are not correlated at all and that the obtained coefficient is a result of chance factors. In other words, is an $r$ of .30 large enough to make the hypothesis of no relation unlikely?

The strategy of testing such a hypothesis is similar to that used in the difference-of-means test; the null hypothesis states that the correlation in the population is zero, and the research hypothesis, that it is different from zero:

$$H_0: \rho = 0$$
$$H_1: \rho \neq 0$$

***Testing the Significance of* r *When* $\rho$ *Is Zero.***    When $\rho$ is assumed to be zero under the null hypothesis, the researcher can test the statistical significance of $r$ by converting $r$ to a standard score using the t test statistic with $n - 2$ degrees of freedom. Thus $t$ is defined as follows:

$$t = \frac{r\sqrt{n - 2}}{\sqrt{1 - r^2}} \tag{19.5}$$

To illustrate the use of $t$ in testing the significance of Pearson's $r$, let us suppose that we have obtained a correlation of .30 between income and years of schooling from a sample of $n = 24$ ($df = 22$). The $t$ is equal to

$$t = \frac{.30\sqrt{22}}{\sqrt{1 - .30^2}} = 1.475$$

From the distribution of $t$ in Appendix F, we see that at the .05 level of significance for a two-tailed test and with 22 $df$, the value of $t$ required to reject the null hypothesis is 2.074. As the obtained $t$ is smaller than this value, the null hypothesis cannot be rejected, and the relationship between income and years of schooling is said to be not significant.

Researchers can also test the significance of $r$ by using a test statistic called $F$. The $F$ statistic is based on the ratio of the explained ($r^2$) to the unexplained ($1 - r^2$) variance. It is defined in Equation (19.6), where $n - 2$ stands for the degrees of freedom:

$$F = \frac{r^2}{1 - r^2} (n - 2) \tag{19.6}$$

Using the data from our example on income and years of schooling, we have

$$F = \frac{.30^2}{1 - .30^2} (24 - 2) = 2.17$$

To evaluate the $F$ statistic, we use the $F$ distribution given in Appendix G. $F$ values are given for $\alpha = .05$ (light numbers) and $\alpha = .01$ (bold numbers). The degrees of freedom for the explained variance (across the top of the table) is equal to the number of groups we are comparing $- 1$ (in our example we are comparing two groups, thus degrees of freedom is $2 - 1 = 1$) and the degrees of freedom for the unexplained variance is equal to $n - 2$ (left-hand column); $24 - 2 = 22$ in our example. $H_0$ is rejected when $F$ is larger than or equal to the $F$ value appearing in the table. Thus to find the significance of $F = 2.17$, we locate the $F$ value corresponding to 1 (across the top) and 22 (left-hand column); there are two $F$ values,

---

**Parametric Tests of Significance**

*Assumptions basic to parametric tests:* The observations must be randomly drawn from a normally distributed population and the variables are measured on at least an interval scale.

- *Difference-between-means:* Researchers use the *t* test to assess the significance of differences between the means of samples drawn from different populations. The probability of the difference between the sample means occurring by chance if the null hypothesis is true is calculated using Formula (19.1). If we can assume that the population variances are equal, we calculate the standard error using Formula (19.2). When there is no reason to assume the population variances are the same, we must use Formula (19.3), the equation for standard error. When both sample sizes are at least 30, we use the normal curve table to evaluate *t*. If either sample size is less than 30, we use the *t* table to evaluate *t*.
- *Significance Tests for Pearson's* r: There are two tests researchers can use to test the significance of a correlation coefficient. When the null hypothesis assumes that the correlation in the population is zero ($\rho = 0$), the *t* distribution can be used to determine the significance of the correlation and is calculated with Formula (19.5). Researchers can also use the *F* distribution to assess the significance of a correlation. The *F* statistic is based on the ratio of the explained to the un-explained variance, using Formula (19.6).

---

$F = 4.30$ corresponding to $\alpha = .05$ and $F = 7.94$ corresponding to $\alpha = .01$. In either case, the obtained value of $F = 2.17$ is smaller than the $F$ required to reject $H_0$, and we must conclude that the relationship between income and years of schooling is not significant.

## Selected Nonparametric Tests

***The Mann-Whitney Test.***    The **Mann-Whitney test** is applicable whenever we wish to test the null hypothesis that two samples have been drawn from the same population against the alternative research hypothesis that the populations differ from each other.[7] The only assumptions required in making this test are that the two samples are independently and randomly drawn and that the level of measurement of the variables under investigation is at least ordinal.

Suppose that we have sampled 13 males ($n_1 = 13$) and 14 females ($n_2 = 14$) and have given each one a score reflecting their level of alienation:

Male sample: 5, 7, 10, 13, 19, 24, 25, 28, 30, 32, 33, 36, 37
Female sample: 1, 3, 4, 6, 9, 12, 14, 15, 17, 18, 20, 21, 22, 23

If we assume that the population of females is identical to the population of males with respect to level of alienation, we expect that the values in the two samples

---

7. Siegel, *Nonparametric Statistics,* pp. 116–126.

will be similar. If the values have similar magnitudes, males will have larger alienation scores in approximately one-half of the male-female pairs; in the rest of the pairs, the females' scores will exceed the males'. We can count the number of pairs in which the scores of males exceed the scores of females and designate it as $U$; the number of pairs for which the opposite is true is designated $U'$. If the null hypothesis of identical populations were true, we would expect $U$ and $U'$ to be approximately equal.[8]

$$H_1: U \approx U'$$
$$H_0: U \neq U'$$

To determine $U$, we can use the following equation:

$$U = n_1 n_2 + \frac{n_2(n_2 + 1)}{2} - R_2 \qquad (19.7)$$

where $n_1$ = the sample size of sample 1

$n_2$ = the sample size of sample 2

$R_2$ = the sum of ranks for sample 2

We obtain the ranks by arranging all the scores in order of magnitude. For instance, the first three females (1, 3, 4) head the scale, with rank 4 being the first male (score 5). Thus the ranks for males are 4, 6, 8, 10, 15, 20, 21, 22, 23, 24, 25, 26, 27, and the ranks for females are 1, 2, 3, 5, 7, 9, 11, 12, 13, 14, 16, 17, 18, 19. To determine $U'$, we subtract $U$ from the total number of pairs

$$U' = n_1 n_2 - U \qquad (19.8)$$

For our data,

$$U = (13)(14) + \frac{14(14 + 1)}{2} - 147 = 140$$

$$U' = (13)(14) - 140 = 182 - 140 = 42$$

To evaluate the significance of $H_0$, we compare the smaller of the two values $U$ and $U'$ with the significant values of the sampling distribution of $U$ in Appendix H.[9] At the .05 level, we need a $U$ of 50 or smaller when direction is not predicted or 56 or smaller when direction is predicted. In either case, the obtained value (42) is smaller and enables us to reject the null hypothesis that men and women are equally alienated.

The sampling distribution of $U$ approaches normality when the samples' size increases. When either of the samples is larger than 20, we can compute standard scores and use the normal distribution. The mean of the sampling distribution would then be

8. John H. Mueller, Karl F. Schuessler, and Herbert L. Costner, *Statistical Reasoning in Sociology* (Boston: Houghton Mifflin, 1970), p. 423.

9. For situations in which one of the samples is smaller than 9, another table for probabilities is used.

$$\mu_u = \frac{n_1 n_2}{2}$$

and the standard error would be

$$\sigma_u = \frac{\sqrt{n_1 n_2 (n_1 + n_2 + 1)}}{12}$$

Z is obtained using the following formula:

$$Z = \frac{U - \dfrac{n_1 n_2}{2}}{\sqrt{\dfrac{n_1 n_2 (n_1 + n_2 + 1)}{12}}} \tag{19.9}$$

***The Chi-Square Test ($\chi^2$).*** Chi-square is a general test designed to evaluate whether the difference between observed frequencies and expected frequencies under a set of theoretical assumptions is statistically significant. Researchers most often apply the **chi-square test** to problems in which two nominal variables are cross-classified in a bivariate table. The data summarized in Table 19.6 are an example of a research problem to which the chi-square test is applicable. Table 19.6 is a bivariate table of mens' attitudes toward traditional gender roles during the 1970s and the 1980s. When the frequencies are converted to percentages (in parentheses), it is observed that in the 1970s 69 percent of the men believed it was better if men worked outside the home and women cared for the home and family; in the 1980s only 47 percent of the men held this belief. We want to examine whether such differences are statistically significant. Under the null hypothesis, we assume that there are no differences in beliefs between men surveyed in 1970 and those surveyed during 1980. We then compute the frequencies, given this assumption, and compare them with the observed frequencies. If the differences between the observed and expected frequencies are so large as to occur only rarely (5 percent or 1 percent of the time), the null hypothesis is rejected.

**Table 19.6**
Percentage of Men Supporting and Opposing Traditional Male
Provider Role in the 1970s and 1980s

| Better if man achieves outside and woman takes care of home and family | Year | | |
| --- | --- | --- | --- |
| | 1970s | 1980s | Total |
| Yes | 36 (69%) | 80 (47%) | 116 |
| No | 16 (31%) | 90 (53%) | 106 |
| Total | 52 | 170 | 222 |

Adapted from Jane Riblett Wilkie, "Changes in U.S. Men's Attitudes Toward the Family Provider Role, 1972–1989," *Gender and Society,* Vol 7, No 2 (June 1993): pp. 261–279.

The statistic used to evaluate these differences is chi-square ($\chi^2$), which is defined as

$$\chi^2 = \sum \frac{(f_o - f_e)^2}{f_e} \tag{19.10}$$

where $f_o$ = observed frequencies and $f_e$ = expected frequencies.

To compute the expected frequencies for any cell, use the following formula:

$$f_e = \frac{(\text{row total})(\text{column total})}{n} \tag{19.11}$$

For Table 19.6, the expected frequency for men who responded "yes" in the 1970's (Row 1, Column 1) is equal to

$$f_e = \frac{(116)(52)}{222} = 27$$

Table 19.7 is the reconstructed table containing frequencies we would expect if men's attitudes towards traditional gender roles had not changed from the 1970s to the 1980s.

*Calculating Chi-Square ($\chi^2$).* To compute $\chi^2$, we subtract the expected frequencies of each cell from the observed frequencies, square them, divide by the expected frequency of the cell, and then sum for all cells. These calculations are summarized in Table 19.8. Note that $\chi^2$ would be zero if the observed frequencies were identical with the expected frequencies. That is, the larger the difference between what is observed and what would be expected were the hypothesis of no relations true, the larger will be the value of $\chi^2$.

To evaluate the $\chi^2$ statistic obtained, we need to compare it to the sampling distribution of $\chi^2$ and to observe whether the value of 8.1 is large enough and thus unlikely if the null hypothesis is true. The sampling distribution of $\chi^2$ is reproduced in Appendix I. Two factors determine the distribution: the level of significance ($\alpha$) and the number of degrees of freedom. Thus $\chi^2$ is really a family of distributions, each determined by different parameters. We shall select for this problem a level

**Table 19.7**

Percentage of Men Supporting and Opposing Traditional Male Provider Role in the 1970s and 1980s: Expected Frequencies

| Better if man achieves outside and woman takes care of home and family | Year | | |
| --- | --- | --- | --- |
| | 1970s | 1980s | Total |
| Yes | 27 | 89 | 116 |
| No | 25 | 81 | 106 |
| Total | 52 | 170 | 222 |

**Table 19.8**

Calculation of $\chi^2$ for the Data of Tables 19.6 and 19.7

| $f_o$ | $f_e$ | $f_o - f_e$ | $(f_o - f_e)^2$ | $\dfrac{(f_o - f_e)^2}{f_e}$ |
|-------|-------|-------------|-----------------|------------------------------|
| 36 | 27 | 9 | 81 | 3.0 |
| 16 | 25 | −9 | 81 | 3.2 |
| 80 | 89 | −9 | 81 | .9 |
| 90 | 81 | 9 | 81 | 1.0 |
|    |    |    |    | $\chi^2 = 8.1$ |

of significance of .01, which means that only if we obtain a $\chi^2$ larger than what we would expect to find in no more than 1 out of 100 of our samples will the null hypothesis be rejected.

The number of degrees of freedom of the $\chi^2$ sampling distribution is set by the number of cells for which expected frequencies can be selected freely. For any bivariate table, the cells that can be determined arbitrarily are limited by the marginal total of both variables. Thus in a 2 × 2 table, for instance, only one cell is free to vary, the three others being predetermined by the marginal totals. Generally, we can compute the number of degrees of freedom using the following formula:

$$df = (r - 1)(c - 1) \tag{19.12}$$

Where $r$ = the number of rows and $c$ = the number of columns. Thus

In a 2 × 2 table: $df = (2 - 1)(2 - 1) = 1$
In a 3 × 3 table: $df = (3 - 1)(3 - 1) = 4$
In a 4 × 3 table: $df = (4 - 1)(3 - 1) = 6$

The probabilities under $H_0$ are given at the top of each column in Appendix I, and the row entries indicate the number of degrees of freedom.

The sampling distribution of $\chi^2$ is positively skewed, with higher values in the upper tail of the distribution (to the right). Therefore, with the $\chi^2$ test, the critical region is located at the upper tail of the sampling distribution.

For our example, with 1 $df$ and a .01 level of significance, the entry is 6.635, indicating that a value of 6.635 will occur in only 1 percent of the samples. Our obtained sample result of 8.1 is larger than 6.635 and is unlikely under the null hypothesis. However, at higher levels of significance—of .001, for example ($\chi^2 = 10.827$)—we would not reject the null hypothesis. Researchers generally choose the level of significance prior to calculating statistics by considering the consequences of Type I and Type II errors. Most researchers in the social sciences set their significance levels at .05 or .01. Using this as a rule of thumb, we would reject the null hypothesis that men's attitudes toward traditional gender roles did not change from the 1970s to the 1980s.

## Nonparametric Tests of Significance

- *Mann-Whitney Test:* Researchers can apply the Mann-Whitney test if the two samples have been independently and randomly drawn and the variables have been measured on at least the ordinal level. The Mann-Whitney test compares pairs of observations to test the null hypothesis that two samples have been drawn from the same population against the research hypothesis that the populations differ from each other. The observations for each sample are arranged in order of magnitude, and all observations are then ranked by magnitude. When both sample sizes are under 20, $U$ and $U'$ are calculated using Formulas (19.7) and (19.8). To evaluate the null hypothesis, researchers compare the smaller of the two values $U$ and $U'$ to the critical value of $U$ in the table (see Appendix H), finding the appropriate critical value by using the sample sizes and the desired level of significance. If either $U$ or $U'$ is smaller than the number in the table, the null hypothesis can be rejected. When either of the sample sizes is larger than 20, researchers can compute standard scores and use the normal distribution.
- *The Chi-Square Test:* The chi-square test may be used with nominal variables cross-classified in a bivariate table to determine whether the difference between the observed and expected frequencies is statistically significant. Chi-square is obtained using Formulas (19.10) and (19.11). Using the chi-square distribution, we locate the appropriate minimum value needed to reject the null hypothesis in the table in Appendix I. We determine the minimum value by locating the row containing the appropriate degrees of freedom and the column containing the desired level of significance. The obtained chi-square value can then be compared to the minimum value. If the obtained value is larger, we can reject the null hypothesis.

## Summary

**1.** Statistical inference refers to a procedure that allows the investigator to decide between two hypotheses about a population parameter on the basis of a sample result.

**2.** The first step in testing a hypothesis is to formulate it in statistical terms. The statistical hypothesis always applies to the population of interest. Two statistical hypotheses are involved in hypothesis testing. The first is the research hypothesis, symbolized by $H_1$. The second, symbolized by $H_0$, is the null hypothesis, which is set up for logical purposes. The null hypothesis is the one that is tested directly. When the null hypothesis is rejected as being unlikely, the research hypothesis is supported.

**3.** The need for two hypotheses arises out of a logical necessity. The null hypothesis is based on negative inference in order to avoid the fallacy of affirming the consequent; that is, the researcher must eliminate false hypotheses rather than accept true ones.

**4.** After formulating a specific null hypothesis, the investigator proceeds to test it against the sample result. The researcher does this test by comparing the sample result to a statistical model that gives the probability of observing such a result. Such a statistical model is called a sampling distribution. A sampling distribution of a statistic is obtained by drawing a large number of random samples of the same size from the defined population, computing the statistic for each sample, and plotting the frequency distribution of the statistic.

**5.** The sampling distribution allows us to estimate the probability of obtaining the sample result. This probability is called the level of significance, or $\alpha$, which is also the probability of rejecting a true hypothesis (Type I error). When the likelihood of obtaining the sample result is very small under the assumptions of the null hypothesis, $H_0$ is rejected, and the rejection adds to our confidence in the research hypothesis.

**6.** Statistical tests are divided into two major groups: parametric tests and nonparametric tests. A parametric test is a statistical test based on several assumptions about the parameters of the population from which the sample was drawn. One of the most important assumptions is that the observations have been drawn from a normally distributed population and that the variables were measured on at least an interval scale. A nonparametric statistical test is one whose model does not specify that the population be normally distributed nor does it require an interval-level measurement. The difference-between-means test and a significance test for Pearson's $r$ are parametric tests. The Mann-Whitney test and chi-square are nonparametric tests of significance.

---

### Key Terms for Review

---

chi-square test (p. 496)
degrees of freedom (*df*) (p. 491)
difference-between-
    means test (p. 488)
level of significance (p. 483)
Mann-Whitney test (p. 494)
nonparametric test (p. 487)
null hypothesis (p. 480)
one-tailed test (p. 485)

parametric test (p. 487)
region of rejection (p. 483)
research hypothesis (p. 480)
sampling distribution (p. 481)
*t* test (p. 491)
two-tailed test (p. 485)
Type I error (p. 486)
Type II error (p. 486)

---

### Study Questions

---

1. Discuss the role of the null hypothesis and the research hypothesis in the logic of hypothesis testing.
2. What is the difference between using a level of significance of .50 and using one of .05?

3. What is the difference between one-tailed and two-tailed tests?
4. Show in a diagram the difference between Type I and Type II errors.
5. Distinguish between parametric and nonparametric tests of significance.

## Computer Exercises

1. Using the GSS file, or a dataset of your own, generate a chi-square statistic on two nominal level variables (the STATISTICS are associated with the CROSS-TABS procedure). Is the relationship you find statistically significant? On what do you base your answer? (See Appendix A, pp. 518–521.)
2. Using the *t* test procedure, examine the difference of means of an interval level variable based on a nominal level grouping variable. Is the difference statistically significant and at what level? Did you use a one-tailed or two-tailed test? Why? (The *t* test procedure is described in your SPSS manual.)

## Additional Readings

Bohrnstedt, George W., and David Knoke. *Statistics for Social Data Analysis.* Itasca, Ill.: Peacock, 1988.
Healey, Joseph F., *Statistics: A Tool for Social Research.* Belmont, Calif.: Wadsworth, 1993.
Runyon, Richard P., Audrey Haber, and Kay A. Coleman. *Behavioral Statistics: The Core.* New York: McGraw-Hill, 1994.
Walsh, Anthony. *Statistics for the Social Sciences.* San Francisco: Harper & Row, 1990.

# APPENDIX A    Introduction to SPSS

*Claire L. Felbinger and Stephen F. Schwelgien*

The Statistical Package for the Social Sciences (SPSS), Release 4 is one of the most popular and widely available software packages for preparing and executing computerized data analysis. SPSS was designed especially for the analysis of social science data and contains most of the routines social scientists employ. Indeed, all the data analysis procedures described in this text can be executed by SPSS subprograms. In particular, social scientists value the program's capacity to handle with ease the recurring needs of data analysis. For instance, SPSS enables the researcher to recode variables; to deal with missing values; to sample, weight, and select cases; and to compute new variables and effect permanent or temporary transformations.

In this appendix we will supply you with the tools necessary to set up an SPSS file and execute basic analyses. The appendix is not by any means an exhaustive display of either the variety of subprograms available or the intracacies of the more highly powered types of analyses possible with SPSS. Rather, the examples we will use parallel the work covered in this text. Refer to the appropriate *SPSS User's Guide* for information on other available subprograms and for a more detailed explanation of the ones covered in this appendix.[1]

The three main environments within which SPSS operates are on a mainframe computer, on a PC, and in Windows. In addition to the full service programs, there are abbreviated *Studentware* versions for the PC and Windows. We will assume usage of the more general versions in this appendix. You can operate the *Studentware* packages with minor adjustments—they tend to provide fewer subprograms, allow for a smaller data matrix, and allow fewer options. However, you should be able to execute all the procedures described here on *Studentware*. Since the operation and commands used for the mainframe tend to be more similar to the PC environment than the PC ones are to Windows, we will describe the mainframe (SPSS) and PC (SPSS PC+) applications first and then discuss Windows adaptations.

The data set used in the examples that follow is from the General Social Survey (GSS) of 1993. If you have access to the diskette that accompanies this text, you will find that the examples included in this appendix are from a subset

---

1. Marija J. Norusis/SPSS Inc., *SPSS Base System User's Guide* (Chicago: SPSS Inc., 1990). Norusis/SPSS Inc., *SPSS PC+ Base System User's Guide Version 5* (Chicago: SPSS Inc., 1992). Norusis/SPSS Inc., *SPSS Base System Syntax Reference Guide* (Chicago: SPSS Inc., 1993).

of the data on that diskette. A sample codebook containing the subset of variables used is found in Exhibit A.1 at the end of this appendix (pages 547–551).

The GSS examines social indicators and issues over time. The first survey was conducted in 1972. Questions are either permanent (occuring on every survey), rotating (appearing on two out of three surveys), or occasional (occuring in a single survey). The data are collected by interviewing a sample of English-speaking persons 18 years of age or older who live in noninstitutional settings in the United States. We have drawn a sample of 1,500 respondents for the analyses reported here. As you can see from the codebook, we have selected demographic and opinion questions that will help us explain opinions on government activism and personal happiness. We will use these data to build a permanent SPSS file, clean the data, and execute statistical procedures in much the same way as if we were actually involved in a research project. Hence we will assume that the data are prepared in machine-readable form (see Chapter 14), clean the data by examining univariate distibutions (Chapter 15), perform bivariate (Chapter 16) and multivariate (Chapter 17) analyses with hypothesis testing (Chapter 19), and construct scales (Chapter 18).

# Mainframe and PC Versions

## Preparing the Data

Preparation of the data is discussed in Chapter 14. The data can be prepared and stored on tape or disk (on the mainframe) or on a diskette or hard drive (on a PC). There are two formats for including raw data: from a standard text file or from a spreadsheet.

*Standard Text Files.*    Data entered from a standard text file can be imported from a word-processed or edited file or entered directly into the runstream using the SPSS internal editor. In SPSS PC+ you can use the REVIEW editor to build your data set. The easiest way to format the data is to use a *fixed format*. In the simplest example of fixed format data entry, the information for each case is contained on one line or row of text. SPSS refers to this line as a record. In fixed format, each variable's value for every case is contained in the same column locations. For example, the GSS subset used for this appendix contains 1,500 cases with one 80-column line per case. Each line is called a *record*. The variable ID is located in the first four columns of each record. It is typical to identify a case by number and include that information at the beginning of a data set (you will see its utility when you "clean" the data). The information for the variable AGE is located in columns five and six and so on.

When the data for a case includes more information than one record will hold, begin a second record with a new variable. We suggest that the first variable that appears on each record be a duplication of the identification information with a new variable name like ID2 for the second record and ID3 for the third record.

All the records associated with each case are together in order (case 1, record 1; case 1, record 2; and so on to case *n,* record *last*).

*Spreadsheet Data.*    SPSS has adapted to the widespread use of spreadsheets by allowing them to be input directly into your setup runstream. You should organize your data so that each row contains all the information for a case and that each column contains a particular variable's value. For example, column A would contain each case's ID while column B would contain each case's AGE and so on. If you place variable names in row one and begin the data for the first case in row two, SPSS will read and assign both the variable names and their associated values for each case. Be sure to save the contents of your spreadsheet. You may have to refer to it when you "clean" the data.

*Accessing SPSS on the Mainframe.*    To access the mainframe version of SPSS from your computing services facility, you must supply commands known as *Job Control Language,* or JCL. These commands are unique to your mainframe computer system and to your facility. They grant access to the computer, initiate accounting procedures, assign disk or tape space, access the SPSS software, and perform other functions, including the important file handling services you will need to input data and save system files you have set up. Contact the consultants at your facility to learn the proper JCL since site requirements vary from facility to facility.

## Setting Up an SPSS System File

The language of SPSS is logical and quite simple. You will usually find that the language and patterns employed by SPSS match your expectations. For example, when you wish to generate univariate frequencies you ask for the procedure FREQUENCIES. If you are providing a list of your data, you designate its format in a DATA LIST. However, in order to operate SPSS, you will need to become familiar with a number of files by name:

1. *Command files* contain the SPSS commands you wish to execute in any particular run. These commands are known as the *runstream.* We will assume in this appendix that your commands will be stored in a file (and that you will not be using menus from the SPSS Manager). For those of you using SPSS PC+, you can use the INCLUDE command to process the runstream of a command file or submit a command file directly from REVIEW.

2. *Data files* contain your raw data. The data can be stored on any readable medium. SPSS can accommodate virtually any form of stored data. However, since coding is traditionally done using the 80-column format, we will use that format here.

3. *Listing files* contain the results or output associated with your executed procedures that were stored in a command file. This is the output that can be viewed on a screen or printed at a remote printer.

4. *SPSS system files* contain the information about the data from the input file defined uniquely by the series of commands executed in the command file used

to set up the system file plus any permanent transformations stored at a later time. As such, the system file contains a *dictionary* that defines variables and contains information concerning labels, missing values, and the like. This is the file most easily used by students since you do not have perform all the set up commands each time you do a run. All the information on the set up run is stored for you in the system file. When a system file is in use, it is called an *active file*.

**Data and File Definition.** We will now describe the commands necessary to set up an SPSS system file. Commands are executed line by line, starting with commands beginning in column 1 of a line. In this appendix we will denote commands with UPPERCASE LETTERS. (In this example, we will again use an 80-column line to define a line of text submitted in an SPSS run. This is the most common length of an input line; however, most systems will accept longer lines.) You can use as many lines as necessary to specify a command. The command field is the collection of columns, starting from column 1, that contain the SPSS commands for data handling, modification, and procedures.

Terms that "specify" what to do with the commands are found in the specification field. Specifications must not occupy column 1. In other words, indent continuations of specifications at least one column on lines following the command. You may continue specifications on the next line provided that you begin in column 2 and that you do not break within a word or logical connector (such as "and" or "or"). Remember, a computer cannot read English and interpret your needs; it reads only signals (characters) for which it has been programmed. Therefore, be careful to key in commands and specifications exactly as designated. SPSS will accept commands in either upper- or lowercase letters.

In SPSS PC+ all specifications must end with a period (.). This alerts the program that you have ended the specification for the command regardless of the number of lines you have used to specify the command.

The first step in analyzing your data is to set up and SAVE a file containing not only the data but also details about the type of information contained, where it is located, and what you plan to call it—this is the system file. One thing to keep in mind is that a variable must be defined before it is used.

**Commands.** *File definitions* provide basic information about files handled in the process of setting up the system file—where the data are stored, where you want the resulting system file to be stored, and so on. *Variable definitions* provide information concerning the location, structure, and meaning of the data on your input file. Table A.1 lists the following file and variable definition commands for a hypothetical file:

1. TITLE. This optional feature allows you to label your run with a title of up to 60 characters that is printed across the top of each page of your output in the listing file.

2. FILE HANDLE. [SPSS mainframe command] The *handle* identifies a file already stored or to be stored as a result of the commands in your command file. File handles must not exceed eight characters and must begin with a letter of the

alphabet or another symbol accepted by your computer or at your computing facility. You will have enough FILE HANDLE lines to identify each file used in the process of the run, for example, raw data files or SPSS system files.[2] The "file specifications" refers to the facility-specific specifications that define files stored on the mainframe.

3. DATA LIST. This command, discussed in detail in the next section, describes the variable names, location, type of data, and number of records associated with your input file.

4. MISSING VALUES. This optional command defines the values (a maximum of three) for variables that are designated as missing. SPSS will automatically assign a system missing value for blank fields. The SET command allows blanks on the input file to be read as either system missing or as some other value you SET. The ability to declare MISSING VALUES enables the researcher either to include variables that contain missing values in statistical procedures or to exclude them.

5. VARIABLE LABELS. This optional command allows you to describe your variables further. It augments the variable names on the DATA LIST by associating a label with the name. This option is quite handy if you choose to assign v-numbers as variable names (such as v1, v2, v3 and so on). It is also helpful when you are interpreting your output since the label descriptor will be listed beside your much smaller variable name. As shown in Table A.1, the format consists of your

**Table A.1**
Format Specification for SPSS Data Definition Commands

| Command Field (must begin in column 1) | Specification Field (no specifications or continuations appear in column 1) |
|---|---|
| TITLE* | Text up to 60 characters |
| FILE HANDLE** | Handle/file specifications |
| [additional FILE HANDLES if necessary] | |
| DATA LIST | FILE = [name] |
| | RECORDS = [N] |
| | /1 VARLIST$_1$ column number—column number, VARLIST$_2$ ... |
| | [/2 ... /N ...] |
| MISSING VALUES* | VARLIST$_1$ (value list$_1$)/[VARLIST$_2$ (value list$_2$)] |
| VARIABLE LABELS* | VARNAME$_1$ 'label$_1$' [/VARNAME$_2$ 'label$_2$'] |
| VALUE LABELS* | VARLIST$_1$ value$_1$ 'label$_1$' value$_2$ 'label$_2$' [/VARLIST$_2$ ...] |
| [additional modifications and then procedures may be placed here] | |
| SAVE | OUTFILE = [name] |

* Optional commands.
** Only on SPSS mainframe.

2. Note that some operating systems use JCL to identify files and hence in some cases a FILE HANDLE is not necessary. Your facility's consultants can tell you when a FILE HANDLE is necessary.

VARIABLE NAME, a space, then the descriptive VARIABLE LABEL inside single or double quotation marks. The label is followed by a slash (/)—which SPSS interprets as a sign for more specifications to follow.

6. VALUE LABELS. This optional command allows you to associate a label with each value of a variable. For example, if the coded values 1, 2, 3 stand for the terms *low, medium,* and *high,* respectively, then when that particular variable is used in a procedure, its coded value will have its associated label next to it on the listing file. If you have a number of variables that have the values of low, medium, and high, then you can list them all or access contiguous variables with the keyword "TO" and assign the numerals to the values once. Continuations of the VALUE LABELS' specifications are denoted by using a slash (/). Remember, in SPSS PC+ the specification ends with a period (.).

7. SAVE. This command saves your data and their labels or modifications as a permanent system file. We SAVE a file when we know we will want to access it at a later time for other purposes. Then we can eliminate many of the steps used to set up the file and begin with executing procedures via a FILE HANDLE and/or GET command. The GET command will be described shortly. The MAP specification on the SAVE command displays the order and complete list of variables SAVEd. In the case of the hypothetical file that is set up in Table A.1, once we GET the file SAVEd on the OUTFILE = specification, we never need to define the file again.

Table A.1 lists command keywords in the order of their inclusion in the command file. The inclusion order is relatively flexible in SPSS; however, one thing to keep in mind is that a variable must be defined before it is used. The inclusion order shown in Table A.1 is an example of a successful run.

DATA LIST *Command.* The DATA LIST command identifies your input file and indicates the format of the file and the number of records to be read per case from fixed-format data files. SPSS can read from a variety of data file types; the following example, from the GSS data set for this appendix, follows the fixed-field format discussed in Chapter 14:

```
FILE HANDLE GSS93/file specifications [mainframe]
DATA LIST FILE = GSS93 FIXED RECORDS= 1
    /1 ID 1–4 AGE 5–6 SEX 7 . . .
```

The FILE subcommand that appears after DATA LIST indicates either the file handle of your input file as it was defined in an earlier FILE HANDLE command on the mainframe or the file name on a diskette (e.g., "a:\gss93.dat") in SPSS PC+. The file handle is GSS93.

The keyword FIXED indicates that your data appear in a fixed-field format. FIXED is the format default in SPSS. By *default* we mean that in the absence of the specification, SPSS will assume a FIXED field "by default."

The RECORDS subcommand indicates the number of records, decks, or lines of input associated with each case for FIXED-format files. In the example, the input file GSS93 has one record per case.

The remainder of the specification refers to the variable definition. The number after the slash (/) refers to the number of the record on which SPSS is to find the variables described in the specification that follows. The first variables are to be read from record number 1 (the only one in this subset). Three variables, ID, AGE, and SEX, can be found on record 1 in the fields containing columns 1 through 4, 5 and 6, and 7, respectively.

As you can see from the example, each variable has a name designated in the DATA LIST command. Variable names have a maximum length of eight characters and must begin with a letter of the alphabet or with the character @, #, or $. If you are a beginner, avoid using special characters if at all possible as these characters refer to special types of variables. Variable names must be unique. That is, a variable cannot be named twice. If you do this accidentally, you will get an error message. Select names that reflect the nature of your variables, such as GENDER, AGE, and ID; as long as the names are unique and they do not exceed eight characters, they are acceptable. Otherwise, you can use a prefix (e.g., Q- for question number or v- for variable number). SPSS will then name your variables with the prefix and attach ascending numbers.

One of the easiest ways to identify the location of your variables on a record is to use the column numbers. In our example, SPSS expects to find the variable named ID in columns 1 through 4 on the first record of each case, AGE is found in columns 5 and 6 on the first record of each case, and so on. Our DATA LIST command defines the first three variables in our codebook. Compare the DATA LIST with the information found in the codebook in Exhibit A.1.

Some data require the use of decimal points. For instance, you can have percentages rounded to one decimal place or have dollars and cents (two decimal points). You must specify in your DATA LIST whether decimals in your data set are implied or are directly keyed into your input file. Consider the following hypothetical specification:

```
DATA LIST FILE = HYPSET RECORDS = 2
     /1 IDNUMBER 1–5 Q2 6–11 Q3 12
     /2 PCTSPENT 1–3 (1) TOTSPENT 4–9 (2)
```

The parentheses following the column numbers on the second record indicate that the variable PCTSPENT has one implied decimal place in the field and TOTSPENT has two. Therefore, when SPSS encounters the following on the second record of a case

```
231028954
```

it will list the value for PCTSPENT as 23.1, while the value for TOTSPENT would be 289.54. If SPSS encounters decimals on the input file, it will ignore the implied decimals (the number in parentheses) and instead add a decimal in the place specified by the decimal point (i.e., the number implied will be overridden).

SPSS also allows you to specify multiple adjacent variables with a shorthand notation. For example, if you have a list of ten adjacent variables, each with the same number of columns (two), you can name these contiguous variables

/3 V1 TO V10 1–20

SPSS will name these variables v1, v2, and so on to v10 and identify each as being located in two-column fields beginning with the field 1–2 for v1 and ending with the field in columns 19–20 for v10. In other words, the columns allocated will be divided equally among the v variables. The number of columns must be divisible by the implied number of variables. If you have five expenditure variables in a row, each with an equal number of columns to a field, you could follow a similar procedure, using the convention SPEND1 TO SPEND5 to name SPEND1, SPEND2, and so on, with SPSS allocating column fields if the number of columns you designated is divisible by 5. Note that you must know the final column number for the end of records when using this shorthand approach.

***Data Modifications and Procedures.***   Once you have assembled the necessary JCL and SPSS data definition information, you are ready to take the final step in the process of setting up the file: instructing the computer to do something with the information you have supplied. The two generic processes you will be concerned with in this treatment are DATA MODIFICATIONS and PROCEDURES.

In general, you employ DATA MODIFICATIONS when you wish to manipulate or transform your data in any way. PROCEDURES, by contrast, instruct the computer to calculate statistics. The DATA MODIFICATIONS available for our purposes are RECODE, COMPUTE, IF, SELECT IF, and LIST. The procedures are FREQUENCIES, CONDESCRIPTIVE, CROSSTABS, CORRELATIONS, SCATTERGRAM, PARTIAL CORR, RELIABILITY, and REGRESSION.

***Initial Run.***   The initial run should be executed with two goals in mind. First, you must determine whether the input data have been read into the SPSS system file exactly as you planned. Second, you must determine whether any stray or illegal codes were keyed in and not caught in the verification process. During the initial run, SPSS will display the information contained on your DATA LIST lines in a table that includes your list of variables, the record and columns on which each variable is found, the width of the field, and the number of decimal places the variable contains. Check this information carefully to ensure that you have properly transferred the data onto the system file. Assuming that the format is correct, the next step is to insert a PROCEDURE to provide FREQUENCIES, or univariate distributions, for each variable. The output you will get as a result of this procedure will enable you to determine the extent of cleaning the data will need prior to generating statistical information (see Chapter 14).

The general format of the FREQUENCIES command is

FREQUENCIES VARIABLES = VARNAME$_1$, VARNAME$_2$, ... VARNAME$_n$

where adjacent variables may be accessed by stating VARNAME$_{1st}$ TO VARNAME$_{last}$ and where all variables can be included by simply keying the word ALL after the equal sign. Table A.2 shows the actual setup of the GSS93 data set we are using in this appendix.

**Table A.2**

SPSS System File Setup for 1993 GSS Data Subset

|  |  |
|---|---|
|  | [Insert initial JCL here for mainframe] |
| TITLE | SETTING UP 1993 GSS DATA SUBSET SYSTEM FILE |
| FILE HANDLE | DATA/[file specifications] |
| FILE HANDLE | GSS93/[file specifications] |
| DATA LIST | FILE = DATA RECORDS = 1 |
|  | /1 ID1–4, AGE 5–6, SEX 7, RACE 8, REGION 9, MARITAL 10, |
|  | EDUC 11–12, DEGREE 13, INCOME 14–15, PARTYID 16, |
|  | EQWLTH 17, CAPPUN 18, RACSEG 19, HAPPY 20, HOMOSEX 21, |
|  | HELPPOOR 22, HELPNOT 23, HELPSICK 24, HELPBLK 25, |
|  | POLVIEWS 26, NATFARE 27, NATCITY 28, NATRACE 29 |
| VARIABLE LABELS | SEX 'RESPONDENTS SEX' |
|  | /RACE 'RESPONDENTS RACE' |
|  | /REGION 'REGION OF INTERVIEW' |
|  | [additional labels here] |
|  | /NATRACE 'IMPROVING THE CONDITION OF BLACKS' |
| VALUE LABELS | SEX 1 'MALE' 2 'FEMALE' / REGION 0 'NOT ASSIGNED' |
|  | 1 'NEW ENGLAND' 2 'MIDDLE ATLANTIC' 3 'E.NOR.CENTRAL' |
|  | 4 'W.NOR.CENTRAL' 5 'SOUTH ATLANTIC' |
|  | 6 'E.SOU.CENTRAL' 7 'W.SOU.CENTRAL' 8 'MOUNTAIN' |
|  | 9 'PACIFIC' |
|  | [additional labels here] |
|  | / NATFARE TO NATRACE 0 'NAP' 1 'TOO LITTLE' |
|  | 2 'ABOUT RIGHT' 3 'TOO MUCH' 8 'DK' 9 'NA' |
| MISSING VALUES | AGE, INCOME (0, 98, 99)/ EDUC (97, 98, 99)/ REGION (0) |
|  | / MARITAL (9)/ DEGREE (7, 8, 9)/ PARTYID (8, 9) |
|  | / EQWLTH TO NATRACE (0, 8, 9) |
| FREQUENCIES | VARIABLES = ALL |
| SAVE | OUTFILE = GSS93/MAP |

***Subsequent Runs.*** Once you have created an SPSS system file, you can access it by beginning the runstream with appropriate JCL and FILE HANDLE commands [mainframe] followed by the GET command. The GET specifies the active SPSS system file you want to use to perform the operations in your runstream. The format of the GET command is

GET FILE = [handle or file specification]

## Cleaning the Data

Once you have verified that the DATA LIST is correct and that all the data were read in their intended formats, use the output generated from the FREQUENCIES procedure to determine whether there are any illegal responses listed for each of the variables.

For example, the variable MARITAL is coded: 1 = MARRIED, 2 = WIDOWED, 3 = DIVORCED, 4 = SEPARATED, 5 = NEVER MARRIED and 9 = NOT APPLICABLE. If you find a 7 listed in the FREQUENCIES for that variable, you can either declare the 7 a MISSING VALUE on a subsequent run or replace the 7 with the actual value from the questionnaire or coding sheet used to input these data. If you do not have the original coding source and cannot verify what a 7 is supposed to mean, you could use the following runstream to purge this inappropriate response:

```
GET FILE = [handle]
MISSING VALUES MARITAL (7, 9)
[insert remaining modifications, then procedures]
SAVE OUTFILE = [handle]
```

With this runstream, you make any modifications or permanent changes to your system file via the SAVE command. In this case, anytime you use MARITAL, SPSS will consider a 7 a MISSING VALUE and will treat it as you specify for MISSING VALUES. For example, it will not be used in any statistical calculations unless you directly specify to use it as such. Note that some facilities do not allow GET and SAVE on the same file name or handle in one runstream. Check with a consultant as to the most efficient way you can eliminate inappropriate responses at your facility. For the remainder of the examples in this appendix, we will assume that the appropriate JCL, FILE HANDLE and GET commands are included in your runstream.

If you are setting up your own data and encounter an invalid response category, you can use the SELECT IF and LIST commands to identify and list the errant cases. Once you have the list, you can determine what the correct responses are and permanently change the values using the IF or RECODE command in combination with the SAVE command (this sequence is discussed later).

The SELECT IF command allows you to isolate a subset of cases for investigation. Often in the social sciences, researchers wish to look only at the responses of "women" or "old people" or "Democrats" who are included with persons having different attributes in the data set. The SELECT IF command allows you to easily group respondents on the desired attribute. This is the most common usage for the SELECT IF. However, you can also use the SELECT IF while cleaning the data. Let's say that you found two responses of 7 to MARITAL (also assume there were no other errant codes). You can isolate those incorrect responses by using SELECT IF. The format of the SELECT IF command is

SELECT IF VARNAME [logical connector] value

where the logical connectors are

| Connector | Meaning |
| --- | --- |
| EQ *or* = | equal to |
| LT *or* < | less than |
| LE *or* < = | less than or equal to |
| GT *or* > | greater than |
| GE *or* > = | greater than or equal to |
| NE *or* < > | not equal to |

and the value can be a number or another variable name. You can make the SELECT IF command more complex by forming logical compound sentences connected by AND (meaning that all conditions must apply for case inclusion), OR (any condition can be met for case inclusion), or NOT (reverses the outcome of an expression).

Just isolating the errant cases for MARITAL is not sufficient for cleaning the data, of course. You can use LIST to list the cases you have selected and their values on a number of variables. In the example, all you need to identify and clean MARITAL is the case ID. Then you can consult your coding source (questionnaire or coding sheet) to find the correct values. The general format of the LIST command is

    LIST VARIABLE = [variable list]

The runstream to clean MARITAL would be

    SELECT IF MARITAL EQ 7
    LIST VARIABLES = ID

Let's say that the output indicates that ID numbers 24 and 87 have the value 7 for MARITAL and we find that the values should have been 1 and NOT APPLICABLE, respectively. We therefore need to change the 7 in the first instance to a 1 and to declare the 7 in the second instance as a MISSING VALUE. On a subsequent run, we could make the permanent transformations by using the IF command to isolate conditions that must exist for the transformation. The general format of the IF statement is

    IF [logical condition] target variable = value

where the *logical condition* and *value* are the same as defined in the SELECT IF specification field and the *target variable* is the variable to which you wish to attach the value. The runstream to clean our two cases would be

    IF ID EQ 24 MARITAL = 1
    MISSING VALUES MARITAL (7, 9)
    [any other permanent modifications]
    SAVE OUTFILE = [handle]

The IF statement changes the value of 7 for MARITAL to 1 for case number 24. The MISSING VALUES line includes the miscode of 7 for case number 87 as a missing value. This cleaning of the data permanently changes the system file when you use the SAVE command.

When you are confident that all your variables are clean, you can generate a complete and up-to-date data definition description of your system file by a procedure called DISPLAY, keyed in the form

    DISPLAY DICTIONARY

The more completely you define your data via the optional labeling, the better the DISPLAY output functions as a revised codebook. (In fact, the information generated using this command was used to construct the codebook in Exhibit A.1.) Also, the more carefully you key in the raw data and data definition commands, the less time you will spend cleaning the data. At this point, you are ready to begin your analysis of the data.

## Univariate Distributions (Chapter 15)

If you examine the output from the FREQUENCIES command, you will recognize it as a univariate distribution of groups of responses for each variable. Now that the data are clean, you can repeat this procedure to generate summary statistics including the mean, standard error, median, mode, standard deviation, variance, kurtosis, skewness, range, minimum, and maximum values. If you wish to generate all of these statistics for a subset of your variables, the runstream would include

```
FREQUENCIES VARIABLES = DEGREE, HAPPY
    /STATISTICS = ALL
```

If you wish to select only some of the available statistics, thus saving some computer time, you may specify the name of the statistics you require in the field after the STATISTICS = specification. The specification lists the statistics of interest, for example, mean, mode.

If you wish to generate summary statistics (e.g., mean, standard error) on interval-level variables (e.g., age, salary, city populations) and do not need to see the actual frequency distribution, use the subprogram called DESCRIPTIVES. The DESCRIPTIVES procedure has this format:

```
DESCRIPTIVES VARIABLES = VARLIST
    /STATISTICS = ALL
```

A DESCRIPTIVES command without a STATISTICS subcommand will generate the mean, standard deviation, minimum, maximum, standard error of the mean, kurtosis, skewness, range, and sum.

You can do some elementary graphics in SPSS and SPSS PC+. However, you must have the graphics portion of the packages to get any that are comparable in quality to even a basic PC graphics package. The graphics that are available with the Windows version are much better. See the display on pages 541–542 of this appendix to see what Windows will do with univariate graphics.

## Measurement: Scale and Index Construction (Chapter 18)

In Chapter 18, we discussed methods for measuring respondents' attitudes by constructing scales and indexes with indicators of particular attitudes. SPSS has the facility to assist scientists in a variety of ways in constructing unidimensional and multidimensional scales. As your expertise in methodology and statistics increases, you are encouraged to explore options in FACTOR analysis for multidimensional scaling. However, for purposes of this treatment, we will explore some basic operations with the COMPUTE, RELIABILITY, and IF commands.

COMPUTE *Command.*    Often social science researchers find it convenient to create or transform variables, for example, by weighting, percapitizing, or otherwise performing mathematical operations on existing variables. Researchers frequently use the COMPUTE transformation to satisfy these needs. The format of the COMPUTE command is quite simple: you use logical mathematical expressions to create your composite measures. For instance, you can add (+), subtract (−), multiply (*), divide (/), and exponentiate (**N). The command is also quite flexible—the operands may be variable names, real numbers, or integers. The general format of the COMPUTE command is

COMPUTE COMPUTED VARNAME = ARITHMETIC EXPRESSION

For the interval level statistics used in this Appendix, we COMPUTEd several new variables. For example, GOVACT is a scale that measures respondents' attitude toward overall governmental activism—a high score means one is opposed to activism. This variable is a combination of the responses to the survey items represented by the variables EQWLTH, HELPBLK, HELPNOT, HELPPOOR, and HELPSICK. We initially selected these variables along with the variable NATCITY because their survey descriptions suggested that they could contribute to a single scaled concept of governmental activism. Before doing the actual COMPUTing, however, we recognized that we were in an exploratory stage and wished to examine the extent to which our variables of interest actually contributed to our underlying unidimensional concept of antigovernmental activism. We wish only to retain those variables that contribute strongly to our scale and reject those that fail to meet a criteria of acceptability.

RELIABILITY *Analysis.*    To assess the variables' contribution to our scale, we need to measure the average intercorrelation among the variables and to relate this to the actual number of variables comprising our index. The statistic that is available to accomplish this is called Cronbach's alpha and the SPSS procedure that provides this reliability estimate is RELIABILITY.

Before running a RELIABILITY analysis with our proposed scale, however, we have to be sure that all the component variables are coded in the same direction, that is, that a high value (4 or 5) on any one of the variables indicates an attitude opposed to governmental activism. For our proposed scale, GOVACT, we find that all the variables we are considering are already coded in the same direction. That is, a low score on every variable that is a candidate for the index indicates an attitude favoring high governmental involvement; whereas, a high score indicates an attitude that is opposed to governmental involvement. Therefore, no recoding was required.

We did, however, create another index where RECODing was first required. This index, LIBERAL, portrays an underlying latent attitude of liberalism through scaling the following variables: CAPPUN, HOMOSEX, NATCITY, NATFARE, NATRACE, POLVIEWS, and RACSEG. Initially all of the variables were not coded in the same direction: a low score for four of the variables indicated a liberal response whereas a low score on the other three indicated a conservative response. We chose to RECODE the low/liberal measures to be directionally consistent with low/conservative measures. In the example that follows, the lower scores on the variables identified on the RECODE lines indicate liberalism, whereas lower scores on all the other variables indicate conservatism. Therefore, we have to use a RECODE to change the values on those low/liberal variables to be consistent with the other component variables. The following lines were used to RECODE the variables:

```
RECODE NATCITY
   (1=3) (2=2) (3=1) INTO NATCITY2
RECODE NATFARE
   (1=3) (2=2) (3=1) INTO NATFARE2
RECODE NATRACE
   (1=3) (2=2) (3=1) INTO NATRACE2
RECODE POLVIEWS
   (1=7) (2=6) (3=5) (4=4) (5=3) (6=2) (7=1) INTO POLVIEW2
```

We could have changed the initial variables by using the RECODE without the "INTO" specification. By using INTO we maintained both the original and new variables in the system file.

After we are sure that all of our candidate variables for the index are coded in the same direction, we can submit them to RELIABILITY testing. The basic format of the RELIABILITY command is:

```
RELIABILITY /VARIABLES = VARNAME1, VARNAME2, ETC.
   /SUMMARY = TOTAL
```

For our first RELIABILITY run we used all of our candidate variables for GOVACT in the following statement:

```
RELIABILITY /VARIABLES = EQWLTH HELPBLK HELPNOT
                         HELPPOOR HELPSICK NATCITY
   /SUMMARY = TOTAL
```

Our resultant output is in Table A.3.

The key statistical figure in interpreting the reliability of our scale is the alpha listed under the reliability coefficients section at the end of our output. The value of coefficient alpha can range from zero (no internal consistency) to one (complete internal consistency). How large must our coefficient be to suggest an acceptable level of internal consistency? Nunnally suggests a value of no less than .70 as a quick rule.[3] As you can see in the first output of our RELIABILITY for our index GOVACT, the coefficient alpha was .6814. This does not quite meet acceptable reliability according to our quick rule. However, if we look at the section of output entitled "Item-total Statistics" and under the column labeled "Alpha if Item Deleted," we see that the alpha if NATCITY is deleted would be .6841—somewhat higher than the current scale alpha of .6814. This means that if we take NATCITY

---

3. J. Nunnally. *Psychometric Theory* (New York: McGraw-Hill, 1978).

**Table A.3**
Reliability Analysis: Scale (All)

Item-Total Statistics

| | Scale Mean if Item Deleted | Scale Variance if Item Deleted | Corrected Item—Total Correlation | Alpha if Item Deleted |
|---|---|---|---|---|
| EQWLTH | 13.3485 | 12.4605 | .4460 | .6611 |
| HELPBLK | 13.5379 | 17.2821 | .3772 | .6513 |
| HELPNOT | 13.9520 | 16.0863 | .5281 | .6033 |
| HELPPOOR | 14.0354 | 16.5608 | .5511 | .6025 |
| HELPSICK | 14.6187 | 16.9656 | .4304 | .6350 |
| NATCITY | 15.4571 | 20.2842 | .2529 | .6841 |

Reliability Coefficients

N of Cases = 396.0    N of Items = 6
Alpha = .6814

out of consideration for our index, the index would become more reliable. Although the magnitude of the difference between .6841 and .6814 is not great, in our experience we have found that the actual alpha you will obtain if you run RELIABILITY again after removing a "weak" item may be somewhat different than that suggested in the "Alpha if Item Deleted" column states.

The runstream below yields the output in Table A.4.

```
RELIABILITY /VARIABLES = EQWLTH HELPBLK HELPNOT
                         HELPPOOR HELPSICK
         /SUMMARY = TOTAL
```

**Table A.4**
Reliability Analysis: Scale (All)

Item-Total Statistics

| | Scale Mean if Item Deleted | Scale Variance if Item Deleted | Corrected Item—Total Correlation | Alpha if Item Deleted |
|---|---|---|---|---|
| EQWLTH | 11.9288 | 11.6635 | .4517 | .6948 |
| HELPBLK | 12.0825 | 16.4242 | .3610 | .6923 |
| HELPNOT | 12.5684 | 14.6144 | .5739 | .6141 |
| HELPPOOR | 12.6418 | 15.2754 | .5716 | .6225 |
| HELPSICK | 13.1740 | 15.7457 | .4589 | .6583 |

Reliability Coefficients

N of Cases = 885.0    N of Items = 5
Alpha = .7040

Indeed, as can be seen in the second RELIABILITY output, our alpha without the variable NATCITY is .7040. By dropping NATCITY out of consideration, our pooled number of cases changed from 396 to 885. The increase in the number of cases accounts for the difference between the magnitude of this coefficient and the .6841 suggested by the previous output. In other words, dropping NATCITY not only improved our alpha because it had relatively low inter-item correlations (an improvement from .6814 to .6841) but also because it was suppressing cases as missing that otherwise would have remained in our pooled sample and that just happen to contribute to greater reliability (an improvement from .6841 to .7040).

COMPUTE *after* RELIABILITY.    Now that we are confident that our index, GOVACT, meets an acceptable level of reliability with a coefficient alpha of .7040, we need only COMPUTE it into a new variable. The command we use to accomplish this is:

COMPUTE GOVACT = EQWLTH + HELPBLK + HELPNOT + HELPPOOR
+ HELPSICK

If you COMPUTE new variables or indexes you can SAVE them and make them permanent variables in your system file. When new variables are computed, cases with missing data on any variable operand will be assigned the system missing value.

IF *Statements.*    IF statements are especially useful when constructing indexes, or typologies (combinations of characteristics that are usually referred to with labels rather than values, such as an ideal type in sociology), using nominal or ordinal variables (or both). The format of IF was discussed earlier. Let's say that you wish to construct a measure of the socioeconomic status of your respondents. We could use the IF statements and VALUE LABELS thus:

IF EDUC LE 8 AND INCOME LE 8 SES = 1
IF EDUC GE 9 AND EDUC LT 16 AND INCOME LE 8 SES = 2
[proceed until all combinations have been exhausted]
VALUE LABELS SES (1) LOWEST (2) LOW . . .

Note that you need to consider all possible combinations of your component variables. In other words, the typology must be mutually exclusive and exhaustive— every respondent must be able to be classified under a type, but in one category only. Also note that you can code different combinations into the same category, such as medium education and low income. In this case, both categories receive the same code.

## Bivariate Distributions (Chapter 16)

As you learned in Chapter 16, bivariate analysis enables us to see the association or relationship between two variables; we can observe how one variable covaries with another. Using bivariate statistics, we can determine not only whether a relationship exists at all (significance test) but also the strength and direction of such a relationship (measures of association).

*Nominal and Ordinal Measures.*    In SPSS the CROSSTABS procedure is specifically designed to generate bivariate tables and statistics for nominal and ordinal variables and takes the form

CROSSTABS TABLES = VARNAME$_1$ BY VARNAME$_2$ [BY VARNAME$_3$]
/VARNAME$_4$ BY VARNAME$_5$ [BY VARNAME$_6$]

VARNAME$_1$ and VARNAME$_4$ will be treated as dependent variables (printed down the left-hand column, or $Y$ axis, as has been the convention in this book) of individual tables; VARNAME$_2$ and VARNAME$_5$ are the independent variables of their respective tables; and VARNAME$_3$ and VARNAME$_6$ function as control variables, generating one table for each value of the control. The use of controls is optional.

Suppose that you wish to examine the relationship between educational level and opinions regarding how happy people are with their lives in general. To test this relationship, you would use the following command:

CROSSTABS TABLES = HAPPY BY DEGREE
/CELLS = ROW, COL, TOT/STATISTICS = ALL

which would produce Table A.5. The outlined cell presents the numbers for persons with a bachelor's degree (DEGREE = 3) who are pretty happy with their lives (HAPPY = 2). The uppermost left-hand description cell (COUNT, ROW PCT, COL PCT,

---

**Table A.5**
Crosstabulation of Happy and Degree

HAPPY    GENERAL HAPPINESS    by    DEGREE    RS HIGHEST DEGREE

| | | DEGREE | | | | Page 1 of 1 | |
|---|---|---|---|---|---|---|---|
| | Count | | | | | | |
| | Row Pct | LT HIGH | HIGH SCH | JUNIOR C | BACHELOR | GRADUATE | |
| | Col Pct | SCHOOL | OOL | OLLEGE | | | Row |
| | Tot Pct | 0 | 1 | 2 | 3 | 4 | Total |
| HAPPY | | | | | | | |
| | 1 | 80 | 234 | 26 | 91 | 44 | 475 |
| VERY HAPPY | | 16.8 | 49.3 | 5.5 | 19.2 | 9.3 | 31.8 |
| | | 28.8 | 30.1 | 28.9 | 38.9 | 39.3 | |
| | | 5.4 | 15.7 | 1.7 | 6.1 | 2.9 | |
| | 2 | 152 | 459 | 56 | 122 | 60 | 849 |
| PRETTY HAPPY | | 17.9 | 54.1 | 6.6 | 14.4 | 7.1 | 56.9 |
| | | 54.7 | 59.0 | 62.2 | 52.1 | 53.6 | |
| | | 10.2 | 30.8 | 3.8 | 8.2 | 4.0 | |
| | 3 | 46 | 85 | 8 | 21 | 8 | 168 |
| NOT TOO HAPPY | | 27.4 | 50.6 | 4.8 | 12.5 | 4.8 | 11.3 |
| | | 16.5 | 10.9 | 8.9 | 9.0 | 7.1 | |
| | | 3.1 | 5.7 | .5 | 1.4 | .5 | |
| Column | | 278 | 778 | 90 | 234 | 112 | 1492 |
| Total | | 18.6 | 52.1 | 6.0 | 15.7 | 7.5 | 100.0 |

## Table A.5 (continued)

| Chi-Square | Value | DF | Significance |
|---|---|---|---|
| Pearson | 20.06834 | 8 | .01008 |
| Likelihood Ratio | 19.24346 | 8 | .01361 |
| Mantel-Haenszel test for linear association | 13.84328 | 1 | .00020 |

Minimum Expected Frequency -   10.134

| Statistic | Value | ASE1 | Val/ASE0 | Approximate Significance |
|---|---|---|---|---|
| Phi | .11598 | | | .01008 *1 |
| Cramer's V | .08201 | | | .01008 *1 |
| Contingency Coefficient | .11520 | | | .01008 *1 |
| Lambda : | | | | |
| symmetric | .00000 | .00000 | | |
| with HAPPY     dependent | .00000 | .00000 | | |
| with DEGREE    dependent | .00000 | .00000 | | |
| Goodman & Kruskal Tau : | | | | |
| with HAPPY     dependent | .00585 | .00308 | | .02593 *2 |
| with DEGREE    dependent | .00354 | .00186 | | .00692 *2 |
| Uncertainty Coefficient : | | | | |
| symmetric | .00576 | .00267 | 2.15880 | .01361 *3 |
| with HAPPY     dependent | .00693 | .00320 | 2.15880 | .01361 *3 |
| with DEGREE    dependent | .00493 | .00228 | 2.15880 | .01361 *3 |
| Kendall's Tau-b | -.08272 | .02350 | -3.50764 | |
| Kendall's Tau-c | -.07555 | .02154 | -3.50764 | |
| Gamma | -.13496 | .03810 | -3.50764 | |
| Somers' D : | | | | |
| symmetric | -.08246 | .02343 | -3.50764 | |
| with HAPPY     dependent | -.07638 | .02173 | -3.50764 | |
| with DEGREE    dependent | -.08960 | .02546 | -3.50764 | |
| Pearson's R | -.09636 | .02585 | -3.73680 | .00019 *4 |
| Spearman Correlation | -.09237 | .02624 | -3.58084 | .00035 *4 |
| Eta : | | | | |
| with HAPPY     dependent | .09859 | | | |
| with DEGREE    dependent | .09703 | | | |

*1 Pearson chi-square probability
*2 Based on chi-square approximation
*3 Likelihood ratio chi-square probability
*4 VAL/ASE0 is a t-value based on a normal approximation, as is the significanc

Number of Missing Observations:   8

TOT PCT) tells the order of the numbers within each internal cell. For the highlighted cell, the number 122 means that 122 respondents (count) have both of these characteristics. Of all respondents who are pretty happy, 14.4 percent have a bachelor's degree (row percent), and 52.1 percent of respondents with a bachelor's degree are pretty happy with their lives (column percent). The $N$ of 122 out of the total $N$ of 1492 accounts for 8.2 (total) percent of the respondents in the survey.

Notice that Table A.5 has three rows and five columns. We know that the value of our coefficients, for example, chi-square ($\chi^2$), are a function of the number of cells in the table. Since there are 112 respondents with graduate degrees, we can reduce the number of cells by excluding those with a graduate degree, using the command:

```
SELECT IF DEGREE LE 3
```

Another option would be to collapse the categories so that those with graduate degrees would be grouped with those having bachelor's degrees since they are all college graduates. You can collapse categories using RECODE:

```
RECODE DEGREE (3, 4 = 3)
```

We could go even further and collapse the categories so that all who have not graduated from college are in one category and all who have graduated from college are in the other:

```
RECODE DEGREE (0 THRU 2 = 1) (3, 4 = 2)
```

Often social scientists wish to examine the relationships among a subset of respondents. In CROSSTABS, this can be accomplished by including a third (control) variable in the TABLES = specification. However, if we are interested in only one category of the control variable (or if we are using a procedure that does not allow a method of control), SELECT IF is the handiest way to segregate such a subset. We can use SELECT IF and RECODE together to select cases and collapse categories. For example, the runstream

```
SELECT IF SEX EQ 2 AND MARITAL EQ 1
RECODE DEGREE (O THRU 2 = 1) (3, 4 = 2)
CROSSTABS TABLES = HAPPY BY DEGREE
   /STATISTICS ALL
```

would produce a table of married female respondents only. (Note that the variables in the SELECT IF command need not appear in CROSSTABS or any other PROCEDURE command.)

*Interval Measures.*   The subprogram CORRELATIONS calculates the Pearson product-moment correlation coefficient (Pearson's $r$), an association statistic appropriate for interval-level variables, and tests for significance using a two-tailed $t$ test. In most cases, coefficients generated by CORRELATIONS are equivalent to the Spearman rank-order coefficients produced by the procedure NONPAR CORR as appropriate for ordinal-ordinal, ordinal-interval, and interval-interval variables. The series

```
CORRELATIONS VARIABLES = AGE, EDUC, INCOME, LIBERAL, GOVACT
   /STATISTICS = ALL
```

will produce one table showing the means and standard deviations of the variables, a variance-covariance table, one table featuring the coefficients, the $N$ on which the calculations were based, and the significance level. This is illustrated in Table A.6.

The cell outlined in Table A.6 is the correlation between AGE and a LIBERAL scale where a higher score on LIBERAL the respondent is more liberal. On the second-to-the-last line from the bottom of the table we find the legend for this table, where the first line in each cell is the Pearson's $r$ (coefficient), the second line is the $N$ (cases), and the third line is the two-tailed significance. In this example, the higher the age of the respondent, the less liberal the person is. The strength of the relationship is $-.2784$ (not very strong). However, the relationship is statistically significant at the p=.000 level. (Recall that the higher the $N$, the greater the probability of there being a statistically significant relationship. It is more "significant" in this case to discuss the strength of the relationship rather than the statistical significance.)

You may wish to plot a scatter diagram to visually assess the relationship between two of your variables. The subprogram PLOT will plot these relationships for you if your SPSS installation has graphics capacity. The series

    PLOT PLOT= AGE WITH␣LIBERAL

will produce the output graphically, displaying the relationship between age and the liberalism score (Figure A.1).

## Multivariate Analysis (Chapter 17)

The three major functions of multivariate analysis, as we learned in Chapter 17, are control, interpretation, and prediction. Mechanically, the first two functions are covered by using control variables in the equations; the subprograms CROSSTABS and PARTIAL CORR can provide for these controls. Prediction is enhanced by REGRESSION.

*Multivariate* CROSSTABS.    We have already presented the basic format of the CROSSTABS procedure. The portion of the specification in brackets indicates the control variable(s). For instance, if you are controlling for the variable "gender of respondent," the resultant output will consist of two tables having the same dependent and independent variables but differing as to respondents' gender: for the first table, all cases reported will be men, and for the second, they will all be women. Of course, the $N$s for each table will be different, but the structure of the rows and columns will be the same.

PARTIAL CORR.    Partial correlations are conceptually similar to multivariate CROSSTABS in that the effects of other variables are controlled when analyzing the relationship between the original variables. Whereas CROSSTABS physically removes the effects by portioning the cases based on the values of the control, PARTIAL CORR removes the effects statistically. This difference can be very impor-

**Table A.6**
Correlation Ouput Using Interval Level Variables

| Variable | Cases | Mean | Std Dev |
|---|---|---|---|
| AGE | 1495 | 46.2268 | 17.4180 |
| EDUC | 1496 | 13.0374 | 3.0741 |
| INCOME | 1434 | 10.4777 | 2.6535 |
| LIBERAL | 345 | 16.7797 | 3.4427 |
| GOVACT | 885 | 15.5989 | 4.6315 |

| Variables | | Cases | Cross-Prod Dev | Variance-Co· |
|---|---|---|---|---|
| AGE | EDUC | 1491 | -20667.0463 | -13.8· |
| AGE | INCOME | 1429 | -6186.9643 | -4.3· |
| AGE | LIBERAL | 345 | -5541.2029 | -16.1· |
| AGE | GOVACT | 882 | 13315.5556 | 15.1· |
| EDUC | INCOME | 1430 | 4446.1888 | 3.1· |
| EDUC | LIBERAL | 344 | 803.3663 | 2.3· |
| EDUC | GOVACT | 882 | 2713.3039 | 3.0· |
| INCOME | LIBERAL | 334 | -49.4072 | -.1· |
| INCOME | GOVACT | 849 | 2242.5830 | 2.6· |
| LIBERAL | GOVACT | 159 | -1224.7107 | -7.7· |

- - Correlation Coefficients - -

| | AGE | EDUC | INCOME | LIBERAL | G( |
|---|---|---|---|---|---|
| AGE | 1.0000 ( 1495) P= . | -.2593 ( 1491) P= .000 | -.0949 ( 1429) P= .000 | -.2784 ( 345) P= .000 | ( P= |
| EDUC | -.2593 ( 1491) P= .000 | 1.0000 ( 1496) P= . | .3819 ( 1430) P= .000 | .2205 ( 344) P= .000 | . ( P= |
| INCOME | -.0949 ( 1429) P= .000 | .3819 ( 1430) P= .000 | 1.0000 ( 1434) P= . | -.0168 ( 334) P= .760 | . ( P= |
| LIBERAL | -.2784 ( 345) P= .000 | .2205 ( 344) P= .000 | -.0168 ( 334) P= .760 | 1.0000 ( 345) P= . | -. ( P= |
| GOVACT | .1929 ( 882) P= .000 | .2227 ( 882) P= .000 | .2181 ( 849) P= .000 | -.4807 ( 159) P= .000 | 1. ( P= |

(Coefficient / (Cases) / 2-tailed Significance)

" . " is printed if a coefficient cannot be computed

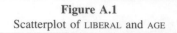

**Figure A.1**
Scatterplot of LIBERAL and AGE

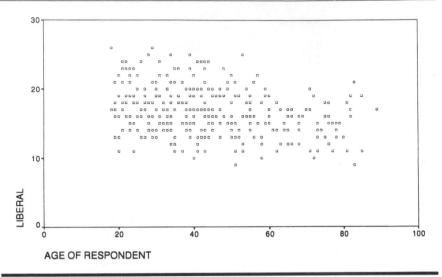

tant when you are controlling for more than one variable because separating the cases reduces the cell frequencies. Thus when the analysis involves interval-level variables, you should use PARTIAL CORR.

The following lines in your command file

```
PARTIAL CORR GOVACT WITH AGE BY LIBERAL, INCOME (1, 2)
    /STATISTICS = ALL
```

calculate the zero-order, first-order, and second-order partial for each unique combination of the dependent variable (GOVACT) and the independent variable (AGE). The controls will be for LIBERAL and INCOME individually and simultaneously. Recall that zero-order partials are the same as the Pearson's $r$ correlation between the independent variable and dependent variable. The first-order partial is the correlation controlling for the first control variable, while the second-order is when you also control simultaneously for the second control variable. A maximum of five orders may appear within the parentheses. The order may not exceed the number of control variables. An example of PARTIAL CORR is presented in Table A.7.

REGRESSION *(Multiple Relationships).*    Often a researcher will hypothesize that a number of independent variables contribute to the explained variance of a

**Table A.7**
Partial Correlation Output

| Variable | Mean | Standard Dev | Cases |
|---|---|---|---|
| GOVACT | 15.4091 | 4.4511 | 154 |
| AGE | 44.5519 | 17.1083 | 154 |
| LIBERAL | 16.8571 | 3.6343 | 154 |
| INCOME | 10.6364 | 2.4755 | 154 |

- - - P A R T I A L    C O R R E L A T I O N    C O E F F I C I E N T S - - -

Zero Order Partials

|  | GOVACT | AGE | LIBERAL | INCOME |
|---|---|---|---|---|
| GOVACT | 1.0000 | .2337 | -.4707 | .0943 |
|  | ( 0) | ( 152) | ( 152) | ( 152) |
|  | P= . | P= .004 | P= .000 | P= .245 |
| AGE | .2337 | 1.0000 | -.3031 | -.1638 |
|  | ( 152) | ( 0) | ( 152) | ( 152) |
|  | P= .004 | P= . | P= .000 | P= .042 |
| LIBERAL | -.4707 | -.3031 | 1.0000 | .0647 |
|  | ( 152) | ( 152) | ( 0) | ( 152) |
|  | P= .000 | P= .000 | P= . | P= .426 |
| INCOME | .0943 | -.1638 | .0647 | 1.0000 |
|  | ( 152) | ( 152) | ( 152) | ( 0) |
|  | P= .245 | P= .042 | P= .426 | P= . |

(Coefficient / (D.F.) / 2-tailed Significance)

" . " is printed if a coefficient cannot be computed

- - - P A R T I A L    C O R R E L A T I O N    C O E F F I C I E N T S - - -

Controlling for..    LIBERAL

|  | AGE |
|---|---|
| GOVACT | .1083 |
|  | ( 151) |
|  | P= .183 |

(Coefficient / (D.F.) / 2-tailed Significance)

" . " is printed if a coefficient cannot be computed

---

**Table A.7** *(continued)*

---

```
- - - P A R T I A L   C O R R E L A T I O N   C O E F F I C I E N T S   -

Controlling for..    INCOME

                AGE

GOVACT          .2537
               (  151)
               P=  .002

(Coefficient / (D.F.) / 2-tailed Significance)

" . " is printed if a coefficient cannot be computed
```

```
- - - P A R T I A L   C O R R E L A T I O N   C O E F F I C I E N T S   -

Controlling for..    LIBERAL    INCOME

                AGE

GOVACT          .1326
               (  150)
               P=  .103

(Coefficient / (D.F.) / 2-tailed Significance)

" . " is printed if a coefficient cannot be computed
```

---

single dependent variable. Multiple REGRESSION is the SPSS subprogram that handles such simultaneous effects.

The commands for REGRESSION feature a declaration of the variables included in the analysis and a description of how the processing should take place. The following lines produced the output in Table A.8:

REGRESSION /VARIABLES = GOVACT, LIBERAL, INCOME, EDUC
    / DESCRIPTIVES / STATISTICS = ALL / DEPENDENT = GOVACT
    / METHOD=STEPWISE

In the sequence of lines, we asked SPSS to compute descriptive statistics for all the variables on the VARIABLES = list. Because REGRESSION is an asymmetrical statistic, we must state which of our variables is dependent so that we can regress $Y$ on $X$. We chose a STEPWISE procedure so that we can see the results at each step. Notice that you receive an analysis of variance for the set of variables, the standard error, some summary statistics, the Pearson's $r$ between each independent variable and the dependent variable, each $b$, beta, and the intercept $a$.

## Table A.8
### Regression Output with GOVACT as the Dependent Variable

```
* * * *   M U L T I P L E   R E G R E S S I O N   * * * *
```

Listwise Deletion of Missing Data

```
              Mean  Std Dev  Label

GOVACT       15.409   4.451  Scale of Government Inactivism
LIBERAL      16.857   3.634  Scale of Liberal Attitudes
INCOME       10.636   2.476  TOTAL FAMILY INCOME
EDUC         13.442   3.160  HIGHEST YEAR OF SCHOOL COMPLETED
```

N of Cases =   154

Correlation:

```
              GOVACT    LIBERAL     INCOME      EDUC

GOVACT        1.000     -.471       .094        .141
LIBERAL       -.471     1.000       .065        .267
INCOME        .094      .065        1.000       .311
EDUC          .141      .267        .311        1.000
```

```
* * * *   M U L T I P L E   R E G R E S S I O N   * * * *
```

Equation Number 1    Dependent Variable..   GOVACT   Scale of Government In

Block Number  1.  Method:  Stepwise      Criteria   PIN  .0500   POUT  .1000

Variable(s) Entered on Step Number
   1..    LIBERAL    Scale of Liberal Attitudes

```
Multiple R            .47071
R Square              .22156          R Square Change    .22156
Adjusted R Square     .21644          F Change           43.26314
Standard Error        3.94003         Signif F Change    .0000
```

Analysis of Variance
```
                   DF      Sum of Squares     Mean Square
Regression          1        671.60858        671.60858
Residual          152       2359.61869         15.52381
```

```
F =      43.26314      Signif F =  .0000
AIC          424.31262
PC             .79892
CP           16.80225
SBC          430.38652
```

Var-Covar Matrix of Regression Coefficients (B)
Below Diagonal: Covariance    Above:  Correlation

```
              LIBERAL

LIBERAL       .00768
```

## Table A.8 *(continued)*

XTX Matrix

|          | LIBERAL  | GOVACT  | INCOME  | EDUC    |
|----------|----------|---------|---------|---------|
| LIBERAL  | 1.00000  | .47071  | -.06466 | -.26731 |
| GOVACT   | -.47071  | .77844  | .12469  | .26670  |
| INCOME   | .06466   | .12469  | .99582  | .29328  |
| EDUC     | .26731   | .26670  | .29328  | .92855  |

```
* * * *   M U L T I P L E   R E G R E S S I O N   * * * *
```

Equation Number 1    Dependent Variable..   GOVACT   Scale of Government Inactiv

---------------------- Variables in the Equation ----------------------

| Variable   | B         | SE B     | 95% Confdnce Intrvl B |           | Beta     |
|------------|-----------|----------|-----------------------|-----------|----------|
| LIBERAL    | -.576488  | .087646  | -.749649              | -.403327  | -.470705 |
| (Constant) | 25.127032 | 1.511187 | 22.141389             | 28.112676 |          |

------------------------ Variables in the Equation ---------------------------

| Variable   | SE Beta | Correl Part Cor | Partial  | Tolerance | VIF   | T      |
|------------|---------|-----------------|----------|-----------|-------|--------|
| LIBERAL    | .071563 | -.470705 -.470705 | -.470705 | 1.000000 | 1.000 | -6.577 |
| (Constant) |         |                 |          |           |       | 16.627 |

------ in -------

| Variable   | Sig T |
|------------|-------|
| LIBERAL    | .0000 |
| (Constant) | .0000 |

----------------------- Variables not in the Equation -----------------------

| Variable | Beta In | Partial | Tolerance | VIF   | Min Toler | T     | Sig T |
|----------|---------|---------|-----------|-------|-----------|-------|-------|
| INCOME   | .125216 | .141624 | .995820   | 1.004 | .995820   | 1.758 | .0808 |
| EDUC     | .287220 | .313694 | .928548   | 1.077 | .928548   | 4.060 | .0001 |

Collinearity Diagnostics

| Number | Eigenval | Cond Index | Variance Proportions Constant | LIBERAL |
|--------|----------|------------|-------------------------------|---------|
| 1      | 1.97768  | 1.000      | .01116                        | .01116  |
| 2      | .02232   | 9.413      | .98884                        | .98884  |

**Table A.8** *(continued)*

```
        *  *  *    M U L T I P L E    R E G R E S S I O N    *  *  *  *

Equation Number 1    Dependent Variable..   GOVACT   Scale of Government Inactiv


Variable(s) Entered on Step Number
    2..    EDUC       HIGHEST YEAR OF SCHOOL COMPLETED


Multiple R            .54604
R Square              .29816          R Square Change    .07660
Adjusted R Square     .28887          F Change          16.48071
Standard Error       3.75352          Signif F Change     .0001

Analysis of Variance
                      DF       Sum of Squares      Mean Square
Regression             2           903.80358        451.90179
Residual             151          2127.42369         14.08890

F =       32.07503       Signif F =   .0000
AIC             410.36002
PC                 .72972
CP                2.38831
SBC             419.47087
```

Var-Covar Matrix of Regression Coefficients (B)
Below Diagonal: Covariance    Above: Correlation

|         | LIBERAL | EDUC    |
|---------|---------|---------|
| LIBERAL | .00751  | -.26731 |
| EDUC    | -.00231 | .00993  |

XTX Matrix

|         | LIBERAL  | EDUC     | GOVACT   | INCOME   |
|---------|----------|----------|----------|----------|
| LIBERAL | 1.07695  | -.28787  | .54748   | .01977   |
| EDUC    | -.28787  | 1.07695  | -.28722  | -.31585  |
| GOVACT  | -.54748  | .28722   | .70184   | .04046   |
| INCOME  | -.01977  | .31585   | .04046   | .90319   |

```
        *  *  *  *    M U L T I P L E    R E G R E S S I O N    *  *  *  *

Equation Number 1    Dependent Variable..   GOVACT   Scale of Government Inactiv


--------------------- Variables in the Equation ----------------------
```

| Variable   | B         | SE B     | 95% Confdnce Intrvl B | | Beta     |
|------------|-----------|----------|-----------|-----------|----------|
| LIBERAL    | -.670518  | .086650  | -.841721  | -.499315  | -.547481 |
| EDUC       | .404545   | .099650  | .207656   | .601433   | .287220  |
| (Constant) | 21.274394 | 1.724302 | 17.867519 | 24.681268 |          |

## Table A.8 *(continued)*

```
--------------------- Variables in the Equation --------------------------
```

| .able | SE Beta | Correl | Part Cor | Partial | Tolerance | VIF | T |
|---|---|---|---|---|---|---|---|
| :RAL | .070750 | -.470705 | -.527559 | -.532873 | .928548 | 1.077 | -7.738 |
| | .070750 | .140876 | .276769 | .313694 | .928548 | 1.077 | 4.060 |
| stant) | | | | | | | 12.338 |

```
-- in -------
```

| able | Sig T |
|---|---|
| :RAL | .0000 |
| | .0001 |
| stant) | .0000 · |

```
-------------------- Variables not in the Equation ----------------------
```

| able | Beta In | Partial | Tolerance | VIF | Min Toler | T | Sig T |
|---|---|---|---|---|---|---|---|
| ME | .044793 | .050814 | .903188 | 1.107 | .842174 | .623 | .5341 |

inearity Diagnostics

| er | Eigenval | Cond Index | Variance Proportions Constant | LIBERAL | EDUC |
|---|---|---|---|---|---|
| 1 | 2.94402 | 1.000 | .00350 | .00464 | .00545 |
| 2 | .03566 | 9.086 | .01361 | .46364 | .78741 |
| 3 | .02032 | 12.035 | .98289 | .53173 | .20714 |

Block Number   1   PIN =    .050 Limits reached.

```
* * * *   M U L T I P L E   R E G R E S S I O N   * * * *
```

tion Number 1   Dependent Variable..   GOVACT   Scale of Government Inactiv

Summary table
-------------

| MultR | Rsq | F(Eqn) | SigF | | Variable | BetaIn |
|---|---|---|---|---|---|---|
| .4707 | .2216 | 43.263 | .000 | In: | LIBERAL | -.4707 |
| .5460 | .2982 | 32.075 | .000 | In: | EDUC | .2872 |

# SPSS for Windows

The following section deals exclusively with SPSS for Windows—both Professional and Student versions. The information presented customizes the previous section's discussion of SPSS procedures and their outcomes to the popular Windows environment. While Windows has many features and capabilities unique to its operating system, the basic procedures and commands available to the SPSS user in the mainframe and DOS (PC) environments are also available in the Windows operating system. In this section, then, we will not "reinvent the wheel" by portraying Windows as a completely different way of doing SPSS. Instead, we will build upon your understanding of the basic SPSS functions and procedures described in the previous section and demonstrate how you can perform comparable operations in your Windows environment. In fact, as you will see, if you have the SPSS Professional version, you can employ practically the same syntax of the SPSS command statements presented to you in the previous section to obtain precisely the same output in your Windows version. Therefore, we will not recreate output examples in this section that are an exact match for output demonstrated in the previous section. Rather, we will relate the "Windows way of doing SPSS" to the standard output you have already encountered, referring you, when appropriate, to the previous sections of this appendix.

## Getting Acquainted with SPSS for Windows

SPSS for Windows Version 6 is a well-integrated Windows program that adheres to many typical Windows conventions and commands. For instance, the main application window contains the usual menu bar at the top with several conventional menu items such as **File, Edit,** and **Help.** Clicking once with a mouse or trackball on a menu item opens it, for example, clicking on **File** opens the File menu. The File menu itself contains such command items as **New, Open, Save,** and **Exit,** which an experienced Windows user expects to encounter. Clicking once again on any of these will perform the command or open a dialog box where further optional commands may be performed. Alternately, you can use the ALT key in combination with the underlined letter of the command (e.g., ALT + F for the **File** command) to activate the desired menu command. For purposes of instruction, however, we will assume that everyone using Windows will have access to a mouse or pointer device and that it will be the preferred method for maneuvering in SPSS. Hence, in the subsequent discussion, while references to SPSS menu items will be given in bold type, the ALT key combination letter of the command (e.g., the **F** in **File**) will not be underlined.

If you are using SPSS for Windows Student Version 6, you will find that it looks and behaves for the most part exactly as the full professional version of SPSS for Windows does. Hence the instructions that follow (which describe the SPSS professional system) are usually applicable to the Student Version. The Student Version is, however, a "restricted version of the system," and the following are the major limitations that apply to it: 1) Data files with more than 50 variables or more than 1,500 cases cannot be created or read into the application; 2) certain SPSS add-on options such as Professional Statistics or Trends are not available; and 3) the ability to write, paste, or run syntax commands using the SPSS Syntax window is not available. Additionally, certain minor limitations to the Student Version appear within some procedures. Where applicable, such minor limitations will be noted in the information that follows.

*Preferences.*    When first opening SPSS for Windows, you need to get acquainted with the configuration settings under which you run your SPSS sessions. To view your default settings, select the menu item **Edit,** then select **Preferences. . . .** The most important setting in the subsequently displayed dialog box (see Figure A.2) that you may need to alter in order to optimize the use of the program on your system is the **Working Memory.** You can change this value by clicking on the associated value box and entering an appropriate value (in kilobytes). There is no particular value that we can suggest for this setting since it must reflect the memory available to your system after invoking Windows. However, it is our experience that the initial default is less than optimal and that by fine-tuning this value you should be able to substantially improve the performance of your PC while executing SPSS programs. If you are working with the Professional version, you will also be able to effect the following options in the Preferences dialog box: 1) open a Syntax window at startup to run SPSS syntax, 2) display SPSS commands in the Output window along with procedure results, and 3) customize your session journal (your log for the session) within the default journal file or as a filename of your choice.

In the Student Version these conditions apply: 1) as previously mentioned, there is no Syntax window, 2) SPSS commands that are invoked by your menu choices cannot be displayed in the Output window, and 3) the session journal cannot be changed from the default as C:\WINDOWS\TEMP\SPSS.JNL . For the Student Version, however, the syntax commands *are* recorded in the session journal in an appended format. If you are using the Student Version, are familiar

**Figure A.2**
Preferences Dialog Box

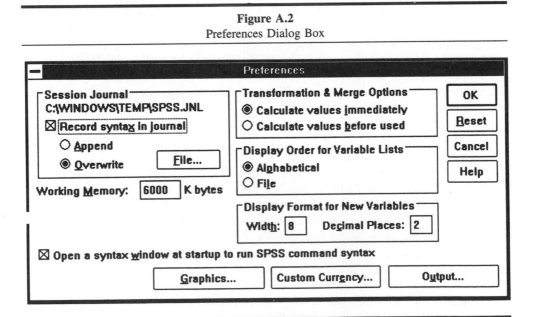

with SPSS syntax, and wish to check your Windows work for correspondence with your syntactical expectations, look in the session journal. If, however, you wish to use your knowledge of SPSS syntax to create programs in the Windows version, you will only be able to do so in the unrestricted Professional version.

***Entering Data.***    When you start SPSS for Windows, a data editor window with the default name **Newdata** and an empty **!Output** window are opened. A **!Syntax** window will also open if you have selected this option in the Professional version (see Figure A.3). If you are interested in entering data manually, this is the point where you begin. Make sure your data editor window, **Newdata,** is active (if so, it will be in the forefront and its title bar—the long bar at the top with the title "Newdata"—will be highlighted). You can make this or any other window showing on the screen active by clicking once on any part of the target window.

Entering data in the editor window is very similar to entering in any typical Windows spreadsheet program. You enter data one cell at a time into the current *active* entry cell. The *active cell* is so-called because it is always the immediate target cell for data entry or editing. It is always clearly identifiable by the thicker border surrounding it. And while any cell can be made the active cell simply by clicking upon it, the default active starting cell is always at row one, column one.

In SPSS Windows, a column contains all of a single variable's values and a row contains all of a single case's values. So you begin, as is natural, by entering a value for the first case upon the first variable. To do so, with the *active cell* in

---

**Figure A.3**
Windows Data Editor Window

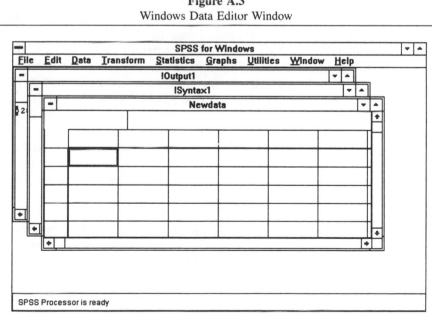

SPSS Processor is ready

the default position of row one/column one, you only need to type the appropriate numerical value and then hit Enter. You will notice that as you type, the value appears in the elongated cell editor at the top of the sheet where the cursor is blinking. Upon hitting Enter the first time, three things happen: 1) the value you typed enters into the first cell; 2) the column label above the cells in column one, which was previously displaying a generic "var" label is now labeled as "var00001" and 3) the next cell immediately below the first in column one—the cell for the second case value (row 2) upon the first variable (column 1)—now becomes the active cell and awaits your next entry. You may now enter another value, or if, for instance, the second case lacks a value, just hit the down arrow (⇓) key. Skipping an entry in a cell will cause a period to be displayed instead. This period represents a system-missing value and will be treated by all SPSS procedures as missing.

***Simple Editing: Correcting a Wrong Entry or Updating a Cell Entry.*** If you should happen to enter a wrong value in a cell or if the value in a particular cell requires updating, you simply need to click once on the desired cell to make it active and then retype. Press Enter and the job is done.

***Labeling Your Variable.*** At some point as—or after—you enter the data values for a variable, you will probably want to assign a name to the variable. Labeling in SPSS for Windows is remarkably easy. Moreover, in the dialog box you access to rename a variable, you can also: 1) change the variable's type, logical width, and the number of decimal places; 2) add, change, and remove variable and value labels; 3) set missing values; and 4) define the column format (width and alignment). To access this dialog box you can click on the menu bar item **Data, Define Variable . . .** or more simply you can just double click on the column label header "var00001," "var00002," and so forth. After the Define Variable dialog box appears, you can immediately change the variable name and select other options, which access further dialog boxes that allow you to define all of the other variable characteristics mentioned above (see Figure A.4). In the middle of this dialog box is a Variable Description area that informs you of your variable's current descriptive characteristics (type, label, missing values, alignment). As you change any of these characteristics for a variable, the information in this area is updated. To confirm all of the changes you define for a variable, click the **OK** button in the main dialog box. You will return to the main data window, where all of your customizations will have taken effect.

***Variable Information.*** At some point after you have spent time creating variables, you may want to look again at information concerning label, type, missing values, and value labels for a particular variable. You could call up a Define Variable dialog box, which contains a description of the variable. However, an easier and faster method is to click on **Utilities, Variables. . . .** You will get a Variables box that presents summary variable information for any variable you select (see Figure A.5). Moreover, as you scroll through the variable list on the

**Figure A.4**
Define Variables Dialog Box

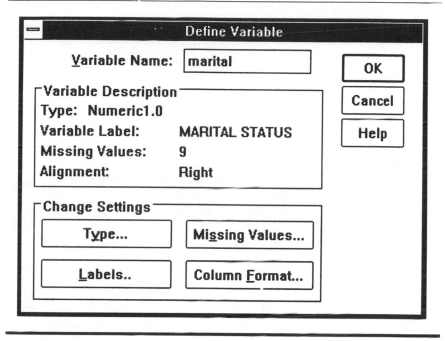

left of the box, you can instantly view the associated information for that variable on the right side.

You can also use this dialog box to move your active cell to other variables in your datasheet. This is especially useful if you have created a large datasheet composed of many columns—most of which are off the screen and out of sight. To use this feature, select the variable you are interested in by clicking on it once, click on the **Go To** button, and then click on the **Close** button. Your active cell will now reside in the column of the variable you selected.

*Saving Your Data.*   As you record your data or perform transformations upon it, you should save it periodically so that you won't lose your work in the event of a computer mishap. Give your data a unique and descriptive name so that you can refer to it readily. You need provide only the first part of the DOS name for your data file since the SPSS System provides an **.sav** extension as a default for data files. Once you have decided upon a name for your file (e.g., **mydata.sav**), click on **File, Save As . . .**, and provide the name as a replacement for the place-holding *\*.sav* that appears by default in the **File Name** box. Now just click on the **OK** button and your data is saved.

*Opening Saved Data.*   At any point after your data has been saved, you can leave the SPSS System and later return to it to open your data just as you left it

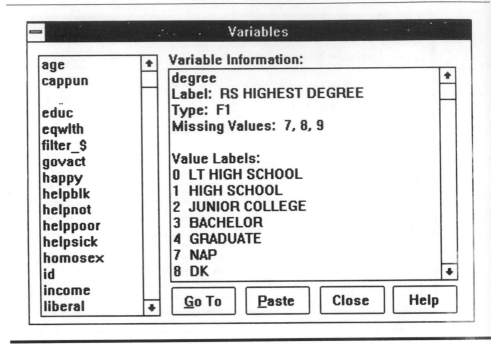

after your last save. To do so, click on **File, Open, Data . . . ,** and then select your file from the file list. If you saved your data as a file in a place other than the default SPSS directory, you will first need to select the drive and directory where your saved file resides. Once you have selected your data file, click **OK** and your data should load into a data window. You should, however, be aware that you can only open one data window at a time. If you have an open data window and decide to load another, the open one will close in order to accommodate your new request.

*Organizing and Saving Your Output.* If you are conducting a large number of output-generating procedures during any one session, all your output will load by default into your current Output window. To avoid creating an Output window with an unwieldy profusion of procedural output, you may want to direct selected output to additional Output windows. At any time during your session you can open an additional Output window by clicking on **File, New, SPSS Output.** A new Output window—sequentially numbered—will be displayed. However, it will not become your *active* Output window until you click on the **! button** that appears at the far right of its menu bar. When you do so, you will notice that the Output window you have selected changes—for example, from **Output2** to **!Output2,** with the **!** indicating that it is the actively selected window.

System output that has been generated and displayed in your current !Output window can be saved in the same fashion that you save data in a data window. With the !Output window you wish to save active, click on **File, Save As . . . ,** and provide a unique file name. You need to provide only the first part of the DOS name for your output file since the SPSS System provides a **.lst** extension as a default for output files. Once you have decided upon a name for your file (e.g., **newout.lst**), click on **File, Save As . . . ,** and provide the name **newout.lst** as a replacement for the placeholding **\*.lst** that appears by default in the **File Name** box. Now just click on the **OK** button and your output is saved.

To open saved output, click **File, Open, SPSS Output . . .** and select your output file.

## Running SPSS Procedures from Your Syntax Window

In the Professional version of SPSS only, a Syntax window is available in which you can create SPSS command language, to which you can paste SPSS commands from your menu selections, and from which you can run your SPSS syntax commands. As was discussed earlier, you can set your **Preferences** to open a Syntax window at startup. You can also open a new Syntax window at any time by clicking **File, New, SPSS Syntax.** See the manual for further information on using the Syntax window to create your own commands.

## Running SPSS for Windows by Menuing

Of course, you don't *have to use* the Syntax window *at all* to use the Windows program. Changing syntax is an option available to you if it is suitable to your work style. If you prefer to use only the Windows menus and dialog boxes to accomplish your work, the following will provide instructions for doing so that match the specific procedure commands discussed in the previous section of this appendix. Be aware, however, that running the precise syntax of SPSS commands described in the previous section through the use of a !Syntax window will *always* generate the *same* output that we have discussed and displayed in the previous section, while recreating those syntax commands through Windows menuing alone will *sometimes* generate *slightly different* output.

## Cleaning the Data

MISSING VALUES.    (See pages 510–513.) To declare a missing value for a variable, double-click on the variable name in the column header cell, click on the **Missing Values . . .** button, and then define your missing value in the Define Missing Values dialog box. When you are done, first click on the **Continue** button and then on the **OK** button. For the example on page 512:

1. Double click on the column header with the variable name MARITAL.
2. Click on the **Missing Values . . .** button and then click on a blank box under the **Discrete missing values** category.

3. Type in the new missing value of **7** (the missing value of **9,** already declared, appears in another adjacent box).
4. Click on the **Continue** and **OK** buttons.

SELECT IF / LIST.    (See pages 512–513.) The SELECT IF and LIST commands are used in the previous section to guide you through cleaning the data. You can use these same two commands in combination in Windows to achieve the same task. Or, alternatively, you can use a different and unique Windows command, **Search for Data . . . ,** to do the same thing.

If you choose to use the combination of SELECT IF and LIST to assist you in cleaning your data, you will execute the following sequence of menus:

1. Click on **Data,** and **Select Cases. . . .**
2. In the **Select Cases** dialog box, click on the **If condition is satisfied** option button.
3. Click on the **If . . .** button. A working box appears that contains a list of all of your variables, a calculator-like button keyboard of values and operators, and an insertable functions list (see Figure A.6).
4. Select the variable of interest (MARITAL) by clicking on it once and then click on the right arrow button ($\Rightarrow$) to move it over to the operations area, or simply click twice on your variable to move it over.
5. Now using the calculator-like button keyboard, click in sequence on those operators and those values required to isolate a subset of cases. For our example, click on the equals (=) operator and then click on the **7** number button.

**Figure A.6**
SELECT IF Working Box

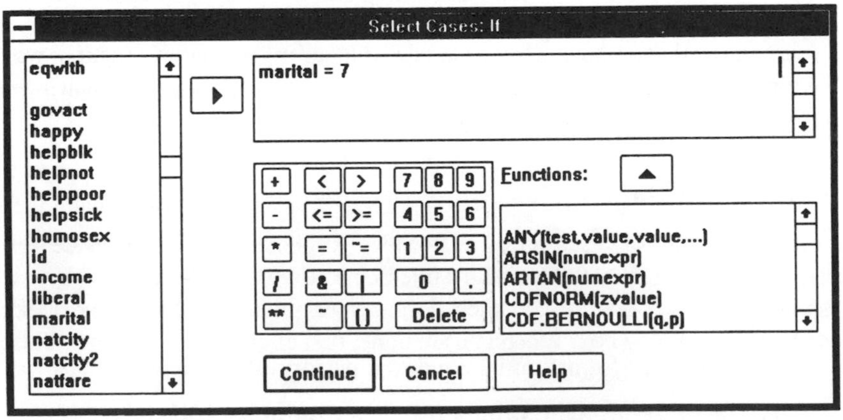

6. When done, click on the **Continue** button and then the **OK** button. *Note:* If you do nothing else, any further commands or procedures you execute during this session upon a variable you have subsetted with **If . . .** will act only upon that subset. If, at some point, you wish to execute procedures on all cases, return to the **Select Cases** dialog box, select the subsetted variable, and click on the **All cases** option button to remove the subsetting **If . . .** condition.

7. Next, click on **Statistics, Summarize, List Cases. . . .** You will be presented with a **List Cases** dialog box.

8. Select the identification variable of your choice (ID, in our case) and then click on the **Number cases** selection box so that an **x** appears in it. Then click **OK.** The identification variable for those value(s) you have previously subsetted, along with the associated case number(s), appear in a list in your Output window.

Instead of using the SELECT IF / LIST method of locating faulty (offending) values, you may wish to try the following method:

1. Click on any cell in the column of the variable (MARITAL) you wish to examine.

2. Click on **Edit, Search for Data. . . .** This presents you with a **Search for Data** dialog box.

3. Type in the value for which you wish to search (7). Then click on either the **Search Forward** or **Search Backward** buttons depending on how you want to proceed with your search. *Hint:* To conduct a more methodical search, in step 1 above click on the topmost cell (case 1) in the column of your variable of interest and then always proceed to **Search Forward.**

4. Since the **Search for Data** dialog box remains open until you click on the **Close** button, you can proceed from one case search to another by repeatedly clicking on one of the **Search** buttons. *Note:* You may have to reposition the **Search for Data** dialog box to see the results of your search on your Data window. To do so, click on the title bar of the dialog box and, while holding the click button down, **drag** the whole box to a more convenient location in your workspace; then **drop** it there by releasing the mouse button.

IF *transformation.*   (See page 518.) The IF transformation command is handled by the Windows program as a special case of the COMPUTE command. For instance, consider the command:

IF ID EQ 33 EDUC = 1

To achieve this transformation in Windows, perform the following steps:

1. Click on **Transform, Compute. . . .** A **Compute** dialog box appears that is very similar to the **Select Cases** dialog box.

2. In the **Target Variable** box, type the name of the variable whose value you want to transform for a particular case or number of cases. For this example, we type: **EDUC.**

3. In the **Numeric Expression** box type the value to which you wish to set a particular case or number of cases. For this example, we type: **1.**

4. Next click on the **If . . .** button. Make sure the **Include if case satisfies condition** option button is selected.

5. Now define the logical condition by which you intend to designate a subset for your transformation. For this example, we click, in the following order, on:

   ■ the variable **ID** from the variable list
   ■ the right arrow ($\Rightarrow$) to move **ID** over to the operation area
   ■ the = sign button
   ■ the number **33** button
   ■ the **Continue** button

   You will notice, as you return to the previous screen, that the condition **ID = 33** is now coded next to the **If . . .** button.

6. Now click on the **OK** button to launch the transformation.

DISPLAY *Dictionary.* (See page 513.) To output key information on all the variables in your entire data set, click on **Utilities, File Info.**

## Univariate Distributions

FREQUENCIES. (See page 514.) To generate FREQUENCIES statistics for your data, follow these steps:

1. Click on **Statistics, Summarize, Frequencies. . . .**
2. Select the variable or variables you are interested in examining (by example, DEGREE and HAPPY).
3. Make sure the **Display frequencies tables** is xed.
4. Click on the **Statistics . . .** button.
5. Select all options under the **Dispersion, Distribution,** and **Central Tendency** category boxes.
6. Click on **Continue** and then **OK.**

DESCRIPTIVES. (See page 514.) To generate DESCRIPTIVES statistics for your data, follow these steps:

1. Click on **Statistics, Summarize, Frequencies. . . .**
2. Select the variable or variables you are interested in examining.
3. Make sure the **Display labels** box is xed.
4. Click on the **Options . . .** button.
5. Select all options available.
6. Click on **Continue** and then **OK.**

**GRAPH.**     You can make barcharts and pie charts of univariate distributions using GRAPH. This subprogram produces graphics that are much better than any graphics available in SPSS or SPSS PC+. The graphics in Figures A.7 and A.8 were produced by this sequence

GRAPH / BAR (SIMPLE) = COUNT BY DEGREE / MISSING = REPORT.
GRAPH / PIE = COUNT BY HAPPY / MISSING = REPORT.

## Measurement: Scale and Index Construction

**RECODE** *before* **RELIABILITY.**     (See pages 515–516.) As explained in the previous section, all variables that are scaled into one index need to be coded in the same direction. We found that the variables NATCITY, NATFARE, NATRACE, and POLVIEWS were not coded in the same direction as other candidate variables for our scale of LIBERAL. Therefore, we recoded them to reverse the direction of their values. The following steps RECODE the three of these variables that have the same values and value range.

1. Click on **Transform, Recode, Into Different Variables. . . .** This invokes the **Recode into Different Variables** dialog box.
2. Select the first of the variables (NATCITY) and click on the right arrow button ($\Rightarrow$) to move it into the **Numeric Variable $\Rightarrow$ Output Variable** box.

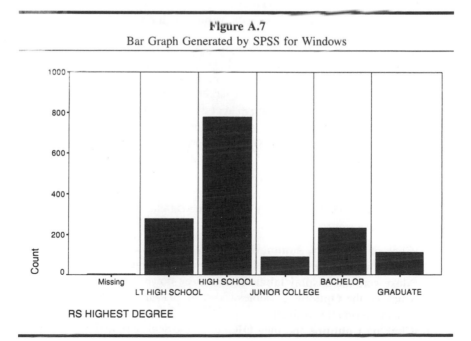

**Figure A.7**
Bar Graph Generated by SPSS for Windows

**Figure A.8**
Pie Chart Generated by SPSS for Windows

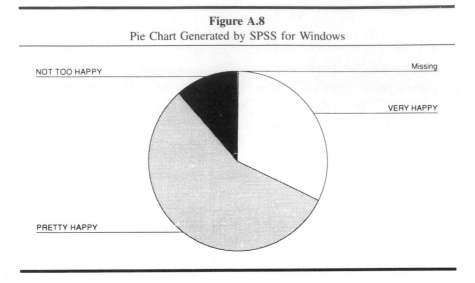

3. In the **Output Variable** section, click in the **Name** box and type the new name for your recoded variable (NATCITY2). Then click on the **Change** button.
4. Repeat step 3 for both NATFARE and NATRACE, renaming them as NATFARE2 and NATRACE2.
5. Click on the **Old and New Values** button. Click in the **Old Value—Value** box and type: **1.** Click in the **New Value—Value** box and type: **3.** Now click on the **Add** button.
6. Repeat step 5 matching the values **2** with **2** and **3** with **1.**
7. When finished, click on the **Continue** and **OK** buttons.

The fourth variable, POLVIEWS, has a larger range and needs recoding as a separate entity. Following the steps above, recode POLVIEWS as POLVIEW2 matching the values as: **1=7, 2=6, 3=5, 4=4, 5=3, 6=2,** and **7=1.**

*Note:* Remember that the above variables were recoded for the scale LIBERAL. No recoding was necessary for the candidate variables for the scale GOVACT, which is discussed next.

**RELIABILITY.**    (See pages 515–518.) For the RELIABILITY analysis, follow the following steps:

1. Click on **Statistics, Scale, Reliability Analysis....** You immediately obtain the **Reliability Analysis** dialog box (see Figure A.9).
2. Make sure that the **Model** option on the drop-down menu displays **Alpha.**
3. Select all the candidate variables (EQWLTH, HELPBLK, HELPNOT, HELPPOOR, HELPSICK, and NATCITY).
4. Click on the **Statistics . . .** button and select the **Scale if item deleted** option.
5. Click on the **Continue** and **OK** buttons.

**Figure A.9**
Reliability Analysis Dialog Box

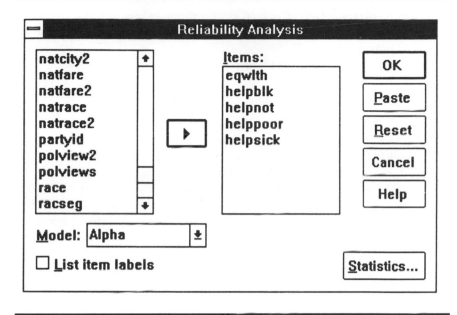

COMPUTE *after* RELIABILITY.   (See page 518.) To COMPUTE the scale GOVACT by Windows menuing:

1. Click on **Transform, Compute. . . .**
2. Click in the **Target Variable** box and type the name of your new variable (GOVACT).
3. Select the first variable from the variable list (EQWLTH), use the right arrow button ($\Rightarrow$) to move it into the **Numeric Expression** box, and click on the plus button (+).
4. Repeat step 3 for HELPBLK, HELPNOT, HELPPOOR, and HELPSICK—except omit the plus (+) after the last variable, HELPSICK.
5. When done, click on the **OK** button.

## Bivariate Distributions

*Nominal and Ordinal Measures*—CROSSTABS.   (See pages 519–521.) In Windows, the CROSSTABS procedure discussed in the previous section is accomplished by the following steps:

1. Click on **Statistics, Summarize, Crosstabs. . . .**
2. Select your dependent variable (HAPPY) and click on the right arrow button ($\Rightarrow$) to place it into the **Row(s)** box.

3. Select your independent variable (DEGREE) and click on the right arrow button ($\Rightarrow$) to place it into the **Column(s)** box.
4. Click on the **Cells . . .** button and select the **Counts—Observed** and all **Percentages** options. Click on the **Continue** button.
5. Click on the **Statistics . . .** button and select all options. Click on the **Continue** button.
6. Click on the **OK** button to launch the procedure.

RECODE *into the Same Variable.*   (See page 521.) To RECODE in order to collapse categories of a target variable, perform the following steps:

1. Click on **Transform, Recode, Into Same Variables. . . .**
2. Select your target variable (in our case, DEGREE) from the variable list and move it into the **Numeric Variables** list by clicking on the right arrow ($\Rightarrow$).
3. Click on the **Old and New Values . . .** button. Type one old value (**3**) in the **Old Value** box, type the new corresponding value (**3**) in the **New Value** box, and then click on the **Add** button. Repeat this last operation as necessary to recode another old value (**4**) into the same corresponding new value (**3**).
4. Click on **Continue** and **OK** to put your transformative commands into effect. *Note:* To Recode the additional example from the previous section, repeat step 3 above but for *all* the old values of 0 through 4.

*Interval Measures*—CORRELATIONS.   (See pages 521–522.) To conduct bivariate correlational runs:

1. Click on **Statistics, Correlate, Bivariate. . . .**
2. Select your variables (AGE, EDUC, INCOME, LIBERAL, and GOVACT) and click on the right arrow button ($\Rightarrow$) to move them over to the **Variables** list.
3. Make sure that the **Display actual significance level** box is xed and that the **Two-tailed** option button is selected.
4. Click on the **Options . . .** button and select all **Statistics.**
5. Click on the **Continue** and then the **OK** buttons.

GRAPH.   (See page 522.) To plot a scatter diagram to assess the relationship between two variables:

1. Click on **Graphs, Scatter . . . , Simple,** and **Define.**
2. Select your dependent variable (LIBERAL) from the variable list and click the right arrow ($\Rightarrow$) to move it into the **Y Axis** box. Then select your independent variable (AGE) and move it over to the **X Axis** box.
3. Click on the **OK** button.
4. The chart should appear in a separate window called the **Chart Carousel** (see Figure A.10). If the **Chart Carousel** initially appears as an icon, double click the icon to open it as a window.

**Figure A.10**
Chart Carousel Window

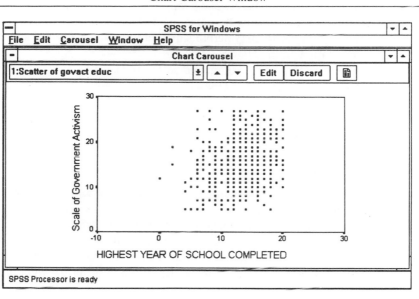

## Multivariate Analysis

PARTIAL CORR. (See pages 522–524.) Creating partial correlations by SPSS Windows menuing only provides you with the precise-order partials for all control variables you introduce. For example, if you attempt to recreate the syntax of the example on page 524 of

PARTIAL CORR GOVACT WITH AGE BY LIBERAL, INCOME (1, 2)

you cannot select the (1, 2) option that allows for zero-order, first-order, and second-order partials by using the menus. So instead of obtaining three partial correlations of GOVACT with AGE controlling for 1) both LIBERAL and INCOME, 2) only LIBERAL, and 3) only INCOME, the best you can do in one run in Windows is a single second-order partial correlation of GOVACT with AGE controlling for both LIBERAL and INCOME. You can, of course, do separate Windows runs to recreate all the other different-order partial scenarios. However, if you have SPSS Professional, it is certainly easier to run this command from a Syntax window with your order specifications included in just one command.

The following steps create a partial correlation for GOVACT with AGE controlling for both LIBERAL and INCOME simultaneously (second-order):

1. Click on **Statistics, Correlate, Partial. . . .**

2. Move the variables GOVACT and AGE from the variable list to the **Variables** box using the right arrow button ($\Rightarrow$).
3. Move the variables LIBERAL and INCOME from the variable list to the **Controlling for** box using the same method as above.
4. Make sure that the **Display actual significance level** box is xed and that the **Two-tailed** option button is selected.
5. Click on the **Options ...** button and select all statistics.
6. Click on the **Continue** and **OK** buttons.

REGRESSION.   (See pages 524–530.) Although running REGRESSION through the Windows menuing system provides slightly different output than that produced by the syntax on page 526, the core of the REGRESSION output remains the same. The steps are:

1. Click on **Statistics, Regression, Linear** to open the **Linear Regression** dialog box (see Figure A.11).
2. Select your dependent variable (GOVACT) and move it from the variable list to the **Dependent** box using the right arrow button ($\Rightarrow$).
3. Select your independent variables (LIBERAL, INCOME, EDUC) and move them from the variable list to the **Independent(s)** box using the right arrow button ($\Rightarrow$).
4. Click on the **Statistics** button and select all statistics.
5. Insure that the **Method** drop-down menu shows **Stepwise** as the selection.
6. Click on the **OK** button.

**Figure A.11**
Linear Regression Dialog Box

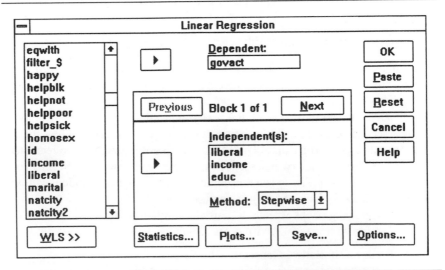

# Conclusion

The SPSS and other statistical package manuals may seem complicated and imposing on first inspection, but they will make your life easier in the long run. This appendix was designed to assist you in taking that first big step into computerized data analysis. We hope that this treatment will encourage researchers to pick and choose portions of those packages that lend themselves to their data analysis needs and methodological expertise. As you work with a package like SPSS, you will learn more about its many capabilities and potentials. As your skills increase, we encourage you to explore these potentials with the help of the manual.

---

**Exhibit A.1**
Codebook for Subset of GSS93

---

| Variable Name | | | | Column Numbers |
|---|---|---|---|---|
| ID | RESPONDENT ID NUMBER | | | 1–4 |
| AGE | AGE OF RESPONDENT | | | 5–6 |
| | Missing Values: 0, 98, 99 | | | |
| | Value | | Label | |
| | 98 | M | DK | |
| | 99 | M | NA | |
| SEX | RESPONDENTS SEX | | | 7 |
| | Value | | Label | |
| | 1 | | MALE | |
| | 2 | | FEMALE | |
| RACE | RACE OF RESPONDENT | | | 8 |
| | Value | | Label | |
| | 1 | | WHITE | |
| | 2 | | BLACK | |
| | 3 | | OTHER | |
| REGION | REGION OF INTERVIEW | | | 9 |
| | Missing Values: 0 | | | |
| | Value | | Label | |
| | 0 | M | NOT ASSIGNED | |
| | 1 | | NEW ENGLAND | |
| | 2 | | MIDDLE ATLANTIC | |
| | 3 | | E. NOR. CENTRAL | |
| | 4 | | W. NOR. CENTRAL | |
| | 5 | | SOUTH ATLANTIC | |
| | 6 | | E. SOU. CENTRAL | |
| | 7 | | W. SOU. CENTRAL | |
| | 8 | | MOUNTAIN | |
| | 9 | | PACIFIC | |

## Exhibit A.1 *(continued)*

| Variable Name | | | | Column Numbers |
|---|---|---|---|---|
| MARITAL | MARITAL STATUS | | | 10 |
| | Missing Values: 9 | | | |
| | Value | | Label | |
| | 1 | | MARRIED | |
| | 2 | | WIDOWED | |
| | 3 | | DIVORCED | |
| | 4 | | SEPARATED | |
| | 5 | | NEVER MARRIED | |
| | 9 | M | NA | |
| EDUC | HIGHEST YEAR OF SCHOOL COMPLETED | | | 11–12 |
| | Missing Values: 97, 98, 99 | | | |
| | Value | | Label | |
| | 97 | M | NAP | |
| | 98 | M | DK | |
| | 99 | M | NA | |
| DEGREE | RS HIGHEST DEGREE | | | 13 |
| | Missing Values: 7, 8, 9 | | | |
| | Value | | Label | |
| | 0 | | LT HIGH SCHOOL | |
| | 1 | | HIGH SCHOOL | |
| | 2 | | JUNIOR COLLEGE | |
| | 3 | | BACHELOR | |
| | 4 | | GRADUATE | |
| | 7 | M | NAP | |
| | 8 | M | DK | |
| | 9 | M | NA | |
| INCOME | TOTAL FAMILY INCOME | | | 14–15 |
| | Missing Values: 0, 98, 99 | | | |
| | Value | | Label | |
| | 0 | M | NAP | |
| | 1 | | LT $1000 | |
| | 2 | | $1000 TO 2999 | |
| | 3 | | $3000 TO 3999 | |
| | 4 | | $4000 TO 4999 | |
| | 5 | | $5000 TO 5999 | |
| | 6 | | $6000 TO 6999 | |
| | 7 | | $7000 TO 7999 | |
| | 8 | | $8000 TO 9999 | |
| | 9 | | $10000 – 14999 | |
| | 10 | | $15000 – 19999 | |
| | 11 | | $20000 – 24999 | |
| | 12 | | $25000 OR MORE | |
| | 13 | | REFUSED | |
| | 98 | M | DK | |
| | 99 | M | NA | |

| Variable Name | | | Column Numbers |
|---|---|---|---|
| PARTYID | POLITICAL PARTY AFFILIATION | | 16 |

Missing Values: 8, 9

| Value | | Label |
|---|---|---|
| 0 | | STRONG DEMOCRAT |
| 1 | | NOT STR DEMOCRAT |
| 2 | | IND,NEAR DEM |
| 3 | | INDEPENDENT |
| 4 | | IND,NEAR REP |
| 5 | | NOT STR REPUBLICAN |
| 6 | | STRONG REPUBLICAN |
| 7 | | OTHER PARTY |
| 8 | M | DK |
| 9 | M | NA |

| EQWLTH | SHOULD GOVT REDUCE INCOME DIFFERENCES | | 17 |
|---|---|---|---|

Missing Values: 0, 8, 9

| Value | | Label |
|---|---|---|
| 0 | M | NAP |
| 1 | | GOVT REDUCE DIFF |
| 7 | | NO GOVT ACTION |
| 8 | M | DK |
| 9 | M | NA |

| CAPPUN | FAVOR OR OPPOSE DEATH PENALTY FOR MURDER | | 18 |
|---|---|---|---|

Missing Values: 0, 8, 9

| Value | | Label |
|---|---|---|
| 0 | M | NAP |
| 1 | | FAVOR |
| 2 | | OPPOSE |
| 8 | M | DK |
| 9 | M | NA |

| RACSEG | WHITES HAVE RIGHT TO SEG. NEIGHBORHOOD | | 19 |
|---|---|---|---|

Missing Values: 0, 8, 9

| Value | | Label |
|---|---|---|
| 0 | M | NAP |
| 1 | | AGREE STRONGLY |
| 2 | | AGREE SLIGHTLY |
| 3 | | DISAGREE SLIGHTLY |
| 4 | | DISAGREE STRONGLY |
| 8 | M | DK |
| 9 | M | NA |

| HAPPY | GENERAL HAPPINESS | | 20 |
|---|---|---|---|

Missing Values: 0, 8, 9

| Value | | Label |
|---|---|---|
| 0 | M | NAP |
| 1 | | VERY HAPPY |
| 2 | | PRETTY HAPPY |
| 3 | | NOT TOO HAPPY |
| 8 | M | DK |
| 9 | M | NA |

---

## Exhibit A.1 *(continued)*

---

| Variable Name | | | | Column Numbers |
|---|---|---|---|---|
| HOMOSEX | HOMOSEXUAL SEX RELATIONS | | | 21 |

Missing Values: 0, 8, 9

| Value | | Label |
|---|---|---|
| 0 | M | NAP |
| 1 | | ALWAYS WRONG |
| 2 | | ALMST ALWAYS WRG |
| 3 | | SOMETIMES WRONG |
| 4 | | NOT WRONG AT ALL |
| 5 | | OTHER |
| 8 | M | DK |
| 9 | M | NA |

| | | | | |
|---|---|---|---|---|
| HELPPOOR | SHOULD GOVT IMPROVE STANDARD OF LIVING? | | | 22 |

Missing Values: 0, 8, 9

| Value | | Label |
|---|---|---|
| 0 | M | NAP |
| 1 | | GOVT ACTION |
| 3 | | AGREE WITH BOTH |
| 5 | | PEOPLE HELP SELVES |
| 8 | M | DK |
| 9 | M | NA |

| | | | | |
|---|---|---|---|---|
| HELPNOT | SHOULD GOVT DO MORE OR LESS? | | | 23 |

Missing Values: 0, 8, 9

| Value | | Label |
|---|---|---|
| 0 | M | NAP |
| 1 | | GOVT DO MORE |
| 3 | | AGREE WITH BOTH |
| 5 | | GOVT DOES TOO MUCH |
| 8 | M | DK |
| 9 | M | NA |

| | | | | |
|---|---|---|---|---|
| HELPSICK | SHOULD GOVT HELP PAY FOR MEDICAL CARE? | | | 24 |

Missing Values: 0, 8, 9

| Value | | Label |
|---|---|---|
| 0 | M | NAP |
| 1 | | GOVT SHOULD HELP |
| 3 | | AGREE WITH BOTH |
| 5 | | PEOPLE HELP SELVES |
| 8 | M | DK |
| 9 | M | NA |

| | | | | |
|---|---|---|---|---|
| HELPBLK | SHOULD GOVT AID BLACKS? | | | 25 |

Missing Values: 0, 8, 9

| Value | | Label |
|---|---|---|
| 0 | M | NAP |
| 1 | | GOVT HELP BLKS |
| 3 | | AGREE WITH BOTH |

| Variable Name | | | | Column Numbers |
|---|---|---|---|---|

|  | 5 |  | NO SPECIAL TREATMENT | |
|  | 8 | M | DK | |
|  | 9 | M | NA | |
| POLVIEWS | THINK OF SELF AS LIBERAL OR CONSERVATIVE | | | 26 |

Missing Values: 0, 8, 9

| Value | | Label |
|---|---|---|
| 0 | M | NAP |
| 1 |  | EXTREMELY LIBERAL |
| 2 |  | LIBERAL |
| 3 |  | SLIGHTLY LIBERAL |
| 4 |  | MODERATE |
| 5 |  | SLGHTLY CONSERVATIVE |
| 6 |  | CONSERVATIVE |
| 7 |  | EXTRMLY CONSERVATIVE |
| 8 | M | DK |
| 9 | M | NA |

| NATFARE | WELFARE | | | 27 |
|---|---|---|---|---|

Missing Values: 0, 8, 9

| Value | | Label |
|---|---|---|
| 0 | M | NAP |
| 1 |  | TOO LITTLE |
| 2 |  | ABOUT RIGHT |
| 3 |  | TOO MUCH |
| 8 | M | DK |
| 9 | M | NA |

| NATCITY | SOLVING PROBLEMS OF BIG CITIES | | | 28 |
|---|---|---|---|---|

Missing Values 0, 8, 9

| Value | | Label |
|---|---|---|
| 0 | M | NAP |
| 1 |  | TOO LITTLE |
| 2 |  | ABOUT RIGHT |
| 3 |  | TOO MUCH |
| 8 | M | DK |
| 9 | M | NA |

| NATRACE | IMPROVING THE CONDITIONS OF BLACKS | | | 29 |
|---|---|---|---|---|

Missing Values: 0, 8, 9

| Value | | Label |
|---|---|---|
| 0 | M | NAP |
| 1 |  | TOO LITTLE |
| 2 |  | ABOUT RIGHT |
| 3 |  | TOO MUCH |
| 8 | M | DK |
| 9 | M | NA |

# APPENDIX B   Writing Research Reports

## Nina Reshef

Research report writing is a specialized skill, but one that can easily be learned. Although academic disciplines may vary somewhat in the details required for the presentation of their subject, the basic elements are quite consistent for the full range of reports from take-home tests to doctoral dissertations and scholarly journal articles. The goal of this appendix, then, is to provide the guidelines that simplify the writing of research reports.

The purpose of a research report dictates its structure. Here, again, form follows function. The function of research reports, as differentiated from other reports, is not only to relay findings but to link those findings directly to a theoretical model or to one or more empirically testable hypotheses. The structure of research reports has become standardized into models that shape the presentation into a consistent, logical framework. This makes reporting and writing easier.

## Why Write a Research Report?

The basic question preceding any activity is why do it? In scholarly research, the answer is the desire to expand the horizons of human knowledge, to enhance methodologies, and to increase the incisiveness of analysis. These lofty aims are, however, insufficient to guarantee a well-written report; nor are they always a student's primary motivation.

If we consider instead how successful reports are written, two themes become apparent. The first is how much the writer is involved with the subject or excited about the process and product of research. The second is how well the subject is defined and presented. If the topic is interesting to the author, it may very well be interesting to the reader, at first the course instructor and then, perhaps, a wider audience. In addition, readers will be more readily convinced of the value of the report if the organization of the ideas, the presentation of findings, and the quality of the writing are professional. Our purpose, then, is to provide the guidelines for effectively communicating the results of your research effort to another person.

## Matching Your Format to Your Audience

In effective report writing, the character of the reading audience is just as important to the writer as the character of the listening audience is to the speaker when preparing a presentation. The more general the audience, the more general the content will be and the looser the format. Reports geared to professional audiences should be highly technical and specialized. That is, with the audience in mind, the writer can choose the appropriate format, the degree of detail to include, and the subject-related vocabulary. Keeping the audience in mind also helps the writer to determine whether the assumptions underlying the report will be perceived and understood. In short, the writer's strategy—as expressed by the report's internal structure—should be geared to a specific target audience and never left to chance.

## Types of Reports

Social science research is generally divided into two main types: qualitative and quantitative. Qualitative research can include quantitative elements such as diagrams and flow charts, and quantitative research can move beyond numbers to analyze the link between a formula and the place of the variable measured within the theory. Therefore, it is important not to confuse the devices used to present findings with the character of the report. Nonetheless, despite the difference in their focus and content, the principles dictating the structure of both qualitative and quantitative reports are basically the same.

*Qualitative Reports.*    Qualitative research, an outgrowth of the *Verstehen* tradition of empathic comprehension of social phenomena, is inductive in nature. Qualitative researchers use field research methods, primarily case studies and participant observation, within natural settings (see Chapter 12). The researcher interferes as little as humanly possible in the course of events. Consequently, the report will present much descriptive material. The report should also show how the observations prompted the researcher to analyze and isolate variables (induction) and how, in turn, these variables may be developed into a theory. The important points to remember when writing a report based on qualitative research are to stick to the main theoretical themes or concepts and to avoid including too many details taken from the field research. These can be distracting and interfere with your line of argument.

*Quantitative Reports.*    Because quantitative research is deductive, researchers deal directly with operationalization, the manipulation of empirical variables, prediction, and testing. Quantitative research therefore places great emphasis on methodology, on procedure, and on statistical measures of validity. Consequently, quantitative research reports should be organized to show a clear progression from theory to operationalization of concepts; from choice of methodology and procedures to the data collected; from statistical tests to findings and, ultimately, conclusions.

If the report entails hypothesis testing, each hypothesis should be clearly labeled (e.g., 1, 2, and so on; or A, B, and so on) and even set off by using a different typeface or by underlining. This method makes it easier for the reader to identify the question asked and its relation to the research findings. Highlighting the question helps you to organize your thoughts as well as hold the reader's attention. This is important because much of the text of quantitative research reports contains verbal elaboration of the data presented in the tables. Therefore, clearly marking the research questions helps the reader keep track of the exposition as well as the conclusion, in which the findings are evaluated within both methodological and theoretical contexts.

*Oral Reports.*    Oral reports in the classroom have become accepted tools for introducing the student not only to report writing but to the give and take of academic judgment. When you give a short oral report on your research, you need to organize your material not only in terms of content but also in terms of tone and audience. In short, oral presentations may be perceived as abstracts, or prologues, of the final written paper. Therefore, everything we have said about the organization of written reports applies, but with a change in emphasis. In an oral presentation, you need to pay more attention to the main point of your report and to your pace and tone—you don't want your audience to fall asleep or to be aroused into excessive criticism. Practicing your report helps you not only to control the amount of material you present in the time available, but it also helps you to develop techniques for maintaining a good rapport with your audience.

Oral presentations made during conferences for professional audiences follow the same basic rules but on a more sophisticated level. Therefore, you should think of classroom reports as opportunities to hone your speaking and presentation skills.

## Choosing the Topic

Choosing a topic for research is the most important, and perhaps the most difficult, stage in the research process. Current events, life experiences, or intellectual puzzles stimulate curiosity and yield original research topics. Avoid topics that have been extensively researched by other students or by scholars, no matter how enticing they appear at first glance. When in doubt, consult your instructor. In any case, even overworked topics, such as alchoholism, can be interesting if approached with ingenuity.

You can test both your understanding of the topic and its appropriateness by attempting to convert the purpose of your paper into one of these questions: What are you trying to learn, to explore, to promote? Can the topic be stated as a "who," "what," or "when" question and answered in a linear, analytical manner or as an historical narrative? Can it be stated as a hypothesis, to be tested according to strict experimental methods? Avoid topics that cannot be translated into a clear and precise research question—such topics are either muddled, too broad, or not amenable to study in the manner you have chosen.

For the student, the two most important criteria for choice are the topic's relevance to the course and the empirical data to be collected. A quick review of the available literature will not only introduce the topic and stimulate ideas, it will also help the student ascertain if the topic, as originally conceived, is manageable or if it has to be redefined or limited. A great deal of precious time and effort can be saved by doing background reading first.

*Manageability.*   The term *manageability* is often mentioned as a criterion for selecting a topic, but what does it actually mean? Basically, manageability in research refers to the theoretical complexity of an event or concept to be explained, to the amount and availability of pertinent data, and to the time it takes to collect and analyze the data before writing can begin. For the student, manageability may also be translated into the number of books and journal articles that should be read as part of the literature review; to the academic scholar, manageability may mean the number of trips abroad needed to collect sources stored in government archives, or the number and complexity of the theoretical models needed to explain the phenomenon of interest.

Every researcher must ask just how manageable the topic is, given the confines of the report. It is always preferable to limit a topic and investigate it thoroughly rather than expand its scope to the point where you have neither the time, the resources, nor the space to adequately present a reasoned argument. As a hypothetical example, for a researcher at the University of Chicago, an analysis of income collected from property taxes in the State of Illinois from 1919–1929 may be a more manageable topic than property tax collection in pre–Depression Chicago. In this case, if the Illinois data is better organized within existing files, the greater accessibility would simplify the analytic and statistical procedures the researcher would have to employ even if it might take him or her more time to collect all the data.

## The Direct Aim of the Report

After choosing the research topic, a writer has to decide on the direct aim of the report. If the aim is kept specific and focused, organizing the material and writing the report become much easier.

Research reports aim at answering five basic questions: "who," "what," "where," "when," and "how." Underlying these is a sixth question: "why." That is, the purpose of a research report is to relay findings that are empirically and logically related to some conception of causation, to a theory. The writer is free to emphasize only one of these questions in any particular piece. The choice of aims should be dictated by personal interests (even though, in some cases, the topic may be assigned by the instructor) and, of course, the data available.

The purpose of most research reports can also be conceptualized according to three general categories: *description* of an incident or a research technique; *exploration* of a new idea or unusual event; and *explanation* of causal relationships.

A fourth category, one that encompasses both your findings and your opinions, is *submission of proposals* for solving social problems.[1]

Your goals and assumptions should be clearly communicated in the introduction to the report. For example, exploratory reports present tentative findings about what occurred and set the stage for further research. The content and legitimacy of proposals for change may be based on assumptions and values not universally held. By clearly stating your goals and assumptions, you will ensure that the report is placed in its proper context. Readers can therefore judge your report in a more balanced way.

## Organizing the Report

Research reports are organized in fairly consistent formats in order to facilitate communication. Nothing is more frustrating than trying to read a muddled report about an interesting study or finding. Therefore, although every author has a degree of freedom in his or her style and choice of devices (e.g., tables, figures) for conveying information, all writers should follow this outline when reporting their research.

*Introduction.* The introduction should clearly and concisely state your purpose in writing the report. It should relate the type of report (e.g., exploratory) and the specific research question asked as well as your conclusions. (An abstract is an even more concise introduction and generally precedes the text in published articles.) The introduction, therefore, presents an overview of the content and, most important, the contribution of the study to your discipline. Although the latter may seem to be beyond the scope of a student report, it relates directly to the scientific value of the question or issue explored.

Use your imagination in writing your opening sentence, the main attention-getting device after the title.[2] Your skills as a stylist are most important here. Many strategies are available: you can cite a dramatic event in the news, quote a pointed but relevant comment, state the paradox your study resolves, or make a particularly forceful statement of your purpose. You should then state the purpose of your report succinctly. Avoid lengthy explanations of your purpose until you reach the discussion section of the text. You should also state the methodological or theoretical limitations of your report but in a way that does not disparage your contribution. For the student, if your instructor thinks the study was worth doing, that should be enough.

Many beginning writers feel that because the introduction opens the report, it should be written first. This is not true. For many writers, the first words of a document are major stumbling blocks and can delay the whole process. If you have

1. Earl Babbie, *The Practice of Social Research* (New York: Wadsworth, 1995), Appendix B, p. A–10.
2. Michael Meyer, *The Little, Brown Guide to Writing Research Papers* (New York: HarperCollins, 1991), pp. 113–114.

organized your work properly and outlined the text, and if you are fairly sure of what you are going to say (although there may be interesting surprises in store—writing always involves thinking, and thinking can lead you anywhere), try waiting until you have drafted the rest of the report to write the introduction.

*Literature Review.*    Due to the systematic nature of science, scholarly research rests on the findings and insights of others. In other words, research is never conducted in a vacuum, no matter how innovative the topic or the procedure. Therefore, a literature review is necessary to set the stage for your study.

Literature reviews summarize past research and can be presented in a number of ways. The strategy behind the review can vary, but it should be logically connected with the purpose of the report. For example, if you are exploring the validity of a particular statistical test, you may want to review when the test was used according to subject area. After clearly and briefly citing its successes and failures, you should concisely state how your study fits into the debate surrounding its validity. A review can also be organized according to schools of thought, such as Freudian, Jungian, and Skinnerian in psychology; approaches to reducing inflation; or historical period, for instance the Vietnam War. But whatever the strategy, the review should be selective, including only the sources most pertinent to your report and its conclusions.

What you should bear in mind is that not all sources can be legitimately used in writing literature reviews. Always use scholarly texts, those that directly involve theories or that test hypotheses. Newsmagazine articles, therefore, are inappropriate in this section.[3] Their place is in the data collection stage of research precisely because their purpose is to relay rather than interpret events. Therefore, they can be used as sources for noting when an event occurred or for statistical data when other, more methodologically appropriate resources are unavailable.

*Methodology and Findings.*    This section is devoted to transmitting the details of your procedure, its methodological foundations, the reasoning behind your choice of case or procedure, and the findings. It is not necessary to repeat your research purposes unless it helps the reader to follow the methodology. The more empirical, or quantitative, the research, the more this section will be devoted to the orderly presentation of hypotheses; the equations employed to test the findings; and tables containing the statistical results of the tests of the data (see p. 562 for a discussion of tables). As we noted above, numbering the hypotheses makes it easier to organize the material. Because tables should be inserted in the order in which the variables are discussed, you only need to refer to the table number (e.g., see Table 3) when integrating the relevant data into the text.

Qualitative research findings can be organized according to their historical development or the concepts explored, depending on the type of methodology employed.

---

3. Ibid.

*Discussion.*    This section of the report contains the bulk of your analysis—your interpretations of the findings, their integration with the research question(s) posed, their relationship to previous research (supportive and nonsupportive alike), and their implications for further research. In this section you can employ all your analytic skills and imagination to ask additional questions, draw conclusions, and qualify the applicability of your method or your findings. Therefore, begin with a brief restatement of your purpose and then indicate whether or not your findings support your original hypothesis or validate your line of research. You should also evaluate your contribution without placing undue emphasis on negative results or problems. In short, your presentation should be to the point—clearcut, concise, and balanced.

*Conclusion.*    The purpose of the conclusion is to close the circle of research, moving from past research to the place of your report in the stock of scientific knowledge. This requires you to link your theoretical or methodological conclusions with the current state of research. But the conclusion also presents an opportunity to suggest new avenues of research—ideas on how to follow up on what you have discovered. Although recommendations for further research may seem to be a heavy burden for the beginner, they present an opportunity to use your investigative imagination; they help place your findings within the continuing flow of research; and they indicate humility, the admission that the report's contribution represents only one addition to the expanding reservoir of knowledge. This section may be only a paragraph long, but without it your work lacks closure. If your conclusion is very short, it can be integrated with the discussion section.

## Writing the Report

*Drafting the Report.*    After all the effort you put into the research, writing the report may still present the greatest obstacle. Writing is a challenge because it forces you to think and be self-critical. In the following section, we will not emphasize writing style, other than to state that simple, shorter sentences are better, especially when you are trying to communicate complex ideas or procedures.

One good way to begin writing your report is to start early. Write up descriptions of your procedures and what you've discovered more or less as you go along. Besides providing summaries and keeping the material fresh in your mind, this strategy gives you the opportunity to begin checking your original ideas as well as developing new ones. These summaries become, in fact, the first drafts of the final report.

After you have completed your first draft, the next step is to review it several times, revising as necessary. During at least one review of your draft, take the position of the reader, not the writer. If, as a reader, you can't follow the line of argument, then you should look for flaws in your thinking as well as in your style. This review may lead you to reassess your argument and perhaps improve it. It may also inspire new ideas that you can mention and develop in another paper. Therefore, write as many drafts as you see fit and have time for.

*Editing.*    A research report must not only be written according to the structure we have described, it must also be edited or rewritten. Editing means making sure that only the details most relevant to your method and your argument appear. However, be aware that there is a point of no return, where you've read the text so often you can't see the problems. This is the point to stop.

Editing should take place with your audience in mind. For example, suppose you are reporting a study using survey research methods to investigate attitudes toward flexible working hours. If your report is geared to survey researchers and statisticians, you will probably include many more methodological details and more mathematical logic than you would if your audience was composed of personnel managers. For the latter, you might include more information about the populations surveyed and the types of questions asked.

Finally, once you are satisfied with your complete draft, you should review it for style and for errors in grammar and spelling. Personal computers make these tasks easier by providing programs for correcting spelling and style and by making the shifting of paragraphs technically much easier. Nevertheless, despite technology, the process still requires a good deal of concentration. If you don't have a printer readily available and must do at least some of your corrections by hand, remember that too many handwritten corrections, even if they're only typing errors, make the text look unprofessional and hint at a lack of concern on your part. If you have more than two corrections on a page, you should reprint or retype it.

*Length.*    Two factors control the length of a research report: its aims and its topic. The aims of a report are varied and, for the student, may include the improvement of personal research skills. Another factor bearing on length may be the influence of the paper on the final grade. An instructor may require only three pages for an exercise but up to 30 pages for a paper that serves as the sole basis for a grade. Master's and doctoral theses are of course much longer. Journal articles may be limited by the editors to 40 manuscript pages, and monographs to perhaps 50 typewritten pages. Papers dealing with statistics may be shorter because so much information is summarized in an equation. If you have a length limitation, use shortcuts for presenting material, such as flow charts to illustrate causal models.

*Tone and Sexist Language.*    Two stylistic factors should be considered in planning your report—tone and sexist language. Keep your audience in mind when you decide how formal or informal your style should be. Formality assumes a more rigid sentence structure and internal organization. Neither formal nor informal style precludes humor, but both demand consistency. Whichever you choose, make sure you are comfortable in your choice in order to avoid slipping into ponderous, awkward prose or losing a sense of your subject or its academic purpose.

Sexist language, on the other hand, is something to be avoided throughout your report, whether you are using a formal or informal style. The current manuals of style offer alternatives that should be adopted in place of traditional male-oriented phrasing.

*Plagiarism.*[4]    Why should a text in social science research methodology include a section on plagiarism? Isn't it already clear that it is immoral and illegal to use another person's ideas and phrases without giving direct credit? Unfortunately, plagiarism keeps cropping up in academia and elsewhere. Due to the pressure to publish or to pass a course, people are often tempted to "borrow" from others, on the assumption that no one will catch on. However, as stated above, the development of knowledge is based on the work of forerunners. It tends to be incremental, progressing piece-by-piece; hence it really is difficult to "get away" with plagiarism. In addition, an instructor is likely to be sufficiently familiar with the level of work expected from students, as well as the material concerning an approved research topic, to catch on. Therefore, not only is plagiarism wrong, it is also a risky strategy.

For most students, plagiarism may be unintentional. It isn't always absolutely clear when quotation marks should be used or when a page number must be cited in addition to the text author and title. Therefore, we present the following basic rules for avoiding plagiarism to assist those who are baffled and to discourage those who are tempted.

1. Always use quotation marks and cite the author, text, and page number when incorporating another author's exact words into your text. In general, U.S. federal copyright laws are infringed whenever a string of at least eight words is used without citing the source. The following examples, taken from Item 69 in Exhibit 4.1 of this text, can be used as guides.

*Plagiarism:* When relating research findings, the procedures should be described fully and accurately in reports, including all evidence regardless of whether it supports the research hypotheses.

*Correct:* In reporting findings, "[research] procedures should be described fully and accurately in reports, including all evidence regardless of the support it provides for the research hypotheses. . . ." (Reynolds, 1979, pp. 447–448).

2. If you paraphrase an author, cite the author's name and the text.

*Correct:* Whether or not the evidence supports the hypothesis investigated, the procedures should be accurately and completely described in the concluding report (Reynolds, 1979, pp. 447–448).

3. Another author's ideas, even if rephrased, should never be presented as your own; you should state that you accept them and cite the original source. If you have independently reached the same conclusions found in the literature, state so clearly and cite the supporting author.

*Correct:* Following the normative principles of scientific methodology presented in Frankfort-Nachmias and Nachmias (1995), I would conclude that all the procedures used in collecting evidence, whether or not they support the original

---

4. This section incorporates many ideas and examples to be found in Babbie, pp. A11–A12 and Meyer, pp. 109–114.

hypothesis, should be reported. In fact, this concept was stated as an ethical principle by Paul Davison Reynolds (1979, pp. 447–448).

4. Common knowledge does not have to be attributed as long as you are confident that the information is in fact commonly known. For example, the fact that Washington, D.C., the nation's capital, has no representation in the Senate may be common knowledge for students in American history or American politics, but the reasons behind that status may not be. Therefore, a source should be cited when giving those reasons.

Perhaps the best way to avoid plagiarism is simply to be honest. When in doubt, cite your sources. Remember that you demonstrate your research skills by knowing when and where to give credit.

## Tables

Tables and figures are really highly succinct summaries of your findings. They are used in all quantitative research but may also be used in qualitative research to simplify the presentation of a theoretical argument—see, for example, Figures 1.1 and 2.1. These figures use only words—concepts—to summarize the information or ideas discussed in the text.

Following are some basic technical guidelines for constructing tables:[5]

1. Tables should be self-explanatory, that is, understandable without reference to the text. Therefore, they must be clear, logically planned in terms of the relationships examined, and accurate. Summary columns should appear last.
2. Each table or graph should be given its own number (e.g., Table 1, Figure 2), placed at the top and, for most academic reports, centered.
3. The title should clearly and succinctly refer to the table's contents (what, where, when). Underneath the title, indicate the type of table entries (e.g., percents, frequencies, currency base). If not indicated under the title, then each designation should be entered in the appropriate column. The table title and related information should be centered.
4. Column and row headings should be clearly distinguishable from each other and may be numbered for clarity. Text references to table entries should refer to the headings in the table.
5. Column headings should refer to independent variables; row headings to dependent variables.
6. Column figures should be centered, aligned on decimal points, and aligned with the row headings.
7. The only abbreviations that are generally permitted are "n.a." (not available) and $N$ (frequency). The $N$ may appear in parentheses directly below calculated percentages if they are small but should always appear as part

5. Adapted in part from guidelines prepared by David G. Wegge, St. Norbert College.

of the column summary below the total of 100 percent (see Table 16.6 as an example).

8. Asterisks or other symbols may be used as indicators of footnotes or of unique data entry sources. Keep these to a minimum to avoid clutter and confusion on the part of the reader. (See Table 18.5 as an illustration.)

9. Explanatory footnotes appear directly under the table, in full citation form. Sources of data, also in complete citation form, appear underneath the footnotes.

The point to remember is that a table is used to assist the reader; therefore, the number of tables, figures, or other visual devices used is a direct consequence of your argument as well as of the amount of data collected. Use your judgment and don't overburden the reader by introducing tables that don't really contribute to your presentation.

## Documentation

Many disciplines have their own format for documenting sources. The following books provide guidelines for three common documentation styles:

American Psychological Association. *Publication Manual of the American Psychological Association,* 4th ed. Washington, D.C.: APA, 1994.

*The Chicago Manual of Style,* 14th ed. Chicago: University of Chicago Press, 1993.

Gibaldi, Joseph. *MLA Handbook for Writers of Research Papers,* 4th ed. New York: The Modern Language Association of America, 1995.

In addition, many journals have developed their own style of documentation. The basic manuals are available in your college bookstore and library. The choice of format will usually be made by your instructor. Although different disciplines prefer different formats, the rule of thumb is to be consistent.

---

## Additional Readings

---

Meyer, Michael. *The Little, Brown Guide to Writing Research Papers.* New York: HarperCollins, 1991.

The Sociology Writing Group. *A Guide to Writing Sociology Papers,* 3d ed. New York: St. Martin's Press. 1994.

# APPENDIX C   Σ: The Summation Sign

In statistics, it is frequently necessary to make use of formulas involving sums of numerous quantities. As a shorthand substitute for writing out each of these sums at length, the Greek letter Σ (capital sigma), which means to summate or add, is used. As a rule, whenever Σ appears, it means that *all* quantities appearing to the right of it should be summed.

If you want to add ten scores, we can always write

$$X_1 + X_2 + X_3 + X_4 + X_5 + X_6 + X_7 + X_8 + X_9 + X_{10}$$

or the same expression can be shortened to

$$X_1 + X_2 + \cdots + X_{10}$$

which means the same thing. The three dots ($\cdots$) mean "and so on." This same instruction may be put in still another way:

$$\sum_{i=1}^{10} X_i$$

Σ instructs us to add up everything that follows ($X_i$), starting with the case specified below the symbol ($i = 1$) and ending with the case specified above (10). This example may be read as follows: add up (Σ) all the observations ($X_i$) ranging from the first ($i = 1$) through the tenth (10). If we want only to sum the observations 4 and 5 ($X_4 + X_5$), we can write

$$\sum_{i=4}^{5} X_i$$

and if we wish to indicate that all of some unspecified number of cases should be added together, we can use $N$ to symbolize the unspecified number of cases and write

$$\sum_{i=1}^{N} X_i$$

This says to sum all the observations from the first to the $N$th; it is a general instruction for the addition of all cases regardless of their number. When this general instruction is intended, and when the range of values to be summed is obvious, it is customary to omit the notation of limits and write

$$\Sigma X_i$$

or even

$$\Sigma X$$

This indicates that the summation is to extend over all cases under consideration.

## Rules for the Use of Σ

There are a number of rules for the use of $\Sigma$. For example,

$$\sum_{i=1}^{N} (X_i + Y_i) = \sum_{i=1}^{N} X_i + \sum_{i=1}^{N} Y_i$$

which says that the summation of the sum of the two variables ($X$ and $Y$) is equal to the sum of their summations. It makes no difference whether one adds each $X_i$ to each $Y_i$ and then sums their total from 1 to $N$ or sums all $X_i$ and then all $Y_i$ and adds their sums; the result is the same.

Another rule is expressed in the following equation:

$$\sum_{i=1}^{N} kX_i = k \sum_{i=1}^{N} X_i$$

A constant $k$ may be moved across the summation sign. That is to say, if we are instructed to multiply each of a series of numbers by a constant

$$kX_1 + kX_2 + \cdots + kX_N$$

we can simply sum our numbers and multiply that sum by the constant; the result is the same.

A third rule is the following:

$$\sum_{i=1}^{N} k = kN$$

The summation of a constant is equal to the product of that constant and the number of times it is summed.

Another rule states that

$$\left( \sum_{i=1}^{N} X_i \right)^2 = (X_1 + X_2 + \cdots + X_N)^2$$

$$= X_1^2 + X_2^2 + \cdots + X_N^2 + 2X_1X_2$$

$$+ 2X_1X_3 + \cdots + 2X_{N-1}X_N$$

$$\neq X_1^2 + X_2^2 + \cdots + X_N^2$$

That is, we must distinguish between

$$\sum_{i=1}^{N} X_i^2$$

and

$$\left( \sum_{i=1}^{N} X_i \right)^2$$

# APPENDIX D   Random Digits

| Line/Col. | (1) | (2) | (3) | (4) | (5) | (6) | (7) | (8) | (9) | (10) | (11) | (12) | (13) | (14) |
|---|---|---|---|---|---|---|---|---|---|---|---|---|---|---|
| 1 | 10480 | 15011 | 01536 | 02011 | 81647 | 91646 | 69179 | 14194 | 62590 | 36207 | 20969 | 99570 | 91291 | 90700 |
| 2 | 22368 | 46573 | 25595 | 85393 | 30995 | 89198 | 27982 | 53402 | 93965 | 34095 | 52666 | 19174 | 39615 | 99505 |
| 3 | 24130 | 48360 | 22527 | 97265 | 76393 | 64809 | 15179 | 24830 | 49340 | 32081 | 30680 | 19655 | 63348 | 58629 |
| 4 | 42167 | 93093 | 06243 | 61680 | 07856 | 16376 | 39440 | 53537 | 71341 | 57004 | 00849 | 74917 | 97758 | 16379 |
| 5 | 37570 | 39975 | 81837 | 16656 | 06121 | 91782 | 60468 | 81305 | 49684 | 60672 | 14110 | 06927 | 01263 | 54613 |
| 6 | 77921 | 06907 | 11008 | 42751 | 27756 | 53498 | 18602 | 70659 | 90655 | 15053 | 21916 | 81825 | 44394 | 42880 |
| 7 | 99562 | 72905 | 56420 | 69994 | 98872 | 31016 | 71194 | 18738 | 44013 | 48840 | 63213 | 21069 | 10634 | 12952 |
| 8 | 96301 | 91977 | 05463 | 07972 | 18876 | 20922 | 94595 | 56869 | 69014 | 60045 | 18425 | 84903 | 42508 | 32307 |
| 9 | 89579 | 14342 | 63661 | 10281 | 17453 | 18103 | 57740 | 84378 | 25331 | 12566 | 58678 | 44947 | 05585 | 56941 |
| 10 | 85475 | 36857 | 53342 | 53988 | 53060 | 59533 | 38867 | 62300 | 08158 | 17983 | 16439 | 11458 | 18593 | 64952 |
| 11 | 28918 | 69578 | 88231 | 33276 | 70997 | 79936 | 56865 | 05859 | 90106 | 31595 | 01547 | 85590 | 91610 | 78188 |
| 12 | 63553 | 40961 | 48235 | 03427 | 49626 | 69445 | 18663 | 72695 | 52180 | 20847 | 12234 | 90511 | 33703 | 90322 |
| 13 | 09429 | 93969 | 52636 | 92737 | 88974 | 33488 | 36320 | 17617 | 30015 | 08272 | 84115 | 27156 | 30613 | 74952 |
| 14 | 10365 | 61129 | 87529 | 85689 | 48237 | 52267 | 67689 | 93394 | 01511 | 26358 | 85104 | 20285 | 29975 | 89868 |
| 15 | 07119 | 97336 | 71048 | 08178 | 77233 | 13916 | 47564 | 81056 | 97735 | 85977 | 29372 | 74461 | 28551 | 90707 |
| 16 | 51085 | 12765 | 51821 | 51259 | 77452 | 16308 | 60756 | 92144 | 49442 | 53900 | 70960 | 63990 | 75601 | 40719 |
| 17 | 02368 | 21382 | 52404 | 60268 | 89368 | 19885 | 55322 | 44819 | 01188 | 65255 | 64835 | 44919 | 05944 | 55157 |
| 18 | 01011 | 54092 | 33362 | 94904 | 31273 | 04146 | 18594 | 29852 | 71585 | 85030 | 51132 | 01915 | 92747 | 64951 |
| 19 | 52162 | 53916 | 46369 | 58586 | 23216 | 14513 | 83149 | 98736 | 23495 | 64350 | 94738 | 17752 | 35156 | 35749 |
| 20 | 07056 | 97628 | 33787 | 09998 | 42698 | 06691 | 76988 | 13602 | 51851 | 46104 | 88916 | 19509 | 25625 | 58104 |
| 21 | 48663 | 91245 | 85828 | 14346 | 09172 | 30168 | 90229 | 04734 | 59193 | 22178 | 30421 | 61666 | 99904 | 32812 |
| 22 | 54164 | 58492 | 22421 | 74103 | 47070 | 25306 | 76468 | 26384 | 58151 | 06646 | 21524 | 15227 | 96909 | 44592 |
| 23 | 32639 | 32363 | 05597 | 24200 | 13363 | 38005 | 94342 | 28728 | 35806 | 06912 | 17012 | 64161 | 18296 | 22851 |
| 24 | 29334 | 27001 | 87637 | 87308 | 58731 | 00256 | 45834 | 15398 | 46557 | 41135 | 10367 | 07684 | 36188 | 18510 |
| 25 | 02488 | 33062 | 28834 | 07351 | 19731 | 92420 | 60952 | 61280 | 50001 | 67658 | 32586 | 86679 | 50720 | 94953 |

| 26 | 81525 | 72295 | 04839 | 96423 | 24878 | 82651 | 66566 | 14778 | 76797 | 14780 | 13300 | 87074 | 79666 | 95725 |
|----|-------|-------|-------|-------|-------|-------|-------|-------|-------|-------|-------|-------|-------|-------|
| 27 | 29676 | 20591 | 68086 | 26432 | 46901 | 20849 | 89768 | 81536 | 86645 | 12659 | 92259 | 57102 | 80428 | 25280 |
| 28 | 00742 | 57392 | 39064 | 66432 | 84673 | 40027 | 32332 | 61362 | 98947 | 96067 | 64760 | 64584 | 96096 | 98253 |
| 29 | 05366 | 04213 | 25669 | 26422 | 44407 | 44048 | 37937 | 63904 | 45766 | 66134 | 75470 | 66520 | 34693 | 90449 |
| 30 | 91921 | 26418 | 64117 | 94305 | 26766 | 25940 | 39972 | 22209 | 71500 | 64568 | 91402 | 42416 | 07844 | 69618 |
| 31 | 00582 | 04711 | 87917 | 77341 | 42206 | 35126 | 74087 | 99547 | 81817 | 42607 | 43808 | 76655 | 62028 | 76630 |
| 32 | 00725 | 69884 | 62797 | 56170 | 86324 | 88072 | 76222 | 36086 | 84637 | 93161 | 76038 | 65855 | 77919 | 88006 |
| 33 | 69011 | 65795 | 95876 | 55293 | 18088 | 27354 | 26575 | 08625 | 40801 | 59920 | 29841 | 80150 | 12777 | 48501 |
| 34 | 25976 | 57948 | 29888 | 88604 | 67917 | 48708 | 18912 | 82271 | 65424 | 69774 | 33611 | 54262 | 85963 | 03547 |
| 35 | 09763 | 83473 | 73577 | 12908 | 30883 | 18317 | 28290 | 35797 | 05998 | 41688 | 34952 | 37888 | 38917 | 88050 |
| 36 | 91567 | 42595 | 27958 | 30134 | 04024 | 86385 | 29880 | 99730 | 55536 | 84855 | 29080 | 09250 | 79656 | 73211 |
| 37 | 17955 | 56349 | 90999 | 49127 | 20044 | 59931 | 06115 | 20542 | 18059 | 02008 | 73708 | 83517 | 36103 | 42791 |
| 38 | 46503 | 18584 | 18845 | 49618 | 02304 | 51038 | 20655 | 58727 | 28168 | 15475 | 56942 | 53389 | 20562 | 87338 |
| 39 | 92157 | 89634 | 94824 | 78171 | 84610 | 82834 | 09922 | 25417 | 44137 | 48413 | 25555 | 21246 | 35509 | 20468 |
| 40 | 14577 | 62765 | 35605 | 81263 | 39667 | 47358 | 56873 | 56307 | 61607 | 49518 | 89656 | 20103 | 77490 | 18062 |
| 41 | 98427 | 07523 | 33362 | 64270 | 01638 | 92477 | 66969 | 98420 | 04880 | 45585 | 46565 | 04102 | 46880 | 45709 |
| 42 | 34914 | 63976 | 88720 | 82765 | 34476 | 17032 | 87589 | 40836 | 32427 | 70002 | 70663 | 88803 | 77775 | 69348 |
| 43 | 70060 | 28277 | 39475 | 46473 | 23219 | 53416 | 94970 | 25832 | 69975 | 94884 | 19661 | 72828 | 00102 | 66794 |
| 44 | 53976 | 54914 | 06990 | 67245 | 68350 | 82948 | 11398 | 42878 | 80287 | 88267 | 47363 | 46634 | 06541 | 97809 |
| 45 | 76072 | 29515 | 40980 | 07391 | 58745 | 25774 | 22987 | 80059 | 39911 | 96189 | 41151 | 14222 | 60697 | 59583 |
| 46 | 90725 | 52210 | 83974 | 29992 | 65831 | 38857 | 50490 | 83765 | 55657 | 14361 | 31720 | 57375 | 56228 | 41546 |
| 47 | 64364 | 67412 | 33339 | 31926 | 14883 | 24413 | 59744 | 92351 | 97473 | 89286 | 35931 | 04110 | 23726 | 51900 |
| 48 | 08962 | 00358 | 31662 | 25388 | 61642 | 34072 | 81249 | 35648 | 56891 | 69352 | 48373 | 45578 | 78547 | 81788 |
| 49 | 95012 | 68379 | 93526 | 70765 | 10592 | 04542 | 76463 | 54328 | 02349 | 17247 | 28865 | 14777 | 62730 | 92277 |
| 50 | 15664 | 10493 | 20492 | 38391 | 91132 | 21999 | 59516 | 81652 | 27195 | 48223 | 46751 | 22923 | 32261 | 85653 |

## Appendix D (continued)

| Line/Col. | (1) | (2) | (3) | (4) | (5) | (6) | (7) | (8) | (9) | (10) | (11) | (12) | (13) | (14) |
|---|---|---|---|---|---|---|---|---|---|---|---|---|---|---|
| 51 | 16408 | 81899 | 04153 | 53381 | 79401 | 21438 | 83035 | 92350 | 36693 | 31238 | 59649 | 91754 | 72772 | 02338 |
| 52 | 18629 | 81953 | 05520 | 91962 | 04739 | 13092 | 97662 | 24822 | 94730 | 06496 | 35090 | 04822 | 86774 | 98289 |
| 53 | 73115 | 35101 | 47498 | 87637 | 99016 | 71060 | 88824 | 71013 | 18735 | 20286 | 23153 | 72924 | 35165 | 43040 |
| 54 | 57491 | 16703 | 23167 | 49323 | 45021 | 33132 | 12544 | 41035 | 80780 | 45393 | 44812 | 12515 | 98931 | 91202 |
| 55 | 30405 | 83946 | 23792 | 14422 | 15059 | 45799 | 22716 | 19792 | 09983 | 74353 | 68668 | 30429 | 70735 | 25499 |
| 56 | 16631 | 35006 | 85900 | 98275 | 32388 | 52390 | 16815 | 69298 | 82732 | 38480 | 73817 | 32523 | 41961 | 44437 |
| 57 | 96773 | 20206 | 42559 | 78985 | 05300 | 22164 | 24369 | 54224 | 35083 | 19687 | 11052 | 91491 | 60383 | 19746 |
| 58 | 38935 | 64202 | 14349 | 82674 | 66523 | 44133 | 00697 | 35552 | 35970 | 19124 | 63318 | 29686 | 03387 | 59846 |
| 59 | 31624 | 76384 | 17403 | 53363 | 44167 | 64486 | 64758 | 75366 | 76554 | 31601 | 12614 | 33072 | 60332 | 92325 |
| 60 | 78919 | 19474 | 23632 | 27889 | 47914 | 02584 | 37680 | 20801 | 72152 | 39339 | 34806 | 08930 | 85001 | 87820 |
| 61 | 03931 | 33309 | 57047 | 74211 | 63445 | 17361 | 62825 | 39908 | 05607 | 91284 | 68833 | 25570 | 38818 | 46920 |
| 62 | 74426 | 33278 | 43972 | 10119 | 89917 | 15665 | 52872 | 73823 | 73144 | 88662 | 88970 | 74492 | 51805 | 99378 |
| 63 | 09066 | 00903 | 20795 | 95452 | 92648 | 45454 | 09552 | 88815 | 16553 | 51125 | 79375 | 97596 | 16296 | 66092 |
| 64 | 42238 | 12426 | 87025 | 14267 | 20979 | 04508 | 64535 | 31355 | 86064 | 29472 | 47689 | 05974 | 52468 | 16834 |
| 65 | 16153 | 08002 | 26504 | 41744 | 81959 | 65642 | 74240 | 56302 | 00033 | 67107 | 77510 | 70625 | 28725 | 34191 |
| 66 | 21457 | 40742 | 29820 | 96783 | 29400 | 21840 | 15035 | 34537 | 33310 | 06116 | 95240 | 15957 | 16572 | 06004 |
| 67 | 21581 | 57802 | 02050 | 89728 | 17937 | 37621 | 47075 | 42080 | 97403 | 48626 | 68995 | 43805 | 33386 | 21597 |
| 68 | 55612 | 78095 | 83197 | 33732 | 05810 | 24813 | 86902 | 60397 | 16489 | 03264 | 88525 | 42786 | 05269 | 92532 |
| 69 | 44657 | 66999 | 99324 | 51281 | 84463 | 60563 | 79312 | 93454 | 68876 | 25471 | 93911 | 25650 | 12682 | 73572 |
| 70 | 91340 | 84979 | 46949 | 81973 | 37949 | 61023 | 43997 | 15263 | 80644 | 43942 | 89203 | 71795 | 99533 | 50501 |
| 71 | 91227 | 21199 | 31935 | 27022 | 84067 | 05462 | 35216 | 14436 | 29891 | 68607 | 41867 | 14951 | 91696 | 85065 |
| 72 | 50001 | 38140 | 66321 | 19924 | 72163 | 09538 | 12151 | 06878 | 91903 | 18749 | 34405 | 56087 | 82790 | 70925 |
| 73 | 65390 | 05224 | 72958 | 28609 | 81406 | 39147 | 25549 | 48542 | 42627 | 45233 | 57202 | 94617 | 23772 | 07896 |
| 74 | 27504 | 96131 | 83944 | 41575 | 10573 | 08619 | 64482 | 73923 | 36152 | 05184 | 94142 | 25299 | 84387 | 34925 |
| 75 | 37169 | 94851 | 39117 | 89632 | 00959 | 16487 | 65536 | 49071 | 39782 | 17095 | 02330 | 74301 | 00275 | 48280 |

| | | | | | | | | | | | | | |
|---|---|---|---|---|---|---|---|---|---|---|---|---|---|
| 76 | 11508 | 70225 | 51111 | 38351 | 19444 | 66499 | 71945 | 05422 | 13442 | 78675 | 84081 | 66938 | 93654 59894 |
| 77 | 37449 | 30362 | 06694 | 54690 | 04052 | 53115 | 62757 | 95348 | 78662 | 11163 | 31651 | 50245 | 34971 52924 |
| 78 | 46515 | 70331 | 85922 | 38329 | 57015 | 15765 | 97161 | 17869 | 45349 | 61796 | 56345 | 81073 | 49106 79860 |
| 79 | 30986 | 81223 | 42416 | 58353 | 21532 | 30502 | 32305 | 86482 | 05174 | 07901 | 54339 | 58861 | 74818 46942 |
| 80 | 63798 | 64995 | 46583 | 09785 | 44160 | 78128 | 83991 | 42865 | 92520 | 83531 | 80377 | 35909 | 81250 54238 |
| 81 | 82486 | 84846 | 99254 | 67632 | 43218 | 50076 | 21361 | 64816 | 51202 | 88124 | 41870 | 52689 | 51275 83556 |
| 82 | 21885 | 32906 | 92431 | 09060 | 64297 | 51674 | 64126 | 62570 | 26123 | 05155 | 59194 | 52799 | 28225 85762 |
| 83 | 60336 | 98782 | 07408 | 53458 | 13564 | 59089 | 26445 | 29789 | 85205 | 41001 | 12535 | 12133 | 14645 23541 |
| 84 | 43937 | 46891 | 24010 | 25560 | 86355 | 33941 | 25786 | 54990 | 71899 | 15475 | 95434 | 98227 | 21824 19585 |
| 85 | 97656 | 63175 | 89303 | 16275 | 07100 | 92063 | 21942 | 18611 | 47348 | 20203 | 18534 | 03862 | 78095 50136 |
| 86 | 03299 | 01221 | 05418 | 38982 | 55758 | 92237 | 26759 | 86367 | 21216 | 98442 | 08303 | 56613 | 91511 75928 |
| 87 | 79626 | 06486 | 03574 | 17668 | 07785 | 76020 | 79924 | 25651 | 83325 | 88428 | 85076 | 72811 | 22717 50585 |
| 88 | 85636 | 68335 | 47539 | 03129 | 65651 | 11977 | 02510 | 26113 | 99447 | 68645 | 34327 | 15152 | 55230 93448 |
| 89 | 18039 | 14367 | 61337 | 06177 | 12143 | 46609 | 32989 | 74014 | 64708 | 00533 | 35398 | 58408 | 13261 47908 |
| 90 | 08362 | 15656 | 60627 | 36478 | 65648 | 16764 | 53412 | 09013 | 07832 | 41574 | 17639 | 82163 | 60859 75567 |
| 91 | 79556 | 29068 | 04142 | 16268 | 15387 | 12856 | 66227 | 38358 | 22478 | 73373 | 88732 | 09443 | 82558 05250 |
| 92 | 92608 | 82674 | 27072 | 32534 | 17075 | 27698 | 98204 | 63863 | 11951 | 34648 | 88022 | 56148 | 34925 57031 |
| 93 | 23982 | 25835 | 40055 | 67006 | 12293 | 02753 | 14827 | 23235 | 35071 | 99704 | 37543 | 11601 | 35503 85171 |
| 94 | 09915 | 96306 | 05908 | 97901 | 28395 | 14186 | 00821 | 80703 | 70426 | 75647 | 76310 | 88717 | 37890 40129 |
| 95 | 59037 | 33300 | 26695 | 62247 | 69927 | 76123 | 50842 | 43834 | 86654 | 70959 | 79725 | 93872 | 28117 19233 |
| 96 | 42488 | 78077 | 69882 | 61657 | 34136 | 79180 | 97526 | 43092 | 04098 | 73571 | 80799 | 76536 | 71255 64239 |
| 97 | 46764 | 86273 | 63003 | 93017 | 31204 | 36692 | 40202 | 35275 | 57306 | 55543 | 53203 | 18098 | 47625 88684 |
| 98 | 03237 | 45430 | 55417 | 63282 | 90816 | 17349 | 88298 | 90183 | 36600 | 78406 | 06216 | 95787 | 42579 90730 |
| 99 | 86591 | 81482 | 52667 | 61582 | 14972 | 90053 | 89534 | 76036 | 49199 | 43716 | 97548 | 04379 | 46370 28672 |
| 100 | 38534 | 01715 | 94964 | 87288 | 65680 | 43772 | 39560 | 12918 | 86537 | 62738 | 19636 | 51132 | 25739 56947 |

Abridged from William H. Beyer, ed., *Handbook of Tables for Probability and Statistics*, 2d ed. (Cleveland: Chemical Rubber Company, 1968). Copyright © The Chemical Rubber Co., CRC Press, Inc. Reprinted with permission.

# APPENDIX E  Areas under the Normal Curve

Fractional parts of the total area (10,000) under the normal curve, corresponding to distances between the mean and ordinates that are Z standard deviation units from the mean.

| Z | .00 | .01 | .02 | .03 | .04 | .05 | .06 | .07 | .08 | .09 |
|---|-----|-----|-----|-----|-----|-----|-----|-----|-----|-----|
| 0.0 | 0000 | 0040 | 0080 | 0120 | 0159 | 0199 | 0239 | 0279 | 0319 | 0359 |
| 0.1 | 0398 | 0438 | 0478 | 0517 | 0557 | 0596 | 0636 | 0675 | 0714 | 0753 |
| 0.2 | 0793 | 0832 | 0871 | 0910 | 0948 | 0987 | 1026 | 1064 | 1103 | 1141 |
| 0.3 | 1179 | 1217 | 1255 | 1293 | 1331 | 1368 | 1406 | 1443 | 1480 | 1517 |
| 0.4 | 1554 | 1591 | 1628 | 1664 | 1700 | 1736 | 1772 | 1808 | 1844 | 1879 |
| 0.5 | 1915 | 1950 | 1985 | 2019 | 2054 | 2088 | 2123 | 2157 | 2190 | 2224 |
| 0.6 | 2257 | 2291 | 2324 | 2357 | 2389 | 2422 | 2454 | 2486 | 2518 | 2549 |
| 0.7 | 2580 | 2612 | 2642 | 2673 | 2704 | 2734 | 2764 | 2794 | 2823 | 2852 |
| 0.8 | 2881 | 2910 | 2939 | 2967 | 2995 | 3023 | 3051 | 3078 | 3106 | 3133 |
| 0.9 | 3159 | 3186 | 3212 | 3238 | 3264 | 3289 | 3315 | 3340 | 3365 | 3389 |
| 1.0 | 3413 | 3438 | 3461 | 3485 | 3508 | 3531 | 3554 | 3577 | 3599 | 3621 |
| 1.1 | 3643 | 3665 | 3686 | 3718 | 3729 | 3749 | 3770 | 3790 | 3810 | 3830 |
| 1.2 | 3849 | 3869 | 3888 | 3907 | 3925 | 3944 | 3962 | 3980 | 3997 | 4015 |
| 1.3 | 4032 | 4049 | 4066 | 4083 | 4099 | 4115 | 4131 | 4147 | 4162 | 4177 |
| 1.4 | 4192 | 4207 | 4222 | 4236 | 4251 | 4265 | 4279 | 4292 | 4306 | 4319 |
| 1.5 | 4332 | 4345 | 4357 | 4370 | 4382 | 4394 | 4406 | 4418 | 4430 | 4441 |
| 1.6 | 4452 | 4463 | 4474 | 4485 | 4495 | 4505 | 4515 | 4525 | 4535 | 4545 |
| 1.7 | 4554 | 4564 | 4573 | 4582 | 4591 | 4599 | 4608 | 4616 | 4625 | 4633 |
| 1.8 | 4641 | 4649 | 4656 | 4664 | 4671 | 4678 | 4686 | 4693 | 4699 | 4706 |
| 1.9 | 4713 | 4719 | 4726 | 4732 | 4738 | 4744 | 4750 | 4758 | 4762 | 4767 |
| 2.0 | 4773 | 4778 | 4783 | 4788 | 4793 | 4798 | 4803 | 4808 | 4812 | 4817 |
| 2.1 | 4821 | 4826 | 4830 | 4834 | 4838 | 4842 | 4846 | 4850 | 4854 | 4857 |
| 2.2 | 4861 | 4865 | 4868 | 4871 | 4875 | 4878 | 4881 | 4884 | 4887 | 4890 |
| 2.3 | 4893 | 4896 | 4898 | 4901 | 4904 | 4906 | 4909 | 4911 | 4913 | 4916 |
| 2.4 | 4918 | 4920 | 4922 | 4925 | 4927 | 4929 | 4931 | 4932 | 4934 | 4936 |
| 2.5 | 4938 | 4940 | 4941 | 4943 | 4945 | 4946 | 4948 | 4949 | 4951 | 4952 |
| 2.6 | 4953 | 4955 | 4956 | 4957 | 4959 | 4960 | 4961 | 4962 | 4963 | 4964 |
| 2.7 | 4965 | 4966 | 4967 | 4968 | 4969 | 4970 | 4971 | 4972 | 4973 | 4974 |
| 2.8 | 4974 | 4975 | 4976 | 4977 | 4977 | 4978 | 4979 | 4980 | 4980 | 4981 |
| 2.9 | 4981 | 4982 | 4983 | 4984 | 4984 | 4984 | 4985 | 4985 | 4986 | 4986 |
| 3.0 | 4986.5 | 4987 | 4987 | 4988 | 4988 | 4988 | 4989 | 4989 | 4989 | 4990 |
| 3.1 | 4990.0 | 4991 | 4991 | 4991 | 4992 | 4992 | 4992 | 4992 | 4993 | 4994 |
| 3.2 | 4993.129 | | | | | | | | | |
| 3.3 | 4995.166 | | | | | | | | | |
| 3.4 | 4996.631 | | | | | | | | | |
| 3.5 | 4997.674 | | | | | | | | | |
| 3.6 | 4998.409 | | | | | | | | | |
| 3.7 | 4998.922 | | | | | | | | | |
| 3.8 | 4999.277 | | | | | | | | | |
| 3.9 | 4999.519 | | | | | | | | | |
| 4.0 | 4999.683 | | | | | | | | | |
| 4.5 | 499.966 | | | | | | | | | |
| 5.0 | 4999.997133 | | | | | | | | | |

From Harold O. Rugg, *Statistical Methods Applied to Education* (Boston: Houghton Mifflin, 1917), pp. 389–390. Reprinted by permission of the publisher.

## APPENDIX F    Distribution of $t$

| df | Level of significance for one-tailed test | | | | | |
|---|---|---|---|---|---|---|
| | .10 | .05 | .025 | .01 | .005 | .0005 |
| | Level of significance for two-tailed test | | | | | |
| | .20 | .10 | .05 | .02 | .01 | .001 |
| 1 | 3.078 | 6.314 | 12.706 | 31.821 | 63.657 | 636.619 |
| 2 | 1.886 | 2.920 | 4.303 | 6.965 | 9.925 | 31.598 |
| 3 | 1.638 | 2.353 | 3.182 | 4.541 | 5.841 | 12.941 |
| 4 | 1.533 | 2.132 | 2.776 | 3.747 | 4.604 | 8.610 |
| 5 | 1.476 | 2.015 | 2.571 | 3.365 | 4.032 | 6.859 |
| 6 | 1.440 | 1.943 | 2.447 | 3.143 | 3.707 | 5.959 |
| 7 | 1.415 | 1.895 | 2.365 | 2.998 | 3.499 | 5.405 |
| 8 | 1.397 | 1.860 | 2.306 | 2.896 | 3.355 | 5.041 |
| 9 | 1.383 | 1.833 | 2.262 | 2.821 | 3.250 | 4.781 |
| 10 | 1.372 | 1.812 | 2.228 | 2.764 | 3.169 | 4.587 |
| 11 | 1.363 | 1.796 | 2.201 | 2.718 | 3.106 | 4.437 |
| 12 | 1.356 | 1.782 | 2.179 | 2.681 | 3.055 | 4.318 |
| 13 | 1.350 | 1.771 | 2.160 | 2.650 | 3.012 | 4.221 |
| 14 | 1.345 | 1.761 | 2.145 | 2.624 | 2.977 | 4.140 |
| 15 | 1.341 | 1.753 | 2.131 | 2.602 | 2.947 | 4.073 |
| 16 | 1.337 | 1.746 | 2.120 | 2.583 | 2.921 | 4.015 |
| 17 | 1.333 | 1.740 | 2.110 | 2.567 | 2.898 | 3.965 |
| 18 | 1.330 | 1.734 | 2.101 | 2.552 | 2.878 | 3.922 |
| 19 | 1.328 | 1.729 | 2.093 | 2.539 | 2.861 | 3.883 |
| 20 | 1.325 | 1.725 | 2.086 | 2.528 | 2.845 | 3.850 |
| 21 | 1.323 | 1.721 | 2.080 | 2.518 | 2.831 | 3.819 |
| 22 | 1.321 | 1.717 | 2.074 | 2.508 | 2.819 | 3.792 |
| 23 | 1.319 | 1.714 | 2.069 | 2.500 | 2.807 | 3.767 |
| 24 | 1.318 | 1.711 | 2.064 | 2.492 | 2.797 | 3.745 |
| 25 | 1.316 | 1.708 | 2.060 | 2.485 | 2.787 | 3.725 |
| 26 | 1.315 | 1.706 | 2.056 | 2.479 | 2.779 | 3.707 |
| 27 | 1.314 | 1.703 | 2.052 | 2.473 | 2.771 | 3.690 |
| 28 | 1.313 | 1.701 | 2.048 | 2.467 | 2.763 | 3.674 |
| 29 | 1.311 | 1.699 | 2.045 | 2.462 | 2.756 | 3.659 |
| 30 | 1.310 | 1.697 | 2.042 | 2.457 | 2.750 | 3.646 |
| 40 | 1.303 | 1.684 | 2.021 | 2.423 | 2.704 | 3.551 |
| 60 | 1.296 | 1.671 | 2.000 | 2.390 | 2.660 | 3.460 |
| 120 | 1.289 | 1.658 | 1.980 | 2.358 | 2.617 | 3.373 |
| ∞ | 1.282 | 1.645 | 1.960 | 2.326 | 2.576 | 3.291 |

Abridged from R. A. Fisher and F. Yates, *Statistical Tables for Biological, Agricultural and Medical Research*, 6th ed. (London: Longman, 1974), tab. III. Used by permission of the authors and Longman Group Ltd.

# APPENDIX G  Critical Values of $F$

.05 level of significance (light numbers)
.01 level of significance (heavy numbers)

## Degrees of Freedom in Numerator

| Degrees of Freedom in Denominator | 1 | 2 | 3 | 4 | 5 | 6 | 7 | 8 | 9 | 10 | 11 | 12 | 14 | 16 | 20 | 24 | 30 | 40 | 50 | 75 | 100 | 200 | 500 | ∞ |
|---|---|---|---|---|---|---|---|---|---|---|---|---|---|---|---|---|---|---|---|---|---|---|---|---|
| 1 | 161 | 200 | 216 | 225 | 230 | 234 | 237 | 239 | 241 | 242 | 243 | 244 | 245 | 246 | 248 | 249 | 250 | 251 | 252 | 253 | 253 | 254 | 254 | 254 |
|   | 4,052 | 4,999 | 5,403 | 5,625 | 5,764 | 5,859 | 5,928 | 5,981 | 6,022 | 6,056 | 6,082 | 6,106 | 6,142 | 6,169 | 6,208 | 6,224 | 6,258 | 6,286 | 6,302 | 6,323 | 6,334 | 6,352 | 6,361 | 6,366 |
| 2 | 18.51 | 19.00 | 19.16 | 19.25 | 19.30 | 19.33 | 19.36 | 19.37 | 19.38 | 19.39 | 19.40 | 19.41 | 19.42 | 19.43 | 19.44 | 19.45 | 19.46 | 19.47 | 19.47 | 19.48 | 19.49 | 19.49 | 19.50 | 19.50 |
|   | 98.49 | 99.00 | 99.17 | 99.25 | 99.30 | 99.33 | 99.34 | 99.36 | 99.38 | 99.40 | 99.41 | 99.42 | 99.43 | 99.44 | 99.45 | 99.46 | 99.47 | 99.48 | 99.48 | 99.49 | 99.49 | 99.49 | 99.50 | 99.50 |
| 3 | 10.13 | 9.55 | 9.28 | 9.12 | 9.01 | 8.94 | 8.88 | 8.84 | 8.81 | 8.78 | 8.76 | 8.74 | 8.71 | 8.69 | 8.66 | 8.64 | 8.62 | 8.60 | 8.58 | 8.57 | 8.56 | 8.54 | 8.54 | 8.53 |
|   | 34.12 | 30.82 | 29.46 | 28.71 | 28.24 | 27.91 | 27.67 | 27.49 | 27.34 | 27.23 | 27.13 | 27.05 | 26.92 | 26.83 | 26.69 | 26.60 | 26.50 | 26.41 | 26.35 | 26.27 | 26.23 | 26.18 | 26.14 | 26.12 |
| 4 | 7.71 | 6.94 | 6.59 | 6.39 | 6.26 | 6.16 | 6.09 | 6.04 | 6.00 | 5.96 | 5.93 | 5.91 | 5.87 | 5.84 | 5.80 | 5.77 | 5.74 | 5.71 | 5.70 | 5.68 | 5.66 | 5.65 | 5.64 | 5.63 |
|   | 21.20 | 18.00 | 16.69 | 15.98 | 15.52 | 15.21 | 14.98 | 14.80 | 14.66 | 14.54 | 14.45 | 14.37 | 14.24 | 14.15 | 14.02 | 13.93 | 13.83 | 13.74 | 13.69 | 13.61 | 13.57 | 13.52 | 13.48 | 13.46 |
| 5 | 6.61 | 5.79 | 5.41 | 5.19 | 5.05 | 4.95 | 4.88 | 4.82 | 4.78 | 4.74 | 4.70 | 4.68 | 4.64 | 4.60 | 4.56 | 4.53 | 4.50 | 4.46 | 4.44 | 4.42 | 4.40 | 4.38 | 4.37 | 4.36 |
|   | 16.26 | 13.27 | 12.06 | 11.39 | 10.97 | 10.67 | 10.45 | 10.27 | 10.15 | 10.05 | 9.96 | 9.89 | 9.77 | 9.68 | 9.55 | 9.47 | 9.38 | 9.29 | 9.24 | 9.17 | 9.13 | 9.07 | 9.04 | 9.02 |
| 6 | 5.99 | 5.14 | 4.76 | 4.53 | 4.39 | 4.28 | 4.21 | 4.15 | 4.10 | 4.06 | 4.03 | 4.00 | 3.96 | 3.92 | 3.87 | 3.84 | 3.81 | 3.77 | 3.75 | 3.72 | 3.71 | 3.69 | 3.68 | 3.67 |
|   | 13.74 | 10.92 | 9.78 | 9.15 | 8.75 | 8.47 | 8.26 | 8.10 | 7.98 | 7.87 | 7.79 | 7.72 | 7.60 | 7.52 | 7.39 | 7.31 | 7.23 | 7.14 | 7.09 | 7.02 | 6.99 | 6.94 | 6.90 | 6.88 |
| 7 | 5.59 | 4.47 | 4.35 | 4.12 | 3.97 | 3.87 | 3.79 | 3.73 | 3.68 | 3.63 | 3.60 | 3.57 | 3.52 | 3.49 | 3.44 | 3.41 | 3.38 | 3.34 | 3.32 | 3.29 | 3.28 | 3.25 | 3.24 | 3.23 |
|   | 12.25 | 9.55 | 8.45 | 7.85 | 7.46 | 7.19 | 7.00 | 6.84 | 6.71 | 6.62 | 6.54 | 6.47 | 6.35 | 6.27 | 6.15 | 6.07 | 5.98 | 5.90 | 5.85 | 5.78 | 5.75 | 5.70 | 5.67 | 5.65 |

| | | | | | | | | | | | | | | | | | | | | | | | | |
|---|---|---|---|---|---|---|---|---|---|---|---|---|---|---|---|---|---|---|---|---|---|---|---|---|
| **8** | 2.93 | 2.94 | 2.96 | 2.98 | 3.00 | 3.03 | 3.05 | 3.08 | 3.12 | 3.15 | 3.20 | 3.23 | 3.28 | 3.31 | 3.34 | 3.39 | 3.44 | 3.50 | 3.58 | 3.69 | 3.84 | 4.07 | 4.46 | 5.32 |
| | 4.86 | 4.88 | 4.91 | 4.96 | 5.00 | 5.06 | 5.11 | 5.20 | 5.28 | 5.36 | 5.48 | 5.56 | 5.67 | 5.74 | 5.82 | 5.91 | 6.03 | 6.19 | 6.37 | 6.63 | 7.01 | 7.59 | 8.65 | 11.26 |
| **9** | 2.71 | 2.72 | 2.73 | 2.76 | 2.77 | 2.80 | 2.82 | 2.86 | 2.90 | 2.93 | 2.98 | 3.02 | 3.07 | 3.10 | 3.13 | 3.18 | 3.23 | 3.29 | 3.37 | 3.48 | 3.63 | 3.86 | 4.26 | 5.12 |
| | 4.31 | 4.33 | 4.36 | 4.41 | 4.45 | 4.51 | 4.56 | 4.64 | 4.73 | 4.80 | 4.92 | 5.00 | 5.11 | 5.18 | 5.26 | 5.35 | 5.47 | 5.62 | 5.80 | 6.06 | 6.42 | 6.99 | 8.02 | 10.56 |
| **10** | 2.54 | 2.55 | 2.56 | 2.59 | 2.61 | 2.64 | 2.67 | 2.70 | 2.74 | 2.77 | 2.82 | 2.86 | 2.91 | 2.94 | 2.97 | 3.02 | 3.07 | 3.14 | 3.22 | 3.33 | 3.48 | 3.71 | 4.10 | 4.96 |
| | 3.91 | 3.93 | 3.96 | 4.01 | 4.05 | 4.12 | 4.17 | 4.25 | 4.33 | 4.41 | 4.52 | 4.60 | 4.71 | 4.78 | 4.85 | 4.95 | 5.06 | 5.21 | 5.39 | 5.64 | 5.99 | 6.55 | 7.56 | 10.04 |
| **11** | 2.40 | 2.41 | 2.42 | 2.45 | 2.47 | 2.50 | 2.53 | 2.57 | 2.61 | 2.65 | 2.70 | 2.74 | 2.79 | 2.82 | 2.86 | 2.90 | 2.95 | 3.01 | 3.09 | 3.20 | 3.36 | 3.59 | 3.98 | 4.84 |
| | 3.60 | 3.62 | 3.66 | 3.70 | 3.74 | 3.80 | 3.86 | 3.94 | 4.02 | 4.10 | 4.21 | 4.29 | 4.40 | 4.46 | 4.54 | 4.63 | 4.74 | 4.88 | 5.07 | 5.32 | 5.67 | 6.22 | 7.20 | 9.65 |
| **12** | 2.30 | 2.31 | 2.32 | 2.35 | 2.36 | 2.40 | 2.42 | 2.46 | 2.50 | 2.54 | 2.60 | 2.64 | 2.69 | 2.72 | 2.76 | 2.80 | 2.85 | 2.92 | 3.00 | 3.11 | 3.26 | 3.49 | 3.88 | 4.75 |
| | 3.36 | 3.38 | 3.41 | 3.46 | 3.49 | 3.56 | 3.61 | 3.70 | 3.78 | 3.86 | 3.98 | 4.05 | 4.16 | 4.22 | 4.30 | 4.39 | 4.50 | 4.65 | 4.82 | 5.06 | 5.41 | 5.95 | 6.93 | 9.33 |
| **13** | 2.21 | 2.22 | 2.24 | 2.26 | 2.28 | 2.32 | 2.34 | 2.38 | 2.42 | 2.46 | 2.51 | 2.55 | 2.60 | 2.63 | 2.67 | 2.72 | 2.77 | 2.84 | 2.92 | 3.02 | 3.18 | 3.41 | 3.80 | 4.67 |
| | 3.16 | 3.18 | 3.21 | 3.27 | 3.30 | 3.37 | 3.42 | 3.51 | 3.59 | 3.67 | 3.78 | 3.85 | 3.96 | 4.02 | 4.10 | 4.19 | 4.30 | 4.44 | 4.62 | 4.86 | 5.20 | 5.74 | 6.70 | 9.07 |
| **14** | 2.13 | 2.14 | 2.16 | 2.19 | 2.21 | 2.24 | 2.27 | 2.31 | 2.35 | 2.39 | 2.44 | 2.48 | 2.53 | 2.56 | 2.60 | 2.65 | 2.70 | 2.77 | 2.85 | 2.96 | 3.11 | 3.34 | 3.74 | 4.60 |
| | 3.00 | 3.02 | 3.06 | 3.11 | 3.14 | 3.21 | 3.26 | 3.34 | 3.43 | 3.51 | 3.62 | 3.70 | 3.80 | 3.86 | 3.94 | 4.03 | 4.14 | 4.28 | 4.46 | 4.69 | 5.03 | 5.56 | 6.51 | 8.86 |
| **15** | 2.07 | 2.08 | 2.10 | 2.12 | 2.15 | 2.18 | 2.21 | 2.25 | 2.29 | 2.33 | 2.39 | 2.43 | 2.48 | 2.51 | 2.55 | 2.59 | 2.64 | 2.70 | 2.79 | 2.90 | 3.06 | 3.29 | 3.68 | 4.54 |
| | 2.87 | 2.89 | 2.92 | 2.97 | 3.00 | 3.07 | 3.12 | 3.20 | 3.29 | 3.36 | 3.48 | 3.56 | 3.67 | 3.73 | 3.80 | 3.89 | 4.00 | 4.14 | 4.32 | 4.56 | 4.89 | 5.42 | 6.36 | 8.68 |
| **16** | 2.01 | 2.02 | 2.04 | 2.07 | 2.09 | 2.13 | 2.16 | 2.20 | 2.24 | 2.28 | 2.33 | 2.37 | 2.42 | 2.45 | 2.49 | 2.54 | 2.59 | 2.66 | 2.74 | 2.85 | 3.01 | 3.24 | 3.63 | 4.49 |
| | 2.75 | 2.77 | 2.80 | 2.86 | 2.89 | 2.96 | 3.01 | 3.10 | 3.18 | 3.25 | 3.37 | 3.45 | 3.55 | 3.61 | 3.69 | 3.78 | 3.89 | 4.03 | 4.20 | 4.44 | 4.77 | 5.29 | 6.23 | 8.53 |
| **17** | 1.96 | 1.97 | 1.99 | 2.02 | 2.04 | 2.08 | 2.11 | 2.15 | 2.19 | 2.23 | 2.29 | 2.33 | 2.38 | 2.41 | 2.45 | 2.50 | 2.55 | 2.62 | 2.70 | 2.81 | 2.96 | 3.20 | 3.59 | 4.45 |
| | 2.65 | 2.67 | 2.70 | 2.76 | 2.79 | 2.86 | 2.92 | 3.00 | 3.08 | 3.16 | 3.27 | 3.35 | 3.45 | 3.52 | 3.59 | 3.68 | 3.79 | 3.93 | 4.10 | 4.34 | 4.67 | 5.18 | 6.11 | 8.40 |
| **18** | 1.92 | 1.93 | 1.95 | 1.98 | 2.00 | 2.04 | 2.07 | 2.11 | 2.15 | 2.19 | 2.25 | 2.29 | 2.34 | 2.37 | 2.41 | 2.46 | 2.51 | 2.58 | 2.66 | 2.77 | 2.93 | 3.16 | 3.55 | 4.41 |
| | 2.57 | 2.59 | 2.62 | 2.68 | 2.71 | 2.78 | 2.83 | 2.91 | 3.00 | 3.07 | 3.19 | 3.27 | 3.37 | 3.44 | 3.51 | 3.60 | 3.71 | 3.85 | 4.01 | 4.25 | 4.58 | 5.09 | 6.01 | 8.28 |

# Appendix G (continued)

Degrees of Freedom in Numerator

| Degrees of Freedom in Denominator | 1 | 2 | 3 | 4 | 5 | 6 | 7 | 8 | 9 | 10 | 11 | 12 | 14 | 16 | 20 | 24 | 30 | 40 | 50 | 75 | 100 | 200 | 500 | ∞ |
|---|---|---|---|---|---|---|---|---|---|---|---|---|---|---|---|---|---|---|---|---|---|---|---|---|
| 19 | 4.38 | 3.52 | 3.13 | 2.90 | 2.74 | 2.63 | 2.55 | 2.48 | 2.43 | 2.38 | 2.34 | 2.31 | 2.26 | 2.21 | 2.15 | 2.11 | 2.07 | 2.02 | 2.00 | 1.96 | 1.94 | 1.91 | 1.90 | 1.88 |
|    | 8.18 | 5.93 | 5.01 | 4.50 | 4.17 | 3.94 | 3.77 | 3.63 | 3.52 | 3.43 | 3.36 | 3.30 | 3.19 | 3.12 | 3.00 | 2.92 | 2.84 | 2.76 | 2.70 | 2.63 | 2.60 | 2.54 | 2.51 | 2.49 |
| 20 | 4.35 | 3.49 | 3.10 | 2.87 | 2.71 | 2.60 | 2.52 | 2.45 | 2.40 | 2.35 | 2.31 | 2.28 | 2.23 | 2.18 | 2.12 | 2.08 | 2.04 | 1.99 | 1.96 | 1.92 | 1.90 | 1.87 | 1.85 | 1.84 |
|    | 8.10 | 5.85 | 4.94 | 4.43 | 4.10 | 3.87 | 3.71 | 3.56 | 3.45 | 3.37 | 3.30 | 3.23 | 3.13 | 3.05 | 2.94 | 2.86 | 2.77 | 2.69 | 2.63 | 2.56 | 2.53 | 2.47 | 2.44 | 2.42 |
| 21 | 4.32 | 3.47 | 3.07 | 2.84 | 2.68 | 2.57 | 2.49 | 2.42 | 2.37 | 2.32 | 2.28 | 2.25 | 2.20 | 2.15 | 2.09 | 2.05 | 2.00 | 1.96 | 1.93 | 1.89 | 1.87 | 1.84 | 1.82 | 1.81 |
|    | 8.02 | 5.78 | 4.87 | 4.37 | 4.04 | 3.81 | 3.65 | 3.51 | 3.40 | 3.31 | 3.24 | 3.17 | 3.07 | 2.99 | 2.88 | 2.80 | 2.72 | 2.63 | 2.58 | 2.51 | 2.47 | 2.42 | 2.38 | 2.36 |
| 22 | 4.30 | 3.44 | 3.05 | 2.82 | 2.66 | 2.55 | 2.47 | 2.40 | 2.35 | 2.30 | 2.26 | 2.23 | 2.18 | 2.13 | 2.07 | 2.03 | 1.98 | 1.93 | 1.91 | 1.87 | 1.84 | 1.81 | 1.80 | 1.78 |
|    | 7.94 | 5.72 | 4.82 | 4.31 | 3.99 | 3.76 | 3.59 | 3.45 | 3.35 | 3.26 | 3.18 | 3.12 | 3.02 | 2.94 | 2.83 | 2.75 | 2.67 | 2.58 | 2.53 | 2.46 | 2.42 | 2.37 | 2.33 | 2.31 |
| 23 | 4.28 | 3.42 | 3.03 | 2.80 | 2.64 | 2.53 | 2.45 | 2.38 | 2.32 | 2.28 | 2.24 | 2.20 | 2.14 | 2.10 | 2.04 | 2.00 | 1.96 | 1.91 | 1.88 | 1.84 | 1.82 | 1.79 | 1.77 | 1.76 |
|    | 7.88 | 5.66 | 4.76 | 4.26 | 3.94 | 3.71 | 3.54 | 3.41 | 3.30 | 3.21 | 3.14 | 3.07 | 2.97 | 2.89 | 2.78 | 2.70 | 2.62 | 2.53 | 2.48 | 2.41 | 2.37 | 2.32 | 2.28 | 2.26 |
| 24 | 4.26 | 3.40 | 3.01 | 2.78 | 2.62 | 2.51 | 2.43 | 2.36 | 2.30 | 2.26 | 2.22 | 2.18 | 2.13 | 2.09 | 2.02 | 1.98 | 1.94 | 1.89 | 1.86 | 1.82 | 1.80 | 1.76 | 1.74 | 1.73 |
|    | 7.82 | 5.61 | 4.72 | 4.22 | 3.90 | 3.67 | 3.50 | 3.36 | 3.25 | 3.17 | 3.09 | 3.03 | 2.93 | 2.85 | 2.74 | 2.66 | 2.58 | 2.49 | 2.44 | 2.36 | 2.33 | 2.27 | 2.23 | 2.21 |
| 25 | 4.24 | 3.38 | 2.99 | 2.76 | 2.60 | 2.49 | 2.41 | 2.34 | 2.28 | 2.24 | 2.20 | 2.16 | 2.11 | 2.06 | 2.00 | 1.96 | 1.92 | 1.87 | 1.84 | 1.80 | 1.77 | 1.74 | 1.72 | 1.71 |
|    | 7.77 | 5.57 | 4.68 | 4.18 | 3.86 | 3.63 | 3.46 | 3.32 | 3.21 | 3.13 | 3.05 | 2.99 | 2.89 | 2.81 | 2.70 | 2.62 | 2.54 | 2.45 | 2.40 | 2.32 | 2.29 | 2.23 | 2.19 | 2.17 |
| 26 | 4.22 | 3.37 | 2.98 | 2.74 | 2.59 | 2.47 | 2.39 | 2.32 | 2.27 | 2.22 | 2.18 | 2.15 | 2.10 | 2.05 | 1.99 | 1.95 | 1.90 | 1.85 | 1.82 | 1.78 | 1.76 | 1.72 | 1.70 | 1.69 |
|    | 7.72 | 5.53 | 4.64 | 4.14 | 3.82 | 3.59 | 3.42 | 3.29 | 3.17 | 3.09 | 3.02 | 2.96 | 2.86 | 2.77 | 2.66 | 2.58 | 2.50 | 2.41 | 2.36 | 2.28 | 2.25 | 2.19 | 2.15 | 2.13 |
| 27 | 4.21 | 3.35 | 2.96 | 2.73 | 2.57 | 2.46 | 2.37 | 2.30 | 2.25 | 2.20 | 2.16 | 2.13 | 2.08 | 2.03 | 1.97 | 1.93 | 1.88 | 1.84 | 1.80 | 1.76 | 1.74 | 1.71 | 1.68 | 1.67 |
|    | 7.68 | 5.49 | 4.60 | 4.11 | 3.79 | 3.56 | 3.39 | 3.26 | 3.14 | 3.06 | 2.98 | 2.93 | 2.83 | 2.74 | 2.63 | 2.55 | 2.47 | 2.38 | 2.33 | 2.25 | 2.21 | 2.16 | 2.12 | 2.10 |
| 28 | 4.20 | 3.34 | 2.95 | 2.71 | 2.56 | 2.44 | 2.36 | 2.29 | 2.24 | 2.19 | 2.15 | 2.12 | 2.06 | 2.02 | 1.96 | 1.91 | 1.87 | 1.81 | 1.78 | 1.75 | 1.72 | 1.69 | 1.67 | 1.65 |
|    | 7.64 | 5.45 | 4.57 | 4.07 | 3.76 | 3.53 | 3.36 | 3.23 | 3.11 | 3.03 | 2.95 | 2.90 | 2.80 | 2.71 | 2.60 | 2.52 | 2.44 | 2.35 | 2.30 | 2.22 | 2.18 | 2.13 | 2.09 | 2.06 |
| 29 | 4.18 | 3.33 | 2.93 | 2.70 | 2.54 | 2.43 | 2.35 | 2.28 | 2.22 | 2.18 | 2.14 | 2.10 | 2.05 | 2.00 | 1.94 | 1.90 | 1.85 | 1.80 | 1.77 | 1.73 | 1.71 | 1.68 | 1.65 | 1.64 |
|    | 7.60 | 5.42 | 4.54 | 4.04 | 3.73 | 3.50 | 3.33 | 3.20 | 3.08 | 3.00 | 2.92 | 2.87 | 2.77 | 2.68 | 2.57 | 2.49 | 2.41 | 2.32 | 2.27 | 2.19 | 2.15 | 2.10 | 2.06 | 2.03 |

| | | | | | | | | | | | | | | | | | | | | | | | | |
|---|---|---|---|---|---|---|---|---|---|---|---|---|---|---|---|---|---|---|---|---|---|---|---|---|
| **30** | 4.17 | 3.32 | 2.92 | 2.69 | 2.53 | 2.42 | 2.34 | 2.27 | 2.21 | 2.16 | 2.12 | 2.09 | 2.04 | 1.99 | 1.93 | 1.89 | 1.84 | 1.79 | 1.76 | 1.72 | 1.69 | 1.66 | 1.64 | 1.62 |
| | 7.56 | 5.39 | 4.51 | 4.02 | 3.70 | 3.47 | 3.30 | 3.17 | 3.05 | 2.98 | 2.90 | 2.84 | 2.74 | 2.66 | 2.55 | 2.47 | 2.38 | 2.29 | 2.24 | 2.16 | 2.13 | 2.07 | 2.03 | 2.01 |
| **32** | 4.15 | 3.30 | 2.90 | 2.67 | 2.51 | 2.40 | 2.32 | 2.25 | 2.19 | 2.14 | 2.10 | 2.07 | 2.02 | 1.97 | 1.91 | 1.86 | 1.82 | 1.76 | 1.74 | 1.69 | 1.67 | 1.64 | 1.61 | 1.59 |
| | 7.50 | 5.34 | 4.46 | 3.97 | 3.66 | 3.42 | 3.25 | 3.12 | 3.01 | 2.94 | 2.86 | 2.80 | 2.70 | 2.62 | 2.51 | 2.42 | 2.34 | 2.25 | 2.20 | 2.12 | 2.08 | 2.02 | 1.98 | 1.96 |
| **34** | 4.13 | 3.28 | 2.88 | 2.65 | 2.49 | 2.38 | 2.30 | 2.23 | 2.17 | 2.12 | 2.08 | 2.05 | 2.00 | 1.95 | 1.89 | 1.84 | 1.80 | 1.74 | 1.71 | 1.67 | 1.64 | 1.61 | 1.59 | 1.57 |
| | 7.44 | 5.29 | 4.42 | 3.93 | 3.61 | 3.38 | 3.21 | 3.08 | 2.97 | 2.89 | 2.82 | 2.76 | 2.66 | 2.58 | 2.47 | 2.38 | 2.30 | 2.21 | 2.15 | 2.08 | 2.04 | 1.98 | 1.94 | 1.91 |
| **36** | 4.11 | 3.26 | 2.86 | 2.63 | 2.48 | 2.36 | 2.28 | 2.21 | 2.15 | 2.10 | 2.06 | 2.03 | 1.98 | 1.93 | 1.87 | 1.82 | 1.78 | 1.72 | 1.69 | 1.65 | 1.62 | 1.59 | 1.56 | 1.55 |
| | 7.39 | 5.25 | 4.38 | 3.89 | 3.58 | 3.35 | 3.18 | 3.04 | 2.94 | 2.86 | 2.78 | 2.72 | 2.62 | 2.54 | 2.43 | 2.35 | 2.26 | 2.17 | 2.12 | 2.04 | 2.00 | 1.94 | 1.90 | 1.87 |
| **38** | 4.10 | 3.25 | 2.85 | 2.62 | 2.46 | 2.35 | 2.26 | 2.19 | 2.14 | 2.09 | 2.05 | 2.02 | 1.96 | 1.92 | 1.85 | 1.80 | 1.76 | 1.71 | 1.67 | 1.63 | 1.60 | 1.57 | 1.54 | 1.53 |
| | 7.35 | 5.21 | 4.34 | 3.86 | 3.54 | 3.32 | 3.15 | 3.02 | 2.91 | 2.82 | 2.75 | 2.69 | 2.59 | 2.51 | 2.40 | 2.32 | 2.22 | 2.14 | 2.08 | 2.00 | 1.97 | 1.90 | 1.86 | 1.84 |
| **40** | 4.08 | 3.23 | 2.84 | 2.61 | 2.45 | 2.34 | 2.25 | 2.18 | 2.12 | 2.07 | 2.04 | 2.00 | 1.95 | 1.90 | 1.84 | 1.79 | 1.74 | 1.69 | 1.66 | 1.61 | 1.59 | 1.55 | 1.53 | 1.51 |
| | 7.31 | 5.18 | 4.31 | 3.83 | 3.51 | 3.29 | 3.12 | 2.99 | 2.88 | 2.80 | 2.73 | 2.66 | 2.56 | 2.49 | 2.37 | 2.29 | 2.20 | 2.11 | 2.05 | 1.97 | 1.94 | 1.88 | 1.84 | 1.81 |
| **42** | 4.07 | 3.22 | 2.83 | 2.59 | 2.44 | 2.32 | 2.24 | 2.17 | 2.11 | 2.06 | 2.02 | 1.99 | 1.94 | 1.89 | 1.82 | 1.78 | 1.73 | 1.68 | 1.64 | 1.60 | 1.57 | 1.54 | 1.51 | 1.49 |
| | 7.27 | 5.15 | 4.29 | 3.80 | 3.49 | 3.26 | 3.10 | 2.96 | 2.86 | 2.77 | 2.70 | 2.64 | 2.54 | 2.46 | 2.35 | 2.26 | 2.17 | 2.08 | 2.02 | 1.94 | 1.91 | 1.85 | 1.80 | 1.78 |
| **44** | 4.06 | 3.21 | 2.82 | 2.58 | 2.43 | 2.31 | 2.23 | 2.16 | 2.10 | 2.05 | 2.01 | 1.98 | 1.92 | 1.88 | 1.81 | 1.76 | 1.72 | 1.66 | 1.63 | 1.58 | 1.56 | 1.52 | 1.50 | 1.48 |
| | 7.24 | 5.12 | 4.26 | 3.78 | 3.46 | 3.24 | 3.07 | 2.94 | 2.84 | 2.75 | 2.68 | 2.62 | 2.52 | 2.44 | 2.32 | 2.24 | 2.15 | 2.06 | 2.00 | 1.92 | 1.88 | 1.82 | 1.78 | 1.75 |
| **46** | 4.05 | 3.20 | 2.81 | 2.57 | 2.42 | 2.30 | 2.22 | 2.14 | 2.09 | 2.04 | 2.00 | 1.97 | 1.91 | 1.87 | 1.80 | 1.75 | 1.71 | 1.65 | 1.62 | 1.57 | 1.54 | 1.51 | 1.48 | 1.46 |
| | 7.21 | 5.10 | 4.24 | 3.76 | 3.44 | 3.22 | 3.05 | 2.92 | 2.82 | 2.73 | 2.66 | 2.60 | 2.50 | 2.42 | 2.30 | 2.22 | 2.13 | 2.04 | 1.98 | 1.90 | 1.86 | 1.80 | 1.76 | 1.72 |
| **48** | 4.04 | 3.19 | 2.80 | 2.56 | 2.41 | 2.30 | 2.21 | 2.14 | 2.08 | 2.03 | 1.99 | 1.96 | 1.90 | 1.86 | 1.79 | 1.74 | 1.70 | 1.64 | 1.61 | 1.56 | 1.53 | 1.50 | 1.47 | 1.45 |
| | 7.19 | 5.08 | 4.22 | 3.74 | 3.42 | 3.20 | 3.04 | 2.90 | 2.80 | 2.71 | 2.64 | 2.58 | 2.48 | 2.40 | 2.28 | 2.20 | 2.11 | 2.02 | 1.96 | 1.88 | 1.84 | 1.78 | 1.73 | 1.70 |
| **50** | 4.03 | 3.18 | 2.79 | 2.56 | 2.40 | 2.29 | 2.20 | 2.13 | 2.07 | 2.02 | 1.98 | 1.95 | 1.90 | 1.85 | 1.78 | 1.74 | 1.69 | 1.63 | 1.60 | 1.55 | 1.52 | 1.48 | 1.46 | 1.44 |
| | 7.17 | 5.06 | 4.20 | 3.72 | 3.41 | 3.18 | 3.02 | 2.88 | 2.78 | 2.70 | 2.62 | 2.56 | 2.46 | 2.39 | 2.26 | 2.18 | 2.10 | 2.00 | 1.94 | 1.86 | 1.82 | 1.76 | 1.71 | 1.68 |
| **55** | 4.02 | 3.17 | 2.78 | 2.54 | 2.38 | 2.27 | 2.18 | 2.11 | 2.05 | 2.00 | 1.97 | 1.93 | 1.88 | 1.83 | 1.76 | 1.72 | 1.67 | 1.61 | 1.58 | 1.52 | 1.50 | 1.46 | 1.43 | 1.41 |
| | 7.12 | 5.01 | 4.16 | 3.68 | 3.37 | 3.15 | 2.98 | 2.85 | 2.75 | 2.66 | 2.59 | 2.53 | 2.43 | 2.35 | 2.23 | 2.15 | 2.06 | 1.96 | 1.90 | 1.82 | 1.78 | 1.71 | 1.66 | 1.64 |
| **60** | 4.00 | 3.15 | 2.76 | 2.52 | 2.37 | 2.25 | 2.17 | 2.10 | 2.04 | 1.99 | 1.95 | 1.92 | 1.86 | 1.81 | 1.75 | 1.70 | 1.65 | 1.59 | 1.56 | 1.50 | 1.48 | 1.44 | 1.41 | 1.39 |
| | 7.08 | 4.98 | 4.13 | 3.65 | 3.34 | 3.12 | 2.95 | 2.82 | 2.72 | 2.63 | 2.56 | 2.50 | 2.40 | 2.32 | 2.20 | 2.12 | 2.03 | 1.93 | 1.87 | 1.79 | 1.74 | 1.68 | 1.63 | 1.60 |

# Appendix G (continued)

Degrees of Freedom in Numerator

| Degrees of Freedom in Denominator | 1 | 2 | 3 | 4 | 5 | 6 | 7 | 8 | 9 | 10 | 11 | 12 | 14 | 16 | 20 | 24 | 30 | 40 | 50 | 75 | 100 | 200 | 500 | ∞ |
|---|---|---|---|---|---|---|---|---|---|---|---|---|---|---|---|---|---|---|---|---|---|---|---|---|
| 65 | 3.99 | 3.14 | 2.75 | 2.51 | 2.36 | 2.24 | 2.15 | 2.08 | 2.02 | 1.98 | 1.94 | 1.90 | 1.85 | 1.80 | 1.73 | 1.68 | 1.63 | 1.57 | 1.54 | 1.49 | 1.46 | 1.42 | 1.39 | 1.37 |
|  | 7.04 | 4.95 | 4.10 | 3.62 | 3.31 | 3.09 | 2.93 | 2.79 | 2.70 | 2.61 | 2.54 | 2.47 | 2.37 | 2.30 | 2.18 | 2.09 | 2.00 | 1.90 | 1.84 | 1.76 | 1.71 | 1.64 | 1.60 | 1.56 |
| 70 | 3.98 | 3.13 | 2.74 | 2.50 | 2.35 | 2.23 | 2.14 | 2.07 | 2.01 | 1.97 | 1.93 | 1.89 | 1.84 | 1.79 | 1.72 | 1.67 | 1.62 | 1.56 | 1.53 | 1.47 | 1.45 | 1.40 | 1.37 | 1.35 |
|  | 7.01 | 4.92 | 4.08 | 3.60 | 3.29 | 3.07 | 2.91 | 2.77 | 2.67 | 2.59 | 2.51 | 2.45 | 2.35 | 2.28 | 2.15 | 2.07 | 1.98 | 1.88 | 1.82 | 1.74 | 1.69 | 1.62 | 1.56 | 1.53 |
| 80 | 3.96 | 3.11 | 2.72 | 2.48 | 2.33 | 2.21 | 2.12 | 2.05 | 1.99 | 1.95 | 1.91 | 1.88 | 1.82 | 1.77 | 1.70 | 1.65 | 1.60 | 1.54 | 1.51 | 1.45 | 1.42 | 1.38 | 1.35 | 1.32 |
|  | 6.96 | 4.88 | 4.04 | 3.56 | 3.25 | 3.04 | 2.87 | 2.74 | 2.64 | 2.55 | 2.48 | 2.41 | 2.32 | 2.24 | 2.11 | 2.03 | 1.94 | 1.84 | 1.78 | 1.70 | 1.65 | 1.57 | 1.52 | 1.49 |
| 100 | 3.94 | 3.09 | 2.70 | 2.46 | 2.30 | 2.19 | 2.10 | 2.03 | 1.97 | 1.92 | 1.88 | 1.85 | 1.79 | 1.75 | 1.68 | 1.63 | 1.57 | 1.51 | 1.48 | 1.42 | 1.39 | 1.34 | 1.30 | 1.28 |
|  | 6.90 | 4.82 | 3.98 | 3.51 | 3.20 | 2.99 | 2.82 | 2.69 | 2.59 | 2.51 | 2.43 | 2.36 | 2.26 | 2.19 | 2.06 | 1.98 | 1.89 | 1.79 | 1.73 | 1.64 | 1.59 | 1.51 | 1.46 | 1.43 |
| 125 | 3.92 | 3.07 | 2.68 | 2.44 | 2.29 | 2.17 | 2.08 | 2.01 | 1.95 | 1.90 | 1.86 | 1.83 | 1.77 | 1.72 | 1.65 | 1.60 | 1.55 | 1.49 | 1.45 | 1.39 | 1.36 | 1.31 | 1.27 | 1.25 |
|  | 6.84 | 4.78 | 3.94 | 3.47 | 3.17 | 2.95 | 2.79 | 2.65 | 2.56 | 2.47 | 2.40 | 2.33 | 2.23 | 2.15 | 2.03 | 1.94 | 1.85 | 1.75 | 1.68 | 1.59 | 1.54 | 1.46 | 1.40 | 1.37 |
| 150 | 3.91 | 3.06 | 2.67 | 2.43 | 2.27 | 2.16 | 2.07 | 2.00 | 1.94 | 1.89 | 1.85 | 1.82 | 1.76 | 1.71 | 1.64 | 1.59 | 1.54 | 1.47 | 1.44 | 1.37 | 1.34 | 1.29 | 1.25 | 1.22 |
|  | 6.81 | 4.75 | 3.91 | 3.44 | 3.14 | 2.92 | 2.76 | 2.62 | 2.53 | 2.44 | 2.37 | 2.30 | 2.20 | 2.12 | 2.00 | 1.91 | 1.83 | 1.72 | 1.66 | 1.56 | 1.51 | 1.43 | 1.37 | 1.33 |
| 200 | 3.89 | 3.04 | 2.65 | 2.41 | 2.26 | 2.14 | 2.05 | 1.98 | 1.92 | 1.87 | 1.83 | 1.80 | 1.74 | 1.69 | 1.62 | 1.57 | 1.52 | 1.45 | 1.42 | 1.35 | 1.32 | 1.26 | 1.22 | 1.19 |
|  | 6.76 | 4.71 | 3.88 | 3.41 | 3.11 | 2.90 | 2.73 | 2.60 | 2.50 | 2.41 | 2.34 | 2.28 | 2.17 | 2.09 | 1.97 | 1.88 | 1.79 | 1.69 | 1.62 | 1.53 | 1.48 | 1.39 | 1.33 | 1.28 |
| 400 | 3.86 | 3.02 | 2.62 | 2.39 | 2.23 | 2.12 | 2.03 | 1.96 | 1.90 | 1.85 | 1.81 | 1.78 | 1.72 | 1.67 | 1.60 | 1.54 | 1.49 | 1.42 | 1.38 | 1.32 | 1.28 | 1.22 | 1.16 | 1.13 |
|  | 6.70 | 4.66 | 3.83 | 3.36 | 3.06 | 2.85 | 2.69 | 2.55 | 2.46 | 2.37 | 2.29 | 2.23 | 2.12 | 2.04 | 1.92 | 1.84 | 1.74 | 1.64 | 1.57 | 1.47 | 1.42 | 1.32 | 1.24 | 1.19 |
| 1000 | 3.85 | 3.00 | 2.61 | 2.38 | 2.22 | 2.10 | 2.02 | 1.95 | 1.89 | 1.84 | 1.80 | 1.76 | 1.70 | 1.65 | 1.58 | 1.53 | 1.47 | 1.41 | 1.36 | 1.30 | 1.26 | 1.19 | 1.13 | 1.08 |
|  | 6.66 | 4.62 | 3.80 | 3.34 | 3.04 | 2.82 | 2.66 | 2.53 | 2.43 | 2.34 | 2.26 | 2.20 | 2.09 | 2.01 | 1.89 | 1.81 | 1.71 | 1.61 | 1.54 | 1.44 | 1.38 | 1.28 | 1.19 | 1.11 |
| ∞ | 3.84 | 2.99 | 2.60 | 2.37 | 2.21 | 2.09 | 2.01 | 1.94 | 1.88 | 1.83 | 1.79 | 1.75 | 1.69 | 1.64 | 1.57 | 1.52 | 1.46 | 1.40 | 1.35 | 1.28 | 1.24 | 1.17 | 1.11 | 1.00 |
|  | 6.64 | 4.60 | 3.78 | 3.32 | 3.02 | 2.80 | 2.64 | 2.51 | 2.41 | 2.32 | 2.24 | 2.18 | 2.07 | 1.99 | 1.87 | 1.79 | 1.69 | 1.59 | 1.52 | 1.41 | 1.36 | 1.25 | 1.15 | 1.00 |

From George W. Snedecor and William G. Cochran, *Statistical Methods*, 7th ed. © 1980 by the Iowa State University Press, 2121 South State Avenue, Ames, Iowa 50010.

# APPENDIX H    Critical Values of $U$ in the Mann-Whitney Test

Critical values of $U$ at $\alpha = .001$ with direction predicted or at $\alpha = .002$ with direction not predicted.

| $N_1$ \ $N_2$ | 9 | 10 | 11 | 12 | 13 | 14 | 15 | 16 | 17 | 18 | 19 | 20 |
|---|---|---|---|---|---|---|---|---|---|---|---|---|
| 1 | | | | | | | | | | | | |
| 2 | | | | | | | | | | | | |
| 3 | | | | | | | | | 0 | 0 | 0 | 0 |
| 4 | | 0 | 0 | 0 | 1 | 1 | 1 | 2 | 2 | 3 | 3 | 3 |
| 5 | 1 | 1 | 2 | 2 | 3 | 3 | 4 | 5 | 5 | 6 | 7 | 7 |
| 6 | 2 | 3 | 4 | 4 | 5 | 6 | 7 | 8 | 9 | 10 | 11 | 12 |
| 7 | 3 | 5 | 6 | 7 | 8 | 9 | 10 | 11 | 13 | 14 | 15 | 16 |
| 8 | 5 | 6 | 8 | 9 | 11 | 12 | 14 | 15 | 17 | 18 | 20 | 21 |
| 9 | 7 | 8 | 10 | 12 | 14 | 15 | 17 | 19 | 21 | 23 | 25 | 26 |
| 10 | 8 | 10 | 12 | 14 | 17 | 19 | 21 | 23 | 25 | 27 | 29 | 32 |
| 11 | 10 | 12 | 15 | 17 | 20 | 22 | 24 | 27 | 29 | 32 | 34 | 37 |
| 12 | 12 | 14 | 17 | 20 | 23 | 25 | 28 | 31 | 34 | 37 | 40 | 42 |
| 13 | 14 | 17 | 20 | 23 | 26 | 29 | 32 | 35 | 38 | 42 | 45 | 48 |
| 14 | 15 | 19 | 22 | 25 | 29 | 32 | 36 | 39 | 43 | 46 | 50 | 54 |
| 15 | 17 | 21 | 24 | 28 | 32 | 36 | 40 | 43 | 47 | 51 | 55 | 59 |
| 16 | 19 | 23 | 27 | 31 | 35 | 39 | 43 | 48 | 52 | 56 | 60 | 65 |
| 17 | 21 | 25 | 29 | 34 | 38 | 43 | 47 | 52 | 57 | 61 | 66 | 70 |
| 18 | 23 | 27 | 32 | 37 | 42 | 46 | 51 | 56 | 61 | 66 | 71 | 76 |
| 19 | 25 | 29 | 34 | 40 | 45 | 50 | 55 | 60 | 66 | 71 | 77 | 82 |
| 20 | 26 | 32 | 37 | 42 | 48 | 54 | 59 | 65 | 70 | 76 | 82 | 88 |

Critical values of $U$ at $\alpha = .01$ with direction predicted or at $\alpha = .02$ with direction not predicted.

| $N_1$ \ $N_2$ | 9 | 10 | 11 | 12 | 13 | 14 | 15 | 16 | 17 | 18 | 19 | 20 |
|---|---|---|---|---|---|---|---|---|---|---|---|---|
| 1 | | | | | | | | | | | | |
| 2 | | | | | 0 | 0 | 0 | 0 | 0 | 0 | 1 | 1 |
| 3 | 1 | 1 | 1 | 2 | 2 | 2 | 3 | 3 | 4 | 4 | 4 | 5 |
| 4 | 3 | 3 | 4 | 5 | 5 | 6 | 7 | 7 | 8 | 9 | 9 | 10 |
| 5 | 5 | 6 | 7 | 8 | 9 | 10 | 11 | 12 | 13 | 14 | 15 | 16 |
| 6 | 7 | 8 | 9 | 11 | 12 | 13 | 15 | 16 | 18 | 19 | 20 | 22 |
| 7 | 9 | 11 | 12 | 14 | 16 | 17 | 19 | 21 | 23 | 24 | 26 | 28 |
| 8 | 11 | 13 | 15 | 17 | 20 | 22 | 24 | 26 | 28 | 30 | 32 | 34 |
| 9 | 14 | 16 | 18 | 21 | 23 | 26 | 28 | 31 | 33 | 36 | 38 | 40 |
| 10 | 16 | 19 | 22 | 24 | 27 | 30 | 33 | 36 | 38 | 41 | 44 | 47 |
| 11 | 18 | 22 | 25 | 28 | 31 | 34 | 37 | 41 | 44 | 47 | 50 | 53 |
| 12 | 21 | 24 | 28 | 31 | 35 | 38 | 42 | 46 | 49 | 53 | 56 | 60 |
| 13 | 23 | 27 | 31 | 35 | 39 | 43 | 47 | 51 | 55 | 59 | 63 | 67 |
| 14 | 26 | 30 | 34 | 38 | 43 | 47 | 51 | 56 | 60 | 65 | 69 | 73 |
| 15 | 28 | 33 | 37 | 42 | 47 | 51 | 56 | 61 | 66 | 71 | 76 | 82 |
| 16 | 31 | 36 | 41 | 46 | 51 | 56 | 61 | 66 | 71 | 76 | 82 | 87 |
| 17 | 33 | 38 | 44 | 49 | 55 | 60 | 66 | 71 | 77 | 82 | 88 | 93 |
| 18 | 36 | 41 | 47 | 53 | 59 | 65 | 70 | 76 | 82 | 88 | 94 | 100 |
| 19 | 38 | 44 | 50 | 56 | 63 | 69 | 75 | 82 | 88 | 94 | 101 | 107 |
| 20 | 40 | 47 | 53 | 60 | 67 | 73 | 80 | 87 | 93 | 100 | 107 | 114 |

Critical values of $U$ at $\alpha = .025$ with direction predicted or at $\alpha = .05$ with direction not predicted.

| $N_1$ \ $N_2$ | 9 | 10 | 11 | 12 | 13 | 14 | 15 | 16 | 17 | 18 | 19 | 20 |
|---|---|---|---|---|---|---|---|---|---|---|---|---|
| 1 | | | | | | | | | | | | |
| 2 | 0 | 0 | 0 | 1 | 1 | 1 | 1 | 1 | 2 | 2 | 2 | 2 |
| 3 | 2 | 3 | 3 | 4 | 4 | 5 | 5 | 6 | 6 | 7 | 7 | 8 |
| 4 | 4 | 5 | 6 | 7 | 8 | 9 | 10 | 11 | 11 | 12 | 13 | 13 |
| 5 | 7 | 8 | 9 | 11 | 12 | 13 | 14 | 15 | 17 | 18 | 19 | 20 |
| 6 | 10 | 11 | 13 | 14 | 16 | 17 | 19 | 21 | 22 | 24 | 25 | 27 |
| 7 | 12 | 14 | 16 | 18 | 20 | 22 | 24 | 26 | 28 | 30 | 32 | 34 |
| 8 | 15 | 17 | 19 | 22 | 24 | 26 | 29 | 31 | 34 | 36 | 38 | 41 |
| 9 | 17 | 20 | 23 | 26 | 28 | 31 | 34 | 37 | 39 | 42 | 45 | 48 |
| 10 | 20 | 23 | 26 | 29 | 33 | 36 | 39 | 42 | 45 | 48 | 52 | 55 |
| 11 | 23 | 26 | 30 | 33 | 37 | 40 | 44 | 47 | 51 | 55 | 58 | 62 |
| 12 | 26 | 29 | 33 | 37 | 41 | 45 | 49 | 53 | 57 | 61 | 65 | 69 |
| 13 | 28 | 33 | 37 | 41 | 45 | 50 | 54 | 59 | 63 | 67 | 72 | 76 |
| 14 | 31 | 36 | 40 | 45 | 50 | 55 | 59 | 64 | 67 | 74 | 78 | 83 |
| 15 | 34 | 39 | 44 | 49 | 54 | 59 | 64 | 70 | 75 | 80 | 85 | 90 |
| 16 | 37 | 42 | 47 | 53 | 59 | 64 | 70 | 75 | 81 | 86 | 92 | 98 |
| 17 | 39 | 45 | 51 | 57 | 63 | 67 | 75 | 81 | 87 | 93 | 99 | 105 |
| 18 | 42 | 48 | 55 | 61 | 67 | 74 | 80 | 86 | 93 | 99 | 106 | 112 |
| 19 | 45 | 52 | 58 | 65 | 72 | 78 | 85 | 92 | 99 | 106 | 113 | 119 |
| 20 | 48 | 55 | 62 | 69 | 76 | 83 | 90 | 90 | 105 | 112 | 119 | 127 |

Critical values of *U* at $\alpha = .05$ with direction predicted or at $\alpha = .10$ with direction not predicted.

| $N_1$ \ $N_2$ | 9 | 10 | 11 | 12 | 13 | 14 | 15 | 16 | 17 | 18 | 19 | 20 |
|---|---|---|---|---|---|---|---|---|---|---|---|---|
| 1 | | | | | | | | | | | 0 | 0 |
| 2 | 1 | 1 | 1 | 2 | 2 | 2 | 3 | 3 | 3 | 4 | 4 | 4 |
| 3 | 3 | 4 | 5 | 5 | 6 | 7 | 7 | 8 | 9 | 9 | 10 | 11 |
| 4 | 6 | 7 | 8 | 9 | 10 | 11 | 12 | 14 | 15 | 16 | 17 | 18 |
| 5 | 9 | 11 | 12 | 13 | 15 | 16 | 18 | 19 | 20 | 22 | 23 | 25 |
| 6 | 12 | 14 | 16 | 17 | 19 | 21 | 23 | 25 | 26 | 28 | 30 | 32 |
| 7 | 15 | 17 | 19 | 21 | 24 | 26 | 28 | 30 | 33 | 35 | 37 | 39 |
| 8 | 18 | 20 | 23 | 26 | 28 | 31 | 33 | 36 | 39 | 41 | 44 | 47 |
| 9 | 21 | 24 | 27 | 30 | 33 | 36 | 39 | 42 | 45 | 48 | 51 | 54 |
| 10 | 24 | 27 | 31 | 34 | 37 | 41 | 44 | 48 | 51 | 55 | 58 | 62 |
| 11 | 27 | 31 | 34 | 38 | 42 | 46 | 50 | 54 | 57 | 61 | 65 | 69 |
| 12 | 30 | 34 | 38 | 42 | 47 | 51 | 55 | 60 | 64 | 68 | 72 | 77 |
| 13 | 33 | 37 | 42 | 47 | 51 | 56 | 61 | 65 | 70 | 75 | 80 | 84 |
| 14 | 36 | 41 | 46 | 51 | 56 | 61 | 66 | 71 | 77 | 82 | 87 | 92 |
| 15 | 39 | 44 | 50 | 55 | 61 | 66 | 72 | 77 | 83 | 88 | 94 | 100 |
| 16 | 42 | 48 | 54 | 60 | 65 | 71 | 77 | 83 | 89 | 95 | 101 | 107 |
| 17 | 45 | 51 | 57 | 64 | 70 | 77 | 83 | 89 | 96 | 102 | 109 | 115 |
| 18 | 48 | 55 | 61 | 68 | 75 | 82 | 88 | 95 | 102 | 109 | 116 | 123 |
| 19 | 51 | 58 | 65 | 72 | 80 | 87 | 94 | 101 | 109 | 116 | 123 | 130 |
| 20 | 54 | 62 | 69 | 77 | 84 | 92 | 100 | 107 | 115 | 123 | 130 | 138 |

From D. Auble, "Extended Tables for the Mann-Whitney Statistic," *Bulletin of the Institute of Educational Research at Indiana University*, 1:2 (1953): tab. 1, 3, 5, and 7, with the kind permission of the publisher; as adapted in Sidney Siegel, *Nonparametric Statistics for the Behavioral Sciences* (New York: McGraw-Hill, 1956), tab. K.

# APPENDIX I    Distribution of $\chi^2$

| df | .99 | .98 | .95 | .90 | .80 | .70 | .50 | .30 | .20 | .10 | .05 | .02 | .01 | .001 |
|---|---|---|---|---|---|---|---|---|---|---|---|---|---|---|
| | | | | | | | Probability | | | | | | | |
| 1 | .0³157 | .0³628 | .00393 | .0158 | .0642 | .148 | .455 | 1.074 | 1.642 | 2.706 | 3.841 | 5.412 | 6.635 | 10.827 |
| 2 | .0201 | .0404 | .103 | .211 | .446 | .713 | 1.386 | 2.408 | 3.219 | 4.605 | 5.991 | 7.824 | 9.210 | 13.815 |
| 3 | .115 | .185 | .352 | .584 | 1.005 | 1.424 | 2.366 | 3.665 | 4.642 | 6.251 | 7.815 | 9.837 | 11.341 | 16.268 |
| 4 | .297 | .429 | .711 | 1.064 | 1.649 | 2.195 | 3.357 | 4.878 | 5.989 | 7.779 | 9.488 | 11.668 | 13.277 | 18.465 |
| 5 | .554 | .752 | 1.145 | 1.610 | 2.343 | 3.000 | 4.351 | 6.064 | 7.289 | 9.236 | 11.070 | 13.388 | 15.086 | 20.617 |
| 6 | .872 | 1.134 | 1.635 | 2.204 | 3.070 | 3.828 | 5.348 | 7.231 | 8.558 | 10.645 | 12.592 | 15.033 | 16.812 | 22.457 |
| 7 | 1.239 | 1.564 | 2.167 | 2.833 | 3.822 | 4.671 | 6.346 | 8.383 | 9.803 | 12.017 | 14.067 | 16.622 | 18.475 | 24.322 |
| 8 | 1.646 | 2.032 | 2.733 | 3.490 | 4.594 | 5.527 | 7.344 | 9.524 | 11.030 | 13.362 | 15.507 | 18.168 | 20.090 | 26.125 |
| 9 | 2.088 | 2.532 | 3.325 | 4.168 | 5.380 | 6.393 | 8.343 | 10.656 | 12.242 | 14.684 | 16.919 | 19.679 | 21.666 | 27.877 |
| 10 | 2.558 | 3.059 | 3.940 | 4.865 | 6.179 | 7.267 | 9.342 | 11.781 | 13.442 | 15.987 | 18.307 | 21.161 | 23.209 | 29.588 |
| 11 | 3.053 | 3.609 | 4.575 | 5.578 | 6.989 | 8.148 | 10.341 | 12.899 | 14.631 | 17.275 | 19.675 | 22.618 | 24.725 | 31.264 |
| 12 | 3.571 | 4.178 | 5.226 | 6.304 | 7.807 | 9.034 | 11.340 | 14.011 | 15.812 | 18.549 | 21.026 | 24.054 | 26.217 | 32.909 |
| 13 | 4.107 | 4.765 | 5.892 | 7.042 | 8.634 | 9.926 | 12.340 | 15.119 | 16.985 | 19.812 | 22.362 | 25.472 | 27.688 | 34.528 |
| 14 | 4.660 | 5.368 | 6.571 | 7.790 | 9.467 | 10.821 | 13.339 | 16.222 | 18.151 | 21.064 | 23.685 | 26.873 | 29.141 | 36.123 |
| 15 | 5.229 | 5.985 | 7.261 | 8.547 | 10.307 | 11.721 | 14.339 | 17.322 | 19.311 | 22.307 | 24.996 | 28.259 | 30.578 | 37.697 |
| 16 | 5.812 | 6.614 | 7.962 | 9.312 | 11.152 | 12.624 | 15.338 | 18.418 | 20.465 | 23.542 | 26.296 | 29.633 | 32.000 | 39.252 |

| | | | | | | | | | | | | | |
|---|---|---|---|---|---|---|---|---|---|---|---|---|---|
| 17 | 6.408 | 7.255 | 8.672 | 10.085 | 12.002 | 13.531 | 16.338 | 19.511 | 21.615 | 24.769 | 27.587 | 30.995 | 33.409 | 40.790 |
| 18 | 7.015 | 7.906 | 9.390 | 10.865 | 12.857 | 14.440 | 17.338 | 20.601 | 22.760 | 25.989 | 28.369 | 32.346 | 34.805 | 42.312 |
| 19 | 7.633 | 8.567 | 10.117 | 11.651 | 13.716 | 15.352 | 18.338 | 21.689 | 23.900 | 27.204 | 30.144 | 33.687 | 36.191 | 43.820 |
| 20 | 8.260 | 9.237 | 10.851 | 12.443 | 14.578 | 16.266 | 19.337 | 22.775 | 25.038 | 28.412 | 31.410 | 35.020 | 37.566 | 45.315 |
| 21 | 8.897 | 9.915 | 11.591 | 13.240 | 15.445 | 17.182 | 20.337 | 23.858 | 26.171 | 29.615 | 32.671 | 36.343 | 38.932 | 46.797 |
| 22 | 9.542 | 10.600 | 12.338 | 14.041 | 16.314 | 18.101 | 21.337 | 24.939 | 27.301 | 30.813 | 33.924 | 37.659 | 40.289 | 48.268 |
| 23 | 10.196 | 11.293 | 13.091 | 14.848 | 17.187 | 19.021 | 22.337 | 26.018 | 28.429 | 32.007 | 35.172 | 38.968 | 41.638 | 49.728 |
| 24 | 10.856 | 11.992 | 13.848 | 15.659 | 18.062 | 19.943 | 23.337 | 27.096 | 29.553 | 33.196 | 36.415 | 40.270 | 42.980 | 51.179 |
| 25 | 11.524 | 12.697 | 14.611 | 16.473 | 18.940 | 20.867 | 24.337 | 28.172 | 30.675 | 34.382 | 37.652 | 41.566 | 44.314 | 52.620 |
| 26 | 12.198 | 13.409 | 15.379 | 17.292 | 19.820 | 21.792 | 25.336 | 29.246 | 31.795 | 35.563 | 38.885 | 42.856 | 45.642 | 54.052 |
| 27 | 12.879 | 14.125 | 16.151 | 18.114 | 20.703 | 22.719 | 26.336 | 30.319 | 32.912 | 36.741 | 40.113 | 44.140 | 46.963 | 55.476 |
| 28 | 13.565 | 14.847 | 16.928 | 18.939 | 21.588 | 23.647 | 27.336 | 31.391 | 34.027 | 37.916 | 41.337 | 45.419 | 48.278 | 56.893 |
| 29 | 14.256 | 15.574 | 17.708 | 19.768 | 22.475 | 24.577 | 28.336 | 32.461 | 35.139 | 39.087 | 42.557 | 46.693 | 49.588 | 58.302 |
| 30 | 14.953 | 16.306 | 18.493 | 20.599 | 23.364 | 25.508 | 29.336 | 33.530 | 36.250 | 40.256 | 43.773 | 47.962 | 50.892 | 59.703 |

For larger values of $df$, the expression $\sqrt{2\chi^2} - \sqrt{2df - 1}$ may be used as a normal deviate with unit variance, remembering that the probability for $\chi^2$ corresponds to that of a single tail of the normal curve.

Reprinted from R. A. Fisher and F. Yates, *Statistical Tables for Biological, Agricultural and Medical Research*, 6th ed. (London: Longman, 1974), tab. IV. Used by permission of the authors and Longman Group Ltd.

# GLOSSARY

*Glossary terms are cross-referenced to text discussions, indicated by the boldface text page number following each term.*

**accretion measures** Unobtrusive measures using deposited physical material (**316**)

**actuarial records** Public records concerning the demographic characteristics of the population served by the record-keeping agency (**318**)

**ad hoc classificatory system** A level of the theory comprised of arbitrary categories constructed to organize and summarize empirical observations (**37**)

**analytic induction** A theoretical approach to field research where a researcher begins with a tentative hypothesis explaining the phenomenon observed and then attempts to verify the hypothesis by observing a small number of cases. If the hypothesis does not fit these cases, it is either rejected or reformulated so that the cases account for it (**294**)

**anonymity** The protection of research participants by separating specific identities from the information given (**88**)

**arithmetic mean** The sum total of all observations divided by their number (**367**)

**assumptions of science** The fundamental premises, unproven and unprovable, which are prerequisite for the conduct of scientific discourse (**5**)

**attitude** All of a person's inclinations, prejudices, ideas, fears, and convictions about any specific topic (**252**)

**attitude index** A series of questions selected on a priori basis, the scores of which are interpreted as indicating the attitude of the respondent (**464**)

**authenticity** The genuineness of private records (**321**)

**axiomatic theory** A theoretical system containing a set of concepts and operational definitions; a set of statements describing the situations in which the theory can be applied; a set of relational statements (axioms and theorems); and a system of logic employed to relate *all* concepts within statements and deduce theorems (**40**)

**bar chart** A graphic device used for displaying nominal or ordinal data. Researchers construct bar charts by labeling the categories of the variable along the horizontal axis and drawing rectangles of equal width for each category. The rectangles are separated by spaces, and the height of each rectangle is proportional to the frequency percentage of the category (**360**)

**census block** The smallest geographic area for which census data is collected (**311**)

**Census Designated Places (CDP)** Densely settled population centers lacking legally defined corporate limits or powers (**311**)

**census tract** A small, locally defined statistical area in metropolitan areas and counties with an average population of 4,000 (**311**)

**chi-square test ($\chi^2$)** A test statistic that allows one to decide whether observed frequencies are essentially equal to or significantly different from frequencies predicted by a theoretical model. The outcome of the test allows decisions as to whether or not frequencies are distributed equally among categories, whether or not a distribution is normal, or whether or not two variables are independent (496)

**classic experimental design** An experimental design format, usually associated with research in the biological and social sciences, that consists of two comparable groups: an experimental group and a control group. These two groups are equivalent except that the experimental group is exposed to the independent variable and the control group is not (101)

**closed-ended question** A question that offers respondents a set of answers from which they are asked to choose the one that most closely reflects their views (253)

**cluster sample** Type of probability sampling, frequently used in large-scale studies because it is the least expensive sample design, that involves selecting layer groupings (clusters) and selecting sampling units from the clusters (190)

**code** The number assigned to an observation. A code should be consistent across cases or units of analysis when the same condition exists (335)

**codes of ethics** Regulations developed by major professional societies that outline the specific problems and issues that are frequently encountered in the types of research carried out within a particular profession, which serve as a guide to ethical research practices (90)

**codebook** A book compiled by the researcher identifying a specific item of observation and the code number assigned to describe each category included in that item (340)

**coding** Assigning codes in the form of numerals (or other symbols) for each category of each variable in a study (334)

**coding reliability** The extent of agreement between different coders when classifying their individual responses according to the coding scheme (342)

**coding scheme** A system of categories used to classify responses or behaviors that relate to a single item or variable (335)

**coefficient of multiple correlation** The correlation between a number of independent variables with a dependent variable (444)

**coefficient of reproducibility (CR)** A measure that indicates how precisely a score on a Guttman scale can be used to reproduce the total response pattern on the items that compose the scale; the fewer the number of errors in predicted item scores, the higher the coefficient of reproducibility (468)

**coefficient of variation** A measure of variation based on the standard deviation and the mean and reflects relative variation. It is defined as the ratio of the standard deviation to the mean of the distribution (379)

**combined designs** The merging of two or more research designs into a single study to increase the inferential powers of that study (144)

**comparison** The operational process required to demonstrate that two variables are correlated (105)

**competence** The assumption that any decision made by a responsible, mature individual who is given relevant information will be the correct decision (83)

**complete count census** The census of population and housing taken every ten years intended to reach every household in the country. Includes only basic demographic information on each member of the household plus a few questions about the housing unit (310)

**complete participant** A role taken by the observer where the observer is wholly concealed; the research objectives are unknown to the observed, and the researcher attempts to become a member of the group under observation (282)

**comprehension**    An important element of informed consent that refers to the confidence that the participant has provided knowing consent when the research procedure is associated with complex or subtle risks **(85)**

**computer-assisted telephone interviewing (CATI)**    Type of telephone survey where the interviewer sits at a computer terminal and, as a question flashes on the screen, asks it over the telephone. Respondents' answers are typed and coded directly on a disk, and the next question comes up on the screen **(243)**

**concept**    An abstraction representing an object, a property of an object, or a certain phenomenon that scientists use to describe the empirical world **(26)**

**conceptual definition**    A definition that describes a concept by using primitive and derived terms **(29)**

**conceptual framework**    A level of theory in which descriptive categories are systematically placed within a broad structure of explicit and assumed propositions **(38)**

**conditional variable**    A contingency necessary for the occurrence of the relationship between the independent and dependent variable **(436)**

**confidence interval**    A measure that specifies the range of values within which a given percentage of the sample means falls **(196)**

**confidentiality**    Protection of the identity of research participants **(89)**

**congruence**    The agreement between the conceptual and the operational definitions **(34)**

**construct validity**    A process that involves relating a measuring instrument to a general theoretical framework in order to determine whether the instrument is tied to the concepts and theoretical assumptions that are employed **(168)**

**content analysis**    The systematic, quantitative analysis of observations obtained from archival records and documents **(324)**

**context of discovery**    Activities that lead toward discovery; at the initial stages of exploration, no formalized rules or logic can be formalized as guides **(19)**

**context of justification**    Activities of scientists as they attempt logically and empirically to verify claims for knowledge **(19)**

**context unit**    The largest body of content that may be examined when characterizing a recording unit **(327)**

**contingency question**    A question that applies only to a subgroup of respondents because it is relevant only to certain people **(255)**

**continuous variable**    A variable that does not have a minimum-sized unit **(58)**

**contrasted groups**    Comparison of groups that are known to differ in some important attributes **(132)**

**control**    A procedure designed to eliminate alternative sources of variation that may distort the research results. Methods of control include holding variables constant under experimental conditions or during statistical analysis **(106)**

**control group**    The group in an experimental research design that is not exposed to the independent variable **(101)**

**control-series design**    A quasi-experimental design that attempts to control the aspects of history, maturation, and test-retest effects shared by the experimental and comparison groups **(142)**

**control variable**    A variable that is controlled for, or held constant, in order to examine whether it affects the relationship between independent and dependent variables; used to test whether the observed relations between independent and dependent variables are spurious **(57, 428)**

**controlled observation** A method typified by clear and explicit decisions as to what, how, and when to observe; as the method is highly systematized, it allows for little flexibility **(213)**

**correlation coefficient** A measure of linear association between two interval variables. Pearson's product-moment correlation coefficient ($r$) estimates the direction and magnitude of the association **(400)**

**correlational design** The most predominant research design employed in the social sciences, most often identified with survey research, where data are used to examine relationships between properties and dispositions, establish causal relations between these properties and dispositions, or to simply describe the pattern of relation before any attempt at causal inference is made **(129)**

**covariation** When two or more phenomena vary together **(59, 104)**

**cover letter** The letter that accompanies a mail questionnaire **(266)**

**criterion of least squares** The criterion that minimizes the sum of the squared vertical distances between the regression line and actual observations **(416)**

**cross-sectional design** A research design most predominant in survey research and used to examine relations between properties and dispositions. A cross-sectional design can approximate the posttest-only control group design by using statistical data analysis techniques **(129)**

**cross-tabulation** A table showing the relationship between two or more variables by presenting all combinations of categories of variables **(428)**

**data cleaning** A process that precedes analysis of collected information whereby data is proofread to catch and correct errors and inconsistent codes. Most data cleaning is performed by special computer programs that are designed to test for logical consistency set up in the coding specifications **(347)**

**data editing** Process performed by coders both during and after the data coding phase of data processing that involves checking for errors and omissions and making sure that all interview schedules have been completed as required **(347)**

**deductive coding** Requires that data be recorded to some preconceived scheme that is constructed before the measurement instrument is administered **(337)**

**deductive explanation** An explanation that accounts for a phenomenon by demonstrating that it can be deduced from an established universal generalization **(9)**

**degrees of freedom ($df$)** A characteristic of the sample statistics that determines the appropriate sampling distribution **(491)**

**demand characteristics** A bias that may occur when individuals know that they are in an experimental situation, are aware that they are being observed, and believe that certain responses are expected from them. Consequently, they may not respond to the experimental manipulation at face value but rather to their interpretation of the responses that these manipulations are intended to elicit **(215)**

**dependent variable** The variable that the researcher wishes to explain **(56)**

**derived term** A term that can be defined by the use of a primitive term **(29)**

**descriptive statistics** Statistical procedures used for describing and analyzing data that enable the researcher to summarize and organize data in an effective and meaningful way. These procedures provide tools for describing collections of statistical observations and reducing information to an understandable form **(355)**

**difference-between-means test** A test used to assess the significance of a difference between means to reflect the amount of relationship between two variables **(488)**

**discrete variable** A variable with a minimum-sized unit **(58)**

**discriminative power (*DP*)**    The ability of a test to locate items that consistently distinguish those that are high on the attitude continuum from those that are low **(466)**

**double-barreled question**    A question combining two or more questions, thus confusing respondents who might agree with one aspect of the question but disagree with the other **(266)**

**ecological fallacy**    The inappropriate generalization from more complex to a simpler unit of analysis **(54)**

**elaboration**    A method of introducing other variables to the analysis in order to determine the links between the independent and dependent variables **(435)**

**empirical**    Relying on perceptions, experience, and behavior **(6)**

**epistemology**    The study of the foundations of knowledge **(5)**

**erosion measures**    Unobtrusive measures employed to examine the signs left after use of an object **(316)**

**error of prediction**    The deviation of the actual observations from the ones predicted by the regression line **(416)**

**ethical dilemma**    Arises when a decision is made to conduct research despite an ethically questionable practice **(81)**

**exhaustiveness**    The rule of exhaustiveness dictates that the enumeration of categories is sufficient to exhaust all the relevant categories expected of respondents **(337)**

**experimental group**    The group exposed to the independent variable in an experimental research design **(101)**

**experimental mortality**    Refers to the dropout problems that prevent the researcher from obtaining complete information on all cases. When individuals drop out selectively from the experimental or control group, the final sample on which complete information is available may be biased **(108)**

**experimental realism**    The extent to which an experimental situation is experienced as real to the research participants **(215)**

**experimenter bias**    A situation that occurs when an experimenter unintentionally communicates his or her own expectations onto the participants being studied. This behavior, though not intended to be part of the experimental manipulation, influences the participants **(216)**

**explanation**    A systematic and empirical analysis of the antecedent factors that caused the event or behavior **(8)**

**explanatory variable**    Also called the "independent variable," it is the variable the researcher presumes is the cause of changes in the values of the dependent variable **(56)**

**extended time-series design**    A research design that presents the data as part of a broadened time series and therefore controls for maturation **(139)**

**external validity**    The extent to which the research findings can be generalized to larger populations and applied to different settings **(113)**

**extralinguistic behavior**    The noncontent aspects of behavior, such as rate of speaking, loudness, tendency to interrupt, and pronunciation peculiarities, often referred to as or paralanguage or body language **(209)**

**extrinsic factors**    Biases resulting from the differential recruitment of research participants to the experimental and control groups **(106)**

**face validity**    The investigators' subjective evaluation as to the validity of a measuring instrument. It concerns the extent to which the measuring instrument appears to measure the researcher's subjective assessment **(165)**

**factor analysis**    A statistical technique for classifying a large number of interrelated variables into a limited number of dimensions or factors **(471)**

**factor loading**    The correlation coefficient between a variable and a factor **(471)**

**factor scores**    A case's score on a factor obtained by multiplying the factor score coefficient for each variable by the standardized value of that variable obtained for that case **(473)**

**factorial design**    A research design that allows one to examine simultaneously the effects of two or more independent variables on the dependent variable and also to detect interaction between the variables **(120)**

**factual question**    A question designed to elicit objective information from respondents regarding their background, environment, and habits **(251)**

**fallacy of reification**    The error of treating abstractions as real rather than the outcome of thinking **(27)**

**field experimentation (research)**    Research taking place in a *natural* setting, in which the investigator can manipulate one or more independent variables under conditions that are as carefully controlled as the situation permits **(218, 281)**

**filter question**    In questionnaire design, the question that precedes a contingency question: the relevance of the contingency question is contingent on the response to the filter question **(255)**

**focused interview**    Type of personal interview (following an interview guide) that specifies topics related to the research hypothesis and gives considerable liberty to the respondents to express their views. The interview focuses on the subject's experiences regarding the situation under study **(234)**

**follow-up**    In mail questionnaires, a strategy used to secure an acceptable response rate (e.g., sending a series of reminder postcards and/or a replacement questionnaire) **(229)**

**frequency distribution**    The number of observations of each value of a variable **(355)**

**funnel sequence**    A technique of questionnaire construction in which the questionnaire begins with general queries and then "funnels down" to more specific items **(260)**

**gamma**    A coefficient of association indicating the magnitude and direction of the relationship between ordinal variables **(410)**

**generalizability**    The extent to which the research findings can be generalized to larger populations and applied to different settings **(173)**

**grounded theory**    In field research, the development of a theory that is closely and directly relevant to the particular setting under study whereby the researcher first develops conceptual categories from data and then makes new observations to clarify and elaborate these categories. Concepts and tentative hypotheses are then developed directly from data **(294)**

**Guttman scale**    Scaling method designed to incorporate an empirical test of the unidimensionality of a set of items and employed as an integral part of the scale-construction process. If the items comprising the scale tap the same attitudinal dimension, they can be arranged so that there will be a continuum that indicates varying degrees of the underlying dimension **(467)**

**histogram**    A graphic device used to display frequency distributions of interval or ratio level data. The histogram looks like a bar chart with no spaces between the rectangles. The rectangles are constructed contiguously and their heights reflect the percent or frequency of the interval **(362)**

**history**    All events occurring during the time of the research study that might affect the individuals studied and provide a rival explanation for the change in the dependent variable **(107)**

**hypothesis**    A tentative answer to a research problem, expressed in the form of a relationship between independent and dependent variables (**62**)

**independent variable**    The explanatory variable, that is, the hypothesized or presumed cause of changes in the values of the dependent variable (**56**)

**index**    A composite measure of two or more indicators or items (**457**)

**indicator**    The empirical, observable element of a concept (**158**)

**indirect effect**    When the effect of one variable on another is mediated through a third intervening variable (**449**)

**individualistic fallacy**    Inferences about groups, societies, or nations inappropriately drawn directly from evidence gathered about individuals (**55**)

**inductive coding**    When the coding scheme is designed on the basis of a representative sample, responses, or other kinds of data, and is then applied to the remainder of the data (**337**)

**inference**    A claim for knowledge logically derived, or inferred, from prior assumptions (**13**)

**inferential statistics**    Allows the researcher to make decisions or inferences about characteristics of a population based on observations from a sample taken from the population (**355**)

**informed consent**    The agreement of an individual to participate in a study after being informed of facts that would be likely to influence his or her willingness to participate (**81**)

**instrumentation**    A process that designates changes in the measuring instrument between the pretest and the posttest. To associate the difference between posttest and pretest scores with the independent variable, one must show that repeated measurements with the same measurement instrument under unchanged conditions will yield the same result (**108**)

**interaction**    A difference in the relationship between two variables within different categories of a control variable (**436**)

**interaction process analysis (IPA)**    A set of 12 categories used to code interaction in groups. The analysis is a highly structured observational technique, using both structured observational categories and a structured laboratory setting (**210**)

**internal validity**    The evidence required in experiments to rule out the possibility that factors other than the independent variable are responsible for variation in the dependent variable (**106**)

**interpretive approach**    Belief that the phenomena of focal concern to the sociobehavioral scientist are far less stable then those of interest to the natural scientist (**12**)

**interquartile range**    The difference between the lower and upper quartiles ($Q_1$ and $Q_3$). It measures the spread in the middle half of the distribution and is less affected by extreme observations (**375**)

**intersubjectivity**    The ability to share knowledge that permits a scientist to understand and evaluate the methods of others and to conduct similar observations so as to validate empirical facts and conclusions (**15**)

**interval level**    The level of measurement at which the distance between observations are exact and can be precisely measured in constant units (**162**)

**intervening variable**    An intermediate variable between an independent variable and a dependent variable; the independent variable affects the dependent variable through the intervening variable (**435**)

**intrinsic factors**    Changes in units under study that occur during the study period, changes in the measuring instrument, and the reactive effect of the observation itself (**107**)

**isomorphism**    Similarity or identity in structure (**157**)

**Kendall's tau-*b***    A coefficient of association between ordinal variables incorporating ties (**413**)

**known-groups technique**    When a measuring instrument is administered to groups of people with known attributes, and the direction of difference is predicted (**169**)

**lambda (Guttman coefficient of predictability)**    A measure of association indicating the magnitude and direction of the relationship between nominal variables (**403**)

**leading question**    A question phrased in such a manner that the respondent believes that the researcher expects a certain answer (**263**)

**level of measurement**    The degree to which typical numbers describe characteristics of the measured variable; the higher the level of measurement, the greater the number of applicable statistical methods (**158**)

**level of significance**    The probability of rejecting a true null hypothesis; that is, the possibility of making a Type I error (**483**)

**Likert scale**    A summated rating scale designed to assist in excluding questionable items (**465**)

**linear relation**    A relation between two variables $X$ and $Y$ of the form $Y = a + bX$, where $a$ and $b$ are constant values; the graph of a linear relation is a straight line (**414**)

**linguistic behavior**    The content of speech and the structural characteristics of talking (**209**)

**log**    A record of events, meetings, visits, and other activities of an individual over a given period of time (**323**)

**logic**    Statements that are universally valid, certain, and independent of the empirical world (**14**)

**logical empiricists**    Researchers who take the position that objective knowledge can be attained in the study of the social as well as the natural world (**12**)

**magnitude of a relation**    The extent to which variables covary positively or negatively (**62**)

**mail questionnaire**    An impersonal survey method in which questionnaires are mailed to respondents, whose responses constitute the data on which research hypotheses are tested (**225**)

**mainframe computer**    A large computer that controls and coordinates activities of the computer system, such as executing the program instructions and monitoring the operation of the input and output devices (**348**)

**manipulation**    A procedure that allows the researcher in experimental settings to have some form of control over the introduction of the independent variable. This procedure allows for the determination that the independent variable preceded the dependent variable (**106**)

**Mann-Whitney test**    A nonparametric test that is applicable whenever researchers wish to test the null hypothesis that two samples have been drawn from the same population against the alternative research hypothesis that the populations differ from each other (**494**)

**matching**    A method of control that involves equating the experimental and control groups on extrinsic variables that are presumed to relate to the research hypothesis (**110**)

**matrix question**    A method of organizing a large set of rating questions that have the same response categories (**258**)

**maturation**    Biological, psychological, or social processes that produce changes in the individuals or units studied with the passage of time. These changes could possibly influence the dependent variable and lead to erroneous inferences (**108**)

**mean deviation**    Computed by taking the differences between each observation and the mean, summing the absolute value of these deviations, and dividing the sum by the total number of observations **(376)**

**measure of qualitative variation**    An index of heterogeneity based on the ratio of the total number of differences in the distribution to the maximum number of possible differences within the same distribution **(372)**

**measurement**    The assignment of numbers or other symbols to empirical properties according to rules **(155)**

**measurement artifacts**    The biased results that occur when measurement procedures or instruments such as cameras or test schedules give participants hints about what is really going on in the experiment **(217)**

**measurement errors**    Differences in measurement scores that are due to anything other than real differences between the variables **(164)**

**measures of central tendency**    Statistical measures that reflect a typical or an average characteristic of a frequency distribution **(363)**

**measures of dispersion**    Statistical measures that reflect the degree of spread or variation in a distribution **(371)**

**median**    A measure of central tendency defined as the point above and below which 50 percent of the observations fall **(364)**

**methodology**    A system of explicit rules and procedures on which research is based and against which claims for knowledge are evaluated **(13)**

**Metropolitan Statistical Areas (MSA)**    One or more counties, including a large population nucleus and nearby communities, having a high degree of interaction **(311)**

**mode**    A measure of central tendency defined as the most frequently occurring observation category in the data **(364)**

**model**    An abstraction from reality that orders and simplifies a view of reality by representing its essential characteristics **(43)**

**multiple regression**    A statistical technique that allows us to assess the relationship between an interval variable and two or more interval, ordinal, or nominal variables **(441)**

**mundane realism**    The degree to which an experimental situation is experienced as real or likely to occur in the real world **(215)**

**mutual exclusivity**    Under the rule of mutual exclusivity, the coding categories for each variable must be designed so that each case or unit of analysis can be coded into one and only one category of the variable **(336)**

**negative case**    Actions and statements that refute a field researchers' hypothesis. Researchers compare positive and negative cases to determine whether the hypothesis can be modified to better fit all of the data or if the hypothesis must be rejected entirely **(293)**

**negative relation**    An association whereby as the value of one variable increases, the value of another decreases **(60)**

**nominal level**    The level of measurement at which the properties of objects in one category are identical and mutually exclusive for all its cases; the lowest level of measurement **(159)**

**noncontrolled observation**    A rather flexible observational method in which samples are rarely taken and which is often associated with qualitative research **(213)**

**nondirective interview**    The least structured form of interviewing; no prespecified set of questions is employed, nor is an interview schedule used. The interviewer has a great deal of freedom to probe various areas and to raise specific queries during the course of the interview **(235)**

**nonparametric test**    A statistical test that requires either no assumptions or very few assumptions about the population distribution (**487**)

**nonprobability sample**    A sampling method in which there is no way of specifying the probability of each unit's inclusion in the sample (**183**)

**nonresponse error**    Bias that occurs when persons do not respond to a survey and are therefore not represented in the total sample (**199**)

**nonverbal behavior**    Body movements such as facial expressions that convey a wide range of emotions, such as anger, surprise, and fear (**208**)

**normal curve**    A theoretical distribution of great significance in the field of statistics. Some of its major properties are (1) it is symmetrical and bell-shaped; (2) the mode, the median, and the mean coincide at the center of the distribution; (3) the curve is based on an infinite number of observations; (4) a single mathematical formula describes how frequencies are related to the values of the variable; and (5) in any normal distribution, a fixed proportion of the observations lie between the mean and fixed units of standard deviations (**382**)

**normal distribution**    A type of symmetrical distribution of great significance in the field of statistics. It is a mathematically defined curve. Under certain circumstances, it is permissible to treat frequency distributions of variables as close approximations of the normal distribution (**382**)

**normal science**    The routine verification of dominant paradigms in any historical period (**16**)

**null hypothesis**    A statement of no relationship between variables; the null hypothesis is rejected when an observed statistic appears unlikely under the null hypothesis (**480**)

**one-tailed test**    A statistical test where extreme results leading to rejection of the null hypothesis can be located at either tail (**485**)

**one-shot case study**    An observation of a single group or event at a single point in time, usually subsequent to some phenomenon that allegedly produced change (**146**)

**open-ended question**    A question that is not followed by any kind of specified choice; the respondents' answers are recorded in full (**254**)

**operational definition**    A set of procedures that bridges the conceptual-theoretical and empirical-observational levels by describing the activities needed to empirically observe a phenomenon empirically (**30**)

**opinion**    The verbal expression of an attitude (**252**)

**optical scanning**    A method used to translate data into machine-readable format. Optical scanning machines read black pencil marks and produce data files automatically (**345**)

**ordinal level**    The level of measurement in which all sets of observations generate a complete ranking of objects (e.g., from "the most" to "the least"), although the distances cannot be precisely measured (**159**)

**ostensive definition**    A definition that conveys the meaning of a concept through examples; as such, it can be used as a primitive term in theorizing and research (**29**)

**panel**    A design in survey research that offers a close approximation of the before-and-after condition of experimental designs by interviewing the same group at two or more points in time (**137**)

**paradigm**    The theory dominant in any historical period (**17**)

**paralanguage**    The noncontent aspects of behavior, such as the rate of speaking and tendency to interrupt. Also referred to as "extralinguistic behavior" (**209**)

**parallel-forms technique**    A means to counter the limitations of the test-retest method; a researcher develops two parallel versions of a measuring instrument, which are then administered to the same group of persons. The researcher then correlates the two sets of measures (scores) to obtain an estimate of of the instrument's reliability **(172)**

**parameter**    A specified value of a variable to be found in the population **(179)**

**parametric test**    A hypothesis test based on assumptions about the parameter values of the population **(487)**

**partial correlation**    A statistical control that involves a mathematical adjustment of the bivariate correlation, designed to cancel out the effect of other variables on the independent and dependent variables **(440)**

**partial tables**    Tables that reflect only part of the total association between the independent and dependent variables **(429)**

**participant-as-observer**    Role most often assumed by contemporary fieldworkers, where the researcher's presence is made known to the group being studied, and the researcher becomes an active member and a participant in the group being observed **(285)**

**participant observation**    A method of data collection most closely associated with contemporary field research whereby the investigator attempts to attain some kind of membership in or close attachment to the group that he or she wishes to study **(282)**

**path analysis**    Technique that uses both bivariate and multiple linear regression techniques to test the causal relations among the variable specified in the model. It involves three steps: drawing of a path diagram based on theory or a set of hypotheses, the calculation of path coefficients (direct effects) using regression techniques, and the determination of indirect effects **(448)**

**path coefficient**    A standardized regression coefficient that reflects the causal relationship between two variables in path analysis **(448)**

**Pearson's *r***    The Pearson product-moment correlation coefficient, a statistic that specifies the magnitude and direction of relation between two interval-level variables, is the most commonly used statistic in correlational analysis **(420)**

**personal interview**    A face-to-face situation in which an interviewer asks respondents questions designed to obtain answers pertinent to the research hypotheses **(232)**

**physical location analysis**    The investigation of the ways in which individuals use their bodies in a naturally occurring social space **(317)**

**pie chart**    A graphic device used to show differences in frequencies or percentages among categories of nominal or ordinal variables. The frequencies or percentages of different categories are shown as segments of a circle **(359)**

**planned variation**    A research design that exposes individuals to stimuli (the independent variables) that have been systematically varied in order to assess their causal effects **(134)**

**population**    The entire set of relevant units of analysis **(179)**

**positive relation**    An association whereby as the value of one variable increases, the value of another also increases **(60)**

**posttest**    The measurement taken after exposure to the independent variable **(101)**

**prediction**    The process of seeking a future event implied by known former events **(10)**

**predictive validity**    The assessment of a measuring instrument by comparing the outcomes of one instrument against another in reference to an external measure, referred to as a *criterion* **(167)**

**pretest**    The measurement taken prior to the introduction of the independent variable **(101)**

**pretest-posttest design**    A preexperimental design that compares the measures of the dependent variable before and after exposure to the independent variable **(101)**

**primitive term**     A concept so basic that it cannot be defined by any other concept (**29**)

**probabilistic explanation**     Use of generalizations that express either an arithmetic ratio between phenomena (*n* percent of *X* = *Y*) or generalizations that express tendencies (*X* tends to cause *Y*) (**9**)

**probability sample**     A sample that permits specifying the probability that each sampling unit will be included in the sample; this ensures that the findings from different samples drawn from a given population will not differ from the population parameters by more than a specified amount (**183**)

**probing**     The technique used by an interviewer to stimulate discussion and obtain more information (**241**)

**property-disposition relationship**     The relationship between some characteristic or quality of a person (property) and a corresponding attitude or inclination (disposition) (**127**)

**proportional reduction of error**     A method used to measure the magnitude of the relations between two variables wherein one variable is used to predict the values of another (**402**)

**quantifiers**     The responses categories of the rating scale that reflect the intensity of the particular judgement involved (**258**)

**question**     The foundation of all questionnaires. The questionnaire must translate the research objectives into specific questions; answers to such questions will provide the data for hypothesis testing (**250**)

**quota sample**     The selection of a nonprobability sample that is as closely as possible a replica of the population (**185**)

**random-digit dialing (RDD)**     Drawing a random sample of telephone numbers by selecting an exchange and then appending random numbers between 0001 and 9999 (**242**)

**randomization**     A method of control that helps to offset the confounding effects of known as well as unforseen factors by randomly assigning cases to the experimental and control groups (**112**)

**range**     Measure of the distance between the highest and lowest values of a distribution (**375**)

**ranking**     In questionnaire research, when researchers obtain information regarding the degree of importance of the priorities that people have given to a set of attitudes or objects. This procedure is a useful device in providing some sense of relative order among objects or judgments (**260**)

**rating**     A judgment made by the respondent in terms of sets of ordered categories such as "strongly agree," "favorable," or "very often" (**258**)

**ratio level**     The level of measurement that has a unique zero point (**162**)

**rationalism**     Use of statements that must be true in principle and that are logically possible and permissible (**4**)

**reasonably informed consent**     The six basic elements of information that must be communicated to the participant in situations where fully informed consent would make it impossible to conduct the research (**84**)

**recording unit**     The smallest body of content in which the appearance of a reference is noted (a reference is a single occurrence of the content element) (**327**)

**region of rejection**     The area under the sampling distribution specified by the null hypothesis that covers the values of the observed statistic that led to the rejection of the null hypothesis. In a one-tailed test, there is one region of rejection; in a two-tailed test, there are two regions of rejection (**483**)

**regression artifact**    An error that occurs when individuals have been assigned to the experimental group on the basis of their extreme scores on the dependent variable. When this happens, and measures are unreliable, individuals who scored below average on the pretest will appear to have improved upon retesting. Conversely, individuals who scored above average on the pretest would appear to have done less well upon retesting **(108)**

**regression line**    A line based on the least squares criterion that is the best fit to the points in a scatterplot **(415)**

**relation**    Joint occurrence or covariation between two or more variables **(59)**

**reliability**    The consistency of a measuring instrument, that is, the extent to which a measuring instrument contains variable error **(170)**

**reliability measure**    A statistical measure varying on a scale from 0 to 1; the value 0 indicates that the measurement includes that nothing but error, the value 1 indicates that there is no variable error at all **(172)**

**replication**    The repetition of an investigation in an identical way as a safeguard against unintentional error or deception **(14)**

**representative sample**    A segment of a population being studied chosen because it is as representative as possible of the population from which it is drawn. Said to be representative of the analyses made on its sampling units and to produce results similar to those that would be obtained had the *entire* population been analyzed **(183)**

**research design**    The program that guides the investigator in the process of collecting, analyzing, and interpreting observations **(99)**

**research hypothesis**    Used in statistical hypotheses-testing, the research hypothesis states what the researcher is attempting to show in the study. The research hypothesis is not directly tested, however it is supported when the null hypothesis is rejected **(480)**

**research problem**    An intellectual problem calling for an answer in the form of a scientific inquiry **(52)**

**research process**    The overall scheme of activities in which scientists engage in order to produce knowledge; the paradigm of scientific inquiry **(20)**

**research-then-theory strategy**    A research plan beginning with empirical observation, description of attributes, measurement, and analysis of the resulting data before the researcher attempts to construct a theory **(46)**

**response rate**    The percentage of individuals who respond to a given questionnaire **(226)**

**revolutionary science**    The abrupt development of a rival paradigm that is accepted only gradually by a scientific community **(18)**

**right to privacy**    The freedom of individuals to choose for themselves the time, circumstances, and extent to which their beliefs and behavior are to be shared or withheld from others **(86)**

**sample**    Any subset of a population **(179)**

**sampling distribution**    A theoretical distribution that can be specified for any statistic that can be computed for samples from a population **(481)**

**sampling frame**    The list of the sampling units that is used in the selection of the sample **(181)**

**sampling unit**    A single member of a sampling population or, in cluster sampling, a collection of sampling units **(180)**

**sampling validity**    The degree to which a given population (i.e., the total set of cases having the property in question in the real world) is adequately sampled by the measuring instrument **(166)**

**schedule-structured interview**    An interview in which the questions (their wording and their sequence) are fixed and identical for every respondent (**232**)

**science**    All the knowledge collected by the means of scientific methodology (**2**)

**semantic differential**    A rating scale that measures the respondent's reaction to some object or concept in terms of rating on bipolar scales defined with contrasting adjectives at each end (**259**)

**sensitivity of information**    Refers to how personal or potentially threatening is the information being collected by the researcher. The greater the sensitivity of the information, the more safeguards are called for to protect the privacy of the research participants (**87**)

**simple observation**    An unobtrusive measurement made in a situation in which the observer remains unnoticed by the observed (**316**)

**simple random sample**    A basic probability sampling design that gives each of the sampling units of the population an equal chance of being selected for the sample (**186**)

**skewed distribution**    A distribution in which more observations fall to one side of the mean than the other (**382**)

**spatial behavior**    The attempts people make to structure the space around them, such as attempts to control the amount of their personal space (**208**)

**split-half method**    A method of assessing the reliability of an instrument by dividing items into two equivalent parts and correlating scores in one part with scores in the other (**173**)

**spurious relation**    An apparent relation between the independent and dependent variables that is found to be false because it can be explained by variables other than those stated in the hypothesis (**57, 427**)

**standard deviation**    A commonly used measure of variability whose size indicates the dispersion of a distribution (**377**)

**standard error**    A statistical measure indicating how closely sample results reflect values of a parameter. It is calculated from the distribution of all the sample means about the mean of the total of those samples; the standard deviation of a sampling distribution (**194**)

**standard score**    An individual observation that belongs to a distribution with a mean of zero and a standard deviation of one (**383**)

**statistic**    A value of a parameter obtained from a sample rather than the population (**179**)

**stimulus-response relationship**    A relationship characterized by an independent variable that can be manipulated by the reseacher (**127**)

**stratified sample**    A probability sampling design in which the population is first divided into homogeneous strata within each of which sampling is conducted (**188**)

**subset**    Any combination of sampling units that does not include the entire set of sampling units that has been defined as the population (**194**)

**systematic sample**    A sample in which every *k*th case is selected (usually with a random start) where *k* is a constant (**187**)

**t test**    A hypothesis test that uses the *t* statistic and the *t* distribution to determine whether to reject or retain the null hypothesis (**491**)

**tautology**    A statement that is true by virtue of its logical form alone (**5**)

**taxonomy**    A level of theory that consists of a system of categories constructed to fit the empirical observations so that relationships among categories can be described (**37**)

**test-retest method**    A method of assessing the reliability of an instrument by administering it twice to the same group of people and correlating the scores (**172**)

**theoretical import**    The meaning concepts acquire only in the context of the theory in which they are introduced (**35**)

**theoretical system**    Systematic combinations of taxonomies, conceptual frameworks, descriptions, explanations, and predictions in a manner that provides structure for a complete explanation of empirical phenomena (**39**)

**theory-then-research strategy**    A research plan beginning with the development of ideas and followed by the attempt to confirm or refute those ideas through empirical research (**46**)

**threatening question**    A question that respondents may find embarrassing or sensitive (**264**)

**time sampling**    The process of selecting observation units at different points in time in order to ensure the representativeness of the chosen ongoing activities (**210**)

**time-series design**    A quasi-experimental design in which pretest and posttest measures are available on a number of occasions before and after exposure to an independent variable (**138**)

**topical autobiography**    A private record that focuses on a limited aspect of a person's life (**322**)

**triangulation**    Use of more than one form of data collection to test the same hypothesis within a unified research plan (**204**)

**two-tailed test**    A statistical test where extreme results leading to the rejection of the null hypothesis will be located at both left and right tails (**485**)

**Type I error**    The rejection of a true null hypothesis (**486**)

**Type II error**    The acceptance of a false null hypothesis (**486**)

**unidimensionality**    Principle that implies that the items comprising a scale reflect a single dimension and belong on a continuum that reflects one and only one theoretical concept (**457**)

**unit of analysis**    The most elementary part of the phenomenon to be studied; its character influences subsequent research design, data collection, and data analysis decisions (**53**)

**unobtrusive measures**    A method of observation in which the subjects are not aware they are being observed, with little danger that the act of measurement will introduce a change in behavior that might bias the data (**315**)

**validity**    The degree to which a measuring instrument measures what it is supposed to measure (**165**)

**variable**    An empirical property that can take on two or more values (**55**)

**variance**    A measure of quantitative variation reflecting the average dispersion in the distribution; the square of the standard deviation (**376**)

*Verstehen*    Empathic understanding of human behavior (**11**)

**voluntarism**    The freedom of participants to choose whether or not to take part in a research project; guarantees that exposure to known risks is voluntarily undertaken (**83**)

**weighted aggregate**    Component in constructing an index specifying the relative influence of each indicator or item (**462**)

**Ackonwledgments** *(continued from copyright page)*

**Table 10.1** adapted from Don A. Dillman, James A. Christensen, Edward H. Carpenter, and Ralph M. Brooks, "Increasing Mail Questionnaire Response: A Four-State Comparison," *American Sociological Review*, 39 (1974): 755, and Don A. Dillman and Dan E. Moore, "Improving Response Rates to Mail Surveys: Results from Five Surveys," unpublished paper presented at the annual meeting of the American Association for Public Opinion Research, Hershey, Pa., 1983. Reprinted with the permission of the American Sociological Association and Don A. Dillman.

**Exhibit 10.1** from Samuel Devons, "A Questionnaire for Questioners," *Public Opinion Quarterly*, 39 (1975): 255–256. Reprinted with the permission of The University of Chicago Press.

**Exhibits 10.2, 10.3, and 10.4** adapted from Raymond L. Gorden, *Interviewing: Strategy, Techniques, and Tactics, Third Edition* (Homewood, Ill.: Dorsey Press, 1980), pp. 48–50. Copyright © 1975 by Raymond L. Gorden. Reprinted with the permission of the author.

**Exhibit 11.4** based on Angus Campbell and Howard Shuman, *Racial Attitudes in Fifteen American Cities* (Ann Arbor: Social Science Archive, 1973). Reprinted with the permission of the Institute for Social Research, Center for Political Studies, University of Michigan.

**Exhibit 13.1** from Inter-university Consortium for Political and Social Research, *Guide to Resources and Services, 1994–1995* (Ann Arbor: University of Michigan, Institute for Social Research, Center for Political Studies, 1994), p. xxiii. Reprinted with the permission of ICPSR.

**Table 14.1** from Paul F. Lazarsfeld and Alan Barton, "Qualitative Measurement in the Social Sciences: Classification, Typologies, and Indices" in *The Policy Sciences*, edited by Daniel Lerner and Harold D. Lasswell (Stanford, Calif.: Stanford University Press, 1951), p. 161. Reprinted with the permission of Stanford University Press.

**Exhibit 14.2** from the National Opinion Research Center, University of Chicago, *General Social Survey, 1972–1989: Cumulative Codebook* (Storrs, Conn.: Roper Center for Public Opinion Research, 1989). Reprinted with the permission of the publishers.

**Figure 14.1** from James L. Gibson and Richard D. Bingham, *Civil Liberties and the Nazis*. Copyright © 1985 by Praeger Publishers. Reprinted with the permission of the publishers.

**Table 15.2** adapted from Alison Landes, Jacquelyn Quiram, and Nancy R. Jacobs, editors, *Child Abuse: Betraying a Trust* (Wylie, Tex.: Information Plus, 1995), p. 33. Reprinted with the permission of Information Plus.

**Table 16.5** from Susan J. Carroll, "The Personal Is Political: The Intersection of Private Lives and Public Roles among Women and Men in Elective and Appointive Office," *Women and Politics* 9, no. 2 (1989). Reprinted with the permission of Haworth Press, Inc.

**Table 16.7** adapted from Elizabeth Addel Cook, Ted G. Jelen, and Clyde Wilcox, "The Social Bases of Abortion Attitudes" from *Between Two Absolutes: Public Opinions and the Politics of Abortion* (Boulder, Colo.: Westview Press, 1992). Copyright © 1992 by Westview Press. Reprinted with the permission of the publishers.

**Table 16.10** from *Social and Political Survey: Winter 1989*, Social Science Research Facility, University of Wisconsin, Milwaukeee. Reprinted by permission.

**Figures 17.8 and 17.9** adapted from Gary L. Tompkins, "A Causal Model of State Welfare Expenditures," *Journal of Politics*, 37 (1975): 406, 409. Copyright © 1975 by the University of Texas Press. Reprinted with the permission of the author and the publishers.

**Table 18.7** based on Jules J. Wanderer, "An Index of Riot Severity and Some Correlates," *American Journal of Sociology*, 74 (1969): 503. Reprinted with the permission of The University of Chicago Press.

**Table 19.6** adapted from Jane Riblett Wilkie, "Changes in U.S. Men's Attitudes Toward the Family Provider Role, 1972–1989," *Gender and Society*, 7, no. 2 (June 1993): 261–279. Copyright © 1993 by Sage Publications, Inc. Reprinted with the permission of the publishers.

**Figures A.2 through A.6 and A.9 through A.11** (all generated figures from SPSS for Windows Release 5.0). Reprinted with the permission of SPSS Inc.

**Appendix B** (guidelines for preparing tables) adapted from classroom handout prepared by David Wegge of St. Norbert College. Reprinted with the permission of the author.

**Appendix D** abridged from William H. Beyer, editor, *Handbook of Tables for Probability and Statistics, Second Edition* (Cleveland: Chemical Rubber Company, 1968). Copyright © 1968 The Chemical Rubber Company, CRC Press, Inc. Reprinted with the permission of the publishers.

**Appendix E** from Harold O. Rugg, *Statistical Methods Applied to Education* (Boston: Houghton Mifflin Company, 1917), pp. 389–390. Reprinted with the permission of the publishers.

**Appendixes F and I** abridged from Ronald A. Fisher and Frank Yates, *Statistical Tables for Biological, Agricultural, and Medical Research, Sixth Edition*, Tables III and IV. Reprinted with the permission of Longman Group, Ltd. on behalf of the Literary Executor of the late Sir Ronald A. Fisher, F.R.S. and Dr. Frank Yates, F.R.S.

**Appendix G** from George W. Snedecor and William G. Cochran, *Statistical Methods, Seventh Edition*. Copyright © 1980 by Iowa State University Press. Reprinted with the permission of the publisher.

**Appendix H** from D. Auble, "Extended Tables for the Mann-Whitney Statistic," *Bulletin of the Institute of Educational Research at Indiana University* 1, no. 2 (1953), tables 1, 3, 5, and 7. Reprinted with the permission of the Department of Education, Indiana University.

# AUTHOR INDEX

Abramson, Paul R., 133*n*
Ackoff, Russell, 192
Aiello, A. J., 209*n*
Ailkins, Winona, 347*n*
Alker, Hayward R., 57
Allport, Gordon W., 322*n*
Alreck, Pamela L., 228*n*, 231*n*
Anderson, Theodore R., 393*n*
Angell, Robert, 320
Aristotle, 4, 36
Aronson, Elliot, 215*n*, 219
Asch, Solomon E., 214

Babad, E. Y., 99*n*
Babbie, Earl, 557*n*, 561*n*
Bailey, Kenneth D., 227*n*, 238*n*, 263*n*
Bainbridge, William Sims, 467
Balay, Robert, 67
Bales, Robert, 209–10, 211
Baron, Robert A., 204*n*
Bart, Pauline, 71
Barton, Alan, 338, 339
Baumrind, Diana, 79*n*
Baxter, Janeen, 426*n*
Becker, Howard S., 293*n*
Belson, William A., 261*n*
Bensman, Joseph, 88
Berelson, Bernard, 328*n*
Berger, Michael A., 147*n*
Berk, Richard A., 133*n*
Biles, George E., 334*n*
Bingham, Richard D., 268*n*, 270*n*
Blackwood, Larry G., 261*n*
Blalock, Hubert M., Jr., 42, 446
Bogdan, Robert, 293–94
Bohrnstedt, George W., 422
Bolton, Alfred A., 334*n*
Boruch, Robert F., 80*n*, 90*n*, 138*n*
Botein, Bernard, 102*n*
Bradburn, Norman M., 243*n*, 258*n*, 261*n*, 265, 266*n*
Braithwaite, Richard, 8
Brecht, Arnold, 36

Brewer, John, 144*n*
Brewer, Marilynn B., 215*n*, 219
Bridgman, P. W., 31
Brim, Oliver G., 86*n*
Bronfen, Marna I., 204*n*
Bronfenbrenner, Urie, 88*n*
Brooks, Ralph M., 229*n*, 230
Brooks-Gunn, J., 435*n*
Brown, Samuel, 224
Brownlee, K. A., 144*n*
Burnim, Mickey L., 228*n*, 267*n*
Byrne, Bryan, 98*n*

Campbell, Angus, 271*n*
Campbell, Donald, 89, 106*n*, 116*n*, 138*n*, 140, 143*n*, 169*n*, 170*n*
Cannell, Charles F., 264*n*
Carlsmith, J. Merrill, 216*n*
Carlsmith, James, 215*n*, 219
Carpenter, Edward II., 229*n*, 230
Carpenter, Edwin H., 261*n*
Carroll, Susan J., 394
Chapin, Stuart F., 322*n*
Chein, Isidor, 179*n*, 183
Childers, Terry L., 231*n*
Christensen, James A., 229*n*, 230
Cloud, Monique Y., 133*n*
Cochran, William, 188*n*
Cohen, Morris R., 13*n*
Cohen, Reuben, 245–46
Collins, Barry E., 216*n*
Consorte, Josildeth Gomes, 98*n*
Cook, Elizabeth Adell, 396, 488*n*
Cook, Thomas D., 143*n*
Costner, Herbert L., 402*n*, 403*n*, 410*n*, 495*n*
Coughlin, Ellen K., 2*n*
Crandall, Rick, 81*n*, 82*n*, 83, 86*n*, 88*n*
Cressey, Donald R., 295*n*
Cronbach, Lee J., 168, 169*n*, 173

Daddario, Gina, 321
Dalphin, John R., 238*n*

# SUBJECT INDEX